MASTERS OF THE AMERICAN CINEMA

MASTERS OF THE

AMERICAN CINEMA

LOUIS GIANNETTI

Case Western Reserve University

Prentice-Hall, Inc., Englewood Cliffs, New Jersey 07632

Library of Congress Cataloging in Publication Data

GIANNETTI, LOUIS D
    Masters of the American cinema.

    Includes bibliographies and index.
    1. Moving-pictures—United States.   2. Moving-pic-
ture producers and directors—United States.   I. Title.
PN1993.5.U6G49 1981   791.43′0233′0922   80-28887
ISBN 0-13-560102-9 (pbk.)
ISBN 0-13-560110-X

MASTERS OF THE AMERICAN CINEMA
Louis Giannetti

Printed in the United States of America

10   9   8   7   6   5   4   3   2

Editorial/production supervision by Robert Hunter
Interior and cover design by Mark A. Binn
Manufacturing buyer: Harry Baisley

Prentice-Hall International, Inc., *London*
Prentice-Hall of Australia Pty. Limited, *Sydney*
Prentice-Hall of Canada, Ltd., *Toronto*
Prentice-Hall of India Private Limited, *New Delhi*
Prentice-Hall of Japan, Inc., *Tokyo*
Prentice-Hall of Southeast Asia Pte. Ltd., *Singapore*
Whitehall Books Limited, *Wellington, New Zealand*

For the women in my life—
Christina and Francesca

Contents

Introduction

Art, Industry, Audience 3

Representative Artists

Foreword

The American cinema can be analyzed from a number of different perspectives. I have chosen an eclectic method, though with emphasis on major figures. Part I is an overview. The individual filmmakers of Part II are representative artists. That is, in addition to being distinguished filmmakers in their own right, they were also chosen because they made important contributions in a given genre, style, or studio, or their work is typical of a given era. Because of the limitations of space, a number of equally gifted artists have been left out, only because they happen to be less representative in these respects. I have tried to synthesize as much of the available literature as possible, without sacrificing my own opinions. Above all, however, I have been influenced in my thinking about the American cinema by the writings of three of its finest critics: Pauline Kael, Andrew Sarris, and James Agee.

LOUIS GIANNETTI
CLEVELAND, OHIO

Acknowledgments

I would like to thank the following friends for offering me their reactions and insights. Their encouragement meant a lot to me: Scott Eyman, Paula Cohen, Gary Engle, Tom and Terri Mester, and especially David Mallery, who gave me the best advice of all. I am grateful to William H. Oliver and Robert Hunter of Prentice-Hall for their patience and support. I'm indebted to my students for allowing me to test much of this material on them in the classroom, and to the Case-Western Reserve University Film Society for helping me research the project. I owe a special debt to the following for supplying me with the still photos: Gwen Feldman of the Larry Edmunds Bookshop in Hollywood, The Memory Shop West in San Francisco, Cinemabilia in New York City, and especially Paula Klaw Kramer and the indefatigable David Noh of Movie Star News in New York. Other stills were provided by my friends and colleagues, Carmie Amata, Scott Eyman, and Gary Engle.

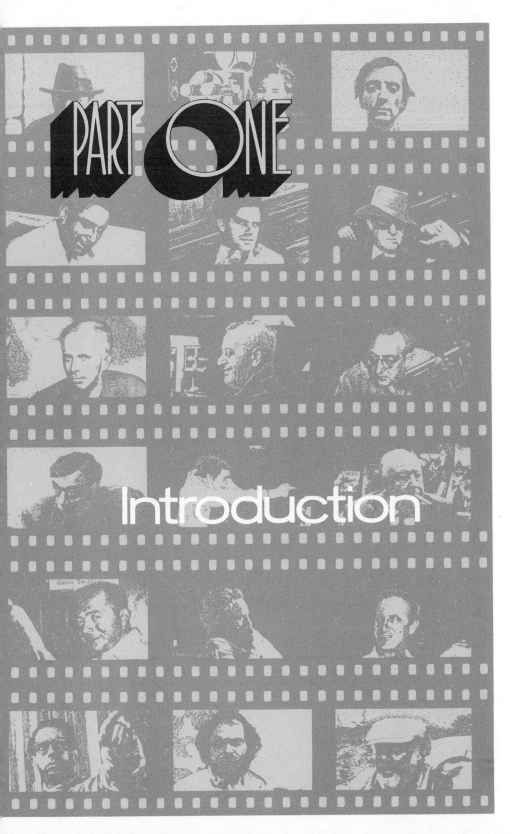

PART ONE

Introduction

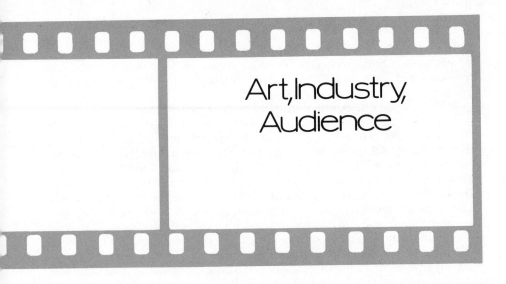

Art, Industry, Audience

> *I believe that we respond most and best to work in any art form (and to other experience as well) if we are pluralistic, flexible, relative in our judgments, if we are eclectic.*
>
> —*Pauline Kael,* I Lost It at the Movies

BOX OFFICE

Cinema is the most expensive artistic medium in history, and its development has been largely determined by those who paid the bills. Fiction filmmakers need cameras, actors, film stock, sound and editing equipment, costumes, lights, and so on. Like all artists, they've got to earn a living, and they do so by providing a product which has a cash value to its consumers. In most European countries the cinema in its early stages of development fell into the hands of artists who shared most of the values and tastes of the educated elite. European movie houses before World War I were usually located in fashionable districts and catered to the cultivated classes—the same patrons who attended the legitimate theatre and the opera. In the Soviet Union and other Communist countries, film production has been carefully regulated by the government, and the movies produced in these countries reflect most of the values of the political elite.

In the United States, which quickly became the leading film-producing nation in the world, motion pictures developed as a popular art within a capitalistic system of production. The industry catered primarily to patrons of the lower social echelons, who likewise wanted to see their values, tastes, and aspirations sympathetically portrayed. Before 1900, when movies were in their infancy, 90 percent of the American population had never been exposed to any form of enacted drama.

Within a decade, as historian Benjamin Hampton noted, the small coins of the masses had created a business larger in volume than the live theatre, vaudeville, museums, lecture bureaus, concert halls, circuses, and carnivals combined.

Movies were a boom industry in the United States primarily because audiences were getting what they really wanted. The American cinema was the most democratic art in history, reflecting most of the strengths and failings of the society that nurtured it. In order to guarantee their continued employment in this expensive medium, fiction filmmakers had to be sensitive to the demands of the box office, to the tastes of those anonymous millions who cared little for "culture," "edification," and other such lofty abstractions. Above all, audiences wanted to be entertained, and only at his own peril would a Hollywood film artist ignore this fundamental commandment of the box office. The best as well as the worst American movies have been produced within this commercial framework of a mass audience and a competitive marketplace.

Of course Hollywood films are hardly unique in this respect. Shakespeare, Dickens, and Mark Twain, to name only a few, also appealed primarily to "vulgar" audiences, and like the earliest American

Figure I.1. *Star Wars* **(1977), directed by George Lucas, special effects by John Dykstra, produced by 20th Century-Fox.** Almost from the beginning, American movies were big business, with the profit motive preeminent. But art, entertainment, and profit are not necessarily exclusive characteristics. Lucas' charming sci-fi fantasy broke every box office record in history, grossing a staggering $216 million in its first year of release in Canada and the United States alone. For a discussion of the relationship of art to commerce in the American cinema, see Pauline Kael, "Trash, Art, and the Movies," in *Going Steady* (New York: Bantam, 1971). Photo: Gary Engle.

moviemakers, they were harshly criticized by the cultural establishments of their day for pandering to the low tastes of the mob. In fact, the Renaissance scholar Mario Praz has pointed out that the unruly patrons who thronged to Shakespeare's plays were very much like American movie audiences, especially in their fondness for the spectacular and the sensational. The staples of the American cinema—violence, sex, comedy, fantasy, and "heart interest" (sentimental melodramas)—were also the staples of the Elizabethan drama. Sex and violence have always headed the list.

Particularly before World War II, most American intellectuals lamented the state of the Hollywood cinema. Movies were routinely dismissed as "cheap shows for cheap people" and "the flimsy amusement of the mob." With dubious logic, cultural commentators insisted that art had nothing to do with commerce, with "show business." Whatever their individual merits or failings, American pictures were automatically suspect because even the most serious artists were required to work within commercially viable formats—as though this weren't true for all artists in

Figure I.2. James Cagney in *The Public Enemy* (1931), with Mae Clarke, directed by William Wellman, produced by Warner Brothers. Sex and violence have always been the two most popular subjects of American movies; only the degree of explicitness has varied from period to period. Gangster films of the early depression era were particularly violent and provoked outcries from spokesmen of public morality. Over two hundred gangster films were made between 1930 and 1932, many of them by Warners, which came to be known as "the depression studio" because its films picked up on the crisis of confidence of this era. The Catholic Legion of Decency threatened massive boycotts against the industry unless it changed its ways. In 1934 the studios capitulated to these demands and imposed a policy of "self-censorship" known as the Production Code.

Figure I.3.   Publicity photo of Mae West and Cary Grant in *She Done Him Wrong* (1933), written by Mae West, based on her play, *Diamond Lil*, produced by Paramount. West made her debut on the screen with her persona (not to speak of her ample person) totally developed. For years she had been a stage star who wrote and even produced her own plays. America responded enthusiastically to Mae's insolence and snappy wisecracks. In *She Done Him Wrong* she's at her outspoken best: cool, lecherous, cynical. In her opening scene, she saucily proclaims herself to be "one of the finest women who ever walked the streets." West preferred playing outcasts, like showgirls and kept women. This afforded her the opportunity of satirizing sexual hypocrisies. Her one-liners are legendary, like the famous "It's not the men in my life, it's the life in my men that counts." Mae's "lewd" comic style—almost exclusively verbal—fueled the wrath of the Legion of Decency. The Production Code killed her comedy, for after 1934, when it was strictly enforced, the laughs were laundered right out of her scripts.

all mediums. (In our own time, television is often condemned with these same objections.)

The reasons for this hostility are understandable, for out of the five hundred or so pictures produced yearly in Hollywood between the two world wars, only a relative handful were of enduring aesthetic value. Because of this sheer volume, the best movies were often overshadowed by the worst, or at least by the merely routine. Conversely, only the most prestigious foreign movies were exported to the United States, amounting roughly to 2 percent of the pictures exhibited in this country. For the most part these dealt with subjects that rarely attracted American filmmakers, particularly that virtually taboo theme, honest failure. Popular audiences regarded foreign movies as arty, downbeat, and very slow—at least when contrasted with American pictures, which were usually unpretentious, optimistic, and fast-moving. Only box office hits were widely imitated in Hollywood, and since foreign films seldom attracted large audiences, American producers were content to leave "highbrow" subjects to European and Japanese filmmakers.

These cinematic differences were based on totally different social conditions. After World War I, the major film-producing nations of Europe were spiritually exhausted, their economies in shambles. Disillusionment and pessimism were in the air, traditional standards of morality were collapsing, and absolute values were viewed as naive. While Europe was plunged in chaos and despair, the United States was thriving, immersed in the gaudiest spree of its history, to use Scott Fitzgerald's famous phrase. Millions of destitute immigrants were pouring into the country, eager to make it in the Land of Opportunity. In greater numbers than ever before, rural Americans streamed to the cities in search of excitement and wider options. These were the major patrons of the movies during this formative stage, and what they wanted to see above all were success stories. It wasn't for nothing that the American film industry was sometimes called the Hollywood dream factory.

Because the best European movies during this era generally dealt with pessimistic themes, they were regarded by naive intellectuals as innately more "artistic" than American pictures. (Only after the late 1960s did such themes become popular in the United States, thanks to America's tragic Vietnam adventure and the jarring Watergate revelations of the early 1970s.) Furthermore, unlike the foremost European filmmakers, who considered themselves serious artists, almost all Hollywood artists preferred to think of themselves as professional entertainers, though in fact a good number of them were well educated and cultivated people, especially those who had emigrated from Germany and Austria. Nonetheless, the stereotype persisted. "The people who make films don't do it to ennoble man," wrote the novelist André Malraux; "they are there to make money. Consequently, inevitably, they work upon man's lower insticts." Perhaps what was most galling—though it was seldom openly acknowledged—was that the best American movies often did both: They made money *and* ennobled man.

This hostility was economically motivated as well, for between the two world wars, American movies dominated over 80 percent of the world's screens and were more popular with foreign mass audiences

Figure I.4. Harold Lloyd in *Safety Last* (1923). The American success ethic was Lloyd's principal theme in nearly 200 movies (over 180 of them shorts). Though his career spanned the years 1915–1947, the era of his greatest popularity—the 1920s—coincided with a period of extraordinary economic prosperity in the United States. Lloyd's persona was the embodiment of the bustling go-getter on the way up. All his films end with the brash hero "making good." Lloyd's character is a gainfully employed and industrious upholder of the system. He is the most normal and average of the silent clowns—eager to succeed, perseverent, and incorrigibly middle class. See Lloyd's 1928 autobiography, *An American Comedy* (New York: Dover, 1971); and Adam Reilly, *et al., Harold Lloyd: The King of Daredevil Comedy* (New York: Collier Books, 1977).

than all but a few natively produced movies. As much as 40 percent of the grosses of American pictures were earned abroad, especially in Great Britain, which accounted for nearly half the total foreign revenue of American films. Thus, foreign producers and directors complained bitterly that they were being closed out of their own markets, that they were being oppressed by a form of "cultural colonization." Various theories were offered concerning the "mystery" of American movies, but film historian Hampton claimed that the explanation was perfectly obvious: "The mystery is nothing but a willingness to give the public what it is willing to pay for instead of a desire to 'educate' the public against its will."

THE STUDIO SYSTEM

During their primitive phase (roughly from 1896 to 1908), American movies were aesthetically crude, devoid of serious artists, and immensely popular. Exhibitors clamored for more "product," and still the demand swallowed up the supply. New production and distribution companies sprang up, until by 1915 there were over two hundred of them in the United States. As the industry and the art grew more complex, the production of movies became more specialized. The earliest filmmakers were former actors, mechanics, and cameramen who improvised as they went along. The most successful of these eventually became directors, supervising the actual making of a movie from the creation of the story line to the coaching of the actors to the placement of the camera to the final assembly of shots into a coherent continuity.

Eventually producers developed a factory system of production. With the rise of the star system in the early teens, movies soon centered on a popular player, with stories especially tailored by studio scenarists to enhance a star's box office appeal. Set designers, cinematographers, and specialized technicians relieved the director of many of his former responsibilities, allowing him to concentrate on the players and the placement of the camera. With the exception of the most prestigious directors and stars, who insisted upon greater artistic autonomy or simply went into independent production, movies by committee become the general rule.

Under the factory system, the key figure was usually the producer, who by controlling the financing of a film also exercised significant control over how it would be made, although the director generally still commanded the camera, and hence, the mise-en-scène (that is, the photographed images). By the mid-1920s, movies were big business, with a total capital investment of over two billion dollars and an annual commerce of about one and one-quarter billion. The film industry was one of the top ten in America, a prominence it maintained for twenty-five years, a period which industry regulars refer to wistfully as the golden age of the studio system.

The three main branches of the industry—production, distribution, and exhibition—were controlled by different interests in the earliest years. Movies were sold outright by the linear foot, regardless of quality. The original distributors were called exchanges and were set up in key cities where, for a fee, exhibitors could swap their used prints for those of other theatre owners. This system eventually proved too crude for the burgeoning industry, and by the late teens, the most aggressive exhibitors and producers had begun to integrate all three phases of the business under one directorship—a method of consolidation known as vertical integration. This movement was spearheaded by such daring and cunning businessmen as Adolph Zukor of Paramount Pictures, William Fox of the Fox Film Corporation, and Marcus Loew of Loew's Inc., the parent firm of what eventually became Metro-Goldwyn-Mayer.

Under Zukor's shrewd leadership, Paramount became the leading film company of the teens and twenties, with most of the biggest stars of the period under contract. As early as 1921, the company owned over four hundred theatres, most of them first-run city houses, which commanded the highest ticket prices and the largest audiences. Zukor also introduced such concepts as blind and block booking, whereby even independent exhibitors were required to rent Paramount films—sight unseen—as a package rather than individually. The studio thus reduced

Figure I.5. *Greed* (1924), written and directed by Erich von Stroheim, based on the novel *McTeague*, by Frank Norris. Stroheim was one of the first casualties of the studio system. He began *Greed* in 1923 for the Goldwyn Company just before it merged with Metro Pictures, with Louis B. Mayer as chief executive. Stroheim was determined to preserve every word of Norris' pessimistic novel, a classic document of American literary naturalism. The director shot forty-two reels (approximately nine hours), which even the impractical Stroheim realized was excessive, so he cut the movie to twenty-four reels. Mayer and his production chief Irving Thalberg loathed the film because it had no stars, no glossy production values, no glamor, no sentimental affirmations, and no happy ending—all MGM trademarks. Fiercely opposed to a director-oriented cinema and determined to humble the haughty Stroheim, Mayer and Thalberg had the movie cut to ten reels, its present form. All the discarded footage was burned and lost forever. Though the two-hour version of *Greed* is still regarded as a masterpiece, Stroheim disowned the work, referring to it as his "mutilated child."

its risk on any single production and also guaranteed a constant supply of product for exhibitors. (It wasn't until the late 1940s that the U.S. Supreme Court declared this system a monopoly and in restraint of trade. The court ordered the studios to divest themselves of their theatre chains and to cease the practices of blind and block booking.)

Other producers and exhibitors followed Zukor's example by merging their considerable resources. By 1929 only five companies, known in the trade as the Big Five or the majors, had a virtual monopoly on the industry, producing over 90 percent of the fiction films in America. Paramount was responsible for about 25 percent of this output, a percentage matched by Warner Brothers, which had forged into prominence in 1927 with the introduction of talkies. Fox and MGM produced about 40 percent of the movies that year. Radio-Keith-

Orpheum, commonly known as RKO, was established in 1928 as a subsidiary of RCA, but despite this late start, it was capitalized at $80 million, boasted four production facilities, and like the other majors, was fully integrated, with a chain of over 300 theatres. These five companies controlled over 50 percent of the seating capacity in America, mostly in urban first-run houses, where the big money was earned. Of the remaining 10 percent of the movies made in 1929, most were produced by the so-called Little Three: Universal, Columbia, and United Artists.

The Hollywood studio system was modeled along the lines of "the American system of manufacture," introduced by Eli Whitney in the mass production of rifles. Henry Ford's concept of the assembly line in the manufacturing of autos was clearly derived from Whitney's ideas, and today, of course, these techniques are commonplace in virtually all forms of industrial mass production. The main features of this system are as follows: A product can be manufactured with greater efficiency and in

Figure I.6. United Artists was established in 1919 by D. W. Griffith, Mary Pickford, Charles Chaplin, and Douglas Fairbanks. Strictly speaking, UA was not a production company but a distributor of the independently produced movies of its four principal stockholders, who were the top box office personalities of the American cinema of that era. "So the lunatics have taken charge of the asylum," one wag quipped at the founding of the company. UA sold and promoted its films individually, not in blocks. It had no contract players or directors, no company-owned studio. Eventually other important independent producers—like Sam Goldwyn, Walt Disney, and David O. Selznick—also distributed their product through UA. Although the output of this company was small in its earliest years, the quality of its movies was generally high. See Tino Balio, *United Artists: The Company Built by the Stars* (Madison: University of Wisconsin Press, 1975).

far greater numbers if it's broken down into standardized interchang-able parts. These parts are assembled not by a single skilled craftsman but by ordinary workers who are responsible only for adding a simple component to the product, which is then passed along for ultimate com-pletion by other workers in the assembly line. Except for an overseer of some sort, no one handles the product from beginning to end.

As a number of critics have pointed out, this system works admirably in the production of rifles and autos, where uniformity and predicta-bility are desirable. In the production of movies, however, standardiza-tion is inimical to artistic excellence, and often even to commercial suc-cess. Assembly-line methods worked most efficiently in the production of the so-called program films. Over half the movies of the majors con-sisted of these routine formula pictures, which were also known as B movies. Program films were seldom box office hits, but they were con-sidered safe investments by the studios. Some interesting movies were produced in this form, but in general they were regarded even by the industry as its filler product.

Figure I.7. *D-Day on Mars* **(1945), produced by Republic Pictures, reedited from the Republic serial,** *The Purple Monster Strikes.* From the early 1930s to the decline of the studio system in the 1950s, B movies were commonly shown on the second half of double bills and were especially popular in provincial markets. "Poverty Row" studios like Monogram and Republic concentrated almost exclusively on the production of these cheapies, but the majors used them as testing grounds for the raw talent under contract. For the most part these pictures featured lurid and infantile titles, were made on minus-cule budgets, included lots of stock footage, and rarely featured important stars. Most of them took the form of staple genres, like westerns, thrillers, and science-fiction and horror movies.

Though all the studios attempted to standardize production as much as possible even for their important A films, intelligent producers realized that the key ingredients of box office hits were usually style, boldness, and originality—hardly the qualities encouraged by the assembly-line method of production. In general, studio executives tried to steer a middle course, allowing their most prestigious (that is, commercially successful) employees greater artistic autonomy, whereas their less accomplished colleagues were expected to do what they were told. Realizing that the studio system was the only ballgame in town, most ambitious artists resigned themselves to this situation in the hopes that eventually they too would be successful enough to demand more creative independence.

Figure I.8. *Pat and Mike* **(1953), produced by Metro-Goldwyn-Mayer.** From the early 1930s to the 1950s, MGM was the most successful and powerful studio in Hollywood. Though it rarely deviated from an assembly-line method of production, even at this studio rank had its privileges. Its top stars, directors, and writers were sometimes allowed more artistic freedom, providing their movies made money. At its best, the studio functioned like a cinematic repertory company, allowing a variety of artists to collaborate in a common enterprise. *Pat and Mike* was the seventh pairing of Spencer Tracy and Katharine Hepburn, two of the studio's box office magnets. Like most of their joint vehicles, it was directed by the highly respected George Cukor, who was on Metro contract for much of his career and was known as a "woman's director" because so many of MGM's stars—mostly glamorous females—had done their best work with him. The script to *Pat and Mike* was written by the husband-wife team Garson Kanin and Ruth Gordon, who wrote seven screenplays for Cukor, most of which dealt with the chemistry of the couple. For a history of MGM, see Bosley Crowther, *The Lion's Share* (New York: Dutton, 1957). See also Gavin Lambert, *On Cukor* (New York: Putnam's, 1972); and Gary Carey, *Cukor & Co.* (New York: Museum of Modern Art, 1971).

Studio chiefs were often under fire from two flanks. Serious artists complained they were being forced to make cheap compromises in their work, and company officers in New York (where most of the studios had their financial headquarters) lamented the reckless extravagance of their West Coast executives, the flamboyant "moguls." The moguls responded to these accusations by pointing out that box office hits were produced by instinctive gamblers rather than cautious businessmen. Conservatives almost invariably disappeared from the industry, for the public was notoriously fickle, subject to radical shifts in taste from year to year. For example, in 1930, mighty Paramount was sinking into insolvency, but by the middle of the decade, the studio's net earnings were up 820 percent, thanks largely to the films of Mae West. Similarly, in 1929, Warner Brothers was the top studio in Hollywood, with a net profit of over $17 million. Two years later it showed a deficit of almost $8 million. Little wonder, anthropologist Hortense Powdermaker observed, that Hollywood movies were produced in an atmosphere of constant crisis.

Each of the majors during the era of studio dominance was a virtual city-state, with vast holdings in land and buildings, standing back lots, and sound stages. Technical staffs and creative personnel were under long-term contract, and in such tightly organized studios as Warners and Columbia, employees often ran rather than walked to their next assignments, so "efficiently" were they scheduled. Each studio had an array of specialized departments, such as publicity, costumes, art design, story, and so on. Most of the decision-making power rested with the front office, which consisted of the studio head, the production chief, the producers, and their assistants.

To such rebellious artists as Warner Brothers' Bette Davis, the front office symbolized cautious mediocrity, for she had to fight to make most of her best films (often on loan-out to more adventurous producers), and she was frequently put on suspension by the equally intransigent Jack Warner for refusing to act in routine studio projects. Ironically, the movies she fought for usually made more money than the potboilers favored by the front office. At this time most film stars were under exclusive seven-year contracts which the studios could cancel after six months' notice. Suspended employees were legally barred from working for others, and their suspension time was cruelly added to their seven-year terms. Davis claimed—with some justice—that she was trapped in perpetual servitude.

The front office of each studio was determined in part by the personality and tastes of the colorful moguls who ran the studios autocratically. Virtually all of them were Jewish immigrants, or the sons of Jewish immigrants, from eastern Europe. Most of them were born in poverty and became self-made men whose tastes didn't differ radically from those of the masses who flocked to their movies. All the moguls were shrewd businessmen, even though some, like William Fox, were barely literate. Others, like MGM's Louis B. Mayer, were incredibly philistine in their taste in movies. A few—like production chief Hunt Stromberg, Thalberg's successor at MGM; RKO's Pandro S. Berman; Hal B. Wallis of Warners and later Paramount—were men of considerable intelligence and taste. Such independents as David O. Selznick and

Samuel Goldwyn were also admired for the quality of their films. Darryl F. Zanuck, one of the few gentiles among the moguls, headed "the goy studio," 20th Century-Fox, which in the late 1940s and 1950s became one of the most progressive studios in Hollywood, a distinction it shared with Harry Cohn's Columbia Pictures, which also produced some excellent movies during this era of changing tastes.

The production chief was the front office executive who made most of the important decisions concerning what movies to make and

Figure I.9.   Fred Astaire and Ginger Rogers in *Top Hat* (1935), directed by Mark Sandrich. Depression-weary America responded enthusiastically to RKO's nine Astaire-Rogers musicals, which were among the top-grossing films of the 1930s and helped keep the studio afloat during troubled times. Style, wit, and grace blend with a breezy innocence in these escapist vehicles. The dance numbers were worked out in detail by Astaire and choreographer Hermes Pan, then photographed in a few uninterrupted shots to capture an effortless lyricism. See Arlene Croce, *The Fred Astaire & Ginger Rogers Book* (New York: Vintage Books, 1977).

how. He was sometimes given the title of vice-president in charge of production. Generally he supervised about fifty films per year and was responsible for all the main assignments, budget allocations, and the selection of key personnel for each project. He also made the important decisions concerning potential properties (that is, novels, plays, and stories which might serve as sources for movies) and the principal emphasis of scripts. Furthermore, he had the final say about how a movie ought to be reshot, edited, scored, and publicized. All these decisions were based on such considerations as the types of stars and directors under studio contract, the genres that were enjoying the greatest popularity during any given period, and the production chief's gut instincts about the box office.

The title of producer was one of the most ambiguous of the studio era and could refer to a prestigious mogul or a glorified errand boy, depending on the individual involved. As a class, however, producers enjoyed more power within the industry than any other group. They were also among the highest paid, accounting for nearly 19 percent of the net profits of a studio, according to sociologist Leo Rosten. The rise to power of producers coincided with the rise of the studio system. In the mid-1920s, for example, there were only about 34 major producers in the industry. Ten years later, when the studio system was firmly entrenched, there were over 220 of them, even though the studios produced 40 percent fewer pictures. Nepotism was common in the front offices of many studios, and a good number of associate and assistant producers were talentless relatives of the company top brass. In order to justify their high salaries, many of them threw their weight around by obstructing the work of others, often out of envy and spite. Directors were especially loud in their complaints that they weren't able to perform their duties because of the interference of these minions.

Depending on the complexity of the studio, each front office had a number of producers, most of them specialists in a particular type of work: A productions, star vehicles, B films, musicals, short subjects, serials, newsreels, and so on. These producers usually shaped the writing and rewriting of the script, had a major say in the casting, and often selected the cameraman, composer, and art designers. The producer and his assistants oversaw the director's day-to-day problems of filming, smoothing out difficulties if they were good at their jobs, creating more if they weren't. Producers superceded directors in the final cut of a film. If a director was sufficiently prestigious, he was at least consulted on many of these decisions; if he wasn't, he was informed of them.

There were two other types of Hollywood producers, and though they were few in number, they accounted for much of the best work in the industry. The so-called creative producer was usually a powerful mogul who supervised the production of a film in such exacting detail that he was virtually its artistic creator. David O. Selznick was the most famous of these, for his *Gone with the Wind* (1939) was the top-grossing movie in history, a supremacy that remained unchallenged for years. "Great films, successful films, are made in their *every detail* according to the vision of one man," Selznick insisted, and in his own case, that man was David O. Selznick.

Figure I.10. Publicity photo of Gene Kelly in *Singin' in the Rain* (1952), directed by Kelly and Stanley Donen, produced by Arthur Freed for MGM. All fiction films are collaborative at least to some degree, but the musical requires a coordination of talent on the most sophisticated level—a level admirably maintained by the celebrated Freed Unit at MGM. During its golden age of musicals in the 1940s and 1950s, Metro had under contract virtually every major singer and dancer; such gifted directors as Kelly, Donen, and Vincente Minnelli; and choreographers Michael Kidd, Bob Fosse, and Gower Champion. For a discussion of the Freed Unit see Hugh Fordin, *The World of Entertainment* (New York: Equinox Books, 1975).

Figure I.11 Clark Gable and Vivien Leigh in *Gone with the Wind* (1939), produced by David O. Selznick. "The difference between me and other producers," Selznick once said, "is that I am interested in the thousands and thousands of details that go into the making of a film. It is the sum total of all these things that either makes a great picture or destroys it." A brilliant publicist, Selznick had the public buzzing with speculation for months concerning the casting of his film. Though Sidney Howard was officially credited with adapting Margaret Mitchell's best-selling novel, Selznick himself wrote much of the script—with the help of over a dozen writers and rewrite specialists. The producer also closely supervised the sets, the costumes, the photographic style of the movie, and the editing. So precise were his ideas about the mise-en-scène that even though the movie was directed by five different men (Victor Fleming received official credit), there were no disjunctions in style and overall tone. Interestingly, although these facts were common knowledge within the industry, Howard and Fleming both received Academy Awards for their work—a striking instance of the irrationality and arbitrariness of many academy selections.

Most of the artistically significant works of the American cinema have been created by the top-echelon producer-directors. By controlling the financing of their movies, producer-directors control virtually every aspect of their work, without making crippling concessions and compromises. During the studio era there were about thirty producer-directors, most of them working independently in the majors. They were among the most admired artists in the industry—and also the most commercially successful, or they wouldn't have remained independent for long. In addition to controlling the staging and the placement of the camera (which was true even of most studio-employed directors), producer-directors had the final say about scripts, which they often wrote themselves, or at least closely supervised. In addition, they controlled the casting, scoring, and editing of their movies. Such autonomy was rare during the studio era, as producer-director Frank Capra pointed out in 1939 in the *New York Times:* "I would say that 80% of the directors today shoot scenes exactly as they are told to shoot them without any changes whatsoever, and that 90% of them have no voice in the story or in the editing." Among the most distinguished producer-directors of the studio era, in addition to most of the filmmakers included in this volume, were such figures as Leo McCarey, George Stevens, Joseph Mankiewicz, William Wellman, King Vidor, and Preston Sturges, to mention only some of the most prominent.

The studio system began its slow decline in the late 1940s, after the Supreme Court ordered the majors to divest themselves of their theatre chains. Deprived of a guaranteed outlet for their product, the majors gradually were supplanted by more aggressive producers, most of them independents. One by one the stars left the studios, some to drift into

Figure I.12. *The King of Kings* (1926), produced and directed by Cecil B. DeMille. Most of the movies admired by serious critics have been created by producer-directors, but not all producer-directors have been critically admired. DeMille's pictures were so popular at the box office that his name was almost universally recognized by American moviegoers, especially for his Biblical spectacles, which combined generous dollops of sin, sex, and salvation—the latter usually in the final reel. Within the industry, he was thought to have the golden touch, at least by those who measured success in commercial rather than aesthetic terms. His huge grosses allowed him to remain independent for virtually his entire career, which began in 1913 and ended with his death in 1959. Except for his Jazz Age comedies, which are as likable as his spectacles are vulgar, DeMille's works have not prompted much critical attention except as triumphs of kitsch.

obscurity, others to free-lance successfully, a few into independent production. In the early 1950s, television supplanted movies as the country's leading mass medium, siphoning off most of the so-called family audience, which had been the mainstay of the industry during the studio era. Film attendance began to shrink precipitously. In 1946, the industry's peak year, ninety million Americans went to the movies each week—nearly 75 percent of the population. In 1955, this figure had dwindled to forty-six million. By 1973, only twenty million patrons attended weekly—about 10 percent of the population. Though still a big industry, movies have become a minority art, catering to a variety of specialized audiences, most of them young and educated.

Scholars and historians have noted other reasons for the waning of the studios. After World War II, American audiences began to develop more mature tastes in themes, but studio regulars were inclined to favor the romantic, sentimental, and escapist themes of the prewar cinema. MGM, the most prosperous studio since the early 1930s, began to lose touch with the audience's tastes, and except for its excellent musicals of the 1950s, the studio never regained its former eminence. Another factor contributing to the deterioration of the studios was the increasing tendency of filmmakers to shoot on location rather than in Hollywood.

Figure I.13. *Wild in the Streets* **(1968), with Christopher Jones, directed by Barry Shear, produced by American International Pictures.** After the advent of television, family audiences began to desert movie theatres. Those who remained loyal to the older medium were primarily young people. The youth films of the poststudio period tended to focus on conflicts between generations. The image of the American family—virtually unassailable in the American cinema of the prewar era—was denigrated and in some cases flagrantly attacked. *Wild in the Streets,* for example, deals with a rock singer who becomes President of the United States, lowers the voting age to fourteen, and incarcerates all citizens over thirty in concentration camps. The kids loved it.

The huge back lots and sound stages thus became white elephants, too expensive for the studios to maintain, especially during a period of rapidly escalating production costs. Eventually these facilities were sold or rented out, mostly to television production companies.

By the mid-1950s, most of the old moguls had been replaced by younger men, but it became increasingly apparent that the new era belonged to the independents. They were producing not only the best movies but also the lion's share of the box office hits as well. (Of course the two are by no means incompatible and never have been: Some of the greatest films of the American cinema are also its box office champions.) European movies were beginning to make sizable inroads into the

Figure I.14. Sidney Poitier and Tony Curtis in *The Defiant Ones* (1958), produced and directed by Stanley Kramer, released through United Artists. Spearheaded by such socially-conscious producer-directors as Kramer, filmmakers of the 1950s increasingly turned to social problems like racial prejudice for their materials. Poitier, the pre-eminent black star of the American cinema, was the first Negro player to rise to the top not as a singer, dancer, or comedian, but as a straight leading man. His goal was to play the kind of roles traditionally denied to black actors: doctor, teacher, psychiatrist, detective. As the Civil Rights Movement gained momentum in the 1960s, Poitier favored more militant roles which consciously reflected the frustrations and aspirations of black Americans: jazz musician, revolutionary, urban hustler. In the 1970s, he turned to producing and directing, and joined forces with Paul Newman, Barbra Streisand, Steve McQueen and Dustin Hoffman to form First Artists Presentations Company. Such comedies as *Uptown Saturday Night* (1974), *Let's Do It Again* (1975), and *A Piece of the Action* (1977)—which Poitier produced and directed as well as starred in—were popular with white and black audiences alike. Three studies of blacks in American movies are: Donald Bogle, *Toms, Coons, Mulattoes, Mammies, & Bucks* (New York: A Bantam Book, 1974); James Murray, *To Find an Image* (Indianapolis: The Bobbs-Merrill Company, 1973); and Thomas Cripps, *Slow Fade to Black* (New York: Oxford University Press, 1977).

American market, and the so-called art theatres catered primarily to these more sophisticated audiences. By the 1960s, the studios were producing only a few expensive "blockbuster" films, leaving the rest of the field to the independent producers, who often distributed their products through the majors. In the area of production, however, the heyday of the studios was clearly over.

Today, American movies are financed through a variety of methods. Many important stars and directors act as their own producers, assuming the financial risks in order to guarantee their artistic autonomy—somewhat in the manner of the founders of United Artists. Others employ a method favored by many important European directors, who relegate the financing and business details to professional producers. Artists can thus concentrate on artistic decisions. A number of independent producers are former agents, who secure their financing by presenting package deals to potential investors. Such packages often include the story property, the director, and one or more "bankable" stars, that is, proven box office magnets. Frequently these artists prefer a

Figure I.15 Melanie Mayron in *Girl Friends* (1978), directed by Claudia Weill, distributed by Warner Brothers. After the collapse of the studio system, a few fiction filmmakers, working primarily out of New York City, managed to break into the industry independently. Among those who entered the field in this manner was Claudia Weill, who began making short movies while still in college, generally on budgets of a few hundred dollars. Eventually she made several documentaries for PBS television. She received a $10,000 grant from the American Film Institute to make a short movie about two women artists, which eventually became the basis for the low-budget feature, *Girl Friends*. She managed to acquire other grants and loans in order to finish the movie—a process that took two years. For a discussion of the perils and joys of independent filmmaking, see William Bayer, *Breaking Through, Selling Out, Dropping Dead* (New York: Macmillan, 1971). See also Karyn Kay and Gerald Peary, eds., *Women and the Cinema* (New York: Dutton, 1977).

percentage of the net profits rather than a straight salary. There are also a few production companies, like AIP, that concentrate on low-budget films—the last vestige of the B tradition. Today the majors—Warner Brothers, Paramount, 20th Century-Fox, Columbia, UA, and Universal—are primarily distributing companies and film investment firms.

THE STAR SYSTEM

The star system isn't unique to the movies. Virtually all the performing arts—live theatre, television, opera, dance, concert music—have exploited the box office popularity of a charismatic performer. In America, the star system has been the backbone of the film industry since the mid-teens. Stars are the creations of the public, its reigning favorites. Their influence in the fields of fashion, politics, and public behavior has been enormous. They confer instant consequence to any film they appear in. Their fees have staggered the public. In the teens, Pickford and Chaplin were the two highest paid employees in the world. Contemporary stars like Robert Redford and Marlon Brando command salaries of $2 million plus per film, so popular are these box office giants. Some have reigned five decades: Henry Fonda, Bette Davis, and John Wayne, to name a few. Like the ancient gods and goddesses, stars have been adored, envied, and venerated as mythic and psychic icons.

Before 1910, actors' names were almost never included in movie credits, for producers feared the players would then demand higher salaries. But the public named their favorites anyway. Mary Pickford, for example, was first known by her character's name, Little Mary. From the beginning the public often fused a star's artistic persona with his or her private personality, and in Pickford's case, as with many others, the two were radically dissimilar.

Carl Laemmle, the diminutive and likable mogul who eventually ran Universal Studios, is credited with introducing the star system. In 1910 he staged one of his flamboyant publicity stunts by announcing that he had hired away the Biograph Girl, who was identified as Florence Lawrence. Adolph Zukor also contributed to the star craze. In 1911 he secured the distribution rights to the French movie, *Queen Elizabeth,* featuring the aging Sarah Bernhardt, the most famous stage star of her generation. With the profits from this film Zukor established the Famous Players Company in 1912, and he soon was able to hire some of the most prestigious stage stars of that era to perform before his cameras. But most of these actors were too old for the movies and too stagey in their techniques. Film-trained actors were younger, better looking, and more natural in their gestures. "In the cinema the actor must think and let his thoughts work upon his face. The objective nature of the medium will do the rest," wrote the French stage star, Charles Dullin. "A theatrical performance requires magnification, a cinema performance requires an inner life." Overwhelmingly, the best movie-trained players were able to convey this inner life. Stage-trained actors usually appeared hammy and insincere.

By the mid-teens, the desperate scramble for stars was on. Pro-

Figure I.16. **Mary Pickford in** *Little Annie Rooney* **(1925), produced by the Mary Pickford Corporation, released by United Artists.** Pickford was the most powerful woman in the American film industry of the silent era. "My career was planned," she insisted; "there was never anything accidental about it." In 1914 she was neck and neck with Chaplin in the star salaries sweepstakes. She commanded from $300,000 to $500,000 per picture between the years 1917 and 1919. After she went into independent production in 1919, she grossed as much as $1,200,000 per film. Reputedly she was the business brains behind United Artists. She also directed many of her own films, though never with official credit. Pickford specialized in playing waggish juveniles—bouncy, high-spirited, and sentimental, like the pubescent heroines of such popular hits as *Rebecca of Sunnybrook Farm* (1917) and *Pollyanna* (1920) in which her blonde curls were her trademark. By 1923, at the age of thirty, she was weary of playing wide-eyed innocents, and urged her fans to suggest possible new roles. The response: Cinderella, Heidi, Alice in Wonderland, ad nauseum. She was a prisoner of her public. In desperation, she defiantly cut off her curls in 1929—at the age of thirty-seven. Her new flapper's bob was her emancipation proclamation, but she appeared in only a few more films after that, and none of them was popular with the public. Her last movie was *Secrets* (1933). She retired from acting at the age of forty. See Mary Pickford (with Cameron Shipp), *Sunshine and Shadow* (New York: Doubleday, 1955).

ducers plundered each others' stables like bandits. Stars grew giddy with their sudden wealth and power. Intoxicated by the opulence of Hollywood's new royalty, the public was hungry to learn more of its favorites. Fan (short for fanatic) magazines sprang up by the dozens, and the burgeoning studios churned out a steady stream of publicity—most of it fabricated—to feed this insatiable curiosity. Fabulous legends circulated in the 1920s concerning the lavish parties and palaces of such celebrities as Pickford, Lloyd, DeMille, and a host of others. Paramount's rival queens, Gloria Swanson and Pola Negri, vied with each other in the extravagance of their life-styles. Both of them married many times, and each managed to snare at least one petty nobleman among her stable of rapt admirers. Swanson's contract stipulated that she could be seen only

Figure I.17.   Publicity photo of Theda Bara in *Cleopatra* (1917), produced by the Fox Film Corporation. Not to be outdone by Laemmle and Zukor, William Fox manufactured his own star, Theda Bara, in 1915. Her name was said to be an anagram of Arab Death. She gave birth to the term *vamp*—short for vampire. To audiences of this era, she was the incarnation of forbidden sexuality, insatiable in her lust, indifferent to the misery she inflicted on her adoring slaves. This first in a long line of sex queens was later found to be the former Theodosia Goodman, whose father was a tailor in Ohio.

in the most expensive designer clothes. "I have gone through a long apprenticeship," Swanson said. "I have gone through enough of being nobody. I have decided that when I am a star I will be every inch and every moment the star. Everyone from the studio gateman to the highest executive will know it." She boasted such yearly expenditures as $50,000 for gowns, $25,000 for furs, $10,000 for lingerie, and $9,000 for silk stockings.

Few of the stars of the silent cinema survived the transition to talkies. Most of them had risen to fame on the basis of their good looks, but after 1927 they were regarded, rather unfairly in some cases, as so many pretty faces. The problem wasn't just their voices. Sound made movies startlingly realistic, and the exaggerated gestures that silent

Figure I.18. Greta Garbo in *Anna Christie* (1929), directed by Clarence Brown, produced by MGM. The talkie revolution cut short the careers of many silent stars, especially those with heavy accents. Garbo was an exception. Her throaty, world-weary voice enhanced her allure, and her accent lent her an exotic aura. Like her famous face, her voice conveyed a sense of exhaustion, concealed suffering, and a noble stoicism. Sound made most players instantly more realistic, but Garbo's voice, tinged with regret and longing, made her even more mysterious and inaccessible. "Garbo Talks!" was the famous slogan used by the MGM Publicity Department to promote their film. She remained the preeminent *femme fatale* throughout the 1930s and made fourteen talkies before retiring into seclusion in 1942.

players had developed to compensate for their lack of voices now appeared florid and old-fashioned. Audiences laughed at their former deities.

The talkie stars came from the live theatre primarily. Such important newcomers as James Cagney, Bette Davis, Edward G. Robinson, Cary Grant, Katharine Hepburn, and James Stewart became popular in part because of their distinctive manner of speaking—the so-called "personality voices," as they were known in the trade. In their first years under studio contract, they were given maximum exposure. For example, Clark Gable appeared in fourteen movies in 1930, his first year at MGM. Each of his roles represented a different type, and the studio kept varying them until one clicked with the public.

The majors viewed their stars as valuable investments, as "properties." Promising neophytes served an apprenticeship as "starlets," a term reserved for females, though male newcomers were subjected to the same treatment. They were often assigned a new name; were taught how to talk, walk, and wear costumes; and frequently had their social schedules arranged by the publicity department to insure maximum press exposure. Suitable "romances" were arranged to fuel the columns of the four hundred and more reporters who covered the Hollywood beat during the studio era. A few zealous souls even agreed to marry a studio-selected spouse if such an alliance would further their careers. Of course there were always some who disdained such folly, generally the most self-respecting. For example, both Davis and Hepburn refused to pose for cheesecake photos, and they insisted that their private lives remain private.

Though stars were often exploited by the studios, there were some compensations. As a player's box office power increased, so did his or her demands. Top stars often had script approval stipulated in their contracts, as well as approval of director, producer, and co-star. Glamorous stars insisted upon their own cameramen, who knew how to conceal physical defects and enhance virtues. Many insisted upon their own clothes designers, hair stylists, and lavish dressing rooms. The biggest stars had movies especially tailored for them, thus guaranteeing maximum camera time, and in some cases even a specified number of closeups—the favored shot of the stars. And of course, they were paid enormous sums of money. In 1938, for example, there were over fifty stars who earned more than $100,000 a year. But the studios got much more. Shirley Temple made over $20 million for 20th Century-Fox in the late 1930s. Another juvenile, Deanna Durbin, saved Universal from bankruptcy during this same period. Furthermore, though there were a few important exceptions, movies without stars generally failed at the box office. Most serious stars used money and power to further their art, not just to gratify their vanity. Bette Davis was considered difficult during her stormy tenure at Warners because she insisted upon better scripts, more sensitive directors, and stronger co-stars (she was often paired with the serviceable George Brent as her leading man).

During the big studio era, most of the majors had a characteristic style, determined in part by the stars under contract. During the early 1930s, sophisticated Paramount could boast such polished players as

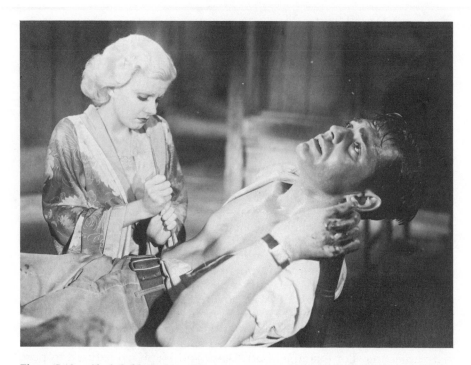

Figure I.19. Clark Gable and Jean Harlow in *Red Dust* (1932), directed by Victor Fleming, produced by MGM. "They were born to co-star!" proclaimed the studio's publicity blurbs about its two sexiest stars. Top stars attracted the loyalty of both men and women, though as sociologist Leo Handel pointed out, 65 percent of the fans preferred stars of their own sex. The studios received up to 32 million fan letters per year, 85 percent of them from young females. Major stars received about 3,000 letters per week, and the volume of their mail was regarded as an accurate barometer of their popularity. The studios spent as much as $2 million a year processing these letters, most of which asked for autographed photos. Box office appeal was also gauged by the number of fan clubs devoted to a star. By 1934 there were already 535 of these clubs, with a total membership of over 750,000. During this period, the stars with the greatest number of fan clubs were Gable, Harlow, and Joan Crawford—all of them under contract to MGM, "The Home of the Stars." Gable alone had 70 clubs, which partly accounted for his supremacy as the top male star of the 1930s.

Claudette Colbert, Marlene Dietrich, Carole Lombard, Frederic March, and Cary Grant, who eventually became the finest light comedian of the big studio period. Warners was a male-dominated studio, with an emphasis on fast-moving urban melodramas. Many of their stars were the famous tough guys: Edward G. Robinson, James Cagney, Paul Muni, and Humphrey Bogart. At MGM, both Mayer and Thalberg preferred glamorous female stars, Mayer because he could bully most of them, Thalberg because he had a romantic sensibility—so romantic, in fact, that F. Scott Fitzgerald used him as a model for the wistful hero of Fitzgerald's Hollywood novel, *The Last Tycoon*.

After the 1950s, stars could no longer count on the studios to mold their careers. Marilyn Monroe at 20th Century-Fox was perhaps the last to benefit from—or endure—the buildup techniques developed by the

Figure I.20. Katharine Hepburn in *Long Day's Journey Into Night* (1962), with Jason Robards and Ralph Richardson, directed by Sidney Lumet, based on the play by Eugene O'Neill, an Embassy Pictures Release. Hepburn was considered "difficult" by her studio bosses for much of her career. Like her greatest rival, Bette Davis, who was less fortunate in her rebellion, Hepburn refused to act in dumb, demeaning roles—but she got away with it. Occasionally she bought a property with her own money to guarantee her artistic independence. As a free lance, she has accepted minimum-scale salaries and even deferred payment of her fees in order to act in established classics, like O'Neill's masterpiece. A star for nearly five decades, she has been nominated for Academy Awards twelve times and has won four. See Charles Higham, *Kate* (New York: Signet Books, 1975).

majors. After nearly a quarter of a century, Gable left the security of MGM in 1954, but he never regained his former eminence. The great prewar icons were fading, and such new stars as Marlon Brando, James Dean, and Montgomery Clift openly sneered at the Hollywood studio system, making even such long-time rebels as Bogart look docile by comparison. Acting in movies was no longer considered second best to the live theatre, and besides, many of the new stars had conquered both. Glamor was increasingly considered old-fashioned and tinselly. During the 1960s even such strikingly attractive stars as Elizabeth Taylor and Paul Newman coarsened their images to demonstrate their considerable talent as actors. After 1970, few of the top stars were conventionally glamorous, and many of them were first-rate actors pursuing distinguished careers. Such stars as Dustin Hoffman, Al Pacino, and Jane Fonda are among the most respected performers in the world.

From the beginning, stars were commonly classified into character types: virgins, vamps, romantic leading men, swashbucklers, flappers,

Figure I.21. A twenty-fifth anniversary photo of "The MGM Family," 1949. No other studio could match MGM's enormous stable of contract players, which included over eighty stars and character actors. The motto of the studio was "More Stars than there are in Heaven." (Later this was amended to "More Stars than in the Heavens"—apparently for fear of offending God.) Front row: Lassie, Arlene Dahl, James Craig, Spring Byington, Ethel Barrymore, Mary Astor, Edward Arnold, Fred Astaire, Leon Ames, June Allyson, Lionel Barrymore. Second row: Van Heflin, Kathryn Grayson, Edmund Gwenn, Betty Garrett, Judy Garland, Ava Gardner, Clark Gable, Errol Flynn, Vera Ellen, Jimmy Durante, Tom Drake, Gloria DeHaven. Third row: Janet Leigh, Mario Lanza, Angela Lansbury, Christian Kent, Gene Kelly, Howard Keel, Louis Jourdan, Jennifer Jones, Van Johnson, Claude Jarman, Jr., John Hodiak, Katharine Hepburn. Fourth row: Red Skelton, Frank Sinatra, Ginger Rogers, Jane Powell, Walter Pidgeon, Reginald Owen, George Murphy, Jules Munshin, Ricardo Montalban, Ann Miller, Jeanette MacDonald, Peter Lawford. Top row: Kennan Wynn, Esther Williams, Spencer Tracy, Audrey Totter, Robert Taylor, Clinton Sundberg, Lewis Stone, Dean Stockwell, J. Carrol Naish, Ann Sothern, Alexis Smith. Not included in this photo are such important MGM contract players as Cyd Charisse, Greer Garson, Lena Horne, Deborah Kerr, Margaret O'Brien, William Powell, James Stewart, Elizabeth Taylor, and Lana Turner. See James Robert Parish and Ronald L. Bowers, *The MGM Stock Company: The Golden Era* (New York: Bonanza Books, 1972).

and so on. At Mack Sennett's Keystone Studio, the leading clowns were classified by physical type—fat, tall, skinny, cross-eyed, and so forth. Over the years, a vast repertory of types evolved: the Latin lover, the he-man, the heiress, the good bad girl, the cynical reporter, the career girl, and many others. Of course all great stars are unique, even though they might fall under a well-known category. For example, the cheap blonde has long been one of America's favorite types, but such important stars as Mae West, Jean Harlow, and Marilyn Monroe are highly distinctive as individuals. A successful type was always imitated. In the mid-1920s, for example, the Swedish import Greta Garbo supplanted such passé vamps as Bara and Negri in favor of a more sophisticated and complex type, the *femme fatale*. Garbo inspired many imitations, including such important stars as Marlene Dietrich and Carole Lombard, who

Figure I.22. Paul Newman and Robert Redford in *Butch Cassidy and the Sundance Kid* (1969), directed by George Roy Hill, released by 20th Century-Fox. Good looks and sex appeal are the most conspicuous characteristics of most stars, both male and female. Especially at the beginning of their careers, stars generally allow themselves to be exploited as sex objects, for eroticism has always been a compelling aphrodisiac at the box office. Newman and Redford both began as conventional pretty boys, and for some years they weren't allowed to break out of this mold, the assumption being, apparently, that such striking men couldn't possibly be talented actors as well. Once they were able to take charge of their careers, both expanded their range considerably—as occasional producers and directors as well as actors.

were first touted as "Garbo types," only with a sense of humor. In the 1950s Sidney Poitier became the first black star to attract a wide following outside of his own race. In later years a number of other black performers attained stardom in part because Poitier had established the precedent. He was one of the great originals and hence worthy of imitation.

Stars commonly refuse all parts that go against their type, especially if they're leading men or leading ladies. Performers like Barbra Streisand would never play cruel or psychopathic roles, for example, because such parts would conflict with her sympathetic image. If a star is locked into his or her type, any significant departure can result in box office disaster. For example, when Pickford tried to abandon her little girl roles in the 1920s, her public stayed at home: They wanted to see Little Mary or nothing. Similarly, when such nice guy types as Gregory Peck attempt roles outside the standard leading man range, the response is usually lukewarm or even hostile.

Many top stars stay on top by being themselves, by not trying to

Figure I.23. Publicity photo of Rudolph Valentino and ravishee in *Son of the Shiek* (1926), released by United Artists. No other Latin lover type could equal the popularity of the original, Valentino. His eroticism was almost as flagrant as Bara's, stimulating the fantasies of an enraptured following of women, who were enjoying the cinematic fruits of the sexual revolution of the Jazz Age. Though he was not much of an actor, Valentino's brilliantined beauty became an icon of his era. He moved gracefully and wore clothes well. He also had a sleek, androgynous body, which was displayed to maximum advantage. His career as a star lasted only from 1921 to 1926, when he died at the age of thirty-one of peritonitis. At his funeral, thousands of women vented their grief hysterically; it was one of the gaudier spectacles of a gaudy age. Reputedly, men considered Valentino's sexuality too exotic and "feminine." Most subsequent male sex symbols, like Clark Gable, emphasized a more conventional, macho form of virility, avoiding even a hint of sexual ambiguity. Interestingly, both Valentino and Gable were personally insecure and had their careers molded for them by forceful older women.

impersonate anyone. Gable insisted that all he did in front of the camera was to "act natural." Gary Cooper's sincerity and homespun decency attracted audiences for over three decades, and the persona he projected on the screen was virtually identical with his actual personality. Similarly, Marilyn Monroe was always at her best when she played roles that exploited her indecisiveness, her vulnerability, and her pathetic eagerness to please. Such contemporary charmers as Woody Allen and Burt Reynolds are never so attractive as when they play variations of their own personalities. Critics sometimes refer to this type of player as a personality-star.

On the other hand, there have been many stars who refuse to be

Figure I.24. Publicity photo of Elizabeth Taylor in *Cat on a Hot Tin Roof* (1958), directed by Richard Brooks, adapted by Brooks and James Poe from the play by Tennessee Williams. The public's affection for its favorites has often been based on personality rather than artistry, though the two aren't necessarily exclusive. Despite the fact that Taylor made only a handful of good movies, she remained among the top ten box office attractions from 1958 to 1970. Throughout her adult life, her many romances and marriages were constantly in the headlines. She was also the most classically beautiful sex queen since the heyday of Garbo, and considerably more earthy in her eroticism. She never took her acting very seriously during her MGM years (1943–1960), where her scripts—and her performances—were generally mediocre. One of her finest performances, however, was in *Cat*, which was MGM's top-grossing film in 1958 and established her as an accomplished actress.

typed and deliberately attempt the widest array of roles possible. Such actor-stars as Davis, Hepburn, Brando, and De Niro have sometimes undertaken unpleasant character roles rather than conventional leads in order to expand their range, for variety and breadth have traditionally been the yardsticks by which great acting is measured. Many stars consider the live theatre technically challenging, and they've suffered considerable financial sacrifice in order to act in both mediums. Stars like Orson Welles have worked successfully in four performing mediums—radio, stage, movies, and television.

The distinction between a professional actor and a star is not based on technical skill but on mass popularity. By definition, a star must have enormous personal magnetism, a riveting quality which commands our attention. Few public personalities have inspired such deep and widespread affection as the great movie stars. Some are adored because they're fun-loving and generous: The doings of "Doug and Mary at Pickfair" were as fascinating to audiences in the 1920s as those of "Liz and Richard" four decades later. Some stars are loved because they embody such traditional American values as plain speaking, integrity, and idealism: Jimmy Stewart and Henry Fonda are examples of this type. Others are identified with antiestablishment images, and include such celebrated loners as Bogie, Clint Eastwood, and Jack Nicholson.

Figure I.25. Al Pacino in *Dog Day Afternoon* (1975), directed by Sidney Lumet, released by Warner Brothers. Some stars are so winning in their charm that they can stretch the public's tolerance far beyond its conventional parameters, forcing viewers to reevaluate their prejudices. In this movie, for example, Pacino plays a childishly inept bank robber who is also a homosexual. Few male stars would have risked alienating their public by attempting such a role, but like most serious artists, Pacino thrives on risks. *Dog Day Afternoon* was a huge box office success.

Players like Cary Grant and Carole Lombard are so captivating in their charm that they're fun to watch in almost anything. And of course many of them are spectacularly good-looking: Names like Garbo and Redford are virtually synonymous with godlike beauty.

Sophisticated filmmakers exploit the public's affection for its stars by creating ambiguous tensions between a role as written, as acted, and

Figure I.26. Humphrey Bogart and Ingrid Bergman in *Casablanca* (1943), directed by Michael Curtiz, produced by Warner Brothers. Bogie is one of the most universally recognized icons of American culture. His persona evolved slowly and incorporated elements from his actual personality as well as his screen performances. In his early years at Warners, he was repeatedly typecast as a gangster—tough, cynical, antisocial. His persona became more humanized and sympathetic in the early 1940s, though his shadowy association with violence was never abandoned, and he remained more of an antihero than a conventional leading man. A loner, Bogie seldom got the girl in his films, nor was he swayed by the opinions of others. He followed a private code of honor rather than the dictates of social convention. Above all, he was his own man—cool, sardonic, contemptuous of all forms of hypocrisy. In private life he was outspoken and refused to allow others to define his nature. He loved to needle authority figures. *Casablanca* is perhaps his most popular movie, because his performance synthesized the associations of his earlier roles and also revealed a more tender sensibility and heroic stoicism. Beneath the tough exterior lurked a melancholy, vulnerable idealist, capable of the ultimate romantic gesture—self denial. He has inspired such diverse artists as Woody Allen and Jean-Luc Godard, who paid homage to him in *Play It Again Sam* and *Breathless*. *Casablanca* was produced during the darkest days of World War II, when Americans were being called upon to make personal sacrifices for a higher cause. One critic has suggested that the movie is not a portrait of the way we were, but of the way we wanted to be.

directed. "Whenever the hero isn't portrayed by a star the whole picture suffers," Alfred Hitchcock observed. "Audiences are far less concerned about the predicament of a character who's played by someone they don't know." When a filmmaker selects a star rather than a conventional actor to play a role, much of the characterization is fixed by the casting; but what he and the star then choose to add to the written role is what constitutes its full dramatic meaning. Some directors have capitalized on the star system with great artistic effectiveness, particularly studio-nurtured filmmakers like Capra, Hawks, and Huston. The most perceptive film critics and commentators on the American cinema have also been exceptionally sensitive to the complexities of the star system.

Perhaps the ultimate glory for a star is to become an icon in American popular mythology. Like the gods and goddesses of ancient times, some stars are so universally known that merely one name is enough to evoke an entire complex of symbolic associations—like *Marilyn* for example. Unlike the conventional actor (however gifted) the star automatically suggests ideas and emotions that are deeply embedded in his or her persona. These undertones are determined not only by the star's previous roles but often by his or her actual personality as well. Naturally, over the course of many years this symbolic information can begin to drain from public consciousness, but the iconography of a great star like Gary Cooper becomes part of a shared experience. As the French critic Edgar Morin has pointed out, when Cooper played a character, he automatically "garycooperized" it, infusing himself into the role and the role into himself. Since audiences felt a deep sense of identification with Coop and the values he symbolized, in a sense they were celebrating themselves—or at least their spiritual selves. The great originals are cultural archetypes, and their box office popularity is an index of their success in synthesizing the aspirations and anxieties of an era. As a number of cultural studies have shown, the iconography of a star can involve communal myths and symbols of considerable complexity and emotional richness.

STORIES

With surprisingly few exceptions, the best American movie artists have been excellent storytellers. In fact, even modestly talented filmmakers have at least mastered the craft—if not the art—of narrative action. Stories are seductive, and many viewers have known the experience of getting hooked on an otherwise banal picture because they want to see how it turns out. Elements such as character, theme, and mood are all subsumed within the story line—the structural spine of virtually all American movies. Seldom does the narrative drift, or the pace of the action slacken. Dull stretches are edited out. Characters are almost invariably doers rather than thinkers or dreamers, and what they do constitutes the story. American movies *move*. Within the first few minutes we're presented with a clearcut conflict that's intensified according to classical conventions of dramaturgy: the introduction of a protagonist

Figure I.27. Stan Laurel and Oliver Hardy in _Brats_ (1930), story by Leo McCarey and Hal Roach, dialogue by H. M. Walker, directed by James Parrott. The soul of silent comedy was improvization: The story was simply a container. Once provided with a narrative premise, Laurel and Hardy embroidered on their basic situation until its comic possibilities were exhausted. They were among the few silent clowns to cross the talkie barrier, and in fact, are respected as masters of both mediums, for they used dialogue only for punctuation. They were a team from 1926 to 1955, though their golden age was roughly 1927 to 1937. Laurel was the creative force behind the team and invented most of the gags. Astonishingly, the modest Oliver Hardy always regarded himself as a straight man rather than a great comedian in his own right. The personas they evolved were sunny, warm, and endearing. "We were dignified but dumb," Laurel said. "I haven't a lick of common sense, and Ollie is just as dumb, but he _thinks_ he's smarter." They are the most innocent of the talkie clowns. Like children, they renew their harmless schemes against a hostile society with hope undeterred. In _Brats_ they even play their own children. Usually they're affectionate with one another, but boys will be boys, and they do have their occasional tiffs. Ollie, fussy, dainty, self-important, the insufferable know-it-all, often gets impatient with the eternally vacuous Stan. Their comedies are filled with rituals of revenge and slow escalations of hostility, snowballing finally into total mass destruction—a story formula they employed many times with brilliant results. See John McCabe, _Mr. Laurel and Mr. Hardy_ (New York: Signet Books, 1968); Charles Barr, _Laurel & Hardy_ (Berkeley: University of California Press, 1968).

versus an antagonist, a progressive escalation of their conflict, and a climactic clash leading to a resolution.

Since the publication in 1835 of Alexis de Tocqueville's _Democracy in America,_ the French have been among the most perceptive commentators on American culture, perhaps because it's so radically different from their own. In striking contrast to the American cultural establishment, French enthusiasm for American movies sometimes bordered on idolatry, especially after World War II. Influential critics like François Truffaut, Jean-Luc Godard, and Claude Chabrol were awed by the narrative vitality of the American cinema, and when they became filmmakers themselves, they imitated American models. Interestingly (and perhaps inevitably) they drifted away from action in favor of character delineation, atmosphere, and the exploration of ideas—essentially static elements. "If you want to say something," Godard once remarked of his movies, "there is only one solution: say it." An American filmmaker would have said "show it."

The earliest American movies centered on such nonnarrative subjects as sporting events, vaudeville acts, and public ceremonies. Shortly after 1900, the first story films made their appearance in the United States. Most of these short works were innocent comedies and didactic allegories of good versus evil. The range of characters included a few basic types, most of them borrowed from the live theatre of that era: the boy, the girl, the villain, the mother, and a handful of others. Eventually three genres became especially popular: slapstick comedies, westerns, and melodramas. Fantasy elements played an important role in these movies, and the happy ending was almost invariable. Many of them centered on such rags-to-riches myths as the Horatio Alger story and its feminine counterpart, the Cinderella story. Almost all of these movies were violent, grossly sentimental, and aesthetically crude.

Eventually more gifted artists filtered into the industry, and by the mid-teens, stories had become more sophisticated, characters more fully rounded. The range of dramatic materials was radically expanded, thanks largely to D. W. Griffith. Filmmakers learned to sharpen the narrative thrust of their movies by focusing almost exclusively on goal-oriented characters in a hurry to succeed. American movies generally open with an implied dramatic question: how will the protagonist get what he or she wants in the face of considerable opposition? These dramaturgical conventions are used in the best as well as the worst American films.

For example, in Orson Welles's *Citizen Kane* (which many critics regard as the greatest movie of all time), the story materials are innately rambling and unfocused. The film traces the life of Charles Foster Kane from the time he was a young boy until shortly after his death as an old man. In order to give these materials a narrative urgency, Welles and his coscenarist Herman Mankiewicz scrambled the chronology of events and introduced a note of suspense. At his death, Kane utters the word *Rosebud.* No one seems to know what it means, and its significance piques the curiosity of a newspaper reporter who spends the remainder of the movie questioning Kane's former associates about this mystery. Only at the end of the movie do we finally learn its significance, though we also discover that it's merely one piece of an infinitely complex jigsaw puzzle. Welles claimed that the Rosebud motif was merely a plot gimmick, intended to hook the audience on a dramatic question that's really a red herring. But the gimmick works. Like the hopeful reporter, we too think that Rosebud will provide us with a key to Kane's ambiguous and contradictory personality. Without this gimmick, the story would have re-

Figure I.28. Publicity photo of Henry Fonda and Barbara Stanwyck in *The Lady Eve* (1941), written and directed by Preston Sturges. Sturges began his career as a writer at Paramount, and like many scenarists, he complained bitterly that the studio's directors were ruining his work. By 1940 he was among the industry's top writers, powerful enough to insist on directing his own screenplays. From 1940 to 1945 he wrote and directed a string of hits, mostly screwball comedies. Sturges' success as a writer-director inspired other scenarists to take over the direction of their scripts, most notably John Huston, Joseph Mankiewicz, and Billy Wilder. See James Ursini, *Preston Sturges: An American Dreamer* (New York: Curtis Books, 1973).

mained sprawling and far less urgent. This is what the French mean by the American genius for storytelling.

In the earliest years of the silent cinema, filmmakers seldom worked from scripts, preferring to improvise around the sketchiest of story outlines, which they often carried in their heads. With the introduction of the studio system, the producer usually insisted that stories be outlined in greater detail, for in this way he could guarantee the box office appeal of the narrative elements before the director began the actual filming. Eventually the construction of the story line was taken over by the producer and his hired scenarists, and the director was relegated to matters of execution. Even in the silent period, multiple authorship of scenarios was common. Under the studio system, it was almost invariable. Scripts were assembled rather than written, the collaboration of producers, directors, stars, and writers. Specialists were called in to doctor specific narrative ailments. Some of these writers were

Figure I.29.   Bette Davis in *All About Eve* (1950), with Marilyn Monroe and George Sanders, written and directed by Joseph L. Mankiewicz, produced by 20th Century-Fox. Mankiewicz is one of the most literary of filmmakers. "Old Joe, the Talk Man," as one critic fondly described him, is above all a *verbal* stylist, a master of sophisticated dialogue and repartee. He is conservative in his use of the camera, which is placed at the disposal of talking actors, who are usually seen up close. *All About Eve,* one of the best-written movies of the American cinema, is a witty commentary on the mores and manners of its theatrical milieu. See *More About All About Eve* (New York: Bantam, 1974), which contains Mankiewicz's script to the movie and a lengthy interview. See also Kenneth L. Geist, *Pictures Will Talk: The Life and Films of Joseph L. Mankiewicz* (New York: Scribner's, 1978).

Figure I.30. Marlene Dietrich in *Blonde Venus* (1932), directed by Josef von Sternberg, produced by Paramount Pictures. When asked what value he placed on his stories, Sternberg replied that narrative was of "no importance whatsoever" to him. Mise-en-scène was his obsessive concern. Unlike most American filmmakers, he actually deemphasized action in order to create a dreamlike atmosphere of rich textures, suggestive camera movements, and evocative lights and shadows. He abhorred everything "natural" and pursued a goal of art-for-art's-sake. He was concerned not with authenticity but with visual lyricism: "There is nothing authentic about my pictures," he boasted. When asked why he preferred the studio to actual locations, he said, "Because I am a poet." He made seven movies with Dietrich in the 1930s, mostly at Paramount, mostly at her behest. Her screen character is revealed not by what she says or does so much as by how she's photographed. "Everything I have to say about Miss Dietrich I have said with the camera," he replied when asked about his famous protégée. See Josef von Sternberg, *Fun in a Chinese Laundry: An Autobiography* (New York: Collier Books, 1965). Three critical studies of his works are Andrew Sarris, *The Films of Josef von Sternberg* (New York: Museum of Modern Art, 1966); Herman G. Weinberg, *Josef von Sternberg* (New York: Dutton, 1967); and John Baxter, *The Cinema of Josef von Sternberg* (Cranbury, N.J.: A. S. Barnes, 1971).

idea people, others genre experts, dialogue writers, plot carpenters, comic relief specialists, and so on.

Producer-directors often scoffed at this assembly-line method of scriptwriting, for they believed that a story ought to be dominated by a single personality—the storyteller's. But the issue is more complex. In the first place, even the greatest filmmakers sometimes rely on the assistance of writers to elaborate their story ideas—Fellini, Kurosawa, Truffaut, to name a few. Others insist that the effectiveness of a movie depends on the way the story is told, not on the subject matter per se, which can be quite simple. Critics like Andrew Sarris have pointed out that movie scripts seldom are interesting reading precisely because they're mere blueprints of the finished product. Even studio-employed directors controlled the staging of the action and the placement of the camera, and according to Sarris these two factors (constituting the mise-en-scène) are the crucial artistic elements in most movies:

> The choice between a close-up and a long-shot, for example, may quite often transcend the plot. If the story of Little Red Riding Hood is told with the Wolf in close-up and Little Red Riding Hood in long shot, the director is concerned primarily with the emotional problems of a wolf with a compulsion to eat little girls. If Little Red Riding Hood is in close-up and the Wolf in long shot, the emphasis is shifted to the emotional problems of vestigial virginity in a wicked world. Thus, two different stories are being told with the same basic anecdotal material. What is at stake in the two versions of Little Red Riding Hood are two contrasting directorial attitudes toward life. One director identifies more with the Wolf—the male, the compulsive, the corrupted, even evil itself. The second director identifies with the little girl—the innocence, the illusion, the ideal and hope of the race. Needless to say, few critics bother to make any distinction, proving perhaps that direction as creation is still only dimly understood. ["The Fall and Rise of the Film Director," in *Interviews with Film Directors* (New York: Avon Books, 1967)].

But of course a director must have a fighting chance. As critic Pauline Kael has pointed out, when a gifted filmmaker is strapped with trashy materials, untalented stars, philistine producers, or various combinations of these, all he can hope for is to make an entertaining bad movie.

During the big studio era, each of the majors had a story editor who headed the story department. His or her job was to scout potential properties for movies—mostly novels, plays, short stories, and magazine articles. During this period, literary properties were generally more prestigious than original screenplays because a novel or a stage drama was thought to have a presold audience. The most popular stories by far dealt with American life. For example, 481 of the 574 features produced in 1938 and 1939 were set in the United States. Literary sources were generally loosely adapted and made to conform to box office realities and the talent available to the producer.

The assembly-line method was employed with a vengeance in the construction of studio screenplays. During the script conference, the producer (and sometimes the director and stars, depending on their power) outlined what the principal emphasis of the story should be. A studio scribe then worked out a first draft. This was duly criticized and sent back for revision, often to another writer, and then to another, and so on. Action and plot generally took precedence over all, even at the expense of character consistency and probability. After the rough draft was completed, additional writers were instructed to sharpen the dialogue, speed up the story, add comic relief, and provide a host of other finishing touches.

Little wonder that studio writers enjoyed scant fame in the world of *belles lettres*. Many thought of themselves as whores, hired hacks who wrote to order. Anthropologist Powdermaker observed that writers were

Figure I.31. Richard Dreyfuss and Marsha Mason in *The Goodbye Girl* (1977), written by Neil Simon, directed by Herbert Ross, released by Warner Brothers. Simon's name has usually been the main box office attraction in the movies he's been associated with. For example, this film was publicized as "Neil Simon's *The Goodbye Girl,*" and like virtually all his other works, was considered "a writer's film" not only by most critics but also by much of the public. Only a relative handful of American movies have been dominated by writers, and those few have been produced primarily in the postwar era.

the least powerful and least respected group in Hollywood. They were also the best educated: Over 80 percent of them had college degrees. Torn by conflicting desires of greed and literary ambition, writers took masochistic delight in mocking themselves. A famous writer's lament has been attributed to a number of Hollywood wits: "They ruin your stories. They massacre your ideas. They prostitute your art. They trample on your pride. And what do you get for it? A fortune."

The most successful writers were seldom such distinguished novelists as Fitzgerald and Nathanael West, who both failed as scenarists, but people who had previously been salaried writers in such areas as journalism, advertising, and public relations. Writers from the live theatre tended to be too talky. Those who had been novelists were inclined toward beautifully phrased descriptive passages and interior motivations, but they often lacked a sense of action. Within the industry, writers were widely regarded as highbrows, with little or no sensitivity to the demands of the box office. They in turn complained that their scripts were vulgarized by trite formulas. With rare exceptions, studio scribes weren't even allowed on the set while the director was filming the script.

Figure I.32. Woody Allen and Diane Keaton in _Annie Hall_ (1977), written (with Marshall Brickman) and directed by Woody Allen, released by United Artists. Allen is a great favorite with literary intellectuals, and his humorous essays have been published by such prestigious literary magazines as _The New Yorker_. Much of his work has been autobiographical and is steeped in New York Jewish humor, which became a dominant comic mode in the American cinema after the late 1960s. It's a self-lacerating type of comedy, emphasizing guilt, neurosis, and ethnic stereotypes. Allen's screen characters are generally anti-intellectual intellectuals—skeptical, ironic, and paralyzed with indecision. Beneath the comic masochism and self-mockery is a substratum of anxiety and alienation. His themes characteristically revolve around moral and philosophical ideas, though they are treated from an ironic perspective. "I took all the abstract philosophy courses in college," he once mused, "like Truth and Beauty and Advanced Truth and Beauty, and Intermediate Truth, Introduction to God, Death 101." See Eric Lax, _On Being Funny: Woody Allen & Comedy_ (New York: Manor Books, 1977); and Bill Adler and Jeffrey Feinman, _Woody Allen: Clown Prince of American Humor_ (New York: Pinnacle Books, 1975). Allen's humorous essays are collected in _Getting Even_ (New York: Warner Books, 1972), and _Without Feathers_ (New York: Warner Books, 1976).

Some of the best Hollywood writers eventually became directors to protect their scripts, especially after the success of writer-director Preston Sturges. Other important scenarists produced much of their finest work collaborating with producer-directors, who were usually more receptive to fresh story ideas. They were also more likely to prefer the writer to remain on the set in case of last-minute adjustments in the script. A number of scenarists frequently teamed with prestigious directors: Robert Riskin with Capra, Ben Hecht with Hawks and Hitchcock, Dudley Nichols and Frank Nugent with Ford.

American movies commonly fall into well-known story types—genres. In fact, sociologist Leo Handel pointed out that genre was second only to stars in box office appeal. Genres are distinguished by a characteristic set of conventions in style, values, and subject matter. Many of these conventions can be artificial and stylized. For example, musicals require the audience to accept song and dance as the major means of artistic expression, much like the opera and ballet. Genre is also a method of organizing and focusing the story materials. Virtually all westerns, for instance, deal with a specific era of American history—the western frontier of the late nineteenth century. The stylized conventions and archetypal story patterns of genres encourage viewers to participate ritualistically in the basic beliefs, fears, and anxieties of their culture.

The major shortcoming of genre pictures, of course, is that they're easy to imitate and have been debased by stale mechanical repetition. Genre conventions are mere clichés unless they're united with significant innovations in style or content. But this is true of all the arts, not just movies. As Aristotle notes in *The Poetics,* genres are qualitatively neutral: The conventions of classical tragedy are basically the same whether they're employed by a genius or a forgotten hack. Certain genres enjoy more cultural prestige because they've attracted the most gifted artists. Genres that haven't are widely regarded as innately inartistic, but in many cases their déclassé status is caused by neglect rather than an intrinsic inferiority. For example, the earliest film critics considered slapstick comedy an infantile genre—until such important comic artists as Chaplin and Keaton entered the field. Today, no critic would malign the genre, for it boasts a considerable number of masterpieces.

The most critically admired genre films strike a balance between the form's preestablished conventions and the artist's unique contributions. The artists of ancient Greece drew upon a common body of mythology, and no one thought it strange when dramatists and poets returned to these tales again and again. Incompetent artists merely repeat. Serious artists reinterpret. By exploiting the broad outlines of a well-known tale or story type, the storyteller can play off its main features, creating provocative tensions between the genre's conventions and the artist's inventions, between the familiar and the original, the general and the particular. Myths embody the common ideals and aspirations of a civilization, and by returning to these communal tales, the artist becomes, in a sense, a psychic explorer, bridging the chasm between the known and the unknown.

Moviemakers are attracted to genres for the same reason they're attracted to stars: A genre automatically synthesizes a vast amount of iconographical information, freeing the filmmaker to explore more personal concerns. A nongeneric movie must be more self-contained. The artist is forced to communicate virtually all the major ideas and emotions within the work itself—a task that preempts much of his screen time. On the other hand, the genre artist never starts from scratch. He can build upon the accomplishments of his predecessors, enriching their ideas or calling them into question, depending upon his inclinations.

The most enduring genres tend to adapt to changing social conditions. Most of them begin as naive allegories of good versus evil. Over the years they become more complex in both form and thematic range.

Figure I.33.   Publicity photo of Bette Davis in *Dark Victory* (1939), directed by Edmund Goulding, produced by Warner Brothers. Genres specialize in certain types of dramatic situations. The so-called woman's picture, for example, is usually strongly emotional in emphasis and centers on a top female star. Also known as *weepies,* these movies often feature scenes of thrilling self-sacrifice, separations, and tearful reconciliations. In this movie Davis plays a headstrong heiress who is dying of brain cancer. The production values in women's pictures tend to be glossy, the costumes chic and numerous. The woman's picture seldom explores the male psyche in much detail. For the most part, men are conventionalized and kept at the fringes, the unworthy but grateful recipients of a woman's gift of love. (Action movies, the masculine counterpart of the woman's picture, tend to conventionalize women in much the same manner.) A 1943 industry survey confirmed

Finally they veer into an ironic mode, mocking many of the genre's original values and conventions. Some critics claim that this evolution is inevitable and doesn't necessarily represent an aesthetic improvement. Genres at the beginning of their development tend to be simple, direct, and powerful in their emotional impact. A genre in its intermediate stage is often said to embody such classical ideals as balance, richness, and poise. In its ironic phase, the same genre is often self-conscious, stylistically nuanced, and more intellectual in its appeal. For example, the western's naive phase is exemplified by Edwin S. Porter's *The Great Train Robbery* (1903). Its classical phase could be typified by John Ford's *Stagecoach* (1939). A transitional western like Fred Zinnemann's *High Noon* (1952) features many ironic elements, though it's still essentially in the heroic mold. Arthur Penn's *Little Big Man* (1970) is virtually a parody of the genre. A number of cultural theorists insist that questions of individual value in a genre's evolution are largely matters of taste and fashion.

Some of the most suggestive critical studies have explored the relationship of a genre to the society that nurtured it. The very success of Hollywood, according to Leo Rosten, was in the skill with which it reflected the assumptions, the fallacies, and the aspirations of an entire culture. This sociopsychic approach was pioneered by the French literary critic Hippolyte Taine in the nineteenth century. Taine claimed that the social and intellectual anxieties of a given era and nation will find expression in its art. The implicit function of an artist is to harmonize and reconcile cultural clashes of value. He believed that art must be analyzed both for its overt and its covert meaning, that beneath its explicit content there exists a vast reservoir of latent social and psychic information. In the area of film, for example, genre critics have pointed out how gangster movies are often vehicles for exploring rebellion myths and are especially popular during periods of social breakdown.

The ideas of Sigmund Freud and Carl Jung have also influenced many genre theorists. Like Taine, both psychiatrists believed that art is a reflection of underlying structures of meaning, that it satisfies certain subconscious needs in both the artist and his audience. For Freud, art was a form of daydreaming and wish-fulfillment, vicariously resolving urgent impulses and desires that can't be satisfied in reality. Pornographic films are perhaps the most obvious example of how anxieties can be assuaged in this indirect manner, and in fact Freud believed that most neuroses were sexually based. He thought that art was a by-product of neurosis, though essentially a socially beneficial one. Like neurosis, art is characterized by a repetition compulsion, the need to go over the same stories and rituals in order to reinact and temporarily resolve certain psychic conflicts, which are rooted in childhood traumas.

---

many sexual stereotypes about story preferences. Females overwhelmingly preferred such genres as women's pictures, love stories, and serious dramas. Males were more attracted to war movies, westerns, and gangster films. Both sexes enjoyed comedies and musicals. However, the poll also showed that the particular movie rather than the genre alone is what excited the audience's interest. See Bette Davis, *The Lonely Life* (New York: Putnam's, 1962).

Figure I.34. Publicity photo of Sissy Spacek in *Carrie* (1976), directed by Brian De Palma, released by United Artists. Ritual plays an important role in genre films, channeling communal impulses into a prescribed symbolic form. Artistic rituals are often tied to supernatural beliefs: Classical tragedy, for example, evolved from religious ceremonies, as did the communal drama of medieval Europe. *Carrie* is a horror movie that exploits the concept of ritual in a number of ways. The film deals with a rite of passage, emphasizing social, sexual, and religious ideas which are all associated with the motif of blood. The young heroine undergoes the passage from girlhood to womanhood, and her transformation is heralded with the beginning of her menstrual cycle—a terrifying experience for her. There are also ceremonies revolving around high school rites, like the crowning of a king and queen at the senior prom—treated here as a primitive blood sacrifice at an alter.

Figure I.35. *The Great Train Robbery* **(1903), directed by Edwin S. Porter, produced by the Edison Company.** Porter's ten-minute western was immensely popular with the public and inspired many imitations. Within a decade, the genre was one of the staples of the American cinema. Westerns are often vehicles for exploring clashes of value between East and West. Critics like Wollen and Kitses have pointed out how each cultural polarity symbolizes a complex of positive and negative traits:

West	East
Wilderness	Civilization
Individualism	Community
Self-interest	Social welfare
Freedom	Restriction
Anarchy	Law and Order
Savagery	Refinement
Private honor	Institutional justice
Paganism	Christianity
Nature	Culture
Masculine	Feminine
Pragmatism	Idealism
Agrarianism	Industrialism
Purity	Corruption
Dynamic	Static
Future	Past
Experience	Knowledge
American	European

See Peter Wollen, *Signs and Meaning in the Cinema* (Bloomington: Indiana University Press, 1969); and Jim Kitses, *Horizons West* (Bloomington: Indiana University Press, 1969).

Figure I.36. Al Pacino and Robert Duvall in _The Godfather, Part II_ (1974), directed by Francis Ford Coppola, distributed by Paramount Pictures. Popular genres usually reflect the shared values and fears of the public: They are contemporary myths, lending philosphical meaning to the facts of everyday life. As social conditions change, genres often change with them, challenging some traditional customs and beliefs, reaffirming others. Gangster movies, for example, are often covert critiques of American capitalism. The protagonists—usually played by small men—are likened to ruthless businessmen, their climb to power a sardonic parody of the Horatio Alger myth. During the Jazz Age, gangster films like _Underworld_ (1927) dealt with the violence and glamor of the Prohibition era in an essentially apolitical manner. During the harshest years of the depression, in the early 1930s, the genre became subversively ideological. Movies like _Little Caesar_ (1930) reflected the country's shaken confidence in authority and traditional social institutions. In the final years of the depression, gangster films like _Dead End_ (1937) were pleas for liberal reform, arguing that crime was the result of broken homes, lack of opportunity, and slum living. Gangsters of all periods tend to suffer from an inability to relate to women, but during the 1940s, movies like _White Heat_ (1949) featured protagonists who were outright sexual neurotics. In the 1950s, partly as a result of the highly publicized Kefauver Senate Crime Investigations, gangster movies like _The Phoenix City Story_ (1955) took the form of "confidential exposés" of syndicate crime. Coppola's two _Godfather_ films are a virtual recapitulation of the history of the genre, spanning three generations of characters and reflecting the weary cynicism of a nation still numbed by the impact of the hearts-and-minds hoax of Vietnam and the Watergate conspiracy. See Robert Warshow's classic essay, "The Gangster as Tragic Hero," in _The Immediate Experience_ (New York: Atheneum, 1970); John Gabree, _Gangsters: From Little Caesar to The Godfather_ (New York: Pyramid Books, 1973); Jack Shadoian, _Dreams and Dead Ends: The American Gangster/Crime Film_ (Cambridge, Mass.: M.I.T. Press, 1977); and Eugene Rosow, _Born to Lose: The Gangster Film in America_ (New York: Oxford University Press, 1978).

Figure I.37. Dustin Hoffman and Katharine Ross in *The Graduate* (1967), directed by Mike Nichols, an Embassy Release. An underlying structure of *The Graduate* is the Oedipus complex, which Freud believed was the paradigm of prepubescent human sexuality. Its feminine form is known as the Electra complex, also derived from Greek myth. The protagonist in this film has an affair with a jaded older woman, a friend of his parents. Midway through the story, he transfers his affection to her daughter, whose values are closer to his own. Like many movies centering on youth, *The Graduate* also employs a rite-of-passage structure, wherein an untried youth passes from innocence to experience, boyhood to manhood. The film is one of the all-time box office champions and was particularly popular with young audiences.

Jung began his career as a disciple of Freud, but eventually he broke away, believing that Freud's theories lacked a communal dimension. Jung was fascinated by myths, fairy tales, and folklore, which he believed contained symbols and story patterns that were universal to all individuals in all cultures and periods. According to Jung, unconscious complexes consist of archetypal symbols that are as deeply rooted and as inexplicable as insticts. He called this submerged reservoir of symbols the collective unconscious, which he thought had a primordial foundation, traceable to primitive times. Many of these archetypal patterns are bipolar and embody the basic concepts of religion, art, and society: god-devil, light-dark, active-passive, male-female, static-dynamic, and so on. Jung believed that the artist consciously or unconsciously draws on these archetypes as raw material, which must then be rendered into the generic forms favored by a given culture. For Jung, every work of art (and especially generic art) is an infinitesimal exploration of a universal psychic experience—an instinctive groping toward an ancient wisdom. He also believed that popular culture offers the most unobstructed view of archetypes and myths, whereas elite culture tends to submerge them beneath a complex surface detail.

A story can be many things. To a producer it's a property that has a box office value. To a writer it's a script. To a star it's a vehicle. To a director it's an artistic medium. To a genre critic it's an objective, classifiable narrative form. To a sociologist it's an index of public sentiment. To a psychiatrist it's an instinctive exploration of hidden fears or communal ideals. To a moviegoer it can be all of these, and more.

Figure I.38. *Snow White and the Seven Dwarfs* **(1937), released by RKO.** © **Walt Disney Productions.** Disney's work draws heavily from fairy tales, myths, and folklore, which are profuse in archetypal elements. *Snow White,* based on a complex of tales collected by the Grimm Brothers, features many nightmarish scenes derived from the Sleeping Beauty myth: storms, magical transformations, a poisoned apple, forbidden gardens, enchanted palaces, a wicked stepmother, and so on. According to scholar Joseph Campbell, the folktale is "the primer picture-language of the soul," an art form on which the whole community of mankind has worked and which draws on universal, deeply rooted impulses. "The folk tale survives not simply as a quaint relic of days childlike in belief," Campbell has observed. "Its world of magic is symptomatic of fevers deeply burning in the psyche: permanent presences, desires, fears, ideals, potentialities, that have glowed in the nerves, hummed in the blood, baffled the senses, since the beginning." See Joseph Campbell, *The Masks of God: Primitive Mythology* (New York: Viking, 1959); Christopher Finch, *The Art of Walt Disney* (New York: Harry W. Abrams, 1975); and Richard Schickel, *The Disney Version* (New York: Avon Books, 1968).

SUMMING UP

As even this brief outline may suggest, the American cinema is immensely complex, subject to a variety of often conflicting generalizations. Its follies and vices have been amply documented. At their worst, American movies can be shallow, gaudy, and cheaply sensational. Few of our film artists have matched the intellectual subtlety and wit of the greatest French moviemakers or the political sophistication of the Italians at their best. Nor can we boast such great contemplative artists as the Japanese Yasujiro Ozu. Unlike the works of the Swedish Ingmar Bergman, the darker side of the human psyche has been consistently minimized by most American moviemakers. Except for a rare figure like Orson Welles, they tend to lack a mature sense of evil, falling back on glib and evasive formulas. Even some of the better American films can be sentimental, antiintellectual, or stylistically overwrought.

Figure I.39. Robert De Niro in *Taxi Driver* (1975), written by Paul Schrader, directed by Martin Scorsese, released by Columbia Pictures. Although there have been important exceptions, one of the major weaknesses of the American cinema had been its unwillingness to go beyond formulaic conventions in its portrayal of evil. Vietnam and Watergate changed that: Americans finally relinquished their most cherished illusion—innocence. A bleak vision characterized many of the best American movies of the post-Vietnam, post-Watergate era. Young filmmakers like Scorsese rejected the good-guys-vs-bad-guys clichés of the past, insisting that evil is inherent in the human condition. Scorsese's urban infernos are steeped in violence, complicity, and guilt. Moral distinctions are blurred, and innocence is portrayed as a form of self-deception. Characters act upon impulses they scarcely perceive, much less understand.

On the other hand, the American cinema is unmatched in emotional intensity, excitement, and narrative verve. Even its harshest detractors concede its technical brilliance. Nor can any other nation approach the richness and variety of American film comedy. It's a profoundly democratic cinema, overtly hostile toward rank, privilege, and authority. Almost invariably its sympathies are with the underdog and the oppressed. Conflicts between the individual and society are usually resolved in favor of individuals. In fact, if there's one overriding subject that American filmmakers return to with compulsive regularity, it's the theme of individualism. The cult of personality is a national characteristic and can be traced back to the very founding of the country. In 1865, for example, journalist Edwin Godkin noted,

> A society composed at the period of its formation mainly of young men, coming from all parts of the world in quest of fortune, released from the ordinary restraints of family, church, and public opinion, even of the civil law, naturally and inevitably acquires a certain contempt for authority and impatience with it, and individualism among them develops itself very rapidly.

Figure I.40. Jack Nicholson in *One Flew Over the Cuckoo's Nest* (1975), directed by Milos Forman, released by United Artists. Like the romantic revolution that swept across Europe and the Americas in the nineteenth century, American movies have repeatedly glorified nonconformists and outsiders. Romantics of all periods advocate the overthrow of stultifying convention and decorum. Social institutions are portrayed as antihuman and tyrannical. Above all, romantic art is an art of revolt against the Establishment, and its characteristic hero is the rebel.

The protagonists of American movies are often rebels, outsiders, and inner-directed loners. Their goals are personal rather than social, and their morality is often based on a private code rather than a consensus.

The American cinema is also deeply romantic, like most of the best art produced in this country. Detachment and objectivity are rare. The characters and events are dramatized in a frankly partisan manner, and film artists employ every technique at their command to encourage the viewer to identify with the characters and their goals. A romantic yearning for the extraordinary is the rule rather than the exception, and this theme is frequently expressed with lyrical fervor. American movies are encumbered by few traditions of restraint, decorum, or "good taste"; genres are mixed with casual nonchalance; the fantastic and the real are fused with matter-of-fact facility. Impatient of nuances, our filmmakers prefer bold, sweeping themes and strident clashes. Even our comedies tend more toward physical mayhem than to sophisticated wit, though there are important exceptions, such as the polished comedies of Lubitsch.

There have always been important exceptions.

SELECTED BIBLIOGRAPHY

Cultural Studies

HANDEL, LEO A. *Hollywood Looks at its Audience: A Report of Film Audience Research*. Urbana: University of Illinois Press, 1950.

JOWETT, GARTH. *Film: The Democratic Art*. Boston: Little, Brown, 1976.

KOUWENHOVEN, JOHN A. *The Arts in Modern American Civilization*. New York: The Norton Library, W. W. Norton & Co., Inc., 1967. (Originally published in 1948 as *Made in America*.)

MacCANN, RICHARD DYER, *et al. Film and Society*. New York: Scribner's, 1964.

SKLAR, ROBERT. *Movie-Made America*. New York: Random House, 1975.

THORP, MARGARET FERRAND. *America at the Movies*. New Haven, Conn.: Yale University Press, 1939.

WOLFENSTEIN, MARTHA, and NATHAN LEITES. *Movies, A Psychological Study*. New York: Free Press, 1950.

WOOD, MICHAEL. *America in the Movies*. New York: Delta Books, 1975.

Industry Studies

BALIO, TINO, *et al. The American Film Industry*. Madison: University of Wisconsin Press, 1976.

HAMPTON, BENJAMIN B. *History of the American Film Industry from Its Beginnings to 1931*. New York: Dover, 1970. (Published originally in 1931 as *History of the Movies*.)

MacCANN, RICHARD DYER, *et al. Hollywood in Transition*. Boston: Houghton Mifflin, 1962.

MAYERSBERG, PAUL. *Hollywood: The Haunted House*. New York: Ballantine, 1967.

MONACO, JAMES. *American Film Now: The People, the Power, the Money, the Movies*. New York: Oxford University Press, 1979.

POWDERMAKER, HORTENSE. *Hollywood: The Dream Factory.* Boston: Little, Brown, 1950.

ROSTEN, LEO. *Hollywood: The Movie Colony, The Movie Makers.* New York: Harcourt Brace, 1941.

STANLEY, ROBERT. *The Celluloid Empire.* New York: Hastings House, 1978.

TAYLOR, THEODORE. *People Who Make the Movies.* New York: Avon Books, 1967.

ZIEROLD, NORMAN. *The Moguls.* New York: Avon Books, 1969. See also Philip French, *The Movie Moguls* (London: Weidenfeld & Nicholson, 1969).

The Star System

AFFRON, CHARLES. *Star Acting: Gish, Garbo, Davis.* New York: Dutton, 1977.

HASKELL, MOLLY. *From Reverence to Rape: The Treatment of Women in the Movies.* New York: Penguin, 1974.

MORIN, EDGAR. *The Stars.* New York: Grove Press, 1960.

ROSEN, MARJORIE. *Popcorn Venus: Women, Movies, and the American Dream.* New York: Coward, McCann & Geoghegan, 1973.

SCHICKEL, RICHARD. *The Stars.* New York: Bonanza Books, 1962.

SHIPMAN, DAVID. *The Great Movie Stars.* Vol. I. *The Golden Years.* New York: Crown Publishers, 1970. Vol. II. *The International Years.* New York: St. Martin's Press, 1972.

THOMPSON, DAVID. *A Biographical Dictionary of Film.* New York: Morrow, 1976.

WALKER, ALEXANDER. *Stardom.* Briarcliff Manor, N.Y.: Stein & Day, 1970.

Stories, Genres, and Myth

BLUESTONE, GEORGE. *Novels Into Film.* Berkeley: University of California Press, 1957.

CORLISS, RICHARD. *Talking Pictures: Screenwriters in the American Cinema.* New York: Penguin, 1975.

GRANT, BARRY K., ed. *Film Genre: Theory and Criticism.* Metuchen, N.J.: Scarecrow, 1977.

JUNG, CARL G., et al. *Man and His Symbols.* New York: Dell Pub. Co., Inc., 1968.

KAMINSKY, STUART M. *American Film Genres.* Dayton, Ohio: Pflaum Publishing, 1974.

SOLOMAN, STANLEY J. *Beyond Formula: American Film Genres.* New York: Harcourt Brace Jovanovich, Inc., 1976.

TYLER, PARKER. *Magic and Myth of the Movies* (1947) and *The Hollywood Hallucination* (1944). New York: Simon & Schuster.

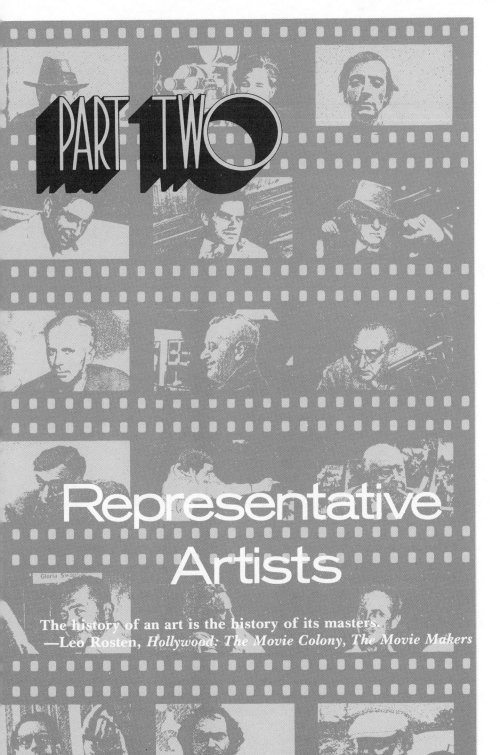

PART TWO

Representative Artists

The history of an art is the history of its masters.
—Leo Rosten, *Hollywood: The Movie Colony, The Movie Makers*

1

The Fountainhead

The Cinema of D. W. Griffith

Figure 1.1. Publicity photo of Griffith and G. W. "Billy" Bitzer (behind camera), during the production of *Way Down East* **(1920).** Bitzer, who photographed virtually all of Griffith's movies, is the first great cinematographer of the American cinema. Together they popularized many of the standard optical techniques of their medium, including the fade-out, iris-in and iris-out, double and multiple exposures, and all kinds of masking devices to alter the shape of the screen. He and Bitzer developed soft focus and "mist" (filtered) photography, back lighting, side lighting, and tinting. They introduced the point-of-view shot (photographing events as though through a character's eyes) and many types of moving camera shots. See G. W. Bitzer, *Billy Bitzer: His Story* (New York: Farrar, Straus & Giroux, 1973).

Griffith is almost universally regarded as the father of the American cinema. When he entered the movie industry in 1908, the new medium was largely a crude working-class entertainment. Within a few years, he had perfected a mature storytelling form of such force, complexity, and expressiveness that every filmmaker since his time has been in his debt. Because of his conspicuous brilliance, Griffith has been credited with "inventing" virtually every cinematic technique. Subsequent scholars have discovered isolated precedents for many of his self-proclaimed innovations, but though the director wasn't always the first, he was certainly the best. That is, he consolidated and expanded the piecemeal accomplishments of his predecessors, fusing them into a language of extraordinary richness and complexity. Though his movies have dated badly in many respects, his masterpieces, especially *The Birth of a Nation* (1915) and *Intolerance* (1916), are still regarded as among the finest achievements of the silent cinema. Scholars have estimated that Griffith directed approximately 525 movies, most of them one-reelers (a reel was between ten and fourteen minutes long). Most of these and virtually all of his 30 features (a film of over an hour's length) still exist. Many of these movies are of interest only to scholars and film buffs, and even Griffith frankly admitted that his perfunctory "sausages" were concocted only to raise some quick cash or to stall for time while he devoted his energies to his more ambitious projects. General audiences are likely to find these minor works disappointing, for they contain little of enduring value, either in terms of subject matter or style. During his artistic maturity, Griffith was able to work virtually without interference. In addition to directing, he also wrote, produced, edited, and supervised the music for most of his major films. True, producers complained of his extravagance, but he was usually allowed to go his own way—as long as his movies continued to make money. Actors who became popular stars—like the clever and headstrong Mary Pickford—were never allowed to dominate his movies: They were "Griffith films, with Mary Pickford," not "Pickford films, directed by D. W. Griffith."

The motion picture, although a growth of only a few years, is boundless in its scope and endless in its possibilities. The whole world is its stage, and time without end its limitations.

—D. W. Griffith

David Wark Griffith was born in 1875 in Crestwood, Kentucky. Though his family lived in genteel impoverishment, they prided themselves on their quasi-aristocratic heritage. As a child, Griffith was regaled with chivalrous tales of the Old South and sentimental homilies culled from Victorian literature—the worst as well as the best. Early in life, he decided that he wanted to be a great author. He was especially attracted to the drama and decided to take Shakespeare's route of learning stagecraft through acting. For twelve years Griffith traveled with various stock companies, performing mostly with second-rate troupes specializing in Victorian melodramas and farces. Throughout his acting years, he continued to write plays, poems, and stories, though not with much success.

In 1908, at the age of thirty-three, Griffith was broke, jobless, and desperate. At the time, no actor with any pretentions to dignity would condescend to appear in "the flickers," which stage people regarded—if at all—with contemptuous sneers. Though Griffith shared this snobbery, he couldn't afford to be so fastidious, and with some mortification he eventually went to the American Mutoscope and Biograph Company, commonly known as Biograph, and was hired as an actor and occasional writer. Actors were paid five dollars a day at this time, and treatments (a rough outline of a story) commanded fifteen dollars. When he was asked to direct, he was skeptical at first but decided that it might be a profitable way of supporting himself until he received his due fame as an author. Until then, he would continue to use his stage name, Lawrence Griffith.

It's impossible to gauge Griffith's contributions to the cinema without a knowledge of its downright pathetic beginnings. Around 1900, when it became apparent that "picture shows" might develop into profitable commodities, a motley assortment of semiliterates, exbookies, and other marginal types were irresistibly drawn to the field. For the most part, respectable businessmen loftily snubbed the chaotic new industry as beneath their notice. For exhibition halls, these hustling entrepreneurs rented vacant stores, located usually in the crowded working-class districts of America's cities. Filthy, cramped, smelly, and unventilated, these "theatres"—which were not unlike our sleazier porno parlors of today—charged only a nickel admission, and hence were called *nickelodeons*. At this price, almost everyone could afford to attend, though audiences of this period consisted almost exclusively of immigrants and laborers. Between 1895 and 1908, nickelodeons proliferated rapidly in America, until even small towns featured at least one storefront theatre. Scholars have estimated that at the time Griffith entered the field, there were about nine thousand nickelodeons in the United States, serving approximately three million viewers a week.

Programs were generally about thirty minutes long and consisted of several single-reel movies, mostly melodramas and boisterous farces. These were often plagiarized from the same kind of plays Griffith had acted in during his touring days. Above all, these movies emphasized action—usually violent action. One would search in vain for a hint of subtlety, understatement, or restraint. Many of these films, reflecting the biases of both their producers and audiences, were innately democratic, antiauthoritarian, and strongly working class in their style and ethical values. Because these movies contained few if any genteel refinements, middle-class Americans and their cultural spokesmen regarded them as dangerous, unwholesome, and even subversive.

Technically, these crude one-reelers weren't much more than photographed stage playlets. The camera passively recorded the action from a stationary long-shot position, the actors and set in full view. Performers made entrances and exits from the right and left of the frame (stage), even in scenes with exterior locations. Photographing a single action from different angles and distances was virtually unheard of: If the story called for twelve scenes, it was photographed in twelve shots, all of them with the camera in the same stationary position. Not every movie of this period was so stagey, but the few attempts to break out of this mold were regarded as eccentric aberrations. Until Griffith refined the art of editing in his popular Biograph films, most producers assumed that audiences paid their money to see *all* of the sets and actors, not just parts of them. Since performers weren't seen in closeup, they tended to use broad, theatrical gestures, with much flailing of arms and hysterical tearing of hair.

Soon after joining Biograph, Griffith came to the conclusion that the aesthetic conventions of movies ought to be different from those of the stage. Films, he believed, were closer to novels and epics than to the live theatre, in which the restrictions of space and time are far more severe. Between *The Adventures of Dollie* (1908), the first movie he directed, and *Judith of Bethulia* (directed in 1913), his first feature and last assignment for Biograph, Griffith revolutionized the medium, establishing virtually the entire gamut of techniques in the construction of silent story films. He set himself a torturous pace, working fourteen to sixteen hours a day, seven days a week—a regimen he continued for the remainder of his active career.

Dissatisfied with the one-scene/one-shot principle, Griffith decided to cut to a closer shot *within* a continuous scene in order to emphasize a character's reaction. Before long, he began using a variety of shots to convey a single action, thus establishing the shot—and not the "continuous" scene—as the basic unit of movie construction. Film time could therefore be condensed, a technique that allowed him to preserve the fluidity of an action without literally showing all of it. In order to make his transitions smooth and continuous, he carefully established his scenes in a long shot at the opening. Then he cut to various medium and close shots, occasionally reminding the viewer of the wider context by reestablishing it with a return to the opening setup. Editing allowed him to exclude dull inessentials and to condense and expand time subjectively. Thanks to the closeup, actors could now modify their exaggerated gestures and behave more like people than gesticulating puppets.

By breaking down an action into a series of fragmentary shots, Griffith achieved a far greater degree of control, not only over the story materials, but also over the audience's reactions. In carefully selecting and juxtaposing long, medium, and close shots, he constantly shifted the viewer's point of view within a scene—excluding here, emphasizing there, consolidating, contrasting, connecting, and so on. He justified these shifts in camera placement as a means of achieving a greater dramatic impact than an unedited long shot could possibly convey. Eventually this editing style came to be called classical cutting, and in the following decades it became the standard method of editing in the American film industry. What Griffith conveyed, then, was not an objectively presented event but a selective *interpretation* of the event.

Most of Griffith's innovations were vociferously opposed by the Biograph officials, and even by Billy Bitzer, the director's gifted but stodgy cameraman. In *After Many Years* (1908), Griffith used a closeup of a wife longing for her marooned husband on a desert isle. The director followed this with a shot of the husband himself, who is thousands of miles away. The front office insisted that viewers would be confused by this jump in continuity. But they weren't: The movie was a box office success. The far-ranging implications of Griffith's discovery were not lost on him. He realized that cinematic continuity is not necessarily determined by the continuity of literal time and space but by the association of ideas and feelings which are linked in the spectator's mind. "A film is a cooperative effort between the director and the audience," he insisted, a view that was to exert a profound influence on the Soviet filmmakers of the 1920s.

In such works as *The Lonely Villa* (1909) and *The Lonedale Operator* (1911), Griffith perfected his famous last-minute rescue sequences. The same formula was used in many of his movies: Shots of a besieged heroine are crosscut with shots of her stalwart preserver in a different location, racing to her rescue. As the sequence peaks to its climax, the shots get shorter and usually closer in, thus intensifying the suspense. These intricately crosscut rescue scenes were widely imitated by other directors. Griffith claimed he derived the technique from literature:

> I borrowed the "cut-back" from Charles Dickens. Novelists think nothing of leaving one set of characters in the midst of affairs and going back to deal with earlier events in which another set of characters is involved.... I found that the picture could carry not merely two, but even three or four simultaneous threads of action—all without confusing the spectator.

Griffith was chafing to expand the single-reel format to two. He believed that the length of a movie ought to be governed organically by the subject matter and not arbitrarily imposed by mere custom. His bosses argued that audiences would never sit still for a movie beyond fifteen minutes, and they refused him permission. Despite this injunction, he was encouraged by his box office success, and at the end of 1911, when he signed his fourth contract (at an astonishing $3,000 a month),

Figure 1.2. *The Musketeers of Pig Alley* **(1912), with Lillian Gish, produced by Biograph.** Photographed in the slums of New York City, this movie has been called the first gangster film. Griffith's vision of urban life was usually nightmarish—steeped in terror, crime, and poverty. The city is characteristically portrayed as a maelstrom of impersonal forces which suffocate the human spirit.

he crossed out *Lawrence* and penned in *David W. Griffith.* He no longer spoke of becoming a famous author.

Griffith was now directing most of Biograph's movies, and though some of these were pretty conventional, in others he continued to explore the expressive range of his medium. He made a number of romantic costume pictures, dealing with various historical periods. He made movies centering on contemporary social problems, especially poverty, prejudice, and economic exploitation. Many of his films were adaptations of well-known literary works by Tennyson, Tolstoy, Poe, and others. His productions grew more ambitious, and finally he was allowed to expand to two reels. Biograph movies were widely praised as the best-produced films in America. Though three-reelers were the coming vogue, the executives of the company refused to allow Griffith to expand beyond two, a limitation that galled him more than all others.

The art of editing is generally regarded as Griffith's greatest contribution to the movies, but he was also responsible for introducing or reviving many other techniques as well. He was almost universally considered the best director of actors in the film industry, and he trained many ambitious newcomers who later became famous personalities, most notably Mary Pickford, Lillian Gish, Mack Sennett, and Erich von Stroheim. He often had his actors stream in and out of the set past the camera, rather than having them make "stage" entrances from the right or left of the frame. His mise-en-scène became increasingly more complex, sometimes with simultaneous actions occuring in the back-, mid-, and foregrounds of his compositions.

In 1913, Griffith wired his Biograph bosses from Los Angeles (where he and his regulars were now working permanently), asking permission to make a feature-length movie, in imitation of such popular Italian imports as the eight-reel *Quo Vadis.* But New York wired back that their limit was still two reels. He decided to proceed anyway and began preparations for *Judith of Bethulia*, his most ambitious project to date. A biblical walled city was erected, encompassing an area of twelve square miles. Costs escalated rapidly, totaling finally $36,000— astronomical by Biograph standards. The front office was furious when Griffith turned in a four-reel film, the first of the American cinema. Angered by the stubborn independence of their house genius, Biograph refused to release *Judith* until 1914, after Griffith had already left the company in disgust.

Once he gained total independence, even his impressive one- and two-reelers were destined to seem crude in comparison with the masterworks that lay ahead. His apprenticeship over, in the next few years he quickly established himself as the foremost artist not only in the American film industry but also in the international cinema as well. When he left Biograph, he depleted it of its finest talent, for most of his regulars—including Bitzer, Mae Marsh, Dorothy and Lillian Gish—left with him. Biograph lost its preeminence and soon disappeared from the industry. Distributing through Mutual, Griffith and his loyalists dashed off four features in 1914: *The Battle of the Sexes, Home Sweet Home, The Escape,* and *The Avenging Conscience,* none of them of the first rank, according to Griffith specialists.

Figure 1.3.   A 1915 publicity photo of Lillian Gish at the age of nineteen. Critics, historians, and scholars are virtually unaminous in their agreement that Griffith's greatest performer was Lillian Gish. John Barrymore compared her with Bernhardt and Duse. Critics rhapsodized over her "Dresden porcelain" beauty. She started with Griffith in 1912 at the age of sixteen and became his preeminent interpreter in such major works as *The Birth of a Nation, Broken Blossoms, Way Down East,* and *Orphans of the Storm.* See Lillian Gish, *The Movies, Mr. Griffith & Me* (New York: Prentice-Hall, 1969). Photo: Scott Eyman.

Astonishingly, during this same year the director was working on *The Birth of a Nation* (1915), which is widely regarded as the most important silent movie of the American repertory. An encyclopedic work, it consolidated the techniques Griffith had evolved in his Biograph days on a scale so vast and intense that the nation was staggered by its impact. The film's total cost was approximately $100,000—a figure that amazed industry regulars, who confidently proclaimed that no movie with such an enormous budget could possibly hope to recover its investment. But once again Griffith challenged their complacency, and once again he was right. *Birth* was the top-grossing movie in silent film history. Its exact receipts have been impossible to determine, but estimates have ranged from $5 million to $50 million. At twelve reels, its running time was nearly three hours, easily the lengthiest movie ever made up to that time. In its long New York City run it commanded a top price of $2 per ticket. It was seen—and reputedly praised—by President Wilson in the White House. According to Lillian Gish, it was viewed by approximately 25 million people within its first two years of release. It seduced millions of new middle-class patrons, who soon developed the habit of moviegoing.

Figure 1.4. *The Birth of a Nation* **(1915).** Though Griffith boasted that the battle scenes required 30,000 to 35,000 extras, Miss Gish dismissed such exaggerations as mere press-agentry. Actually, no more than 500 extras were ever employed—a far more impressive achievement, as she has pointed out, for the military scenes never look skimpy or undermanned.

In the South alone, it played consecutively for twelve years. In Boston and other northern cities, its racism provoked riots.

A saga of the Civil War and Reconstruction periods, *Birth* is a diseased masterpiece, steeped in racial bigotry. Griffith was incapable of portraying black people with the same compassion he had demonstrated toward other oppressed minorities. As film historian Alan Casty has pointed out, Griffith's racial stereotypes were really no different from his treatment of *all* his villains: "His was a world without mixtures—of black and white in more ways than one—a world of certitudes absolutely expressed." But the movie caused irreparable social damage. It was widely used throughout the 1920s by the KKK at recruiting rallies and was responsible for fixing many of the degrading Negro stereotypes that dominated the American cinema for at least the next four decades.

The fierce controversy surrounding the movie's bigotry was an indirect testimony to its artistic power; there had been racist films before *Birth*, but none of them provoked such visceral responses. From a purely aesthetic point of view, no one had approached the brilliance of Grif-

Figure 1.5. *The Birth of a Nation.* Griffith was obsessed with authenticity. Many books were consulted to verify the costumes, the weaponry, and the architecture. He modeled his visual style on the Civil War photographs of Mathew Brady. Actual veterans of the war were hired to scout authentic-looking locations. The director also included many "historical facsimiles" in his film—brief tableaux that come to life, modeled on actual photographs of such events as Lee's surrender at Appomattox, and (shown here) Ford's Theatre, where Lincoln was assassinated. Photo: Scott Eyman.

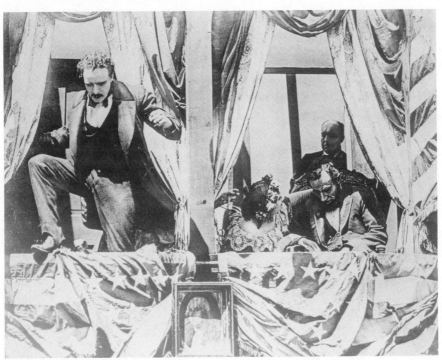

fith's direction in this movie. It was at once audaciously daring, yet poised, mature, and assured. Audiences thrilled to its vastness of scope and its justly famous battle scenes, more spectacular than anything that had ever been done before. Almost overnight, Griffith became a national celebrity. Cultural commentators began to suggest that the lowly flickers might now have to be taken more seriously as an art form. More than any other movie of its time, *Birth* jolted the film industry into a new awareness of its awesome influence over the American public.

The editing in the film was a calculated display of virtuosity. The movie contains about 1,375 shots—a staggering number when we consider that the average European spectacles of the time featured only about 100 separate setups. Astonishingly, every shot but one was captured in a single take, for stock was expensive, and actors who screwed up shots seldom prospered. The cutting rhythms are still impressive: The languorous love scenes are gracefully edited at a leisurely pace, and the shots in the multiple rescue sequences erupt in staccato explosions.

But Griffith was also able to achieve some powerful effects without the aid of editing. The celebrated homecoming scene is conveyed with

Figure 1.6. *The Birth of a Nation.* Griffith took great care in his selection of music, but today his films are usually shown silent, thus draining them of much of their charm and excitement. Viewers who have seen the famous battle scenes of *Birth* accompanied by a soundtrack of appropriate music have testified to the brilliance of these sequences—as fine as anything that's been done in the medium. Projected without music, these same scenes can seem remote, academic, uninvolving.

Figure 1.7. *Intolerance* **(1916) set construction by Frank Wortman, produced by the Wark Producing Corporation.** The Babylonian story is primarily what skyrocketed Griffith's budget to an all-time high of $1,900,000. The banquet scene for Belshazzar's feast alone cost a reputed $250,000 and employed over 4,000 extras. The story required the construction of a walled city, extending nearly three-quarters of a mile in length. The court was flanked by enormous colonnades with pillars 50 feet high, each supporting a huge statue of an elephant-god. Behind the court were towers and ramparts, their tops planted with cascading flowers and exotic trees, representing Belshazzar's famous hanging gardens. The outer walls of the city were 200 feet high, yet were wide enough so that two chariots were able to roar past each other on the road that perched on top.

only a few lengthy shots. After being released from a military hospital, the hero (Henry Walthall) returns home, where he is met outside the house by his young sister (Mae Marsh). Standing on the threshold, they joke briefly, then he sadly gazes at the now-grown woman who used to be his little pet. With barely restrained tears, they look off-camera and survey the wreckage of their once lovely plantation. Suddenly she bursts into sobs, and he clasps her to his chest, choked with emotion. As they part, their mother's arms reach out from the open door, enfolding her son within the house, where they disappear from view. It is one of Griffith's most tender scenes—simple, understated, poetic.

His next movie was based on a concept he believed would make even *Birth* seem modest in comparison. By using the principle of the association of ideas implicit in the art of editing, he wanted to explore a single theme within a variety of different settings. The result was *Intolerance* (1916), still one of the most awesome spectacles in the history of the cinema. Griffith intercut four separate stories, all of them unified—more or less—by the theme of intolerance. A contemporary story of social injustice was crosscut with an epic tale set in ancient Babylon, with the story of Jesus, and with a love tragedy which is culminated by the massacre of the Huguenots in sixteenth-century Paris. The movie leaps over thousands of years and over as many miles. The "connections" between the four stories are entirely mental and emotional and have nothing to do with literal continuity. Griffith tied them together with a recurrent image of The Eternal Mother rocking a cradle, accompanied by Walt Whitman's famous line, "Out of the cradle, endlessly rocking. . . ."

At the beginning of the movie, Griffith announces his theme: "Each story shows how hatred and intolerance, through the ages, have battled against love and charity." Each of the four stories is introduced and developed briefly. As the audience becomes more familiar with each set of characters, Griffith dispenses with title transitions and cuts directly from story to story, accelerating the pace of the editing radically as the movie builds to its multiple climaxes. As Alan Casty has pointed out, Griffith often favored a triadic pattern of cutting, and in *Intolerance* he magnified this technique to produce a veritable torrent of images. Three of the four stories are cut to this pattern, each involving a last-minute rescue attempt. In the contemporary story the Boy (Robert Harron) is being prepared for execution by the state, while his wife, the Dear Little One (Mae Marsh), races in a car to obtain a last-minute pardon from the governor, who is speeding away in a train. The French plot is also characterized by three-way cutting: The Catholic hero races to the rescue of his Protestant fiancée, who along with her family is slated to be murdered by the king's troups, who are maurauding in the streets. These shots are intercut with a three-way sequence in the Babylonian story, in which the loyal Mountain Girl (Constance Talmadge) races in a chariot to warn her Prince and his revelling subjects of an impending attack by the Persian army. These three hair-breadth sequences are intercut in turn with shots of the crucifixion of Jesus. Only in the contemporary story does justice prevail. In the others, the forces of "love and charity" are tragically defeated.

From the point of view of technique, *Intolerance* is a veritable feast. The original print was tinted: blue for the Judean scenes, sepia for the French plot, grayish-green for the Babylonian story, and amber for the contemporary sequences. Griffith altered his tinting internally as well: Many of the evening scenes were blue, the daytime exteriors yellow, and the night battle scenes red. The director designed many of the opulent sets and costumes of the Babylonian sequences. He also used a wide variety of masking devices to alter the screen's size: irises to pinpoint details, vertical masks to emphasize steepness, and horizontal masks to create thrilling widescreen panoramas. The battle scenes are even more monumental than those of *Birth*. Thousands of extras were employed to represent the clashing armies of Cyrus and Belshazzar. The weapons and strategies of war are fascinating. Enormous ladderlike towers are used by the Persians to scale Belshazzar's mountainous walls. Boiling oil is poured over the invading Persian hoards. Primitive flamethrowing tanks repeatedly batter the Babylonian fortifications, while catapults hurl enormous rocks over the walls of the city. It was many years before the American cinema produced a spectacle of comparable dimensions.

Some critics complained that Griffith's elephantine scale reduced the human dimension to virtual insignificance. Unlike *Birth*, in which the viewer is encouraged to identify emotionally with individual problems as well as larger political issues, in *Intolerance* the sheer awesomeness of the production values tends to sweep everything else away. Many spectators found it difficult to care about the characters, who on the whole are less compelling and individualized than those in *Birth*. In part this inadequacy was caused by Griffith's decision to cut the movie to thirteen reels, about three hours. Originally he planned to release the film in two four-hour sections, to be shown on two consecutive evenings. In effect, five-eighths of the picture is missing. Miss Gish, who was intimately connected with the movie on the production level, believes that the original version would have been an enormous success.

There are other flaws in the film that contributed to its box office failure. Griffith sometimes informs us how to respond to the characters instead of dramatizing them effectively. Most of the villains—always a weakness in his works—are unconvincingly motivated and crudely acted. The lovers in the French story don't do much of anything except smile goonily at one another, and Belshazzar and his Princess Beloved merely drape the furniture, declaring their undying love. Similarly, Jesus is only a "presence," gliding mysteriously over the landscape. The characters in the modern story are developed in greater detail, but even here we're given labels rather than rounded characters: The Friendless One, The Musketeer of the Slums, and so on. Even some of the movie's enthusiasts have admitted that its four stories aren't very organically related to the ostensible theme of intolerance. Edward Wagenknect, who regarded the film as "incontestably the greatest motion picture ever made," nonetheless lamented Griffith's clumsy titles, which keep harping on intolerance as if he knew his theme was not sufficiently dramatized to stand on its own. Despite all these flaws, however, the film remains a towering achievement, if for nothing else because of its undeniable grandeur. Though Griffith continued to make films of high artistic merit, none of them could equal the sheer majesty of *Intolerance*.

Most of the actors working with him during this period had been with him for years, forming a kind of cinematic repertory company. With the exception of Mary Pickford, Griffith's players adored him and stood in awe of his genius, even though their names never appeared on the credits of his films until after 1915, and they were paid surprisingly meagre wages for the time. The director affectionately called his players children, and he often treated them as such, advising them in his fatherly fashion, instigating rivalries among them in order to get better performances, studying their behavior in their off-hours in order to exploit any mannerism for a scene in a movie, and casting them in minor roles to avoid creating his own star system. Everyone, including Bitzer, called him Mr. Griffith. Few claimed to know him well, not even Lillian Gish, perhaps his closest confidant during their years together. He was aloof, mysterious, and gallantly polite to all.

Today the acting in Griffith's movies tends to look rather stagey, but in his own time his players were often praised for their realism and authenticity. Acting styles change from period to period, of course, and

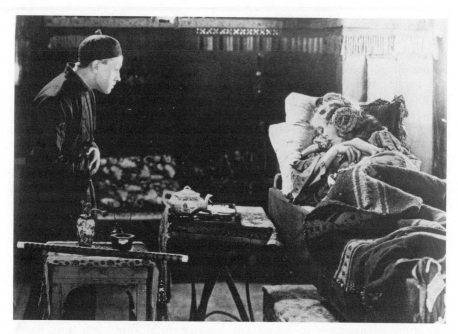

Figure 1.8. *Broken Blossoms* **(1919), with Lillian Gish and Richard Barthelmess, distributed by United Artists.** This film allowed Griffith to reveal another side of his genius, one that's often neglected by critics in favor of the editing virtuosity of his earlier works. The movie contains no flashy cutting, no thrilling last-minute rescue, and no happy ending. It was shot in a studio rather than on location, for Griffith wanted to create a poetic, dreamlike atmosphere. Griffith's use of fog, smoke, and shimmering pools of light in this movie influenced the German studio films of the 1920s.

Griffith himself predicted that future generations would probably consider his performers stilted and artificial. Eventually he avoided using stage-trained actors, preferring to mold his own. He generally cast according to type. Thus, Miss Gish usually played ethereal, frail young virgins, and the muscular Donald Crisp played virile middle-aged men.

Griffith was regarded as eccentric because he rehearsed his players extensively, a practice that industry sages considered wasteful and extravagant. His frequent use of the closeup allowed his actors to "behave" rather than perform before the cameras. According to Miss Gish, he would often restrain his performers while a scene was being photographed: "Not so much, not so much. Less, less—simple, simple, *true*. Don't act it, feel it." He taught his players the value of repose, of poetic delicacy, and how to exploit small authentic gestures in order to particularize their frankly allegorical roles. The camera, he believed, ferrets out all insincerity and calculation.

Griffith is widely regarded as a great "woman's director." That is, his heroines embody the spiritual core of most of his best works. He identified intensely with his female protagonists: Their emotional range is deeper, more complex, and more artistically satisfying than that of his males. These pale, quivering creatures were derived from the idealized females of the Victorian era, which he viewed as the highest expression of the feminine spirit. But feminist critics like Molly Haskell and Marjorie Rosen, although acknowledging Griffith's undeniable sensitivity to women, have also criticized their narrow psychological and social range. His heroines feel deeply, yes, but they don't seem to do much of anything else. Chaste, wide-eyed, and fawnlike in their tremulous innocence, they are usually presented as victims of their own sexuality, unwittingly inflaming the passions of the males who invariably prey upon them. As Rosen has pointed out, rarely do Griffith's heroines behave as fully developed women with identities other than sexual, and rarely are they allowed to fulfill their sexuality without disastrous consequences. Above all, his heroines suffer—innocently, nobly, sublimely.

Griffith's artistic flaws are as conspicuous as his genius and often spring from the same source—his extravagantly romantic sensibility. Perhaps his most serious shortcoming is his sentimentality. No major American director is so mawkish in his veneration for mothers, children, animals, and benevolent authority figures. Like the late nineteenth-century stage which nurtured him, and the Victorian literature that thrilled him as a child, Griffith's movies are dominated by a "high moral tone" and by such pre-World War I themes as duty, chastity, self-sacrifice, mother love, family solidarity, and the brotherhood of man.

Figure 1.9. *Way Down East,* **with Richard Barthelmess, distributed by United Artists.** Griffith's associates thought he had taken leave of his senses when he paid $175,000 for the rights to an old melodrama of wronged womanhood—the highest price ever paid for a property up to that time. But his magic touch had not yet deserted him: The movie version was second only to *Birth of a Nation* in its box office receipts. The brilliantly edited rescue on an ice floe of a river is one of his most powerful sequences, thanks to its extraordinary realism.

His values were essentially agrarian, and he viewed urban life with a deeply engrained skepticism, derived no doubt from his southern rural heritage.

On the other hand, like his favorite novelist, Dickens, Griffith was unmatched in his emotional intensity and his compassion for the dispossessed. His universe, like that of Dickens, is viewed essentially from a child's perspective—steeped in dread, anxiety, and menace. The tranquil openings of his movies are often shattered by nightmarish outbursts of violence and terror. His stories characteristically revolve around such childhood fears as abandonment, the loss of parents, wrenching separations, wars and social upheavals, sudden impoverishment, and the threat of physical violation. Unlike Dickens, however, Griffith was relatively humorless, and consequently, his scenes of terror are usually unrelieved by any effective comic contrast, which does much to mitigate the melodrama of Dickens's novels.

Edward Wagenknecht has observed that Griffith lived closer to the

Figure 1.10. *True Heart Susie* **(1919), with Lillian Gish.** Like many of his audiences, Griffith was born and raised in the country, and he emigrated to the city in search of fortune and wider opportunities. Though he eventually found—and lost—both, he almost invariably sentimentalized the virtues of rural life and minimized its shortcomings. His idyllic pastorals are filled with simple homely pleasures, caring families, and decent neighbors. Like his spiritual disciples Ford and Capra, Griffith's values were conservative, Christian, and humanist—values rarely encountered in his cities of dreadful night.

world of *The Faerie Queene* than that of *Madame Bovary*; that is, the director was drawn to the general type rather than the concrete particular, to allegory rather than strict realism. Hence, the proliferation of labels rather than names for his characters: The Dear One, The Uplifters, Lilywhite, The Evil One, and so on. He inherited this allegorical convention from the pre-1908 cinema, but even into the 1920s, when other filmmakers began to particularize their characters with more individual details, he continued to employ this hackneyed symbolism.

Many of Griffith's movies are also marred by their preachiness. "I believe in the motion picture not only as a means of amusement," he proclaimed, "but as a moral and educational force." Although movies were often attacked for their trashiness by cultural spokesmen, Griffith's films were generally exempted. Indeed, he yearned for bourgeois respectability and often trumpeted the propagandistic potential of his medium, which he described as "the greatest spiritual force the world has ever known." Above all, he was an incorrigible moralist: "A film without a message is just a waste of time," he claimed, and in some of his titles particularly, he was prone to bludgeoning his viewers with his "message" instead of allowing them to arrive at their own conclusions. Griffith's gifts were instinctive rather than intellectual. Even his most fervent partisans have lamented the "culture-vulture" side of his personality. Of his contemporaries, no one was his equal in portraying the extremities of emotion, but as critic Dwight Macdonald observed, "when he thought, he was a child." To a large extent, Griffith's ideas consisted of threadbare Victorian pieties, larded with high-sounding phrases.

Like all original geniuses, Griffith was widely imitated, and this tends to diminish his stature and the scope of his achievement. Viewed out of historical context, his films can seem trite, both in terms of subject matter and technique. Although it's true that Griffith tended to favor conventional and even banal stories, the manner in which he conveyed them was radically new, and this audacious originality is lost to viewers who have been desensitized by decades of second-rate imitations. Perhaps this is the inevitable fate of an original artist: In time his innovations are absorbed by others and become part of an anonymous universal language. When the innovator's works are compared with later, more refined imitations, the originals can seem crude and obvious. But as Swift observed of the ancients and moderns in literature, today's artists often seem superior to their predecessors because they are pygmies standing on the shoulders of giants.

Griffith's artistic powers declined after the mid-1920s. Lewis Jacobs has argued that audiences found his movies naive and old-fashioned, totally out of keeping with the Jazz Age, a view shared by Miss Gish, who claimed Griffith "didn't understand what audiences of the time required." One of his associates observed that "D. W. made the virginal the vogue, and it reigned until Volstead, gin, and F. Scott Fitzgerald gave birth to the flapper." Sex, money, fun, and booze were the fashionable topics of the 1920s, and directors like Lubitsch, Stroheim, and Cecil B. DeMille were more attuned to these vogues than Griffith, whose tastes were still rooted in a prewar sensibility.

After Griffith's movies began to fail commercially, he lost his artis-

Figure 1.11. *Isn't Life Wonderful* **(1924), with Carol Dempster (third from left), distributed by United Artists.** This was Griffith's last independently produced movie until the end of the decade. Many critics regard it as his final great work, though in its own day the director was criticized for his sentimentality and "splendid unsophistication." The movie failed at the box office.

tic autonomy. Once again he went to work for others, for the most part with disappointing results. Before this period, Griffith "wrote" his films only in his head. He never bothered with scripts, not even for the original eight-hour version of *Intolerance*. But once the director was deprived of his creative freedom, he was required to use shooting scripts (not always written by himself), and the result was a startling impoverishment: His inventiveness and spontaneity evaporated. In a desperate attempt to revive his flagging fortunes, he directed a number of quickies in the late 1920s—all of them flops. His second talkie, the crudely outdated *The Struggle* (1931), was ravaged by the critics and died a humiliating if quick death at the box office. It was his last movie. Shortly afterward, when the Griffith Corporation went into bankruptcy, the rights to twenty-one of his films were auctioned off to the highest bidder. A broken Griffith bought them for a measley $500. For the next seventeen years, until his death in 1948 at the age of seventy-three, Griffith lived in seclusion—lonely, embittered, and forgotten.

His legacy to the cinema is incalculable. More than any other single individual, he provided those who followed him with the very grammar of their medium. As James Agee observed, "There is not a man working in movies, nor a man who cares for them, who does not owe Griffith more than he owes anyone else." The classical cutting style of such direc-

Figure 1.12. *Abraham Lincoln* **(1930), with Walter Huston and Una Merkel, distributed by United Artists.** Griffith's penultimate film was his first talkie, and like most movies of this transitional era, it talked and talked and talked. Shot mostly on studio sets, the picture allowed Griffith few opportunities to open up the action. The best episodes take place out of doors, as in this lyrical love scene between Lincoln and Ann Rutledge. Like his fellow Populists Ford and Capra, Griffith idolized Lincoln, regarding him as the highest embodiment of American Populist values. (For a discussion of Populism, see Chapter 5.)

tors as Ford, Huston, and Hawks can be traced back to Griffith's innovations. Pudovkin and Eisenstein based their theories of radical montage on Griffith's audacious cutting techniques in *Intolerance,* which these Soviet moviemakers referred to as their bible. He nurtured an entire generation of film artists, including such giants as John Ford and Erich von Stroheim. "He was the teacher of us all," DeMille said of him. "He was my day school, my adult education program, my university," Mack Sennett claimed. To the brilliant Stroheim, he was simply "The Master."

BIBLIOGRAPHY

ARVIDSON, LINDA. *When the Movies Were Young.* New York: Dutton, 1925. An account of Griffith's early years, narrated by his first wife and sometimes actress.

BARRY, IRIS, AND EILEEN BOWSER. *D. W. Griffith: American Film Master.* New York: Museum of Modern Art, 1965. An updated revision of Barry's classic 1940 study.

CASTY, ALAN. "The Films of D. W. Griffith: A Style for the Times," in *The Journal of Popular Film* (Spring, 1972), pp. 67–79. One of the best short discussions of Griffith's style and values, with major emphasis on *Birth* and *Intolerance.*

EISENSTEIN, SERGEI. "Dickens, Griffith, and the Film Today," in *Film Form.* London: Dennis Dobson, 1951. A classic theoretical essay on Griffith's borrowings from literature.

GEDULD, HARRY M., ed. *Focus on D. W. Griffith.* Englewood Cliffs, N.J.: Prentice-Hall, 1971. A collection of useful articles by and about Griffith. Annotated bibliography. See also Fred Silva, ed., *Focus on "The Birth of a Nation"* (Englewood Cliffs, N.J.: Prentice-Hall, 1971): reviews, commentaries, and essays, with much material on the racial controversy.

HENDERSON, ROBERT M. *D. W. Griffith: The Years at Biograph.* New York: Farrar, Straus & Giroux, 1970. A scholarly account of Griffith's apprenticeship years. Filmography. Henderson has also written the standard biography, *D. W. Griffith: His Life and Work* (New York: Oxford University Press, 1972).

HUFF, THEODORE. *A Shot Analysis of D. W. Griffith's "The Birth of a Nation."* New York: Museum of Modern Art, 1961. See also Huff's *"Intolerance": The Film by David Wark Griffith: Shot-by-Shot Analysis* (New York: Museum of Modern Art, 1966).

JACOBS, LEWIS. *The Rise of the American Film.* New York: Teachers College Press, 1968. (Originally published in 1939.) Contains three fine chapters on Griffith, with emphasis on his innovations. See also Anthony Slide, *Early American Cinema* (Cranbury, N.J.: A. S. Barnes, 1970).

O'DELL, PAUL. *Griffith and the Rise of Hollywood.* Cranbury, N.J.: A. S. Barnes, 1970. A descriptive analysis, with extended coverage of *Birth* and *Intolerance.*

WAGENKNECHT, EDWARD, AND ANTHONY SLIDE. *The Films of D. W. Griffith.* New York: Crown Publishers, 1975. Filmography of features, with brief critical comment and copious illustrations. See also Wagenknecht's *The Movies in the Age of Innocence* (New York: Ballantine, 1962), which contains essays on Pickford and Miss Gish as well as Griffith. See also Kevin Brownlow, *The Parade's Gone By . . .* (New York: Ballantine, 1968): one of the most interesting accounts of the American silent cinema, with a chapter on Griffith. The standard study of the influence of nineteenth-century melodrama on the early American cinema is Nicholas A. Vardac, *Stage to Screen* (Cambridge, Mass.: Harvard University Press, 1949).

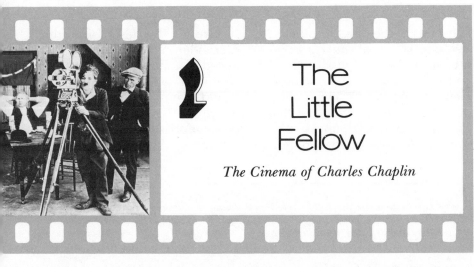

The Little Fellow

The Cinema of Charles Chaplin

Figure 2.1. Chaplin directing *Sunnyside* (1919), with cinematographer Rollie Totheroh (wearing cap). Chaplin's works often have a home-movie look, in part because he regarded the camera merely as a recording machine and not an expressive medium in its own right. Most of his images are photographically plain, and in some instances even ugly. In 1966, when the American Society of Cinematographers was compiling a documentary on the innovations of cameramen, Chaplin's films were flatly rejected on the grounds that Totheroh's cinematography added nothing to the art of the camera. Chaplin's concern was with ideas and with the art of acting, rarely with the art of mise-en-scène. Photo: Scott Eyman.

harlie Chaplin was not only the most popular personality in the history of the cinema but also the most universally recognized comic figure the world had ever known. We have nothing today to compare with the "Chaplin craze" that swept the globe in the late teens and twenties. Theodore Huff, Chaplin's biographer, has estimated that some 300 million people had seen every Chaplin comedy. In New York City alone, one theatre showed only Chaplin movies from 1913 to 1923. But his popularity was—and still is—international: Over 70 percent of his grosses were earned abroad. He was easily the most copied comedian in history: Virtually every studio in Hollywood had its Chaplin imitator, and in France, Germany, England, and elsewhere, ambitious newcomers impersonated him shamelessly. As early as 1916 he was receiving fan mail by the truckloads. Chaplin toys and dolls were mass produced, and photographs, cartoons, and look-alike contests proliferated everywhere. In his celebrated European tour of 1921, he was innundated with letters (73,000 in London alone) and swamped by hysterically adoring fans wherever he went. He was eagerly pursued and lionized by the most distinguished personalities of the day. Despite the déclassé status of movies as an art form, intellectuals rhapsodized over his comedies. George Bernard Shaw, the greatest living playwright of this era, described Chaplin as "the only genius developed in motion pictures." The fastidious critic Alexander Woolcott, who believed that movies were beneath contempt, went even further: "I would be prepared to defend the proposition that this darling of the mob is the foremost living artist."

I've known humiliation. And humiliation is a thing you never forget. Poverty—the degradation and helplessness of it! I can't feel myself any different, at heart, from the unhappy and defeated men, the failures.

—Charles Chaplin

Chaplin's art is emotionally based on personal experiences, especially of his childhood, which for sheer squalor rivals the novels of Dickens. Charles Chaplin, Jr., was born in 1889 in London. His parents were both music-hall performers, though not very successful for the short time they remained together. Chaplin, Sr., was a wastrel and womanizer who died at the age of thirty-seven of alcoholism. After Mrs. Chaplin separated from him, her health began to fail and she became increasingly unstable mentally. Her two children, Sydney and Charlie, were often left to fend for themselves. The family led a humiliating, hand-to-mouth existence. They were almost always hungry. Charlie and his older half-brother became street urchins, begging or stealing money for the barest necessities, filching food from vendors, and sleeping occasionally in public parks.

Both youngsters adored their mother, who was a clever mimic and taught them how to act, sing, and dance. But as the family's situation grew more desperate, Mrs. Chaplin's mind deteriorated. The boys returned home one day to find her totally withdrawn and suffering from malnutrition. She was taken away to a mental asylum for the indigent. Charlie was only seven at the time, but the terror of that experience was seared into his memory. For many years Mrs. Chaplin was in and out of asylums and workhouses. Occasionally she was able to earn a few pennies taking in sewing and working in sweatshops. But for the remainder of her life, she was lucid only for relatively brief intervals, a casualty of Victorian social indifference.

The youngsters were incarcerated at the Hanwell School for Orphans and Destitute Children for about a year and a half. While there, Charlie received the only formal education of his life. But he was miserable at Hanwell, where flogging was still the official punishment for virtually any infringement. Finally his mother was released, and once again the family was united, however briefly. During the next few years, Charlie found occasional work as a juvenile performer in touring reviews. When she was able, Mrs. Chaplin coached him. By the time he was ten, Charlie was already a skillful singer, dancer, acrobat, juggler, pantomimist, and comic improviser. At the age of twelve, he joined a touring stock company and specialized in playing tough Cockneys. Still almost illiterate, he was able to memorize his roles only after his mother drilled him in private. Throughout this period, he was barely able to eke out a subsistence. Sydney had gone off to sea, and sent back what little he could.

Eventually Sydney managed to get a job with the prosperous Karno Company, which specialized in such music-hall entertainment as acrobatics, juggling, song and dance, and slapstick skits. He wheedled Karno into giving seventeen-year-old Charlie an audition. After a rather inauspicious beginning, the youth gradually worked his way up from bit roles, until at the age of nineteen, Charlie was Karno's principal comedian. In the following year he was receiving top billing and earning the equivalent of $75 a week—a handsome salary in 1910. During this period, he was morose and withdrawn, ashamed of his ignorance, and too shy and proud to make friends. He taught himself how to play the violin and cello and practiced four to six hours a day in his room, a regimen he continued for many years. He began to read voraciously, and was particularly drawn to American literature and the pessimistic philosophy of Schopenhauer. He lived simply, saving two-thirds of his salary: He never forgot the terrors of poverty, notwithstanding his considerable success.

The Karno Company actually consisted of several troups of performers who regularly toured the major cities of Europe, Canada, and the United States. In 1910 Chaplin made his first trip to America, and he was favorably impressed: "I felt at home in the states—a foreigner among foreigners, allied with the rest." During his second tour in 1912, he received a telegram from the representatives of Mack Sennett, who had recently set up his Keystone Studio in Los Angeles. Sennett offered the young English comedian a one-year contract at $150 a week. Like Griffith, Chaplin was contemptuous of "the flickers" and reluctant to relinquish the prestige of being a music-hall headliner. But the money was too tempting, and he reasoned, "A year at that racket and I could return to vaudeville an international star." With great trepidation, Chaplin signed with Sennett.

Even within the trade, the Keystone Studio was viewed as something of a sausage factory, grinding out 140 one-reelers in its first year of existence. But the Canadian-born Sennett had a shrewd box office instinct, and over the years he gave employment to some of the finest comic talent in America, including such gifted performers as Mabel Normand, Roscoe "Fatty" Arbuckle, Harry Langdon, and—briefly—Harold Lloyd. Other Keystone graduates included Gloria Swanson, Marie Dressler, Carole Lombard, and the directors Leo McCarey and Frank Capra. Sennett is regarded as the Griffith of American film comedy because he established many of the basic conventions of the slapstick form. "Our specialty was exasperated dignity and the discombobulation of Authority," he boasted. Every sacred cow of respectable society was burlesqued with gleeful vulgarity, much to the delight of the spectators, who were almost exclusively from the lowest social echelons. Spokesmen

Figure 2.2. Chaplin and Marie Dressler in *Tillie's Punctured Romance* (1914), directed by Mack Sennett. The characters Chaplin played in his Keystone period were obnoxious but likable. His year at the studio culminated with this six-reel feature in which he plays Dressler's larcenous boyfriend who swindles her out of her money. Like many of Sennett's comedies, it parodies a popular dramatic formula of the era—the country virgin who's deceived by a city slicker. Like all of Sennett's movies, it's fast, robust, and shamelessly vulgar in its exuberance.

of bourgeois culture criticized these movies in large part because the rich and powerful were Sennett's most frequent targets.

Violent and unpredictable, the Keystone one-reelers featured chases of truly demented proportions, epic pie battles, and monumental traffic collisions—usually photographed in fast motion. No one agonized much over such aesthetic niceties as unity or coherence. The "stories" generally centered on a specific place, event, or occupation. Working without scripts, Sennett's cheery lunatics would often descend upon a location and improvise madly before being evicted as undesirables. Virtually every movie ended with a chase. Speed, spontaneity, and bad taste were the watchwords, and if things got dull, the zany Keystone Kops and Sennett's famous Bathing Beauties could be counted on to enliven the show.

When Chaplin arrived at the studio in 1913, he was terrified. After observing the bedlam for several days, he was sure he had made a horrible mistake. He was appalled by the speed and total lack of restraint of the Keystone style. He detested chase scenes, believing they dissipated one's personality. "Little as I knew about movies," he later recalled, "I knew that nothing transcended personality"—a conviction that was to become his central credo in the years ahead. Finally Sennett persuaded

Chaplin to give the new medium a try. The results were disappointing. He simply couldn't work in such a chaotic and undisciplined style.

He explained his dilemma to the charming and sympathetic Mabel Normand, Sennett's lover and the reigning comedienne at Keystone. Both of them convinced Sennett to allow the newcomer to develop his own slower style. The results produced a bonanza at the box office, and

Figure 2.3. Charlie, also known as Charlot, Carlino, Carlos, Carlitas, and so on. No other movie clown could boast such an enormous international following: Charlies's appeal was virtually universal. Said Chaplin of his persona, "You know this fellow is many-sided, a tramp, a gentleman, a poet, a dreamer, a lonely fellow, always hopeful of romance and adventure. He would have you believe he is a scientist, a musician, a duke, a polo-player. However, he is not above picking up a cigarette butt or robbing a baby of its candy." Chaplin claimed that his size (he was five feet four inches tall and weighed 130 pounds) contributed greatly to his popularity, for "everyone knows that the little fellow in trouble always gets the sympathy of the mob." He developed the Tramp's costume with an eye for incongruity, a mixture of the fastidious dandy and the scruffy street urchin—with a touch of the poet. Photo: Carmie Amata.

exhibitors clamored for more comedies with "the little fellow." Before long, Chaplin persuaded Sennett to allow him to direct his own films. Once again Sennett acquiesced, though harboring many doubts about the Englishman's extravagant methods. Chaplin insisted on photographing all rehearsals so that he could subsequently edit out unsuccessful improvisations and correct mistakes in timing and technique. Since film stock was expensive, Sennett considered this practice wasteful. But like every other forceful genius of the American cinema, Chaplin was allowed to go his own way as long as the box office hummed. It not only hummed, it positively sang: Audiences couldn't see enough of the sensational new clown.

Viewed from today's perspective, Chaplin's Keystone shorts aren't very impressive except to idolotors. Most of these early efforts seem crude, though a few of them contain flashes of brilliance. In all, he made thirty-four shorts (mostly one-reelers) and one feature at Keystone, all released in 1914. He wrote and directed most of these and never relinquished authorial control after this period. He played a variety of roles, drawing from his vast music-hall repertory. Most of the characters he created were cocky and insolent and included such staple vaudeville types as the drunk, the rich "swell," the con man, the philandering husband, the boor, and so on. In playing a seedy dandy in *Kid Auto Races at Venice* (1914), Chaplin accidentally stumbled onto a tramplike costume, complete with baggy pants, derby, and oversized shoes. Sennett had a genius for attracting and nurturing talent, but a fatal inability to hold on to it. Many fine comedians left his studio in disgust because he refused to pay them what they were worth. Chaplin was no exception.

In 1915 the Essanay Company offered him a one-year contract at $1,250 a week. Astonished by such a fantastic sum, he signed eagerly. In his year at Essanay he produced fifteen films, most of them two-reelers. During this period his work habits began to settle into a fixed pattern, for he enjoyed considerable creative independence. The placid beauty, Edna Purviance, became his leading lady and remained with him for his next thirty-four movies. Rollie Totheroh became his regular cameraman, a function he performed for over three decades. The Essanay films are mostly transitional works, more carefully produced, slower, and more subtle than the Keystone shorts, but still somewhat primitive compared to his mature films. Working from a general outline which allowed for considerable improvisation, Chaplin retained the Keystone formula of unifying his movies around a location, a personality type, or a situation.

The most important works of the Essanay period are *The Bank* and *The Tramp* (1915), his first movies to introduce elements of irony and pathos—characteristics which later gave birth to the phrase *Chaplinesque*. Indeed, *The Tramp* is regarded by many as Chaplin's first masterpiece. Complete with tragic undercurrents and an unhappy ending (which was unheard of in slapstick comedy), this is the movie that fixed the cinema's most famous persona. The celebrated conclusion conveyed an emotional richness not even Chaplin fully appreciated until later. Rejected by the woman he loves, unemployed, and utterly alone, the Tramp is photographed from behind, his shoulders slumped in dejection. Meandering aimlessly on a barren country road that stretches on endlessly, he is a figure of pathetic vulnerability. Suddenly he stops, considers, then shrugs his shoulders stoically. He kicks up his heels, twirls his cane, then waddles jauntily toward his uncertain destiny on the horizon, an iris closing in on his receding figure. This classic final shot was to become a ritualistic feature in many of Chaplin's movies in the years ahead.

In 1916, at the age of twenty-six, Chaplin signed a one-year contract with Mutual. He was now the most popular box office attraction in the world, commanding a salary of $10,000 a week, plus a bonus of $150,000. The twelve Mutual shorts, all of them two-reelers, were painstakingly created. Though dazzled by Chaplin's unprecedented string of hits, industry regulars considered him extravagant, for each short cost about $100,000—more than most features of the time. But Chaplin considered himself an artist first and a businessman only incidentally. He scorned petty economies where his art was concerned and often shot as much as 90,000 feet of stock from which he would sculpt a 2,000-foot two-reeler.

Several of the Mutual shorts are now considered classics. *Easy Street* and *The Immigrant* (both released in 1917) include a good deal of social criticism, a characteristic that was to become increasingly prominent in

Figure 2.4. *The Immigrant* **(1917), with Edna Purviance (center).** Chaplin's comedy is steeped in social comment, which is often presented from a wryly ironic perspective. In this film, the Tramp and other impoverished refugees aboard ship are roped off like cattle the very moment they sail past America's most famous symbol of liberty in New York harbor. The movie is unrelenting in its picture of social squalor; yet it's also one of Chaplin's funniest comedies. Photo: Scott Eyman.

Chaplin's works. *Easy Street* is set in a slum, swarming with underfed children, bullies, and lurking opportunists. Into this unsavory milieu waddles Charlie—as a cop! Touched by the plight of a mother who steals food for her starving children, he innocently gazes the other way. When Edna is almost raped by a drug-crazed addict, Charlies gallantly rushes to her rescue—only to inject the narcotic accidentally. Stoned out of his

Figure 2.5.   Publicity photo for *Shoulder Arms* (1918). This three-reel comedy was made during the final months of World War I and was released three weeks before the Armistice. It ridiculed the absurdity of war and the dehumanizing regimentation of military life. Chaplin feared the movie might be criticized for its bad taste, a charge that had been leveled at him many times before. But the film proved to be his most popular work to date.

Figure 2.6. Publicity photo from *The Kid* (1921), with Jackie Coogan as the kid. A powerful Dickensian work partly based on Chaplin's childhood experiences in the London slums, *The Kid* was his first self-directed feature (six reels). The police in his works are almost invariably portrayed as bullies whose main purpose is to protect the interests of the propertied classes. *The Kid* netted Chaplin a personal profit of over a million dollars and considerably more for its distributor, First National.

mind, Charlie swiftly subdues the burly assaulter, and even manages to hold back a threatening mob.

When Chaplin signed with First National Films in 1917, he was paid a cool $1 million, a sum that sent a thrill of amazement throughout the industry. During this period, he had his own studio constructed and used this modest facility for shooting most of his subsequent movies. As his art grew more complex, he produced fewer works and devoted increasingly more time to preparations. The eight movies for First National took him five years to complete. (In 1919 he joined with Griffith and his two close friends, Mary Pickford and Douglas Fairbanks, to form United Artists, but he was unable to distribute through their joint company until he fulfilled his obligation to First National in 1922.) The movies produced during this period are unquestionably the work of a mature artist and include such masterpieces as the three-reelers, *A Dog's Life* and *Shoulder Arms* (both 1918), and his first feature, *The Kid* (1921).

Beginning in 1923, Chaplin was totally independent, answerable to no one: "I aimed exclusively at pleasing myself. For when I gave the subject thought, I became convinced it was the average man I tried to please. And was I not that average man?" Critics sometimes designate the years between 1923 and 1952 as his United Artists period, for all his works were released through this parent firm. Though he produced only eight features in these three decades, most of them are works of the first rank and include such masterpieces as *The Gold Rush* (1925), *The Circus* (1928), *City Lights* (1931), *Modern Times* (1936), and *Monsieur Ver-*

Figure 2.7. *The Gold Rush,* **"A Dramatic Comedy" (1925).** In this movie Charlie's vulnerability and solitude are conveyed by the mise-en-scène as well as the acting. The Tramp's small, gallant figure is often contrasted with the sterility of the epic setting, a flimsy shawl his only additional protection against the arctic harshness. The comedy contains fewer laughs than his previous works, and its undercurrents of pessimism are only partly mitigated by its upbeat ending. Contemporary critics regarded this as his greatest work, and even Chaplin referred to it as "the picture I want to be remembered by."

doux (1947). His two all-time box office hits were also made within this period: *The Great Dictator* (1940) and *Limelight* (1952). He directed only two movies after then, both of them unsuccessful: *A King in New York* (1957) and *A Countess from Hong Kong* (1967).

Chaplin is a sublimely egotistical artist, and his fierce individuality is central to an appreciation of his art. In the first place, he realized early in his career that artistic control was predicated on financial independence; accordingly, he kept fluid reserves of two to three million dollars throughout his mature career, allowing him to produce his own movies. He never had to battle with the front office because he *was* the front office. Though he never used shooting scripts until 1936, he "wrote" all his movies in the sense that only he decided what the subject matter would be. As a great actor-director, he controlled all decisions both in front of and behind the camera. In addition, he carefully controlled the music of his movies, supervising the cue sheets for his silents and composing and even conducting the music for most of his talkies. (His most famous composition is the melancholy tune, "Smile," used in *Modern Times*.) As part owner of United Artists, he could even control how his movies would be distributed and where they would be exhibited. In short, he is unique in the American cinema. Throughout his career, he scorned the Hollywood studio system of filmmaking, insisting that standardization and mass production are admirable methods for the manufacture of tractors but hardly conducive to the creation of movie masterpieces.

This same egocentric principle applies to the films themselves: Chaplin is almost never off-camera, and in those few instances where he is, he's sorely missed. He made only two films in which he didn't star—*A Woman of Paris* (1923) and *A Countess from Hong Kong*—neither of them popular. Furthermore, like most great comic creations—Don Quixote, Falstaff, Tartuffe—the Tramp is an egregious egomaniac. He will go to almost any lengths to get what he wants, will undertake any enterprise however forbidding, and views any failure of cooperation as a personal malicious affront. Precisely because Charlie is so monomaniacal, his failures seem all the more unjust: A person of such fervent determination clearly *deserves* to win.

The Tramp's complexity is due in part to the fact that he was developed serially. Each movie, in effect, represents a slice of life from his continuing story, somewhat like a sitcom character within an open-ended television series. Though Chaplin continued to play other roles even into the 1920s, the Tramp was his principal persona for over twenty years. He made his final appearance in 1936 in *Modern Times*, after which Chaplin felt compelled to create speaking characters. (His private experiments with allowing the Tramp to talk met with failure.) Over the years, as his environment grows more complex, so does the Tramp. In the beginning, he is preoccupied primarily with survival, his need for food, warmth, and shelter. His adversaries are "respectable citizens," bullies, and cops. Gradually he yearns for higher things: respect, affection, love. Toward the end, he becomes more politicized: The bullies are now institutions rather than individuals—big business, big labor, big government.

Winston Churchill, a Chaplin enthusiast, pointed out that his comedy was far more American than English, particularly in its rejection of social conformity. "Behind his wandering," Churchill wrote, "was something of the old adventurous urge that sent the covered wagons lumbering across the prairie towards the sunset." The fact that Charlie is so obviously competent in a variety of skills—with awesome ease, he can be a waiter, preacher, boxer, cook, mechanic, paperhanger, and so on—suggests that he *prefers* the excitement and freedom of the open road to the fixed routines of bourgeois life. Charlie is not so much an outcast from middle-class society as a rebel against it. These antiestablishment sentiments were probably absorbed at Keystone, and they became more pronounced over the years. The Tramp is cynically irreverent toward authority. He despises cant and people who are pompous, domineering, and snooty. Custodians of public morality often complained of his vulgar displays of disrespect—like sticking out his ass and wiggling it at his adversaries in malicious triumph.

Chaplin never abandoned the engaging villains of his Keystone period; he simply incorporated them into his persona of the Tramp. A larcenous heart beats beneath that sweetly benign exterior. He's never above cheating people, especially if they are rich or stupid. If they're both, he swindles them as though it were a matter of eminent domain. While sidling up to his mark, he often feigns a cool disinterest, with only his darting eyes betraying his excitement. If the intended victim responds with suspicion, Charlie will flash a toothy smile that's the very quintessence of calculated "sincerity." He's the coolest of hustlers and will brazen out any accusation—however just—with either astonished innocence or glacial hauteur.

Much of Charlie's appeal lies in his attempts to preserve his dignity. Chaplin had a vast repertory of gestures to convey the Tramp's persnickety side. To express disapproval, he purses his lips prudishly and arches his eyebrows in unfeigned disgust. His double- and tripletakes of wide-eyed amazement have been imitated by many, but seldom equaled and never surpassed. In his dealings with bullies, Charlie will often tip his hat prissily—as if to say, "Well, at least *I* am a gentleman"—click his heels, pivot smartly, and stride away, all accompanied by an expression of unutterable disdain. Sometimes he gets carried away by his own grandeur: When offered a handout he will refuse the small change imperiously, stop, reconsider, then snatch up the offering before the bewildered giver has a chance to repocket it.

But it was the introduction of pathos that most endeared the Tramp to hundreds of millions. When he lets down his guard; when he allows himself to feel; above all, when he falls in love, Charlie's vulnerabilities are as sensitive as nerve endings. Always compassionate toward the helpless and oppressed, he's especially gallant toward women and defends them with a courage that borders on folly. He's particularly drawn to girlish women, innocent gamines who seem utterly incapable of caring for themselves. Like a moonstruck boy, his love is shy, asexual, idealistic. The object of his devotion is often worshipped from afar: He suffers secretly, hopelessly. Only his goony listlessness—so strangely untypical—betrays his condition. He sometimes misinterprets the pity of

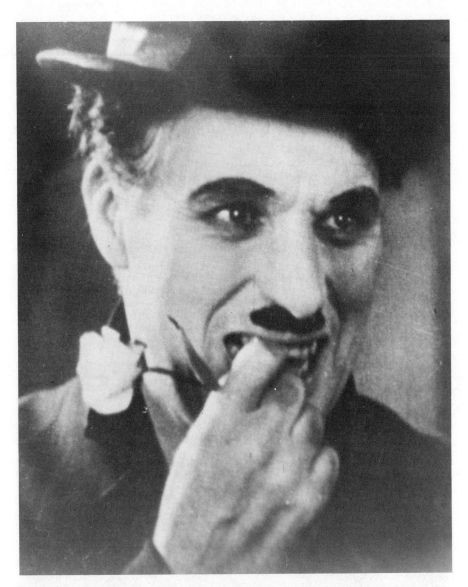

Figure 2.8. *City Lights*, **"A Comedy Romance in Pantomime" (1931).** One of Chaplin's most famous pronouncements was "Long shot for comedy, closeup for tragedy." When the camera is relatively distant from Charlie, we tend to be objective and detached and are more likely to laugh at his predicaments. As the famous final shot of *City Lights* illustrates, when the camera moves in for a closeup, in effect *we* get close to the character and identify more with his feelings, which are difficult to ignore at this range. Chaplin used closeups sparingly for this very reason: As long as the Tramp remains at a distance, we're likely to be amused by his antics. In scenes of greater emotional impact, however, he moved his camera closer in, and the effect is often devastating on the audience, for we suddenly realize that the situation we've been laughing at is no longer funny. Photo: Scott Eyman.

mature women for love. The mortification he suffers upon realizing his error is poignant. Chaplin was occasionally sentimental in his treatment of other characters, but never the Tramp: His pain and humiliation are conveyed with exquisite tact.

Perhaps the most famous example of Chaplinesque pathos is found at the conclusion of *City Lights.* Charlie has fallen in love with an impoverished flower vendor who is blind. She believes him to be an eccentric millionaire, and out of vanity he allows her to continue in this delusion. By engaging in a series of monumental labors—love has reduced him to work—he manages to scrape together enough money for her to receive an operation to restore her sight, but he's dragged off to jail before she can scarcely thank him for the money. The final scene takes place several months later. The young woman can now see and owns her own modest flower shop. Charlie is released from prison, and disheveled and dispirited, he meanders past her shop window. She sees him gazing at her wistfully and jokes to an assistant that she's apparently made a new

Figure 2.9. *Modern Times* **(1936).** Originally entitled *The Masses,* this was Chaplin's most overtly political feature to date and the Tramp's final appearance. The movie is an impassioned defense of the human spirit in the face of increasing mechanization and regimentation. In this scene Charlie goes beserk while toiling on an assembly line, and in a demented ballet he whirls and twirls like a loon around the gears and levers of an enormous factory generator. *Modern Times* is also Chaplin's last silent movie—nine years after the talkie revolution.

conquest. Out of pity she goes out to the street and offers him a flower and a small coin. Instantly she recognizes his touch, and scarcely able to believe her eyes, she can only stammer, "You?" In a series of alternating closeups, their embarrassment is unbearably prolonged. Clearly he is not the idol of her romantic dreams, and he's painfully aware of her disappointment. Finally he stares at her with an expression of shocking emotional nakedness. The film ends on this image of sublime vulnerability.

Unlike the performances of even some of the greatest silent movie players, Chaplin's acting has dated very little. Today's viewers find him almost as fresh and spontaneous as his original audiences, despite the fact that many of his gags have been copied ad nauseum by other comedians. The wide variety of skills he acquired in his music-hall years made him the most versatile of all film actors. In the area of pantomime, no one approaches his discipline and inventiveness. Critics waxed eloquently on his balletic grace, and even the brilliant dancer Nijinsky proclaimed Chaplin his equal. Nor was his genius as an actor confined to silents. In *Verdoux*, a rather talky talkie, his range is breathtaking, extending from the mincing effeminacy of his opening scenes to the tragic grandeur of the conclusion.

His body was as finely tuned as any instrument, and he was able to control it with precision. His expressive hands, small and delicate, had a life of their own: In *A Dog's Life* he uses them to carry on an elaborate conversation while the remainder of his body is totally hidden from view. Over the years he developed a number of specialties, like hopping and "skidding" too far on one leg while rounding a corner trying to escape a pursuer. Or pratfalling to the floor while carrying a cup of tea, somersaulting over, and landing neatly on his feet, the cup and tea totally intact, all in one fluid motion—known in the trade as "the teacup roll." The boxing matches in such movies as *The Knockout* (1914), *The Champion* (1915), and *City Lights* are exquisitely timed and choreographed. In addition, he was an expert skater, juggler, acrobat, and aerialist and used these skills in many of his movies.

Chaplin was also brilliant with props, as can be seen in a famous sequence from *The Gold Rush*. Stranded in a tiny cabin in the Yukon during a blizzard, Charlie and his starving companion are reduced to eating one of the Tramp's shoes for Thanksgiving. He boils it in a pot, tests it for tenderness, and announces that dinner is almost ready. Before bringing it to the table, he lovingly bastes it with its "juices." While his skeptical companion looks on, Charlie separates the nail-studded sole from the more "tender" top, which he slyly sets aside for himself. But his burly cabin-mate insists on the more delicate portion. Like a fastidious gourmand, Charlie takes a bite from the sole, chews it tentatively, then expresses satisfaction with its flavor. On a side dish are the shoelaces, which he nonchalantly twirls on his fork as though they were strands of spaghetti. He gnaws and sucks each of the nails clean, as though they were succulent chicken bones, and extending his pinky, he even offers to split the "wishbone" for good luck—a suggestion that's received with stoney incredulity. Grudgingly impressed by the Tramp's weird trans-

Figure 2.10. *The Great Dictator* **(1940), with Jack Oakie (right).** Chaplin played two roles in this, his first talkie: a meek Jewish barber who bears a slight resemblance to Charlie the Tramp; and Adenoid Hynkel, dictator of Tomania, who bears a strong resemblance to Adolph Hitler. In a delicious parody of Mussolini, Oakie is nearly as funny in his role of Benzino Napaloni, dictator of Bacteria.

formations, and too hungry to care anymore, the companion finally nibbles on his own portion, doubtlessly stifling some gloomy forebodings about his own mental health.

"Comedy is the most serious study in the world," Chaplin was fond of saying. He believed that the funniest situations were taken from everyday life, and weren't comical in themselves. Cold, hunger, and the shame of poverty formed the basis for much of his humor. *The Gold Rush,* for example, was based on a notorious incident involving cannibalism, and Chaplin's movie contains many scenes that allude to or actually involve eating. Whereas other comedians like Keaton and Lloyd modeled their characters on the mythic success hero, Horatio Alger, Chaplin's persona was shaped by oppression and failure. Even when his films end happily, success is shown to be the result of fate and dumb luck, seldom of perseverance, justice, or hard work. He focused his art on many of the social issues of the day, especially with the problems of survival and preserving one's individuality in an increasingly regimented world. Over the years his movies grew more sophisticated, yet he remained in step with popular tastes for over three decades, until 1947, when mass audiences rejected the bitterly pessimistic *Monsieur Verdoux.*

Chaplin's work methods were characteristically egocentric. The first stage was the "incubation period," which could last for months or even years. During this phase, he would explore a theme or situation in his mind, testing ideas on a few trusted friends or associates. Often he would perform a scene at social gatherings to gauge its effect. When the rough outline of the story was fixed in his mind, he would instruct his staff to prepare for production, which he closely supervised, including the design and construction of the costumes and sets. (He disliked working on location, claiming such methods were distracting and hard to control.) When his cast was assembled, he enacted all their roles for them: Their job was to imitate his performances. He allowed himself considerable room for improvisation, photographing every rehearsal so that he could evaluate the results the following morning when he viewed the rushes. Seldom did he experiment with the camera: Most of the scenes were photographed in master shots, with closer shots added later. He could be patient with his actors, but also autocratic, imperious, and demanding. One scene from *A Woman of Paris* was shot two hundred times before he was satisfied. An average eight-reel feature ate up as much as a half million feet of stock. After he edited and scored the

Figure 2.11. *Monsieur Verdoux,* **"A Comedy of Murders" (1947), with Martha Raye.** Banned and picketed in a number of American cities, this was Chaplin's most controversial movie and his least successful commercially. Its black comedy was many years ahead of its time. The film is his most sardonic critique of capitalism. "Von Clausewitz said that war is a logical extension of diplomacy," Chaplin observed; "M. Verdoux feels that murder is the logical extension of business." Though Chaplin's treatment of his own character is not without sympathy, his principal symbol of the life force centers around the Martha Raye character—the vulgar, slobbering, and sublimely indestructible Annabella, who escapes Verdoux's malevolent machinations through sheer blundering luck.

movie, he would test it with an audience at a sneak preview—virtually a universal practice in Hollywood at this time and almost essential for comedy. Carefully noting which scenes were effective and which weren't, he would then return to the editing bench to excise the offending footage. Only then was the movie ready for release.

Chaplin's artistic flaws stem from this same obsession with control. As a directorial technician, he was frankly pedestrian and sometimes downright crude. He disliked "tricky effects" with the camera. His concern was with people—principally his own character—not with the aesthetic subtleties of mise-en-scène. He seldom used suggestive camera movements or unusual angles, insisting they were distracting: "*I* am the unusual," he argued, "I do not need camera angles." He disdained what he called "prosaic realism," stressing a "poetic effect" in his lighting, sets, and costumes. But too often this "poetic effect" is banal. The "Parisian" sets of *Verdoux* are so patently phony that some viewers wince at their tackiness. When he needed to use miniatures or special effects, as in the cabin-tilting scene from *Gold Rush*, the results often look amateurish. Except for his unerring instincts in the use of closeups, which are as powerful as they are rare, his editing is functional and unexciting. He never bothered to explore the expressive possibilities of sound: Like the camera, the microphone was a mere recording machine.

For such a brilliant actor, Chaplin was shockingly mechanical in his direction of other performers. His staging is often stiff and theatrical, as though the players had learned their movements by rote—which, of course, they had. He frequently cautioned his players with the injunction: "And above all, don't *act!*" But there's little that's truly spontaneous in the other performers. Even Marlon Brando, widely regarded as the most gifted American film actor of his generation, looks like a harassed automaton in *A Countess from Hong Kong*. The heavies in Chaplin's movies look big, burly, and dumb; little else was expected, and little else was exhibited. He was something of a Svengali with his leading ladies. Rarely using established actresses, he preferred to mold his own, and few of them continued their careers after working with him. The handsome but stolid Edna Purviance, who played opposite him for nine years, was as dull as he was charismatic. Co-star Paulette Goddard often looks as though she had been programmed by computer in *Modern Times* and *The Great Dictator,* yet in her subsequent movies with other directors, she displays considerable talent. Only a few exceptions stand out, most notably Clair Bloom's sensitive performance in *Limelight* and Sophia Loren's irresistible vitality in *A Countess*.

Many commentators have criticized Chaplin's deficient narrative sense, charging that his movies are episodic and lacking in structural rigor. The "stories" are merely a tandem collection of two-reelers, mechanically unified by the nearly continual presence of the Tramp, these critics have complained. But in this respect, the charges against Chaplin seem superficial. In the first place, the Tramp is a vagabond, a wanderer; and the essence of such a character, like the protagonist of a picaresque novel, lies in his constant search for novelty. This characteristic necessarily precludes the likelihood of a single locale or occupation, an overriding goal, or a permanent relationship. In short, the episodic

Figure 2.12. *Limelight* **(1952), with Buster Keaton.** Chaplin's last major work was condemned by some critics for its talkiness and didacticism. Others praised it as his *Tempest,* a mellow, philosophical meditation on life's eternal truths. The movie concludes with this superb (and essentially nontalking) sequence between two old vaudevillians. The sequence culminates with the Chaplin character's death.

structures of the Tramp features are governed by the personality of the protagonist. Most of the features are unified instead by a central symbolic concept. In *Gold Rush,* for example, the governing metaphor is hunger; in *City Lights,* the symbolism revolves around various kinds of blindness; *Modern Times* is unified by the central motif of machinery; and so on. Chaplin's talkies, which center on more goal-oriented protagonists, are more tightly constructed. For example, the plot to *Verdoux* is exceptionally intricate, and it's as disciplined as any in the American cinema.

In the 1940s, the American public turned against Chaplin with such ferocity that a lesser person would have been destroyed by the experience. Although he detested scandal, his private life constantly invited it. His numerous love affairs, marriages, and divorces provided a steady stream of gaudy headlines. He was involved in a humiliating paternity suit in 1943, and though he was finally acquitted (blood tests proved he couldn't possibly have been the child's father), various women's organizations conducted "morality" campaigns against him. As his movies became more explicitly critical of social conditions, he was accused by right-wing organizations of being a Red or at least a fellow traveler. Chaplin was passionately interested in political and philosophical ideas, and among his friends were a number of Marxist freethinkers, like Max Eastman, Upton Sinclair, and H. G. Wells. But as Eastman pointed out, Chaplin's political views were vague and inconsistent. His sympathies were with the poor and oppressed, but he never joined any political party; and as Eastman drily observed, Chaplin's minuscule financial contributions to leftist causes were hardly the effusions of a fervent revolutionary.

Few of his critics bothered to recall the millions of dollars in U.S. bonds that he helped to sell in various tours during both world wars. Furthermore, in the late 1930s, when precious few were speaking out against the impending Holocaust in Europe, Chaplin was preparing the grimly prophetic anti-Nazi satire, *The Great Dictator,* a film he was told by industry sages would be too controversial and would almost certainly be a flop. But he went ahead anyway, declaring on its release, "I made this film for the Jews of the world." At a time when anti-Semitism was still a commonplace in America, he stubbornly refused to deny he was a Jew. (He wasn't.)

Above all, then, Chaplin was an indomitable individualist. He refused to be cowed by bullies, no matter how powerful. He insisted—and of course rightly—that his private life, however screwed up, was his own concern. When asked why he never became an American citizen, he replied that he was "a citizen of the world" and owed his allegiance to all humanity, not to one country alone. In 1952 he and his young wife Oona (the daughter of Eugene O'Neill) sailed for Europe to launch a publicity tour for *Limelight.* He was cabled by the U.S. Immigration Department that he would be refused reentry into the United States until he satisfactorily answered "charges of a political nature and moral turpitude." Angry, hurt, and disgusted, Chaplin neither answered nor returned.

He was a man of great cunning as well as courage, and he managed to outlive and outfox them all. For over twenty years the Chaplins remained outside the United States. He and Oona settled in Switzerland, where they purchased an isolated estate and raised eight children in lofty tranquility, far removed from the petty conniving of political bureaucrats and the venom of self-righteous moralists. But eventually the political paranoia in America subsided. In 1972, Chaplin was invited back to receive a special Oscar at the Academy Awards. In his celebrated tour of that year, he was greeted with thunderous adulation. Deeply moved by his reception, Chaplin forgave and forgot. Shortly afterward, he was knighted in the country of his birth by Queen Elizabeth. In his declining years, Sir Charles Chaplin lived quietly in Switzerland, no doubt deriving considerable satisfaction from the knowledge that his "radical" views were almost universally shared by compassionate and humane people everywhere. He died in his sleep at the age of eighty-eight on Christmas morning of 1977. He was buried in Switzerland.

Chaplin's influence on other comic artists has been enormous, not only in the American cinema, with such gifted comedians from Harry Langdon to Woody Allen, but also in Europe and elsewhere. In Italy, Federico Fellini and Vittorio De Sica both admitted a major indebtedness, and in France, René Clair, Jean Vigo, and François Truffaut were obviously influenced by Chaplin's bitter-sweet comedy. Some of the finest comic actors have been described as "Chaplinesque," including Giulietta Masina, Jean-Pierre Léaud, and Giancarlo Giannini. In his famous essay, "Comedy's Greatest Era," perhaps James Agee best summed up Chaplin's achievement:

> Of all comedians he worked most deeply and most shrewdly within a realization of what a human being is, and is up against. The Tramp is as centrally representative of humanity, as many-sided and as mysterious, as Hamlet, and it seems unlikely that any dancer or actor can ever have excelled him in eloquence, variety or poignancy of motion.

BIBLIOGRAPHY

AGEE, JAMES. "Comedy's Greatest Era," in *Agee on Film*. Boston: Beacon Press, 1958. An affectionate and beautifully written appreciation of American silent comedy, with emphasis on Chaplin, Keaton, Lloyd, and Langdon. This volume also contains Agee's three-part encomium on *Monsieur Verdoux*.

CHAPLIN, CHARLES. *My Autobiography*. New York: Simon & Schuster, 1964. An indispensible though surprisingly humorless book, written in Chaplin's old age. Other autobiographical books, apparently more fanciful than factual, are *Charlie Chaplin's Own Story* (Indianapolis, Ind.: Bobbs-Merrill, 1916); and *My Trip Abroad* (New York: Harper & Row, Pub., 1922).

COTES, PETER, AND THELMA NIKLAUS. *The Little Fellow*. New York: Citadel Press, 1965. An illustrated biography and critical study.

HUFF, THEODORE. *Charlie Chaplin*. New York: Henry Schuman, 1951. A classic biography and critical study, though the book doesn't cover Chaplin's later years. Filmography.

KERR, WALTER. *The Silent Clowns*. New York: Knopf, 1975. A well-written and lavishly illustrated analysis of the silent comic cinema, with several chapters on Chaplin.

LYONS, TIMOTHY J. *Charles Chaplin: A Guide to References and Resources*. Boston: G. K. Hall & Co., 1978. The most extensive bibliography and filmography.

MCCABE, JOHN. *Charlie Chaplin*. New York: Doubleday, 1978. Biography and critical study.

MCCAFFREY, DONALD, ed. *Focus on Chaplin*. New York: Prentice-Hall, 1971. A useful collection of essays, written by a variety of hands. See also McCaffrey's *4 Great Comedians* (Cranbury, N.J.: A. S. Barnes, 1968), which contains a lengthy section on Chaplin.

MANVELL, ROGER. *Chaplin*. Boston: Little, Brown, 1974. A comprehensive biography, with selective bibliography.

SOBEL, RAOUL, AND DAVID FRANCIS. *Chaplin: Genesis of a Clown*. London and New York: Quartet Books, 1977. A study of the origins of Chaplin's art. Bibliography and filmography.

The Poetics of Space

The Cinema of Buster Keaton

Figure 3.1. Publicity photo of Keaton relaxing between shots with co-star Marian Mack, during the production of *The General* (1926). Keaton liked a happy set, where work procedures were informal, efficient, and fun. Though he was invariably cordial with all the members of his company, most of his spare time during production was devoted to playing baseball with the boys—especially his regulars, like Clyde Bruckman, who was hired in 1921 as "outfielder and writer." Photo: Scott Eyman.

Thanks largely to the pioneering work of the French critics of the 1960s, Buster Keaton is now regarded as a unique comic genius, not merely as Chaplin's greatest rival. No one was more surprised than Keaton himself when the French wrote so admiringly of his movies, for he was a modest, unpretentious man who thought of himself as a professional entertainer rather than a self-conscious artist. Totally apolitical, Keaton seldom dealt with serious social themes, nor was he interested in a wide range of ideas. In his interviews, he became excited only when discussing the mechanics of a gag or the intricacies of a shot. But style is the man, despite Keaton's self-effacing disclaimers. His style has been called classic: poised, sophisticated, and elegant, yet at the same time functional, simple, direct. There are few "beautiful shots" in Keaton's works, only superlatively intelligent ones. Though he was trained in vaudeville, he expressed himself in almost purely cinematic terms. He used fewer titles than any other American silent filmmaker: His shots are composed and edited with such self-evident lucidity that words are usually unnecessary. Keaton was a physical comedian rather than a traditional pantomimist. His was a comedy of mise-en-scène as well as character and situation: We laugh not only at Buster's indomitable pluck but also at the "perverse" objects which loom threateningly in his environment. The French surrealist Jean Cocteau once remarked, "The more one touches mystery, the more important it becomes to be realistic." This observation might well serve as Keaton's artistic credo, for his filmworld is both dreamlike and concrete. Rejecting trick editing, he insisted that most gags are funnier when they're presented in a matter-of-fact, documentary style and when they occur in space that's not been artificially manipulated at the editor's bench. In fact, his gags are mounted with such cinematic mastery that they would retain much of their wit even if someone else performed them.

> *For a real effect and to convince people that it's on the level,* do *it on the level. No faking. Move the camera back and take it all in one shot.*
> —*Buster Keaton*

Joseph Frank Keaton was born in 1895 in the tiny town of Piqua, Kansas. When he was six months old he fell down a flight of stairs, and his godfather Harry Houdini, who later gained fame as an escape artist, dubbed the child *Buster* because he could take such a fall without busting anything. The name stuck. The boy's parents, Joe and Myra, were variety performers with a number of traveling tent shows in the midwest. Eventually they worked their way up to vaudeville, and for over a decade they were a headliner act. Fortunately the Keatons were a hearty lot, for they were oddly accident-prone: They were nearly trapped in three separate hotel fires; their two-year-old daughter stepped out of an open window and plunged two stories to the pavement below without killing herself; and weirdest of all, three-year-old Buster was lifted out of a hotel room by a cyclone which flattened the entire town of Piqua. A gentle downwind deposited him—without a scratch—four blocks away. Not surprisingly, Keaton developed a fatalistic attitude toward life long before he reached his maturity.

As a child, Buster begged his parents to let him join the act. By the time he was three, he knew all Joe's routines by heart. The child was a natural acrobat and enjoyed roughhousing with his father, who tossed him so high in the air that Myra was unnerved by their recklessness. Unable to leave the child alone for fear he'd get into mischief, Joe and Myra finally let Buster join their act when he was five. His contribution was to allow Joe to hurl him into the wings, against the scenery, even into the orchestra pit! Apparently The Three Keatons was one of those you-had-to-be-there kind of acts, for it was enormously popular. At the age of eleven, Buster was perhaps the best-known juvenile comedian in America, and by the time he was sixteen, the act was built primarily around his acrobatic feats. Billed as The Human Mop, the resiliant youth never seriously injured himself in all his years in vaudeville. In

Figure 3.2. Buster and Joe Keaton in vaudeville costumes, circa 1906. Even as a boy, Buster had already fixed that melancholy, stoical gaze which later gave him the nickname, The Great Stoneface. Deadpan humor was a staple technique in vaudeville, but when used by a child, its effect was doubly funny. "If I laughed at what I did," Keaton later recalled, "the audience didn't. The more serious I turned the bigger laugh I could get. I didn't even know I was doing it." Photo: Scott Eyman.

addition to acrobatics, The Three Keatons also featured such standard fare as musical interludes, satirical sketches, pantomime, standup comedy, improvisations, recitations, and parodies. All of this experience proved invaluable when Keaton later turned to performing in movies.

He had an exceptionally happy childhood, for in addition to being a traveling entertainer, he amused himself by building fantastically intricate Rube Goldberg machines. He also loved athletics, especially baseball, a passion he never abandoned. His only day in school proved disastrous when he parried the teacher's questions with zippy one-liners—much to the delight of the other children, who were vastly impressed by his wit. Myra took over his formal education, though she had gone only as far as the third grade herself. Keaton's real schoolroom was the vaudeville stage, and he enjoyed the instruction of some of the most talented entertainers in show business.

The act broke up in 1917, after Joe's heavy drinking began to affect his work. Keaton was twenty-one at the time. He was soon offered $250 a week as a solo act, with his name up in lights. But Fate intervened. While pondering his future, Keaton ran into an old vaudeville friend who was now working for Roscoe "Fatty" Arbuckle. Fresh from his Keystone triumphs, Arbuckle had just formed a new company and planned to go into independent production. Keaton accompanied them to the studio, and immediately he became fascinated by the camera and the elaborate technology involved in producing movies. When Arbuckle offered him a job as second comic lead, Keaton accepted without hesitation, even though movies were far less prestigious than vaudeville. Later he learned that his salary would be $40 a week.

Keaton admired and respected Arbuckle, who taught the newcomer everything he knew about filmmaking. The boss ran a loose ship, with lots of practical joking and impromptu baseball games between scenes. Everyone enjoyed working there because Arbuckle believed that work should be fun. Within three months, Keaton became his assistant director, and increasingly, Arbuckle was turning to him for advice. Both of them were expert improvisors, and the generous star allowed his assistant to take the spotlight on many occasions. Some of the films they produced have been lost, but scholars have estimated that Keaton made from fourteen to seventeen two-reelers in his two years with Arbuckle. They became close personal friends, and several years later, when the fat clown was implicated in a rape and homocide scandal, Keaton was one of the few to stand by his old friend, lending him money and securing him employment as a director. Though the ill-fated comedian was legally acquitted, his acting career was finished.

In 1920, as a result of his box office popularity and on the advice of his business manager and brother-in-law Joseph Schenck, Keaton went into independent production. Never very concerned with the business aspects of his career, the comedian allowed Schenck to manage the Keaton Film Company for him. In the early years, Keaton drew a salary of $1,000 per week, plus 25 percent of the net profits. As usual, he didn't bother with a written contract: All agreements were oral. Later his salary was raised to $2,000, then to $3,000 per week, 25 percent of the net, plus occasional bonuses. Most important of all, Keaton had total artistic autonomy. Schenck handled only the business affairs and never interfered with artistic matters.

The 1920s was to be Keaton's golden era. During this period, he made nineteen two-reelers and twelve features. Encouraged by his box office popularity, he continued refining his art and accelerating his pace. Within a five-year period, he made nine first-rate features: *Our Hospitality* (1923), *Sherlock Junior* (1924), *The Navigator* (1924), *Seven Chances*

(1925), *Go West* (1925), *Battling Butler* (1926), *The General* (1926), *College* (1927), and *Steamboat Bill Jr.* (1928). Each movie cost about $210,000 and each grossed about $1½ to $2 million. Keaton's two favorites, *The Navigator* and *The General,* are regarded as his masterpieces.

In his first three years as an independent artist, Keaton concentrated on perfecting his craft. Several of his two-reelers of this period are frankly experimental and aren't always artistically successful. Some of the gags seem to be included only to raise an easy laugh. A few of the films are based on vaudeville routines and employ a variety of comic personas. The casts were usually kept small: "the villain, myself, and the girl, and she was never important," as Keaton once remarked. Eventually the comedian learned to unify his shorts around a central premise, perhaps a prop as in *The Boat* (1921), special effects as in *The Playhouse* (1921), or a villain or group of heavies as in *Cops* (1922). Discarding unmotivated gags, Keaton and his regulars were careful to include only organically related humor. Given a central concept, they then outlined what they called "the main laughing sequences," which were developed in a cause-effect pattern from the initial premise. Each sequence builds to a rising climax, culminating finally in a chase. This formula allowed

Figure 3.3. *Day Dreams* **(1922), directed by Keaton and Edward Cline, distributed by First National.** Most of the great silent clowns preferred the camera at the full shot range, the distance ideally suited to the art of pantomime. But Keaton's physical comedy had an epic dimension, and hence he frequently moved the camera back in order to capture all the dramatic variables. In this distant long shot, for example, three gag components are presented simultaneously: Buster clinging to the revolving paddlewheel, the two policemen gaping from the windows on the left, and the cold churning water below. Such epic long shots tend to diminish the hero, dwarfing him into visual insignificance. Of course, the smaller the hero and the larger the obstacles, the greater his ultimate triumph.

Keaton sufficient room for improvisation—still the soul of his comedy—yet also provided a sense of coherence and dramatic inevitability. When Keaton graduated to full-length movies, he retained many of these structural principles.

Critic Daniel Moews has pointed out that most of Keaton's features employ the same basic comic formula. Buster begins as a callow greenhorn who bungles every attempt to ingratiate himself with a person he holds in awe—usually a pretty girl. At the conclusion of the day, he often falls asleep, lonely, depressed, and discouraged. When he awakens he's spiritually invigorated and goes on to succeed, usually at the same or parallel activities of the earlier portions of the movie. Most of the films open with an expository prologue establishing the comic premise. In *College*, for example, the bookworm hero must prove to the girl that he's a "real man" and hence is worthy of her affection. "When you change your mind about athletics," she informs him haughtily, "then I'll change my mind about you." The rest of the movie is devoted primarily to Buster's efforts on the athletic field of battle. Similarly, in *The General*, a Civil War comedy, the battle is for real, and Buster must prove himself a brave soldier before the heroine will consider him for marriage. Keaton almost always ended his films happily, for to violate the American myth of success was to court box office disaster.

Most of the features are highly symmetrical, with the second half of the film a virtual recapitulation of the first half. Of course this formula allows for considerable variation: Occasional successes are permitted in the earlier sections, just as Buster sometimes suffers temporary setbacks in the second half. In general, however, the narratives follow an elaborately counterbalanced pattern, in which most of the earlier humiliations are triumphantly cancelled out on the second day. Keaton often ended his movies with a chase, which he believed was the most effective form of climax: "It works so well because it speeds up the tempo, generally involves the whole cast, and puts the whole outcome of the story on the block."

Described thus schematically, Keaton's narrative structures sound excessively mechanical. But as his French admirers have pointed out, his architectural rigor can be likened to the works of the great neoclassical artists of the eighteenth century, with their intricately worked out parallels and neatly balanced symmetries. Unlike most of his contemporaries, Keaton avoided seamless transitions. Instead, each self-contained gag sequence is a witty variation on a larger theme. The comic formula is not submerged beneath the surface details, hidden from view. It's deliberately heightened and meant to withstand our scrutiny. It's part of the show.

As gagman and codirector Clyde Bruckman pointed out, the story itself was an aesthetic pretext, "as important as a tune to a jazz band, and no more." The artistry lay in what Keaton invented to embellish his stories. The gags were determined by the premise of each movie. Hence, in *The Navigator*, they revolve primarily around nautical situations, as they do in *Steamboat Bill Jr.* In *Battling Butler*, the comic situations deal mostly with boxing and physical prowess; in *Go West* with western movie clichés; and so on. The actual routines were never scripted. Keaton had to know only a movie's premise and conclusion: The middle sections could be improvised.

A number of his works are parodies of other movies and moviemakers. Since many of his satiric targets are no longer familiar to present-day audiences, some of the humor is inevitably diminished, though Keaton usually insisted that a gag ought to be funny even to viewers who didn't recognize what was being travestied. In *Our Hospitality*, for example, he lampooned D. W. Griffith's fondness for historical facsimiles (see Fig. 1.5). A title card announces the setting: "Broadway and 42nd Street as it was in 1830. From an old print." What follows is not a shot of Times Square as we think of it, but a dusty country crossroad with a solitary farmer leading a cow. The shot was, in fact, modeled on an 1830 print of what is now Times Square. *The Frozen North* (1922) burlesques the popular western star William S. Hart, who was famous for his "sensitive" crying jags on screen. Hart refused to speak to Keaton for several years after the movie's release.

Keaton was fascinated with the possibilities of special effects in the cinema. Like the early French surrealists, he believed that no medium

Figure 3.4. Buster Keaton in *The Three Ages* (1923), directed by Keaton and Eddie Cline, distributed by Metro Pictures Corporation. Keaton's first feature is a delicious parody of Griffith's *Intolerance,* intercutting love stories from three historical periods: contemporary America, imperial Rome, and (shown here) the Stone Age.

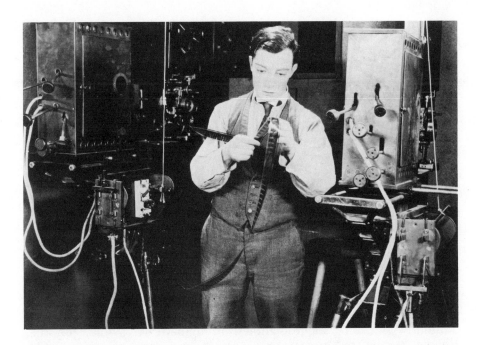

Figure 3.5.   Buster Keaton in *Sherlock Junior* (1924), distributed by Metro Pictures. "A film is a ribbon of dreams," Orson Welles has observed. "The camera is much more than a recording apparatus, it is a medium via which messages reach us from another world that is not ours and that brings us to the heart of a great secret. Here magic begins." Keaton would certainly have agreed, for his movies are steeped in the fantastic—even if he always presents it realistically. This film contains a celebrated special effects sequence in which Buster, a movie projectionist, falls asleep during the show. In a double-exposure shot, his spirit rises from his slumbering body to join the action on the screen. Trapped in the cinematic time-space continuum, he suddenly finds himself catapulted with each change of scene to a desert, an ocean, a snowdrift, and a den of lions. The French surrealists were delighted by such matter-of-fact outrageousness and regarded Keaton as an inspirational figure.

was so well suited to capturing the "concrete irrationality" of dreams and fantasies. A number of movies, like *The Playhouse* and *Sherlock Junior*, contain supernatural sequences. Wish-fulfillment plays a major role in his movies, and as critic Moews has pointed out, the fact that Buster's reversals of fortune are usually preceded by a long, deep sleep suggests that the comically farfetched triumphs of even the more realistic films might be interpreted as adolescent fantasies.

The more unreal the material, the more Keaton insisted it be presented "realistically." In *The Three Ages*, for example, he combined live action with animation in a shot that shows the Stone Age hero riding a dinosaur. In *The Playhouse*, Keaton plays every role: the ticket seller, all the spectators, the performers, and so on. In one scene, he plays nine minstrel players simultaneously: All are on stage at the same time and are photographed in one shot. No one could figure out how he managed to photograph this extraordinary scene. Later Keaton explained that he had a special lens box constructed, with nine separate shutters, allowing only one-ninth of the film emulsion to be exposed to light. Each time Keaton played one of the nine minstrels, the film was recranked back to the original starting point. Needless to say, the synchronization had to be split-second perfect. The director gave much of the credit for such brilliant special effects to his regular cinematographer, Elgin Lessley, whom Keaton described as "a human metronome."

Critical commentators often refer to Keaton's persona as Buster as a matter of convenience. In fact, the characters he plays are more varied than is generally acknowledged. His French admirers have stressed Buster's grace and resourcefulness; others have defined him in terms of his ineptitude; still others have concentrated on his dogged courage in the face of danger. Keaton himself described his persona as the classic slow thinker and emphasized his delayed reactions to life's maddening fluctuations. "The audience wants the comic to be human, not clever," Keaton explained. There's considerable evidence in the movies that Buster can be both: first human, *then* clever. Of the silent clowns, only Harry Langdon's persona seemed younger and more naive than Keaton's. Though clearly an adult, Buster has the social poise of a shy fifteen-year-old boy. The hero of the features is generally given a name in a diminutive form to suggest adolescent immaturity: Willie, Johnnie, Jimmie, Junior (two times), or simply the boy (also two times). The persona is defined somewhat by his work: a railroad engineer, a cowboy, a would-be detective, a college student, and so on. Nor is he always from the same social class: In several movies he's rich and spoiled; in others he's comparatively poor and must work for a living. In films like *Battling Butler, The Navigator,* and *Steamboat Bill Jr.,* he begins as a hopeless wimp, whereas in *The General,* he's unusually competent right from the beginning.

In most cases, as Moews has pointed out, Buster is something of a split personality. At the beginning of the majority of the features, he's passive and fatalistic, hardly bothering to defend himself even against unjust accusations. Once he decides to take control of his life, he's galvanized into action—suddenly quick-witted and aggressive, where previously he was timid, tentative, or just plain dumb. At the beginning he often tries to conform to the prevailing social mores, and the gags are based on his zombielike attempts to appear "normal." In his opening scenes with the heroine, he's the quintessential gawky suitor, determined to court her in the most ploddingly "correct" manner. He's almost totally insensitive to the vibrations of others. Females are especially unfathomable, and he seems to court them not out of any genuine ardor but because it's the expected thing for an elegible young bachelor to do. After his transformation, he demonstrates more naturalness and common sense. The callow Buster is languid to the point of somnambulism; the heroic Buster is adventurous and alert, his eyes blazing with determination where previously they were scarcely visible beneath their heavy lids. Buster the rookie is impractical, abstract, and formalistic; Buster the veteran is pragmatic, concrete, and flexible in his responses. The kid insists on being "logical," even if logic doesn't work; the man is shrewd enough to realize that instincts are often superior to mechanistic thinking.

Figure 3.6. Buster Keaton in *The Navigator* (1924), directed by Keaton and Donald Crisp, distributed by Metro-Goldwyn Pictures. The dim and pampered hero of this movie is introduced with the title, "Rollo Treadway—heir to the Treadway fortune—a living proof that every family tree must have its sap." Many of the gags revolve around contrasts in size, for Rollo and his girl are stranded at sea, the only two passengers aboard a drifting luxury liner. The visual gags in Keaton's works are impeccably framed, without an inch of wasted space. In this shot of Rollo cooking his breakfast, for example, the camera is distant enough to include the enormous pot, yet sufficiently close to reveal the incongruously tiny egg and stopwatch.

As an actor, Keaton displays a relatively narrow range, but within that range, he's superb. The labels of "the Great Stoneface" and "the man who never smiles" have done him a disservice, suggesting that his face is inexpressive. A number of commentators have remarked on its ethereal beauty. The exquisitely chiseled features suggest classical sculpture; the melancholy eyes are dreamy, innocent, and vulnerable. As David Robinson has pointed out, there's a soul behind those eyes. His face recalls the tragicomic Pierrot of the canvasses of Picasso and the sad White Clown so tenderly extolled by Fellini in his nostalgic *The Clowns*. In his early movies particularly, Keaton powdered his face to suggest a fragile, porcelain effect. As Robinson points out, Keaton's face is far from immobile: "He is the only silent comedian with whom you are never for a moment in doubt as to what his thoughts are." His acting genius is expressed primarily in terms of understatement, for modest Buster constantly tries to stay cool.

Keaton's economy as an actor is admirably demonstrated in a scene from *The General*. The railroad engineer hero is impeded in his chase by a rickety boxcar which groans ahead of his train at a snail's pace. He tries several ploys to derail the car so that he can again accelerate his engine, but without success. While he's distracted by other matters, the boxcar veers off the tracks by itself. When Buster returns to his problem, he discovers to his astonishment (conveyed by a slow, uncomprehending blink of his eyes) that he no longer has a problem—a typical instance of the awesome, inexplicable mysteries of his universe. When asked why he remained so sober faced, Keaton replied, "I concentrated on what I was doing." And of course this solemn concentration is what makes him so funny. Only once was he persuaded to smile, and the preview audience booed, hissed, and groaned in response. The smile was cut.

The finest acrobat and athlete of all the movie clowns, Keaton insisted on performing his own stunts. Surprisingly, he injured himself only twice in his career. His range is breathtaking: He leaps from bridges and steep waterfalls, swims against ferocious currents, climbs mountains and dangerous cliffs, falls off of all kinds of speeding vehicles, and even flies through the air during a hurricane. His athletic activities include baseball, football, swimming, boxing, rowing, and virtually every kind of track event. Incredibly, he almost always executed his stunts correctly on the first take. He insisted in the name of realism that whenever possible the stunts be photographed in a continuous shot, or the audience would think that the event was faked through ingenious splicing.

Keaton's movements are usually sharp, virile, and trajectorylike, seldom insinuating or conventionally graceful. Critic J.-P. Lebel has described his body as "coiled like a spring," ready to pounce into action on the slightest cue. His motions are generally rapid and efficient, and he seldom exhibits any panic or dissipates his energies. An incurable optimist, Buster believes that every problem has a logical solution. As Lebel has pointed out, the hero first analyzes the problem with a prodigious amount of attention to its mechanical dynamics. His curiosity satisfied, he then quickly calculates a logical solution. Only then does he spring into action—often with hilariously anticlimactic results, for nothing's as logical as Buster thinks it is. When he finds himself in a totally unfamiliar situation, he often shades his eyes with one hand, arches his body forward, and intently scans the horizon in an effort to get his bearings (see Fig. 3.7). Only after repeated failures will he become discouraged, at which point his body seems to collapse, and he sits down in disgust, his repertory of solutions totally exhausted.

Above all, Keaton's comedy is spatial. Most of the gags center on the way objects and people are positioned and manipulated within the mise-en-scène. Buster's body is seldom funny in itself but in the way it's juxtaposed with other physical elements within the frame. Keaton often used the distant long shot because it allows the viewer to see simultaneously all the relevant variables of a gag. In *The Navigator*, for example, we see the hero and heroine engaged in a futile search for each other on an otherwise abandoned ocean liner. Keaton shoots the scene from a considerable distance away, allowing us to view all three levels of the ship's decks. The comedy is both spatial and temporal, for the two bewildered searchers just miss each other by a matter of seconds as they wander from level to level.

Figure 3.7. Buster Keaton in *The Navigator*. Keaton's artistry often functions on several levels at once. In this shot, for example, elements of design, character, and narrative are fused. Its visual wit results from the juxtaposition of Buster's rigid body with the taut ropes of the ship, forming a perfect V-shape. His scanning of the horizon is a variation of shtick comedy: Contemporary audiences immediately recognized this as one of Buster's quintessential gestures. Yet the shot is also totally integrated within the dramatic context, for Buster and his girl are lost at sea, and he's trying to get his bearings.

Often the gags revolve around contrasts in size. No comedian ever worked with larger props: cars, buses, bridges, railroads, ships. Buster is sometimes photographed as a speck in the mise-en-scène, fighting valiantly against monstrous odds: a herd of cattle, a gang of bootleggers, a precinct of cops, a tribe of Indians, even the Union and Confederate Armies. The conflicts sometimes assume elemental proportions: Buster contends against winds, fires, oceans, deserts, waterfalls, and storms of every variety. Keaton manipulated these spatial conflicts brilliantly. The shots aren't just photographed; they're composed. The visual weights, shapes, and kinetic shifts are choreographed with balletic grace.

"We get it in one shot, or we throw out the gag," the comedian often instructed his staff. Once he had to repeat a gag seventy-five times before it was completed to his satisfaction. But in some cases one shot was all he could command. In *The General,* for example, he wanted to show a train—a real train, not a miniature—toppling off a high burning bridge into a river far below. He photographed the scene from hundreds of yards away, documenting its authenticity by including within the frame several cavalry soldiers on the banks of the river. The contrast in scale between the enormous falling train and the mounted soldiers provides the movie's most thrilling—and funny—epic spectacle.

On a number of occasions, Keaton even risked his life in the name of greater realism. Perhaps the most famous instance of his daring can be seen in the hurricane sequence of *Steamboat Bill Jr.* Fierce gales whip the inhabitants of the small town like puny splinters, uprooting trees and collapsing $100,000 worth of sets. While Buster surveys the wreckage to the town in front of a two-story building, its facade suddenly crashes over him *en bloc,* but a tiny second-story window which happily was left open leaves him still standing at the conclusion of the shot, gazing at the debris of the façade enveloping him. The breakaway front weighed two tons, and Keaton allowed himself only three inches of clearance at his head and shoulders. Audiences gasp rather than laugh at such realistically staged gags. Or rather, they gasp; *then* they laugh.

A number of commentators have remarked on Keaton's fascination with machinery and anything involving mechanistic systems. He was a well-known bridge enthusiast, and some of his plays have been included in bridge manuals. Buster's behavior is often machinelike, and in most of the movies he's associated with a characteristic vehicle. Trains are the favorite by far and are included in most of the features. Several films contain Rube Goldberg machines whose baroque networks of wires, levers, weights, and counterweights perform such functions as preparing and serving breakfast for two. The machines can take on a life of their own. In *The General,* for instance, Buster throws dirt under the train's skidding wheels to get it moving forward again. When he turns his back on the train for a moment, its wheels begin to function properly, and driverless, it chugs out of frame. When Buster returns to his problem, once again he discovers that it's mysteriously disappeared.

Keaton was a master at snowballing a gag until it acquired monumentally threatening proportions. In *Seven Chances,* for example, Buster must marry within a few hours in order to inherit a vast fortune. He randomly approaches over a dozen women, who all reject him. The news about his inheritance later becomes public, and the second half of the movie is devoted to Buster's attempts to escape the importunities of a flotilla of ludicrously veiled would-be brides. Some of Keaton's gag chains are almost dominolike in their inexorability. In *College,* Buster tries to impress the heroine by attempting a number of track and field sports, which of course he bungles dismally. Later in the movie, she calls him up in a panic, for the villain—with obviously nefarious intentions— has locked himself in her dormitory room. Before she can finish, the rotter yanks out the telephone wire, leaving Buster to imagine the worst. Like a bolt he flies to her rescue, cancelling out in the process all his earlier athletic failures: He leaps out of the window, sprints toward her dormitory, feints through a crowd, high jumps a tall shrubbery and then a series of lesser hurdles, broad jumps across a small pond, snatches a clothesline pole just outside her dormitory, vaults up to her second-story window, and lands squarely on his feet inside her room. Once there, it's only a matter of seconds before the villain is meted his comeuppance.

Lebel and other French commentators have been intrigued by the

Figure 3.8. Publicity photo of Keaton in *Seven Chances* (1925), directed by Keaton, distributed by Metro-Goldwyn Pictures. Buster's clothes are usually symbolic and vary from film to film. The flat porkpie hat (see Fig. 3.7) is his most persistent sartorial trademark, but in many of the movies he doesn't wear it. In the earlier comedies he sometimes wears oversized slapshoes, but they're seldom seen in the more realistic features. Buster usually sports a necktie, a symbol of his bourgeois aspirations. If the character is rich, he dresses expensively, if not outright foppishly. If he has to earn his living, he generally wears the uniform of his profession, and proudly. But Buster's clothes are mere coverings, divorced from his actual merit.

fatalism of many of Keaton's movies. His is a universe dominated by whimsical shifts in fortune, and this constant flux of objects and relationships makes it difficult for Buster to master the rules of the game. Indeed, the mechanistic rigor of Keaton's comic formula suggests a kind of structural destiny, as though the hero has no choice but to retrace his previous steps. Moews points out a certain treadmill principle, in which the hero exerts a tremendous amount of energy that's often wasted or reversed. But in general, Moews finds the films good-natured and cheerily optimistic. Fate, for the most part, seems ultimately benevolent. Defeats are provisional, and even when Buster seems totally helpless—as at the conclusion of *The Navigator*—a "miracle" usually pulls him through. Somebody Up There is watching over Buster. A few of Keaton's earlier works—most notably *Day Dreams* (1922), *Cops,* and *The Boat*—end in failure, but the conclusions lack a metaphysical dimension. There's no sense of the movies being *shaped* toward a preordained destiny, as there usually is in the happy endings of the features.

Keaton had a small staff of regulars who worked closely with him on most of his movies. Clyde Bruckman was his right-hand man, helping with the gags and with directorial duties. Other major writers were Jean Havez, Joe Mitchell, and Edward Cline. Keaton's gifted special effects technician was Fred Gabouri, who also helped research the period of the films, scout locations, and supervise the set construction. The underrated Elgin Lessley was the cameraman for most of the features. Working without scripts, Keaton and his regulars improvised around the comic formula for about eight weeks, making due allowances for occasional baseball games. Everyone contributed, and gags were gratefully accepted from all. According to Bruckman, however, Keaton thought up 90 percent of the gags, and though he often allowed someone else to take directorial credit, the comedian chose virtually every camera setup. He also decided on the final cut of each movie.

Incredibly enough, Keaton seldom rehearsed even the most complicated stunts in advance, for he believed that rehearsals produced an effect that looked too calculating and mechanical. Most of his shots were captured on the first take, and he almost never repeated a shot more than once. Generally he would shoot enough material for five or six movies. Later the worst footage was discarded, and Keaton would edit together a preliminary print. All the films were sneak previewed, recut according to audience response, and only then released to the general public.

Even if Keaton never appeared before a camera, he would still be regarded as a great director. He was the first comic to discard the use of fast motion, which he thought threw off the timing of a gag. Later Chaplin and Lloyd followed suit. Most of Keaton's movies were shot on location, and the historical details and costumes of the period comedies provide the mise-en-scène with an authenticity that few of his peers could match. In the staging of complicated scenes, he was the equal of virtually any director. *The General* required 4,000 extras, and they're deployed with impeccable skill. Critic Kevin Brownlow described the hurricane in *Steamboat Bill Jr.* as "the most astonishing special-effects sequence ever attempted." Most of Keaton's shots are in deep focus, and

Figure 3.9. Buster Keaton in *The General* (1926), with Marian Mack, directed by Keaton and Clyde Bruckman, released by United Artists. One has to mine a Keaton shot for its artistry, because function always takes precedence to form. Or rather, form is the embodiment of function: There's no misalignment. In this shot, for example, the human material is paramount—as it almost always is in the classical American cinema. The dramatic context of the shot is a chase, and Buster and his girl are alarmed because their pursuers are catching up with them. But the shot can also be viewed as an almost abstract design. Its underlying structure is triangular, with the topmost circular shape forming its apex. Within this design, Keaton includes an array of geometrical shapes and patterns and subtle gradations of black, grays, and white. The shot is exquisitely balanced in its visual weights and symmetries, yet for all its elegance, there's nothing arty about it. It's too simple and functional. Keaton's genius at design was purely instinctual. He almost never talked about such matters.

usually the staging is also in depth, with important information on a variety of visual planes. No one used the frame more organically: Almost any random shot demonstrates an acute sensitivity to how much—or how little—visual information is necessary to maximize the shot's impact. Keaton disliked overacting, and despite the stock characters most of his performers were required to play, they're almost always convincing and natural in their roles.

Keaton was also a first-rate editor. He didn't use the flamboyant cutting techniques of Griffith, but favored a functional, economical style. The shots are never merely decorative: Each contributes its unique visual information. Closeups are rarely used and generally only for small props, so that the audience will recognize their relevance as comic variables. The logic of Keaton's cutting is precise and inexorable, especially on repeated viewing. The scenes are never rushed: The pacing, whether jaunty or stately, is geared to the psychological effect of the gags. Some of his sequences, like the canon gag from *The General,* are classic examples of the art of editing at its cleanest.

Keaton had his shortcomings as an artist. Some of his gags no longer seem funny, in part because they've been copied to death. A few of the jokes lack bite, either because they're too contrived or self-consciously cute. In an underwater sequence from *The Navigator,* for instance, Buster uses the claws of a live lobster as wirecutters. He also converts a passing swordfish into a rapier in order to ward off a hostile denizen of the deep. A number of commentators have lamented the ethnic stereotyping of some of Keaton's humor. Inherited from the vaude-ville stage, this kind of comedy was popular in the early twentieth century, when immigration was at its peak. Present-day audiences tend

Figure 3.10. Buster Keaton in *The General.* Keaton was a virtuoso improviser and could spin off a variety of gags from a single prop, almost like musical variations on a theme. These gag sequences are miniature dramas, with their own introductory exposition, com-plications that build up to a climax, and quick comic resolution. Such gag chains are funny in themselves, but they're also brilliantly integrated into the dramatic context. In the famous sequence pictured here, for example, our hero's pursuit of the villains is impeded by a railroad tie that they have dumped on the tracks. He slows his engine down to a crawl and scampers off to remove the obstruction. But it proves more unwieldy than he antici-pated, and while he struggles to lift it, the train slowly chugs forward and sweeps him off his feet. A number of comic variations result, as Buster precariously tries to balance the tie in this humiliating posture. While attempting to recover his equilibrium, he sees another tie sprawled across the tracks ahead of him. In a burst of inspiration, he converts his tie into a flying lever by strategically bouncing it off the edge of the other tie, thus hurtling them both off the tracks. Two problems are deftly cancelled out with one stroke. Audiences often burst into spontaneous applause at such resourceful mechanical conversions.

to find it repugnant, but Keaton never employed such gags maliciously. Jews, Italians, and Negroes were widely accepted as comic "types," and Keaton's occasional ethnic slurs exploited these conventions casually, without any meanness of spirit. A few of the movies are structurally lumpy, and some of the concluding chases don't evolve organically out of the materials at hand.

Keaton's heroines are seldom very interesting in their own right: They simply provide a pretext for Buster to surpass himself. Pretty, diminutive, and incurably bourgeois, they're usually portrayed conventionally; they're there only to observe, and occasionally to encourage, the hero in his gallant efforts. "There's no sex, no passion for the comic actor," Keaton once said; "when a woman kissed me I became a father to her. I wanted to protect her for the rest of my life." The two most interesting leading ladies are in *The Navigator* and *The General:* Their flakey ineptitude exceeds even that of the hero. Much of the charm of these comedies derives from the incompetence of these well-intentioned but exasperating creatures.

In 1928, Joseph Schenck persuaded Keaton to join with Metro-Goldwyn-Mayer, a move the comedian later referred to as "the biggest

Figure 3.11. Buster Keaton in *College* (1927), directed by Keaton and James W. Horne, distributed by United Artists. Keaton's features are profuse in elaborate symmetries, parallels, and comic recapitulations. In this film, Buster works at a lunch counter to finance his way through college. While applying for the job, he observes another soda jerk mixing a milkshake with extravagant virtuosity. Pictured here, the same customer enters and asks Buster for a milkshake. Naturally he attempts to duplicate the other soda jerk's bravura style, naturally with disastrous results.

mistake of my life." Appalled by his naiveté, Chaplin and Lloyd both warned him of the dangers of such a move. But unhappily Keaton lacked their shrewdness and cunning. After a half-hearted attempt to seek out alternative options, he signed with MGM for $3,000 a week plus occasional bonuses. The studio absorbed his regulars into its vast bureaucracy. Keaton was told by Irving Thalberg, the famous Boy Wonder of the studio, that the entire scenario department was at the comedian's disposal. No less than twenty-two writers were assigned to work on the script of his first MGM-produced film. In addition, a number of studio executives insisted on improving the script even more with ideas of their own. Thalberg was constantly worried that there wasn't enough story, and when Keaton explained that he preferred to improvise the story, the youthful production chief merely humored him. Thalberg was privately convinced that the factory system of production was more efficient. Finally a script was produced, complete with camera instructions for director Edward Sedgwick. Keaton sincerely tried, but he couldn't work under such conditions. Finally, Thalberg agreed to let Keaton do the movie *his* way, and the first thing he did was throw away the script. *The Cameraman* (1928) is admired by many, but few would rank it with the earlier comedies.

In *Spite Marriage* (1929) the strain was clearly beginning to show. Thalberg never again allowed Keaton independence in his work. The classic yielding nice guy, Keaton always allowed Thalberg—who knew very little about slapstick comedy—to have the final say. The scripts got worse and worse. There followed a succession of glossy and forgettable movies, some of them with songs and dance, others with numerous subplots in which Keaton wasn't even featured. Under these pressures, his spirit shrivelled; increasingly he turned to alcohol for solace. His marriage to Natalie Talmadge—incompatible even in the best of times—was in shambles. Keaton was not the first great artist destroyed by the studio system. That distinction probably belongs to the reckless Stroheim, who was also axed at MGM, also at the hands of their Boy Wonder.

In 1933, at the age of thirty-eight but looking many years older, Keaton was fired by MGM, divorced, and penniless. He was also a drunk. Throughout the next two decades, he was in and out of bars, drying-out homes, and mental institutions. A succession of ambitious, anonymous women took up his evenings. One bleary bloodshot morning he found himself in a cheap hotel with a stranger sharing his bed. Upon awakening, she triumphantly brandished a marriage certificate under his nose. In his autobiography, Keaton doesn't even mention his second wife's name. From time to time he was able to pull himself together, and he was usually able to support himself by the countless hack films he appeared in.

When he married the young dancer Eleanor Norris, his life improved considerably. A devoted and supportive companion, she solaced him through periods of near despair. Throughout the 1950s and 1960s, he made guest appearances on a number of television shows. He also played in summer stock and appeared in the Paris circus. As a result of the many television commercials he made in the 1960s, he lived his final

Figure 3.12.   Buster Keaton in *The Cameraman* (1928), with Marceline Day, directed by Keaton and Edward Sedgwick, produced by MGM. Buster courts his girl (and she's always a girl, never a woman) in regulation fashion: with jacket and tie, hat properly doffed, manner properly sober. Love is a serious—indeed solemn—matter. For Buster, it's like a foreign country, and he doesn't know a word of the language. In the early stages, he's more secure with a protective buffer between himself and the awesome object of his affections. His manner is tentative, his motives unimpeachably chaste. Often he requires a gentle nudge to give him courage, like the discreet digital maneuvering pictured here.

years in comparative comfort, though nowhere near the opulence of his life in the 1920s. Only one performance of his later years displays the old genius: the brilliant vaudeville routine with Chaplin in *Limelight* (see Fig. 1.12). In 1966, at the age of seventy, Buster Keaton died of lung cancer.

His comedies were always admired in Europe, and in the Soviet Union his popularity even exceeded that of Chaplin and Mary Pickford—the box office monarchs of the 1920s. Several commentators have pointed out Keaton's influence on the early French surrealists, especially the movies of Luis Buñuel, and on such absurdist dramatists as Eugene Ionesco and Samuel Beckett. Beckett even wrote a short film— cutely entitled *Film*—for the great clown. Keaton's influence can also be seen in the comedies of Jacques Tati, Red Skelton, Richard Lester, and Jerry Lewis. Perhaps his greatest disciple is Lucille Ball, whose *I Love Lucy* series was indebted to Keaton's comedy, a debt she always acknowledged with pride. Keaton's biographer, Rudi Blesh, summed up his achievement with eloquence: "Beyond the man whom time inevitably had corroded is the figure that time has burnished—the beautiful mime, the tragic clown, the artist, speaking clearly through the silence."

BIBLIOGRAPHY

ANOBILE, RICHARD J., ed. *The Best of Buster*. New York: Crown Publishers, 1976. Frame enlargements of several gag sequences from six Keaton comedies. Anobile has also assembled a continuity of frame enlargements from *The General,* also published by Crown.

BISHOP, CHRISTOPHER. "The Great Stone Face" and "An Interview with Buster Keaton," in *Film Quarterly* (Fall, 1958). A revealing interview and useful short introduction.

BLESH, RUDI. *Keaton*. New York: Collier Books, 1966. The standard biography, written in a lively show-biz style.

KEATON, BUSTER, WITH CHARLES SAMUELS. *My Wonderful World of Slapstick*. New York: Doubleday, 1960. An amiable if modest show-biz life, less complete than Blesh's biography.

LEBEL, J.-P. *Buster Keaton*. Cranbury, N.J.: A. S. Barnes, 1967. The only French critic whose book has been translated into English, especially perceptive on Keaton's persona and mise-en-scène. Contains a filmography, covering the period from 1917 to 1966.

MAST, GERALD. *The Comic Mind*, rev. ed. Chicago: University of Chicago Press, 1979. Contains a lengthy chapter on Keaton.

MOEWS, DANIEL. *Keaton: The Silent Features Close Up*. Berkeley: University of California Press, 1977. The most detailed critical analysis, especially valuable for its insights about Keaton's comic structures.

ROBINSON, DAVID. *Buster Keaton*. Bloomington: Indiana University Press, 1969. The most comprehensive critical analysis of Keaton's movies. Contains a filmography of the silent comedies.

RUBINSTEIN, E. *Filmguide to The General*. Bloomington: Indiana University Press, 1973. An outline and analysis of *The General,* with a useful bibliography, which includes some French criticism.

WEAD, GEORGE, AND GEORGE LELLIS. *The Film Career of Buster Keaton*. Boston: G. K. Hall, 1977. Critical study and the most complete bibliography. See also a stylistic analysis in Wead's *Buster Keaton and the Dynamics of Visual Wit* (New York: Arno Press, 1976).

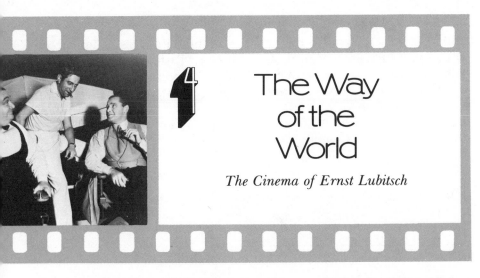

Figure 4.1. **Ernst Lubitsch (center) relaxing with actors Herbert Marshall and Robert Greig during the production of *Trouble in Paradise* (1932).** Lubitsch was one of the most loved directors of his generation. In addition to being kind and generous, he was always good company—charismatic, charming, and witty. In Germany he was known as "the man who never stops smiling," and his exuberence was such that reputedly even Garbo smiled in his presence.

The Way of the World

The Cinema of Ernst Lubitsch

rtistically nurtured in the legitimate theatre, the German-born Lubitsch brought to American movies an unparalleled sophistication, wit, and lightness of touch. His comic roots were not in the native soil of vaudeville or the "vulgar" slapstick tradition of Sennett but in that most aristocratic of genres, the comedy of manners. Lubitsch's idols included such classic comedians as Congreve, Wilde, and Shaw. From the French bourgeois farces of the nineteenth century, Lubitsch lifted many of his comic conventions, including their intricate well-made plots and their risqué themes of sexual itch. His satire of the pretenses, follies, and vanities of the idle class de-

lighted audiences throughout the 1920s and 1930s. His movies were seldom huge box office hits, yet Lubitsch remained one of the most admired of American directors. Industry regulars recognized the famous "Lubitsch touch" even without seeing the credits, so distinctive and personal was his style. He was the darling of clever people everywhere. Reviewers of smart-set magazines like *The New Yorker* and *Vanity Fair* affectionately referred to him as "Herr Lubitsch," and in an unprecedented gesture, included three of his comedies on the ten best list of 1925. International figures like René Clair, Jean Renoir, and Ingmar Bergman paid him the ultimate homage of imitation. Lubitsch was also the favorite with such literary gurus as Edmund Wilson, H. L. Mencken, and the acerbic drama critic George Jean Nathan, who was so disdainful of movies in general that not even Chaplin was exempted from his haughty contempt. Distinguished novelists like Theodore Dreiser and Thomas Mann also included themselves among Lubitsch's loyal band of devotees.

The camera should *comment, insinuate, make an epigram or a* bon mot, *as well as tell a story.*

—*Ernst Lubitsch*

Lubitsch was born in 1892 in Berlin, the son of a Jewish clothing merchant who had hopes that his boy would eventually take over the family business. At sixteen, Lubitsch announced that he wanted to be a stage actor. Aghast by such a whimsical proposal, his father pointed out that the youth was hardly endowed by nature for such a calling, having the misfortune of being short, plump, and far from handsome. For a while the boy served two masters, clerking in his father's store by day, acting in cabarets and cheap dives by night. In 1911 he was finally introduced to Max Reinhardt, the most celebrated theatre director in Germany. Skeptical of the nineteen-year-old's potential, Reinhardt nonetheless took him on as an apprentice. In the following years, Lubitsch played small roles in many of the repertory classics of Shakespeare, Schiller, Goethe, and Shaw.

But he could barely earn a living in Reinhardt's company, and in 1913, young Lubitsch agreed to act in the movies to augment his income. He played a character named Meyer, a good-natured Jewish klutz who bungles even the simplest of tasks but eventually manages to triumph over great odds, for which he is often rewarded with not only the boss's daughter in marriage but also half the business. Drawing heavily on popular Yiddish lore, Lubitsch continued with his persona through a number of cheerful one-reelers, and by 1914 he was one of the most popular movie comics in Germany. In this year too he assumed the duties of writer and director of the Meyer shorts. In 1915 he graduated to feature-length comedies. Few of these earlier works have survived, and those that have are not much admired by movie critics and historians.

In 1918, his producer introduced him to the tempestuous young Polish actress, Pola Negri, and together they persuaded Lubitsch to be her director. Weary of being typecast as the Jewish bumpkin, he finally gave up on his ambition to be an actor and concentrated his energies on directing. Hans Kräly became his regular scenarist and was to remain with him for seventeen years. Another newcomer, Emil Jannings, was also a Lubitsch regular, and eventually Negri and Jannings became important box office attractions in the silent cinema, working in America as well as the Continent. On the basis of their work together, Negri and Lubitsch became a famous star-director team, the most popular in Europe. Their vehicles were mostly costume spectacles, loosely based on historical characters, and directed in the Reinhardt manner, with an emphasis on pictorial richness, striking lighting effects, and a rhythmical stylization of crowd scenes. Such lavishly mounted movies as *Carmen* (1918), *Madame Dubarry* (1919), and *Anna Boleyn* (1920) were immensely popular.

By the early 1920s, Lubitsch was Europe's leading director, working out of UFA, Germany's best-equipped and most prestigious studio. He had directed over three dozen movies, most of them successful and some of them international hits. But he wanted more. In war-devastated Europe, the big time meant Hollywood, which dominated 80 percent of the world's screens. Lubitsch was not long in waiting. In 1922, Mary Pickford, the world's top female star, offered him a contract. She was tired of playing pubescent girls and wanted the sophisticated Lubitsch to guide her through a more mature phase of her career, one more in keeping with the Jazz Age, not to speak of her chronological age. (Little

Figure 4.2. Pola Negri (center scaffold) in *Madame Dubarry* (Germany, 1919). Like most of Lubitsch's spectacle pictures, this was given a racier title in the United States: *Passion.* The movie established Lubitsch as the foremost European director of the period. He was referred to as "the German Griffith" and praised for the opulence of his production values and the mastery with which he deployed his casts of thousands. The director prided himself on treating the intimate sexual nuances of his stories with the same care as the mass movements, a characteristic that prompted critics to describe him as "the humanizer of history."

Mary was thirty.) Lubitsch had proved a sympathetic woman's director in the Negri vehicles, and Pickford had hopes that he could perform a similar function for her.

He accepted her offer, little realizing that America's Sweetheart had a will so fixed that even the imperious Negri paled in comparison. After some disagreement on a story, they finally settled on a romantic Spanish comedy. Although Pickford and Lubitsch liked each other personally, they were unable to agree on an approach: She expected a star vehicle; he wanted to make a Lubitsch film. The result, *Rosita* (1923), satisfied neither of them, and the headstrong star later described it as "the worst picture, bar none, that I ever made." Actually, the film was a modest success at the box office. It taught Lubitsch a valuable lesson early in his American career: The way to make a *Lubitsch* movie is to avoid powerful stars and use unknown actors who'll do what they're told.

The Pickford connection severed by mutual consent, Lubitsch then signed a five-year contract with Warner Brothers, which at this time was not a prestigious studio. The Warners probably hired him to give their organization a touch of class, which it sorely lacked, their claim to fame resting chiefly with their Rin Tin Tin movies. The front office wisely decided to let their house genius make films his own way, as long as they were reasonably commercial. There followed a series of sparkling comedies which firmly established Lubitsch's artistic reputation. Most of them did moderately well at the box office and were praised by respected critics, thus garnering for Warner Brothers a considerable amount of prestige.

Lubitsch was strongly influenced by *A Woman of Paris* (1923), Chaplin's only noncomic film. Upon seeing it, Lubitsch realized that the most telling cinematic effects can be communicated indirectly, by alluding to, rather than dramatizing explicitly, a fact or relationship. Chaplin used understatement throughout the movie, commenting obliquely on the plight of his fate-ridden characters. The story per se isn't what matters most but the subtle intelligence of the storyteller. The camera need not be expository and neutral but could serve as an ironic commentator, pointing out information beyond the consciousness of the characters. "I feel that an intelligent man speaks to me," Lubitsch observed of Chaplin's directorial techniques. Although many of his previous movies contained ironic and satiric touches, it wasn't until seeing Chaplin's film that Lubitsch began to *conceive* of his stories from an ironist's perspective. In short, by intruding overtly into the narrative materials, the director can establish a sly complicity between himself and his audience. The seed of the celebrated "touch" was planted. Beginning with *The Marriage Circle* (1924), it blossomed suddenly and flourished for two decades.

What exactly *is* the Lubitsch touch? Herman Weinberg, the foremost authority on the subject, points out that it's a mock-heroic, skeptical undercutting—a knowing wink to the audience at the expense of the characters. In the credit sequence of *The Merry Widow* (1934), for example, Lubitsch ridicules the insignificance of the tiny principality in which the story is set by showing a map of Europe, with a hand holding a magnifying glass in a futile effort to locate the setting. Lubitsch is seldom severe in his satire: He's too genial and civilized to maintain a hard line.

Figure 4.3. *The Love Parade* **(1929), with Jeanette MacDonald and Maurice Chevalier, released by Paramount Pictures.** Lubitsch's movies mostly revolve around love, marriage, and sex, though rarely in that order. Few filmmakers of his era were so skeptical about romantic attitudes: Lubitsch was inclined to agree with the wag who observed that the matrimonial chains are so heavy, it takes two to carry them, sometimes three.

He punctures the vanities of his characters, not to demean them, but to make them more human, more like us. In the musical, *One Hour With You* (1932), the philandering husband (Maurice Chevalier) sings a song explaining his sexual infidelity of the previous night. "What would *you* do?" he sings plaintively to the camera, to us. "Well, *I* did too!" is his chagrined response—all without losing a beat.

The touch can take many forms: a malicious closeup of an incongruous detail, an edited juxtaposition, a raised eyebrow. Among his favorite targets are sex, money, snobbery, politics, and stuffiness. Though sex was his favorite topic by far, Lubitsch never had problems with censors because he seldom spelled things out. Some of his most risqué scenes are suggestive, not because of what's shown, but because of what's left out. *Trouble in Paradise* (1932), perhaps his greatest film, features a witty juxtaposition of shots to suggest a sexual liaison. The setting is Venice. Two elegantly dressed people (Miriam Hopkins and Herbert Marshall), magnetically attracted to each other, are seen sitting on a couch. Then there is a shot of the empty couch, with the lights dimmed; next a shot of the apartment door, with a "Do Not Disturb" sign hanging on it; a final shot of a gondola plowing into a darkened tunnel of a canal. What was there to censure? The Lubitsch touch is elusive precisely because it's allusive.

At its best, the touch is a way of exposing the inconsistencies of the characters—their vulnerabilities, their low cunning, and their efforts to preserve their dignity. In *Trouble in Paradise,* he reveals these contradictions with rapierlike deftness, often without a word being spoken. In one scene, for example, Lily (Hopkins) is packing a suitcase, preparing to abscond with the riches she and her con-man lover Gaston (Marshall) have taken from the wealthy Mme. Colet (Kay Francis). Lily is happily tra-la-la-ing as she packs. At the appointed time, she calls up Gaston, who is presumably finishing up at Mme. Colet's. No answer. Strange. Lily returns to her packing, her tra-la-las considerably diminished in intensity and brio. She narrows her eyes suspiciously: Mme. Colet is, after all, an extraordinarily beautiful woman . . . indeed, a ravishing creature, truth to tell. The tra-la-las are barely audible, limping after her thoughts. Shaking her head in self-reproach, she resumes her packing and her brisk tra-la-las. But once again she reconsiders, trying to stifle her worst—and well-founded—suspicions about her partner. And so on, through a variety of tra-la-las, each of which reveals yet another facet of this all-too-human charmer.

The legitimate theatre provided most of the major influences on Lubitsch's movies, particularly in terms of genre and style. Once he arrived in America, he abandoned the operatic style of Reinhardt in favor of a simpler, sparer mise-en-scène. Such comedies of manners as Congreve's *The Way of the World,* Wilde's *The Importance of Being Ernest,* and Shaw's *Man and Superman* became his new models. Derived from the works of Molière, this genre flourished on the English stage from the restoration of the Stuarts in 1660 to the middle of the eighteenth century. In a modified form the genre was revived in the late nineteenth century by such dramatists as Wilde and Shaw. It is associated with the upper classes (which comprised its principal audiences) and satirizes their follies in fashions, manners, and values. A few of Lubitsch's works are adaptations of these stage classics: *Lady Windermere's Fan* (1925) is based on an Oscar Wilde play; *Design for Living* (1933), on a comedy by Noël Coward.

Relieved of such mundane considerations as having to earn a living, the characters of the comedy of manners concern themselves with matters of style. Wit, elegance, and urbanity are their ideals, especially in such rituals as courtship and sexual dalliance. The plays are characterized by an air of refined cynicism, most notably in the dialogue, which emphasizes a sparkling, epigrammatic polish. Women are portrayed as the equals of men in most respects, and in their repartee they're often superior. The heroines are sophisticated in sexual matters—at least in word, if not always in deed. Like most neoclassical genres, the theatrical comedy of manners abounds in neat symmetries, ingenious recapitulations, and parallels of every variety. Instead of one pair of lovers, there are usually two and sometimes three. Sexual triangles are common and are often cleverly juxtaposed with other triangles. The rococo plots, despite their complexity, are manipulated with delicacy and finesse. The comedy of manners has seldom enjoyed the patronage of mass audiences, either on the stage or in the movies, in part because of its implicit contempt for middle-class values.

Figure 4.4. *Monte Carlo* **(1930), released by Paramount Pictures.** This was merely one of many films in the early depression era which dealt with the quest for a rich mate. Characteristically, each studio explored this theme in its own idiom: at Paramount, in sophisticated comedies of manners; at Warners, in such proletarian vehicles as the *Gold Diggers* musicals; at MGM, in glossy women's pictures; and so on.

Dramatists catering to bourgeois audiences created a more satisfying imitation of the comedy of manners in the so-called Boulevard Theatre, which flourished in Paris from the middle of the nineteenth century until the 1920s. Such popular playwrights as Sardou, Labiche, Feydeau, and de Najac provided a steady stream of "naughty" farces, revolving usually around themes of marital infidelity. Ingeniously crafted, the *pièce bien faite,* or well-made play, is less literary than the comedy of manners, emphasizing action rather than verbal virtuosity. Farce specializes in a more physical form of humor, in which a desperate urgency propels the characters into increasingly more bizarre situations. Comic props, like letters, a hat, or an incriminating pair of gloves, reappear perversely throughout the action, embarrassing their guilt-ridden owners and forcing them into ever more improbable flights of mendacity. The settings for such farces are often boudoirs or hotel lobbies, where genteel lechers dash behind doors just moments before being discovered by suspicious spouses or lovers or both. The reversals and counterreversals in the plots are dizzying in their rapidity, and most of the laughs are prompted by the adroitness with which the characters keep one step ahead of the game.

Industry regulars were amazed at how Lubitsch would buy up the rights to some obscure eastern European play and transform this sow's ear into a silk purse. Most of these plays were crude imitations of French originals, though Lubitsch sometimes raided the real thing too. *Kiss Me Again* (1925), for example, is based on *Divorçons (Let's Get a Divorce)* by Sardou and de Najac. Lubitsch seldom preserved much from his original sources—an idea, a situation, perhaps an amusing novelty. He was concerned with plots only insofar as they allowed him to reveal character, which was his main interest. The conventions of the *pièce bien faite* are found throughout his movies, sometimes fused with those of other genres. In general, the earlier films tend toward the comedy of manners, whereas the later works, like *Ninotchka* (1939) and *To Be or Not to Be* (1942) are more indebted to the farces of the Boulevard Theatre. Most of the movies are set abroad: Paris, London, Vienna, or a mythical kingdom "somewhere in eastern Europe." Americans liked to believe that they were too wholesome to lead a decadent existence, and Lubitsch, glad to oblige, seldom used native locales. "The American public," he once said, "the American public with the mind of a twelve-year-old, you know—it must have life as it ain't."

Lubitsch lifted the use of doors from classical French farce and transformed this motif into a trademark. Indeed, one of Pickford's pet exasperations about the director concerned his obsession with doors, which are used as comic symbols of concealment, deception, and untold but unseen pleasures. *Monte Carlo* (1930) contains a famous scene in which the lively heroine (Jeanette MacDonald) oohs and ahs voluptuously as her male "hairdresser" casually gives her a massage. Lubitsch then cuts to a shot outside the room, where the maid listens lasciviously at the door, her eyes wide in awe at the presumed debaucheries within. Standard farcical props, like reappearing hats, scarves, canes, and other telltale impedimenta also abound in his movies.

Lubitsch didn't introduce the comedy of manners to the screen; he only refined and polished the genre. Immediately after World War I, films dealing with the absurdities of the idle rich grew in popularity. Before Lubitsch, the genre was dominated by Cecil B. De Mille, whose works in this vein are often amusing, though they lack the elegance and bite of those of Lubitsch. Inspired by the example of De Mille, a number of American filmmakers explored the new sophisticated attitude toward sex in a profusion of Jazz Age comedies. The titles speak for themselves: *Dancing Mothers, Dancing Daughters, Male and Female, Don't Change Your Husband, Why Change Your Wife?, Strictly Unconventional,* and so on. Such flapper stars as Gloria Swanson, Clara Bow, and young Joan Crawford were considered the last word in feminine emancipation. But for all her defiance of social convention, the flapper was a true American innocent—at least on the screen. As critic Molly Haskell has pointed out, the flapper might smoke, drink, and attend wild parties, but beneath the flamboyance, she's as chaste as her prewar mother.

The Lubitsch heroine, on the other hand, is disarmingly lecherous, and there's nothing coy about her either. Like Shaw's New Woman, on whom she's partly modeled, she is often the sexual aggressor in a relationship. Several are rulers of petty principalities, and as such they can select their consorts without the pretense of being "modest" about such

Figure 4.5. *Monte Carlo*, **with Claude Allister.** Lubitsch's musicals rarely feature splashy production numbers. His characters usually burst into song with no transitional bridging material. In this scene, for example, the dim-witted Prince Otto von Seibenheim has just been jilted by his would-be bride. As he sings "Give Me a Moment Please," the bridesmaids close in around him, serving as impromptu chorus girls. Lubitsch delighted in these on-camera regroupings, which spoof the inherent artificiality of the genre's conventions. Until late in his career, he favored a somewhat formal symmetry in his mise-en-scène, even in his nonmusical films.

matters. Social reversals of this sort afforded Lubitsch the opportunity of satirizing sexual role playing and stereotypes. Some of the heroines are married but restless, and they initiate intrigues without embarrassment or such bourgeois encumbrances as a guilty conscience. A few of his characters are older women—poised, mysterious, gently amused at the clumsiness of admiring young males. Even the unmarried females are clearly women and not girls. Unlike the American flapper, the Lubitsch heroine—almost invariably European—doesn't make a rebellious show of her worldliness, which she wears with the same nonchalance as she wears her gowns. Confident and independent, she is almost never conventional in her behavior. At a dinner party he once attended, the director listened impatiently as a British actor extolled the homely virtues of old-fashioned women, especially their artless simplicity and modesty. In his thick German accent, Lubitsch finally quipped, "Who vants dat?" Certainly not Lubitsch, for he preferred women with backbone and bite. The Lubitsch heroine doesn't permit men to define her nature, which is primarily why they find her so alluring. Generally more quick-witted and realistic than the males, they are shrewdly aware of the economic

Figure 4.6. Miriam Hopkins and Herbert Marshall in _Trouble in Paradise_. "In matters of grave importance, style, not sincerity, is the vital thing," opines a character from Oscar Wilde—a sentiment shared by many of Lubitsch's characters as well. In this early scene we're introduced to an impeccably correct baron and an equally fastidious countess. They turn out to be a thief named Gaston and a pickpocket called Lily, and are clearly made for each other—after a few complications.

realities of existence—though there's often a touch of dreaminess about them too.

But to speak of the Lubitsch heroine is to imply a lack of diversity, which is far from true. Few American directors could match the variety of his females, ranging from the slightly bitchy to the sublimely ethereal. A good example of the former is the flirtatious Mizzi in _The Marriage Circle_ and its musical remake, _One Hour with You_. Unhappily married and contemptuous of conventional morality, she seduces her best friend's husband and even taunts him for his guilty scruples. In the middle of a party she lures him off to a darkened terrace, where they embrace and kiss. His bowtie askew from their groping, he asks her to tie it for him, fearful lest his wife or the other guests might become suspicious. With a malicious twinkle in her eye, she reties it, kisses him again, then saucily unties it, leaving him stranded helplessly on the terrace. So much for the hypocrisies of the respectable male.

Not all Lubitsch's heroines are so brazen. Most of them, like the characters played by Miriam Hopkins and the musical heroines played by Jeanette MacDonald, are sportsmanlike and endearingly funny. They're certainly among the most charming heroines of the American cinema—headstrong and not quite ladylike but wonderfully feminine for all their aggressive high spirits. They're quick talkers, especially when they suspect men are trying to take advantage of them, and they're alarmingly prone to calling a spade a spade—usually at some suitably public moment. Resourceful and adventurous, they are basically a romantic lot but smart enough to realize that the doers rather than the dreamers fare best in life. Some are exquisitely subtle in their eroticism, such as the roles played by Kay Francis in *Trouble in Paradise*, Greta Garbo in *Ninotchka*, and Carole Lombard in *To Be or Not to Be*. More sensitive, romantic, and aristocratic than Lubitsch's other heroines, these wistful creatures are also more likely to end with their dignity intact.

Of course the appeal of the Lubitsch heroine is due in large part to the charm of his actresses. After his Pickford fiasco he tended to favor little-known or off-beat performers. Reviewers often noted how his players had never acted so well in the movies of other directors. Irene Rich, who plays the worldly older woman in *Lady Windermere's Fan*, was never lucky enough to get another role requiring so much of her artistry. Kay Francis, the graceful Mme. Colet in *Trouble in Paradise*, was wasted in a series of Warner Brothers potboilers for most of her career. *The Love Parade* (1929) introduced Jeanette MacDonald, who became the director's favorite singing actress, and she performs with engaging spontaneity in a number of Lubitsch musicals. Unfortunately, her artistic reputation and star status were based more on the saccharine operettas she made at MGM later in her career. Teamed with the baritone Nelson Eddy, this glossily embalmed duo became known in the trade as the Iron Butterfly and the Singing Capon.

When Lubitsch worked with established stars, mostly in the later part of his career, the results were mixed. Garbo considered him the only great director she ever worked with. Shrewdly incorporating his star's sober brusqueness as part of her early character in *Ninotchka*, Lubitsch then revealed a facet of her personality few would have expected: "Garbo Laughs!" the advertisements proclaimed, and audiences laughed with her, delighted that such a mysterious woman could also be funny. In other movies, Lubitsch was less fortunate. *The Student Prince* (1927), an Irving Thalberg production for MGM, was badly miscast (by Thalberg), with the unexciting Norma Shearer (Mrs. Thalberg) in the starring role. In his final years, Lubitsch's casting instincts began to desert him. Gene Tierney in *Heaven Can Wait* (1943) is beautiful but dull. Even more disastrous in *Cluny Brown* (1946) is Jennifer Jones, whose neurotic, overwrought mannerisms are at odds with the heroine's whimsical freshness. Never had he been strapped with an actress so utterly humorless.

Lubitsch was immensely good-natured, which in part explains his popularity within the industry. He never did shake his comical German accent, and in his physical demeanor he was what his father stoically prophesied. Like his characters, he was a study in contradictions. Childlike in his enthusiasm, he could also be pretty cynical. He was celebrated for the airiness of his style and his virtuosity as a technician, but his favorite movie was Vittorio De Sica's powerful masterpiece of realism, *Shoeshine*, in which the technique is virtually invisible. Though he projected an air of affable jokiness, Lubitsch was a man of considera-

Figure 4.7. Publicity photo of Kay Francis in *Trouble in Paradise*, gowns by Travis Banton, distributed by Paramount Pictures. Lubitsch was exacting in his ideas about costumes. Some are so elegant they could be worn today and still elicit admiration. He especially favored clingy gowns with an understated eroticism for his leading ladies, who were usually slender and knew how to wear clothes well—an indispensible grace for those who would play high comedy.

ble cultivation. He was interested in new ideas, followed important developments in the arts and in politics, and included among his friends some of the most intellectually stimulating residents of Hollywood—of which there were many, especially during the 1930s, when the community was swelled with well-educated refugees from Hitler's Europe.

Critic Robert E. Sherwood was among the first to point out that Lubitsch's standing within the industry contrasted sharply with the stereotyped image of the Hollywood dream factory: "The veneration that it lavished upon Lubitsch has been out of all proportion to the size of his grosses." He worked for five of the major studios in Hollywood and seldom complained of his treatment, for he was almost always left free from interference. Within the trade, it was clear he was a special case. Several of his movies, including *Trouble in Paradise* and *The Shop Around the Corner* (1940), he produced as well as directed. Among his peers, he was considered a director's director, too subtle perhaps for general audiences, but champagne for the *cognoscenti*.

Much of his mature work was done at Paramount Pictures, widely regarded as the most sophisticated studio in Hollywood and particularly receptive to comedy. In addition to the films of Lubitsch, Paramount could also boast the comedies of De Mille, the movies of Mae West, much of W. C. Fields, the early (and best) Marx Brothers, the screwball comedies of Mitchell Leisen and Preston Sturges, the popular Bing Crosby, Bob Hope vehicles, and the early works of Billy Wilder. Throughout the 1930s, the studio was often in financial difficulties, but it nonetheless refused to skimp on production values. Paramount movies were usually handsomely mounted: Polished but seldom vulgar or overproduced, they emphasized a simple elegance in their design, thanks largely to their

Figure 4.8. Miriam Hopkins in *Design for Living* (1933), scenario by Ben Hecht, based on the play by Noël Coward, distributed by Paramount Pictures. Twenty of Lubitsch's twenty-six American movies are theatrical adaptations, though most of the original stage versions have been long forgotten. Even those films based on distinguished literary sources, like Coward's play, are very loosely adapted.

gifted art director, Hans Dreier. UFA was Paramount's sister studio, and Dreier, like many Paramount regulars, was German-trained. Lubitsch signed with the studio in 1926, and in 1935 he served as production chief for two years, a job he apparently disliked. His contract expired in 1938, at which time he free-lanced with several other studios. He ended his career as a producer-director at 20th Century-Fox.

Of all the American silent directors, Lubitsch was the most graceful in his sound debut. A gifted amateur musician (like Chaplin he was self-taught), he decided in 1929 to make the transition to talkies with a musical, *The Love Parade,* which critic Theodore Huff described as "the first truly cinematic screen musical." Like his French counterpart René Clair, Lubitsch refused to anchor his camera in deference to the microphone. Many of his most clever effects were shot silent, with sound dubbed in later. His editing retained all its pretalkie fluidity. He saw no reason why sound had to be synchronous with the visuals except in important dialogue scenes, and not always even then. Often he used sound in ironic contrast with his images. In short, the Lubitsch touch could be aural as well as visual.

More indebted to the traditions of the Viennese comic operetta

Figure 4.9.   Maurice Chevalier in *The Merry Widow* (1934), produced and distributed by MGM. This movie centers on the on-again off-again romance between a dissipated captain (Chevalier) and a nervous young widow (Jeanette MacDonald). The hero is something of a rake, but his debaucheries are beginning to pall, and like Congreve's Millimant in *The Way of the World,* he is beginning, at long last, to entertain the prospect of dwindling into a spouse.

than to the jazz and Tin Pan Alley idioms of most American musicals, Lubitsch's works in this genre are light, delicate, and incorrigibly parodic. Even while he's exploiting the conventions of the operetta form, he simultaneously zaps their patent silliness. The self-parody of such early musicals as *Monte Carlo* and *The Smiling Lieutenant* (1931) is part of their loony charm. The justly famous "Beyond the Blue Horizon" sequence from *Monte Carlo* is a good example of Lubitsch's mastery of the new mixed medium. While the heroine (Jeanette MacDonald) sings cheerily of her optimistic expectations, Lubitsch provides us with a display of technical bravura. Shots of the speeding train which carries the heroine to her destiny are choreographed with closeups of the whirring locomotive wheels in rhythmical syncopation with the huffing and the tooting and the chugging of the train. Unable to resist a malicious fillip, Lubitsch even has a chorus of suitably obsequious peasants chime in with the heroine in a triumphant reprise as the train plunges past their fields in the countryside. The sequence is both exhilarating and outrageously funny. Observed critic Gerald Mast, "This visual-aural symphony of music, natural sound, composition, and cutting is as complex and perfect an example of montage-in-sound as Eisenstein's editing devices in *Potemkin* were of montage in silents."

Only Hitchcock exceeded Lubitsch in the thoroughness with which his scripts were prepared. He collaborated on the screenplays of all his movies and wanted every detail worked out in advance. "In my mind's eye I can see exactly how that film will appear on the screen," the director once wrote of his working methods, "down to the very last raising of an eyelid." Samson Raphaelson referred to Lubitsch as "the most literary of directors," one who profoundly respected and understood the art of writing. To a great extent, Raphaelson pointed out, the movie was in the screenplay: "Lubitsch prepared a foolproof script that you'd say almost any director could direct." A Broadway dramatist in his own right, Raphaelson wrote or coauthored the scripts to nine of Lubitsch's sound films, including *One Hour with You* and *Trouble in Paradise*. Critic Richard Corliss believes that Raphaelson "created the most highly polished and perfectly sustained comedy style of any Hollywood screenwriter."

Lubitsch's cinematic disciple, Billy Wilder, worked at Paramount as a writer early in his career, and on loanout to MGM, he contributed substantially to the screenplay of *Ninotchka*. Though Lubitsch treated his writers with affection and professional courtesy, he prodded them constantly to refine the dialogue and make the action "more hilarious." Wilder recalled how Lubitsch would use his writers as catalysts:

> When an idea was mentioned which really fertilized his brain, what he could do with it: toss it into the air, make it catch the light one way, then another, spin it out, compress it, try it against this setting, against that, get the nth ultimate out of it.

Ben Hecht, one of the most gifted scenarists in Hollywood during the dominance of the studio system, wrote in 1933, "On the whole, I consider Mr. Lubitsch the best director in the movies."

Acting counted most for Lubitsch. In his silent films, he encour-

Figure 4.10. Greta Garbo in *Ninotchka* (1939), distributed by MGM. Most of the satire in this film is' political. Garbo plays a humorless Soviet commissar who has been sent to Paris to investigate the dubious doings of her comrades (pictured). They have proved all too susceptible to the decadent blandishments of capitalism. "How are things in Moscow?" they ask upon meeting. "Very good," she replies. "The last mass trials were a great success. There are going to be fewer but better Russians."

aged his players to speak in a natural manner, even though they would be unheard on the screen. "I tried to time the speech in such a way that the audience could listen with their eyes," he explained. Like Chaplin, he often played all the roles for his actors. Unlike Chaplin, Lubitsch usually got fresh performances by using this technique, though most trained actors find it constricting and uncreative. In Lubitsch's case, however, even expert performers generally made an exception. The popular radio comic Jack Benny marveled at how natural Lubitsch's instructions seemed for his role as the hammy matinee idol in *To Be or Not to Be*, little realizing perhaps that the director often tailored his characters with the specialties of the performers in mind.

Afraid that his players might dissipate their spontaneity, Lubitsch required few or no rehearsals. He often asked his actors to memorize their scenes several days in advance, however, so they'd feel totally comfortable with their dialogue on camera. Since every detail was planned in advance, Lubitsch never improvised on the set, nor did he deviate from the script's instructions. He generally got what he wanted from his performers on the first take. Unusual for the time, he shot his movies in chronological continuity so there would be no gaps in the characters' curve of development. "I believe in realism," he wrote, "actors should act the way people do in real life. It can be a light film, a comedy, if you like, but it should still be real."

The production values of his movies were often praised by critics. His sets are uncluttered and spacious, with gracefully curving stairways, filligreed Louis Quatorze furniture, majestic draperies sweeping from the ceilings, polished floor tiles, and formal gardens. Rarely gaudy or overlighted, his luxurious décor is presented matter of factly, without bludgeoning the audience with its pricetag. Hans Dreier's sets for *Trouble in Paradise* are triumphs of art deco design. Dwight Macdonald praised them as the finest he had ever seen in this style, either on the stage or the screen. Since so many of Lubitsch's gags revolved around doors, there were usually several of them for each set. In *The Marriage Circle,* the wayward hero (Monte Blue) jilts his lover (Marie Prevost) by striding dramatically through no less than four pairs of them. Doors are also useful for comic servants to eavesdrop at and for women to make stunning entrances from.

Lubitsch seldom needed more than eight weeks to photograph a movie—a short shooting schedule, considering the technical complexity of many of his films. He had a retentive memory and never bothered to

Figure 4.11. Jack Benny (seated on table) in *To Be or Not to Be* (1942). Shakespeare's famous metaphor of the world as a stage is the underlying concept behind this movie, which centers on a group of Polish actors. In no other film does Lubitsch explore the illusion versus reality theme with such exuberence and complexity. Even the audience is deceived. The opening scene shows a Nazi officer tricking a boy into betraying his parents. The officer is played by Jack Benny—whose iconography as a flouncing but good-hearted narcissist was well known to contemporary audiences. Midway through the scene, Lubitsch breaks the illusion by pulling back his camera and revealing the action to be a rehearsal for a play.

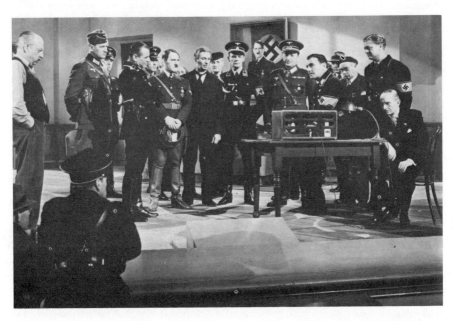

Figure 4.12. Carole Lombard in _To Be or Not to Be_, distributed by United Artists. Of the many gifted comediennes who came into prominence in the American cinema of the 1930s, none was funnier than the captivating Carole Lombard. Her performance in this movie is at once witty, graceful, and sexy. Men are bewitched by her smile, and her air of breathless awe at their fatuous preening has just enough sincerity in it to be irresistible to the masculine ego. Working with Lubitsch was one of Lombard's greatest ambitions. _To Be or Not to Be_ was the happiest experience of her career, the one time, she claimed, when everything began right, stayed right, and ended right. It was her last performance. She died in a plane accident shortly after the picture was completed. See Larry Swindell, _Screwball: The Life of Carole Lombard_ (New York: Morrow, 1975).

consult his script during the actual shooting. Since the screenplay was inviolable, Lubitsch never shot more than he needed. He edited in the camera, and the final assembly of shots was a relatively rapid and easy task. The studio cutter had little alternative footage to choose from and only needed to follow the instructions of the script to the letter.

His few detractors, mostly partisans of the school of social realism, like the English Marxist critic, Paul Rotha, condemned the director for his artistic frivolity. The comedies are clever rather than profound, such critics complained, characterized by a brilliancy of manner rather than brilliance of insight. Though often acknowledging Lubitsch's technical facility, these commentators lamented the director's "desolate sophistication," to use John Grierson's rather grim phrase. But these are largely matters of taste. The genres Lubitsch favored are typified by worldly and even decadent characters; a lack of idealism, sincerity, and passion; a skeptical and intellectual tone; and a certain malice of forethought. To complain that Lubitsch fails to make a profound statement on the human condition is to miss the point, rather like complaining of the song and dance interruptions in a musical or condemning a tragedy for its lack of humor. As a satirist and ironist, Lubitsch hardly subscribes to the trivial values of his characters; he simply refuses to make a cosmic condemnation of them. Furthermore, beneath the glitter, the humanity of his characters is always allowed to come through, though not at the expense of the genre's conventions.

Not that Lubitsch was free of shortcomings. A number of his movies, especially those of the 1940s, are disappointing, like *That Certain Feeling* (1941), a soulless remake of *Kiss Me Again.* His leading men, although usually competent actors, tend to be deficient in sexual vitality, especially when contrasted with the females. Perhaps the most likable was Maurice Chevalier, the bouyant hero of four of the musicals. Lubitsch's jokes—especially his one-liners—are sometimes forced or out of character. Some of his gags are excessively mechanical, a characteristic of many directors who repeatedly favor the same genre.

In the 1940s, Lubitsch's career began to slip, in part because of his failing health. He suffered a number of heart attacks, and several times other directors had to step in and take over his projects. His work began to lose its vitality. *To Be or Not to Be* is the only movie of this period that's widely admired, though some commentators have championed the gentle *Shop Around the Corner.* Unwilling to give up his cigars or to moderate his pace, in 1947 he suffered his sixth heart attack, which proved fatal. He was fifty-five at the time of his death.

Critics have pointed out Lubitsch's influence on isolated movies, like Renoir's *The Rules of the Game* and Bergman's *Smiles of a Summer Night.* The works of René Clair were contemporaneous with those of his American counterpart, and doubtless a certain amount of cross-fertilization took place, especially in the early 1930s. The Paramount farces of Preston Sturges and some of the works of Joseph Mankiewicz (especially *All About Eve*) show a decided Lubitsch influence. Billy Wilder is perhaps his greatest disciple. But when all is said, Lubitsch was unique. No one has made movies with quite the same grace. Wilder has recounted an incident that took place at the funeral. He and William Wyler, who were both close friends of the deceased director, were walking disconsolately back to their cars. "No more Lubitsch," Wilder muttered glumly. "Worse than that," Wyler said, "no more Lubitsch films."

BIBLIOGRAPHY

CARRINGER, ROBERT L., AND BARRY SABATH. *Ernst Lubitsch: A Guide to References and Resources.* Boston: G. K. Hall & Co., 1978. The most comprehensive bibliography and filmography.

CORLISS, RICHARD. "Samson Raphaelson" and "Charles Brackett," in *Talking Pictures.* New York: Penguin, 1975. Articles on two of Lubitsch's writers.

EISNER, LOTTE. "Lubitsch and the Costume Film," in *The Haunted Screen.* Berkeley: University of California Press, 1973. See also Siegfried Kracauer,

From Hitler to Caligari (Princeton, N.J.: Princeton University Press, 1947). Two studies of Lubitsch's German period, with many observations on Reinhardt's influence.

HASKELL, MOLLY. "The Twenties," in *From Reverance to Rape*. New York: Penguin, 1974. Useful discussion of Jazz Age movies, flappers, and the status of women. See also Lewis Jacobs, "Growing Sophistication of Film Content," in *The Rise of the American Film* (New York: Teachers College Press, 1968): Originally published in 1939, it's an interesting survey of Jazz Age themes, films, and directors.

LUBITSCH, ERNST. "Film Directing," in *Hollywood Directors 1914–1940*. Ed. Richard Koszarski. New York: Oxford University Press, 1976. A brief discussion of his working methods.

MAST, GERALD. "Ernst Lubitsch and René Clair," in *The Comic Mind*, rev. ed. Chicago: University of Chicago Press, 1979. A comparative study of two masters of the cinematic comedy of manners. See also Neil D. Isaacs, "Lubitsch and the Filmed-Play Syndrome," in *Literature/Film Quarterly* (Fall, 1975).

POAGUE, LELAND A. *The Cinema of Ernst Lubitsch*. Cranbury, N.J.: A. S. Barnes, 1978. Critical study of the American films. Filmography.

WEINBERG, HERMAN. *The Lubitsch Touch*, 3rd rev. ed. New York: Dover, 1977. Though somewhat idolotrous, required reading for those who would understand Lubitsch and his films. Contains a detailed and annotated filmography and a copious bibliography, which includes some items by German, French, and Italian critics.

WHITTEMORE, DON, AND PHILIP ALAN CECCHETTINI, eds. "Ernst Lubitsch," in *Passport to Hollywood*. New York: McGraw-Hill, 1976. General introduction, with a variety of critical reviews of Lubitsch's movies.

WILDER, BILLY, CHARLES BRACKETT, AND WALTER REISCH. *Ernst Lubitsch's Ninotchka*. Ed. Richard J. Anobile. New York: Darien House, 1975. A reconstruction of the movie with text and 1,500 frame enlargements. An edition of the script in conventional format is also available from Viking Press, 1972.

The Individualist Mystique

The Cinema of Frank Capra

Figure 5.1. Publicity photo of Capra (right), Barbara Stanwyck, and Adolphe Menjou, during the production of *Forbidden* **(1932), distributed by Columbia Pictures.** The budgets at Columbia were too limited to allow for many amenities, but the atmosphere on Capra's sets was usually genial, efficient, and professional. Once shooting began, his involvement was total: He allowed no calls, visitors, or interruptions. Stanwyck was one of his favorite leading ladies and appeared in four other of his films: *Ladies of Leisure* (1930), *The Miracle Woman* (1931), *The Bitter Tea of General Yen* (1932), and *Meet John Doe* (1941).

From 1934 to the end of the decade, Capra was the best-known director in America. Six times during the 1930s his movies were nominated for Academy Awards as best picture. Only three of his thirty-six fiction features lost money, and some of them, like *It Happened One Night* (1934) and *Mr. Deeds Goes to Town* (1936), were spectacular box office successes. A tiny Poverty Row studio called Columbia Pictures was ushered into the majors thanks largely to Capra's work there as an independent producer-director. His classic style is graceful, fast, and light. Though essentially a comic artist, Capra is capable of producing emotional effects of awe-some force. His sentimentality was condemned by some critics as "Capra-corn," but even while carping at it, they often admitted to being moved by it as well. Like Griffith and Ford, Capra was one of the most nationalistic of American filmmakers, championing the cause of "the little people" and such traditional values as freedom, independence, and self-fulfillment. He was fully aware of his enormous influence over the American public, and they responded so enthusiastically to his Populist fables that cultural historians have referred to him as the foremost mythmaker of depression America.

> *I would sing the songs of the working stiffs, of the short-changed Joes, the born poor, the afflicted. I would gamble with the long-shot players who light candles in the wind, and resent with the pushed-around because of race or birth. Above all, I would fight for their causes on the screens of the world. Oh, not as a bleeding-heart with an Olympian call to "free" the masses. Masses is a herd term—unacceptable, insulting, degrading. When I see a crowd, I see a collection of free individuals: each a unique person; each a king or queen; each a story that would fill a book; each an island of human dignity.*
>
> —*Frank Capra*

Capra was born in 1897 in the parched Sicilian village of Bisaquino, near Palermo. He was the youngest of seven children. Like most Sicilians, his heritage consisted of centuries of exploitation and grinding poverty. His entire family was illiterate. Seven of his mother's fourteen children had died in her arms as infants. Somehow the family managed to scratch together enough money to emigrate to America. In 1903 they settled in a shabby Italian ghetto of Los Angeles. Like many immigrants of that era, they believed that money was the key to happiness in America, and one made money by sweating long hours at backbreaking labor. Everyone in the family had to work, even young Frank, who held a variety of jobs while attending public schools.

Eventually he became convinced that only through education would he be able to rise above his squalid surroundings—a notion his family regarded as an excuse for laziness, for they saw no need for schooling as long as jobs were plentiful. No doubt Capra's contempt for materialistic values was fixed during this period. But his parents allowed him to continue his education, and by the time he reached high school, he was totally self-supporting. In the parlance of the times, the diminutive youth was a go-getter. Obsessively ambitious, he wanted to study science in college, but in order to do so, he had to meet his expenses with little help from his family, and even less encouragement. In 1915 he entered the California Institute of Technology, where he quickly rose to the top of his class. Throughout his college years, he supported himself by working two fulltime jobs. He graduated in 1918 with honors in chemical engineering. He entertained hopes that eventually he would earn a doctorate in science.

Despite the postwar boom and Capra's cocksure optimism, he was unable to find an engineering job upon graduation. Broke, humiliated, and scorned by his narrow-minded neighbors in the ghetto, he took to the road. For three years he bummed across the country, living by his wits, sleeping often in flophouses. He scrounged just enough to live by—or nearly enough. At times he was reduced to such extremity that only the kindness of strangers pulled him through. He developed a profound admiration for the generosity of the American character. In the years ahead, Capra was to celebrate that character with many a cinematic valentine.

In 1921 he conned his way into a movie directing job, though it was hardly the big time. He answered a newspaper advertisement which had been placed by an old stage actor who wanted to perform in film versions of popular poems. Capra soon had the terrified old ham convinced that he couldn't possibly succeed in the enterprise without his assistance. At this time Capra had not the least interest in nor knowledge of film. He took a crash course by studying the techniques of several movies that were playing locally. By surrounding the "star" only with nonprofessionals, Capra managed to pull off his bluff. *The Ballad of Fultah Fisher's Boarding House,* a one-reeler, was released in 1922 and fared respectably at the box office. Unfortunately, nothing came of the movie.

Once again he cast about for a job. For a year and a half he was employed as a cutter in a film laboratory. It was here, editing the footage of others, that he learned how to construct stories dramatically and how to enliven the pace by deleting dull transitions. Above all, he learned that what interested people most about movies was people. In 1924 he worked briefly for Hal Roach as a gagman on the *Our Gang* series. Roach was Mack Sennett's greatest rival as a producer of comedies. Roach's stable also included the satiric humorist Will Rogers and the team of Stan Laurel and Oliver Hardy. Leo McCarey was a gagman, writer, and director of many of Roach's films, including some of the finest works of Laurel and Hardy. These artists had a strong influence on Capra's subsequent work as a filmmaker. He was especially attracted to the homespun common sense of Rogers and the warm humanism of McCarey, who long remained one of Capra's favorite directors.

His first big break came when he finagled a job as gagman and writer at Sennett's Keystone Studio. Capra's aggressiveness didn't sit too well with Sennett, who was used to being treated deferentially, but there was no question that the brash newcomer had talent. He was kept on— after a suitable period of public humiliation. When Sennett's famous instinct for talent focused on a pudgy exvaudevillian named Harry Langdon, the producer's associates were bewildered, for the fortyish comic struck them as decidedly unpromising. Neither Sennett nor Langdon had a clue as to what the comedian's strengths were until Capra formulated the sainted moron persona that catapulted Langdon to fame. Director Harry Edwards and co-writer Arthur Ripley were also assigned to the new clown. After a series of enormously successful shorts, critics began comparing Langdon to Chaplin, Keaton, and Lloyd, the big three of American film comedy.

Before coming to Keystone in 1924, Langdon could barely eke out a living performing in honkeytonks. His rise to fame was meteoric. By 1925 he was offered $1 million by First National for three features. When he accepted, he took Capra, Ripley, and Edwards with him. Their first movie was *Tramp, Tramp, Tramp* (1926), which Capra cowrote, coproduced, and codirected. He mastered the fundamentals of the trade, including the importance of keeping to schedules and within budgets. Amazingly, Langdon still failed to understand his persona, and often Capra had to argue strenuously to prevent any violations of character. Intoxicated by his sudden fame, Langdon became obsessed with Chaplin's prestige among intellectuals. Increasingly he argued with Capra that their films ought to have more pathos. The comedian began to womanize, and he surrounded himself with intellectual advisors, who encouraged him to make his comedy more Chaplinesque.

But for the moment, Capra was still the prevailing influence. *The Strong Man* (1926), which he directed alone, was their greatest box office success and was voted one of the ten best films of 1926 in a critics' poll. At the age of twenty-nine, Capra was now earning $600 per week. But Langdon grew increasingly intransigent: Chaplin's phenomenal success became an *idée-fixe*. The star and director argued more and more. *Long Pants* (1927), their last movie together, was a box office hit and was warmly praised by critics. Unable to endure Langdon's monstrous ego, the far-from-shrinking Capra finally told him off. He was fired of course. Langdon subsequently proclaimed that his success was due entirely to his own efforts and had nothing to do with Capra's talents as a

Figure 5.2. Harry Langdon in *The Strong Man* (1926), with Gertrude Astor, distributed by First National Pictures. Capra believed that Langdon's was a comedy of character, not situation. "Only God can help an elf like Langdon," the writer-director insisted: "Harry conquers all with his goodness." The timid and dim-witted hero trusts his way through every crisis, with only Providence to guide him. His gags are delicately nuanced and seldom funny in themselves. The laughs result from Harry's artless, miniaturized reactions to his situations. With his chalk-white puffy face, his fluttery gestures, and his eyes wide in ingenuous absorption, Harry is the most childlike persona of all the great clowns. The workings of his tiny brain are reflected in his tentative, flitting movements. His innocent gaze often passes over a threat several times before he realizes with a thrill of terror that he's in danger. No other movie clown worked so slowly and on so small a scale. The camera is usually close in, capturing every exquisite modulation.

writer-director. Langdon directed himself in his next three pictures. All of them failed dismally. His decline was almost as swift as his ascent. Divorced four times and forgotten by his public, the embittered comedian virtually disappeared from public view. Broke and broken, he died in 1944.

Thanks to Langdon, Capra was unable to find a job. In desperation, he finally turned to Columbia Pictures—The Germ of the Ocean, as he referred to the Poverty Row studio. During this period, it produced mostly B films. It had no stars of its own, though occasionally a performer on the skids could be seduced by the lure of quick cash, and hence the studio was known in the trade as the Home of the Fallen Stars. For Capra, moving from First National to Columbia was like switching from five-star brandy to rubbing alcohol. The studio was presided over by one of the most colorful of the moguls, Harry Cohn—the notorious King Cohn, or White Fang as he was dubbed by scenarist Ben Hecht.

To many, Cohn was a snarling, foul-mouthed bully. He needled his employees sadistically. Even the most jaded industry regulars were shocked by his coarseness. Only the most self-confident could withstand his withering sarcasm, and a number of artists found him so offensive they simply refused to work at Columbia. For example, in the 1930s, the gentle, superstraight Walt Disney was so disgusted by Cohn's grossness that the young animator switched from Columbia to RKO as a distributor of his early shorts. (Later of course Disney built up his own producing and distributing organization, and it preserved a conspicuous aloofness from the Hollywood studio establishment.)

But like many of the moguls, Cohn was a study in contradictions, a *monstre sacré* if there ever was one. He genuinely loved movies, and if he had confidence in someone (sensitive types need not apply), Cohn would support him to the point of recklessness. He was a gambler who played his hunches—though not without considerable grumbling, lamentation, and gloomy prophesies of bankruptcy. Nor was he anybody's fool. Although it was common knowledge that Capra's movies put Columbia on the map in the early 1930s, nonetheless, the fortunes of the studio continued to rise long after Capra's departure, thanks largely to Cohn's shrewd stewardship. He was also something of a wit. For example, he defined a documentary as a movie with no girls in it. If it had one girl, it was a semidocumentary.

Capra the ex-streetfighter was not intimidated. Furthermore, he insisted on total autonomy: He wanted to make movies his way or not at all, including choice of material, casting, execution, and final cut. If the films failed at the box office, Cohn could fire him at any time. Reluctantly impressed by this arrogant "dago"—as Cohn habitually referred to Capra—the mogul agreed to the deal. They didn't bother with a contract. "I knew Harry Cohn," Capra later confided; "I was trading money for power I couldn't get at any other studio." In 1927–1928, Capra directed nine low-budget quickies, all of them popular, all of them in imitation of the formulas of the time. Most of them were fast-paced topical comedies. Though some of these films are no longer extant, few people have lamented their demise, least of all Capra, who frankly used them to perfect his craft. They were made for about $20,000 apiece and were completed in six weeks: two for writing, two for shooting, and two for editing. Capra's salary was about $1,500 per picture.

His skepticism vanquished, Cohn raised Capra's salary, and stopped calling him dago. "The Crude One had confidence in his Cocky One," Capra explained in his autobiography. In 1928 the director was asked to rescue the foundering production of *Submarine,* in which the studio had invested $150,000—astronomical by Columbia standards. The picture returned a large profit. "You little son-of-a-bitch, you can make shit taste like pineapple," Cohn opined in grudging admiration. Capra was offered a new three-year contract—which he signed without reading—at $1,500 per week. Excited by the possibility of crashing the majors, Cohn used Capra as a battering ram, and he in turn used Cohn's ambition to enter the big time on his own terms.

Figure 5.3. *Platinum Blonde* **(1931), with Jean Harlow, Robert Williams, and Louise Closser Hale, released by Columbia Pictures.** Harlow was at the beginning of her career when Capra cast her as an heiress, Anne Schuyler, the only appealing member of a snooty, publicity-shy family. Williams (who died of peritonitis the week this movie was released) plays a breezy reporter, Stew Smith. Newspaper reporters were a popular type in the 1930s, and were almost always portrayed as cynical, citified, and fast talking. A number of Capra's movies deal with a reporter who hustles a gullible innocent in order to get a scoop, and in the process, falls in love with the person he or she is exploiting. Predictably, the lovers in this story marry, but unlike Capra's later films utilizing this formula, all does not end well: The class differences are too great to overcome. Capra retained a distrust of the very rich throughout his career. Though there are some exceptions, tycoons in his films are portrayed as cold, greedy, and isolated from the common experiences of life.

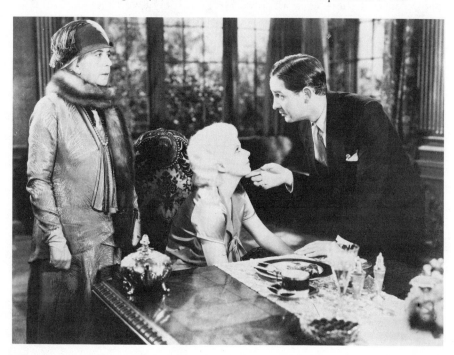

Their joint ascent began in 1930 with the A production of *Ladies of Leisure,* the biggest hit in the studio's history and the first Columbia picture to be praised by critics. Its leading lady was Barbara Stanwyck, who became one of the biggest stars of the following years. Cohn and Capra both developed a case of Academy Award fever. Needless to say, the studio had never even been nominated for an Oscar, nor did it have any votes in the academy. *Lady for a Day* (1933) was their opening wedge. The movie captured four nominations, including best picture, writer, director, and actress. None came through. In the following year, however, *It Happened One Night* swept all five top awards: best picture for Columbia, best director for Capra, best writer for Robert Riskin, and best actor and actress for Clark Gable and Claudette Colbert, who had been on loanout from MGM and Paramount. Not until *One Flew Over the Cuckoo's Nest* (1976) did a single movie make such a clean sweep. Capra

Figure 5.4. Clark Gable and Claudette Colbert in *It Happened One Night* (1934), released by Columbia Pictures. The iconography of both stars was firmly established by this movie, which inaugurated the era of screwball comedy. Gable's macho swagger and tomcat grin became part of his permanent persona. An actor of modest skill, he was nonetheless able to exploit this roguish charm for nearly four decades. Colbert was always at her best playing wealthy, high-spirited women whose warmth was sometimes obscured by a veneer of upper-class fastidiousness. During production, Colbert refused to do a scene requiring her to reveal her legs, in which the heroine demonstrates to the male chauvinist hero that the limb is mightier than the thumb in hitching a ride. Miffed, Capra hired a double, whose legs would be used instead. Colbert checked her out, then haughtily told Capra she'd do the scene after all. "Besides," she sniffed, "my legs are better."

had finally arrived. For the remainder of the decade, he was the most admired and successful filmmaker in America.

"Being a Sicilian, I take a dim view of authority of any kind," Capra has stated. "I don't like anybody telling me what to do." Throughout his career, he was the leading spokesman for a director's cinema. "One man—one film" was his artistic credo. He generously acknowledged the contributions of his collaborators, but he insisted that collaboration didn't mean movies by committee, as in the Hollywood factory system, which he associated especially with MGM. Capra credits Cohn with making a director's cinema viable within the studio system. Beginning in the 1930s, a number of producer-directors worked independently out of Columbia, including such respected figures as Ford, Hawks, and McCarey. Capra believes that other directors could have had the same artistic freedom if they were willing to fight and take responsibility for their failures as well as triumphs. Most directors were afraid to stick their necks out, he claims. Beginning with *Mr. Deeds Goes to Town* (1936), his name was prominently displayed above the title of all his subsequent fiction films. Significantly, he entitled his autobiography *The Name Above the Title*.

Capra's reputation as a fighter was an inspiration to other directors, who turned to him for guidance in gaining a greater measure of artistic autonomy. In 1935 he was elected president of the Academy of Arts and Sciences. He was also elected president of the Screen Directors Guild, which in the late 1930s was engaged in a fierce battle with the Producers Association, representing the interests of the majors. The conflict came to a head in 1939. After being treated in an insolent manner by the spokesmen for the producers, Capra urged his fellow directors to strike and to picket the Academy Award festivities—of which Capra was to be master of ceremonies. He threatened to resign as president of the academy, thus reducing the ceremony to chaos. Horrified at the prospect of a complete shambles, the producers caved in, granting considerable concessions to the Directors Guild, including the right to a first cut, increased salary scales, and improved working conditions. To the chagrin of the producers, the awards for best director and best picture of that year went to Frank Capra's *You Can't Take It with You.*

His ultimate goal was to go into independent production. After the extraordinary success of *It Happened One Night,* Cohn tore up their old contract. Capra subsequently received $100,000 per film, plus 25 percent of the net profits, making him the highest salaried director in the world. "Salaried," there was the rub. Capra wanted to be totally independent, and accordingly he left Columbia in 1939 to set up his own company. Cohn's parting telegram: "You'll be back." (Capra was earning $300,000 per picture at the time.) *Meet John Doe* was his first independent production. It was a hit, netting a $900,000 profit. But the tax laws of that era were such that 90 percent of this amount was eaten up by the IRS. Financially, he had been better off at Columbia, and with fewer production hassles.

Capra tried again after World War II. Along with his former writer, Riskin, and Columbia's production chief, Sam Briskin, Capra set up Liberty Films, which also included as partners the directors William

Wyler and George Stevens. Their movies would be distributed by RKO, which had long been sympathetic to the producer-director system of production (see Chapter 11). But 85 percent of the profits of Liberty Films went to taxes. In 1949, Capra—against the objections of Wyler and Stevens—sold the company to Paramount. (In that same year, seventy-eight other independent producers folded.) Capra claims in his autobiography that abandoning Liberty Films was the blunder of his life, for he made only five fiction films after that. After yielding a number of crucial concessions in the making of *A Pocketful of Miracles* (1961), he realized he was no longer his own man. It was his last movie.

"Maybe there really wasn't an America," filmmaker John Cassavetes mused, "maybe it was only Frank Capra." Cassavetes's wry suggestion is a testimony to Capra's enormous importance as a forger of cultural myths, as commentators like Andrew Bergman and Robert Sklar have demonstrated. Even his detractors, like the social realist critic Richard Griffith, conceded that Capra's movies ought to be evaluated, not as a mirror of American life in the 1930s, but as an index to the

Figure 5.5   Gary Cooper and Jean Arthur in *Mr. Deeds Goes to Town* (1936), distributed by Columbia Pictures. Some of Capra's finest scenes are his impromptu musical interludes, which often symbolize a harmonizing of opposites. Pictured here, Jean Arthur plays "Swanee River" on a trash recepticle in Central Park. The scene is as silly as it is charming—a typical example of the unparaphrasability of Capra's artistry. Arthur was Capra's favorite leading lady, and she appeared in three of his films. She specialized in perky working-girl roles, tender-hearted beneath the flippant cynicism.

temper of the popular mind of that era. After the success of *It Happened,* the director became aware of his immense cultural influence. While still working within a comic idiom, he now became the spokesman for traditional American values: "Beginning with *Mr. Deeds Goes to Town,* my films had to *say* something." Capra's description of the story line of *Deeds* is instructive:

> A simple honest man, driven into a corner by predatory sophisticates, can, if he will, reach deep down into his God-given resources and come up with the necessary handfuls of courage, wit, and love to triumph over his environment. This theme prevailed in all—except two—of my future films. It was the rebellious cry of the individual against being trampled to an ort by massiveness—mass production, mass thought, mass education, mass politics, mass wealth, mass conformity.

In short, Capra's spiritual autobiography.

Cultural historians have identified these sentiments as Populist, though in fact Capra doesn't use the term in his writings or interviews.

Figure 5.6. Gary Cooper in *Mr. Deeds Goes to Town*, cinematography by Joseph Walker. Humiliation and disillusionment are never far off in the Capra universe. Because of his naiveté and idealism, the Capra hero is vulnerable to exploitation, especially by those who pretend to be sympathetic to his values. When he's betrayed by the woman he loves, his anguish is poignant. Like most classicists, Capra preferred a transparent, unobtrusive style, but it's by no means plain, as this evocative, back-lighted shot illustrates. Walker was Columbia's finest cinematographer, and he shot eighteen of Capra's thirty-six features.

Figure 5.7.   James Stewart (center left, wearing hat) in *You Can't Take It with You* (1938), distributed by Columbia Pictures. Instead of two screwballs, this film features an entire household of them. Capra was famous for his mastery with crowds, but unless they are supposed to represent a frenzied mob (see Fig. 5.12), they're portrayed as individuals in groups. He practiced what he preached in his respect for individuals; hence no one could equal the gregarious rapport of his group scenes.

Like many cultural labels, it means different things at different times. Critic Jeffrey Richards points out that Populism is rooted in the very founding of the United States. The revolution was fought in large part to preserve the rights of individuals against the infringements of a ruling class. In the earliest years of the nation's development, two factions evolved: the Federalists, who believed that only a strong centralized power could preserve the fledgling union; and the Anti-Federalists, who believed that centralization would eventually destroy the liberties of individuals. This latter group was associated with the Populist ethic. Its main heroes were Lincoln, Jefferson, and Jackson, who all subscribed to the ideal of a pluralistic society, in which every individual could develop without interference from big business, big government, an established church, or a privileged aristocracy.

Throughout American history, Populism and federalism continued to evolve according to the nation's needs as they were perceived by the spokesmen of both ideologies. In the 1920s, most Americans believed that an untrammeled individualism produced the extraordinary economic prosperity of that decade. Populism was especially embraced by the newly flourishing middle class and also by many immigrants, who had come to the land of opportunity in search of greater self-fulfillment. However, a number of artists and intellectuals during this era were appalled by the rampant materialism which accompanied the economic boom. The journalist H. L. Mencken referred to the grasping middle class as the booboisie, and Sinclair Lewis's corrosively satiric novel, *Babbitt,* established an American archetype—the smug, hypocritical, hick-town booster.

After the crash of 1929, mass sentiment veered sharply toward the Federalist ideal. Vast fortunes crumbled. Millions of Americans were thrown out of work, and crime proliferated in epidemic proportions. The nation seemed on the brink of disintegration. Massive social reorganization seemed increasingly more urgent, especially to intellectuals and America's blue-collar class, which strongly endorsed Roosevelt's New Deal. The need to unify behind a common cause necessarily involved the abridgement of individual liberties, particularly in the economic sphere. Radically diminished in number, the Populists insisted

Figure 5.8. James Stewart in *Mr. Smith Goes to Washington* (1939), distributed by Columbia Pictures. Jefferson Smith (Stewart) is Capra's most idealistic hero. He has faith in the innate goodness of human beings. A romantic, a dreamer, he tries to live by "one plain, simple rule: Love Thy Neighbor." Capra's attitude toward his heroes is by no means a mindless endorsement. He believes they lack a pragmatic sense of reality, but such idealists are necessary in the dialectical search for truth: "Between the idealist and the pragmatist—somewhere in between—lies the truth, and they are often rubbing against each other."

Figure 5.9. Gary Cooper in *Meet John Doe*, distributed by Warner Brothers. This is Capra's least hopeful film, released on the eve of America's entry into World War II. The story deals with the duping of a down-on-his-luck ex-baseball player (Cooper), who's manipulated by a crypto-fascist cartel. The movie ends not with the usual triumph of the "little people" but in a stalemate, and a foreboding one. The reactionary forces in the story are left virtually intact.

that the New Deal was a wolf in sheep's clothing and would eventually devour the rights of individuals.

It was in this context that Capra's idealistic nationalism emerged. In his view, freedom was seriously imperiled by totalitarian ideologies of both the right and left. As early as 1932, his *American Madness,* one of the few movies of this period to deal explicitly with the depression, was in effect a panegyric to individualism, a deliberate attempt to shore up the national morale during a period of spiritual crisis. In *You Can't Take It with You,* Capra's spokesman says, "Whenever things go wrong, people turn to an ism—Fascism, Communism.... Why don't they think of Americanism?" *Meet John Doe,* much less comic, is more overtly didactic and dramatizes the dangers of the Nazi mentality at home.

Capra subscribed to most of the tenets of Populism, including the doctrine of self-help and the insistence that no one has the right to interfere with an individual's self-development unless he obstructs the self-development of others. He was influenced by such writers as Damon Runyon and Clarence Budington Kelland, who often published in *The Saturday Evening Post,* the foremost disseminator of Populist ideas during this era. *Deeds* is an adaptation of a Kelland story, and *Lady for a Day* and its remake, *A Pocketful of Miracles*, are based on a property by Runyon. A character in *You Can't Take It with You* eulogizes such national figures as Washington, Jefferson, Lincoln, and Grant. A number of Capra's heroes are given names evoking American archetypes: John Doe, Jefferson Smith, Longfellow Deeds, Grant Mathews. On his first day in the nation's capital, the hero of *Mr. Smith Goes to Washington* visits the Lincoln Memorial. Similarly, Mr. Deeds visits Grant's Tomb, where he observes that only in America could an Ohio farm boy rise to be President of the United States.

In place of the massive social realignments required by the New Deal, Populist spokesmen advocated a return to such traditions of Americana as good neighborliness, decent and responsible leadership, and social improvement on the community level. They promulgated such middle-class values as hard work, frugality, and healthy competition, but also generosity, compassion, and social purpose. The ethical values of Populism are based on traditional Christian principles. "It may sound sappy," Capra admitted, "but the underlying idea of my movies is actually the Sermon on the Mount." Critic John Raeburn has pointed out that human values always take precedence over material concerns in Capra's movies. A character's wealth is measured in terms of his or her family, friends, and community. Capra's ideal was a sentimentalized past of folksy small towns, close-knit families, and supportive neighbors. "Above all," Capra insisted, "every man is born with an inner capacity to take him as far as his imagination can dream or envision—providing he is *free* to dream and envision." These values are dramatized in all his social movies, but perhaps most explicitly in his favorite film, *It's a Wonderful Life* (1946), which was condemned by some postwar critics for its "Pollyanna platitudes."

Reflecting the left-of-center sentiments of his era, Richard Griffith thought that Capra's movies advocated the preservation of values already lost, thus encouraging audiences to entertain fairytale solutions to urgent social needs. "This ability to express ideas in terms saturated with emotional associations has enabled him to give appropriate form to the fantasy of good will," Griffith scoffed. These criticisms were echoed by others, including the British commentator, Alistair Cooke, who had admired Capra's earlier work: "He's started to make movies about themes instead of people," Cooke wrote of the later social comedies.

More recent commentators, like Andrew Bergman, have criticized Capra for treating class conflicts as mere clashes of personality, with the good guy pitted against the villain. Capra's vision of the American dream is a wide-eyed and affectionate hustle, Bergman has argued. He concedes the director's enormous skill in evoking patriotic emotions, which glow with the successful immigrant's sincerity of conviction. But like Griffith, Bergman believes that the individualist tradition had been too profoundly shaken by the depression to offer any realistic cures for the country's ills. Robert Sklar believes that the key to Capra's popularity was in his ability to fuse audience identification with the larger-than-life "ordinary" heroes on the screen. Americans responded to these movies because they felt that their own worth and dignity as individuals were being affirmed. But like Griffith and Bergman, Sklar believes that Capra's America is a nostalgic experience of art, not an accurate reflection of reality. He refers to the director as a "Jeffersonian agrarian," as a "pastoralist."

In dealing with Capra's social movies, a crucial aesthetic issue hinges on their degree of realism. For example, critic Stephen Handzo claims that Capra's main impact in the 1930s was as a realistic director, not a sentimental fabulist. Griffith's principal complaint was that Capra's surface (that is, stylistic) realism was dangerously misleading, lending his naive social solutions a documentary authenticity. But Capra deliberately embraced mythic materials and was conscious that he was creating cinematic fables, as his allegorical titles suggest, not to speak of his frankly archetypal heroes. When interviewer James Childs asked Capra if he thought his movies were realistic, he replied, "Oh, I don't think so. Not realistic. They're entertainment and they're fantasy and they're comedy." In no way, however, does Capra deny their artistic validity. The Deeds formula, the prototype for all the social movies, is essentially a variation of the Horatio Alger and Cinderella myths, which had been staples of the American cinema almost since its inception. Capra was an artist, not a political analyst; he trafficked in emotional truths, not in sociological facts. Doubtless many confused the two, but many also understood the distinction. After all, the millions who thronged to Capra's Populist parables included many of the same millions who overwhelmingly supported the New Deal.

Most of Capra's social movies deal with values clustering around the two main ideologies of his era and can be broken down into such conflicts as follows:

Federalism	Populism
Conformity	Individualism
City	Small town
Present	Past
Party machines	Participatory democracy
Welfare state	Self-help
Interdependence	Independence
Mass society	Communal society
Cynicism	Innocence
Materialism	Humanism
Sophistication	Simplicity
Alienation	Integration
European intellectualism	Yankee common sense
Secularism	Christianity
Expedience	Loyalty
High art	Popular entertainment

Critic Robert Willson has pointed out that the Capra hero of the social movies is indebted to the childlike holy fools of the silent period. Like them, he is innocent, bumbling, and vulnerable. In addition, Capra's democratic faith in the average man was doubtless influenced by Will Rogers' skepticism toward intellectuals and politicians. All the heroes distrust organized power blocks, be they Democratic, Republican, or Independent. Richards points out that the heroes of the early 1930s movies are generally from the city and are tarnished by its cynicism, but in a crisis their decent impulses triumph. Most of the heroes of the social movies are country boys who against overwhelming odds eventually outsmart the city slickers. These heroes are aided by the Capra heroine, who sometimes begins as a cynical manipulator but eventually becomes converted by the hero's innate goodness. Deeds is the first fully developed Capra hero. He embodies most of the homely virtues associated with Populism: He doesn't smoke or drink, gives his love freely and without ulterior motives, writes corny rhymes for greeting cards, and plays the tuba in his hometown band. This hokum renders him slightly comical, of course, but also endearing, especially as played by Gary Cooper, who as Capra remarked, has integrity written all over him. Deeds is put off by city sophisticates, whom he finds jaded and patronizing. Nor is he particularly impressed by wealth: The $20 million he inherits as a fluke is more of a curse than a windfall.

Throughout his career, Capra wrote or cowrote his own scripts. He found writing laborious, often taking three times longer than shooting. He would rewrite any scene on the set if the script failed to ignite. Robert Riskin was his coscenarist in the 1930s, and during their halcyon years at Columbia, they were among the best paid, most admired teams in Hollywood. Capra especially liked Riskin's bright, crackling dialogue, which is filled with surprises and charming outbursts of whimsy. They wrote in master scenes, for the director preferred selecting his camera setups only after he had seen the actors working on the set. If a performer improved on his written part, Capra willingly preserved the changes during production. The script, in short, was viewed merely as a basic guideline to what eventually went on the screen. He often disliked his scenarios midway through production, dismissing them as "drivel." For him, they were a product of intellect rather than instinct. His artistry lay with the countless gut decisions he made while shooting the script.

In selecting or inventing a story, Capra was concerned primarily with its charm, its capacity to provide "a glow of satisfaction." He called plot a "clothesline" upon which to hang individual episodes. He also referred to scenes as "beads" on the "string" of the storyline. Critic Otis Ferguson pointed out that Capra usually chose a plot with as few restrictions as possible: It has the necessary sentimental angle and forward motion, but is fairly empty of anything else. He then filled it up with situations and characters from life. "It's purely foolish to consider Capra's films in terms of what their story would look like on paper," Ferguson shrewdly observed; "a movie can be made out of anything or nothing so long as it is in the hands of the best picturemakers."

Acting is what counted most for Capra. He would often hold up production for months in order to get the performers he wanted. He believed that casting was the major determinant of characterization. Often he created characters with a specific star in mind. A number of them had their personas established by their roles in Capra's movies:

Figure 5.10. Publicity photo of Capra and Gary Cooper during the production of *Meet John Doe*. "I cast actors that I believed could be living people," Capra said. "Gary Cooper *was* Longfellow Deeds; he *was* Long John Doe. Jimmy Stewart *was* Jefferson Smith and George Bailey." Both Cooper and Stewart are in the Lincoln mold: tall, lean, stammering, WASP. It was Capra's movies that established these stars as icons of traditional Americanism. Capra rarely cast against type: "I cast the person, not the acting ability," he stated. He wanted his players to relax and be themselves. He wanted performances that showed no strain. Cooper was one of the least accomplished actors of the great stars, yet his performances under Capra's direction are powerful and moving. No other leading man of his generation could convey such vulnerability without making a maudlin spectacle of himself.

Gable, Cooper, Stewart, and Jean Arthur, to name a few. Edward Arnold was his favorite villain, and he specialized in playing selfish tycoons. In the late 1930s, Cooper and Stewart accepted roles from Capra scripts unseen—the ultimate compliment for a director. He asked his leading

Figure 5.11. *Prelude to War* **(1942), produced by the U.S. War Department.** World War II interrupted Capra's career as a fiction filmmaker for nearly four years. Though he was forty-four years old, he enlisted in the U.S. Army in 1942. He was personally commissioned by General George C. Marshall to supervise a series of documentaries explaining to American G.I.s why they were fighting. Capra's unifying theme was the contrast between a free and a slave society. *Prelude to War,* the first of the seven *Why We Fight* films, was released theatrically and won an Academy Award as best documentary of 1942.

men to wear no makeup and his leading ladies to use only what they'd wear on the street. He disliked staginess, and he asked his performers not to shout, but to speak softly and intimately, to throw away their lines rather than hammer them home. He kept rehearsals to a minimum, fearing that the actors would tire and dissipate their freshness. He wanted them to look like "real people talking really." He insisted that it was the director's job to convince his players of the reality of their scenes. "There are no bad actors," he claimed, "only bad directors." Few filmmakers could elicit such spontaneity from their players. Capra's camera virtually caresses them. "No matter how small the roles," he has remarked, "I treat all actors as stars." His secondary performers were often praised for their individuality. He gave all of his players some unique characterization to make them seem more real. He never bothered with screen tests, preferring to trust his instincts. He interviewed every actor in his cast, including nonspeaking extras. For example, *Mr. Smith* included 186 speaking parts, and Capra interviewed four or five players for each role.

Even Capra's detractors admitted he was a superlative stylist. He was perhaps the foremost practitioner of what scholars later referred to as the classical narrative cinema of the big studio era. He believed that technique should be unobtrusive, a servant in the presentation of characters in action. "There are no rules in filmmaking, only sins," he said, "and the cardinal sin is Dullness." Often he would improvise on the set, experimenting with various shots, angles, and lighting effects. He could afford this flexibility because he was disciplined in the preproduction phases of his work. Like his friend Howard Hawks, Capra disliked sluggish movies. As early as 1932, he increased the tempo of his films by speeding up the actors' pace 40 percent above normal. He eliminated most entrances and exits, avoided literal transitions and slow dissolves, and asked his players to overlap their lines—thus producing a sense of urgency which is seldom allowed to subside. He often used three cameras even for photographing simple scenes, to assure smooth transitions between long shots and closeups. Using multiple cameras also yielded him considerably more footage, permitting greater creativity at the editing bench. Fearful that his sentimental scenes would degenerate into bathos, he used such understated techniques as having his characters turn their backs to the camera. In their private moments of grief, he tactfully photographs them in the dark or from behind protective obstacles. His love scenes take place in the rain or fog and are often deliberately funny.

Capra regarded editing as the most enjoyable part of filmmaking. The British critic Graham Greene considered him a director of genius, who could edit as brilliantly as Eisenstein. Greene was dazzled by Capra's extraordinary shifts in tone, ranging from despair to hilarity to rapturous lyricism even within a single sequence. Many of his movies contain set pieces within the story, and he punctuates these vignettes with sudden explosions of closeups and witty juxtapositions. Unlike his friend Eisenstein, however, Capra never displays his editing virtuosity for its own sake: Like every other technique, it's subordinated to the needs of the characters in action—the cardinal commandment of classical cutting. The final third of *Mr. Smith* is confined to a single setting, yet the sequence is never static, thanks to Capra's dynamic cutting and counterpointing. In this movie as in others, he employed the concept of a "reactive character," who guides the viewer's response to the action, a technique he probably derived from Lubitsch. For example, if the hero says or does something which might otherwise seem ambiguous, a cutaway to a sympathetic observer's reaction in effect determines how the audience will respond. This technique is especially crucial in sentimental speeches, when an audience is likely to snigger at the hero's naiveté. The same principle is applied when the reactive character frowns at the remarks of an unsympathetic character. In this way, Capra could manipulate the emotional crosscurrents of his scenes with considerable command.

Even more than most directors of his era, he was a stout believer in previewing a movie before releasing it to the public. Too nervous to trust

Figure 5.12. James Stewart in *It's a Wonderful Life* (1946), produced by Liberty Films, distributed by RKO. This film, the favorite work of both Capra and Stewart, has been called "a personal and professional autobiography" by critic Stephen Handzo. A sense of the past and its shared experiences permeate the movie. In this scene depicting a bank run during the early depression period, George Bailey (Stewart) pleads with the despositors of the Bailey Building and Loan not to panic, because by withdrawing their savings, they would foreclose on their neighbors, who are also partners in the building and loan association—a scene that directly parallels Capra's *American Madness*. The footage dealing with World War II recalls the *Why We Fight* series. Bailey's adult life begins with his joining the building and loan company in 1928, the same year Capra joined Columbia Pictures. Bailey gets married in 1932, the same year Capra married his wife of nearly fifty years. The Baileys have four children; the Capras also had four children. In short, the movie represents a kind of summing up: Capra's *Tempest*. See Stephen Handzo, "Under Capracorn," in *Film Comment* (Nov.-Dec., 1972).

his judgments at the screening, he tape-recorded the audience's responses. He then reedited the film according to the duration of the taped laughs. He sometimes repeated this procedure with six or seven audiences before he felt confident of his final version. He believed that the dividing line between the ridiculous and the sublime—a line his movies tread precariously—is vague and imprecise to an individual, no matter how receptive. The larger the audience, the more sensitive the response. He cared about what the critics said of his movies, but he trusted only in the public's response: "I'd read what the gods wrote, but I would listen to what the mortals said. After all, there were more of us."

Capra tends to suffer from the same vices as Griffith and Ford, who had similar sensibilities. Capra's lesser films are often maudlin in their sentiment. When the acting is weak—as in *A Pocketful of Miracles*—all that remains are the mechanical contrivances; without an animating spirit, the archetypes become stereotypes. The gassy philosophizing of *Lost Horizon* (1937) appealed strongly to contemporary audiences, but present-day viewers are likely to find the movie pretentious and arty. Significantly, it's not a comedy, and Capra is seldom at his best outside the comic range. Capra is also inclined to take cheap shots at easy targets: snooty society folk, intellectuals, shyster lawyers, and of course that indispensible figure, the tycoon.

In the early 1950s, Capra returned to his first love—science. Television at that time was still in an experimental stage, and though most movie directors of his stature could scarcely bring themselves to mention the rival medium, let alone work in it, Capra was persuaded to produce and direct a series of science documentaries for children. The results included such charming parables as *Our Mr. Sun, Hemo the Magnificent, The Strange Case of Cosmic Rays,* and *Meteora, the Unchained Goddess.* But that considerable achievement belongs more properly to the history of American television.

Capra's influence on other filmmakers is incalculable, in part because it's so pervasive. In his own day, such directors as Ford, Hawks, and McCarey freely admitted an indebtedness. Among contemporary American filmmakers who have carried on his tradition of comic humanism are such figures as Paul Mazursky, Hal Ashby, and Robert Altman. Capra's friend John Ford ranked him with such giants as De Sica, Renoir, and Fellini. In fact, this director who has been described as the most deeply American of all filmmakers has influenced virtually every major figure of the humanist cinema, including such disparate artists as Ermanno Olmi, Milos Forman, Satyajit Ray, and Yasujiro Ozu.

BIBLIOGRAPHY

BAXTER, JOHN. *Hollywood in the Thirties.* Cranbury, N.J.: A. S. Barnes, 1968. A survey of the major studios, stars, and directors of the decade.

BERGMAN, ANDREW. *We're in the Money: Depression America and Its Films.* New York: Harper & Row, Pub., 1971. A cultural study, with a chapter on Capra and screwball comedy.

CAPRA, FRANK. *The Name Above the Title.* New York: Macmillan, 1971. An unusually candid autobiography.

———, and ROBERT RISKIN. *It Happened One Night,* in *Four Star Scripts.* Ed. Lorraine Noble. New York: Doubleday, 1936. See also *Lady for a Day* in the same collection; and *Mr. Smith Goes to Washington,* in *The Best Pictures: 1939–40,* eds. Jerry Wald and Richard Macauley (New York: Dodd Mead, 1940): reading versions of the screenplays.

Frank Capra: "One Man—One Film." Pamphlet published by the American Film Institute, Number 3 (1971). The longest interview, with brief bibliography and filmography.

Frank Capra: The Man and His Films. RICHARD GLATZER, and JOHN RAEBURN, eds. Ann Arbor: University of Michigan Press, 1975. An excellent collection of articles by various critics and scholars. Bibliography and filmography.

GRIFFITH, RICHARD. "The Film Since Then," in *The Film Till Now*, by Paul Rotha and Griffith. London: Spring Books, 1967. A social realist critique.

LARKIN, ROCHELLE. *Hail, Columbia.* New Rochelle, N.Y.: Arlington House Publishers, 1975. A studio history, with chapters on Capra and screwball comedy. See also Bob Thomas, *King Cohn: The Life and Times of Harry Cohn* (New York: Putnam's 1967).

POAGUE, LELAND A. *The Cinema of Frank Capra.* Cranbury, N.J.: A. S. Barnes, 1975. A critical study. Bibliography and filmography.

RICHARDS, JEFFREY. "Frank Capra and the Cinema of Populism," in *Movies and Methods*, ed. Bill Nichols (Berkeley: University of California Press, 1976). Reprinted from the British journal *Cinema,* the best introduction to Capra's Populism.

WILLIS, DONALD C. *The Films of Frank Capra.* Metuchen, N.J.: Scarecrow, 1974. A critical study of the fiction films, with an annotated filmography.

Leaves of Grass

The Cinema of John Ford

Figure 6.1. John Ford during the production of *Gideon of Scotland Yard* (1959), distributed by Columbia Pictures. A tolerant scowl was about all Ford could muster for studio publicity shots. Actually, this photo captures one of his lighter moments. He was completely in command on his sets: He tolerated no disagreements and didn't suffer fools gladly. Anyone who presumed to question his judgment was subjected to unrelenting humiliation for the duration of the shooting period. During production, he was dour, taciturn, or cantankerous most of the time. When he got mad, he was downright mean. Ford loathed interviews, and rarely granted them. When he did, he was testy and easily irritated. If he didn't want to answer a question, he used his partial deafness as a pretext for not hearing it. He seldom discussed his movies in terms of art, and when interviewers pressed him, he resorted to silence, evasion, or outright lies. It took courage, tenacity, and a tough hide to interview Ford. A certain masochism also helped. Photo: Scott Eyman.

ord was one of the most prolific of all American filmmakers. Scholars have estimated that he directed approximately 112 features. Most of his 61 silent movies are no longer extant, a loss that his admirers have often lamented, though Ford didn't seem to have very high opinion of the majority of his early efforts. A studio contract director for most of his career, he was frequently assigned to inferior projects by his bosses. He viewed such assignments as the necessary price he had to pay in order to make the movies *he* liked. "What I used to do was try to make a big picture, a smash, and then I could palm off a little one on them," he explained. So great was his contempt for these hack projects that he sometimes didn't even bother to look at the finished results. Of course virtually all American moviemakers of his generation began their careers by working on mundane studio assignments. Ford continued to function in this manner even after World War II, though most of his best postwar films were produced by his own company, Argosy Pictures. Certainly few major directors have produced a body of work of such inconsistent artistic merit as Ford. At his best, however, as in such films as *The Grapes of Wrath* and *The Searchers,* Ford was the equal of the finest artists of the movies. Like Walt Whitman, to whom he's often compared, Ford might be regarded as America's cinematic laureate, a bardic poet who celebrates the glories and eulogizes the tragedies of our national heritage. As critic Andrew Sarris has noted,

No American director has ranged so far across the landscape of the American past, the worlds of Lincoln, Lee, Twain, O'Neill, the great wars, the Western and trans-Atlantic migrations, the horseless Indians of the Mohawk Valley and the Sioux and Comanche cavalries of the West, the Irish and Spanish incursions, and the delicately balanced politics of polyglot cities and border states. [From *The American Cinema: Directors and Directions 1929–1968* (New York: Dutton, 1968.)]

Most of Ford's best movies are westerns, a genre that enjoyed little prestige within the movie industry and even less with critics. In all, he received six Academy Awards and four New York Film Critics Awards, but with only one exception (*Stagecoach*), these honors went to his literary adaptations, films of social realism, and his wartime documentaries. It wasn't until the 1950s that these snobbish prejudices against the western were cleared away, mostly by Ford's French admirers. Jean Mitry's pioneering study, *John Ford,* was published in France in 1954. Many others followed.

> *I have never thought about what I was doing in terms of art, or "this is great," or "world-shaking," or anything like that. To me it was always a job of work—which I enjoyed immensely—and that's it.*
>
> —*John Ford*

Sean Aloysius O'Fienne was born in 1894 in Cape Elizabeth, Maine, the thirteenth and last son of Irish immigrant parents. The family was bilingual, speaking Gaelic and English. As a youth, young Jack attended Catholic schools, and he also painted and sketched a great deal. His ambition was to be an artist. His older brother Francis migrated west and got a job as a director at Universal Studio, where they changed his name to Ford. Upon hearing of the opportunities in the West, Jack soon followed. Beginning as a stuntman and sometimes actor (he was one of the klansmen in Griffith's *Birth of a Nation*), Ford (as he too was now called) became friends with the actor Harry Carey. Together they made a number of popular silent westerns at Universal. Ford's early works were mostly one- and two-reelers. His first feature, *Straight Shooting* (1917), was well regarded by his bosses, but it wasn't until the visually sophisticated *The Iron House* (1924) that the director was singled out for more than routine praise.

From 1920 to 1935, Ford was contracted to the Fox Film Corporation. When it merged with 20th Century Films in 1935, with Darryl F. Zanuck as head, Ford remained with the new company for over a decade. (He also free-lanced during this period, mostly at RKO.) Zanuck, one of the most intelligent of the Hollywood moguls, shared many of Ford's patriotic and Populist sentiments, especially his promilitary sympathies and his social consciousness. Among the movies that Zanuck produced for Ford at 20th Century-Fox were *Young Mr. Lincoln* (1939), *Drums Along the Mohawk* (1939), *The Grapes of Wrath* (1940), *Tobacco Road* (1941), and *How Green Was My Valley* (1941).

The early controversy surrounding Ford criticism centered on the

Figure 6.2.   Victor McLaglen (right) in *The Informer* (1935), cinematography by Joseph August, distributed by RKO. This was one of Ford's earliest independent productions and his first big success with critics. The picture was shot entirely in the studio on a small budget and a quickie schedule. Its lighting is moody and richly textured, with many nighttime scenes and expressionistic effects. Throughout the film, Ford used a thick fog to symbolize the isolation of the protagonist (McLaglen), who for personal gain has betrayed his comrades in the cause for Irish independence. Of all his collaborators, Ford was most generous in his praise of his cinematographers. He claimed he never had an argument with any of them. The roster of great cameramen he worked with reads like a Who's Who of American cinematography: Joseph MacDonald, Gregg Toland, Joseph August, Arthur Miller, Bert Glennon, Archie Stout, William Clothier, and the brilliant colorist, Winton Hoch. Ford coyly admitted that he had "an eye for composition," but he attributed much of the credit for the beauty of his images to his cinematographers.

problem of genre. Since the western had never been an important genre in either drama or literature, many commentators, steeped in the critical traditions of these older and more prestigious arts, looked upon the cinematic western as a cliché. But the problem is more complex. In the first place, the western is a relatively recent subspecies of the epic, a genre that enjoys considerable literary prestige. Briefly, the epic is a narrative form which celebrates an historic and/or mythic subject. Generally epics deal with larger-than-life heroes, who embody the highest ideals (but seldom the shortcomings or vices) of a given nation, culture, or religious group. Most epics are psychologically naive, for sweeping events tend to take precedence over nuances of character. Stylistically, epics are elevated, sincere, and lyrical in their fervor. The narrative events of most epics synthesize a cultural epoch. Bold stirring clashes—often of a military nature—tend to predominate. Great epics are usually produced during periods of ascending power and represent the triumph of a given civilization over its adversaries. Many of Ford's westerns, for example, deal with the conquering of the Indian nations of the American West.

Walt Whitman modified the concept of the epic by insisting that each individual, each blade of grass, is the true hero of a democratic

Figure 6.3. *Stagecoach* **(1939), distributed by United Artists.** Ford was a master of the epic long shot, which includes miles of terrain within its purview and dwarfs the inhabitants to virtual insignificance. As Andrew Sarris has noted, Ford rarely lost sight of the human materials even in contexts of epic magnitude, such as Monument Valley (pictured). Ford considered this locale "the most complete, beautiful, and peaceful place on earth," and it was so intimately identified with his westerns that industry regulars referred to it as Ford country. He shot eight other westerns here. André Bazin, the editor of *Cahiers du Cinéma*, considered the western the American genre *par excellence*, and Ford's *Stagecoach* as its most classic embodiment.

civilization, a belief that Ford shared. Both artists idolized Abraham Lincoln, but they viewed him as "the common man raised to the highest," to use Whitman's egalitarian phrase. Like any other genre, the epic isn't necessarily a mode of intrinsic artistic excellence. There are more examples of bad epics than good, but since these inferior works have been lost or neglected over the centuries, the term *epic* (like *tragedy*) tends to connote an innate dignity to many ahistorical commentators. Because westerns were produced with staggering frequency during Ford's era, many viewers were aesthetically desensitized by the artistic vulgarity of most of these works. In a sense, they poisoned people's responses to westerns of genuine artistry. Like any other genre, in short, there are good westerns and bad.

The principal myth underlying virtually all westerns was first enunciated by historian Frederick Jackson Turner in 1893. Turner's thesis was that the great western frontier was finally closed, sealing off America's most pervasive symbol of freedom, innocence, and refuge. Such scholarly works as Henry Nash Smith's *Virgin Land* have demonstrated how Americans viewed the frontier as a Promised Land, a Garden of Eden, free from the rigidities and repressive traditions of the eastern "established" states. Because of its comprehensive range and its innate potential for dramatic conflict, filmmakers have repeatedly turned to the western genre to explore America's historical conflicts of value (see Fig. I.35).

The western is perhaps the most prominent example of America's nostalgia for the innocence and excitement of the past. Not surprisingly, Ford's movies are filled with flashbacks and verbal reminiscences. No other American director was so obsessed with the past. Most westerns take place between the years 1865 and 1890, the Golden Age of westward expansion. This was a period in American history when options for the future still seemed open, and the phrase *Manifest Destiny* was employed to justify the "obvious" and "God-ordained" role of American pioneers to take over and dominate the western wilderness.

Like the early dime novels which featured such dashing heroes as Deadwood Dick and Buffalo Bill, the earliest movie westerns consisted largely of clichés, and characters were manufactured by rote formula. The western hero was virile, brave, and forthright. His adversaries—the "savages" and "outlaws"—were cruel, devious, and depraved. But as Robert Warshow pointed out in his influential essay, "The Westerner," the cinematic western came into the realm of serious art only when the hero's moral code, without ceasing to be compelling and romantic, is also seen to be ambiguous, darkening his morality and saving him from being childishly simple-minded. John Ford was among the first to handle the western with this requisite degree of ambiguity and complexity.

As John Cawelti has pointed out in his important study, *The Six-Gun Mystique,* the most popular western plot deals with the conflict between the eastern pioneers and the savage inhabitants of the western frontier. These antagonistic forces are generally evenly matched. A third force, the western hero, is needed to tip the balance. Divided in his sentiments, he must decide whether to side with the forces of the civilized community, which may destroy or at least confine him, or to allow the renegades and Indians (whose values are not unlike his own) to destroy the community. The western hero is usually a man of violence himself, but by directing his violence against the enemies of the community, he is morally vindicated and in most cases honored as a model of social commitment. Generally such an action on the part of the hero involves some sacrifice of his personal code. In Ford's westerns especially, self-sacrifice to a communal cause is the highest form of heroism. In his later works, the hero sometimes sacrifices himself to a cause he doesn't really believe in.

Over the years, an increased erosion of confidence became apparent in Ford's attitude toward these three forces. In his earlier westerns, like *Stagecoach* (1939), *My Darling Clementine* (1946), *She Wore a Yellow Ribbon* (1949), and especially the unabashedly optimistic *Wagon Master* (1950), the director's sympathies are strongly weighted in favor of the community. The tone of these works is predominantly lyrical, at times soaring with rapturous nationalism. The heroes identify more overtly with the community than those of the later westerns. They also tend to be relatively static in terms of character development, undergoing little internal change. The dramatic tension is created externally, by pitting two forces in a conventional confrontation, usually in the form of a shootout. These earlier works are more concerned with extolling the American Dream and America's legendary heroes than with portraying the actual texture of frontier existence. The idealization is a deliberate attempt to give patriotic myths precedence over literal history. Corruption in these movies is generally treated as an excess of individualism, the result of social irresponsibility, and especially, greed. More than any other classical American filmmaker, Ford is skeptical of individualism. He often treats it as a form of selfishness in his movies. Above all, the family—the minimal communal unit—is given precedence over any single individual.

Ford minimizes the negative effects of the westward expansion in most of these earlier works. Particularly open to criticism is his casual imperialism toward the Indian nations, whose cultures were destroyed by the encroachments of the white victors. Even in these earlier movies, however, Ford's treatment of Indians is more respectful than virtually anything that can be found in the works of his less sensitive contemporaries. Indians are almost always portrayed as heroic adversaries, as courageous as they are dangerous. Furthermore, Ford knew and respected their culture. In private life he championed their cause, long before it became fashionable to do so. He also went out of his way to give them employment as extras in his movies, in some cases rescuing them from desperate poverty.

As the director grew older, his vision—like Whitman's—became increasingly melancholy, dark, and even disillusioned. Social injustices are not so easily glossed over, especially in such works as *The Searchers* (1956), *Sergeant Rutledge* (1960), *Two Rode Together* (1961), and *The Man Who Shot Liberty Valance* (1962). In the bitter *Cheyenne Autumn* (1964), the Indians are portrayed as the civilized force, and most of the whites are the savages. In part, this change was inevitable, both socially and artisti-

Figure 6.4. **Henry Fonda (extreme right) in** *The Grapes of Wrath* **(1940), scenario by Nunnally Johnson, based on the novel by John Steinbeck, produced by 20th Century-Fox.** Many of Ford's works contain funeral scenes: His treatment of death is dignified and solemn. Widely regarded as the greatest film dealing with the depression of the 1930s, *The Grapes of Wrath* centers on a dispossessed family of Okies, the Joads, and their odyssey to California, their Promised Land. Characteristically, Ford transformed Steinbeck's Marxist novel into a masterpiece of Christian humanism. The film's compassion for the victims of oppression is simple, decent, eloquent.

cally. Beginning in the early 1950s, a number of filmmakers began to exploit the western as a vehicle for social protest, emphasizing America's violent heritage and bigotry toward unassimilated minorities, particularly Negroes. Such pro-Indian (and by implication, antiwhite) westerns as Delmer Daves' *Broken Arrow* (1950) and Samuel Fuller's *Run of the Arrow* (1956) nurtured the embryonic civil rights movement, which like the new breed of "antiwestern," was to expose the soft underbelly of the American Dream.

An important source of irony in most westerns derives from the fact that the audience knows that eventually progress and civilization triumphed over the forces of lawlessness. But in the 1960s particularly, Americans were growing increasingly disillusioned with the presumed benefits of progress. Many artists, reflecting this dissatisfaction, began searching for new myths or redefining old ones in order to explore the moral inconsistencies of America's past. Sam Peckinpah was perhaps the most successful film artist to reexamine traditional myths in this way, and his westerns vividly confirmed the once-startling pronouncement of black militant Stokely Carmichael: "Violence is as American as apple pie." (For a discussion of this period, see Chapter 16.)

But the precedent had already been established—in the final works of John Ford. His later westerns are set in an era closer to the neurotic, unheroic twentieth century. Confinement and delimitation characterize these films, not the spaciousness and freedom which typify his earlier westerns. There is an atmosphere of loss in many of these movies, a sense of failure. The heroes are no longer necessarily models of behavior. They view the values of the community with skepticism and sometimes contempt, even though they may finally make extraordinary sacrifices for it. In *The Man Who Shot Liberty Valance*, the protagonist dies a pauper's death, virtually unnoticed and unmourned, though it was he who made the establishment of the community possible, a cause he intuitively sensed was against his own interest. Always sympathetic to outcasts, Ford's compassion for minority figures became more apparent in these later works. Mexicans, Negroes, and Indians figure more prominently, though they are often sentimentalized.

Even in his silent westerns, Ford emphasized the epic grandeur of the American landscape. The Great Plains, the lofty regality of the Rockies, and especially the arid, inhospitable deserts of the West, are exploited as heroic obstacles to be overcome by the pioneers streaming in from the East. The fragile communities are tenuously linked by trails at first, then by coach, and finally—in the later stages of civilization—by the railroad, which connects East with West. Ford's most famous natural landmark is Monument Valley. Located on the Arizona-Utah state line within the Navajo Indian Reservation, it consists of a vast desert plain almost totally devoid of vegetation. The terrain is periodically interrupted by majestically towering buttes and mesas, which were created by centuries of erosion. Ford photographed its primordial mystery lovingly, with its ever-shifting colors, its shadows, and its merciless sun.

Violence in Ford's films is usually underplayed. Seldom does he dwell over gory details, and even in his westerns he never lingers over shootouts, preferring instead to execute them with efficient dispatch. What Ford dwells on most lovingly is the community—its institutions and its spiritual solidarity. Four social institutions are glorified with compulsive regularity: the family, the military, the church, and the saloon. (Social drinking is almost always viewed as a positive value in his movies.) The director also loved to portray community rituals: His films are filled with weddings, funerals, public addresses, dedication ceremonies, dinner scenes, drinking bouts, farewell scenes, and amiable brawls. Many of these rituals are accompanied by two favorite songs, "Red River Valley" and the hymn, "Shall We Gather at the River."

Ford's plots are often deliberately structured to provide ample leeway for the exploration of such community rituals. To be sure, some of his movies, like *The Informer* (1935) and *The Searchers*, are tightly plotted, with hardly any slackening of the narrative thrust. But most of his works are more leisurely structured, and even his westerns—ordinarily an action-oriented genre—are among the loosest of the American cinema. Often Ford introduces a dramatic conflict early in the film, then sus-

Figure 6.5. *How Green Was My Valley* **(1941), with Donald Crisp (extreme left), produced by 20th Century-Fox.** Ford disliked overt emotions in his movies: He preferred conveying feelings through form. Stylized lighting effects and formal compositions such as these almost invariably embody intense emotions. A romantic conservative, Ford was skeptical of the notion of progress. In this film dealing with a Welsh mining community, he nostalgically recreates a world of Edenic innocence and family solidarity. This green world is eventually polluted by industrialization and its by-products—greed and class exploitation. The disintegration of the family was one of Ford's main themes, and in this movie it's treated from an ironic perspective through the use of flashbacks and a voiceover commentary. Photo: Scott Eyman.

pends it until the concluding scenes, when the issue is finally resolved. In *Stagecoach*, for instance, the threat of an Indian attack is brought up almost immediately, but not until near the end of the movie does the threat actually erupt. The middle portions of the film are devoted to a study of the interrelationships among the characters. A number of movies have very little plot at all: *How Green Was My Valley*, *They Were Expendable* (1945), and *The Last Hurrah* (1958), among others, are a series of loosely related vignettes. Of course when the occasion demanded, Ford could direct an action sequence with commanding power, but for the most part his heart lay with the quieter, less theatrical episodes.

Orson Welles once referred to Ford as a great poet and comedian. Often he's both at the same time, as in *My Darling Clementine*. Ostensibly the film deals with the Wyatt Earp story, but Ford uses this mythical material as a pretext for exploring the coming of civilization to a rough frontier community. The arrival of Boston-bred Clementine Carter (Cathy Downs) to Tombstone represents an elusive, oddly moving experience for Wyatt (Henry Fonda). Tremulous and awed, he gawks at her as she delicately descends the stagecoach. He offers to carry her luggage inside the hotel, where his two brothers watch in dumbfounded amazement: Clearly Wyatt has never behaved like this before. One of the funniest episodes takes place later in the movie, after the marshal has begun to fall in love. Unable to keep his mind clear of Tombstone's fair visitor, Wyatt ambles over to the bar, where Mac, the polite middle-aged bartender is standing. With a sigh, the moonstruck marshal asks, "Mac, you ever been in love?" Mac replies matter of factly, "No, I've been a bartender all my life." Pure Ford.

The heart of the film, and one of the most brilliant sequences the director ever created, is the famous Sunday morning church episode. Wyatt is in the barbershop, where he has just received the deluxe treatment, complete with a heavy dosing of flowery cologne. His brothers join him under the covered promenade of the main street, where they watch the graceful procession of buggies filled with townspeople in their best

Figure 6.6. **John Wayne in** *She Wore a Yellow Ribbon* **(1949), distributed by RKO.** Ford was an ardent champion of the military. He made many movies dealing with war—from the Indian Wars and the American Revolution to the Korean conflict of the early 1950s. He believed that military virtues represented the highest form of idealism: the willingness to sacrifice oneself for the preservation of a civilization. Ford also loved military rituals and a tradition of gallantry he associated with the professional soldier. His best characters are rarely the young romantic leads, if any. He preferred extolling the virtues of middle age. He was obsessed with the process of growing older, and some of his finest scenes explore the serenity of late life. In this tender farewell scene between a company commander and his hearty wife, the Wayne character tactfully averts his eyes. Ford's protagonists often do when confronted with naked emotions.

finery. One brother remarks that he can almost smell flowers in bloom. "That's me," Wyatt mutters brusquely. The elderly deacon (Russell Simpson, a Ford regular) stops his wagon and invites the Earps to join the celebration. The floor of the first church in town has been completed, and the community plans to commemorate the event with a dance. Wyatt's brothers respectfully decline, leaving him alone to daydream. Stationed outside the door of the hotel, he occupies an ideal vantage point for meeting the lady of his reveries. Soon she comes out, and after remarking that she can almost smell flowers in bloom, she asks him where all the buggies are going. Amused and touched by his shyness, Clementine hints that she would like to join the celebration. The two walk solemnly toward the church to the stately accompaniment of "Shall We Gather at the River." When they arrive, Wyatt is too reserved to do anything but look. Once again she's forced to resort to gentle hints. Finally he musters enough nerve to ask her to dance, and the townspeople instinctively clear some space for them. Beginning stiffly and with comical formality, Wyatt takes his frail partner in his arms. When the fiddles switch to a more sprightly pace, the two fall in with the music and execute a lively polka. Near the conclusion of the sequence, Ford moves his camera up and back, to a distant long-shot range: While the dancers revel joyfully below, their thumping feet resounding on the crude planks of the church floor, the American flag flutters high above them in an image of piercing majesty.

Ford was politically conservative and Populist in his sympathies. (For a discussion of Populism, see Chapter 5.) Characteristically, when he adapted John Steinbeck's *The Grapes of Wrath*, he cut out most of the Marxist analysis of the original, focusing instead on the personal and familial aspects of the material. In the novel, the exploited Okies are helpless pawns in a vast impersonal social machine. In the movie the members of the Joad family are more resiliant: They may be down, but they're never out. In the final scene, which takes place on the road—they've just accepted a twenty-day job as fruit pickers—Pa Joad (Russell Simpson) admits to his wife (Jane Darwell) that for a while he thought the family was finished. Ma Joad answers, "I know. That's what makes us tough. Rich fellas come up an' they die, an' their kids ain't no good, an' they die out. But we keep a-comin'. We're the people that live. They can't wipe us out. They can't lick us. We'll go on forever Pa, 'cause we're the people." The final image of the film follows: a thrilling extreme long shot, in which the fragile Joad vehicle merges imperceptibly with a procession of other dilapidated trucks and autos, forming an unbroken river of traffic—a visual tribute to the invincibility of the human spirit.

Few directors commanded as much respect as Ford within the film industry. He was the Grand Old Man—eccentric, unconventional, stubbornly independent. His movies usually made money, and they were often praised by critics as well. Although he had made his share of commercial potboilers in his early years, he had paid his proverbial dues. From the mid-1930s until the end of his career, many of his films were regarded as prestige projects, the kind of movies only top-echelon directors could command. Unimpressed by front office minions, he was an old pro, and he knew what he was worth. Although he was authoritarian

Figure 6.7. _Wagon Master_ (1950), released by RKO. "When I pass on, I want to be remembered as 'John Ford—a guy that made westerns.'" Unlike most of his peers, Ford believed the genre was flexible and rich in expressive possibilities. His friend, the French director Jean Renoir, agreed: "The marvellous thing about westerns is that they're all the same film. This gives the director unlimited freedom." Ford exploited the genre as a vehicle of national celebration. The most lyrical rituals are found in his dance scenes—his most pervasive symbol of the harmonious reconciliation of opposites, which Ford felt was the democratic genius of America.

and paternalistic on the set, he despised these qualities in others, especially producers and their flunkeys. He treated them with utmost contempt and rudeness. When such functionaries dared to show up on his set—a rare occurrence—Ford went out of his way to humiliate them publicly. Peter Bogdanovich relates how one foolhardy soul was sent by his boss to speed up production, which had fallen about eight pages (roughly one day's shooting) behind schedule. Ford picked up the script and tore out eight pages. "You can tell your boss we're back on schedule now," he sneered. The intruder never returned, nor did the director ever shoot the offending eight pages.

Ford believed that a filmmaker was more like an architect than a novelist. The director can be creative within certain limits, but essentially he is a coordinator of the individual contributions of others. Next to cinematographers, he believed that writers were the director's most important collaborators. Working closely and in advance with his scenarists, he also liked to have them on the set for last-minute changes.

He often wrote and rewrote lines himself. Though he seldom bothered to take any formal credit for his contributions to the script, he was especially effective in breaking up solemn scenes with a comic piece of dialogue. He regarded comedy as his forte. He affected a disdain for intellectuals but was in fact a knowledgable historian, especially sophisticated in his grasp of the American Civil War period—an invaluable asset for an artist of Ford's nationalistic temperament. He often incorporated this knowledge into his scripts. Twenty-four of his movies were written by Frank S. Nugent and Dudley Nichols, his favorite writers and two of the most literate men in the film industry. Nunally Johnson and Lamar Trotti also wrote a number of Ford's works. These four were among the most respected scenarists in Hollywood, and Ford was frankly envied by other directors for his exceptionally well-crafted scripts.

"There's no such thing as a good script really," he once remarked; "scripts are dialogue, and I don't like all that *talk*. I've always tried to get things across visually." His films are usually best when dialogue is kept to a minimum, as in most of Nugent's scripts. When talk takes precedence, the results can seem didactic and excessively literary. In *Talking Pictures,* critic Richard Corliss is especially harsh on the scripts of Nichols for these failings. At his best, Ford reveals character through actions and gesture rather than dialogue. His outdoor stories are generally superior because there are not so many opportunities for extended conversations. His most admired films are constructed around simple, lean scripts, with an emphasis on behavior. Movies like *Wagon Master, The Quiet Man* (1952), and *The Searchers* might be described as literarily neutral: What makes them impressive is the way in which the screenplays are executed, not the quality of the writing *as* writing. On the other hand, when literary values predominate, Ford's visual style is often reined in, and the results are often dull movies like *Sergeant Rutledge* (script by Willis Goldbeck and James Warner Bellah).

Ford preferred working with an informal company of regulars who appeared in film after film. Among these were the character actors Ward Bond, Victor McLaglen, Ben Johnson, John Qualen, Mildred Natwick, John Carradine, Harry Carey, Jr., and Thomas Mitchell. They were generally cast to type. As several commentators have pointed out, their reappearance in Ford's movies lends them a sense of continuity, as we watch them growing old and mellow, passing on traditions that were passed on to them in the earlier films. His favorite leading lady was the Irish beauty Maureen O'Hara, who was often paired with John Wayne, perhaps most memorably in the Irish comedy, *The Quiet Man.*

The director was somewhat sadistic in his relationship with actors. Even established stars, like Henry Fonda and James Stewart, who were grudgingly fond of the old man (Ford seems never to have been young), felt the sting of his ridicule on more than one occasion. He needled John Wayne mercilessly, referring to him as a "big oaf," among other colorful epithets. Wayne endured these insults with extraordinary good grace, for he loved the old curmudgeon as few others could. Ford's fellow Irish-American, James Cagney, was less generous. After the director had instructed him to perform a dangerous and gratuitous action, an ob-

Figure 6.8. John Wayne and Maureen O'Hara in *The Quiet Man* (1952), with Victor McLaglen (seated) and Barry Fitzgerald, released by Republic Pictures. Next to America, Ford loved Ireland best. He described *The Quiet Man* as "the first love story I've ever tried, a mature love story." He returned to the Ould Sod to shoot it, taking many of his regulars with him. Wayne plays Sean Thornton, an Irish-American ex-boxer who moves back to the land of his ancestors and comes acourtin' in the local forms, complete with a proper broker (Fitzgerald). Almost immediately, there is a clash of cultures—a frequent theme in Ford's work. "I feel I'm essentially a comedy director," he once volunteered; and in this film, he mined the humor mostly from the ritual scenes, with their slightly comical formality. Ford's mise-en-scène is a visual analogue of the human material. The heroine is appropriately garbed in white and carries a symbolic lamp. The enquiring parties are attired in formal black, the hero bearing a modest bouquet, his broker the book of rules and procedures. Only the sharp diagonal of the dinner table and the messy area in front of the master of the house suggest a jarring note, violating the shot's prim correctness.

server wondered aloud why Ford would risk his star's safety in so pointless a manner. "Because he's got the Irish disease," Cagney muttered, "malice."

Ford's tactics might have been his way of humbling his stars to establish who's boss on the set. But—more charitably—the director might have used these devious stratagems as a way of exposing an actor's vulnerabilities on camera, vulnerabilities a star might otherwise conceal for fear that he'd be considered unmanly or less virile. The director preferred a certain edginess in his performers, believing that too much ease drained a scene of its humanity. He would sometimes encourage his players to improvise their dialogue to prevent their performances from getting too precise. Even when actors bungled a scene, Ford often retained their clumsiness as an aspect of characterization. "I don't *want* it to look perfect—like a circus," he growled when an actor asked to repeat a scene in order to improve upon it.

Ford's two favorite leading men were Henry Fonda and John Wayne. Fonda is the gentler of the two, dreamy, poetic, and soft-spoken. His range is also broader: He can play the pragmatic idealist in *Young Mr. Lincoln* (1939) as well as the hardassed professional soldier in *Fort Apache* (1948). He's seldom aggressive, and in some cases he's even shy, but there's never a lack of confidence beneath his surface reserve. He can get most jobs done with casual competence and certainly with no fanfare, which he despises. He's sensitive and intelligent, and he doesn't hide either characteristic behind a macho façade. Whatever the role, there's always a countrified sincerity and decency in Fonda, and Ford exploited these qualities intelligently.

The Wayne character is more volatile. Chary of his personal honor and dignity, he can intimidate by his sheer massive presence. A man of few words and fewer pretensions, he usually does what he says he'll do, and does it forcefully. In the later movies he plays paternalistic figures,

Figure 6.9. John Wayne in *The Searchers* (1956), distributed by Warner Brothers. In their forty-five year association, Wayne always had to play Junior to Ford's Pappy. "You ask a question of Ford," the actor said, "and he looks at you as if you were the stupidest dope in the world." Nonetheless, Ford loved him as much as he needled him. Wayne's performance as Ethan Edwards in *The Searchers* is widely regarded as the finest of his long career—at once powerful, poetic, and funny. Ford described the story as "the tragedy of a loner," of a man who can never really be part of a family, even though he finally yields to the mystic ties of blood over social prejudice. Like Ford, Wayne was strongly promilitary in his sympathies and publically applauded patriotism, courage, and self-sacrifice. His name is virtually synonymous with masculinity, though Wayne's persona suggests more of the warrior than the lover. Ford usually played down eroticism, which he considered inappropriate in males. For that matter, he wasn't too wild about it in his female characters either.

chivalrous to the ladies, though generally ill at ease in their presence. His voice is matter-of-factly wooden, and he defiantly refuses to tone it up. He doesn't walk so much as lumber, with a swagger that became a trademark. Beneath the brusqueness, however, is a mysterious vulnerability. No one was as skillful as Ford in bringing out Wayne's loneliness and isolation, his capacity to suffer without making a federal case out of it. More than any other Ford protagonist, the Wayne character is a tragic loser: At the end of most of the films, he's defeated, excluded, or even killed in defense of a larger cause.

Ford's artistic shortcomings have been severely censured by critic Michael Dempsey and others. Like Griffith, Ford was a romantic conservative. His greatest strengths as well as his failures can be attributed to this characteristic. Even some of his best works are flawed by his sentimentality and his endorsement of the most platitudinous hokum concerning family, country, and God. His worship of the past borders on the reactionary: Seldom does Ford exhibit any curiosity about the future or show any enthusiasm for new ideas. With the exception of Griffith, no major American director was so cloying in his veneration for authority figures and women. Dempsey has deplored what he calls Ford's Victorian "pedestalism." His ingenues are often saccharine abstractions, enacted by simpering starlets. Ford's Mother Earth figures have also been criticized as clichés. For the most part, they exist to service their menfolk—to fuss over them, humor them, and bury them like good grieving widows. The love relationships in most of the director's movies are scrupulously chaste: Sex wouldn't dare rear its head in so wholesome an environment.

Though Ford's comedy is often appealing, especially when underplayed, he occasionally pushed his humorous scenes into farce. Actors mug, grimace, and overact so broadly that these boisterous interludes threaten to snap some of his movies in two. The brawling, drinking Irishman, often played by McLaglen, is an especially offensive comic fixture. The director was also guilty of some disastrous miscasting, as in *Cheyenne Autumn,* in which the principal Indian characters are played by slick Hollywood pros, like Sal Mineo and Ricardo Montalban. The trite performances more than anything else ruin this otherwise noble effort. Even Ford's best movies, like *The Searchers,* are marred by box office concessions. Natalie Wood plays a young woman who has lived most of her life with a savage tribe of Indians, yet she looks remarkably glamorous withal. Allowing his leading ladies to violate the authenticity of a period with incongruously modern coiffures and makeup is another recurrent shortcoming. Perhaps Ford tried to resist some of these compromises: "I can fight like hell," he once complained, "but I always lost." Yet for a director of his enormous prestige within the industry, these lapses of taste were surprisingly frequent.

Ford is one of the few American directors who demonstrated a consistent interest in, and respect for, old people. In movies like *The Last Hurrah* and *How Green Was My Valley,* in which older characters are played by such gifted performers as Spencer Tracy, Donald Crisp, and Sara Allgood, the portrayals are among the most memorable elements of the films. But without tough, disciplined performers, older characters

Figure 6.10. *The Last Hurrah* **(1958), distributed by Columbia Pictures.** Parades are a way of celebrating community solidarity and the wisdom of consensus, traits that are characteristic of most epic artists. This film explores the last political campaign of an old-style city boss and his party machine. The movie is in the elegaical mode: a mournful celebration of a grand spirit, which dies with the protagonist's political defeat. Many of Ford's movies end in failure. He despised conventional happy endings, preferring to stress the nobility of fighting for a lost cause and the glory of a heroic defeat. See also J. A. Place, *The Non-Western Films of John Ford* (New York: Citadel Press, 1979), a companion volume to her book, *The Western Films of John Ford* (New York: Citadel Press, 1974).

tend to slip into doddering stereotypes. Authority figures, especially fathers, military leaders, and clergymen, are often portrayed with Jehovahlike infallibility. Conversely, his young people are presented as warm-hearted but oafish louts, totally inept compared to their wiser elders.

Ford's working methods and his technical expertise were legendary. He was much admired for his flexibility, economy, and simplicity. A believer in preplanning, he could sometimes shoot a movie in three weeks—after six months of careful research. He never bothered with camera directions in his scripts, for he had all the setups in his head or knew instinctively where to place the camera for a shot. Cinematographers expressed amazement at how he always chose the best setup, even though he seldom looked through the viewfinder. He usually shot only one take and almost never more than two. Even action shots were rarely rehearsed in advance. Technical complications were discussed with the appropriate crew members and actors, then shot in a single take.

"The best things in movies happen by accident," Ford insisted. He

Figure 6.11.   James Stewart (left) in *The Man Who Shot Liberty Valance* (1962), with Lee Marvin (right), distributed by Paramount Pictures. "We've had a lot of people who were supposed to be great heroes, and you know damn well they weren't," Ford admitted. "But it's good for the country to have heroes to look up to." In this film, the West is conquered not by the virtues of civilization (represented by the Stewart character) but by the crude force of the western hero (represented by the John Wayne character). The outlaw Liberty Valance (Marvin) is gunned down in the dark, an appropriate medium for the birth of a myth, for the dark obscures facts. When Stewart finally confesses to a newspaper editor that he was falsely credited with killing Valance, the editor replies, "This is the West, sir. When the legend becomes the fact, print the legend." In his earlier westerns, Ford also printed the legend. But as he grew older, he grew more ironic. Characteristically, in this film he offers both the legend *and* the fact, insisting on the validity of each.

was an expert improviser, and if he or his cameraman happened to see a special kind of light, an interesting cloud formation, or an impending storm, they would set up their camera on the spot and adapt a scene to fit the fortuitous circumstances of the locale. Although he complained mightily about the way studio cutters ruined his footage, Ford's custom of editing in the camera usually offered little choice in the way his shots could be assembled. He seldom shot any coverage material. During one project, he debated with himself concerning a closeup, which he didn't think would be necessary. "If I make a closeup," he reasoned, "somebody will want to use it." He decided not to shoot one. Producers were usually unable to recut his films, a shrewd maneuver that Hitchcock also employed to keep busy fingers away from his footage. Ford was usually under schedule and under budget, two incalculable virtues, especially during the cost-conscious period after the decline of the studio system in the 1950s.

Above all, Ford's arrestingly poetic images are what provide the films with their emotional richness. He is a master of the subtle nuances of lighting. His movies are filled with arches, windows, and doorways in which the light source radiates from the center of the image, and the edges are sealed off by the surrounding darkness. He often groups his characters standing in shadows and semisilhouette, lending them a tender, ghostly effect. His sunsets and sunrises are among the most ravishing ever photographed, particularly those of Monument Valley. Many of his westerns feature shots of long columns of mounted troops or wagon trains strung out like fragile beads on a string. Some of his finest shots feature the slanted lights of the late afternoon, when the shadows of his characters are elongated in streams along the ground.

Ford is a master of the classical style. His movies are edited at a tempo that is smooth and fluid, yet unhurried and rather grand. His compositions and framing techniques are usually formally balanced, lending the images an epic dignity, especially in group shots. Traveling shots are rare, generally used when a threatening force disrupts the tranquil stability of the characters' world, as in the comic brawl at the conclusion of *The Quiet Man* or the famous Indian pursuit sequence of *Stagecoach,* in which the camera speeds alongside the careening coach as its horses desperately strain to outpace the pursuing warriors. Most of Ford's communal scenes are photographed with a stationary camera, for a stable image suggests a stable universe.

Figure 6.12. *Cheyenne Autumn* **(1964), distributed by Warner Brothers.** Ford wanted to make this movie to help his Indian friends, who were suffering severe economic distress, thanks to the ever-enlightened policies of the U.S. Bureau of Indian Affairs. (The director was made a member of the Navajo nation and was given the name Natani Nez, the Tall Soldier.) The film is based on an actual event, in which 286 Cheyenne Indians (including women and children) made an 1,800-mile odyssey from a barren Oklahoma reservation to their historic homeground in the Yellowstone region. Despite some mediocre dialogue and several miscasts, *Cheyenne Autumn* is eloquent in its moral outrage, primarily because Ford expresses it visually. The dignity of an oppressed people—a frequent theme in Ford's work—is conveyed through the power of epic images such as these.

Though Ford used many closeups in his indoor dramas, in his outdoor movies he avoided them. The characters are most meaningfully defined by their juxtaposition with their environment. His landscapes are usually shot in deep focus, with delicate filters emphasizing the cloud formations above the terrain. Many shots are taken from a slightly low angle to underline the heroic qualities of the pilgrims. Generally Ford kept his horizons low, especially in his extreme long shots, in which the specklike pioneers or soldiers seem almost in danger of slipping off the bottom of the frame, so precarious is their position in comparison to the vast skies that threaten to overwhelm them from above.

In 1973, at the age of seventy-nine, John Ford died of cancer. Shortly before, he was selected by the American Film Institute to be the first recipient of the Life Achievement Award for contributions to the American cinema. The televised ceremony was attended by the President of the United States. The choice was apt. Like his literary counterpart, Whitman, this great national poet sang of America and its people with a lyric sincerity that has never been surpassed. Other epic filmmakers, like Sergei Eisenstein and Akira Kurosawa, admitted a major indeptedness to Ford's work. Less obviously, he has also influenced Ingmar Bergman, who considers Ford a towering figure. The French filmmakers who began as critics at *Cahiers du Cinéma* were ardent Ford enthusiasts. When asked what he studied in order to learn the art of the movies, Orson Welles replied, "The old masters. By which I mean John Ford, John Ford, and John Ford."

BIBLIOGRAPHY

ANOBILE, RICHARD J., ed. *John Ford's Stagecoach,* New York: Flare Books, 1975. A reconstruction of the film, with over 1,200 frame enlargements. The script is available in conventional format from Simon & Schuster, 1971. See also the screenplays of *Stagecoach, The Grapes of Wrath,* and *How Green Was My Valley* in *Twenty Best Film Plays*, John Gassner and Dudley Nichols, eds. (New York: Crown, 1943). The script to *The Informer* is included in *Theatre Arts* (August, 1951). See also Warren French, *Filmguide to The Grapes of Wrath* (Bloomington: Indiana University Press, 1973).

BAXTER, JOHN. *The Cinema of John Ford.* Cranbury, N.J.: A. S. Barnes, 1971. The most comprehensive examination of John Ford's works.

BOGDANOVICH, PETER. *John Ford.* Berkeley: University of California Press, rev. ed. 1978. Ford's lengthiest interview, with a selected filmography.

CAWELTI, JOHN. *The Six-Gun Mystique.* Bowling Green, Ohio: Bowling Green State University Popular Press, 1970. A useful discussion of the conventions of the western genre. Other cultural studies include Joe B. Frantz and Julian E. Choate, *The American Cowboy: Myth and Reality* (London: Thames and Hudson, 1956); and Henry Nash Smith, *Virgin Land: The American West as Symbol and Myth* (New York: Vintage Books, 1957).

DEMPSEY, MICHAEL. "John Ford: A Reassessment," in *Film Quarterly* (Summer, 1975). A harsh but perceptive discussion of Ford's shortcomings as an artist.

FENIN, GEORGE, AND WILLIAM K. EVERSON. *The Western.* New York: Grossman

Publishers, expanded ed. 1973. The standard history of the movie genre.

FRENCH, PHILIP. *Westerns,* rev. ed. New York: Oxford University Press, 1977. Genre and iconography study.

McBRIDE, JOSEPH, AND MICHAEL WILMINGTON. *John Ford.* New York: Da Capo Press, 1975. A sympathetic exploration of Ford's humanist values, concentrating on fourteen films. Selected filmography.

NACHBAR, JACK, ed. *Focus on the Western.* New York: Prentice-Hall, 1974. A collection of essays, including Robert Warshow's "The Westerner."

SARRIS, ANDREW. *The John Ford Mystery Movie.* Bloomington: Indiana University Press, 1976. A discussion of the sound features, with emphasis on the westerns.

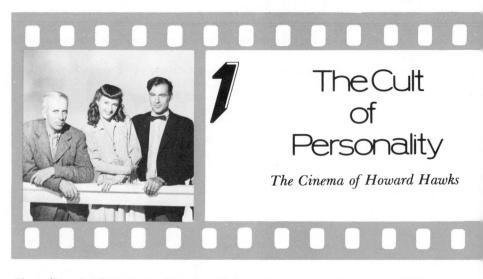

Figure 7.1. Publicity photo of Hawks with Gary Cooper and Barbara Stanwyck during the production of *Ball of Fire* (1941), distributed by RKO. Hawks was famous for his happy sets. Things were seldom dull during production, and actors often turned down more lucrative offers in favor of joining his cheery band. Normally he made about one movie a year, usually with personal friends for collaborators. Reserved and soft-spoken, Hawks despised any kind of "fuss" or pretentiousness and often directed his wry wit against such affectations. He disliked granting interviews or talking about his work at length. To him, a movie was either "good" or "no good." The highest accolade he used in describing one of his films was to call it "fun."

The directing career of Howard Hawks spanned nearly five decades. During this period he made forty-two features. His last movie, *Rio Lobo,* was released in 1970, when he was seventy-four years old. It was a career of remarkable endurance, and if he produced no towering masterpiece, he did at very least create some of the most enjoyable films in America. "I think our job is to make entertainment," he insisted, and he did so by working in close collaboration with the most gifted writers and stars in the industry. Few filmmakers could match Hawks's breadth and versatility. He worked in many genres: aviation and rac-

ing films, prison movies, detective thrillers, newspaper pictures, gangster films, musicals, costume pictures, westerns, safari films, and war movies. Of course he wasn't equally proficient in all these genres, but he made important contributions in several, most notably the gangster film, *Scarface,* the detective thriller, *The Big Sleep,* and the western, *Rio Bravo.* Above all, Hawks was at his best within the comic range. He is the preeminent loon of the American cinema. Some of his comedies are the silliest of the repertory, especially *Twentieth Century, Bringing Up Baby,* and *His Girl Friday.* Though Hawks was sufficiently prestigious to work as a producer-director for most of his career, he never won an Academy Award and was scarcely ever nominated. The French changed all that. In the 1950s Hawks became the darling of the highly influential *Cahiers du Cinéma*. Critics like Godard and Truffaut rhapsodized over his works, and when these young Frenchmen turned to making movies themselves, they imitated Hawks. Soon critics in England and America reevaluated his work. By 1975, even the industry acknowledged its oversight by awarding him an honorary Academy Award. Hawks's movies are built on actors and actions, not themes, plots, or ideas. Personality is what interested him most, and for Hawks, personality meant an attractive star doing things that are goofy, courageous, and sometimes touching—but never normal.

> *If I like somebody and think they're attractive, I can make them attractive. If I think a thing's funny, then people laugh at it.*
> —*Howard Hawks*

Hawks was born in 1896 in Goshen, Indiana. His family moved to California when he was ten. His parents were wealthy, with considerable holdings in the lumber industry and in paper manufacturing. Their three sons enjoyed many of the prerogatives of the rich. Howard, the oldest, attended Phillips-Exeter Academy, and went on to Cornell University, where he took a degree in mechanical engineering in 1917. During summer vacations, he worked as a prop boy for Famous Players-Lasky, which eventually became Paramount Pictures. Between the ages of sixteen and twenty-one, Hawks was a barnstorming pilot, and when the United States entered World War I, he enlisted in the fledgling Army Air Corps. After the war he returned to work for Jesse Lasky, who put him in charge of the story department at Paramount. Even at this early date, Hawks's tastes ran to action and adventure tales, and he turned to such distinguished authors as Jack London and Joseph Conrad for story ideas.

Thanks to an inheritance, Hawks became a small-time producer-director in 1922. Most of his productions were two-reel comedies. He also worked as a scenarist at the Fox Film Corporation during this period. In 1926 the studio allowed him to direct his first feature, *The Road to Glory*. He stayed with Fox until 1929, directing a total of eight silent features, primarily comedies and action films. He wrote as well as produced most of these movies, which were successful at the box office. After 1929 he refused to sign any more long-term contracts, and throughout his lengthy career, he worked at virtually every major studio as a producer-director. He occasionally helped write the films of others, however, and he would also undertake directing studio projects from time to time if a friend asked for help or if he needed cash.

Hawks was able to work independently within the industry because his movies were popular with the public. To be sure, almost none of them was a huge box office hit, but most of them turned in a respectable profit. "Fortunately, I have found that what I like, most people also like," Hawks explained, "so I only have to let myself go and do what interests me." He selected his studio on the basis of which stars it had under contract, and the front office rarely interfered with the way he worked. Hawks chose the writers and casts, he personally shaped the story materials, and he enjoyed the privilege of final cut. Within the industry he was regarded as a competent professional. He was respected, but not highly touted. Since his métier was comedy and genre pictures—which enjoyed comparatively little prestige within the industry—his movies were seldom cited for their artistic excellence. Only *Sergeant York* (1941) was a big critical and popular success, and it was also the only Hawks film to win an important Academy Award (Gary Cooper, for best actor). Interestingly, this somewhat pretentious war movie is untypical of Hawks's output, nor is it much admired by critical commentators today.

Personality is what interested Hawks as an artist, and his own was appealing. Scenarist Ben Hecht, who was not given to gushing, described Hawks as "mysteriously romantic." His rugged appearance appealed strongly to women: He was married and divorced three times and had many attractive female friends. He dressed conservatively, though with an elegant flair. Tall (6 feet, 3 inches) and well built, the athletic Hawks excelled in many sports. He loved speed and was a professional racer for several years after he graduated from college. In 1936 he built an eight-cylinder car that won at Indianapolis. He was a lifelong motorcycle enthusiast and continued riding until he was seventy-six years old. In addition, he was an aviator, skier, and horseman. In the movie colony, only Gary Cooper surpassed him as a marksman. Hawks was also an accomplished silversmith and gunsmith. A "man's man," he frequently went off on hunting and fishing trips with such friends as Ernest Hemingway and William Faulkner. Ordinarily these writers hated talking about their books, but both men enjoyed discussing literature with Hawks because they respected his judgment. He was also a successful businessman and died richer than he was born. In short, he embodied those virtues he admired above all others: competence and style.

Hawks enjoyed working in genres. For him, it was simply a convenient way of organizing and focusing the story materials. He often turned to pulp subjects as a starting point, but the story was essentially a pretext for exploring some personalities that intrigued him. He delighted in scrambling the conventions of genres. For example, instead of boy chases girl, he often reversed the formula. He decided that the Hecht-MacArthur play, *The Front Page,* would make a better movie if the ace reporter were switched from a man to a woman and the central plotline converted to a love story. Most commentators are agreed that Hawks's film (retitled *His Girl Friday,* 1940) is the finest of the three versions of the play. "All that stuff is kind of fun," Hawks said of his formula reversals; "it taxes your imagination to try to do something no one else has done." He often repeated a successful gimmick even in dissimilar genres, and he was pleased when people recognized his self-plagiarisms.

"I love to copy myself," he cheerfully admitted. Unfortunately, when his inspiration flagged, and especially when his comic sense deserted him, he often fell back on genre clichés, particularly in the action films.

Hawks insisted that the only difference between comedy and drama is the point of view: In his action movies, the situations are dangerous; in the comedies, they're embarrassing. As critic Robin Wood has pointed out, the action films can be viewed as inversions of the comedies. In the adventure movies, rugged males master their work and environment through their professional competence; in the comedies, hapless males are stripped of their competence through a series of humiliations. Hawks introduced comic elements into virtually all his movies. *Scarface* is such a gleeful takeoff that Wood categorizes it with the overt comedies. Similarly, both *The Big Sleep* and *Rio Bravo* are among the funniest of their genres.

"Whenever I hear a story, my first thought is how to make it into a comedy," Hawks claimed, "and I think of how to make it into a drama only as a last resort." His sense of humor was bizarre. He was fond of recounting a story which took place during the filming of *Red River,* a western starring John Wayne, one of Hawks's favorite players. The direc-

Figure 7.2. *Scarface, Shame of a Nation* **(1932), released by United Artists.** Hawks's comedy is usually based on dialogue, but some of his funniest touches are purely visual. Note the crossed-bones motif on the flag in the upper left corner of this photo. The protagonist of the film was loosely based on the gangster Al Capone and has a crosslike scar on his face. Whenever a rival mobster is rubbed out, Hawks managed to work in a cross motif as a symbol of death: The victim is metaphorically crossed off the killer's enemy list. Since there are fifteen murders in the story, Hawks was hard pressed not to repeat himself.

tor told his star that a funny scene could be built around Wayne's getting drunk and having his finger amputated. Somehow the finger gets lost near the campfire, and the other characters then have to search on their hands and knees for the missing member. Understandably, Wayne thought the idea wasn't funny. In fact, he thought it was weird. Hawks didn't press it. Instead, he included the scene in another western, *The Big Sky* (1952), with Kirk Douglas. The missing finger episode turned out to be one of Hawks's most celebrated scenes, and after viewing it, Wayne vowed never again to reject Hawks's ideas, no matter how ghoulish.

In fact, it was Hawks more than any other director who encouraged Wayne's considerable comic talents. The two worked together on four westerns, which all begin seriously, then veer off into comedy—sometimes right in the middle of scenes of violence. A line from *Rio Bravo* almost invariably breaks up audiences. Wayne smashes the villain's face with a gunbutt, bloodying him hideously. When his sidekick rushes to restrain him, our hero turns away, drawling contemptuously, "I'm not gonna hurt him." These eruptions of sardonic humor became Hawks and Wayne specialties. The four Wayne westerns might almost be regarded as a personality study in four parts. *Rio Bravo, El Dorado* (1967), and *Rio Lobo* even use the same basic plot. As Hawks explained, the genre artist's creativity lies not so much in inventing narrative materials but in how traditional materials can be treated freshly: "You're telling the same old story, and the only way you can change it is by getting different characters. And the only different characters you can get are funny ones."

Hawks believed that all good directors put their personal stamp on their work. His own output was epitimized by an outlandish craziness. He thought that almost anything had comic possibilities. For example, when he learned that the character actor Walter Brennan wore false teeth, Hawks worked it into Brennan's characterization in *Red River*. Brennan loses his teeth to an Indian in a poker game, and throughout the remainder of the movie, the cantankerous oldtimer must borrow them back each time he has to eat. *Scarface* is steeped in comic grotesqueries. The protagonist, played with strutting flamboyance by Paul Muni, delights in parading his dressing gowns, ties, and garish hankerchiefs. Intoxicated by his swanky apartment, he proudly displays it to a bewildered female guest. "It's kinda gaudy, isn't it?" she ventures, in genuine awe. "Isn't it though? Glad you like it," is his delicious reply.

Hawk's comic brilliance is best represented by his screwball comedies, a genre he and Capra introduced in 1934, with *Twentieth Century* and *It Happened One Night*. The heyday of the genre was roughly 1934 to 1945, though Hawks's postwar comedies, like *I Was a Male War Bride* (1949) and *Monkey Business* (1952), contain many screwball elements. Essentially love stories, these films featured zany but glamorous lovers, often from different social classes. Capra and Hawks were the foremost practitioners of the genre, which became the most popular type of comedy in the American cinema of the later depression era. In part, this was because it was a "healing" type of humor, emphasizing the unity of all social strata, as cultural historian Andrew Bergman has pointed out.

Figure 7.3.   Paul Muni (center) in *Scarface, Shame of a Nation.* Like many gangster films of the early 1930s, *Scarface* is a parody of the success ethic, mocking the ruthless ambition of the protagonist in his climb to the top. The gangster's origins are generally working class. He's usually a first- or second-generation American, with ambivalent ties to his ethnic heritage, usually Italian. His chosen milieu is the city, where opportunities for fast money abound. His favorite haunts are nightclubs, gaudy amusement centers, swanky apartments, ethnic restaurants, and the tackier fringes of show business. The gangster revels in his flashy clothes, which are his symbols of achievement. Other icons of the genre are guns, fedora hats (often worn indoors), expensive black sedans, cigars, booze, lots of neon.

Caste conflicts are neutralized into personality antagonisms, and the marriages which conclude these films often symbolize the reconciliation of the classes. Capra's screwball comedies became increasingly social as the decade wore on, but the apolitical Hawks wasn't interested in ideological issues. Since Capra's screwball comedies were more popular with the public, other important directors of the genre—like Mitchell Leisen, Gregory La Cava, William Wellman, and Preston Sturges— tended to explore it along the social lines of Capra rather than the formalist vein of Hawks.

More realistic than the slapstick of the silent era, screwball comedy is also more collaborative: The contributions of the director and writer are as crucial as those of the actor. The genre attracted the most gifted comic scenarists of the period, including Ben Hecht, Robert Riskin, Charles MacArthur, and Charles Lederer. The sophisticated dialogue crackles with cynicism, witty repartee, and proletarian wisecracks. Sappy, sentimental speeches are often intended to deceive. Screwball comedy produced a bonanza of charming comediennes, including Jean Arthur,

Figure 7.4. Publicity photo of John Barrymore and Carole Lombard in *Twentieth Century* (1934), distributed by Columbia Pictures. Hawks preferred stars who enjoyed struttin' their stuff, who were *on* most of the time. He cast Barrymore because he thought the actor was the biggest ham he had ever seen. What's more, Hawks *told* him so. Barrymore's performance as the slightly demented theatrical producer, Oscar Jaffee, is outrageously funny. Hawks knew that Lombard was a lively young woman, but her acting during rehearsal was stiff. He took her aside and asked what *she* would do if a monomaniac like the Barrymore character tried to push her around in the manner outlined in the script. Lombard, whose lexicon of four-letter words exceeded even that of Harry Cohn, told Hawks she'd never put up with such treatment. Hawks told her to return to the set and play the character as Carole Lombard. The rest, as they say, is history. The movie was finished in three weeks, and it proved to be Lombard's breakthrough performance.

Figure 7.5. James Cagney (center) in *Ceiling Zero* (1936), distributed by Warner Brothers. Hawks's stories almost invariably revolve around off-beat characters, far removed from the centers of normalcy. His characters are generally gainfully employed but in adventurous professions. In the action films, the occupations are usually dangerous, like aviation. Average people are portrayed as hicks or they're absent altogether. His heroines, who are usually immensely likable, are independent working girls who can hold their own in male-dominated societies. Domestic women and married life in general seldom interested Hawks.

Rosalind Russell, Barbara Stanwyck, Irene Dunne, Claudette Colbert, and Katharine Hepburn. The most famous screwball comedienne was Carole Lombard, who became a major star of the 1930s after her performance in *Twentieth Century*. Beautiful, sexy, and funny, Lombard was also an accomplished dramatic actress. Cary Grant, Hawks's favorite comedian, was the most gifted male actor of screwball comedy. The genre was dominated by Columbia, RKO, and Paramount.

The premises of most screwball comedies are absurdly improbable, and the plots, which are intricate and filled with preposterous twists and turns, tend to snowball out of control. The movies center on a comic and romantic couple rather than a solitary protagonist. Often they are initially antagonistic, with one constantly trying to outwit or outmaneuver the other. In Hawks's comedies, the hero is sometimes a scheming, egregious egomaniac, determined to foist his will on an uncooperative heroine, as in *Twentieth Century* and *His Girl Friday*. In other movies, however, the dim-witted hero is stalked by a clever, resourceful heroine, as in *Bringing Up Baby* and *Ball of Fire*. Much of the comedy results from the utter seriousness of the coprotagonists, who are usually

Figure 7.6. Cary Grant and Katharine Hepburn in _Bringing Up Baby_ (1938), with George Irving, distributed by RKO. _Bringing Up Baby_ is almost like a Shakespearean comedy in its nuttiness—with its "enchanted forest," its whimsy, and its brazen artificiality. The booby country sheriff (Irving) might almost be the American cousin of Dogberry in _Much Ado About Nothing_, a title that suits Hawks's movie as much as Shakespeare's play.

unaware that they're funny, even though they engage in the most loony masquerades and deceptions. Sometimes one of them is engaged to a sexless prude or a humorless bore; this lends an urgency to the attraction between the coprotagonists, who are clearly made for each other. The genre usually includes a menagerie of secondary characters who are as wacky as the lovers.

Hawks's screwball comedies stretched the genre to its utmost limits, and are generally more farcical than the works of other directors in this form. He loved packing his movies with pratfalls, brawls, men dressed in drag, Sennett-like chases, and wildly improbable coincidences. Only Hawks could dream up the scene in _Bringing Up Baby_ in which two zanies (Hepburn and Grant) try to entice "Baby," a stubborn pet leopard, off a roof by singing its favorite song, "I Can't Give You Anything But Love, Baby." In another scene, Grant is deprived of his clothes and is forced to wear Hepburn's frilly negligée until they're returned. Thus attired, he sulks on some stairs until Hepburn's prim matron aunt discovers him and expresses amazement at his sartorial eccentricity. The poor devil leaps to his feet, agitates his arms frantically, and sputters, "I just went _gay_ suddenly!"

In his pre-World War II movies, Hawks tended to prefer tight, compact stories, with plots that are usually clear and straightforward. Often they are organized around a journey of some kind, a job that needs to be done, or a constricting situation that requires immediate relief. In the comedies, the stories usually concern the corralling of a mate. Most of the stories take place over a brief period. Hawks seldom bothered with much exposition or resorted to flashbacks. He was flattered by the adulation lavished on him by his French admirers, who tried to imitate his work, but somewhat impatient with their indifference to plot: "I think a director's a storyteller, and if he tells a story that people can't understand, then he shouldn't be a director."

Consistency, however, was not Hawks's forte. For example, the aviation movie, *Only Angels Have Wings* (1939), is relatively static, with only the barest rudiments of a plotline. On the other hand, critic Donald Willis has called the plot to *The Big Sleep* virtually incoherent: It suffers from too *much* story. "You don't have to be too logical," Hawks instructed his scenarists before they began adapting Raymond Chandler's

Figure 7.7. Cary Grant and Katharine Hepburn in *Bringing Up Baby*. Hawks's comic heroes are often absent-minded professor types whose absorption in their work is so obsessive that they neglect other important facets of their lives—especially fun and romance. These are provided by a high-spirited, dippy heroine, who reduces her swain to a state of thralldom. No one was funnier than Grant in conveying the impotent exasperation of the polite male who does *try* to be understanding. His scenes are profuse in rituals of masculine humiliation, in which he's virtually stripped of his stodgy identity.

Figure 7.8. Cary Grant and Rosalind Russell in *His Girl Friday* (1940), distributed by Columbia Pictures. Above all, Jean-Luc Godard noted, Hawks is the director of the couple. Hawks described most of his movies as "a relationship with two friends"—buddies in the action films, lovers (or would-be lovers) in the comedies. He rarely intercut between the lovers: He wanted them sharing the same space, close enough to respond to each other's physical presence. He favored the medium two-shot because it's best suited to capturing the interplay between personalities. The critics at *Cahiers du Cinéma* considered this camera setup so characteristic of Hawks and the American cinema in general that they called it *le plan américain*, the American shot.

intricately plotted novel; "you should just make good scenes. You follow one scene with another and stop worrying about hooking them together." Like most of Hawks's best movies, *The Big Sleep* has the conviction of immediacy, but no one could figure out who killed one of the eight victims. When Hawks called up Chandler for clarification, even he was unable to identify the killer. The director's later works tend to be more relaxed and informal in their plotting. Even the westerns are loosely structured, especially the final three Wayne pictures. All center around the Wayne hero whose friends come to his assistance. All involve a love story, the rehabilitation of a buddy who has known better times, and that old staple of the genre, the triumph of the good guys over the the bad guys in a shootout. The digressiveness of the plots gives them an almost improvisatory air, as if anything—however outlandish—could happen before the inevitable showdown in the final reel.

Despite his insistence that he was "just a storyteller," in actual practice, Hawks's orientation was generally toward the individual scene rather than the overall structure. He thought in terms of situations and gags and often would save leftover material for his next movie. For example, *El Dorado* contains scenes that were originally conceived for

Rio Bravo. "My recipe for making movies has always been to give an audience two or three really top-notch scenes," Hawks modestly claimed, "and to try not to annoy them the rest of the time." This casual attitude toward plot is what produces the uneven passages in his films. Even his best works have sections that sag: The stories don't always build dramatically, but depend in large part on the inspiration of the moment.

Manny Farber, who was one of the first American critics to champion Hawks's movies, also believes that no artist was less suited to a discussion of profound themes. John Peter Dyer goes even further and insists that Hawks's best films are his most unoriginal thematically. His worst—like *Sergeant York* and *Land of the Pharaohs* (1955)—are his most ambitious. Intellectual and social concerns seldom fired his imagination. For example, in *To Have and Have Not* (1944), the political subplot is formularized, in frank imitation of the earlier Bogart success, *Casablanca,* which was directed for Warner Brothers by Michael Curtiz the year before. To be sure, certain thematic preoccupations recur throughout Hawks's work, most notably the integration of an individual into a group, professionalism as a regenerative force, and the necessity for self-respect. But these are hardly novel themes, especially in the action genres the director favored.

Much of the controversy surrounding Hawks's work centers on the action films. Critics tend to fall into three camps concerning his output in this genre. His French admirers and their Anglo-American disciples enthusiastically applaud these works, especially for their energy, virility, and thematic consistency. Diametrically opposed to this view are such critics as Pauline Kael and Raymond Durgnat, who scoff at Hawks's narrow notions of masculinity, which are steeped in adolescent fantasies and sentimental clichés about "what it is to be a man." Like its feminine counterpart, the woman's picture (contemptuously known in the trade as *weepies*), the genre is simply too corrupted by mawkish platitudes to be taken seriously as art, these critics claim. In fact, one wag described the action film as a "male weepie." The third and perhaps most persuasive group of critics, typified by such commentators as Manny Farber and Donald Willis, agree that Hawks's action films can be childish, banal, and even simple-minded. But they also insist that the movies can be immensely enjoyable, providing a maximum of speed, excitement, and wit, "with the least amount of flat foot," to use Farber's memorable phrase. Willis maintains that the surface excitement is what's best in these movies, not their "depth." Audiences respond to the charm of the performers and the skillful way they carry off the action, not the philosophical significance of the action per se. In short, Hawks was no deep thinker, artistically speaking, and to criticize his action films for their lack of thematic originality is to miss the point.

Like any other genre, the action film has its specialties. It centers on he-men occupations that require courage, skill, and a stoical acceptance of the possibility of injury or death. "The best drama for me is one which shows a man in danger," Hawks claimed. "To live or die. What drama is greater?" Often these movies are based on stories which originally appeared in men's magazines. The films are fast and violent and require a considerable technical proficiency in order to convey the thrills of the

Figure 7.9. Publicity photo of Humphrey Bogart and Lauren Bacall in *To Have and Have Not* (1944), distributed by Warner Brothers. "I have a theory that the camera likes some people," Hawks ventured, "people like Bogart who was not a good-looking man." The director believed that Bogart was the most insolent man on the screen. "I'm going to make a girl a little more insolent than you are," he warned the star before production. Bacall was a Hawks discovery. In this and its companion piece, *The Big Sleep,* she plays a favorite type of the 1940s, the good bad girl—tough on the surface, with a heart of gold underneath. A bit of a vagabond, she's usually sexually worldly. She prefers the company of men to women. Photo: Gary Engle.

action. The subgenres are categorized by occupational emphasis: racing, flying, hunting, and so on. They usually focus on an all-male society, in which a deep respect and camaraderie exist among its members. The highest value is placed on the efforts of the team rather than the contributions of a single member. There is an emphasis on masculine codes of honor and gallantry. A man is measured à la Hemingway, by how "good" he is at his work. That is, how cool, stylish, and professional. Domestic life is viewed with indifference, if not outright hostility. Generally it's portrayed as constricting, compromising, and dull. Except for the female lead, women are usually kept at the peripheries. Sweethearts are normally patient, forgiving, and very nervous. They can also be drags.

Hawks's most entertaining action films are usually in direct proportion to the amount of comedy they contain and the degree of prominence of their female star. As critic Joseph McBride has pointed out, the director's lack of interest in stereotypical female roles allowed him to create unusually strong, independent, yet still emotionally open heroines. Hawks admired women who were direct and aggressive and who enjoyed the same kind of activities as men. Significantly, he is the only action director to evince much sympathetic interest among feminist film critics. Furthermore, as Gerald Peary has noted, a life of action is not sufficient unto itself in most of Hawks's movies. The hero needs both male friends *and* a good strong woman.

Hawks enjoyed writing, and he worked on most of his scripts even in the earliest phases of his career. He seldom took credit for his contributions, however, because of a Screenwriters Guild regulation, which stipulated that a director couldn't receive credit as a scenarist unless he wrote at least 50 percent of the script. Since Hawks preferred working with teams of writers, he never bothered keeping track of who wrote what. His specialty was thinking up bizarre situations for his characters. "I'm interested first in the action and next in the words they speak," he said. However, he also wrote some of the dialogue for his pictures. While working on the script of his first talkie, *The Dawn Patrol* (1930), he emphasized an indirect, understated writing style which the front office at Warners criticized for not being dramatic enough. Hawks claimed he derived this oblique style from his friend Hemingway, who also avoided direct emotional statements in his dialogue. When *The Dawn Patrol* proved popular with the public, Warners periodically screened the movie for its writers as an example of what good dialogue should sound like. In fact, the films Hawks made at this studio in the 1930s helped set many of the conventions of what came to be known as the Warners style during this decade.

Not that Hawks wanted his scripts to sound literary, though he was a lifelong devotee of good literature and had many writers as friends. He simply believed that speech was capable of energy and wit and ought to be entertaining in its own right. Some of his most celebrated passages he wrote himself, like Lauren Bacall's famous "whistle" speech to Bogart in *To Have and Have Not*. "I never follow a script literally," the director claimed, "and I don't hesitate to change a script completely if I see a chance to do something interesting." In *Tiger Shark* (1932), he totally reconceived the hero's characterization when it failed to come to life as

Figure 7.10. John Wayne and Montgomery Clift in *Red River* (1948), distributed by United Artists. Hawks was one of the first directors to appreciate the understated subtlety of Clift. When the director cast him opposite Wayne in this film, the more experienced player expressed some doubt that the frail looking Clift would be able to hold his own againt Wayne's powerful presence. Hawks assured him that he chose Clift because he possessed an inner strength which was equally powerful. Once again, the director's instincts proved correct. Clift rose to stardom with his performance in this film. Personality for Hawks didn't have to be noisy or frenetic to be compelling.

written. His star, Edward G. Robinson, agreed that a new approach was needed, and each morning he was handed new dialogue which Hawks had written the night before. In the comedies particularly, the conflicts are verbal as much as physical, and he was especially stimulated by the challenge of dreaming up *outré* exchanges of dialogue between the lovers.

Several of Hawks's scenarists were successful novelists and dramatists in their own right: Ben Hecht, Charles MacArthur, Jules Furthman, William Faulkner, Charles Lederer, Dudley Nichols, Leigh Brackett, John Huston, Billy Wilder, and many others. Critic Pauline Kael once quipped that Furthman wrote about half of the most entertaining movies to come out of Hollywood, and Hecht wrote most of the other half. Furthman helped create the spirited heroines of such movies as *Only Angels Have Wings, To Have and Have Not, The Big Sleep,* and *Rio Bravo.* The novelist Leigh Brackett, a "fresh-looking girl who wrote like a man," as Hawks described her, contributed substantially to the westerns and action films. Lederer's speciality was deflating pomposity with a well-placed wisecrack. Many of the comedies centering on rituals of male mortification were coscripted by him.

The legendary wit and ex-newspaperman Hecht, who collaborated on at least eight Hawks films, appealed strongly to the director's cynical side. Hecht's sense of humor was brazenly malicious and sardonic. He delighted in satirizing hick values and conventional morality. When Hawks suggested that the gangster hero and his sister in *Scarface* ought to be characterized as a Chicago-style Cesare and Lucrezia Borgia, Hecht was exhilarated by the prospect. The resultant script was one of his most flamboyant literary revels, crammed with outrageous metaphors, incongruous cultural allusions, and racy vulgarisms. Hecht also helped create several of Hawks's other Machiavellian schemers, like the *monstres sacrés* of *Twentieth Century* and *His Girl Friday*. Critic Richard Corliss believes that Hecht's sensational headline style was derived from his experience as a journalist. Some of his best stage and screen writing was created in collaboration with Charles MacArthur, his lifelong friend and fellow zany. Hawks admired their dialogue above all others. Corliss suggests that Hawks's masculine mystique was reinforced by this famous friendship and by Hecht's Chicago pressroom camaraderie.

Faulkner was a special case. Hawks admired his fiction long before he was taken seriously by the American literary establishment or had been "discovered" by the French intelligentsia. He met the novelist in the early 1930s, when he was scratching out a living as a clerk in a bookstore. Although he had already written several volumes, none of them had earned much money. Hawks urged him to go to Hollywood and work as a scenarist. Faulkner accepted, and he worked there on and off for the next twenty-two years. Except for his work with Hawks, he didn't take his film writing very seriously after he noticed that industry regulars were somewhat insensitive to literary excellence. He referred to his tenure in Hollywood as his "sojourn downriver." Not that he despised screenwriting per se. Like Fitzgerald, he thought it was a highly sophisticated art, but he was too committed to his own fiction to ever learn the craft properly. "I don't like scenario writing because I don't know enough about it," he admitted. But Hawks thought that Faulkner's script contributions were inventive, tasteful, and visually exciting. He called Faulkner "a master of his work, who does it without fuss." The novelist made major contributions to the script of *Today We Live* (1933), which was based on his own short story, "Turnabout." He also contributed to the scripts of *The Road to Glory* (1936), *Air Force* (1943), *To Have and Have Not,* and *The Big Sleep.* Hawks even allowed Faulkner to write from his home in Oxford, Mississippi, a privilege seldom allowed even to the most prestigious scenarists. In this way, Faulkner could divide his energies between his own fiction and Hawks's scripts. The two became close friends and often went fishing and hunting together. The novelist remained stolidly loyal to Hawks, and after Faulkner won the Nobel Prize in literature in 1950 and was regarded as America's foremost living author, he would still come to Hawks's assistance to help with story problems, difficult scenes, or additional dialogue. Though Faulkner's royalties now provided him with a handsome income, he would even abandon his own work in progress to help his former mentor, much to the annoyance of Faulkner's publisher. But as the novelist explained, "Mr. Hawks has carried me in pictures, seen that I got screen credits I really did not deserve. Whenever I needed money, he was always very good to me, and if he needs me now, I'm going." Their last collaboration was in 1954, with the writing of *Land of the Pharaohs.*

All Hawks's best films are centered on the personality of his stars. Many of the movies were especially tailored with specific stars in mind, especially the Grant comedies, the Wayne westerns, and the Bogart thrillers. He generally cast only people he liked personally and those performers he thought were naturally funny, like Walter Brennan, one of his favorite character actors. In fact, Donald Willis points out that the credibility of Hawks's work is almost entirely due to the conviction of his players, especially in the action movies. In those few works in which he didn't use stars, like *Red Line 7000* (1965), or in which the acting is weak, like *Hatari!* (1962), there's simply not much to watch, Willis observes, except for the exciting action footage.

An authoritative director, Hawks seldom had to deal with problems of temperament from his stars. Even that notorious prima donna and drunk, John Barrymore, minded his manners on Hawks's set. Bogart was an incorrigible needler and troublemaker who enjoyed testing people's nerve. On his first day of shooting *To Have and Have Not,* Hawks was the recipient of some of Bogart's infamous lip. The director strode up to him, grabbed him by the lapels, lifted him off his feet, slammed him against the wall, and quietly explained that on his sets *he* was accustomed to calling the shots. After that, Bogart was a pussycat. Eventually they became good friends: both men admired a certain forthrightness of manner.

Grant and Wayne were immensely fond of Hawks, and would try anything the director suggested, for they trusted his artistic instincts. His harshest criticism was to call a performance dull. When a scene failed to work in rehearsals—and Hawks rehearsed a lot to get that "unrehearsed" quality—he would often try to make it more comic by thinking up some mad piece of business for his actors. It was he who suggested to Grant that he whinny like a horse whenever he's exasperated in *His Girl Friday.* He encouraged his players to act with their entire bodies, not just their faces and voices. In the comic films especially, much of the humor lies in the way the characters move or stand, the way they talk (usually very fast) the funny clothes they wear, and the way they handle props, like telephones, cigarettes, and hats. Some of the most memorable images of Hawks's movies involve a quintessential gesture, like Cagney sashaying saucily between the racing scenes of *The Crowd Roars* (1932) or the flying episodes of *Ceiling Zero* or Wayne's familiar lumbering gait, as though he were favoring a slight pain in his back but doesn't want to make a fuss about it.

Hawks's visual style is one of the plainest of the American cinema. "I like to tell a story as simply as possible," he explained, "with the camera at eye level." He disliked virtuoso camerawork and showy lighting effects. There are few "memorable shots" in his movies, though occasionally he imitated a poetic effect from the westerns of his friend John Ford. The exquisite lighting of *Scarface* was entirely due to its cinematographer, Lee Garmes, Hawks insisted, almost as though such concerns were rather effete. "I want to see the scene the way it would look if I were looking at it," he said. For Hawks, that usually meant eye-level medium shots. Like many directors of his generation, he believed that the best technique is that which seldom calls attention to itself. As Andrew Sarris has noted,

> Hawks will work within a frame as much as possible, cutting only when a long take or an elaborate track might distract his audience from the issues in the foreground of the action. This is good, clean, direct, functional cinema, perhaps the most distinctively American cinema of all.

Since his films often celebrate the camaraderie of groups, Hawks used many long shots, which allow us to observe simultaneously the give and take of a communal gathering. Close shots are rare. "When you use closeups sparingly," he said, "the public realizes that they are important." Except for epic materials, he disliked CinemaScope, claiming the wide screen drained an image of its intimacy and gave precedence to compositional elements over drama and personality. Hawks's concern was with people, whom he almost always kept in the forefront of his mise-en-scène. He seldom displayed much interest in décor or landscape. His settings are generally neutral: They're simply used as a ground for his figures. Many of his films are visually dull, and *Gentlemen Prefer Blondes* is downright garish.

Hawks's movies are fast paced, especially those of the pre–World War II era. Like Capra, he encouraged his actors to race their delivery, and to overlap their lines as much as possible. His dialogue usually consists of terse sentences, stripped of dependent clauses. "Get the scene over with as soon as possible," was his stated credo. Even violence is over with quickly, which he believed made it more realistic. *His Girl Friday* has been called the fastest of all American talkies. His French admirers were especially enamored of his speed. Indeed, critic Jacques Rivette claimed that Hawks taught the *Cahiers* group "all that was best in the classical American cinema." Hawks's postwar films, however, are less hurried in their pace. The final westerns especially have an easygoing, rambling quality that almost makes them seem like family reunions.

In his editing too, Hawks adhered to a plain, functional style. He disliked cutting his films, because on repeated viewing of his footage he noticed his careless technical mistakes. Like Ford, whenever possible he edited in the camera. He refused to take extra closeups or covering shots in case his footage wouldn't cut smoothly. The result is that some of his movies are marred by awkward inserts, crude transitions, choppy rhythms, and mismatched shots. However, these flaws are generally apparent only on repeated viewing.

Hawks's main artistic shortcoming is his unevenness. Many of his movies suffer from serious lapses in tone and mechanical contrivances in the plotting. He wisely avoided scenes of intense emotion and almost invariably made a mawkish mess of it when he didn't. Actually, Hawks was often his own best critic. He pointed out that in his best films the characters express emotions, not directly, but through action, inaction, hesitation, and outright silliness. His most serious flaws are generally found in the action movies, which are filled with such genre bromides as

Figure 7.11.   Publicity photo of Marilyn Monroe in *Gentlemen Prefer Blondes* (1953), produced by 20th Century-Fox. *Gentlemen Prefer Blondes* was one of the biggest grossers of the year, thanks largely to Marilyn's luminous presence. Audiences responded to her childlike naiveté, even though she wasn't much of an actress at this point in her life. But her inept line readings and desperate eagerness to please were oddly touching. She also photographed beautifully, especially in color. Males comprised the bulk of her following. To them, she was the ultimate unthreatening woman, the mind and soul of a little girl wrapped in the body of a whore. Her private life was already a mess. Paralyzed with a sense of inadequacy, she turned to alcohol and drugs. Hawks didn't understand her very well: He thought her strange, neurotic, and lonely. She was rarely on time for her scenes, and often she was too terrified or drunk, or both, to leave her dressing room. She is one of the most written-about film personalities in history. Two interesting biographies are Maurice Zolotow, *Marilyn Monroe* (New York: Harcourt Brace Jovanovich, Inc. 1960); and Norman Mailer, *Marilyn* (New York: Warner Paperback Library, 1975).

Figure 7.12. John Wayne in *Rio Bravo* (1959), distributed by Warner Brothers. Hawks's mise-en-scène is almost lacklustre in its avoidance of frills. "His films are stripped bare almost to the point of abstraction," observed Henri Langlois, the curator of the Cinémathèque Française, where the American's films were often exhibited. Hawks concentrated on essentials—the human materials. He regarded unusual angles, lighting effects, and complex compositions as superfluous.

a driver (or flyer or hunter) who must expiate a previous act of cowardice; or a last-minute substitution which kills off the second male lead, thus conveniently saving the hero's life; or an insecure youth who proves his manhood by killing someone; and so on.

Hawks died in 1977, at the age of eighty-one, of complications from a concussion caused by a fall. Before he died, he enjoyed the satisfaction of being one of the most imitated of American directors, especially by those who continued in his tradition of genre. In his own day, such filmmakers as Raoul Walsh, William Wellman, Henry Hathaway, and Victor Fleming were clearly influenced by his work. Hawks's action films served as models for many subsequent directors in this genre, most notably Phil Karlson, Robert Aldrich, Don Siegel, Clint Eastwood, and Burt Reynolds—underrated directors all. Hawks regarded Peter Bogdanovich, the Francophile critic turned filmmaker, as something of a protégé. *What's Up Doc?* is a virtual homage to Hawks's screwball comedies of the 1930s. In Bogdanovich's *The Last Picture Show*, he offers a tender tribute to his mentor by including a sequence from Hawks's *Red River*. The early works of such French filmmakers as Godard and Truffaut are deeply influenced by Hawks's movies. Godard claimed that his breakthrough film, *Breathless*, was intended as a remake of *Scarface*. Truffaut's charming gangster picture, *Shoot the Piano Player,* is obviously indebted to the American master's oeuvre. For these young critic-directors, Hawks was the incarnation of American speed, audacity, and wit. He met and talked with them whenever he was in the vicinity of Paris, though he was often flabbergasted by their arcane interpretations, which he thought bordered on the baroque. "I get open-mouthed and wonder where they find some of the stuff they say about me. All I'm doing is telling a story," he insisted. Hawks's self-assessment was characteristically modest.

BIBLIOGRAPHY

BELTON, JOHN. "Howard Hawks," in *The Hollywood Professionals,* Vol. 3. Cranbury, N.J.: A. S. Barnes, 1974. A thematic and stylistic analysis, with filmography.

BLOTNER, JOSEPH. "Faulkner in Hollywood," in *Man and the Movies.* W. R. Robinson, ed. New York: Penguin, 1969. See also Bruce F. Kawin, *Faulkner and Film* (New York: Ungar, 1977); and Richard Corliss, *Talking Pictures* (New York: Penguin, 1975): discussions of several of Hawks's scenarists, including Hecht, Furthman, and Lederer.

FARBER, MANNY, *et al.* "Howard Hawks," in *Great Film Directors.* Leo Braudy and Morris Dickstein, eds. New York: Oxford University Press, 1978. A collection of critical essays.

FAULKNER, WILLIAM, LEIGH BRACKETT, AND JULES FURTHMAN. *The Big Sleep,* in *Film Scripts One.* George P. Garrett, O. B. Hardison, Jr., and Jane Gelfman, eds. New York: Prentice-Hall, 1971. Shooting script.

MCBRIDE, JOSEPH, ed. *Focus on Howard Hawks.* New York: Prentice-Hall, 1972. A collection of articles and interviews, filmography, selected bibliography.

MAYER, WILLIAM R. "Howard Hawks," in *Warner Brothers Directors.* New Rochelle, N.Y.: Arlington House Publishers, 1978. See also Gerald Peary, "Hawks at Warner Brothers: 1932," with Stephen Groark, in *The Velvet Light Trap* (June, 1971).

SARRIS, ANDREW, ed. "Howard Hawks," in *Interviews with Film Directors.* New York: Avon Books, 1967. A brief analysis and interview.

SCHICKEL, RICHARD. "Howard Hawks," in *The Men Who Made the Movies.* New York: Atheneum, 1975. Critical analysis and Hawks's lengthiest interview.

WILLIS, DONALD C. *The Films of Howard Hawks.* Metuchen, N.J.: Scarecrow, 1975. A critical analysis, by genre, with many perceptive observations about Hawks's actors. Filmography and interview.

WOOD, ROBIN. *Howard Hawks.* New York: Doubleday, 1968. A somewhat solemn thematic analysis. Filmography.

The Tradition of Quality

The Cinema of William Wyler

Figure 8.1. Publicity photo of Wyler and Shirley MacLaine during the production of *The Children's Hour* (1962), distributed by United Artists. Like most American filmmakers of Germanic origins, Wyler took himself seriously as an artist, and wanted to make movies of enduring value: "I do not believe great films can be made on a factory-conveyor belt basis, untouched by human hands, as it were. I have always tried to direct my own pictures out of my own feelings, and out of my own approach to life. I have tried to make them 'by hand,' and it has been hard work, work which has left me drained of energy for months after the completion of each film."

In his forty-five years as a director, Wyler made thirty-seven features, many of which were celebrated for qualities seldom seen in American movies: taste, restraint, and subtlety. Though his reputation rests primarily on his prestige pictures, he worked successfully in a wide range of genres: westerns, social dramas, comedies, gangster movies, melodramas, even a musical and two documentaries. Together with the independent producer, Samuel Goldwyn, Wyler produced a string of hits that stunned the industry, for they were based on materials that were regarded as box office poison. He was known as a "dif-

ficult" director because his artistic standards were exacting. His reputation as a perfectionist left actors trembling at the prospect of working with him. Though they complained bitterly of his penchant for repeating scenes time and again in order to refine nuances of characterization, his players usually thanked him in retrospect. No other director could boast so many Academy Award nominations for his actors. Out of thirty-two nominations, fourteen won—an unparalleled accomplishment. He was championed for the purity and transparancy of his style by the great French critic, André Bazin, whose theory of cinematic realism exerted an enormous influence on subsequent theorists. Within the industry, Wyler was regarded as a virtual semideity: Twelve times his directing was nominated for an Academy Award, and he won three times. He also won the New York Film Critics award three times. He was the frequent recipient of foreign honors as well.

> *A movie should not be an advertisement. Drama lies in the subtle complexities of life—in the grays, not the blacks and whites.*
> —*William Wyler*

Willy Wyler was born in 1902 in Mulhouse, located in what is now called Alsace-Lorraine. At the time of his birth, the town was called Mülhousen, and was controlled by the Germans. The Alsace region, located on the border of Germany and France, had long been claimed by both countries. The Wyler family, like most residents of the area, spoke both French and German, in addition to the Alsatian dialect. Since the Wylers were Jewish, they also spoke Yiddish in the home. His father, who ran a prosperous clothing store, was a Swiss national. Willy's mother was from a prominent German family which had produced a number of public figures, including her cousin Carl Lämmle, who eventually emigrated to the United States, where he made his fortune in the motion picture business.

Even as a boy, Willy was considered difficult. Often restless and bored, he was kicked out of several schools for being a hellion. His mother despaired of her son's future but was encouraged by the fact that he enjoyed going with her to concerts, the theatre, operas, and the cinema. During World War I, the Wylers were trapped literally between the crossfire of French and German troops. Young Willy was shaken by the carnage and brutality of the war. Yet he was also amused by the spectacle of watching the city fathers hoist the German or French flag, depending on which way the war was veering. At the age of eighteen, he was sent to Paris, ostensibly to a commercial college to prepare him to enter the family business. He was more drawn to the artists and intellectuals of the Left Bank than to haberdashery. Finally he persuaded his family to allow him to go to America, where he was promised a modest position with his cousin Carl's company, Universal Studios.

In 1920, Wyler arrived in New York, where he worked in Universal's publicity department for a year. He learned to speak English so well that he had only the hint of an accent. In his private hours he took violin lessons. He also became an ardent moviegoer. But he grew restless in New York and asked his cousin if he could transfer to the company's headquarters in Universal City California, the studio-city that Carl Laemmle (as he now spelled it) built in 1915. The diminutive (5 feet, 2 inches) Laemmle was one of the most likable of the moguls. In 1906 he bought a nickelodeon in Chicago, and within a few years he controlled a chain of theatres and exchanges throughout the region. The ex-haberdasher had a flair for publicity and loved getting his name in the papers. Affectionately known as Uncle Carl because he sponsored so many refugees to the United States, Laemmle probably dispensed more jobs to more immigrants than any other mogul. The studio was so rife with cousins and second cousins that even doormen were treated courteously, lest they should turn out to be among the boss's relations. A soft touch, Laemmle extended a helping hand to people outside his family too. Nor were all those he assisted exclusively Jewish and German: Some of his beneficiaries were Catholics and Protestants from all over Europe.

Universal was a notoriously mismanaged studio, with chaotic business procedures, a lack of consistent leadership, and an inflated payroll, even though salaries were low. Laemmle loved to travel, and he often left the country without bothering to designate a chain of command. The studio was essentially a sausage factory, grinding out about two hundred two-reelers per year, mostly low-budget formula pictures and westerns. The early works of Erich von Stroheim constituted an important exception, however, and the studio's Lon Chaney vehicles also brought in a measure of prestige. Stroheim's daring *Foolish Wives* (1921) put Universal on the map, but when the Austrian expatriot grew more reckless in his expenditures, he was fired by Laemmle's protégé, Irving Thalberg, the famous "Boy Wonder," who was not yet twenty-one. (Shortly afterward, Thalberg moved to MGM, where he fired Stroheim a second time for his extravagant overruns in the making of his 1923 masterpiece, *Greed*.)

Laemmle, who enjoyed gambling more than moviemaking, eventually turned the studio over to his son, Carl, Jr. Under his leadership, Universal attempted more ambitious projects. *All Quiet on the Western Front,* based on the respected antiwar novel by Erich Maria Remarque, won the Academy Award for best picture of 1930, as well as an Oscar for its director, Lewis Milestone. Carl, Jr. was also responsible for initiating the cycle of horror films produced at Universal in the 1930s. But despite his efforts, the studio's fortunes continued to slide. Laemmle, Sr. advocated a return to cheap formula pictures but never stayed around long enough to implement any significant changes. By 1936, he decided it wasn't worth the effort, and he sold the company for $5½ million, even though he had been offered $20 million in the early 1930s. When Universal's new managers took over, they fired almost everyone. They even discovered two individuals on the payroll who had been dead for years.

Working at Universal was a mixed blessing for Wyler. Many regarded him as another family freeloader. He began modestly as an assistant director and was given his first solo opportunity, when he was twenty-three, with a two-reel western, *Crook Buster* (1925). Though his legal name was Willy, he used William in his credit title because it sounded more American. (He became a U.S. citizen in 1928.) During his first year as a director, he made twenty-one two-reelers, all of them westerns. He was paid $60 per week. "It was all routine," Wyler later said of these early efforts, "but it taught you the business of movement. It was all action."

In 1926 he graduated to features and made seven full-length westerns, each of them costing about $20,000, and each turning in a tidy profit. His first all-talking movie was *Hell's Heroes* (1930), another western. But on this project, Wyler was given more artistic control, and he decided to shoot much of it on location near Death Valley. The film proved popular at the box office, and the harsh realism of its exterior scenes was praised by critics. Buoyed by his success, Wyler now wanted to make a serious movie about the depression. He became friends with the writer John Huston, and together they worked on several possible projects. But all of them fell through. Universal's prestige policy was leading him to ruination, Uncle Carl lamented. Wyler was told to stick to the tried and true. He returned to directing program films, including a well-received comedy, *Her First Mate* (1933), which several critics regard as the final work of his apprenticeship period.

Finally he was given an opportunity to work on a more personal project. *Counsellor at Law* (1933) was based on a play by Elmer Rice, with John Barrymore playing the leading role of a Jewish attorney. The subject of anti-Semitism was virtually taboo in the movies of this era, despite the fact that almost all the studios were managed by Jews. They preferred to keep a low ethnic profile, however, because anti-Semitism was then a commonplace in Christian America. Barrymore was a problem. Worried that a gentile would appear fraudulent in the role, he began adopting a number of stereotyped Jewish mannerisms. Wyler argued strenuously with him, pointing out that these clichés of characterization made the protagonist appear comical. But the leonine star insisted on doing it his way. Furthermore, he repeatedly blew his lines, requiring many retakes. One scene was shot over forty times before the star got through it correctly. Probably this experience gave birth to the director's nickname, 40-Take Wyler. Despite these problems, the movie was praised by influential critics. But it failed at the box office. The front office decided that serious drama wasn't Wyler's métier, and they refused several of his most ambitious projects. After all, they weren't paying their ace director $1,000 a week to make movies only critics liked. In 1934 he got disgusted and quit. But he was confident of his talent: All he needed was a sympathetic producer to finance his work. Enter Samuel Goldwyn.

Goldwyn was the usual melange of contradictions that went into the making of a mogul, but his ruling passion was his hunger for prestige. Wyler got it for him. Between the years 1935 and 1946, he directed a string of Goldwyn productions that dazzled the industry, including *These Three* (1936), *Dodsworth* (1936), *Dead End* (1937), *Wuthering Heights* (1939), *The Westerner* (1940), *The Little Foxes* (1941), and *The Best Years of Our Lives* (1946). Goldwyn's background was radically different from Wyler's, which in part accounts for their many clashes. The producer was born Samuel Goldfisch in 1881, in the infamous Warsaw ghetto. His family was desperately poor, and like most Polish Jews, had suffered the cruelest persecution. Sam's formal education was finished by the time he was eleven. He left home at the age of twelve and traveled across western Europe on his own, often enduring cold and hunger. When he was

Figure 8.2. Miriam Hopkins, Merle Oberon, and Joel McCrea in *These Three* (1936), screenplay by Lillian Hellman, based on her play *The Children's Hour*, distributed by United Artists. Wyler's stage adaptations are among the best of the American cinema. He had a flair for taking talky properties and converting them into honest movies, without losing the literary virtues of the original. Often he refused to open up stage plays with exterior locations: "I believe that the emotion and conflict between people in a drawing room can be as exciting as a gun battle, and possibly more exciting," he said.

fourteen he managed to scrape up enough money to travel steerage to America—the legendary land of opportunity.

Goldwyn prospered in the United States, primarily because he had a flair for salesmanship. In 1912 he joined forces with his then brother-in-law, Jesse Lasky, and the aspiring director, Cecil B. DeMille, to produce *The Squaw Man* (1913), which made them all rich. But the mercurial Goldwyn quarreled with his partners, and eventually he became an independent producer, or a "lonely wolf," as he once described himself in one of his famous malapropisms, which came to be known as Goldwynisms. Throughout his life he was attracted to cultivated people and was intensely self-conscious about his lack of education. He favored an expensive style of living, and was one of the most fastidiously tailored men in America. He publicized himself as a "prestige producer," and in the nearly eighty movies he financed with his own money, he never stinted on costs. Once he even scrapped a completed film before release because he considered it below his standard of quality. Like many of the moguls, he was a profligate gambler and public benefactor.

Figure 8.3. Bette Davis and Henry Fonda in *Jezabel* (1938). Wyler agreed to produce and direct this film on loanout to Warners. Davis was thrilled with the prospect: "After all these years, I had been given a high-budget film with all the trimmings I had fought for and a talented director that I had been begging for too." Everyone expected fireworks on the set, because both Davis and Wyler had reputations for being difficult. The two got on famously. Davis repeated her opening scene forty-five times before both were satisfied with the results. Wyler had strong praise for her professionalism and artistic commitment. She won her second Academy Award in this film and gave the credit to her director: "It was all Wyler. I had known all the horrors of no direction and bad direction. It was he who helped me realize my full potential as an actress."

Goldwyn loved personal publicity, and for several years his mangled idioms provided amusement to millions. Some claimed that these Goldwynisms were in fact churned out by his own publicity department. Among his choicest were "I can tell you in two words: im possible"; "include me out"; "a verbal contract isn't worth the paper it's written on"; "I read part of it all the way through"; "our comedies are not to be laughed at." Goldwyn also confused proper names and titles: *The Little Foxes* thus became *The Three Little Foxes; Wuthering Heights* was transposed to *Withering Heights;* and so on. Later Goldwyn denied making these slips, claiming they were the inventions of malicious wags. Several perceptive observers insisted that the producer was in fact one of the shrewdest men in the industry and had an excellent if undisciplined mind. Ben Hecht, for example, claimed that Goldwyn, Selznick, and Zanuck were the three brightest producers in Hollywood.

Goldwyn insisted that good writing was the key to successful movie making. Next to himself, he enjoyed publicizing his stable of "Eminent Authors," which included Lillian Hellman, Robert E. Sherwood, S. N. Behrman, Dorothy Parker, and other literary notables. He attempted to hire such Nobel laureates as George Bernard Shaw, Anatole France, Sinclair Lewis, and Maurice Maeterlinck, though not with much success. He gambled on sophisticated literary properties, for which he often paid enormous sums. Industry regulars regarded him as slightly mad for purchasing such uncommercial and censorable properties as *The Children's Hour, The Little Foxes, Arrowsmith,* and *Dodsworth.* Needless to say, writers—who were used to being treated contemptuously in Hollywood—were among Goldwyn's most articulate champions.

He was suspicious and jealous of his directors and seldom credited them for his successes, though he often blamed them for his failures. When Howard Hawks rewrote the script to *Come and Get It* (1936), the producer was furious. "Directors are supposed to direct, not write," he bellowed. Hawks told him what he could do with his script and walked off the project. Wyler was asked to finish it, which he did, though with considerable grumbling. "The trouble with directors," Goldwyn grumbled back, "is that they're always biting the hand that lays the golden egg." Wyler was his joy and his purgatory. Both had strong egos; both were willing to fight like hell for their ideas. Wyler usually won. "In most cases—not all—he seemed to have more confidence in what I thought than in what he thought himself," the director tactfully recalled, "and he let me have my way."

Often Goldwyn would ask Wyler to take over a pet project, and usually the director refused. A shouting match would ensue; then Wyler was duly suspended. The sports-loving director then went off skiing or fishing until the producer assigned the project to another director. When Wyler returned, Goldwyn always took him back. "Somehow all the scripts I turned down were enormous failures," Wyler pointed out. In short, Goldwyn was stubborn, but he wasn't dumb. Furthermore, as Larry Swindell has noted, the eight Wyler-directed films constitute the substance of Goldwyn's reputation as a prestige producer, a view shared by several other critics as well. Goldwyn was as ambivalent about his house genius as Cohn was about Capra. At a press conference a reporter asked Goldwyn, "When Wyler made *Wuthering Heights . . .*" Goldwyn interjected testily: "*I* made *Wuthering Heights,* Wyler only directed it."

Despite their ferocious battles, both men respected each other—in their own fashion. Both wanted to make quality movies and agreed never to cut costs with cheap compromises. Goldwyn usually allowed Wyler freedom in the casting, in shaping the story materials, and in the final cut. Wyler was paid $2,500 per week, and when he was loaned out to other studios, Goldwyn pocketed the additional $1,000 per week he charged for allowing his top director out of the fold. But the mogul liked to keep him close by. When Wyler wanted to shoot *Dead End* and *Wuthering Heights* on location, Goldwyn insisted that his own studio be used instead. In *Wuthering Heights,* the slightly eerie stylization of the sets enhances the romanticism of Emily Brontë's classic novel. But the depression gangster film suffers from its lack of surface realism. Goldwyn's sensibility veered toward the glossy. When he saw the enormous waterfront set for *Dead End,* for example, he complained that it looked dirty. Wyler patiently explained that that's how an East River slum is supposed to look.

Like any other genre, the prestige picture has had its ups and downs. Its antecedents extend back to the silent period, with the literary adaptations of Griffith and with Bernhardt's celluloid immortalization in *Queen Elizabeth,* which inaugurated Zukor's first film company, Famous Players in Famous Plays, in 1912. Prestige films generally took three forms: (1) adaptations of literary classics of the past, especially English, French, and American novels of the nineteenth century; (2) biographies of important public figures, like scientists, inventors, politicians, and artists; and (3) adaptations of novels and plays by prestigious contemporary authors. Though some of the finest works of the American cinema fall into this genre, many of them failed at the box office, including several of Wyler's most critically admired films, as well as such famous movies as Stroheim's *Greed,* Orson Welles's *Citizen Kane* and *The Magnificent Ambersons,* Max Ophüls's *Letter from an Unknown Woman,* and Huston's *The Red Badge of Courage.* The studios that produced the greatest

Figure 8.4. Laurence Olivier and Merle Oberon in *Wuthering Heights* (1939), screenplay by Ben Hecht and Charles MacArthur, based on the novel by Emily Brontë, distributed by United Artists. Wyler took considerable liberties with Brontë's famous novel, cutting out nearly half the story, toning down the book's extravagant romanticism, and sharpening the criticism of the British class system. Though Goldwyn was only half-hearted about the project at first, it eventually became his favorite picture. It failed at the box office.

number of prestige pictures were prosperous and could afford to take risks: MGM, Warners, and 20th Century-Fox. Because RKO encouraged the producer-director system of production, a number of independent filmmakers worked in the genre at that studio too, though often unsuccessfully, thus weakening a financially rocky company. Goldwyn was the most famous independent producer of the genre, with Selznick not far behind. However, most of the majors could boast its prestige producer, like MGM's Thalberg and Sidney Franklin, Warners' Henry Blanke, and Fox's Zanuck.

American prestige pictures are often dominated by British talent, especially in the acting. (In fact, it is perhaps the foremost genre of the English cinema, enlisting the talents of such notable directors as Carol Reed, David Lean, Tony Richardson, Laurence Olivier, Joseph Losey, and others.) The scripts require a high degree of literacy and often tempt writers who have already made their mark in the world of *belles lettres*. Personality-stars are seldom cast in these movies because the roles—often technically difficult—can produce an iconographical incongruity when they are enacted by strongly defined American types. In the studio era, actor-stars like Bette Davis, Katharine Hepburn, Frederic March, and Paul Muni were more likely to be cast, along with other theatre-trained players, such as those who had learned their art in the rigorous British repertory system. In the 1930s, the best American works in this genre were directed by Wyler and Ford, who set the stage for such ambitious directors of the 1940s and 1950s as Welles, Ophüls, Huston, Kazan, and Zinnemann.

The prestige picture is not without its vices, as Higham and Greenberg point out in *Hollywood in the Forties*. Instead of being serious, they are sometimes solemn and overreverent. Some are characterized by good intentions rather than achieved artistic results. Gentility too often is mistaken for delicacy, "class" for taste. The Warner Brothers biography films of the 1930s, which were usually vehicles for Mr. Paul Muni and Mr. George Arliss, as they were pretentiously billed, were often unbearably sanctimonious, with the story materials trivialized and sentimentalized. Thalberg's prestige projects at MGM were generally ponderous, vulgar, and conceptually naive. Most of them are embalmed in gloss and directed in the grand manner: The production values virtually drown the materials in a sea of lavish costumes, pageants, and elephantine sets. Few of Wyler's prestige pictures suffer from these defects, though he wasn't immune to them by any means.

World War II interrupted Wyler's career at its peak. Most of the studios contributed to the war effort by producing propaganda movies that reflected the government's war policies. For example, Wyler directed the immensely popular *Mrs. Miniver* (1942) for MGM to create American sympathy for Roosevelt's Lend Lease assistance to a beleaguered Great Britain. After the picture was completed, he offered his services to the U.S. government. In 1942 he was commissioned a major in the Air Force and was instructed to make a documentary about the B-17 bombing missions over Nazi-occupied territories. With a crude sixteen millimeter camera and some grainy color stock, he flew in actual bombing missions, several times risking his life in order to get authentic

Figure 8.5. Bette Davis in *The Letter* (1940), a Warner Brothers-First National Picture.
As André Bazin pointed out, the constants in Wyler's movies are his intelligence and taste
and a tendency to favor psychological stories in social settings. Otherwise, his dramatic
materials vary considerably. He seldom repeated the same themes, nor did he favor a
single type of setting. His style was dictated by the materials, not by a preconceived concept
of form. His editing changes from film to film, though it tends toward austerity. The
lighting and camerawork are also determined by the unique characteristics of each movie.
Even the acting styles are different. For example, in *The Letter,* Davis's performance is a
triumph of nuance and understatement, perhaps the most subtle of her career—a far cry
from the bravura effulgence she was famous for.

footage. On one mission, Wyler's plane was subjected to intense antiaircraft fire, and the thunderous flak totally deprived him of his hearing.
To this day, he suffers permanent deafness in one ear and can hear out
of the other only with the greatest difficulty. The resultant film, *The
Memphis Belle* (1944), was praised as one of the finest combat documentaries of the war, comparable in its power to Ford's *The Battle of Midway*
and Huston's *The Battle of San Pietro.*

The war profoundly affected Wyler's attitude toward his work.
Like most filmmakers who had witnessed combat at first hand, he was
shaken by what he had seen and believed that the war was the major
experience of his generation. Director George Stevens was appalled by
the inhumanity of the Nazis when he saw the shriveled corpses at
Dachau. Even Capra's postwar work was tinged with new doubts and
undercurrents of despair. When Wyler and Stevens joined forces with
Capra to set up Liberty Films, all three wanted to make movies that
confronted serious issues: "All of us have learned something and gained

a more realistic view of the world," Wyler said. Like many other veterans, he criticized the Hollywood studio establishment for failing to keep up with postwar realities, and he believed that the devastated cinema of Europe was more sensitive to what was really going on in the world.

Wyler's first postwar movie, *The Best Years of Our Lives,* inaugurated a new era in the American cinema, one more attuned to serious social issues. Based on actual case histories, the film deals with the difficulties of civilian readjustment of three American war veterans. "This is not a story of plot," Wyler said of his work, "but a picture of some people, who were real people, facing real problems." To the amazement of the industry, which was still inclined toward escapist entertainment, the movie was an international hit. In Great Britain it outgrossed the box office champion, *Gone with the Wind.* Even in vanquished Germany, which was only beginning to dig itself out from under the debris of massive bombard-

Figure 8.6.   Bette Davis in *The Little Foxes* (1941), screenplay by Lillian Hellman, based on her play, distributed by RKO. Wyler's insistence on complexity of characterization led him to the conclusion that actors should often play somewhat against their material. With melodramatic vehicles especially, villains should never be played as though they were conscious of their villainy. In *The Little Foxes,* Davis believed her role should be played as an outright bitch, smoldering in frustration and fury. Wyler thought the characterization should be more complex: "I wanted her to play it much lighter. This woman was supposed not just to be evil, but to have great charm, humor, and sex. She had some terribly funny lines." But Wyler lost this one: Davis played the role her way. The film was a huge popular and critical success and is regarded as one of Wyler's finest works.

Figure 8.7. Myrna Loy, Teresa Wright, and Dana Andrews in *The Best Years of Our Lives* (1946), cinematography by Gregg Toland, distributed by RKO. "I think that the story dictates its own style rather than the director's style dictating the story," Wyler said. This story ushered in an era of hard-edged realism. Gone was the moody mise-en-scène of Wyler's prewar films. Here was a style for the times: sober, austere, deglamorized. The photography is in razor-sharp deep focus, with no flourishes. Wyler stripped his editing down to essentials: The movie consists of less than 200 shots. (Most features of this period averaged 800 shots.) Above all, as Bazin pointed out, it was a transparent style, a "styleless style." This is precisely what Wyler wanted: "I have never been as interested in the externals of presenting a scene as I have been in the inner workings of the people the scene is about. I am not minimizing the importance of correct use of the camera, or staging of the action. I mean that they are important only as they help the audience understand what the characters are thinking, feeling, saying or doing."

ments, the film struck a responsive chord. It swept both the Academy Awards of 1946 and the New York Film Critics awards. America's finest critic, James Agee, expressed reservations about its sentimental lapses but otherwise had strong praise for the movie and called Wyler one of the greatest of American filmmakers. From today's perspective, *The Best Years of Our Lives* might appear less powerful, but it offered comfort to an entire generation, which had its security disrupted—and in many cases blasted—by the war.

Best Years was Wyler's last Goldwyn-produced work. The director was given 20 percent of the profits from the movie, which netted him over $1 million. But he wanted to be his own producer because he wanted total artistic control. When Liberty Films was sold to Paramount, it was with the understanding that only he would make the decisions on his movies, or he would simply go to another studio. The five pictures he made at Paramount are among his best: *The Heiress* (1949), *Detective Story* (1951), *Carrie* (1952), *Roman Holiday* (1953) and *The Desperate Hours* (1955). When Wyler subsequently went to other studios to work, it was almost always as a producer-director. However, he directed the mammoth spectacle *Ben-Hur* for MGM as a change of pace and because it offered him a chance to return to Italy, where he enjoyed making *Roman Holiday*.

Wyler's perfectionism was famous—or notorious, depending on the point of view. He often went over budget and over schedule, usually because he refused to accept anything he believed was second rate. "Wyler works like a sculptor," wrote Jessamyn West, "molding script, actors, and locale into a form which strikes him at the moment as being significant." Like most directors of his generation, he didn't want his technique to be noticed. But his is an art that conceals art, for in reality, he molded each nuance with utmost precision.

The story was always the central problem in his movies. Though he didn't write his own scripts, he usually outlined what kind of emphasis

Figure 8.8. *The Heiress* **(1949), with Ralph Richardson (seated), distributed by Paramount Pictures.** Wyler's preference for deep-focus photography allowed him to present his scenes more objectively, without the value judgments implicit in a fragmented sequence of close shots. In this scene, for example, an edited sequence would probably focus on the faces of the two characters at the exclusion of the rather undramatic physical context. But Wyler deliberately included the empty tables and chairs as well as the waiting carriage in this shot, thus encouraging the viewer to conclude that there's a subtle interrelationship between them and the heroine's arrogant but lonely father (Richardson).

the story should receive and what kind of scenes would be most effective. He thought that writing and directing were overlapping functions and preferred having his writers on the set in case of last-minute revisions. In making *Friendly Persuasion,* he hired Jessamyn West as a coscenarist to help transfer her stories of Quaker life into a screenplay. He also kept her on as a paid consultant during production to insure against violations of the spirit of her original material. He altered his scripts in mid-production if he believed they could be improved. For example, the aircraft graveyard scene in *Best Years,* which many critics regard as the finest in the movie, was entirely Wyler's invention. Among scenarists, he was one of the most respected of directors. Himself highly articulate, he was an intelligent judge of writing and insisted that the first step in making good movies was a strong script. Among his close friends were such gifted writers as Lillian Hellman, John Huston, and Preston Sturges. Hellman urged Wyler early in his career to work only on projects he felt strongly about. She had a low opinion of most movie people, but regarded Wyler as one of the few serious artists working in Hollywood: "It was Wyler who taught me about movies. It was Wyler who gave me my only happy, hardworking time in Hollywood," she recalled. In fact, Hellman believed that sometimes the director might have been *too* respectful of the writer's art. For example, when he readapted her play *The Children's Hour* in 1962, she suggested that the movie might have been more popular if he had updated the materials rather than remaining so faithful to the 1934 stage original.

Wyler was considered the actor's director *par excellence.* "People who separate directing from acting make a great mistake," he said, "because I consider the first function of a director to be the acting." In the film colony, acting in a Wyler movie was the ultimate mark of accomplishment. Even self-confident players were scared, yet flattered, to work with him. His confrontations with such tempestuous performers as Margaret Sullivan, Miriam Hopkins, and Bette Davis were the stuff of industry legends. Nonetheless, he respected their integrity and was grateful they were as serious about their work as he was about his. In short, he didn't resent "difficult" actors if they were motivated by a desire for artistic excellence. For example, when questioned about Barbra Streisand in her movie debut, *Funny Girl* (1968), Wyler said of her, "She's not easy, but she's difficult in the best sense of the word—the same way I'm difficult." He was always interested in the ideas of his players and would frequently adopt their suggestions. Occasionally he would abandon his own interpretations if he saw they weren't working. Furthermore, he openly admitted his mistakes to his players. He didn't like robots for actors, but if he thought they were wrong, he insisted on doing the scene his way—and he usually got his way.

The most dreaded words on a Wyler set were *once again.* No one shot as many takes, no one seemed as difficult to please. One scene from *Wuthering Heights* was repeated eighteen times, and each time Laurence Olivier thought he got through it without a hitch. When Wyler repeated the dreaded words, Olivier finally snapped, "Good God, man, what do you *want*?" Wyler smiled and replied sadly, "I want you to be better." The twentieth take was tinged with Olivier's frustration. That's what

Figure 8.9. Gregory Peck and Audrey Hepburn in *Roman Holiday* (1953), distributed by Paramount Pictures. This romantic comedy is about as close as any director got to the grace and charm of Lubitsch. Though Wyler was known primarily for his straight dramas, he had directed a number of successful comedies in his apprenticeship period. *Roman Holiday* was very popular with the public and received rave reviews. It also made Audrey Hepburn a star.

Wyler wanted, and he had that take printed. Even the most powerful stars felt humiliated by his exacting standards, and many regarded him as something of a tormentor. Charlton Heston kept a journal during the production of *Ben-Hur*, no doubt to assuage his anger and resentment. "I doubt he likes actors very much," Heston wrote of him in one entry. "He doesn't empathize with them—they irritate him on the set. He gets very impatient, but invariably, they come off well." Later, Heston came to the same conclusion as many of his predecessors when he admitted, "but his taste is impeccable and every actor knows it." When Wyler wanted Myrna Loy for an important role in *Best Years,* she hesitated. Goldwyn subsequently tried to persuade her, assuming she was leery because the role lacked glamor. Finally she confessed, "I hear Willy Wyler is practically a sadist on the set." "That isn't true," Goldwyn insisted, "he's just a very mean fellow." She accepted, and was fine, as usual. Perhaps a bit more than usual. Despite their very real anxieties, Wyler's actors usually came around to defending him. Besides, as Frederic March ruefully conceded, Wyler's release print was his deferred proof.

The director was attracted to characters who are contradictory,

Figure 8.10. Gary Cooper in *Friendly Persuasion* (1956), distributed by Allied Artists.
Wyler made several movies dealing with pacifist themes: "The problem that intrigues me is whether people have faith in a man who *doesn't* punch," the director explained. He was stimulated by the idea of making movies about good people, like the gentle Quaker hero of this film, whose faith in nonviolence is severely strained by the chaos of the Civil War. Warm, sentimental, and decent, *Friendly Persuasion* won the *Palme d'or* at the Cannes Film Festival.

subtle, capable of surprising us. Such a view ruled out one-note performances. He didn't like stars who simply turned on the charm before the camera. He insisted that the camera passively records only what the character does and says, and in order to be believable, the actor must believe his character. He was acutely sensitive to nuances. In *The Heiress,* for example Olivia De Havilland plays a plain spinster who's jilted on the night of her planned elopement. At the scene's conclusion, after it becomes apparent that her lover isn't going to show up for her, she wearily carries her luggage upstairs to her room. Wyler had her repeat the scene many times, but still he wasn't satisfied. Finally it occurred to him: The suitcases were empty. He ordered them filled with books. In the film, when she makes her steep climb up the stairs, she can barely lift the heavy cases. Her exhaustion and humiliation are total. Another director, out of consideration for a star's comfort, probably wouldn't have suggested the idea—which is why Wyler was also regarded as a director's director. His subtlety often went past the critics. For example, he wanted the jilting fortune hunter in *The Heiress* to be played by a warm and charming man. He cast Montgomery Clift because his soulful, boyish sensitivity was hard to resist. The emotional impact of his betrayal of the heroine is all the more powerful because we too have been hoping that this reckless charmer might turn out all right after all. Critics complained because "nobody expected him to be a cad." Apparently movies weren't supposed to be like life.

Wyler seldom began by telling his actors what to do. He wanted to see their ideas first. Then he amplified some elements, softened others. "I think guiding an actor's thinking is the most important thing. If you and the actor agree on what goes on inside the character, then he will have the right expression." With each new scene, the director would explain what it was about in terms of each character's development. "I believe if the actor or actress really understands the scene, and understands the inner motivations of the character, that half the battle for a good performance is won." The other half of the battle involved reminding actors to listen sincerely, to relax, to take their time, and above all, to interact believably with the other characters. He seldom complimented his players, which left them hurt and uncertain of themselves. The frustrated Charlton Heston once ventured a query about his performance. "Look Chuck," he replied, "if I don't say anything after a take, that means it's O.K."

After the main acting problems were ironed out, Wyler turned his attention to the mise-en-scène. He liked his shots to function as miniprosceniums. That is, he positioned his actors within the shot so that the viewer can tell at a glance what any number of them are doing, as in the live theatre, only usually closer in and without the visual artificiality that the conventions of space in the theatre demand. (A good example of this kind of setup is Fig. 8.2.) The interrelationships among the characters are simultaneously presented, allowing us to see the emotional crosscurrents without being nudged with "significant" closeups. Wyler liked to leave it up to the viewer to decide what was significant, and consequently he used very few closeups. Whenever possible, he tried to use lengthy takes, which allowed the players to remain within a scene for long stretches of time. In some lengthy takes Wyler regrouped his characters and the spaces between them to reflect their shifting psychological strategies. In *The Letter,* for example, his takes are unusually long, several lasting over four minutes. He wanted to extend one take for eight minutes, but later decided that it had to be punctuated by an essential closeup. Because lengthy takes are difficult to execute without a hitch, Wyler was often required to repeat them—thus adding to the lore of 40-Take Wyler.

Along with his frequent cinematographer, Gregg Toland, Wyler revived the use of deep-focus photography in the 1930s. Toland, one of the great American cinematographers of the studio era, was under permanent contract to Goldwyn beginning in 1929. Toland died at the age of forty-four of a sudden heart attack in 1948. Deep-focus photography is a method of lighting and shooting interiors which allows objects from five to fifty feet away to remain in sharp focus. The technique tends to encourage a layered effect in the mise-en-scène, with important visual information distributed over a variety of visual planes, commenting obliquely on each other. Wyler worked in close collaboration with Toland, for they varied their visual style even from scene to scene: "You just didn't tell Gregg what lens to use, you told him what mood you were

Figure 8.11. *Ben-Hur* **(1959).** By the mid-1950s, mighty MGM was in serious financial straits. Since this was the era of widescreen epic spectacles, the studio decided to gamble on a remake of its 1926 hit, *Ben-Hur*. Wyler was asked to direct the elephantine project. At first he refused, arguing that the property was more suited to a director like DeMille. But eventually Wyler relented. He was intrigued by the technical challenges of the chariot race (pictured), which is the high point of the film. Ironically, Wyler didn't even get to direct it. Because of the complexities of production, the sequence—which alone cost $1 million— was executed by second-unit directors, though Wyler edited it. *Ben-Hur* grossed an astonishing $80 million. MGM was back in business.

after. When he photographed something, he wanted to go beyond lights and catch feelings." Wyler would ask Toland to look at a scene after it was rehearsed, and together they decided where to put the camera. Both men thought deep-focus photography enhanced the realism of a scene. It also provided exciting challenges in the staging and lighting."I can have action and reaction in the same shot," Wyler pointed out, "without having to cut back and forth from individual cuts of the characters. This makes for smooth continuity, an almost effortless flow of the scene, for much more interesting composition in each shot, and lets the spectator look from one to the other character at his own will, do his own cutting."

André Bazin, the cofounder and editor of *Cahiers du Cinéma,* was Wyler's most fervent champion. In fact, his 1948 essay, "William Wyler, ou le janseniste de la mise en scène," is by far the most sophisticated analysis of the director's style. Unfortunately, this essay has yet to be translated into English. Wyler's oeuvre constituted one of the cornerstones of Bazin's complex theory of cinematic realism. He believed that cinema and photography, unlike the traditional arts, are innately realistic. They reproduce images of reality automatically, without the necessity for a distorting medium, like a writer's words or a painter's pigments, which in effect must *re*-present reality in terms of an alien form of expression. No other art, Bazin believed, can be as faithful as cinema in the presentation of the ambiguities and contradictions of life as it's commonly observed. For Bazin, the best movie artists are those who manipulate their materials the least, who allow life's complexities to remain intact in the visual image. Those who would impose a neat scheme over the pluralistic nature of reality are more concerned with expressing their own particular point of view, rather than letting the materials speak for themselves.

Bazin was leery of editing as a technique of falsification. He disliked the montage theories of such Soviet filmmakers as Pudovkin and Eisenstein, who claimed that film art was based on editing. The raw materials of reality should never be left intact, these Russian filmmakers argued, but should be fragmented and then juxtaposed to show the viewer the underlying relationships that exist beneath the chaotic sprawl of life. (For a discussion of Pudovkin's theories, see Chapter 12.) The art of the film, they claimed, is just as manipulative as any other kind of art. Bazin disagreed. He believed that this technique allows the viewer no choice in deciding for himself. Because ambiguities are ruthlessly eliminated in the editing, the filmmaker coerces us into accepting his forced juxtapositions as the Truth, rather than his particular truth. Soviet montage might be suitable for the black-and-white simplicities of propaganda, but he believed it a bit crude for the gray permutations of art.

Bazin thought that classical editing was less manipulative than Soviet montage but still far from an objective presentation. Classical cutting breaks down a unified scene into a certain number of closer shots

Figure 8.12. *The Collector* **(1965), with Samantha Eggar, distributed by Columbia Pictures.** Essentially a two-actor movie, *The Collector* is confined mostly to a single set—a challenging exercise in austerity for Wyler. Throughout production, he virtually bullied Eggar into a performance, allowing her no amenities and very little freedom. A number of critics remarked on the authenticity of her hysteria, little realizing perhaps that the inexperienced actress wasn't always acting. But like most of Wyler's players, she was comforted by her excellent reviews. She and co-star Terence Stamp swept the two top acting awards at the Cannes Film Festival. See also Michael A. Anderegg, *William Wyler* (New York: G. K. Hall, 1979).

that correspond implicitly to a mental process. But the technique encourages us to follow the shot sequence without our being conscious of its arbitrariness. "The editor who cuts for us makes in our stead the choice which we would make in real life," Bazin pointed out. "Without thinking, we accept his analysis because it conforms to the laws of attention, but we are deprived of a privilege." He believed that classical cutting also tends to eliminate ambiguities and "subjectivises" an event, because each shot represents what the filmmaker thinks is important, not necessarily what we would think.

The realist filmmaker avoids these distortions by minimizing editing and including as many choices as possible within the mise-en-scène. Bazin especially admired Wyler's preference for lengthy takes, deep-focus photography, and long shots that allow us to see the interrelationships between the characters. "His perfect clarity contributes enormously to the spectator's reassurance and leaves to him the means to observe, to choose, and form an opinion." He believed that the director achieved an unparalleled neutrality and transparancy: "Wyler's style is an act of loyalty to the spectator, an attempt at dramatic honesty." It would be naive to confuse this neutrality with an absence of art, Bazin insisted, for all the director's effort tends to hide itself. The visual elements, without seeming to be manipulated, appear in their maximum clarity. Like Wyler, Bazin was a devotee of the live theatre, and he considered the director's techniques especially suited to dramatic adaptations. "There is a hundred times more cinema, and of a better kind, in a shot in *The Little Foxes,*" he claimed, "than in all the outdoor dolly shots, natural locations, exotic geography, and flipsides of sets with which the screen so far has tried to make up for stagey origins." Wyler's directorial brilliance, Bazin concluded, coincides paradoxically with his minimal "direction."

Henri Langlois, the curator of the prestigious *Cinémathèque française,* believed that Wyler's legacy to the cinema was enormous. He influenced filmmakers on four continents. Eisenstein was fascinated by his movies and often screened them for his students and friends. Laurence Olivier claimed that Wyler was the principal influence on his work as a movie director, especially in his handling of actors and in his staging. In 1966, the Directors Guild of America conferred upon Wyler the D. W. Griffith Award for Lifelong Achievement. Wyler's films were generally admired by critics, especially in France. In 1971, the Cannes Film Festival celebrated its twenty-fifth anniversary by awarding trophies to the festival's five most honored directors: René Clair, Ingmar Bergman, Federico Fellini, Luis Buñuel, and William Wyler. The American Film Institute selected him in 1976 to receive their Life Achievement Award for contributions to the art of the American film.

BIBLIOGRAPHY

BAZIN, ANDRÉ. *What is Cinema?* 2 vols. Trans. Hugh Gray. Berkeley: University of California Press, 1967, 1971. Scattered allusions to Wyler throughout these essays, which explore Bazin's theory of cinematic realism.

BLUESTONE, GEORGE. *Novels Into Film.* Berkeley: University of California Press, 1968. Contains a chapter on *Wuthering Heights* and an important theoretical essay on the relationship of movies to novels. See also Ben Hecht and Charles MacArthur, *Wuthering Heights,* in *Twenty Best Film Plays,* John Gassner and Dudley Nichols, eds. (New York: Crown Publishers, 1943): A reading version of the script.

Directed by William Wyler: Life Achievement Award Issue, American Film (April, 1976). Special section devoted to Wyler, with a long interview, excerpts from Heston's *Ben-Hur* journal, and a critical commentary by Larry Swindell.

HESTON, CHARLTON. *The Actor's Life: Journals, 1956–1976.* New York: Dutton, 1978. Much material on the making of *Ben-Hur.*

HIGHAM, CHARLES, AND JOEL GREENBERG. *Hollywood in the Forties.* Cranbury, N.J.: A. S. Barnes, 1968. A survey of the decade, by genre, with a chapter on the prestige picture.

MADSEN, ALEX. *William Wyler: The Authorized Biography.* New York: Thomas Y. Crowell, 1973. An understated account, with a complete filmography and selected bibliography.

MARX, ARTHUR. *Goldwyn.* New York: Ballantine, 1976. Also Richard Griffith, *Samuel Goldwyn: The Producer and His Films* (New York: Simon & Schuster, 1956). See also Michael G. Fitzgerald, *Universal Pictures* New Rochelle, N.Y.: Arlington House Publishers, 1977): A studio history.

REISZ, KAREL, ed. *William Wyler, An Index.* London: British Film Institute, 1958. Filmography and bibliography.

WEST, JESSAMYN. *To See the Dream.* New York: Harcourt Brace Jovanovich, Inc., 1956. Contains an account of the making of *Friendly Persuasion.*

WYLER, WILLIAM. "No Magic Wand," in *Hollywood Directors: 1941–1976.* Richard Koszarski, ed. New York: Oxford University Press, 1977. A brief but lucid discussion of his working methods.

Maschinenwerk

The Cinema of Fritz Lang

Figure 9.1. Production photo of Lang (uplifted finger) while shooting a scene from *The Big Heat* (1953), with Glenn Ford and Gloria Grahame. Lang considered himself a formalist and planned almost every detail in advance. "I like my scripts absolutely ready to shoot," he said, for he had virtually no time to experiment. The alterations he made on the set—if any—were generally minor, like changing an angle for a shot, or rephrasing a line of dialogue. Each night before shooting he worked at least two hours planning his angles, lenses, and lighting effects. He always had exact sketches of his sets and sometimes even small-scale models to work out his shots. Though he claimed to dislike dictatorial personalities, he was widely regarded as inflexible and authoritarian on the set, especially by actors, who generally resented his autocratic manner. In his defense, Lang explained, "Every picture has a certain rhythm which only one man can give it. That man is the director. He has to be like the captain of a ship." See also Scott Eyman, "Fritz Lang Remembered," in *Take One* (March, 1977).

Fritz Lang made major contributions in both the German and American cinemas. His career fell into two roughly equal parts. The violent social upheavals in post-World War I Germany had a lasting effect on the movies he produced in that country. He was also influenced by the revolutionary art movement called German expressionism, and he was regarded as a foremost practitioner of this style in the 1920s. His German period culminated with his masterpiece, *M*. With the rise to power of the Nazis, Lang was forced to flee to the United States, where for many years he was widely regarded as a victim of the Hollywood studio system. Some of his American films were impersonal studio assignments which he directed only because he had no other options. He was never nominated for an Academy Award, nor was he often praised by critics, in part because he favored the déclassé genre of the crime melodrama. In the 1950s, however, Lang's American works were "discovered" by the *Cahiers* critics, who considered his compact American movies his finest achievements. Virtually all of them feature tight, symmetrical plots, which are constructed like machine works, inexorably grinding up their victims. His tone is cold and objective. "He touches one's nerves but never the heart," said critic Arthur Lennig. The characterization in his movies is often weak, probably because he believed that the human spirit is depersonalized by the forces that oppress it. Above all, Lang was a brilliant visual stylist, and he helped to create a new kind of cinema, called *film noir* by the French critics. The style might be regarded as the American cousin of German expressionism.

> *I think there is one thread running through all my pictures: the fight against Destiny or Fate.*
>
> *—Fritz Lang*

Lang was born in 1890, in Vienna. His father was a successful architect, who wanted his son to follow in his footsteps. As a youth, Fritz received a rigorous Catholic education and then studied architecture briefly. But he was more attracted to a career as a painter, a vocation his bourgeois parents viewed as frivolous. Finally he broke away from his home environment and traveled all over the world. He supported himself by selling sketches, drawings, and cartoons. He studied art in both Vienna and Munich and adopted a bohemian lifestyle. In 1912 he took up painting in Paris, living in the artists' quarter in Montmartre. Between 1912 and 1914 Lang became enamored of the cinema, and he saw at least one movie every day. Even at this early date, he believed that film would become *the* art form of the twentieth century. When World War I broke out in 1914, he had to return to Austria, where he was drafted into the army. During the war, he was wounded several times, and while recuperating in the hospital, he began writing movie scenarios, little knowing whether they would ever amount to anything.

Lang's artistic sensibility was forged by the social and intellectual currents of the postwar period in Germany. Between the years 1918 and 1923, German society, which had previously been the most disciplined in Europe, was convulsed by economic chaos and clashes of violence between right- and left-wing extremists. The currency system went beserk. For example, before the war the German mark was worth about 25¢. After the war its value plumeted to less than half that. By 1923 it took 4,200,000,000 marks to equal one American dollar. In Berlin especially, prewar standards of conduct were swept away by a wave of sexual permissiveness that shocked the rest of the world. Disillusioned with all forms of authority, young Germans challenged virtually all absolute values, and found them wanting. Jazz and American movies were all the rage. Freud's revolutionary theories of the subconscious were in the air, and the gloomy fatalism of Spengler's *The Decline of the West* had a profound effect on young artists and intellectuals.

A total rejection of the past also characterized the arts of this period. The new tolerant atmosphere encouraged radical experiments in form, particularly in the visual and performing arts, which embraced the new idiom of distortion called *expressionism,* a style steeped in pessimism, despair, and alienation. "All over the world, young people engaged in the cultural fields, myself among them, made a fetish of tragedy," Lang recalled. These artists viewed themselves as romantic revolutionaries, in revolt against all forms of repression. The popular magazine, *Sturm,* promoted expressionism in the arts and was especially influential with writers, painters, dramatists, and filmmakers. The famous theatrical director, Max Reinhardt, became a leading practitioner of expressionism in the drama, and his ideas influenced many of Germany's movie artists, especially Lang. Expressionism was antibourgeois and antisocial. Its tone was paranoid—mired in anxiety, menace, a vague atmosphere of guilty remorse, and an overwhelming sense of fatalism. Realism was dismissed as a superficial style which could deal with only surfaces, not spiritual essences. Artists can capture the underlying truths of existence only by violating the surface realism of the outside order and by looking within for inspiration. Subjectivity, mysticism, and private fantasies are what lead to the truths of the soul. The stylistic distortion of expressionism was intended as a symbolic projection of spiritual and psychological states.

It was in this cultural climate that Lang began his movie career in Berlin. For three years he had been writing scenarios for producer Joe May. In 1919 he insisted on directing as well as writing *Halbblut (The Halfbreed),* which was popular with the public. In 1920 he went to work for Erich Pommer, the leading producer at Decla Studio, where Lang was a story editor and writer. In this same year Lang married the novelist Thea von Harbou, who collaborated on the scripts of all his German movies after 1920. In the following year, the three major studios in Germany merged under the umbrella of UFA, the largest production facility in Europe.

Critic Paul Jensen, who believes that Lang's German movies are superior to those he made in America, states that the 1920s was the decade of his greatest fame and influence. Though his expressionism was less extreme than that of most of his contemporaries, Lang's movies were still strongly romantic, allegorical, and exotic. They were also imbued with a sense of doleful anxiety. Beginning with *Der Müde Tod* (1921), released in the United States as *Destiny,* he became a leading figure of the German cinema, working in a variety of genres and styles. In 1922 he made a two-part movie dealing with a sinister master criminal, Dr. Mabuse. Another two-part film, *Die Nibelungen* (1924), was based on the thirteenth-century Germanic saga that also inspired Wagner's opera cycle, *Der Ring des Nibelungen.* The Marxist critic, Siegfried Kracauer, criticized the monumentality of these movies, which he thought represented the triumph of the ornamental over the human. Lang's science fiction fantasy, *Metropolis* (1927), was a big-budget project that dealt with the revolt of a slave society against its masters. Kracauer condemned this film as well, calling it an illustration of "Lang's penchant for pompous ornamentation." *Spione* (1928), a master criminal spy melodrama, was more realistic than his previous works. In this movie, expressionist distortions are found in the midst of reality by photographing ordinary objects in disorienting closeups and from strange angles to make them seem more menacing. With *Frau Im Mond* (1929), released in America as *Woman in the Moon,* Lang returned to science fiction fantasy. By this time, he was the most successful and admired filmmaker in Germany, and his movies were considered major artistic events by the cultural élite. Lang's favorite movie, *M*, was his first talkie and introduced Peter Lorre as a compulsive child-murderer. More subdued stylistically than most of his other German movies, *M* is a brilliantly crafted work, especially innovative in its use of sound. It was a big commercial and critical success.

In the early 1930s, Lang, like most German liberals, became alarmed at the rise to power of the Nazi party. He claimed that he made

Figure 9.2.   Peter Lorre in *M* (1931, Germany). The tormented child-killer in this famous film confesses that he's haunted by another self: "Again, again and again I have to walk the streets. And I always feel that somebody is following me.... It is I myself.... Following. Me...." Lang was fascinated by the concept of a double personality, which is known in German culture as the *doppelgänger.* It's a recurrent motif in Lang's movies, both German and American. Mirror shots such as these are common, symbolizing the other self, the subconscious, or in Freudian terms, the driving force of the id.

Das Testament Des Dr. Mabuse (1933) as an anti-Nazi statement. He attacked Hitler's contempt for democracy by having criminals mouth such slogans as "The individual has no existence except as part of the machine—the individual is nothing, the machine everything." Lang believed that the Nazi state was the ultimate mechanized society and Hitler the incarnation of a master criminal. The movie was banned in the Third Reich, and Lang was summoned to the office of Nazi Propaganda Minister Goebbels. During their interview, Goebbels skirted the topic of *The Last Will of Dr. Mabuse;* instead he told the filmmaker how much Hitler had admired *Metropolis* and had suggested that Lang might be put in charge of the German film industry, providing he proved cooperative. Lang agreed to everything, hoping that the interview would be concluded before his bank closed: "I could only think 'How do you get out of here?' I wanted to get some money out of the bank. Outside the window, there was a big clock, and the hands went slowly round." But it was too late. Since his mother was partly Jewish, he decided to take no chances. He returned home, packed a few belongings, and fled to Paris that same night. Shortly afterward, his wife (who was already a member of the Nazi party) divorced him, and his considerable property was confiscated by the state.

In 1934, David O. Selznick, who was then a producer for MGM, signed Lang to a one-picture contract with options for future films. He arrived in the United States at the age of forty-four, speaking not a word of English. He was to remain in America for over twenty years, directing a total of twenty-two movies, mostly on short-term contracts. Though Lang's American films are less overtly stylized than his German works, his vision remained fundamentally intact, as Gavin Lambert has pointed out:

> Fritz Lang's America is not essentially different from Fritz Lang's Germany (or Fritz Lang's London); it is less openly macabre, its crime and terror exist on a comparatively realistic level, but both countries are really another country, a haunted place in which the same dramas constantly recur.

But as Lang noted, his American movies are different in at least one important respect: The protagonists are not larger-than-life heroes or master criminals but ordinary mortals, "Joe Doe" types, as they were known in the trade. "Over here the hero in a motion picture should be a superman, whereas in a democracy he had to be Joe Doe. This was something I learned here for the first time, and I think it's absolutely correct." He believed that a "man of the people" is a more fitting hero for American movies. In Germany, on the other hand, such characters were unthinkable because it was a culture dominated by military traditions of order, absolute obedience to the state, and Nietzsche's philosophy of the *Übermensch*. After Lang arrived in the United States, he even refused to speak German and worked hard to master his new language. He also took immediate steps to become an American citizen. Like most successful immigrants, he was intensely patriotic.

Lang's sensibility was more deeply imbued by the pessimism of his

Figure 9.3.   Henry Fonda and Sylvia Sidney in *You Only Live Once* (1937), distributed by United Artists. This was the first film to deal with the Bonnie and Clyde story, which has inspired a half dozen movies, including Nicholas Ray's *They Live By Night* (1948), Joseph H. Lewis's *Gun Crazy* (1950), William Witney's *The Bonnie Parker Story* (1958), Jean-Luc Godard's *Pierrot le Fou* (1965), Arthur Penn's *Bonnie and Clyde* (1967), and Robert Altman's *Thieves Like Us* (1974). Each director explored the myth from a different perspective. Characteristically, Lang concentrated on the theme of destiny. The doomed lovers (Fonda and Sidney) struggle helplessly in a morally indifferent universe. This love scene takes place just before they are gunned down by the inexorable force of the law. Note the extreme stylization of the set and lighting—a sign of intense emotions in Lang's American movies.

native culture than he realized. He was sometimes instinctively at odds with the basic optimism of American life. He believed that negativism was appropriate to the despairing conditions in Europe but rang false in America, where everyone seemed to prosper freely. He often tried to make his art conform to his conscious convictions rather than his atavistic instincts. For example, his first American movie, *Fury* (1936), was praised by critics for its daring social criticism, but they also condemned its happy ending as a sop to the box office. Similarly, in *The Woman in the Window* (1944), he tried to avoid the negativism of the protagonist's defeat at the hands of fate by concluding the film with the hero waking up from a nightmare, thus undercutting the movie's power. When World War II broke out, however, the real world provided Lang with sinister menaces in abundance. He directed four anti-Nazi melodramas, which allowed him to return to the fearful atmosphere of his earlier work: *Man Hunt* (1941), *Hangmen Also Die* (1943), *Ministry of Fear* (1944), and *Cloak and Dagger* (1946).

Lang's status in the American film industry in no way approached his prominence in Germany. His movies were seldom big hits, and a few lost money. Some of them he directed only because he needed to survive. About all he could do with these projects was to add an occasional directorial touch, but he had few illusions about their artistic value. He was often forced to shoot scenes according to the instructions of his producers—or "so-called producers," as he referred to them. Many of his films were reedited or included additional scenes that were shot by other directors. In none of his American movies did he have total artistic control, and he often quarreled with writers, producers, and stars. He frequently lost these battles. "Look—you sign a contract," he explained; "having signed a contract, you have to do your best." He bitterly complained that there was "no copyright for a director," for the producer ultimately controls the product. In fact, one of his most brilliant sequences, the bank robbery in the rain from *You Only Live Once,* was sold outright to another producer, who included it in an otherwise mediocre gangster film.

Figure 9.4.   Henry Fonda and Sylvia Sidney in *You Only Live Once*. "No shot in Lang is only playful or gratuitous," critic Lotte Eisner has observed; "his compositions always reveal something." He was unmatched in his ability to suggest an atmosphere of menace through purely visual means. His characters are usually dominated by their environment. In this shot, for example, the exhausted fugitives are portrayed as trapped animals, virtually entombed by the massively architecturalized railroad cars that surround them. The foggy atmosphere wraps them in a shroud of mist, nearly obliterating them from view. The shot might almost be entitled No Exit.

Lang's best American movies are often low-budget genre films that weren't considered important enough to meddle with. Most of them are crime melodramas, which commanded little respect from the industry and even less from the critics of that era. He learned to work quickly, for some of his movies were allowed only thirty-six shooting days. There were periods during his career when he couldn't even find hack projects. After World War II, he attempted to go into independent production. Along with the star Joan Bennett and her husband then, producer Walter Wanger, Lang and scenarist Dudley Nichols set up Diana Productions in 1945. The company produced only two movies, the superb *Scarlet Street* (1945) and *Secret Beyond the Door* (1948), which failed at the box office. In the early 1950s, he was unable to find work for a considerable period. Eventually he discovered he was on the infamous blacklist as a Communist sympathizer, because he had once signed a human rights petition. (For a discussion of this period, see Chapter 14.) He was also a close friend of the Marxist dramatist, Bertolt Brecht, who helped write the script to *Hangmen Also Die*. Harry Cohn—whom Lang liked and respected—came to the rescue through the simple expedient of asking him if he was a Communist. When Lang assured him he wasn't, Cohn hired him at Columbia, where the director made one of his finest movies, *The Big Heat* (1953). He followed this with *Human Desire* (1954).

Lang valued his films according to the amount of social criticism they contained. Like his friend Brecht, he believed that the best art combined a "preaching function" with aesthetic pleasure. But Lang was more of an aestheticist than he cared to admit. Fortunately, he was less narrow and didactic in his actual practices. In discussing his movies, however, he often reduced them to clichés. For example, he claimed he made *M* to dramatize the dangers to children in contemporary urban society—a thumping banality, if we were to take it seriously. Paul Jensen has argued that Lang's social themes are often oversimplified. Instead of a consistent ideology he reverts to a consistent set of plot elements that interest him, and their content doesn't really matter. In fact, Jensen claims that Lang's political ideas are so superficial that he inadvertently contradicted himself from movie to movie, especially in his German period. Gavin Lambert shares this view. Lang's films are not so much about social issues, he states, as they are "dramatic abstracts of society's indifference to the outcast, whom it creates, punishes, and then forces back into crime."

Lang probably emphasized the social criticism of his films because it made him look more politically *engagé*—a highly admired trait, especially within the German colony in Hollywood, which was fiercely anti-Nazi and liberal in its values. Paradoxically, Lang's reputation as an arrogant authoritarian was due in part to his Germanic background. When he arrived in 1934, he wore a monocle and was haughty in his manner, recalling such lordly Teutons as the two vons (both phony), Stroheim and Sternberg, who were widely disliked in Hollywood because of their lofty airs. In fact, the entire German colony was viewed with a certain resentment, for it was commonly thought to be aloof, intellectually snobbish, and rather arty. Its members seldom bothered to

Figure 9.5. Joan Bennett and Walter Pidgeon in *Man Hunt* **(1941), produced by 20th Century-Fox.** "I am a visual person," Lang admitted. "I experience with my eyes and never, or only rarely, with my ears." The dialogue in this romantic scene is rather banal, but the mise-en-scène is eloquent. Lang was a master of visual textures, like the lacy shadows thrown against the wall by the light filtering through the curtains on the window. The human materials for Lang weren't usually paramount. Often he would focus on a symbolic detail—like the scar on the protagonist's cheek or the adoring eyes of his companion—leaving the rest in semidarkness.

conceal their contempt for most industry regulars, whose cultural yahooism was a frequent target of their sardonic wit. To be invited to one of Lubitsch's famous Sundays was considered a rare honor, for among those who gathered at his home were such distinguished personalities as Brecht, Thomas Mann, Otto Klemperer, and Bruno Walter. Only the most sophisticated industry regulars were invited, and most of them were German or Austrian in their origins, like the worldly Marlene Dietrich, and the caustic wit, Billy Wilder. Others were eminent scientists, artists, and intellectuals who had fled from Hitler's Holocaust in Europe.

The concept of destiny haunts Lang's work like a recurring nightmare. Even his earliest scenarios for the German producer, Joe May, dealt with isolated individuals trapped in hostile environments. After he arrived in America, Lang tried to deemphasize the negative aspects of this theme by stressing not the outcome of the struggle but the need to fight. Classical tragedy exalted the human spirit even in the face of defeat, and it was this theme of spiritual triumph that he considered the highest achievement in art:

Classic tragedy was negative, in that it showed man trapped by Fate, as personified by the gods, drawn helplessly to his doom. In an age when man was puny in the face of nature, there was a magnificence in this concept which gave man, even in his almost inevitable failures, a sense of dignity. Too often, modern tragedy, unable to draw on a mystic belief in prearranged Fate, is *merely* negative, showing a triumph of evil and a waster of human life *for* nothing and *because* of nothing. It is this negativism which our audience rejects.

Machinery is a persistent motif of destiny in Lang's work. His movies are filled with vehicles, turbines, pistons, trains, and mechanical devices of many types. Machine metaphors were commonly employed by the German expressionists to symbolize the workings of organized society. Lang's German movies contain many images that are geometrically patterned like vast machine works. He also included mechanistic metaphors in his American films, though usually without violating the surface

Figure 9.6. Joan Bennett and Dan Duryea in *The Woman in the Window* (1944), distributed by RKO. Lang made four movies with Bennett as his leading lady. Unlike most of his other players, however, she had some kind words for her director: "Fritz was terribly exacting and demanding and working with him was sometimes abrasive, but he commanded great respect, and I performed better under his direction than at any other time in my career. Almost always I did what I was told, and we developed a great working rapport." Duryea was one of his finest actors, specializing in sleazy punks with a streak of sadism. In this film and *Scarlet Street,* he plays a blackmailer who looks out for Number One.

realism of his scenes. Like Zola, Lang used engines to symbolize forces inside the characters as well, especially the sex drive. Clocks are featured prominently in his films, and disaster is often precipitated by coincidences of timing. Lang's universe is logical and inexorable. "The action is like that of a neatly functioning machine," Paul Jensen has noted, "with each effect inevitably following its cause."

Lang also believed that human behavior is determined by emotional subcurrents that are only dimly understood. He probably derived this idea from Freud's theory of the subconscious. Lang thought that the process of artistic creation was essentially instinctive, and drew upon impulses which the artist probably couldn't explain rationally. "I think every director, subconsciously, imposes his character, his way of thinking, his way of life, his *personality* on his pictures." In his earliest German films, characters are neatly divided into good and evil, but by the time he made *M*, these traits are combined in a single personality who is unable to account for his "other self." In the American movies, double personalities are more common, and the characterization is more complex than the majority of his German works.

Lang is a master of that much-maligned genre, the melodrama. He preferred this form because it allows a high degree of abstraction in the story, without having to make too many concessions in the name of realism. Realism would distract him from his central purpose. Realistic film artists avoid melodramatic conventions because implicit in most forms of realism is a lack of overt manipulation of the narrative materials. Realistic plot structures are generally somewhat random in their development. Conflicts emerge unobtrusively; they aren't presented as *donnés*. Details don't always "mean" anything but are offered for their own sake, to heighten the sense of authenticity. The visual style of most realistic movies is artfully *négligé*, suggesting the casual clutter of everyday reality. Virtually all narrative artists must resort to some kind of abstraction, of course, otherwise their stories would be filled with the same dull stretches that typify everyday reality. The realist eliminates many—not all—of these undramatic elements as unobtrusively as possible.

The melodramatist not only makes no pretence at strict realism he actually heightens the artificiality of his genre in order to convey his vision more forcefully, without irrelevancies, as it were. Of course inferior artists in this genre are concerned with violence, contrivances, and sensation for their own sake. In the hands of a master like Lang, however, melodrama is a form of narrative distortion that can reveal underlying truths otherwise concealed beneath the surface disorder of reality. Lang's best movies are almost machinelike in their symmetry and suggest an air of inevitability. Details in his films are pointedly relevant to the action that follows. The images are seldom casually composed but represent precise symbolic ideas. "The typical Lang film is an exercise in the geometry of tragedy," Whittemore and Cecchettini have written. "Lang lays out his stories very carefully. Organized like mathematical proofs, his films lead toward a single conclusion. It is the careful precision of his construction which marks him as an artist." His best American movies have a well-made, almost schematic quality, allowing for no digressions.

Figure 9.7. Edward G. Robinson in *Scarlet Street* (1945), released by Universal.
Though Lang's American films are superficially more realistic than his German works, he preferred working in the studio to actual locations. Like many German-trained directors, he was strongly influenced by Reinhardt's ideal of "landscapes imbued with soul." The declared aim of most German expressionists was to eliminate nature for a state of absolute abstraction. The spidery branches in this scene suggest a symbolic cobweb, waiting to entangle the unwitting protagonist (Robinson). Lang believed that humans are innately guilty—though not necessarily of the specific crime a person might be accused of. In this movie, for example, moral punishments are meted out to all the major characters, but ironically, a technically innocent person (though a deserving swine) is convicted of a murder he didn't commit; the actual killer (Robinson), tormented with guilt, is not believed by the police when he confesses to the crime.

There are no accidents or extraneous details in his universe: Everything is ultimately relevant, especially apparent irrelevancies. Such isolated details might be likened to individual threads, which in conjunction with other threads, crisscross to imprison its victim in an inescapable web. As Jensen has noted, "These webs of circumstance, coincidence, bad luck, or evil continually ensnare Lang's 'heroes', who are really just specimens being objectively observed under controlled conditions."

Lang got many of his stories out of newspaper accounts. He kept clippings of articles he thought might serve as bases for movies. He worked on most of the scripts to his personal films, even though he didn't do much of the actual writing. He thought of himself as a script doctor rather than a writer. That is, he could detect flaws in the story construction and often suggested revisions or alternate scenes. When he was handed a completed script by his producers, Lang often reshaped it to reflect his thematic interests, unless it was a purely routine assignment. Like Hitchcock, he often thought in terms of striking scenes; then he integrated them into his stories. He preferred his scripts to resemble abstract equations, with the story divided into two sections, the second half neatly paralleling the first. Since his shooting schedules were gener-

Figure 9.8. Gary Cooper and Lilli Palmer in *Cloak and Dagger* (1946), distributed by Warner Brothers. Lang sometimes denied the influence of German expressionism in his movies, claiming each film must evolve its own style according to the subject matter. Though this is true to an extent, it's also not true, as this photo demonstrates. Viewers can judge for themselves: German expressionism rejected the documentary impulse in favor of an artificial stylization. Virtually all expressionist movies were shot in the studio, where visual effects could be controlled with precision, without the contaminations of nature. The style emphasized diagonal and broken lines, with deliberate violations in perspective and weird contrasts in scale. There was an emphasis on jagged, sharp, and pointed shapes, like knife blades. The lighting was dramatic, with high-contrast clashes, low-keyed atmospheric effects, and unreal configurations. Shafts of light and dark tear up the surface of the image. Often lights were placed low or in other off-beat sources, producing sinister, unexpected shadows. Actors were almost always subordinated to the mise-en-scène: Like pawns, they're trapped by their oppressive environments. Scenes were frequently photographed from extreme angles to heighten the sense of dislocation. German expressionism was also strongly symbolic and abstract. Its ideas were stark, with artistic nuances found in the richly textured style rather than the theme or characterization.

ally short, he liked to have his scripts as complete as possible before production.

Lang seldom explored the psychology of his characters in much depth. Usually they are sketchy and stylized, and in some cases, unconvincingly motivated. The workings of the plot take precedence over the workings of the characters' minds, which indeed are often as machinelike as the plots. In the German movies, crowds are often architecturalized into geometrical shapes, and characters are commonly presented as general types. In the American movies they're more concretely developed, in large part because the stars playing these roles brought with them an automatic characterization based on their iconography. Generally Lang remains aloof from his characters and their feelings. Emotions are presented objectively, as scientific variables, as it were. Normal characters—which he claimed didn't exist anyway—seldom excited his curiosity. He was concerned with the emotionally crippled, the driven, the obsessed. Most of his American films focus on tortured individuals, alone or supported only by a woman, struggling against robot-like adversaries.

Actors generally divided directors into two categories: those who were concerned with the performances and those who were obsessed with their visual style. Lang was a stylist. Like most directors of this type, he was considered unsympathetic to the problems of his players. He was overtly hostile to the star system and thought it detracted from the theme of a film, which he claimed was paramount. Needless to say, actors resented his attitude. Edward G. Robinson said of him, "He was autocratic, dominating, and extra-precise. He knew exactly what he wanted and he was going to get it, no matter what." During the production of *Woman in the Window,* Robinson got exasperated when the director spent a whole hour rearranging the folds in Joan Bennett's costume so that she would cast a certain type of shadow he wanted. Robinson also believed that Lang was thoughtless of his crews, who weren't too thrilled with his indifference to their convenience.

Henry Fonda—whose professionalism was praised by such notorious sadists as Ford, Wyler, and Preminger—disliked Lang intensely. "I couldn't get along with him at all," Fonda recounted. "He is an artist certainly. A creative artist. But he has no regard for his actors. It just doesn't occur to him that actors are human beings with hearts and instincts and other things." Lang kept Fonda waiting for three hours in one scene while the director corrected and recorrected the cobwebs on the set. Fonda was fuming in anger, for all the scene required was for him to enter the room, stand there a moment, and walk out. When he did turn his attention to his players, Lang sometimes rushed them, claiming that the shooting schedule didn't allow for frills. After rehearsing, he would shoot an entire scene from one direction; then he repeated the scene with the camera at a 180 degree reverse angle. "He was a master puppeteer," Fonda complained. "He literally tried to manipulate an actor. If he could, and the camera didn't pick it up, he would literally move your hand into a shot with his hand on you. He couldn't talk since it was in sound, but he would be waving his hands frantically at you, and it was very disconcerting."

Lang's insensitivity to actors is amply documented in the films themselves. True, there are some excellent performances in his movies, but for the most part by director-proof actors who are almost invariably good, most notably Fonda, Robinson, Spencer Tracy, Lee Marvin, and Dan Duryea. Most of the protagonists are played by serviceable leading men who generally did better work under other directors. Lang claimed he valued the contributions of his players. "I don't want to have 25 little Fritz Langs running around. I have too much respect for an actor." But the director was often evasive and contradictory in his interviews, which were mostly given in his old age, after he had mellowed somewhat. His highest praise was usually reserved for those players who gave him the least grief rather than their best work. For example, one of his favorite performances was by Marjorie Reynolds in the otherwise excellent *Ministry of Fear*. At best Reynolds is a conventional ingenue, at worst a mannequin on strings. Very likely Lang didn't *want* forceful, attractive stars, for his theme of depersonalization might then be weakened, if not contradicted.

What counted most for Lang was his mise-en-scène. Like a painter, he was acutely sensitive to every nuance of texture and lighting, to the architecture of his sets, to the symbolic implications of shapes, space, and placement within the frame. "Every scene has only one *exact* way it should be shot," he insisted. One reason why actors often complained of his methods was because he made his statements *visually*, by the way the players are positioned within the mise-en-scène. On the other hand, close shots, which he avoided, are favored by performers because these ranges are best suited to capturing acting nuances.

Lang was an important practitioner of a style which the French called *film noir*, or black cinema as it's sometimes referred to by Anglo-American critics. As early as 1937, with *You Only Live Once*, the director introduced certain *noir* elements, though the style is generally associated with the American cinema of the 1940s and early 1950s. *Noir* cuts across generic classifications and can be seen in gangster films, detective thrillers, urban melodramas, and even women's pictures. Its stylistic and psychological antecedents go back to German expressionism, though *noir* usually preserves at least a surface realism. Native influences have been traced to the gangster movies of the early 1930s, especially those produced by Warner Brothers, which were generally more moody and violent than those of other studios. The "hard-boiled" fiction of such novelists as Dashiell Hammett, James M. Cain, and Raymond Chandler also exerted an influence on the development of this style. In fact, several of their novels were adapted by important directors of this era, most notably Huston, Hawks, and Wilder.

The tone of *noir* is nasty, cynical, and paranoid. It's suffused with pessimism, emphasizing the darker aspects of the human condition. Its themes characteristically revolve around violence, betrayal, greed, lust, depravity, and corruption—a far cry from the optimism of the prewar American cinema. This grimness of tone strikes some present-day viewers as lurid, but social conditions during this period hardly encouraged a benevolent view of humanity. It's not coincidental, perhaps, that many of the best American *noir* directors were Jews and political ref-

Figure 9.9. Marlene Dietrich and Arthur Kennedy (standing) in *Rancho Notorious* (1952), distributed by RKO. Lang's French admirers considered this movie an "existential western" because of its emphasis on choice and free will. As Lang explained, "Every human being makes his own fate by the way in which he uses his experience (or does not use his experience), by the choice or rejection of events and situations he partakes in, by what he manages to achieve or not to achieve, for whatever reasons. No mystical fate, no God or whatever is responsible for his fate *except himself*. And this is why one cannot get away from what one has created for oneself." His protagonists are seldom merely victims of fate. They are free to choose their course of action, even if their situations seem hopeless. Many of his characters are motivated by revenge, but they spiritually short-circuit themselves by excluding all other human emotions. Paradoxically, the characters often end up as machinelike as the original perpetrators of evil. In such movies as *Rancho Notorious, Fury,* and *The Big Heat,* Lang explores how an obsessive vengeance can blur the distinctions between good and evil, guilt and innocence, legality and justice.

ugees who had fled from Europe as Hitler's troops goosestepped across the continent. Among these expatriots, in addition to Lang, were Billy Wilder, Fred Zinnemann, Jean Renoir, Otto Preminger, Robert Siodmak, Anatol Litvak, and Max Ophüls. Many of their works of the 1940s are especially gripping in their portrayals of persecutions, manhunts, and frustrated attempts at flight and escape. A deeply felt sense of helplessness and terror characterizes these movies.

Many *films noirs* deal with themes of sexual neurosis. Such perversions as sadism, masochism, and incest are at least hinted at. Repressed homosexual undertones characterize some male relationships. There is also a streak of misogyny that runs through *noir* movies. In fact, the early

Figure 9.10. *The Big Heat*, **with Gloria Grahame and Lee Marvin, produced by Columbia Pictures.** Violence is often perpetrated against women in Lang's films. In this movie, for example, Grahame has half her face hideously disfigured by scalding coffee which Marvin throws at her in a fury. Pictured here, she has just taken her revenge by scalding his face in like savagery and is offering him a closer view of what awaits him. Her mutilated face is a variation of the *doppelgänger* motif—one side of her face is beautiful, the other side terrifying.

1940s saw the creation of a new genre cycle, the "deadly female" films, which centered on corrupt and exploitive seductresses. Some are out-and-out bitches, like the Joan Bennett roles in *Woman in the Window* and *Scarlet Street*. Women in *film noir* are frequently portrayed as tawdry, cheap, and selfish. Few of them can be trusted, especially when money is at stake.

The milieu of *noir* is almost exclusively urban. Titles commonly suggest nightmarish cityscapes by including such words as *street, night, dark, fear, city,* and *sleep.* The films are profuse in images of the city: dark streets glistening after a rain or crouching in the fog; cigarette smoke swirling lazily in dimly lit cocktail lounges; symbols of fragility, such as widowpanes, sheer clothing, glasses, and mirrors. The city is cobwebbed by side streets, alleys, and gutters. There are also many images of entrapment, such as tunnels, subways, elevators, and train cars. Often the settings are locations of transience, like grubby rented rooms, streets, piers, railroad yards, and bus terminals.

Despite the low budgets of many of these films, they are often exquisitely photographed. *Noir* ushered in a decade of brilliant black-

and-white cinematography, for the style attracted some of the most gifted lighting cameramen in the industry: Lee Garmes, Milton Krasner, Lucien Ballard, John Seitz, and Sol Polito, to mention only a few. *Noir* is a world of night and shadow. Some of Lang's most powerful scenes are photographed with the characters seen in silhouette or wrapped in fog. His images are rich in sensuous textures, like neon-lit streets, windshields streaked with mud, and shafts of light streaming through the windows of lonely rooms. Characters are imprisoned behind ornate lattices and grillwork. Foreground elements, like gauzy curtains, potted palms, and drifting cigarette smoke, prevent us from seeing the characters clearly. Visual designs emphasize jagged shapes and violated surfaces. Most of Lang's movies in this style were photographed in the

Figure 9.11. Gloria Grahame in *Human Desire* (1954), screenplay by Alfred Hayes, based on the novel, *La Bête Humaine* (The Human Beast) by Émile Zola, produced by Columbia Pictures. Lang didn't believe that Fate was a supernatural force. His determinism was essentially materialist and dealt with the "real" world of chance, the social order, and human nature itself. The forces that grind humans down are ideological, psychological, and environmental. In this respect he resembled the great French author, Zola, whose pessimistic theory of naturalism was based on the precepts of science. Zola believed that beneath their civilized veneer, all humans are victimized by their animal instincts, their heredity, and their social milieu: "There dwells in each of us a beast, caged only by what we have been taught to believe is right or wrong. When we forget these teachings, the beast in us is unleashed in all its fury." Frequently Lang's protagonists meet their destiny in the form of a *femme fatale,* who sexually ensnares her victim, then leads him to his inevitable destruction.

studio, where he could control his lighting effects with exactitude. But even when he used actual locations in the 1950s, they look forboding and surrealistic, like landscapes recalled from a nightmare.

Few directors could equal Lang's use of the frame as a symbolic device. Sinister shadows often invade the frame before the entrance of the character. Terrifying violence occurs off-screen, while we are presented only with a character's horrified reaction. Off-screen darkness frequently symbolizes a world of guilty secrets and unseen malevolence. In *The Big Heat,* for example, a scheming blackmailer is shot down by an off-screen killer who is "behind" the camera. The camera remains on her inert corpse for a moment; then the gun is thrown into the frame, falling on the floor with a thud of finality. Lang used his frame as a kind of visual prison. The edges are sealed off, suggesting no avenue of escape. He was capable of creating unnerving effects by opening a sequence with the camera in an empty room, "waiting" for someone to enter. These anticipatory setups suggest an eerie vacuum, for we never know what's going to happen. Because we feel more secure in knowing the nature of a threat, no matter how awesome, lack of action can be more fearful than action itself.

Lang was also a master of camera placement. He preferred long shots because they are more objective and permit the viewer to observe events without becoming emotionally involved. (Edited sequences of closer shots tend to draw the viewer into the action.) He insisted that camera movement must express ideas and emotions, and though he preferred stationary setups, he occasionally moved his camera to create a sense of anxiety or a floating, dreamlike effect. He also favored high angles, the angle of destiny as it's been called, because it provides us with a kind of Olympian omniscience in which the characters below seem powerless and vulnerable. Especially in the longer ranges, high-angle shots reduce characters to abstract patterns. Dominated from above, they resemble trapped animals in a maze.

The director's artistic shortcomings usually involved his inability to portray normal life. "Lang functions best with the dark and demonic," Jensen has noted, "and outside this realm he is ill at ease." The director's domestic and love scenes are usually wooden, his rare attempts at humor disastrous. He was too solemn to capture the spontaneity of people and incapable of depicting happiness convincingly. His anti-Nazi movies are flawed by their didacticism, usually in the form of sententious speeches which add little or nothing to the visual presentation of his themes. Lang sometimes had a tin ear for dialogue, especially in his earlier American movies, which were made when his command of English was shaky. In *Hangmen Also Die,* for example, Czech and German characters occasionally speak in an incongruous gangster argot, like "Keep quiet, or you get a slug in the gut." Lang was more eloquent when he used only silence— especially in his sound films, in which the lack of music and dialogue often creates suspenseful, empty spaces in the action.

He ended his career rather ignominiously. He was invited back to West Germany to direct remakes of his earlier successes, but only his final movie, *The Thousand Eyes of Dr. Mabuse* (1961) recaptured some of

Figure 9.12. *While the City Sleeps* **(1956), with John Barrymore, Jr., distributed by RKO.** In this, Lang's last American movie, he explores how a group of newspaper people capitalize on a series of sensational sex murders. "The desire to hurt, the desire to kill," Lang noted, "is closely joined to the sexual urge, under whose dictate no man acts reasonably." Lang refused to divide people into normal and deviant classes. He insisted that these labels merely represent different degrees on the same continuum: "Gradually, and at times reluctantly, I have come to the conclusion that every human mind harbors a latent compulsion to murder." Lang's film doesn't focus on the murderer alone (pictured) but also on those who profit from murder.

his former verve. After that he returned to the United States because his eyesight was failing fast. During his active career, his American films were often condemned by influential critics for their melodramatic contrivances and lack of realism, which they claimed weakened his social criticism. But realism and social commentary are incidental to Lang's art, as the *Cahiers* critics pointed out. In his final years, the director was virtually deified by the French. A profusion of critical articles and interviews was published throughout the later 1950s. In the 1960s, booklength studies of his films were published in France by such critics as Luc Moullet, Francis Courtade, Alfred Eibel, Michel Mourlet, and Lotte Eisner. Unfortunately, only Eisner's volume has been translated into English. But Lang wasn't bitter about his comparative critical neglect in his adopted land. America was the only country where he felt at home. On his tombstone, he had inscribed, "Fritz Lang, born in Vienna 1890, died in Hollywood, 1976."

BIBLIOGRAPHY

ARMOUR, ROBERT A. *Fritz Lang.* Boston: Twayne Publishers, 1978. Critical study. Filmography and selected bibliography.

BOGDANOVICH, PETER. *Fritz Lang in America.* New York: Praeger, 1969. A book-length interview. Filmography.

EISNER, LOTTE H. *Fritz Lang.* New York: Oxford University Press, 1977. Includes discussions of all his films. Bibliography and filmography. See also Eisner's *The Haunted Screen: Expressionism in the German Cinema and the Influence of Max Reinhardt* (Berkeley: University of California Press, 1973).

"Fritz Lang," in *Dialogue on Film.* The American Film Institute (April, 1974). Other interviews include Harry M. Geduld, ed., "Happily Ever After," in *Film Makers on Film Making* (Bloomington: Indiana University Press, 1969); and Andrew Sarris, ed., "Fritz Lang," in *Interviews with Film Directors* (New York: Avon Books, 1967).

JENSEN, PAUL M. *The Cinema of Fritz Lang.* Cranbury, N.J.: A. S. Barnes, 1969. A critical analysis, including both the German and American works. Bibliography and filmography.

KRACAUER, SIEGFRIED. *From Caligari to Hitler.* New York: Noonday Press, 1959. A psychological and sociological study of the German cinema, with much material on Lang and the political context of his films. See also George A. Huaco, "German Expressionism," in *The Sociology of Film Art* (New York: Basic Books, 1965); and Roger Manvell and Heinrich Fraenkel, *The German Cinema* (New York: Praeger, 1971).

LANG, FRITZ, AND BARTLETT CORMACK. *Fury,* in *Twenty Best Film Plays.* John Gassner and Dudley Nichols, eds. New York: Crown Publishers, 1943. See also Lang and Thea von Harbou, *M* (New York: Simon & Schuster, 1969).

McARTHUR, COLIN. *Underworld USA.* New York: Viking, 1972. Contains a chapter on Lang and much material on the iconography of urban melodramas. See also Paul Schrader, "Notes on *Film Noir,*" in *Film Comment* (Spring, 1972); Raymond Durgnat, "The Family Tree of *Film Noir,*" in *Cinema* (Great Britain, August, 1970); Lawrence Alloway, *Violent America: The Movies 1946–1964* (New York: Museum of Modern Art, 1971); and "Film Noir," in *Film Comment* (November-December, 1974): a collection of articles by Stephen Farber and others.

STEEN, MIKE, ed. *Hollywood Speaks.* New York: Putnam's, 1974. Contains an interview with Henry Fonda about Lang and other directors.

WHITTEMORE, DON, AND PHILIP ALAN CECCHETTINI, eds. "Fritz Lang," in *Passport to Hollywood.* New York: McGraw-Hill, 1976. Critical analysis and articles by Gavin Lambert and others. Also include Lang's 1947 article, "The Freedom of the Screen."

Roughing It

The Cinema of John Huston

Figure 10.1 Publicity photo of Huston during the production of *Key Largo* (1948), a Warner Brothers-First National Picture. "John is one of the world's great romantics," said writer Truman Capote, "with *grand luxe* tastes in food, clothes, and women." Huston has always thrived on unpredictability, adventure, anything challenging. Women have found him attractive: He has been married five times and has had a number of highly publicized love affairs. He has also been known to be fickle in his affections, moody, and self-destructive. He is a high-stakes gambler and an even more profligate spender. In 1952 he moved his family to Ireland, where he purchased a princely estate. The manor was superbly furnished with *objects d'art* from all over the world. He owns distinguished works in a variety of styles and periods, and his collection of pre-Columbian art is one of the finest in the world. In his celebrated profile, "Undirectable Director," James Agee expressed amazement at Huston's intellectual breadth. His interviews are sprinkled with allusions to sports, politics, and virtually all the arts. His vocabulary ranges from words of four letters to eight syllables.

uston is one of the legendary personalities of the American cinema. A man of unpredictable extremes, he has been described as part hoodlum, part adventurer, and part intellectual. "Huston has more color than 90 percent of the actors in Hollywood," said his longtime collaborator and fellow rebel, Humphrey Bogart. The director was a child of the Roaring Twenties, and no one roared louder or lived and played harder. He has directed over thirty-five movies, including such classic works as *The Maltese Falcon, The Treasure of the Sierra Madre,* and *The African Queen.* Though his main concern is with revealing character, Huston is a born storyteller who spins a good yarn. His tone is harsh, unsentimental, and often comic. He's had his ups and downs in his career as a writer-director, but he always bounces back. One of his finest works, *The Man Who Would Be King,* was made when he was seventy years old. "Huston has the ability to take life without ducking," said the great

Italian filmmaker, Vittorio De Sica; "the world rushes on and most directors either go dead in the head or lose courage. Huston's got it in the head and his belly's full of courage."

> *The rewards of life are gained in the process of* seeking *a goal, not in the actual attainment.*
>
> —*John Huston*

Huston was born in 1906 in Nevada, Missouri. His father, Walter Huston, was an aspiring actor who achieved fame in the mid-1920s on the New York stage and later in the movies. John's mother was a newspaperwoman, who wrote under the name of Rhea Gore. His parents divorced when he was a boy, and for many years he was shuffled back and forth between them. He traveled a great deal with his father, whose performing at this time was confined to the gaudier branches of the theatrical trade, mostly touring the sticks. But John and his father enjoyed each other's company, and besides, the youth was fascinated by the lowlife he encountered in the various fleapits they called home. His mother enjoyed traveling too, but her tastes ran to swanky hotels. She loved horses and was pleased that her son shared this enthusiasm. A compulsive gambler, she was also often broke. She was a strong-willed woman who disliked any form of fantasy, and she was impatient with the romanticism of her son. Even as an adult, Huston believed that she never really approved of him. He was molded by her, however, and acquired her taste for literature, horses, travel, luxury, and gambling.

When he was a teenager, John was striken by a mysterious ailment which was diagnosed as an enlarged heart "with complications."He was confined to bed and told not to leave it at the risk of death. Before long, he felt himself slipping into a spiritual paralysis. He decided to rebel and damn the consequences. He sneaked off one night to go swimming in a nearby river, which also had a dangerous waterfall. When he survived this ordeal, he reenacted his secret ritual nightly. Several months later, he pronounced himself cured to his astonished mother. He remained a nonconformist from that time onward.

As a youth, Huston leaped from interest to interest, cramming a lifetime of experience into a few years. He attended high school briefly in Los Angeles but quit in order to go to art school, where he became fascinated with modern abstract painting. He developed a taste for Balzac and other French authors, whom he read (in French) on his own. He was also interested in opera and ballet and even hoped to be an opera singer for a brief period. Boxing was another of his passions. By the time he was seventeen, he was the California lightweight amateur champion and had won twenty-three out of twenty-five matches.

When he was nineteen, he accelerated his pace. His father was now in New York, where he was attracting some fame as a stage actor. John joined him there, living in the heady atmosphere of Greenwich Village.

While his father was rehearsing in Eugene O'Neill's new play, *Desire Under the Elms,* John attended the rehearsals, absorbing everything he could about playwriting and performance. O'Neill became his idol and is still his favorite author. Huston's interests remained eclectic. He attended many sporting events, frequented the art galleries, mixed easily with theatre people, and often got spectacularly drunk. He met and talked with some of the most distinguished literary figures of the 1920s, including O'Neill, Theodore Dreiser, Sinclair Lewis, and F. Scott Fitzgerald. The youth tried his hand at many activities, including acting, writing, singing, and painting. He was considered clever, unpredictable, wild. "John will either come into something extraordinary," his father prophesied, "or he'll be no good." He continued his interest in horses and even joined the Mexican cavalry in order to be on their equestrian team.

In the late 1920s, he decided to try his hand at fiction, imitating another idol, Ernest Hemingway. To Huston's surprise, one of his stories, "Fool," was accepted in 1929 by *The American Mercury,* the most prestigious literary magazine in America, which was edited by H. L. Mencken. Soon after, "Figures of Fighting Men," another story, was accepted by *The American Mercury.* Other pieces appeared in *Esquire, Theatre Arts, Sports Illustrated,* and the New York *Times.* He wrote in a lean, virile prose, dealing with his experiences in Mexico and emphasizing such subjects as fighting, whoring, gambling, and drinking. Critic Eugene Archer has pointed out that Huston's artistic sensibility was shaped by this phase of his life:

> His character was clearly formed by the social forces predominant in the twenties, the disillusionment with large causes and the emphasis on experience for its own sake—violent action, boxing, travel, war—expressed in the spare, unadorned prose style typical of the period.

Archer has noted that Hemingway and Huston are very close in their philosophical outlook. "I think Hemingway probably influenced everyone of my generation," Huston said. The two later became friends and occasionally went deep-sea fishing together. The only screenplay of his work that the novelist liked was that of *The Killers,* which Huston had coauthored with Anthony Veiller. Hemingway was pleased when Huston told him he was slated to direct *A Farewell to Arms* in 1957. But his friend David O. Selznick was producing the project as a vehicle for his wife, Jennifer Jones, and when the director realized that the original material was going to be deemphasized as a result, Huston withdrew from the project.

In 1930 he went to Hollywood to work as a scenarist for Goldwyn, but nothing came of the job. Walter Huston was now a star at Universal, and he finagled a writing job there for his son. He was assigned as a dialogue writer for *A House Divided* (1931), which starred the elder Huston and was directed by William Wyler. Wyler became a close friend, advisor, and fellow hellion. But young Huston soon grew restless and bored with the Hollywood scene, so he took off for London, where he nearly starved. Then for a year and a half he lived in Paris, where he studied painting, living in picturesque squalor. Throughout this period, he also wrote stage plays, though none of them was produced.

In 1937, at the age of thirty-one, he returned to Hollywood, where he got a job as a writer at Warner Brothers. His salary was $750 a week, a princely income for a man who had lived a hand-to-mouth existence for several years. Not that Huston held on to his money. He often gambled away his entire paycheck. But his attitude on these matters has always been cavalier: "The one great lesson you've got to learn about gambling," he claimed, "is that money doesn't mean a goddam thing." At Warners, producer Henry Blanke took a fatherly interest in the young writer, though often his protégé resisted Blanke's steadying influence. "Just a drunken boy, hopelessly immature," the producer recalled. "You'd see him at every party, wearing bangs, with a monkey on his shoulder. Charming. Very talented but without an ounce of discipline in his makeup." On many occasions Blanke had to argue with Jack Warner to retain Huston, who refused to abide by the mogul's rigid schedules and regulations.

Warners was known as a good writer's studio. In the early 1930s, its cocky young production chief, Darryl F. Zanuck (a former writer), proclaimed that henceforth the studio would concentrate on contemporary social issues, especially exposé films, gangster movies, and pictures dealing with injustices against "little people"—working-class Americans. Gangsters were often portrayed sympathetically, and the films argued that crime was the result of social exploitation and public indifference to poverty. Warner Brothers was the only major studio that encouraged its writers to deal with social problems. Their movies were publicized with the motto, "Torn from Today's Headlines!" (most of them with an emphasis on the exclamation point). Though Zanuck left the studio in 1933, he was largely responsible for creating the Warners style of this era: fast, gritty, immediate. The lighting was often moody, the décor stripped to starkness. *The Maltese Falcon* (1941) is a classic example of the Warners look of this period.

"We took ourselves very seriously as writers," Huston recalled of his early years at Warners. "There was a good deal of talent in the writers' building there." Though most scripts were written by teams, scenarists took pride in their craftsmanship. Producers like Blanke and Hal B. Wallis were receptive to original story ideas and encouraged writers to experiment with offbeat materials and approaches. Huston's fellow scribes at Warners included his close friend, Howard Koch, as well as Delmer Daves, Casey Robonson, Seton I. Miller, Richard Brooks, William Faulkner, and Julius and Philip Epstein. There were very few women writers at the studio, and those that were felt vaguely unwanted.

Despite this more adventurous atmosphere, writers were subjected to numerous indignities. Jack Warner ran his studio like a prison. Employees were required to punch in and out every day. The writers' building was surrounded by a high fence, thus forcing its inmates to file past Warner's window so he could keep tabs on who came to work late and who left early. Writers dubbed the building "The Buchenwald of Burbank." Huston was almost always late. But talent had its attendant privileges: His scripts were usually successful—as Blanke repeatedly had

Figure 10.2. Humphrey Bogart and Mary Astor in *The Maltese Falcon* (1941), with Peter Lorre and Sydney Greenstreet, produced by Warner Brothers. Huston surprised many industry skeptics by his thoroughness and professionalism in making this famous film. Everything was worked out in advance as much as possible. He made drawings for every setup, complete with camera instructions and details for the mise-en-scène. The movie was completed in two months, at the relatively low cost of $300,000. It was a huge success, both with the public and the critics. James Agee, who was to become Huston's most ardent critical champion, called the film "the best private-eye melodrama ever made," a judgment many critics would be reluctant to dispute even to this day.

to point out to Warner whenever he wanted to fire the rebellious writer. Huston's script for *Dr. Ehrlich's Magic Bullet* won an Academy Award nomination in 1940. His scenario for *High Sierra,* directed by Raoul Walsh in 1941, was a turning point not only for Huston but also for Humphrey Bogart, who was to become one of his closest friends and frequent collaborators in the years ahead. Before this time, Bogart was typecast as villainous gangsters, and though he also played a gangster in *High Sierra,* the role allowed for more subtlety and humanity in the performance. Suddenly Bogart became a viable leading man, and much of his best work after 1941 was done under Huston's direction.

Huston had the foresight to insist that if *High Sierra* proved successful—it was a big hit—he would be allowed to direct as well as write his next picture. He was fortunate to begin his directing career at Warners, for the studio's hard-hitting masculine tradition suited him just fine. Nonetheless, working there was a mixed blessing. Jack Warner was autocratic, and his taste in movies was lamentable, though in no way

Figure 10.3. Humphrey Bogart in *The Treasure of the Sierra Madre* (1948), with Tim Holt, screenplay by Huston, based on the novel by B. Traven, a Warner Brothers-First National Picture. James Agee noted that the better the original material, the better Huston functions as an artist. Of course as a writer himself, Huston is perfectly aware that language can seldom be preserved intact in movies. "I try to penetrate first to the basic idea of the book or the play, and then work with those ideas in cinematic terms." But there is more of Huston than Traven in this film. Huston emphasized the story's universal qualities and turned it into a wry parable of the human condition. Other trademarks include the lack of glamor, the masculine tone, and the ironic "Huston ending." See James Naremore, ed., *The Treasure of the Sierra Madre* (Madison: University of Wisconsin Press, 1979).

approaching the pristine banality of MGM's Louis B. Mayer, as Huston later discovered. Warner at least was willing to trust his producers, whose artistic judgment was much sharper. Furthermore, like many of the moguls, Warner was only partly agrieved by people with guts enough to stand up to him. He complained mightily about Huston's insolence, but he conceded that the firebrand had talent—and especially a talent for aggravating his frayed nerves.

Warner's frayed nerves were legendary. He battled with almost everybody, including his less famous brothers, who often complained of the way Jack ran the studio. There were twelve children in all, though only four of the brothers were in the picture business. They were born of Polish Jewish immigrants and grew up in Youngstown, Ohio. In the teens they invested in a series of nickelodeons. Later they switched to production, and though the studio suffered many financial setbacks, by the 1920s Warner Brothers began its slow ascendency. Its breakthrough into the majors came in 1927, when the studio revolutionized the industry with the introduction of talkies. By 1930, Warners was powerful enough to absorb First National, with its huge chain of eight hundred theatres. It was now the most successful studio in Hollywood.

Jack Warner had every intention of keeping it that way. Employees worked very hard, and salaries were the lowest of the majors. Insurrections erupted periodically, especially among the stars—a feisty lot. Primarily they complained of their trashy roles but also their insufficient compensation. The principal insurrectionists were Bette Davis, James Cagney, Olivia De Havilland, and Bogart. These four incurred more suspensions than any other contract players in Hollywood. Davis, the queen of the lot, was the chief troublemaker. She was Warner's crown of thorns, but her complaints were mostly justified. She was often forced to act in potboilers, supported by tepid leading men and directed by hacks. In desperation she sometimes took over the direction herself, and if anyone interfered, she stormed to the front office, swelling her indignation in waves as she passed each secretary's desk. By the time she reached Jack Warner's office, her fury was full wroth: "Mr. Warner . . ." she inevitably began in launching her tirades. And the mogul was then subjected to another scornful harangue about the lack of creative talent on the lot. Bogart enjoyed tormenting his tormentor by getting mean drunk, calling him up in the middle of the night, and barraging him with such soubriquets as "creep." The next morning, the star duly apologized to his boss—who never could understand Bogart's sardonic rituals of humor. For Warner, such mortifications were all in a day's work. He entitled his autobiography *My First Hundred Years in Hollywood*.

The directors at Warners were also a tempestuous lot—or at least the successful ones were. "Wild Bill" Wellman was known to carry loaded firearms on the set as a warning to recalcitrant actors and crews. The Hungarian immigrant, Michael Curtiz, was a notorious bully who tolerated no interference from anyone. Even Davis was cowed by Curtiz. When she complained that the director hadn't allowed her any break for lunch, he replied majesterially, "When you work with me, you don't need lunch. You just take an aspirin." Warner tolerated these sadists because their pictures usually made money, whereas movies by subservient employees often failed at the box office. He kept the ruffians; the nice guys were let go.

When Huston began his directing career in 1941, he didn't join the Warners' tradition of bullying. Since he didn't like being dictated to himself, he treated his collaborators with courtesy and professional respect—a policy he tried to maintain throughout his career. He decided to make a movie version of Dashiell Hammett's novel, *The Maltese Falcon*, which had been adapted twice before at Warners—twice poorly. Huston wanted to preserve as much of the unsentimental, hard-boiled starkness as the original. His screenplay was virtually a transcription of the novel, with most of the dialogue taken directly from the book. Huston's celebrated brilliance in casting was apparent even in his directorial debut. Bogart played the cynical detective, Sam Spade. Mary Astor, who had been wasted in mediocre films for most of her career, played the trecherously seductive Brigid O'Shaughnessy. In supporting roles were Sydney Greenstreet and Peter Lorre, both first-rate actors who became

Figure 10.4. *The Asphalt Jungle* (1950), with Marilyn Monroe and Louis Calhern, an MGM Picture. One of the most tender relationships in this caper film is between an aging sugar daddy and his childlike mistress. It was Marilyn's first important role, and Huston was pleased with her performance. Generally the director prefers stories that are somewhat allegorical, as his symbolic titles suggest. His best works have the rigor of a cautionary tale. He advocates a graceful and stoical acceptance of life's perverse ironies. His plots are filled with harsh twists of fate or unexpected strokes of good fortune. Huston believes that a person comes to know himself best during a time of crisis or in a threatening environment. "It's how well we behave under duress" that is for him the final gauge of a person's worth. Usually he's drawn to losers and outsiders, and their defeat is all the more poignant because they never seem to expect it. Often they deserve better.

Warner regulars. Huston subsequently directed two other films at the studio, but neither of them approached the stature of *Falcon*.

When World War II broke out, he enlisted in the Army Signal Corps and was sent to the Aleutian Islands to make a documentary on the war in the Pacific. He flew on fifteen attack missions over Japanese controlled territory, and his planes were often fired upon by antiaircraft artillery. *Report From the Aleutians* (1943) was the result. Then he was sent to Italy, where he made the powerful *Battle of San Pietro* (1945), which is perhaps the finest combat documentary of the war. In 1945, he was instructed to make a documentary about war veterans suffering from emotional disorders. *Let There Be Light* was so uncompromising in its authenticity that the War Department refused to release it. To this day, it is banned for public exhibition. Huston regards it as one of his major works. Like many veterans of the war, he was deeply altered, both as a man and as an artist, by what he had seen:

> That whole time was something unforgettable and lives with me. It gave me a sense of the reality of human behavior as against the conventions that the Hollywood screen rather cannibalistically had come to accept as behavior. It also inculcated in me a vast desire to work away from the studios, not within the walls of a sound stage.

After the war, Huston returned to his first love, the live theatre. Actually, he never entirely abandoned his theatrical aspirations. In 1940 he had directed his father on Broadway in *A Passenger to Bali,* which flopped. In 1941 he and Howard Koch wrote *In Time to Come,* which was directed by Otto Preminger. It also failed to attract audiences, though it was a *succès d'estime,* and won the New York Drama Critics Circle Award as the best play of the 1941–1942 season. After he was discharged from

Figure 10.5. *The Red Badge of Courage* **(1951), screenplay by Huston, based on the novel by Stephen Crane.** This film precipitated a power struggle at MGM between Louis B. Mayer and the young production chief, Dore Schary. Mayer detested Huston's previous pictures, which the old mogul thought were "filled with nasty ugly people." He also disliked Crane's novel because it was "full of blood and killing, has got no laughs, no songs, no entertainment value." Who else but Huston would want to direct it, the mogul asked in exasperation. The film was poorly received by preview audiences. The front office panicked, ordered it cut by a third (to a mere sixty-nine minutes), and exhibited it on the lower half of double bills. Though it received excellent critical reviews and is regarded as one of Huston's finest works, the picture lost money. The story behind the movie would make a great Huston movie.

the army, he directed Jean-Paul Sartre's important philosophical play, *No Exit*. But Sartre's existentialism went over the heads of most audiences, and the play closed after only thirty-one performances. It too won critical praise, however, and received the New York Drama Critics Circle Award as best foreign play of 1946.

In 1947, Huston returned to Warner Brothers. His first project was *The Treasure of the Sierra Madre* (1948). It reunited him with Bogart, who played the crafty paranoid, Fred C. Dobbs, and with Walter Huston, who played a garrulous old prospector. The movie was successful, and critics were virtually unanimous in their acclaim. The film's harsh, sardonic humor and its ironic ending (which Jack Warner loathed) were singled out for particular praise by critics. Huston won the New York Film Critics Award as best director of 1948. He also won two Academy Awards, one for directing, the other for his screenplay. His greatest satisfaction came from the Academy Award for best supporting actor, which went to Walter Huston. The director was now firmly reestablished. He stayed at Warners for another year, then free-lanced (usually as a producer-director) with several studios on short-term contracts.

Huston has enjoyed an unusual degree of autonomy within the industry. "I can do pretty much what I set out to do. I've been lucky." Since his early movies were highly successful, he had no need to prove himself. In the 1950s, he set up his own production company, Horizon Films, with the respected producer, Sam Spiegel (also known as S. P. Eagle). Their most distinguished production was the highly acclaimed *The African Queen* (1952). Though some of Huston's later works failed at the box office, he continued to remain his own man. He seldom made compromises in his work, and he claims that most of his errors were his own:

> I've always been a misfit in this industry. They can't quite figure me out. I've made some mistakes, some whoppers. But I hate the system—and I'm free of it so long as I can tell anyone to go to hell in a bucket! I'm free to make a damn fool of myself or to do something wonderful. The choice is mine and that's what counts.

Huston's contempt for bullies has also been directed at political opportunists. During the witch-hunts of the late 1940s and early 1950s (see Chapter 14), he and such fellow liberals as Bogart and Wyler spoke out against the House Committee on Un-American Activities, a committee they considered itself to be un-American. "I'm against *anybody* who tries to tell anybody else what to do," the director said.

Huston was one of the first American directors of the postwar period to shoot on location, mostly in exotic foreign climes. He says that he has always turned to life for truth, not to convention or to his own ego. Sound stages are fine for stylized fantasies but compromising for realistic stories. His mania for realism has been rough on his actors and crews. For example, in shooting *Heaven Knows, Mr. Allison* (1957), Robert Mitchum twisted his ankle, almost drowned when he was dragged underwater by a 300-pound turtle which plunged perilously close to a coral reef, and skinned his chest raw when he was required to

Figure 10.6. Humphrey Bogart and Katharine Hepburn in *The African Queen* (1952), distributed by United Artists. This film was made in the Belgian Congo, where the cast and crew had to endure blistering heat and where the native leprosy rate was seventy percent. The company lived in the jungle for ten weeks, where they encountered dysentery and such unexpected guests as flesh-eating safari ants. Bogart decided to remain soddenly drunk whenever he was off-camera. He had a theory that enormous amounts of alcohol in the bloodstream would repel disease-carrying insects. Interestingly, Huston—also a heavy drinker—and Bogart were the only two members of the company who didn't get sick. "The entire adventure was rather enchanting," Huston cooed at the completion of the project. The public and critics apparently agreed. The film was one of Huston's biggest grossers. Bogart won a well-deserved Academy Award for his performance as the lovable drunk, Charlie Allnutt.

slide down a palm tree. "You work for John, you suffer," said the stoical Mitchum; "what else can you expect?" Sickness and accidents are the only predictable elements on Huston's projects. During the making of *Moby Dick* (1956), actor Richard Basehart broke three bones, Leo Genn slipped a disk in his back and got pneumonia, Gregory Peck damaged his kneecap, and dozens of others were injured at sea. The enormous rubberized whale was lost several times, and the ship's mast snapped three times during turbulent weather. The project took thirty-five weeks to shoot, mostly on the open seas. A crucial scene required Peck to be lashed to the back of the huge artificial whale and repeatedly plunged underwater—an extremely dangerous stunt, especially if the crew failed to bring the whale back to the surface in time for Peck to regain his breath. "I could have *really* come up dead," Peck recalled with a shudder, "which I think would have secretly pleased John—providing the last touch of realism he was after."

Huston's period films are meticulously accurate in their authenticity. During the making of *Moby Dick,* he insisted that real whales had to be hunted in the same manner that they were in 1840. Twenty whales were actually harpooned in the cause of realism. He also wanted the storms to be authentic, even if it meant that their fragile ship would be lacerated by savage waves, rain, and winds. In order to re-create the nineteenth-century Massachusetts port of New Bedford, Huston commandeered an entire Irish seaport village and had false fronts constructed for the buildings. His reconstructions of the past are seldom glossy or glamorized. Even a fabled setting like the kingdom of Kafiristan in *The Man Who Would Be King* (1976) is steeped in the flavor of Kipling's nineteenth century.

Huston's thematic range is more varied than some critics have allowed, though to be sure, certain ideas and motifs recur throughout his works. "The pursuit of the quarry is when a man is most alive," he has claimed; "the rewards or the benefits or the conclusion isn't all that important." Many of his movies are structured around a quest of some kind, which tests the courage and endurance of his characters. Often they fail, especially in their search for riches. The director's bitter and ironic conclusions to such films as *The Asphalt Jungle* (1950) and *Beat the Devil* (1953) came to be known in the trade as "the Huston ending." Characters are often undone by their own psychological failings, as in *The Misfits* (1961) and *Fat City* (1972). Huston is also interested in exploring tensions within groups, as in *Key Largo* (1948) and *The Night of the Iguana* (1964). A number of his protagonists are classic overreachers, men who blasphemously presume to defy God's order, as in *Moby Dick* and *The Man Who Would Be King.*

Huston's stories tend to be strongly masculine. "What attracts me is adventure, and adventure is usually all-male," he's explained. Even Agee pointed out that the director was leery of the "feminine" aspects of art. Emotions are generally underplayed, *à la* Hemingway, whereas danger is romanticized. The virtues Huston celebrates are courage, audacity, stoicism, and personal integrity. His cult of virility has been somewhat exaggerated, however, for these virtues are occasionally found in women as well as men. Several of his films portray admirable females, most notably *The African Queen.* Huston also has a fondness for broken-down drunks, like the Claire Trevor role in *Key Largo* and the Susan Tyrrell character in *Fat City.* Yet undeniably, many of his women invite disaster. According to critic Brendan Gill, Huston's recurring theme is "Beware of Eve." Gill compares the filmmaker with such misogynistic authors as Twain, Kipling, and Hemingway: "How they fear women, these four, and how they rejoice to think of a world of men, from which women are excluded save as a necessary means of procreation!"

Since childhood Huston has been drawn to literature. He was able to read at the age of three and has always been a voluminous reader, even on location. Many of his industry friends—Wyler, Welles, Wilder—are also strongly literary in their sensibilities. Virtually all Huston's movies are based on novels, plays, and short stories. His adapta-

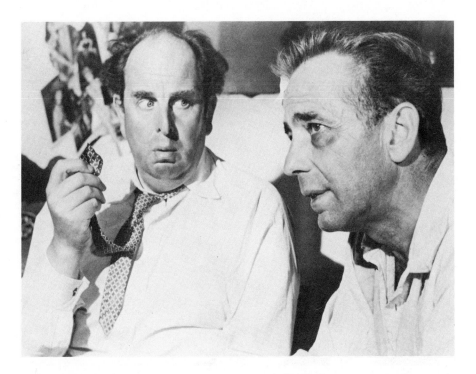

Figure 10.7. Humphrey Bogart in *Beat the Devil* (1953), with Robert Morley, distributed by United Artists. Many of Huston's films failed because they were ahead of their time. Though this black comedy is now considered a classic, when it was first released, audiences found it weird and unpredictable, and it failed at the box office.

tions have encompassed such disparate authors as Hammett, Ellen Glasgow, Traven, Maxwell Anderson, W. R. Burnett, Stephen Crane, Melville, Flannery O'Connor, Arthur Miller, Tennessee Williams, Carson McCullers, Kipling and the writers of the Book of Genesis. "I don't seek to interpret, to put my own stamp on the material," Huston has pointed out. "I try to be as faithful to the original material as I can." He is one of the few American filmmakers who has been praised rather than damned by original authors. For example, Hemingway, Williams, and McCullers all admired Huston's screenplays of their work.

Huston regards himself as a writer-director. "Ideally I think the writer should go on and direct the picture. I think the director is an extension of the writer." But he came to dislike writing alone, which he found too isolating. Most of his scenarios have been written with one other writer. Generally they trade off scenes, polishing each other's copy. Only rarely is a third writer brought in. Huston's collaborators have included such respected authors as James Agee, Truman Capote, Peter Viertel, Ray Bradbury, Arthur Miller, and Christopher Fry. Huston has generally regretted those few occasions when he contributed nothing to the screenplay. He prefers them carefully worked out in advance, though the exigencies of shooting on location have forced him to revise his scripts in mid-production. His coscenarists have been almost

Figure 10.8. Production photo of Marilyn Monroe and Arthur Miller during the shooting of *The Misfits* (1961), distributed by United Artists. This film is based on a short story Miller had written for *Esquire*. It deals with the slaughtering of wild mustangs for dogfood and the cowboys who make their living capturing them. "They represented, to me, the last really free Americans," Miller said. "They were misfits in our modern jet age as were the mustangs they still pursued." Huston asked Miller to write the screenplay, which was expanded to include an important role for his wife, Marilyn Monroe. The production was plagued with difficulties, running its cost up to $4 million. The Miller-Monroe marriage was in its terminal throes. At this point in her life, Marilyn was in an almost constant stupor from drugs and alcohol. Many days she didn't even show up, and when she did, she was usually late or too disoriented to appear before the camera. It was her last completed film. She died in 1962 of an overdose of sleeping pills mixed with alcohol.

unanimous in their praise of his literary craftsmanship. In 1964 he was given the prestigious Laurel Award for distinguished contributions to the art of screenwriting by the Writers Guild.

Huston has been highly praised for his skill in casting. He never creates a character with a specific performer in mind, though he generally casts according to personality rather than technical skill alone. He dislikes being able to see the mechanics of performance, and he insists that the right personality requires very little direction because the player instinctively understands the character's feelings. In secondary and minor roles he often casts the face rather than the talent. He has an aversion to soft, smooth, actorish faces, and on several projects has asked his assistants to round up the local roughnecks for minor roles. "I love to use ugly faces," he cheerfully admits.

He claims that the best performances in his movies were usually the least directed. "When I start a scene I always let the actor show me how he imagines the scene himself." He dislikes telling players what to do or even where to stand. He wants them to "take over" the roles without instruction. When an actor once asked him if he should sit down, Huston responded: "I don't know. Are you tired?" He claims that 50 percent of the time his players choose the same positions he originally had in mind; about 25 percent of the time their placement is superior; and the other 25 percent of the time he has to improve on their ideas. He usually keeps rehearsals to a minimum, since he believes that excessive repetition deadens spontaneity. He almost always treats his actors with respect. Occasionally he will offer suggestions if a player is having difficulties with a role. For example, when Katharine Hepburn's performance in *The African Queen* failed to ignite, Huston suggested she might play the role with an incongruous, ladylike formality—like Eleanor Roosevelt trapped in the tropics with a degenerate. Hepburn's performance turned out to be one of her most brilliant: funny, warm, and full of endearing surprises. Huston's most difficult time with an actor was with Montgomery Clift in *Freud*. Even in the best of times Clift was neurotic, which actually might have helped in the role, for Freud was also a tortured man. But during this production, Clift was on the verge of an

Figure 10.9.   Montgomery Clift in *Freud: The Secret Passion* (1962), with Larry Parks, distributed by Universal-International. Huston described this film as "an intellectual suspense story," exploring Freud's step-by-step formulation of the key concept in his theory of human sexuality, the Oedipus complex.

emotional collapse. Five years before he had been seriously injured in a car accident which left part of his face immoble; his memory was failing him badly; and his eyesight was all but extinguished by cateracts. His personal life was a disaster. He was also an alcoholic and pill addict. Doubtless both actor and director were relieved when the production was finished.

Even in the harshest of locations, Huston seldom loses his temper, and he never loses his control. He is usually calm and efficient. He makes decisions quickly and commands respect from his crews, who are allowed considerable freedom in making technical decisions on their own. "I try to create an atmosphere on the set where everyone feels they can participate. I guess this is as much as I can say in terms of having a basic theory of directing: letting the material have complete freedom, and imposing myself only where necessary."

Huston believes in an organic theory of style. His central preoccupation is always with the idea he's trying to express, and he views everything technical as only a means by which to convey this idea in clear form. There is no such thing as "the Huston style," he insists. Every movie calls for a unique form of expression: "If there's a pattern to my work, it's that I haven't made any two pictures alike. I get bored too

Figure 10.10. *The Bible . . . In the Beginning* **(1966), distributed by 20th Century-Fox.** "And the animals went in unto Noah into the Ark, two and two, male and female, as God commanded him. . . ." Huston wanted to stay very close to the spirit of the original in this movie, which covers about half of the Book of Genesis. The ark was built to biblical specifications: 200 feet long, 60 feet high, and made from hand-hewn logs. (Total cost: $300,000.) The film is steeped in wonder, like a fable. Huston treated the story as a naive, primitive myth. "All these things are strange and have a mysterious beauty as well as a pagan savage spirit," the director marveled.

quickly." He believes that audiences shouldn't be aware of what the camera is doing:

> The means used to convey the idea should be the simplest and the most direct and clear. No extra words, no extra images, no extra music. But it seems to me that this is a universal principle of art.

Nor does he think there's any conflict between his visuals and his dialogue: He views them as complementary forms of expression. He doesn't use a shot to emphasize a certain word; he uses both shots and words to embody the idea he's trying to convey. "Sometimes one single word is enough for this, or even complete silence, if the image is right."

Huston's organic theory of style is a far cry from Hawks's plainness or Wyler's austerity. Huston's movies all have a different look, but they're usually visually sophisticated. He has worked with some of the most gifted cameramen in the world, including the brilliant British cinematographer, Oswald Morris, who has photographed nine of his movies. Huston's other works have been shot by such international figures as Douglas Slocombe, Freddie Francis, Giuseppe Rotunno, Gabriel Figueroa, and Jack Cardiff. Huston works out the lighting and visual style in advance with his cameramen, though rarely in detail. He prefers shots and angles that tell his story as quickly as possible. He tends to frame tightly, excluding all inessentials. He seldom moves his camera during a take, because camera displacement can throw off the composition. He believes that every shot should lead to the next without anyone noticing the seams, like successive positions in ballet. In short, he's a classicist.

The visual richness of Huston's movies is due in large part to his serious interest in the plastic arts. He has also been excellently served by his regular art director, Stephen Grimes. Several films attempt to duplicate the style of painters and photographers. *The Red Badge of Courage* (1951) was modeled on the Civil War photographs of Mathew Brady; *Moby Dick* creates the look of nineteenth-century whaling prints; and *Freud* contains several surrealistic dream sequences, recalling the works of Dali and Buñuel. *Moulin Rouge,* a biography of the French artist, Henri de Toulouse-Lautrec, recreates not only Lautrec's compositions but his color spectrum as well. Huston wanted the movie to look as though Lautrec had directed it himself: "I want it to seem his paintings have come to life in front of the camera," he said. The director is also a superb colorist. In order to get the faded, weatherbeaten look he thought would be appropriate for *Moby Dick,* he had color and black-and-white negatives superimposed on one print. To convey the sense of sexual repression and the drabness of Army life in *Reflections in a Golden Eye,* he shot the film in sepia, with only monochromes of red allowed to seep through the pervasive golden surface. (Thrifty front office executives at Warners regarded this suppression as a waste of Technicolor and later released only full-saturated color prints of the movie.)

Huston commonly edits in the camera, for he believes that there is usually only one way to cut a film. Ordinarily he views the rushes every day, consulting with his actors on which final takes to select. He tries to

Figure 10.11. Jeff Bridges (left) in *Fat City* (1972), distributed by Columbia Pictures.
Unlike most fight films, this doesn't center on a champion or even a potential champion, but on two gentle losers who never manage to climb out of the penny-ante class. Huston's portrayal of the squalid milieu of small-time boxing is masterful. There are many documentarylike scenes that take place in dank working-class bars and gyms reeking of sweat and cigar smoke. Women seem strangely irrelevant in this masculine preserve: Sometimes they wait for their men; more often they drift away.

shoot his movies in chronological order, editing as he goes along, so that by the time the principal photography has been completed, the movie is also essentially in its edited form. In order to work this way, Huston has to be very sure of himself in terms of what the completed film ought to look like. "I've always done this," he said; "I have been told I shoot probably less film than almost any director."

Huston's career took a dip in the later 1950s, and he made only a handful of important films for the next dozen years or so. He has never been particularly sensitive to contemporary trends, and most of his successful movies were made to please himself rather than a particular following. By the late 1960s, however, he needed a hit in order to be commercially viable. Unfortunately, such movies as *Sinful Davey* (1968) and *The Kremlin Letter* (1969) weren't even good commercial entertainments. They seem to have been directed by remote control—very remote. Huston is under no illusions about the artistic quality of most of his late works: "I think I've made only three good films in the last decade," he said in 1976, "*Reflections in a Golden Eye, Fat City,* and *The Man Who Would Be King.*"

During this lean period, Huston took up acting again. Otto Preminger asked him to play a Boston Irish prelate in *The Cardinal,* and his performance was widely praised. Huston also played Noah in *The Bible*. Once again, his performance was winning, filled with fey eccentricities and sly bits of humor. He's a magnificent heavy, primarily because he plays against his material, exploiting his twinkling eyes and jolly extroverted manner to suggest chilling undercurrents of depravity. His portrayal of the sinister tycoon in Roman Polanski's *Chinatown* is one of that movie's many virtues. Oddly, Huston has never regarded himself very seriously as an actor and seems to consider performing in movies as something of a lark.

His critical reputation has fluctuated over the decades. Agee regarded him as second only to Chaplin in the American cinema of the 1940s: "The most inventive director of his generation, Huston has done more to extend, invigorate and purify the essential idiom of American movies, the true visual telling of stories, than anyone since the prime of D. W. Griffith." In later years, critics expressed impatience with what they regarded as Huston's cynical nonchalance about his art. "He is the Hamlet of American directors," said Hollis Alpert, "in that he is still not sure of whether to be or not to be great." His movies have often grossed more abroad than in America, though oddly enough, he was not a favorite with the *Cahiers* critics or their disciples. His works were strongly

Figure 10.12.   Sean Connery (right) in *The Man Who Would Be King* (1976), screenplay by Huston and Gladys Hill, based on a short story by Rudyard Kipling, distributed by Allied Artists. Kipling's tale of overweening pride had appealed to Huston from the time he was fifteen. A rich and complex work, the movie has an epic scope; yet the human dimension is never lost. It's also a handsomely mounted costume picture, filled with stunning visual effects and a genuine sense of mystery. Warm, humorous, and robust, the film was ample proof that the old master was back in top form.

admired, however, at the rival French journal, *Positif,* which was more Marxist in its orientation. Not that Huston has been much altered by what critics say of him, pro or con, as long as they don't accuse him of predictability. Sydney Greenstreet's grudging tribute to Bogart in *The Maltese Falcon* could just as easily apply to Huston:

> By gad, sir, you are a character. That you are! There's never any telling what you'll say or do next, except that it's bound to be something astonishing.

BIBLIOGRAPHY

AGEE, JAMES. *Agee on Film,* 2 vols. Boston: Beacon Press, *Reviews and Comments* (1958) contains "Undirectable Director." *Five Film Scripts* (1960) contains the script to *The African Queen,* with a foreword by Huston.

ARCHER, EUGENE. "A Monograph of John Huston," in two parts, in *Films and Filming* (September, 1959, and October, 1959). Discusses Hemingway's influence, Huston's major themes, and his functional style.

GOODE, JAMES. *The Story of the Misfits.* Indianapolis, Ind.: Bobbs-Merrill, 1963. An account of the making of the film and its many problems.

HUSTON, JOHN. *The Maltese Falcon.* Assembled and edited by Richard J. Anobile. New York: Flare Books, 1974. A reconstruction of the film, with 1,400 frame blowups and all the dialogue. See also "The Courage of Man" (interview) and "Let There Be Light" (script) in Robert Hughes, ed., *Film: Book 2, Films of War and Peace* (New York: Grove Press, 1962); and Arthur Miller, *The Misfits* (New York: Dell Publ. Co., Inc., 1961): a novelized version of the screenplay.

KAMINSKY, STUART. *John Huston: Maker of Magic.* New York: Houghton-Mifflin, 1978. Critical study and biography.

MEYER, WILLIAM R. "John Huston," in *Warner Brothers Directors.* New York: Arlington House Publishers, 1978. Other studio histories are Charles Higham, *Warner Brothers* (New York: Scribners, 1975); Ted Sennett, *Warner Brothers Presents* (New York: Castle Books, 1971); and James R. Silke, *Here's Looking at You, Kid* (Boston: Little, Brown, 1976).

NOLAN, WILLIAM F. *John Huston: King Rebel.* Los Angeles: Sherbourne Press, 1965. A lively biography, though somewhat idolotrous. Selected bibliography and filmography to 1965. See also Axel Madsen, *John Huston* (New York: Doubleday, 1978): biography.

PRATLEY, GERALD. *The Cinema of John Huston.* Cranbury, N.J.: A. S. Barnes, 1977. A book-length interview, with filmography.

RECK, TOM. "Huston Meets the Eye," in *Film Comment* (May-June, 1973). This issue also contains an interview with Huston by Gene Phillips and a reminiscence by Howard Koch.

ROSS, LILLIAN. *Picture.* New York: Avon Books, 1969. About the making and unmaking of *The Red Badge of Courage.* Originally appearing as five articles for *The New Yorker,* Ross's book is now considered a classic.

Paradise Lost

The Cinema of Orson Welles

Figure 11.1. **Publicity photo of Welles and cinematographer Gregg Toland during the production of *Citizen Kane* (1941), released by RKO.** Toland asked Welles to be hired as cinematographer for this project. He often suggested more effective ways of shooting scenes, and Welles was so grateful he gave the cinematographer a conspicuous credit title—unusual in this era. The visual style of *Kane* is eclectic, integrating a variety of influences. Welles was strongly drawn to the lighting theories of such theatrical designers as Gordon Craig and Adolphe Appia and to many of the techniques of the German expressionist movement (see Chapter 9). The young director was also influenced by the artisans at RKO. The studio's special effects department consisted of thirty-five people, most of whom worked on *Kane*. About 85 percent of the movie required some kind of special effects work, such as miniatures, matte shots, and double exposures. See also Peter Bogdanovich, "The Kane Mutiny," in *Esquire* (October, 1972).

Welles is the *monstre sacré* of the American cinema. From the time he was a youth he attracted controversy, inspiring both resentment and adulation. He was commonly called a boy genius after his triumphs on the New York stage as an actor, director, and producer in the late 1930s. He was also a well-known radio personality, and his famous *War of the Worlds* broadcast of 1938 landed him on the front cover of *Time* when he was twenty-two years old. RKO gave him an unprecedented carte blanche contract on the basis of his preco-cious celebrity, hoping he would rescue the foundering studio. But Welles wasn't destined to find a popular audience in movies. By the late 1940s, he was unable to work within the studio system except as an actor, and in desperation he moved to Europe, where his audience was more attuned to his vision. Since then he has made movies in a variety of countries, usually under exasperating conditions. His output has been small. In nearly four decades as a filmmaker he has produced about a dozen completed movies. Many of his projects have been abandoned for lack of funds. He has financed his films primarily from his earnings as a star and has frequently been forced to postpone shooting when his money ran out. To compound his ill fortune, a number of his *finished* works were mutilated after Welles had completed them. Only a handful of filmmakers have attempted such ambitious themes or explored character in such depth. His movies are remarkably free of clichés, and even his failures are usually intelligent failures—complex, provocative, and conceptually inventive but flawed by the frustrating conditions he's forced to work under. "A film is never really good unless the camera is an eye in the head of a poet," he insists. His poetry is best represented by his bravura style, so richly textured that critic James Naremore described it as a "seven-layer cake profusion." Welles's technical brilliance is conceded even by his detractors. His first feature, *Citizen Kane,* is so encyclopedic in its technical range that it's the most frequently cited movie in many of the standard textbooks on film. In Europe, and especially in France, he is regarded as a virtual deity. The *Cahiers* critics considered his works an inexhaustible source of inspiration: "All of us will always owe him everything," gushed Jean-Luc Godard. Even less hyperbolic critics, like Maurice Bessy, said of Welles, "There can be no valid history of the cinema that does not grant him his place as a film director of the very first rank." Incredibly, his two masterpieces, *Citizen Kane* and *The Magnificent Ambersons,* failed at the box office. Properly speaking, the failure belonged to the American public. In a 1962 international critics' poll, which was conducted by the British journal, *Sight and Sound, Citizen Kane* headed the list of the ten greatest films of all time. In a similar poll conducted ten years later, *Kane* was still on top; *Ambersons* placed eighth. The figure who received the most votes as the greatest director in the history of the cinema was Orson Welles.

Almost all serious stories in the world are stories of a failure with a death in it. But there is more lost paradise in them than defeat. To me that's the central theme in Western culture, the lost paradise.

—Orson Welles

Welles was born in 1915 in Kenosha, Wisconsin. His parents were wealthy and traveled a great deal. As a child, Orson spent more time abroad than in the United States. Both of his parents were flamboyant personalities who attracted artists, intellectuals, and eccentrics of every variety. His mother was a concert pianist and something of a political radical, who encouraged her son's interests in painting and books. His father was an inventor, businessman, and playboy. Two of his enthusiasms were magic and the live theatre—which soon became Orson's passions as well. As a boy, he was spoiled and indulged. He adored both parents, who treated him virtually as an adult, as did their friends. He was a child prodigy. He could read when he was two and knew all of Shakespeare's plays by the time he was seven. He could recite *King Lear* by heart, and he loved to draw, perform magic tricks, and write poetry.

This idyll was short-lived. His mother died when he was eight. His father committed suicide in a Chicago hotel when Orson was twelve. He was made the ward of a family friend, Dr. Maurice Bernstein, a Chicago physician, who treated the boy kindly. Young Welles attended the progressive Todd School for Boys in Woodstock, Illinois, where he remained for five years. While he was there, he directed and acted in over thirty plays, mostly from the Elizabethan repertory. Shakespeare was—and still is—his favorite dramatist. Young Welles also coauthored (with the headmaster of Todd) *Everybody's Shakespeare,* a textbook which sold 20,000 copies.

In 1930 he left school permanently, and with a legacy left to him by his father, he embarked on a walking and sketching tour of Ireland. He bluffed his way into the Gate Theatre in Dublin, claiming to be a well-known Broadway star. The managers didn't believe him but were impressed nonetheless, and they hired him. For about a year, Welles directed and acted in many stage classics, mostly Elizabethan. He also performed at the prestigious Abbey Theatre in Dublin. Though he was only sixteen, he was tall (six feet, three inches) and imposing, with a powerful voice. Most of the roles he played were villains and old men. During this same period, the youth tried his hand as a novelist, painter, ballet scenarist, magician, and opera critic. In 1932 he decided to take a sketching tour of Morocco. Then he moved on to Spain, where he tried his hand as a picador. Bullfighting is still one of his passions, and even in Spain he's regarded as something of an authority on the subject.

He returned to the United States in 1933 and finagled an acting job touring with Katharine Cornell, one of the major stage stars of that era. They performed mostly Shakespeare and Shaw. In 1935 in New York, Welles joined forces with the theatrical producer, John Houseman, under the aegis of the Federal Theatre Project, one of many WPA programs of the New Deal. The live theatre of the 1930s was intensely political and leftist in its leanings (see Chapter 14). Welles, a lifelong liberal, was a Roosevelt enthusiast, and like most intellectuals of that era, was strongly pro-New Deal in his sympathies. Throughout the 1930s and 1940s, Welles made many public speeches attacking segregation, anti-Semitism, isolationism, and fascism. He also helped write several of Roosevelt's radio speeches. His stage productions (and later movies) were critical of capitalism, which made him a favorite with Marxist critics.

The first Welles-Houseman venture was a production of *Macbeth* staged in Harlem, with an all-black cast. It was the sensation of the 1936 season, and the twenty-year-old Welles was hailed as a boy wonder. In

1937 he and Houseman formed their own company, the Mercury Theatre, a shoestring venture financed primarily by Welles's earnings as a radio performer. His modern-dress anti-fascist production of *Julius Caesar* was an enormous success. Welles not only starred and directed but also designed the sets, costumes, and lighting. The respected theatre critic, John Mason Brown, pronounced it "a production of genius." Elliot Norton described it as "the most compelling Shakespeare of this generation." Welles and Houseman decided to mount a second New York production of the play, in addition to several road companies.

During this same period, Welles was working in radio. He began in this medium in 1934 and continued on and off until 1952, mostly for CBS. His earnings during his halcyon days in the late 1930s was about $3,000 per week, two-thirds of which was plowed back into the Mercury Theatre. He performed in a variety of shows, including the title role of *The Shadow*. Eventually he formed *The Mercury Theatre of the Air*. Howard Koch and Houseman wrote most of the scripts, which were commonly based on literary classics. Welles would then polish the scripts or rewrite them entirely in some cases. He was notorious for making last-minute changes—this was all live broadcasting— and for improvising brilliantly if he was long or short on time. He insisted on subtle, rich sound effects. The program was widely regarded as the finest dramatic show on the air. Most of the stories featured first-person narrators, but other narrative devices included diaries, interviews, confessions, and stream-of-consciousness monologues. The famous *War of the Worlds* broadcast took place on Halloween, 1938. Welles decided to use a news bulletin format, in which a bland musical program was periodically interrupted by "flashes" about an invasion from Mars. Many listeners had switched their dials after the show had begun, and without knowing its premise, they mistook the "alarm" for the real thing. Thousands panicked. The next morning the headlines of America's newspapers were blazing with tales of mass hysteria. Welles was delighted of course.

Before long, his frenetic pace began to take its toll. In his memoir, *Run-Through,* John Houseman describes how Welles began to sink into profound depressions, tormented by a sense of guilt and impending doom. He seemed to function in only two idioms—manic or depressive. He was often logging twenty-hour days, rushing from radio studio to studio, dashing back to the theatre to perform, rewriting scripts, rehearsing, and designing future productions. He and Houseman quarreled furiously, especially over Welles's indifference to cost and his frequent postponements of their new shows. The exhausted Welles began to believe that his associates were letting him down, and sometimes he accused them of treachery. He withdrew for days at a time, paralyzed by the countless decisions he had to face. He vacillated in his manner—cajoling, charming, or bullying his associates and periodically slipping into remorse and self-reproach. Still he refused to slow down.

Nor was he willing to raise ticket prices at the Mercury, which would have provided the company with some degree of financial stability. A child of the New Deal, the Mercury kept its prices down to an average of one dollar. Many tickets sold for as little as fifty cents in order to encourage working-class audiences to attend, which they did in considerable numbers. When the company had its first flop, the Mercury folded. But Welles was still determined to mount his production of *Five Kings,* a combination of all Shakespeare's history plays except two. Such an enormously ambitious undertaking exhausted Welles's energy and funds. The production was underfinanced, inadequately prepared, and underrehearsed. It proved disastrous in its out-of-town runs. Welles was forced to abandon the project, though he later—much later— incorporated many of his ideas in his movie, *Chimes at Midnight* (1965), also known as *Falstaff.*

In 1939, shortly after the collapse of the Mercury Theatre, RKO offered the twenty-four-year-old Welles an unheard of contract: He was to be paid $150,000 per picture, plus 25 percent of the gross receipts. He could produce, direct, write, or star in any of his films or function in all four capacities if he wished. He was granted total artistic control, answerable only to George Schaefer, the enlightened head of the studio. Before this time, Welles had shot some movie footage but primarily to augment his stage productions. His main interest was still the live theatre: With his earnings from RKO, he hoped to return to New York to revive the Mercury. But another fate awaited him. He was to fall in love with the most expensive artistic medium in history.

RKO was in financial distress, as it had been throughout most of its brief span. The studio was founded in 1928 by the financier Joseph P. Kennedy (the father of the President) and by David Sarnoff, the head of RCA and later NBC. Sarnoff hoped that the studio would become an "NBC with pictures." Kennedy soon withdrew, with a profit of some $5 million. After a promising start, RKO fell on hard times, primarily because of the constant reshuffling of management, which gave it no continuity. Unlike the other majors, RKO had no consistent identity or characteristic style. David O. Selznick was made production chief in 1931, instituting a policy of quality pictures. He encouraged the producer-director system of production, and some of the best filmmakers in the industry worked independently there, though often with disappointing returns. Pandro S. Berman and Merian C. Cooper succeeded Selznick and continued many of his policies, but with uneven results. Sarnoff and his new partner, Nelson Rockefeller, wanted the studio to produce sophisticated and progressive films, but they discovered that artistic worth and box office success were not easily united.

There were some bright spots though. RKO could boast the largest movie palace in America, the opulently appointed Radio City Music Hall in New York's Rockefeller Center. The studio did have some hits, like the charming Astaire-Rogers musicals, *King Kong, Gunga Din,* and the early Disney films. *Snow White and the Seven Dwarfs* grossed an astonishing $8,500,000 in its first run. Though the studio seemed unable to hold onto its talent, it did have under contract—however briefly—such gifted actors as Cary Grant and Katharine Hepburn. Most of its stars were females, and in the 1930s the studio produced many women's pictures, featuring such popular performers as Irene Dunne, Constance Bennett, and Mary Astor. The directors who worked (mostly free lance) at RKO included Ford, Hawks, Hitchcock, George Cukor, King Vidor, William Wellman, and George Stevens. A smallish studio, RKO had some of the finest craftsmen and technical personnel in the industry. Among the most conspicuous was their art director, Van Nest Polglase.

In 1937, George Schaefer was brought in as head of the studio. Sarnoff and Rockefeller encouraged him to continue its prestige policy—only with profits. Floyd Odlum, a new partner, had grave doubts about such a policy, and he preferred low-budget (and low-risk) program films. But for the moment, Odlum held his peace. Rockefeller and Sarnoff were pleased by Schaefer's idea to hire Welles, for they reasoned that if anyone could produce quality movies that also made money, surely it was the boy genius, fresh from his Broadway and radio triumphs. Odlum still held his peace. After Welles's first two films failed at the box office, there was another management struggle, and Odlum emerged triumphant. In 1942, both Welles and Schaefer were out. The studio's most financially successful period ensued, thanks largely to Odlum's schlock policy and the country's apparently inexhaustible appetite for garbage cinema. Most of RKO's movies of this era were cheap B films and "radio dramas," based on such popular programs on the air as *Fibber McGee and Molly.*

When Welles arrived in Hollywood in 1939, the resentment against him was immense. Most directors considered themselves lucky if they were permitted to direct an A production before they were thirty-five, yet here was a mere twenty-four-year-old who was given total autonomy on his first time out. "This is the biggest electric train a boy ever had," he quipped when he saw the production facilities at RKO. Along with a few fellow rebels like Chaplin and Huston, the flamboyant Welles was regarded as arty, supercilious, and arrogant. He didn't help matters by openly sneering at the film colony. "Hollywood is a golden suburb, perfect for golfers, gardeners, mediocre men, and complacent starlets," he announced with obvious delight. He was an incorrigible smartass. He's paid dearly for the flippant wit of his youth.

After a few false starts, he finally decided to make a movie loosely based on the life of the newspaper baron, William Randolph Hearst, entitled *American,* then *John Citizen, U.S.A.,* and finally *Citizen Kane* (1941). Almost from the start, the production was sparked by controversy. A master publicist, Welles had the film colony buzzing with speculation. The movie was shot in "absolute secrecy." Rumors were rife about the identity of the leading character; and when the syndicated gossip columnist, Louella Parsons, heard that the picture was to deal overtly with boss Hearst's private life, a campaign against the movie was launched by La Parsons and others, with Hearst's blessings and full cooperation. Actually, the characters in the film are composites, drawn from the lives of several famous American tycoons, but Hearst was the most obvious.

A controversy also raged around the script's authorship, which is still being argued about. As best as can be determined, the facts seem to be as follows. Scenarist Herman Mankiewicz, a Hollywood regular (and older brother of filmmaker Joseph L. Mankiewicz) approached Welles with the original script of *American.* The writer knew Hearst and was a friend of the old yellow journalist's lover, actress Marion Davies. She was among the best-liked personalities in the film colony and quite

Figure 11.2. Orson Welles in *Citizen Kane*, with Joseph Cotten and Everett Sloane (at far end of the table). Welles's deep focus is meant to be admired for its virtuosity as well as its functionalism. In this shot, for example, the space between Kane (Welles) and his two associates (Cotten and Sloane) suggests a certain estrangement, for they have to shout at each other in order to be heard—a technique the director uses in many scenes. André Bazin, an enthusiastic champion of deep-focus photography, believed that this technique reduces the importance of editing and preserves the cohesiveness of real space and time. Many spatial planes can be captured simultaneously in a single take, maintaining the objectivity of a scene. Bazin felt that audiences were thus encouraged to be more creative—less passive—in understanding the relationship between people and things. In this photo, for example, we are free to look at the faces of over two dozen characters. "The public may choose, with its eyes, what it wants to see of a shot," Welles said. "I don't like to force it." See André Bazin, *Orson Welles: A Critical View* (New York: Harper & Row, Pub., 1978), originally published in 1950.

unlike the Susan Alexander character in *Citizen Kane*. Welles thought the idea was provocative, but he wanted the script rewritten. He suggested that the story be recast in flashback form, with a variety of former associates offering their differing points of view about the central character. Mankiewicz was a notorious drunk—charming, witty, and almost totally unreliable—so Welles asked his former partner, Houseman, to help Mankiewicz rewrite the script in an isolated location. In drafting the second scenario, Mankiewicz and Houseman (who both regarded Welles as an egregious megalomaniac) saw many parallels between him and Kane, and they gleefully incorporated these similarities into the script. After they gave the second draft to Welles, he made extensive revisions—so extensive that Mankiewicz denounced the movie because it departed radically from his scenario. Nor did he want Welles's name to

Figure 11.3. *Citizen Kane. Kane* ushered in an era of flamboyant visual effects in the American cinema, and as such represented an assault on the classical ideal of an invisible style. Lights are often from below or other unexpected sources, creating startling clashes and abstract patterns. Welles has been called a baroque stylist because, as critic Donald Phelps has noted, the director invests each shot with an impact and surprise that are greater than the relationship the shot bears to its dramatic content. There's nothing invisible about the lighting of this shot, for example. As written, the scene is merely exposition, setting up the movie's narrative premise. Some reporters are talking in a screening room, and while they talk, the light from the projection booth splashes into the darkened auditorium, flooding the silhouetted figures in a sea of undulating luminescence. Other stylistic features that might be described as baroque are a tendency toward rich textures and intricate compositions. Overt symmetry is avoided in favor of dynamic contrasts that energize the plastic materials, infusing them with a sense of visual exuberance.

appear on the screenplay credit, and he took his case to the Writers Guild. At this time, a director was not allowed any writing credit unless he contributed 50 percent or more of the screenplay. In a compromise gesture, the guild allowed both of them credit, only with Mankiewicz receiving top billing.

Hearst's campaign against the movie got ferocious. He threatened the industry with a series of scandals and exposés unless the picture was destroyed before release. His stooge, MGM's Louis B. Mayer, the most powerful man in the industry, offered to reimburse RKO's costs, plus a tidy profit, if the studio would destroy the negative. Hearst pressured the other studios to refuse to book the film in their theatres. His newspapers attacked Welles as a Communist and suggested he was a draftdodger. (Welles was rejected for military service for medical reasons.) RKO stalled, paralyzed with indecision. Welles threatened to sue unless his movie was released. Finally, the studio decided to take the risk.

With only a few exceptions, *Citizen Kane* received rave notices.

Bosley Crowther of the New York *Times* called it "one of the greatest (if not the greatest) films in history." It won the New York Film Critics Award as best picture of 1941, which was a very good year for American movies. Even trade publications admitted that *Kane* was an extraordinary achievement. It received nine Academy Award nominations, but at the ceremonies, Welles was booed whenever his name was mentioned. Significantly, the only Academy Award that the movie won was for its screenplay. Critic Pauline Kael suggests that this was intended as a gesture of support for Mankiewicz and as a rebuke to Welles, who lost out on the acting, directing, and best picture awards. The failure of *Citizen Kane* at the box office was received with considerable complacency by most industry regulars.

It was the beginning of the end for Welles in Hollywood. When it failed to please several sneak preview audiences, *The Magnificent Ambersons* (1942) was cut by RKO from its 131-minute length to 88 minutes,

Figure 11.4. ***The Magnificent Ambersons*** **(1942), with Agnes Moorehead and Tim Holt, based on the novel by Booth Tarkington, released by RKO.** Most of Welles's movies are adaptations of novels and plays. He's acutely sensitive to language in cinema, though he regards the medium as essentially dramatic rather than literary. He usually begins his movies with the dialogue rather than the visuals. He claims that the writer should have the first and last word in filmmaking, the only better alternative being the writer-director, but with emphasis on the first word. "I believe you must say something new about a book," he has said, "otherwise it is better not to touch it." The adaptation, in short, should reflect more of the adaptor's vision than that of the original author. In this movie, for example, the tone is less sentimental than Tarkington's, and Welles took considerable liberties with the story. The movie is narrated off-screen by Welles and concludes with a shot of a microphone on a swinging boom, accompanied by his hammy but undeniably effective spoken credit: "I wrote the picture and directed it. My name is Orson Welles."

and a phony happy ending was tacked on. It was released on the second half of a double bill with an Odlum special—*Mexican Spitfire Sees a Ghost*. Except for James Agee, most reviewers were hostile in their notices. Welles directed and starred in *The Stranger* (1946) to prove he could make a commercial picture. He brought it in under budget and under schedule. Though it contains some exciting scenes, the film's story materials are crude, and he considers it his worst movie; but at least it did moderately well at the box office. He conned his way into *The Lady from Shanghai* (1946) because its female lead, Rita Hayworth, was Welles's second wife and Columbia's most important star. Though once again working with inferior materials, Welles managed to convert the property into a silk purse, thanks largely to his technical brilliance. Harry Cohn was furious that Welles included no glamorous closeups of Hayworth, and the mogul ordered many retakes, which were awkwardly inserted into Welles's reedited footage. Welles then turned to lowly Republic Pictures, a Poverty Row studio, where he made *Macbeth* (1948) on a shoestring. Shot in twenty-three days with inadequate facilities and second-rate collaborators, his first Shakespearean adaptation was a commercial and critical disaster. The editing is a mess and the out-of-

Figure 11.5. Rita Hayworth and Orson Welles in *The Lady from Shanghai* (1946), special effects (mirror sequence) by Lawrence Butler, produced by Columbia Pictures. Welles's celebrated mirror shots are a virtual trademark and symbolize the splintered multiplicity of personality. These shots are also visual correlatives of the search for identity—a common theme in his movies. "I believe a work is good to the degree that it expresses the man who created it," Welles once stated.

Figure 11.6. *The Lady from Shanghai,* **with Everett Sloane.** Most of Welles's movies portray a doomed world, where even the arrogant and powerful are brought low. European critics have interpreted his works as critiques of American individualism, which unchecked can degenerate into megalomania. This pessimistic vision is the hallmark of the modernist sensibility, which began to make inroads into the American cinema in the 1940s (see chapter 18).

synch soundtrack garbled. The acting is the weakest of all of Welles's movies. It was his last American film for nearly ten years.

In 1948, Welles left for Europe, where he hoped to work as an independent producer-director. His first movie was to be an adaptation of *Othello* (1951). The project turned out to be a nightmare. It was over three years in the shooting, and Welles had to interrupt production many times to seek additional funding. He lost several players in the process: There were three Desdemonas and four Iagos. Sequences had to be reshot time and again. During this same period, Welles was crisscrossing the globe, acting in other people's movies, on the stage, on radio and television; scrounging funds from the most arcane sources; wheedling and cajoling other directors to let him use their equipment so he could squeeze in a few scenes between acting chores. Not surprisingly, he collapsed from a nervous breakdown. But finally the movie was finished. *Othello,* a Mercury Production, took the Grand Prix at the Cannes Film Festival in 1952. On the Continent the film was enthusiastically praised, but British and American critics complained of its crude soundtrack. This was to be the pattern of virtually all his subsequent work.

Critic Charles Higham and others have suggested that Welles is at least partly to blame for his failures because of his capricious and self-destructive nature. He has been trailed by a stream of creditors who

Figure 11.7. *Othello* **(1951, Morocco), with Micheál MacLiammóir (third from left), distributed by United Artists.** Welles believes that "art surpasses reality" and that film should be a poetic medium, fantastic, and magical, like "a ribbon of dreams." However, he insists that his movies are stylistically unique. Style is governed organically by the nature of the materials. For example, the web and net imagery in *Othello* is derived from Shakespeare's text, which makes frequent use of such symbols. Welles's images are not intended to illustrate the text so much as embody it in cinematic terms. He has compared his Shakespearean adaptations to the operas of Verdi. (Significantly, Verdi's three operas based on Shakespearean materials focus on the same three protagonists as Welles's movies: Macbeth, Othello, and Falstaff.) See Jack J. Jorgens, *Shakespeare on Film* (Bloomington: Indiana University Press, 1977); and Charles W. Eckert, ed., *Focus on Shakespearean Films* (New York: Prentice-Hall, 1972).

claim he's fiscally irresponsible. He has never set roots, preferring the life of a celebrity vagabond, playing the grand seigneur, surrounded by admirers and sycophants. "No one has had to struggle more against his own premature deification than Orson Welles," Charles Silver has noted. As his bulk attests, Welles is a man of large appetites. "He is in love with the physical world," Higham has written, "with the pleasures of eating and drinking, art and women, sculpture and architecture, the theater, the circus and the cinema, travel and financially dangerous living; but he is also tormented with boredom and the distress of the man who fears that the apple he has just eaten may have contained an undetectable poison."

Higham also hypothesizes that Welles has a fear of completion. He has sometimes left his projects early, allowing others to edit his footage, then complaining that it was mutilated by hacks. Others have accused him of slapdash improvisations instead of careful planning. No other director has been jinxed by so many abandoned projects. In *A Ribbon of Dreams,* Peter Cowie lists twenty-five unrealized films, most of which had gotten at least to the scenario stage. Welles began his *Don Quixote* movie in 1955, and he spent ten years shooting bits and pieces. In 1969, the leading actor died of old age before the film could be completed. Welles has not always been a paragon of candor concerning these matters. "I had the worst bad luck in the history of the cinema," he has claimed, with considerable truth. But his explanations are sometimes evasive and contradictory, as are many accounts by others. For some, Welles has inherited the mantle of Erich von Stroheim as "the man you love to hate." His champions argue he's been the victim of malicious enemies. Besides, they point out, when one considers that Welles was an artist of major stature in his early twenties, it's somewhat churlish to complain of his unproductivity in his more advanced years, especially considering the obstacles he's had to surmount. "They don't review my work," Welles has complained of his critics; "they review me." The controversy continues to rage. It has all the makings of a great Welles movie.

Virtually all his films could be entitled *The Arrogance of Power.* He's

Figure 11.8. *Mr. Arkadin* **(1955, Spain), with Robert Arden (right) and Mischa Auer, distributed by Dan Talbot.** Also known as *Confidential Report,* this movie is based on a novel Welles wrote in French. It's one of his most fragmented films: The editing is often confusing, perhaps because he had to interrupt production many times to seek additional financing. (He also had to dub the voices of eighteen of his cast members.) John Houseman has suggested that Welles is essentially an adaptive genius: "His ability to push a dramatic situation far beyond its normal level of tension made him a great director but an inferior dramatist. His story sense was erratic and disorganized; whenever he strayed outside the solid structure of someone else's work, he ended in formless confusion."

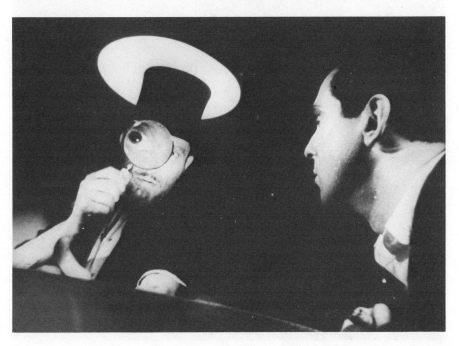

attracted to themes traditionally associated with classical tragedy and the epic: The downfall of a public figure because of arrogance and pride. Power and wealth are corrupting in his films, and the corrupt devour themselves. The innocent usually survive, but they are severely scarred. Many of his protagonists are virtual tyrants: Kane, the wheezing sheriff in *Touch of Evil* (1958), the sinister tycoon in *Mr. Arkadin* (1955), the futile Mr. Clay in *The Immortal Story* (1968). Often Welles portrays their mortal defeat with a symbolic fall: Kane's death is symbolized by a glass globe which shatters on the floor when it falls from his lifeless hand; the neo-Nazi Kindler in *The Stranger* falls from a church tower; Arkadin commits suicide by allowing his private plane to plunge to earth; Quinlan falls to his death into a filthy river in *Touch of Evil*. "All of the characters I've played are various forms of Faust," Welles has stated. All have bartered their souls, and lost.

Welles's sense of evil is mature and complex, seldom conventionalized. He is one of the few American filmmakers of his generation to explore the darker side of the human condition without resorting to a simplified psychology or to moralistic clichés. Though his universe is

Figure 11.9. Orson Welles and Janet Leigh in *Touch of Evil* (1958), with Akim Tamiroff, produced by Universal-International. Welles wasn't paid for his services as a writer-director, but he took on this project because he wanted to stay in shape—artistic shape, that is. *Touch of Evil* turned out to be a masterpiece of *film noir* (see Chapter 9) and swept the Grand Prix at the Cannes Film Festival, where it created a sensation with audiences and critics. In the United States, it failed at the box office.

essentially corrupt, it's shot through with ambiguities, contradictions, and moments of transient beauty. Welles considers himself a moralist, but he's never priggish or sanctimonious, and he detests preaching. Innocence is portrayed as a form of stupidity. His movies often feature a gullible character who fails to perceive evil: Bernstein in *Kane,* O'Hara in *Lady from Shanghai,* Van Stratten in *Arkadin.* Most of his movies are characterized by a nostalgia for a lost innocence. He's obsessed with the past and the cruel ravages of time. Images of decay, disintegration, and old age abound in his films. His tone is sometimes elegaic, as in *Ambersons* and *Chimes at Midnight,* which has been called a lament for the passing of Merrie England. But like Milton's fallen angels, there's a note of grandeur in the downfall of Welles's characters. Even his most corrupt protagonists are tinged by the majestic *hubris* of the classic overreacher. His universe is deceptive and paranoid, perhaps most chillingly in his Kafka adaptation, *The Trial* (1962). The Welles protagonist is often betrayed by those he trusts. Several are unmasked and defeated by a younger man. The source of danger is often the hidden self. Critic Joseph McBride has pointed out that self-deception and the struggle against awareness is one of Welles's main themes. Houses and mansions are exploited symbolically to suggest the bizarre entombment of their owners. His movies also emphasize the importance of the media in creating deceptive public images.

Welles's characters tend to be larger than life. Many are extremists and obsessives. Their power is founded on fraud and human exploitation. Many are incapable of loving, yet they demand love from those around them. Cowie has pointed out that the Welles world is populated by predators and victims. Seldom are his characters merely innocent or damned, however, for Welles usually fuses conflicting traits into one paradoxical personality. Several of his movies are structured around a series of confidential reports, in which informants present divergent points of view about a character. These have been likened to a prism which prevents us from seeing a person in his totality—precisely because Welles believes that the human psyche is too mysterious to be summed up glibly.

Welles is a deeply fatalistic artist. In the title role of *Mr. Arkadin,* he recounts a fable of a scorpion and a frog. The scorpion asks the frog to carry it across a river. The frog refuses, pointing out that he would then be vulnerable to the scorpion's poisonous sting. But what would be the logic of that, the scorpion asks, since then they would both drown? The frog finally agrees, but midway across the river, he feels the sting of the scorpion's venum. "Logic! There is no logic in this!" cries the dying frog. The scorpion answers: "I know, but I can't help it—it's my character." Time and human perversity destroy almost all loving relationships in Welles's movies. "Human nature is eternal," says one of his characters; "therefore one who follows his nature keeps his original nature in the end." Like Hitchcock and Lang, Welles believes in the psychological validity of original sin. In referring to the persecuted protagonist of *The Trial,* for example, Welles stated, "For me he is guilty because he is part of the human condition."

Welles is also an ironist. Many of his movies begin with the end—

usually a death. Then he flashes back to preceeding events, thus emphasizing not only an air of inevitability but also a double perspective, contrasting what is with what was. Since we know the outcome of events in advance in such movies as *Kane, Othello,* and *The Trial,* Welles is also able to present us with the ironic contrast between objective fact and subjective mitigation. As Maurice Bessy has noted, "In Welles' universe, truth is not, after all, either good or beautiful, but, in its own fashion, it is truth."

He structures many of his movies in the form of a search. "If we are looking for something, a labyrinth is the most favorable location for the search," he has observed. But as Jorge Luis Borges pointed out about *Kane,* Welles's labyrinths lack a center. There is a tendency in his movies toward increasing fragmentation. His works are often composed of self-sufficient units which sometimes stray from the story line. It took McBride eight viewings before he could get the plot straight in *The Lady*

Figure 11.10. Anthony Perkins in *The Trial* (1962, France/Italy/West Germany), based on the novel by Franz Kafka, distributed by Astor. Welles took considerable liberties with Kafka's famous novel, though he preserved its allegorical emphasis and its atmosphere of paranoia. Its visual style is surrealistic, with bizarre landscapes, weird disjunctions in scale, and a thick symbolic texture. The plot is a virtual labyrinth, in which the terrified protagonist (Perkins) stumbles from one disjointed location to another in an effort to exonerate himself from a nameless crime.

from Shanghai. *Touch of Evil* observes the unities of time and place, but no one could accuse it of adhering to the unity of action. His plots are almost impossible to paraphrase because of their jigsaw-puzzle structures. Since most of his movies have been pieced together in scraps over lengthy periods, a certain disjointedness is inevitable. But in many cases it's deliberate, as in *The Trial*, in which the story line is intended to have the disconnected logic of a dream.

Welles has acted in all his own movies except *Ambersons*, which he only wrote, directed, produced, and narrated. He became a star after *Jane Eyre* (1943, directed by Robert Stevenson). In all, he's acted in over sixty movies and fifty plays. Most of his film performances have been supporting and cameo roles for European directors. His radio experience provided him with one of the most expressive voices in the cinema: rich, deep, powerful—yet also capable of surprising tenderness. He likes to play with his voice by speaking some words in a caressing whisper, or dropping down vocally on a weirdly off-center phrase to give it surprising new meanings, or simply stopping mid-sentence, as though he has run out of breath—the better to emphasize the final words. Of course he varies his delivery to suit the character. He plays Othello almost exclusively in the lower register and deliberately underplays many scenes. As the sheriff in *Touch of Evil*, he mumbles much of his dialogue and even throws away some of his lines.

Several critics have expressed reservations about his acting, especially in such classical roles as Othello and Falstaff. Dwight Macdonald described him as mannered, especially when he underplays. Walter Kerr believes he's limited to parts that are cold, intellectual, and emotionally dead. But Welles is capable of a surprising degree of humanity in some instances. In *Touch of Evil*, for example, there's a scene in which the fat, sweaty sheriff meanders into a deserted whorehouse which he frequented as a younger man. While chewing on a candy bar, he's sized up by the house madam (Marlene Dietrich), an old flame. When she recognizes who he is—and recalls who he was—she mutters brusquely but without malice, "You're a mess, honey. You'd better lay off those candy bars." In a rare show of vulnerability, Welles's face is flooded with longing, regret, and remembrance. Many regard this as his finest screen performance.

Welles's coactors are seldom on this same high level. His casts tend to be uneven, ranging from the universally acclaimed performance of Agnes Moorehead in *Ambersons* to Jeanette Nolan's inept Lady Macbeth. A few of his regulars, like Everett Sloane and Akim Tamiroff, are always interesting to watch. Others are merely acceptable, like most of his leading ladies. His leading men can be lacklustre, like Robert Arden in *Arkadin*, or miscast, like Anthony Perkins in *The Trial*. Since many of Welles's friends are stars, he occasionally casts them in cameo roles. Though this practice can throw off the dramatic emphasis by suggesting a greater importance than the role can bear, these cameos are often compellingly performed by such veteran scene stealers as Jeanne Moreau, Michael Redgrave, Katina Paxinou, Marlene Dietrich, and John Gielgud. Welles is hard on his actor friends and expects them to be ready to perform on the slightest notice, even though they may be countries away and otherwise occupied. Astonishingly, they usually come. On the set, Welles tends to pamper his actors, encouraging their ideas and urging them to improvise.

He is a dazzling stylist, and as Pauline Kael has noted, his technical virtuosity is part of the show:

> It is Welles' distinctive quality as a movie director—I think it is his genius—that he never hides his cleverness, that he makes it possible for us not only to enjoy what he does but to share his enjoyment in doing it.

Bazin referred to *Citizen Kane* as "a discourse on method," because it synthesizes virtually every technique the medium is capable of. Welles believes that style can't be superimposed in an abstract manner: "I plan every shot then throw all the plans out. The images have to be discovered in the course of work or else they are cold and lack life." His lighting effects and bold compositions derive from an "interior rhythm," which he likens to the shape of poetry or music. He considers some of his movies too explosive stylistically, because he doesn't work enough between pictures and vents his frustration by a tendency to overload each shot. Characteristically, his favorite directors are those who are able to convey powerful effects in a simple, direct manner, like Jean Renoir and Vittorio De Sica. "In handling the camera I feel that I have no peer, but what De Sica can do, that I can't do." He considers De Sica's *Shoeshine* the greatest movie he has ever seen because the screen and camera seem to disappear, allowing the spectator to confront reality without intervention.

Welles is a master of the lengthy take, and his traveling shots are among the most celebrated of the cinema. The interrogation scene in *Touch of Evil* is nearly five minutes long and is captured in a single take so intricately choreographed that the camera was required to make sixty different movements. His crane shots can be deliriously lyrical, like the famous three-minute take in *Touch of Evil,* over which the producer cretinously superimposed the credits. But these shots are seldom merely displays of virtuosity; they convey important symbolic ideas. For example, in *Ambersons* the camera glides through the rooms of the family mansion, suggesting a graceful dying fall and the transience of the family's past glories. In *Kane* a spectacular crane shot through a neon sign on the roof of a nightclub embodies a violent intrusion of privacy. In *Othello,* Welles uses a brisk traveling shot to open the ramparts scene, in which Iago poisons Othello's mind about his wife's fidelity. The camera parallels the workings of his tormented psyche: hesitating, surging forward again, pausing, and finally, fixed in paralysis.

Welles was the most daring sound innovator since the early talkies of Lubitsch. The lessons he learned in his radio years served him well in movies. On the air, sounds must evoke images: An actor speaking through an echo chamber suggests a visual context, a huge auditorium, for instance; a "distant" train whistle evokes a vast landscape; and so on. Welles applied this aural principle to his soundtrack. In *Kane,* for example, almost every visual technique has its sound equivalent. Each shot has an appropriate sound quality, involving volume, degree of definition,

Figure 11.11. Orson Welles (left) in *Chimes at Midnight* (1965, Spain/Switzerland), based on sections from Shakespeare's *Richard II; Henry IV*, Parts I and II; *Henry V;* and *The Merry Wives of Windsor;* distributed by Peppercorn-Wormser. This film, also known as *Falstaff,* was the fulfillment of an old dream. Welles regarded Shakespeare's great comic creation as "the most entirely good man of all dramatic literature. I think Falstaff is like a Christmas tree decorated with vices. The tree itself is total innocence and love." See Pauline Kael, "Orson Welles: There Ain't No Way," in *Kiss Kiss Bang Bang* (New York: Bantam, 1969).

and texture. Long-shot sounds are remote and fragile; closeup sounds, crisp, clean, and generally loud. High-angle shots often feature high-pitched music and sound effects; low angles, brooding and sinister rumblings. Sounds can fade in and out, like images. They can be dissolved and overlapped, as in a montage sequence. Graceful crane movements are sometimes accompanied by glissando passages of music, the jerkiness of hand-held shots is enhanced by staccato noises and musical phrases.

In *Ambersons,* Welles developed a technique he called "sound montage," in which dialogue between several groups of characters is overlapped. The language is not so important for what it expresses intellectually but—like a musical composition—for the emotional tonalities it evokes as pure sound. At the final Amberson ball, for example, clusters of characters are seen in silhouette, while the dialogue of one group gently overlaps with another, which in turn overlaps with a third group. The effect is hauntingly poetic, despite the relative simplicity of the words themselves. Each group is characterized by a particular sound texture: The young people speak rapidly and in a normal to loud vol-

Figure 11.12.   Orson Welles in *The Immortal Story* (1968, France), distributed by Altura Films. "I am one of those who plays kings," Welles once remarked. Jean Renoir said of him, "When he steps before a camera, it is as if the rest of the world ceases to exist. He is a citizen of the screen." He exerts an immensely powerful presence on the screen: intimidating, mocking, theatrical. Welles is not at his best unless there is a larger-than-life quality to his role. He's seldom convincing as an average guy, an innocent, or a self-effacing character. As an icon, he tends to embody ruthlessness, cynicism, and a cold contempt for human rights.

ume; the middle-aged couple whisper intimately and slowly. The shouts of various family members punctuate these dialogue sequences in sudden outbursts. Disembodied phrases float and undulate in the shadows. During quarrels, the family members don't wait patiently for "cues": Accusations and recriminations spew forth simultaneously in spontaneous eruptions of anger and frustration. After Welles left the United States for Europe, the quality of his sound deteriorated badly. He needed the sophisticated technology of the studio system, and deprived of its craftsmen, he was forced to make crippling compromises. Many of his movies made abroad suffer from poor-quality sound, a particularly serious flaw in his Shakespearean adaptations, in which the dialogue is often out of synchronization with the visuals.

Welles has always been a favorite with critics, especially in France. Indeed, McBride points out that there are more books *about* Welles than there are movies *by* him. As early as the 1950s, excerpts from his scripts appeared in France in such journals as *Image et Son* and *Cinéma d'Au-*

jourd'hui. Truffant claimed that *Citizen Kane* inspired the largest number of French filmmakers to begin their own careers, and he included a tender tribute to this famous movie in *La Nuit Américaine* (literally, *The American Night,* though released in the United States as *Day for Night*). By 1971, even the American film industry had relented, when it presented him with an honorary Academy Award for his contribution to the art of the film. Welles also received the prestigious Life Achievement Award from the American Film Institute.

In 1970, Welles began shooting a movie about a controversial film director, with John Huston in the lead. *The Other Side of the Wind* is still incomplete. After Welles shot a few snippets of the movie in 1975, Huston expressed concern about its progress and Welles's perennial problems with raising more funds. "I'll have to find out where Orson is," Huston told Joseph McBride. "I'm going to call him up and say, 'Why the hell don't you finish it?'"

BIBLIOGRAPHY

BESSY, MAURICE, ed. *Orson Welles.* New York: Crown Publishers, 1971. A collection of critical articles and script excerpts from *Cinéma d'Aujourd'hui.* Filmography, selected bibliography.

COWIE, PETER. *A Ribbon of Dreams: The Cinema of Orson Welles.* Cranbury, N.J.: A. S. Barnes, 1973. Critical study, with bibliography, filmography, acting credits, radio and stage credits.

FOWLER, ROY. *Orson Welles, A First Biography.* London: Pendulum Publications, 1946. See also Peter Noble, *The Fabulous Orson Welles* (London: Hutchinson, 1956); and Kenneth Tynan, "Orson Welles," in *Playboy* (March, 1967). Three biographical studies, somewhat idolotrous.

GOTTESMAN, RONALD, ed. *Focus on Orson Welles.* New York: Prentice-Hall, 1976. A collection of critical essays, filmography and bibliography. See also Gottesman's *Focus on Citizen Kane* (New York: Prentice-Hall, 1971). Two excellent anthologies.

HAVER, RON. "The Mighty Show Machine," Part I, and "The RKO Years: Orson Welles and Howard Hughes," Part II, in *American Film* (November, 1977, and December–January, 1978). Studio history. See also *RKO Pictures* in *The Velvet Light Trap* (Fall, 1973): special issue devoted entirely to RKO.

HIGHAM, CHARLES. *The Films of Orson Welles.* Berkeley: University of California Press, 1970. Critical study and psychobiography. Contains a filmography and bibliography. See also James Naremore, *The Magic World of Orson Welles* (New York: Oxford University Press, 1978): a critical study.

HOUSEMAN, JOHN. *Run-Through: A Memoir.* New York: Simon & Schuster, 1972. An account of Welles's years in radio and the New York stage. Contains a somewhat unflattering portrait of Welles. See also Richard France, *The Theatre of Orson Welles* (Lewisburg, Pa.: Bucknell University Press, 1977): the only extensive account of the theatre years.

KAEL, PAULINE. *The Citizen Kane Book.* Boston: Little, Brown, 1971. Includes Kael's controversial essay, "Raising Kane," and the shooting script and a cutting continuity of *Kane.* See also Richard Meryman, *Mank* (New York:

Morrow, 1978): biography of Herman Mankiewicz; and Orson Welles, *The Trial* (New York: Simon & Schuster, 1970): reading version of the script.

MCBRIDE, JOSEPH. *Orson Welles.* New York: Viking, 1972. A perceptive critical study. Filmography. Stage, radio, television acting credits.

MACLIAMMÓIR, MICHEÁL. *Put Money in Thy Purse.* Preface by Orson Welles. London:Methuen, 1952. A diary of the production of *Othello,* by Welles's old Gate Theatre mentor, who also played Iago in the movie.

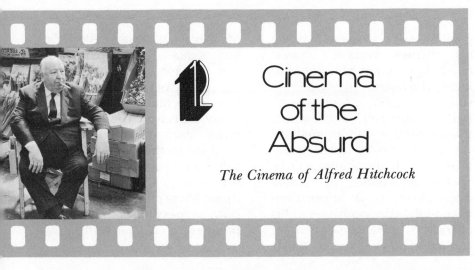

12

Cinema of the Absurd

The Cinema of Alfred Hitchcock

Figure 12.1. Publicity photo of Hitchcock during the production of *Frenzy* (1972). "I wish I didn't have to shoot the picture," Hitchcock admitted. "When I've gone through the script and created the picture on paper, for me the creative job is done and the rest is just a bore." After observing the shooting of several scenes from a Hitchcock movie, critic André Bazin marveled, "I had been watching for a good hour, during which time Hitchcock did not have to intervene more than twice; settled in his armchair, he gave the impression of being prodigiously bored and of musing about something completely different." When asked why he didn't simply let someone else shoot his movies, Hitchcock replied, "They might screw it up."

itchcock began his directing career in England, and when he came to the United States in 1939, he was already a highly respected filmmaker. In America, he publicized himself as the Master of Suspense, specializing in thrillers which combine shock with comedy. As a result of his popular television series in the 1950s, he became well known to the public and a great favorite at the box office. He always regarded himself as a formalist, calculating his effects with an extraordinary degree of control. His bravura editing allowed him to create what he called "pure cinema" which can rivet his audiences in terror even while delighting them with his comic audacity. Within the industry, he was respected as a shrewd professional but was seldom nominated for an Academy Award. Nor was he taken very seriously by critics in his early years. In the mid-1950s, however, he emerged as the favorite American director of the critics at *Cahiers du Cinéma*. No one was more surprised than Hitchcock himself, for he was an unpretentious man of unfeigned humility. He was also a deeply instinctive artist, at least in terms of his thematic obsessions, which he seldom cared to discuss. But his French admirers and their disciples have discussed them in great detail. Characteristically his themes revolve around psychological and philosophical ideas. The *univers hitchcockien* is steeped in guilt, a fundamental trait of virtually all his characters, though they're seldom guilty of the crime they're accused of. Like Lubitsch and Welles, Hitchcock is an ironist. His camera often directs us to information beyond the consciousness of his characters. François Truffaut compared him with such "artists of anxiety" as Dostoyevsky, Poe, and Kafka. Sexual perversion and menace often lie beneath the surface of normality. Characters are victimized by their own dimly perceived desires. When these buried impulses are dredged to the surface, the results can be shocking, macabre, even funny. Often they are all three. Many critics regard this vision as pessimistic. Hitchcock prefered to call it absurd.

The fact is I practice absurdity quite religiously.

—Alfred Hitchcock

Hitchcock was born in 1899 in London, the son of a wholesale vegetable and fruit seller. He never mentioned his mother in his published interviews. Both parents were Roman Catholics, and their only son was brought up in a strict religious environment. As a child he was quiet and almost always well behaved. He was alone most of the time. Since he had no playmates, he invented his own games and fantasies to amuse himself. He was six when he had his first encounter with the police. His father punished him for misbehaving by sending him to the precinct police station with a note instructing the captain to lock him in a cell for a few minutes as a warning to naughty boys. After this experience, he remained fearful of the police for many years, even into adulthood. When he was ten, he was sent to a Jesuit prep school, where the discipline was stern and infractions against Holy Rule were harshly punished. The most common form of retribution for a sinner was to have his hands whipped by a heavy strap. Pain, humiliation, and an intense fear of being involved with evil were what Hitchcock recalled of this period. His French critics insist that his Catholicism is central to his art, but though Hitchcock remained a practicing Catholic until his death in 1980, he never regarded himself as a Catholic artist as such. He did believe, however, that his religious upbringing might have influenced him subconsciously.

He became fascinated with movies at an early age, and by the time he was sixteen, he was already reading trade papers regularly. After the usual number of false starts upon graduation, he managed to get a job with the London branch of Famous Players-Lasky (which later became Paramount). American movies were always his favorites, and he was pleased that his first job was with an American company. Throughout the early 1920s, he learned the rudiments of his craft. He was employed as a title writer and artist, art director, occasional scenarist, and assistant director. He also studied art at the University of London. His private life was austere and circumspect: At twenty-three, he had never tasted alcohol nor been out on a date.

In 1925 he made his feature debut with *The Pleasure Garden,* which was shot in Munich. His producer remarked that it looked like an American film. Hitchcock's assistant director was Alma Reville, who converted to his religion and married him in 1926. She became his frequent coscenarist in the years ahead. Eventually he signed with the British producer, Michael Balcon. Their first project was a thriller, *The Lodger* (1926), which was loosely based on the legend of Jack the Ripper. The movie introduced the wrong-man theme, in which an innocent person is accused of a crime—a recurrent motif in Hitchcock's work. In this film, too, the director began his practice of making a brief (and usually comic) appearance in his movies. *The Lodger* was a big hit. Between 1925 and 1929, Hitchcock made eight other silent films, which were at least modestly popular with the public. Critics often praised his technical virtuosity, especially his editing style, which was influenced by the montage theories of the Soviet filmmaker, V. I. Pudovkin. With *The Man Who Knew Too Much* (1934), Hitchcock established himself as an important British director. Such graceful thrillers as *The Thirty-Nine Steps* (1935) and *The Lady Vanishes* (1938) were very popular in the United States as well as in England. By this time, he was regarded as Britain's foremost fiction filmmaker.

In 1939, Hitchcock signed a seven-year contract with the American independent producer, David O. Selznick. (Selznick was then at the peak of his prestige with his huge hit, *Gone with the Wind.*) Their first project was an adaptation of Daphne du Maurier's best-selling novel, *Rebecca.* It was a popular and critical success, second only to *GWTW* for the triumphant Selznick. *Rebecca* won the Academy Award for best picture in 1940, and Hitchcock received one of his few nominations. His career throughout the 1940s was a series of ups and downs—mostly downs. Because he favored the déclassé genre of the thriller, many top stars refused to work with him. Hitchcock was often forced to make do with lesser talents, like such leading players as Robert Cummings and Laraine Day. *Shadow of a Doubt* (1943), which many critics regard as Hitchcock's first masterpiece, did only so-so at the box office. *Notorious* (1946) reunited him with Cary Grant and Ingrid Bergman, two of his favorite players. It fared much better with the public than most of his movies of this period and is one of his most critically admired films. It's also one of his most romantic works, essentially a love story within a thriller format.

His slump came to an end at the beginning of the next decade, with the dazzling *Strangers on a Train* (1951). The 1950s was to be his greatest period, both commercially and artistically. The movies of this decade are varied and include such elegant entertainments as *To Catch a Thief* (1955), *The Trouble with Harry* (1956), a superior remake of *The Man Who Knew Too Much* (1956), and the stylistic tour de force, *North by Northwest* (1959). He also attempted more thematically ambitious movies, like *Rear*

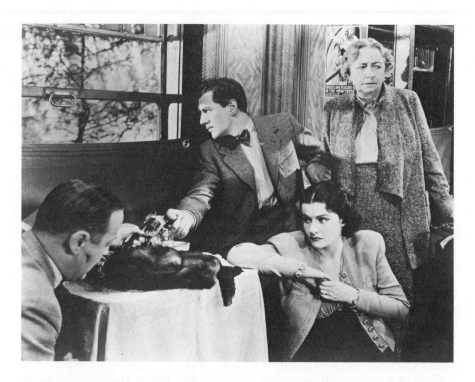

Figure 12.2. *The Lady Vanishes* **(1938, Great Britain), with Michael Redgrave (center), Dame May Whitty (right) and Margaret Lockwood, produced by Gainsborough Pictures.** This is regarded by many critics as Hitchcock's finest English movie. His British period lasted from 1925 to 1939, during which he produced twenty-three films in a variety of genres and styles. The best are thrillers, many of them based on English crime fiction. Many of Hitchcock's movies of this period display the same diabolical whimsy of the novels they're based on. The stories often revolve around ordinary British types who are plunged into bizarre plots in the middle of the most prosaic locales. There is an air of wry absurdity in these neatly crafted tales. The characters are often eccentric and stout hearted, with English pluck to spare. The plots are filled with cheerfully brutal killings, strange disappearances, and devious acts of espionage. A surface realism is preserved to enhance the macabre incongruity of the events. The emphasis is not on profound themes or complexity of characterization so much as the stylistic panache of the execution. See also Maurice Yacowar, *Hitchcock's British Films* (New York: Archon Books, 1977).

Window (1954), *The Wrong Man* (1957), and *Vertigo* (1958). This period culminated with *Psycho* (1960), which is widely regarded as his finest achievement and his most complex work. (It was also his biggest hit, costing $800,000 and grossing over $15 million in its first run.) Hitchcock went into another decline in the 1960s, but in 1972 he came back strong with *Frenzy*. His final work was the impish self-parody, *Family Plot* (1976), which he directed when he was seventy-seven years old.

Early in his American career, Hitchcock became as savvy a self-publicist as Selznick. Beginning with *Saboteur* (1942), he had his name prominently displayed above the title. After his popular television series, he was as well known to the general public as any top star. When his Selznick contract expired, he produced as well as directed most of his subsequent movies. In 1948, he formed an Anglo-American production company called Transatlantic Pictures, releasing primarily through Warners and Paramount. Beginning with *The Birds* (1963), he worked as a producer-director at Universal, where he enjoyed total artistic control, with automatic financing up to $3 million. Hitchcock never regarded movies solely—and certainly not primarily—as a commercial enterprise. But he believed that if a filmmaker is not realistic about his public, he will eventually fail to find work. He was one of the shrewdest analyzers of audience psychology, and he prided himself on being an international artist whose movies were popular all over the world. He thought it was much harder to make a good commercial picture than to make a private statement. Under the best circumstances, the two can be united, but only fools are contemptuous of their public. "You have to design your film just as Shakespeare did his plays," he insisted, "for an audience."

Hitchcock was so successful as a commercial entertainer that for many years he was regarded as only that. Such critics as Lindsay Anderson and Penelope Houston believed that his English movies were superior to those he made in America, which they complained were cynical and sensational. But the French changed all that. As early as 1954, *Cahiers du Cinéma* devoted an entire issue to Hitchcock's works.

Figure 12.3. Laurence Olivier and Joan Fontaine in *Rebecca* (1940), produced by Selznick International. Hitchcock regarded this as Selznick's film. The producer chose the property, wrote much of the script, and did most of the casting. He had to approve some scenes before Hitchcock could go ahead with the shooting, and the glossy photographic style is more typical of Selznick's work than Hitchcock's. The producer liked and respected the odd Englishman, claiming he was the only director he would ever trust with a picture.

Figure 12.4. Teresa Wright and Joseph Cotten in *Shadow of a Doubt* (1943), distributed by Universal. Hitchcock was fascinated by the concept of doubles. His movies are often structured in twos, with parallel scenes and even parallel camera setups, emphasizing complementary pairs. In this film, Hitchcock symbolically explores two sides of the same personality. The charming but evil Uncle Charlie (Cotten) is contrasted with his virginal niece, called young Charlie (Wright). "I think only of that white screen that has to be filled up the way you fill up a canvas," Hitchcock said; "that's why I draw rough setups for the cameraman." In this shot, the table is placed in the exact center of the composition, with Uncle Charlie invading Charlie's space, as well as her world of self-deluded innocence. "Cinema is form," Hitckcock insisted, and as critic Thomas Hemmeter has pointed out, the director's forms are always symbolic: "Hitchcock views the world as a volatile duality of order and chaos, where the forces of order are but a frail hedge against arbitrary eruptions of disorder from nature, society, or from within the mind. The criminal, the psychotic and the demonic intrude with brutal violence into the lives of law-abiding, normal people; they are either destroyed or learn to see the world and themselves as Hitchcock does: as an anxious mixture of normal and abnormal, innocence and guilt, public and private, whose apparent duality is more a conventional illusion than a reality."

Such critics as Truffaut, Claude Chabrol, and Eric Rohmer argued that the American movies were stylistically richer and thematically more complex than his British works. In 1957, Chabrol and Rohmer published their pioneering study, *Hitchcock: The First 44 Films,* emphasizing his Catholic sensibility. Many other reappraisals followed, first in France, then in England with such *Cahiers*-influenced journals as *Movie,* which championed Hawks and Hitchcock above all other filmmakers. In the United States, these revisionist views were popularized by such influential critics as Andrew Sarris, who was the editor of the short-lived *Cahiers du Cinéma in English.* Today, Hitchcock is the subject of doctoral dissertations.

He resisted symbolic interpretations of his work, in part because highbrow labels can be the kiss of death at the box office. Throughout his American career, he promoted himself as the Master of Suspense—no doubt because it sold more tickets. Like many of his characters, however, he was something of a split personality. He *was* the master of suspense, but his movies are also *about* ideas and feelings; they're not exercises in abstract form. As Truffaut notes in his famous book-length interview, to reproach Hitchcock for specializing in suspense is to accuse him of being the least boring of great filmmakers. Truffaut also suggests that Hitchcock's deadpan drollery concealed a profound pessimism, a view shared by many. The American critic Richard Schickel pointed out that the director's persona—the jolly fat man with a macabre, punning sense of humor—was almost entirely fictional.

His persona was developed in his television series, *Alfred Hitchcock Presents,* which began on CBS in 1955 and lasted for ten years. Hitchcock acted as ghoulish master of ceremonies for these hour and half-hour programs, introducing them and offering wry observations at the program's conclusion. The series was produced by his longtime associate, Joan Harrison. Hitchcock directed only twenty episodes—about 12 hours out of a total of 353, according to critic Jack Nolan. Though some of these shows used the same actors and writers as the movies, for the most part the television themes tended to be lighter and treated from a humorously ironic perspective, somewhat in the manner of *The Trouble with Harry,* only better. As a result of the series, Hitchcock became the most famous director in America. The image he projected was only superficially related to the personality behind the mask.

"The man who excels at filming fear is himself a very fearful person," François Truffaut observed. "Under the invariably self-possessed and often cynical surface is a deeply vulnerable, sensitive, and emotional man who feels with particular intensity the sensations he communicates to his audience." Fears and anxieties dominated his life as well as his art. He never took out a driver's license because he was afraid he might be stopped by the police. His mania for order was legendary. He detested surprises and conflicts and tried to regularize his life as much as possible. "I like everything around me to be clear as crystal and completely calm. I don't want clouds overhead," he said. "When I take a bath, I put everything neatly back in place. You wouldn't even know I'd been to the bathroom." He and his wife always lived quietly and modestly. They almost never attended social gatherings in Hollywood, and they had very few friends. New York, Paris, and London were the only cities they visited, and they always reserved the same suites at the same hotels. They seldom ventured out, preferring their friends to visit them at their hotel. Hitchcock owned about a dozen suits, all of the same conservative cut and dark color. His office at Universal—reputedly the most efficiently run studio in Hollywood—was ostentatiously neat and virtually sealed off from the outside. Meals were brought in, even though the studio commissary was nearby. He prefered working with the same associates. Alma Reville and Joan Harrison worked with him since they were all young. Robert Burks photographed twelve of his movies, George Tomasini edited nine, and Bernard Herrmann scored nine. When Hitchcock went out to promote his films, he stuck to a standard routine. In his interviews with critics and scholars, he repeated the same anecdotes and technical details, often phrase for phrase. When interviewers pressed him about his views on the human condition, he shifted the conversation to other topics. He refused to sound pretentious.

In their efforts to shed light on the darker side of Hitchcock's universe, many of his admirers have failed to do justice to the diversity and range of his work. They are also somewhat insensitive to his wit. "Some films are slices of life," he once drawled; "mine are slices of cake." Though he was pleased that critics applauded the thematic complexities of *Psycho,* he was disappointed that they failed to appreciate its grim jokiness. Humorless critics were impatient with his refusal to focus exclusively on the pessimistic implications of his work. They seem to think an artist must be solemn in order to be serious. But like Kafka—who also thought his works were terribly funny—Hitchcock's vision is ironic, rooted in a sense of the comic absurdity of life.

Figure 12.5. Ingrid Bergman in *Notorious* (1946), with Claude Rains and Leopoldine Konstantine, distributed by RKO. "I do not follow the geography of a set, I follow the geography of the screen," Hitchcock pointed out. He insisted that the space around actors must be dramatically meaningful and must be orchestrated from shot to shot. When he directed a scene, he was thinking of the way it would look within the rectangle of the frame, not how it appeared in reality, which was filled with irrelevancies. Here, the mise-en-scène is a perfect analogue of the heroine's sense of entrapment, without violating the civilized veneer demanded by the dramatic context. The dialogue in such instances can be perfectly neutral, for the psychological tensions are conveyed by the placement of the camera and the way the characters are arranged in space.

Actually, the director's ironic vision was closely related to his preference for suspense. Irony depends on a double perspective of some kind, a contrast between what *is* and what's thought to be. Hitchcock was seldom attracted to mystery, claiming it keeps the audience in the dark as much as the characters. Suspense, on the other hand, lets the spectator in on the dramatic variables. "I believe in giving the audience all the facts as early as possible," he pointed out. Though the characters are often unaware of the dangers surrounding them, the spectator almost never is. But unlike Lang, Hitchcock rarely presents the plight of his characters objectively. Rather, we are encouraged to identify strongly with their feelings. Critic Raymond Durgnat claims that in most of Hitchcock's movies, the director plays God, whereas the characters are reduced to insects. The spectator is trapped between these two perspectives—part immune, part victim. In this way, Hitchcock was able "to put the audience through it"—his stated aim—and thereby jolt the spectators out of their smug sense of security.

Hitchcock encourages us to identify with his characters through a variety of techniques. He frequently cast attractive stars, and even though the characters they play are sometimes morally dubious, the good will they generate as cultural icons tends to smother our moral objections. For example, in *Rear Window,* the protagonist is literally a voyeur, snooping on the lives of his neighbors; but because he's played by Jimmy Stewart, the all-American boy, we make generous allowances for his unsavory compulsion. Seldom does Hitchcock attempt to persuade us of the value of what the characters are seeking. He referred to such arbitrary gimmicks as microfilm, government documents, and so on as a MacGuffin—"something the characters in the film care a lot about, but the audience doesn't worry about it too much." Hitchcock also encourages identification by including many subjective techniques; that is, shots that are taken from the point of view of the character, thus implying a certain complicity on our part, since the consciousness of the character is temporarily fused with ours. In *Psycho,* Hitchcock forces us to identify with four successive characters, two of whom are brutally murdered in scenes that are virtually assaults on us as well.

He liked his stories to be tight and clear, and he was seldom at his best when the narrative materials are loosely structured, as in *Topaz* (1969). He insisted that the plot of a good thriller ought to hold up with no gaps in the logic even on repeated viewings. A number of his movies have double structures. That is, the plot seems to end abruptly and a new (though parallel) narrative line is then introduced, as in such works as *Vertigo* and *Psycho.* Several of his movies are overt allegories, most notably *Lifeboat* (1943) and *The Birds.* Others are chase films, in which the hero encounters a series of obstacles in flight. *North by Northwest* is the best example of this type of story. Frequently in these picaresque structures the hero is pursued by both the police and the villains and has nowhere to hide. With these types of plots, Hitchcock was often fearful that the characterization would be thin, for the emphasis is on action per se.

In shaping his plots, the lure of the absurd was hard for Hitchcock to resist. "Logic is dull," he complained. Plugging the loopholes in a plot

Figure 12.6. Robert Walker and Farley Granger in *Strangers on a Train* (1951), distributed by Warner Brothers. Throughout this film, Hitchcock preserves his characteristic motif of doubles: in the characterization, the mise-en-scène, and the very structure of the movie, which is almost schematically split into neatly paralleling scenes. As Jean-Luc Godard pointed out, this narrative symmetry is part of the show: "People say that Hitchcock lets the wires show too often. But because he shows them, they are no longer wires. They are the pillars of a marvellous architectural design made to withstand our scrutiny." Hitchcock's preoccupation with the motif of doubles was probably influenced by Freud. For example, in *Strangers on a Train,* as in many other Hitchcock films, the doubling of characters can be interpreted as the splitting of a single personality: the ostensible hero (Granger) embodies the principle of conscious control; the villain (Walker), the demonic subconscious.

he found tiresome but necessary: Absurdity is more striking when it's placed within a context of surface realism. He insisted that the story construction ought to be visual as well as logical. "You have to be able to see why someone does this, why someone goes there. It is no use *telling* people, they have got to *see*." When he adapted a literary property, his main concern was with its story, not its theme, which always emerged later and is usually more indigenous to Hitchcock's world than to the original material. He and his coscenarists began with the action, then filled in the dialogue later. He kept dialogue to a minimum because he considered "photographs of people talking" uncinematic.

Since the thriller is one of the most popular of genres, and Hitchcock was regularly imitated, his greatest worry was avoiding clichés. Like all genre artists, he was constantly trying to "find new ways to do the same thing." One way of avoiding repetition is to vary the tone. Many of his movies are romantic and explore love relationships, like *Under Capricorn* (1949). *Vertigo* is as dreamlike as an aquarium. *Frenzy* is unremittingly nasty and filled with sudden outbursts of cruelty. Hitchcock liked to shift moods in midscene as well. In *Strangers on a Train,* the tone volleys like a tennis ball in play. At his most perverse, he fuses contradictory emotions to produce a bizarre paradox. His most outrageous sequences—like the famous crop-dusting episode in *North by Northwest*—are simultaneously terrifying and funny.

"I am interested not so much in the stories I tell as in the means of telling them," Hitchcock stated. He described himself as a formalist, and he enjoyed the technical play involved in charging the materials with emotion. Strongly attracted to abstraction in the cinema, he frequently compared movies with music and the plastic arts. "When I say I'm not interested in content, it's the same as a painter not worrying about the apples that he's painting—whether they're sweet or sour. Who cares? It's his style, his manner of painting them—that's where the emotion comes from, same as in sculpture." His favorite artist was the abstractionist Paul Klee, and his art collection included two of Klee's paintings. He believed that subject matter alone is a poor gauge of a picture's worth: "Sometimes you find that a film is looked at solely for its content without any regard to the style or manner in which the story is told and, after all, that basically is the art of the cinema."

The most enjoyable aspect of filmmaking for Hitchcock was creating the script. Since the beginning of his career in the 1920s, he authored or coauthored all his scenarios, without official credit. He preferred working with only one other writer (ideally not a thriller specialist) so they could stimulate each other's imaginations. He often used novelists and dramatists as screenwriters and got them involved with the direction by explaining how he planned to shoot a sequence, what size the images would be, and so on. He worked with many distinguished literary figures, including Thornton Wilder, John Steinbeck, Raymond Chandler, Dorothy Parker, and Robert Benchley. He also worked with such top scenarists as Ben Hecht, John Michael Hayes, and Ernest Lehman.

Hitchcock's precut scripts were legendary. No other director worked from such precisely detailed plans. He often provided frame drawings of his shots (a technique called storyboarding), especially for those sequences involving complex editing. Some of his scripts contained as many as six hundred setup sketches. Every shot was calculated for a precise effect. Nothing was superfluous, nothing left to chance. "I would prefer to write all this down, however tiny and however short the pieces of film are—they should be written down in just the same way a composer writes down those little black dots from which we get beautiful sound." By the time the script was finished, he knew every detail by heart and rarely consulted the scenario during production. He compared himself to a conductor directing an orchestra without a score.

He considered the actual shooting anticlimactic: For him, the creative work was over. Once production began, he almost never deviated from the script, nor did he allow improvisations, which he regarded as wasteful and sloppy. Since the cinematographer lined up his shots in

Figure 12.7. An "edited sequence" from *Rear Window* (1954), starring James Stewart, distributed by Paramount. Hitchcock regarded *Rear Window* as his best example of pure cinema, for the entire movie is conceived in terms of associational montage. The story revolves around a photographic journalist (Stewart), who is confined to his apartment because of a broken leg. Out of boredom, he begins to observe the lives of his neighbors, who live in the apartment building just behind his own. His high-society fiancée (Grace Kelly) wants to get married and sees no reason why marriage should interfere with his work. But he puts her off, filling in his idle hours by speculating on the various problems of his neighbors. Each neighbor's window symbolizes a fragment of his divided sentiments: They are projections of his own anxieties and desires, which center on love, career, and marriage. Each rear window suggests a different option for the protagonist. One neighbor is a desperately lonely woman. Another apartment is occupied by lusty newlyweds. A friendless bachelor musician occupies a third apartment; a shallow and promiscuous dancer another. In still another is a childless married couple, who fawn pathetically over their dog to fill in the vacuum of their lives. In the most sinister apartment (pictured) is a tormented middle-aged man, who is so harrassed by his wife that he eventually murders her. By cutting from shots of the spying protagonist to shots of the neighbors' windows, Hitchcock dramatizes the thoughts going through the hero's mind. The audience is moved by the sheer technique rather than by the material per se or by the actors' performances. Somewhat like the early experiments of Pudovkin and his mentor Kuleshov, who edited together unrelated bits of film to create a new concept, this "edited sequence" is composed of random publicity photos and might be viewed as a kind of guilt by associational montage. Such editing techniques represent a form of characterization. Actors occasionally complained that Hitchcock didn't allow them to *act*. But he believed that people don't always express what they're thinking or feeling, and hence the director must communicate these ideas through his cutting. The actor, in short, provides only a part of the characterization. The rest is provided by Hitchcock's montage.

accordance with the sketches, Hitchcock rarely looked through the viewfinder. Nor did he bother checking the rushes every day: They contained few surprises. He edited in the camera and never shot more footage than the script called for. In his early years, producers were seldom able to reedit his footage. Even Selznick complained of his "godamn jigsaw cutting." The final assembly of his movies was simply a matter of tightening up the shots, a job he regarded as not very exciting, since the finished film was merely "an accurate rendering of the scenario." He rarely had much footage left after the editing. For example, *Rear Window* yielded a stark one hundred feet of outtakes after the final cut.

Hitchcock regarded editing as the foundation of film art, a view he derived from the Soviet theorist, Pudovkin, and his mentor, Lev Kuleshov. Their editing experiments in the silent era are regarded as classic. Pudovkin argued that emotional effects in movies are produced by the juxtaposition of fragmentary shots, not by unified scenes as in the live theatre. On the stage the actor must convey ideas by expressing them in words or pantomime. In movies, these ideas can be synthesized by the way details are arbitrarily linked together in the editing. For example, to convey hunger, a director could juxtapose a closeup of an actor's face, followed by a shot of a bowl of soup, then a return to the closeup of the actor's face. The idea of hunger is filled in by the spectator. This technique, which Pudovkin called "associational montage," also draws the viewer into the experience, since in effect he's creating it in his mind (see Fig. 12.7). If the middle shot were switched to that of a child playing with a toy, the idea conveyed would be one of paternal pride, even though the closeups of the actor might be the same. Similarly, if the shots of the actor's face were joined with a shot of a loved one's corpse, most viewers would interpret the sequence as an expression of grief. Through this linking process, the director not only controls the minutest details of the scene but also is able to manipulate the viewer's emotional response, which was one of Hitchcock's principal concerns. He believed that photographing reality intact is dull:

> The screen ought to speak its own language, freshly coined, and it can't do that unless it treats an acted scene as a piece of raw material which must be broken up, taken to bits, before it can be woven into an expressive visual pattern.

It's this piecing together of fragmentary shots that Hitchcock referred to as "pure cinema." He likened edited shots to individual notes of music that combine to produce a melody. His most famous sequences are essentially silent, with only music and noise to carry the continuity. The highly fragmented shower killing in *Psycho*, for example, took seven days to shoot, consists of seventy-eight shots, and lasts less than a minute on the screen. Some of the cuts are almost subliminal and last for only two or three frames—a fraction of a second. The Albert Hall sequence from the remake of *The Man Who Knew Too Much* is twelve minutes long and contains virtually no dialogue. The audience—but not the heroine—knows that an assassination will occur when the cymbals crash during a symphonic performance. Hitchcock cut to 124 different shots during this sequence, prolonging the suspense brilliantly.

He was challenged by problems of artistic form. For example, he conducted a number of experiments dealing with space. In *Lifeboat,* he confined himself to a single setting: a small boat at sea with eight survivors. In *Rope* (1948) he attempted to stage all the action within one continuous shot, with the characters and camera intricately choreographed in order to vary the size of the images. During shooting, whenever the camera had to be reloaded (every ten minutes), he devised ways to mask the cut between shots, such as having a character's back momentarily darken the screen, and continuing the "uninterrupted" scene when the character moves away from the lens. It's one of the few examples of a literal adherence in film to the unities of time, place, and

Figure 12.8. Henry Fonda in *The Wrong Man* (1957), distributed by Warner Brothers. This film is virtually a documentary on one of Hitchcock's obsessive themes, based on an actual incident, shot on authentic locations, with nonprofessional players in minor roles. Godard pointed out that the entire movie is structured in twos: There are two imprisonments, two handwriting tests, two conversations in the kitchen, two legal hearings, two visits to a clinic, two visits to the lawyer; the hero is arrested twice by two policemen (pictured); he is identified (wrongly) by two witnesses at two different shops. There are even two transfers of guilt: The hero is accused of a crime he didn't commit, and midway through the film, his emotionally disturbed wife (Vera Miles) takes on the guilt, requiring her to be hospitalized in a sanitarium. Chabrol and Rohmer interpreted the film as an example of Hitchcock's Catholic sensibility, for when the hero's crisis seems hopeless, an act of God resolves it in his favor. However, the movie's "happy ending" is highly equivocal. See Eric Rohmer and Claude Chabrol, *Hitchcock: The First 44 Films,* trans. Stanley Hochman (New York: Ungar, 1979).

action. In *Dial M for Murder* (1954), an adaptation of a single-setting play, he decided not to open up the action by staging scenes in various locations. He thought that this arbitrary practice could loosen up the tension of the original: The basic quality of most plays is precisely confinement within an enclosed space, he believed. He was also acutely sensitive to the amount of space included within a shot: The size of an image is closely related to its emotional impact. For example, closeups intensify, long shots relax, extreme long shots diminish, and so on. He calculated the effect of each shot and angle painstakingly.

He was also a master of the moving camera. James Agee believed that no one could surpass Hitchcock's traveling point-of-view shots. Particularly in suspenseful sequences—like Vera Miles's search through the eerie house in *Psycho*—the camera/character virtually drags the fearful spectator where angels fear to tread. His crane shots can be dazzling in their virtuosity. In *Notorious,* for example, a sequence opens with a high-angle extreme long shot of an enormous foyer filled with party guests. The camera slowly cranes down a long stairway—Hitchcock loved stairways and featured them prominently in most of his movies—floating in finally on an extreme closeup of the heroine's hand clasping a key. In love scenes Hitchcock sometimes used graceful traveling shots to suggest a lyrical, unbroken moment, while the embracing lovers glide to another part of the room, as in *Notorious*. While working in *Family Plot,* actor Bruce Dern observed that for Hitchcock movement per se was dramatic: "When he wants the audience emotionally moved, the camera moves."

The director prided himself on his off-beat settings, which contribute substantially to the air of absurdity in his movies. His best films are generally shot on location. "If you have a setting, it should be dramatized, and be indigenous to the whole picture, not just a background," he said. Indeed, some of his movies began with a setting, with the story subsequently fleshed around it. Before writing *Shadow of a Doubt,* he and coscenarist Thornton Wilder lived two months in the California town of Santa Rosa, in order to insure a surface authenticity. Hitchcock often used houses to suggest a place of concealed guilt, as in *Psycho* and *Under Capricorn.* He delighted in trapping his heroes in the middle of the most outlandishly public places, like an auction, a concert hall, even the United Nations lounge. Some of his most celebrated sequences take place at civic monuments, like the famous chase on Mt. Rushmore in *North by Northwest* or the fight scene on the Statue of Liberty in *Saboteur.* Such settings are incongruous symbols of order and stability.

Hitchcock liked to blur moral distinctions between his characters. "All villains are not black and all heroes are not white. There are grays everywhere." His heroes are generally superficially ordinary but with curious—and often kinky—psychological quirks. The heroines tend to be more appealing—instinctive, more emotional, and often victimized by the hero. The villains are almost invariably charming and polite, like the love-smitten and sincere Claude Rains in *Notorious* or the diabolically witty Robert Walker in *Strangers on a Train.* The distinction between the hero and the villain can be entirely academic, as in *Psycho* and *Frenzy,* two of his most misanthropic works. In order not to detract from the villain's charm, his evil is sometimes divided. In *North by Northwest,* for example,

Figure 12.9. James Stewart and Kim Novak in *Vertigo* (1958), distributed by Paramount. Hitchcock's couples are often really triangles, with a missing third party. The director's symbolism is rarely obscure, as Robin Wood has pointed out: "The meaning of a Hitchcock film is not a mysterious esoteric something cunningly concealed beneath a camouflage of 'entertainment'; it is there in the method, in the progression from shot to shot."

the suave James Mason character is provided with two henchmen, one brutal, the other menacing. Hitchcock's supporting characters are often brilliantly etched, like the cheerful middle-aged English couple in the remake of *The Man Who Knew Too Much*—who turn out to be part of the conspiracy. Hitchcock's mother figures constitute a grim gallery of ogres. Mother-son relationships in his movies are generally neurotic, with sadomasochistic undertones. They can also be funny, as in *Strangers on a Train,* in which the villain's mother turns out to be weirder than her son. Family life is seldom a comfort in Hitchcock's oeuvre.

After working on the script of *Strangers on a Train,* Raymond Chandler ridiculed Hitchcock's method of characterization. "His idea of character is rather primitive," the novelist complained: "Nice Young Man," "Society Girl," "Frightened Woman," and so on. Like many inexperienced scenarists, Chandler believed that characterization must be created through language. He was insensitive to the other options available to a filmmaker. In addition to characterization through montage (see Fig. 12.7), Hitchcock was also a cunning exploiter of the star system—a technique that has nothing to do with language. For his leading ladies, for example, the director favored elegant blondes with an

Figure 12.10.   Publicity photo of Cary Grant in *North by Northwest* (1959), distributed by MGM. Hitchcock liked to reverse genre expectations. Dark, sinister alleys often turn out to be comically anticlimactic. In bucolic locations drenched in sunlight the most outrageous acts of violence are perpetrated. Grant was Hitchcock's favorite leading man, and he loved putting the star through his paces.

understated sexuality and rather aristocratic, ladylike manners—in short, the society girl type. But there are great individual differences among such heroines as Joan Fontaine, Ingrid Bergman, and Grace Kelly, to mention only three of Hitchcock's famous blondes. Many of the details of the characterization are provided automatically by the iconography of each actress rather than the roles as written. The director also believed that people don't always discuss their inner thoughts and that a conversation can be quite trivial, but their eyes can reveal what they're really thinking and feeling.

Hitchcock's casting was often meant to deceive. In *Psycho,* for example, he cast the boyishly appealing Anthony Perkins to play the role of Norman Bates. Before this time, Perkins had played several sincere adolescents, like the sensitive Quaker youth in Wyler's *Friendly Persuasion.* Superficially Norman Bates seems to conform to this type, until late in the movie when we discover that he's a psychopath. Similarly, an unquestioned convention of American movies of that era was that a star character stays in the picture until the final reel, at which point it's permissible—though seldom advisable—to kill him or her off. But in *Psycho,* the Janet Leigh character is brutally murdered in the first third of the film, a shocking violation of convention which jolted audiences out of their coziness. The director sometimes cast awkward, self-conscious actors in roles requiring a note of uptight anxiety, like Farley Granger in *Rope* and *Strangers on a Train.* In supporting parts, Hitchcock preferred unfamiliar players, so that the audience is deprived of its iconographical bearings and can only guess at what lies beneath the surface.

Hitchcock had his differences with actors, who sometimes resented his orientation to the camera rather than to themselves. "All actors are cattle," he once joked. When they took umbrage at his remark, he amended it by saying that what he meant was "all actors should be *treated* like cattle." Some actors, like some critics, didn't always appreciate Hitchcock's wit. He disliked working with such Method-trained players as Montgomery Clift and Paul Newman because he regarded their obsession with motivation as irrelevant. (For a discussion of the Method, see Chapter 14.) Generally he discussed characterization with the actors privately in their dressing rooms, seldom on the set. He rehearsed very little, and for some sequences not at all. He explained to his players that they were only one element in the montage, and he let them see the rushes in order to illustrate his method. "I never lose my temper and I hate arguments," Hitchcock remarked, but he insisted on making movies *his* way. The actor had to submit himself to being used as raw material: "Mostly he is wanted to behave quietly and naturally (which of course isn't at all easy), leaving the camera to add most of the accents and emphases. I would almost say that the best screen actor is the man who can do nothing extremely well."

Hitchcock's works are steeped in the ideas of Freud. In fact, *Spellbound* (1945) was one of the earliest movies to deal with psychoanalysis, a popular subject in the American cinema of the 1940s. A central concept of Freudian psychology is the idea of a childhood trauma which produces neurotic—that is, apparently unrelated—behavior in adult life. Like dreams, unresolved neurotic compulsions are symbolic and must be deciphered in order to be cured. Unfortunately, Hitchcock sometimes reduced this concept to a pop formula, and even as late as 1964, in *Marnie,* the title character is instantly "cured" once she understands the origins of her irrational compulsions. In reality, Hitchcock was skeptical about such rehabilitations. For example, he thought his fear of the police was caused by his terrifying experience when he

Figure 12.11. *Psycho* **(1960), distributed by Paramount.** Hitchcock used bird's-eye shots such as these with extreme economy. This camera angle tends to imply destiny or fate, for we're allowed to observe a scene like all-powerful gods. The characters below are reduced to scurrying insects trapped in a maze.

was six. But the miraculous cure never materialized: He remained afraid of the police even in old age. His ironic skepticism is reflected in *Psycho,* in which a glib psychiatrist proffers his theory on the causes of several psychotic murders. But the theory, however accurate, is cold comfort to the victims. Like the police in Hitchcock's movies, the explanation comes too late.

His use of Freudian ideas is generally most effective when it's implicit rather than overt. Dreams and nightmares figure prominently in several films, exploring primitive, archetypal fears which are typical of childhood. His characters are often driven by subconscious sexual drives, like incest, fetishism, and sadomasochism. "Everything's perverted in a different way, isn't it?" he suggested to Truffaut. The protagonist of *Vertigo* is virtually a necrophiliac, as Hitchcock admitted: "To put it plainly, the man wants to go to bed with a woman who's dead." Male pairs are sometimes characterized implicitly as repressed homosexuals, as in *Rope* and *Strangers on a Train.* He believed that most people are voyeuristic and can't resist peeping at what's forbidden. He regarded the cinema as a voyeuristic art, and several of his movies indulge this impulse by opening with a flagrant invasion of privacy. For example, *Psycho, Shadow of a Doubt,* and *I Confess* (1952) all begin with the camera craning into a window (a persistent visual motif in Hitchcock's movies) to reveal its dark, guilty secrets. *Rear Window* is one long peep—with a bang at the end.

Many of Hitchcock's movies explore tensions between the sexes. Several love stories are actually love-hate stories. His protagonists sometimes betray a streak of misogyny (most notably in *Frenzy*), and violence against women is common. The hero of *Marnie* is sexually stimulated by blackmailing a female thief into marriage, and he refers to her as the "wild animal" he has trapped. There is much teasing, punishing, and struggling for dominance between the sexes. Hitchcock believed that human nature is essentially perverse, and he quoted Oscar Wilde's famous line on several occasions: "Each man kills the thing he loves." Chabrol noted a persistent preoccupation with love's rituals of degradation, especially the temptation to self-destruction. Men frequently try to control women: The aptly titled *Man Who Knew Too Much* is virtually a feminist tract, for as Godard noted, feminine intuition is the movie's sole mainspring. Hitchcock's heroines are generally more in touch with their feelings than the males. Women often take the initiative and tend to be less deluded by surface appearance and convention. Even when their instincts seem unreasonable, they prove more reliable than the fatuous logic of the males.

Critic Robin Wood has suggested that Hitchcock's movies are symbolically structured along the lines of Freud's tripartite division of the

Figure 12.12. *Frenzy* (1972), with Jon Finch (second from left) and Alec McCowen (second from right), distributed by Universal. As usual, the police are on the wrong track. But their logic can't be faulted: All the available evidence points indisputably to the hero (Finch). Hitchcock believed that audiences don't necessarily relate to right and wrong, and *Frenzy* contains a scene illustrating his belief. The villain gets trapped in the back of a truck, which is transporting a load of sacked potatoes, including the body of his latest victim. He searches desperately for his diamond stickpin, which he finds locked into her frozen fingers. While he tries to retrieve it, her body is savaged. The scene is both grisly and comic, and to add to its horror, the audience is hoping he'll succeed. Film is stronger than reason or morality, Hitchcock believed, and he used his art to explore even the nastiest recesses of the human condition—both on the screen and in the audience: "My love of film is far more important to me than any considerations of morality."

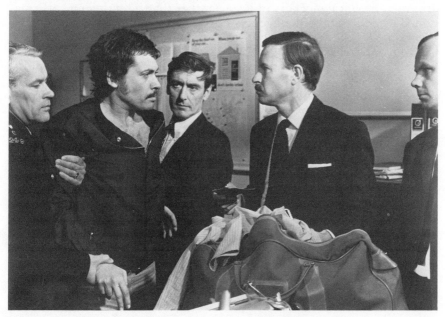

psyche: superego, id, and ego. The superego is an unconscious force which is associated with order and social moral standards. Conscience and a sense of guilt are agents of the superego. The id is also unconscious and is associated with amoral, instinctive impulses which demand immediate satisfaction. It is essentially irrational and selfish, and includes such forces as the sex drive. The ego is a conscious force which regulates the tensions between the superego and the id. Within a healthy psyche, the ego controls most immediate behavior and is most in touch with external reality. Wood believes that the symbolic conflict in Hitchcock's movies is between the ordered world and the chaotic world, between excessively rigid controls and total irrationality. ("Evil is complete disorder," Hitchcock once remarked.) The ideal is the balance provided by the ego, which harmonizes the needs of these two conflicting forces.

Wood also suggests that the action of Hitchcock's films can be likened to "experience therapy": The characters are purged of their obsessions or weaknesses by indulging them and living through the consequences. Since we identify with the protagonists, this "therapeutic theme" applies to the audience as well. We are forced to come to grips with our own hidden impulses, which necessarily produces greater self-awareness and a more realistic view of the human condition. Ian Cameron and Richard Jeffery have pointed out that the key to all the complacency in Hitchcock's films is the desire to pigeonhole experience into tidy categories that make life seem more secure and comprehensible. Whether one views Hitchcock's conflicts in philosophical, religious, or psychoanalytical terms, his main concern was to demolish simpleminded notions of good and evil and to dramatize their inextricability.

The Hitchcock universe at its bleakest is like a perverse machine—inscrutable, implacable, absurd in its whimsy. There is a sense of predestination at work. It's a world where "happy endings" are conspicuously arbitrary, a cynical mockery of justice rather than a sentimental affirmation. The police and other agents of security are almost invariably on the wrong track. They turn up too late to be of much help, and they never inspire confidence. Governments and other social institutions are portrayed as impersonal and repressive, indifferent if not outright hostile to the fate of their charges.

After talking with Hitchcock at some length, André Bazin concluded that the director's thematic obsessions were intuitive rather than consciously worked out. For example, until Bazin pointed it out, Hitchcock was totally unaware of the transfer-of-guilt motif which is found in virtually all his movies: An innocent weak character yields to a stronger evil figure by sharing his guilt. Numerous French critics insist that this idea is the dramatization in psychological and philosophical terms of the Catholic doctrine of original sin. Richard Schickel shares this view, pointing out that though Hitchcock rarely commented directly on these matters, he seemed to believe that he was as guilty as the next person of some vague imperfection for which he deserved punishment. Like the French, Schickel insisted that Hitchcock was not only a supreme stylist but also—in his thematically ambitious works at least—a bleak moralist who offered little hope of spiritual salvation.

BIBLIOGRAPHY

"Alfred Hitchcock," *Dialogue on Film,* No. 5, American Film Institute, 1972. Other interviews include "Alfred Hitchcock," in *Encountering Directors,* Charles Thomas Samuels, ed. (New York: Putnam's, 1972); "Alfred Hitchcock," in *The Men Who Made the Movies,* Richard Schickel, ed. (New York: Atheneum, 1975); and Peter Bogdanovich, *The Cinema of Alfred Hitchcock* (New York: Museum of Modern Art, 1963).

ANOBILE, RICHARD J., ed. *Alfred Hitchcock's Psycho.* New York: Darien House, 1974. Text and 1,400 frame enlargements from the film. See also James Naremore, *Filmguide to Psycho* (Bloomington: Indiana University Press, 1973): Filmography, selected bibliography; and Ernest Lehman, *North by Northwest* (New York: Viking, 1972): Reading version of script.

CAMERON, IAN, *et. al.* "Alfred Hitchcock," in *Movie Reader.* New York: Praeger Publishers, 1972. A collection of articles from the British film journal.

DURGNAT, RAYMOND. *The Strange Case of Alfred Hitchcock.* Cambridge, Mass.: M.I.T. Press, 1974. Critical study, with some perceptive comments on Hitchcock's artistic limitations.

LAVALLEY, ALBERT J., ed. *Focus on Hitchcock.* New York: Prentice-Hall, 1972. An excellent collection of interviews and articles. Filmography and bibliography.

PERRY, GEORGE. *The Films of Alfred Hitchcock.* London: Studio Vista, 1965. Brief survey, well illustrated.

SPOTO, DONALD. *The Art of Alfred Hitchcock.* New York: Hopkinson and Blake, 1976. Critical study of the British and American films; filmography, illustrated.

TAYLOR, JOHN RUSSELL. *Hitch: The Life and Times of Alfred Hitchcock.* New York: Pantheon, 1978. An authorized biography.

TRUFFAUT, FRANÇOIS, WITH HELEN G. SCOTT. *Hitchcock.* New York: Simon & Schuster, 1967. A classic interview, copiously illustrated. Filmography and selected bibliography.

WOOD, ROBIN. *Hitchcock's Films,* 3d rev. ed. Cranbury, N.J.: A. S. Barnes, 1978. Critical study, with excellent chapters on the films of the 1950s and *Psycho.*

Figure 13.1. Publicity photo of Charles Brackett (left), Gloria Swanson, and Wilder during the production of _Sunset Boulevard_ (1950). Famous for his happy sets, Wilder enjoys playing the genial host—with visitors, impromptu parties, and a convivial atmosphere. Said Swanson of her experience, "It went for thirteen weeks, _Sunset Boulevard,_ and all of it full of love and excitement, the crew full of enthusiasm. I wept when it was over for I was so happy during the making of it."

or more than four decades, Wilder has provoked controversy, both as a man and as an artist. His flamboyant personality has already prompted three biographies and innumerable article-length profiles. He has been described as abrasive, cynical, and misanthropic, and his battles with industry bigwigs are legendary. His two dozen or so movies are among the highest grossing in history: Biographer Tom Wood has estimated their total receipts at over $200 million. Wilder has been nominated for twenty-one Academy Awards, and he has won six—as a producer, a director (twice), and a writer (three times). He has worked in a variety of styles and genres, including thrillers,

film noir, social realism, literary and dramatic adaptations. But most of all, comedies. Postwar America witnessed a startling impoverishment in movie comedy, and Wilder was perhaps the only filmmaker of this period who could be ranked with the great prewar comic artists. Reflecting the wary skepticism of the postwar era, his movies are often as acrid as they are funny. He was the leading practitioner of what was later called _black comedy,_ with its emphasis on the cruel, the neurotic, and the grotesque. No other filmmaker was so frequently berated for his lapses in taste. Such classic works as _Double Indemnity, Sunset Boulevard, Some Like It Hot,_ and _The Apartment_ dissect human beings at their worst: brash, exploitive, and heartless, yet vibrantly compelling in their outrageousness. Wilder is ultimately a moralist, but without the smarmy piety that sometimes cheapens the movies of other artists working in this vein. His savage delight in exposing human venality is ambivalent and leaves a bitter aftertaste.

I'm accused of being vulgar. So much the better. That proves I'm close to life.
—*Billy Wilder*

Samuel Wilder was born in 1906 in Vienna. His mother as a young girl had lived in the United States for a few years and adored all things American. She nicknamed her son in honor of Buffalo Bill. As a child, he was regaled with tales of American life, and he vowed at an early age to visit that fabulous land. His father was a prosperous restaurateur who managed a chain of cafés, and later, a hotel and restaurant. It was in the billiard room of the family hotel that little Billy acquired a taste for gambling and competitive games. The poolroom was also educational: "I learned many things about human nature," Wilder recalled, "none of them favorable."

Like many Austrian families, the Wilders were reduced to desperate poverty in the final phases of World War I. In the postwar depression, the country was on the brink of social chaos, until the United States undertook a massive relief program. Once again the youth was dazzled by the apparently limitless wealth and generosity of this legendary utopia. As a teenager, his passion for American culture exceeded even that of his mother. He loved American movies, jazz, autos, and dances. A high school teacher encouraged him as a writer, and upon graduating, he bluffed his way into a reporter's job. In addition to writing about American culture, he also covered crime stories, gossip, scandals, and exposés of all the seven deadly sins. Employed in a traditionally cynical profession and skeptical by temperament, Wilder soon developed a rather jaded view of life. He reveled in exposing the vices of postwar Vienna. He also reveled in indulging in them, and was a profligate fornicator.

When he moved to Berlin, his cynicism deepened. During the 1920s, the German capital was the headiest city in Europe, crowded with innovative artists and intellectuals. An adventurous air of experimentation gave birth to the German expressionist movement, which revolutionized the arts (see Chapter 9). Postwar Berlin was the raunchiest, most vice-ridden city on the Continent. Wilder was intoxicated by it all. For several years he supported himself meagerly as a free-lance journalist, specializing in American topics, which were all the rage. Among his close friends was the worldly young cabaret singer, Marlene Dietrich. He wrote many articles on the corruption, greed, and hypocrisy of the times. He also wrote movie scripts—all unproduced. When he was really down on his luck, he exploited his prowess as a sexual athlete by becoming an *Eintänzer*, euphemistically, a male ballroom dancer. Wilder is characteristically more blunt: "I was a gigolo, dancing for a while at the Eden Hotel. I served as a tea-time partner for lonely ladies." Also characteristically, Wilder subsequently wrote an exposé, entitled "Waiter, Bring Me a Dancer." (Gigolos, prostitutes, and dancing scenes feature prominently in Wilder's movies, and few filmmakers are as cogent in dramatizing the humiliating urgency of the sex drive.)

His first big break came in 1929, when he wrote the script to *Menschen am Sonntag (People on Sunday)*, which was a surprise success. Its codirector, Robert Siodmak, was soon working at UFA, the most prestigious studio in Germany, and he took Wilder with him. Working under the famous producer Erich Pommer, Wilder wrote over a hundred scenarios in a variety of genres. Almost all of them were churned out anonymously, in imitation of the American factory system. At the age of twenty-five, Wilder was suddenly prosperous. He acquired a lavish lifestyle, wore expensive clothes, and maintained an exquisitely furnished apartment. He began collecting contemporary art, which was to remain a lifelong passion. He was also one of the most dissipated young men in Berlin.

All of this came to an end in 1933, when the Nazis came to power. Wilder moved to Paris when Hitler became Chancellor: "It seemed the wise thing for a Jew to do," he later observed. He was forced to abandon his beloved city, his lucrative job, and—the most devastating loss—his native language. Fortunately, he was fluent in French and managed to scrounge a living as a free-lance scenarist. Since he had no work permit, he wrote under pseudonymns. During his brief stay in Paris, he also directed his first movie, *Mauvaise Graine (The Bad Seed,* 1933), a low-budget gangster film with a jazz soundtrack. He disliked directing and resolved never to try it again.

In 1934 Wilder sold a script to Columbia Pictures for $150—just enough to pay his fare to the United States. Unfortunately, he knew very little English, except for swearwords, song titles, and American slang. He studied his adopted language by listening to the radio and cultivating American friends. "It was a most frustrating period," Wilder recalls, "not being able to tell people how wonderful I was." He worked briefly at Columbia, but nothing came of the job. Soon he was broke and unemployed. And hungry.

The land of his childhood fantasies was far from what he expected. He and his fellow expatriot, Peter Lorre, shared a room in a dismal district near Sunset Boulevard. By 1935, Wilder was *very* hungry, and the future looked grim. But like other refugees from Nazism, such as Lang, Preminger, and Zinnemann, Wilder had few options: "For me it was a question of fighting it out here and surviving or going back and winding up like most of my family in the ovens of Auschwitz." He learned to speak English so well that he had only the slightest trace of an accent. (Scenarist Ernest Lehman has observed that he's never regarded Wilder as a European because he seems so totally immersed in American life.) Wilder never rejected his cultural heritage. Rather, he drew from it to provide a wider perspective on his adopted country: "We who had our roots in the European past, I think, brought with us a fresh attitude towards America, a new eye with which to examine this country on film, as opposed to the eye of native-born movie makers who were accustomed to everything around them."

After he met his idol, Ernst Lubitsch, Wilder's luck finally improved. Lubitsch hired him to work on the scenario of *Bluebeard's Eighth Wife* (1938), which was coscripted by Charles Brackett, a Paramount regular. When the movie proved popular, the studio offered Wilder a contract at $125 a week and teamed him permanently with Brackett. "It was an atmosphere of creativity," Wilder said of his Paramount period; "we made pictures then, we didn't just make deals." Together, he and Brackett wrote a string of hits, including Lubitsch's superb *Ninotchka* (1939) and three movies directed by Mitchell Leisen: *Midnight* (1939), *Arise My Love* (1940), and *Hold Back the Dawn* (1941). The Wilder-Brackett team was now one of the highest paid in Hollywood, and they became notorious for their battles with Paramount's front office. They also made life miserable for actors and directors who took liberties with their scripts. Wilder became known as "the Terror," because even though he was barred from the sets, he would waylay the players and criticize their performances. As their power at the studio increased, Wilder and Brackett elbowed their way to artistic independence. To protect their scripts, Wilder decided that he would have to take over the directing. The front office went along with the idea, fully expecting him to fall on his face—a spectacle they anticipated with relish.

The team's first project was a light comedy, *The Major and the Minor* (1942), which was followed by a World War II melodrama, *Five Graves to Cairo* (1943), both box office successes. Made during the darkest days of the war, *Five Graves* is unusual in that it contains a surprisingly human portrait of German Field Marshal Rommel, played by Erich von Stroheim, another Wilder idol. The team was now allowed considerable control over future projects. Brackett bowed out on Wilder's next picture, the corrosive *Double Indemnity* (1944). The team reunited for *The Lost Weekend* (1945), a harshly realistic account of alcoholism, a project the front office regarded as sheer folly. The movie won four Academy Awards: best picture for Paramount, best actor for Ray Milland, best screenplay for Wilder and Brackett, and best director for Wilder. He was now considered in the front rank of American filmmakers. He and Brackett chose to remain in Paramount's Writers' Building, only now they were given lavish suites and commanded top salaries of $5,000 per week apiece. They also enjoyed total artistic autonomy.

"We are Hollywood's happiest married couple," Wilder was fond of telling reporters of his fourteen-year association with Brackett. Actually, as Maurice Zolotow has revealed, the relationship between the two was a stormy one, verging on sadomasochism. They were opposites in terms of temperament and deportment. Brackett, formal, dignified, and professorial, had graduated from Harvard Law School and was a conservative Republican. Before going to Hollywood in 1930 he had been a drama reviewer for the sophisticated *New Yorker* and had also published two satiric novels. The volatile Wilder never badmouthed his collaborator

Figure 13.2. Barbara Stanwyck and Fred MacMurray in *Double Indemnity* (1944), released by Paramount. A classic example of *film noir,* this is also one of several "deadly female" pictures that were made during the war years. It's narrated in flashbacks to emphasize an air of predestination. Cast against type, MacMurray plays a cocky insurance agent who's not as slick as he thinks he is. Stanwyck, looking shockingly cheap in a blonde wig, is his scheming accomplice. Wilder's hustlers are often so engagingly drawn that the audience is seduced into a kind of lax compliance: We find ourselves almost wishing them success. In this way, Wilder forces us to examine our own capacity for dishonesty.

publically, but in private he drove Brackett up the wall. Wilder could never resist needling his partner with cruel and nasty insults. When he could no longer endure these taunts, Brackett would literally hurl objects at his tormentor's head. Frequently they would refuse to speak to each other.

But most of the time they worked together—and reworked together. Before committing anything to paper, they first ironed out the story construction. Sometimes it was months before a single line was written down. Wilder was the talker, pacing furiously around the room while he bounced ideas off his silent partner, who would jot down occasional notes. Both had to agree before anything was written down. They would go through as many as fifteen drafts of a scenario before preparing for production. Most of their stories were angled from an ironic and cynical perspective, and Brackett was often appalled by Wilder's vulgarian sensibility. "It offends me beyond words, Billy," Brackett would moan when Wilder insisted on one of his perverse notions. When Wilder ventured even beyond bad taste, which was his wont, Brackett would stare stonily at him and mutter, "You're sick, Billy, you're very sick."

Brackett considered the *Double Indemnity* project so sordid that the team split up over the issue. They worked together on three more movies, but their quarrels grew more tempestuous, and after *Sunset Boulevard*, their greatest triumph, Wilder broke up the partnership.

Four years later, Wilder left Paramount and free lanced as a producer-director, releasing through a variety of companies. In 1957 he signed a contract with the Mirisch Company, which released through United Artists. It was a profitable and happy association which lasted sixteen years. Wilder had total artistic freedom, and in addition to a standard $100,000 writing fee and $250,000 for directing, he also received a generous percentage of the profits from his films. With such huge hits as *Some Like It Hot* (1959), *The Apartment* (1960) and *Irma La Douce* (1963), he reaped greater profits than the three enterprising Mirisch brothers. (There was plenty to go around: *Irma* alone grossed nearly $25 million.) Wilder has always had his enemies within the industry, particularly in its upper echelons. After he achieved independence as an artist, he enjoyed insulting such powerful moguls as Selznick, Mayer, and Jack Warner. Nonetheless, Wilder has often defended Hol-

Figure 13.3.   Ray Milland in *The Lost Weekend* (1945), released by Paramount. Novelist Joan Didion has observed, "The Wilder world is one seen at dawn through a hangover, a world of cheap *double entendres* and stale smoke, and drinks in which the ice has melted: a true country of despair." Throughout most of his career, Wilder considered himself an iconoclast, exploring controversial materials and treating them in fresh and surprising ways. Industry regulars confidently predicted disaster for most of his projects. In his early years especially, he defied the tradition of American optimism and dared to expose its soft underbelly.

lywood, which he believes has produced most of the world's best films. "I like it here," he told an interviewer, "I feel comfortable. I work with my friends. What more do you want?"

Even with close friends, Wilder can be trying. During the days of his greatest success (roughly from 1943 to 1963), he was overbearing in his arrogance. Like most of his protagonists, he's an obsessive personality: driving, domineering, incorrigibly *de trops*. He loves speed, detests anything slow, and is easily bored. He is a celebrated conversationalist, and his talk ranges over such topics as French novels, football, and Japanese miniature bonsai trees. He can be charming and urbane, and in the same breath, incredibly gross. Biographers have noted his passion for converting—some would say inflicting—his associates with his pet enthusiasms, such as tennis, bridge, crime fiction, Spanish-American history, jazz, Bauhaus furniture, and many others. He loves to lecture his interviewers on wines, haute cuisine, fashion, and art. He dislikes remaining seated for longer than a few minutes. Most of his interviews are granted on the run, while he embarks on a crosstown shopping spree, his exhausted interlocutors gasping for breath in the wake of his torrential energy. Wilder's wife, Audrey (they married in 1949), is much admired for her patience with her husband. When biographer Zolotow marveled at her equanimity, Wilder claimed she could be summed up in one word: "Saint. She is a saint. And I am a shit. The saint and the shit."

Perhaps the most aggrieved victims of Wilder's personality have been his coscenarists. After his parting with Brackett, he worked briefly with a number of them, and they too were stung by Wilder's sadistic jibes. Most of these men grew fond of him despite his jugular compulsions, but not fond enough to repeat the experience. "Billy has to take over your whole life," said Ernest Lehman. "You don't just collaborate on a script with him. He has to change what you wear and what you eat." George Axelrod regards him as the most consummate craftsman he has ever known: "Everything I know about writing films I learned during those five terrible months I was writing with him." Harry Kurnitz claimed that "Billy Wilder at work is actually two people—Mr. Hyde and Mr. Hyde." Kurnitz added that all Wilder's coscenarists "have a hunted look, shuffle nervously, and have been known to break into tears if a door slams anywhere in the same building." Since 1957, his regular coscenarist has been I. A. L. Diamond, who has endured Wilder's mercurial mood shifts better than any other collaborator. Quiet, confident, and intellectual, Diamond somewhat resembles Brackett in his reserved manner. Also like Brackett, he's a gifted writer of dialogue and inventive in the art of story construction. Unlike Brackett, he is relatively unflappable and rarely allows Wilder's insults to perturb him.

Wilder's intimates have argued that his abrasive manner is merely a veneer to mask his embarrassed decency. He is loyal to his friends to an unusual degree and has loaned or given them thousands of dollars when they were in economic distress. He is also a compulsive gift giver. Like many German and Austrian refugees, he's ferociously patriotic. During the war he was a member of the Anti-Nazi League and contributed a great deal of time, money, and organizational skill to the European Refugee Rescue Fund. Marlene Dietrich, ordinarily scornful and con-

Figure 13.4. Publicity photo of Marlene Dietrich in *A Foreign Affair* (1948), released by Paramount. This film was shot in the winter of 1947–1948 in Berlin—or what was left of Berlin after the massive bombardments of the war. Dietrich plays Erika von Schlütow, a former mistress of a high Nazi official, presently the mistress of a hustling American G.I. Considering the fact that most of Wilder's family, including his mother, were murdered in Nazi concentration camps, the treatment of the jaded Dietrich character is surprisingly sympathetic. This is one of Wilder's first explorations of the conflict between innocent Americans and corrupt, disillusioned Europeans. At the age of forty-six, Dietrich was more beautiful than ever, and as this photo irrefutably documents, the famous Dietrich gams still looked sensational.

temptuous of the film colony, regards Wilder as the finest man she has ever met. She was awed by his compassion for the victims of persecution. During the witch-hunts of the McCarthy era, Wilder spoke out against political harrassment when most industry regulars hid their heads in the sand—or joined in the hunt (see Chapter 14).

"I have been pursued for years by that nasty word—vulgarity," Wilder has complained. "They sit there in the movie house and laugh their heads off and then they come out and say 'Cheap! Vulgar!'" By today's tolerant standards, most of Wilder's films might seem relatively benign, but when they were originally released, they were often condemned for their cynicism. Even James Agee, who generally admired Wilder's work, lamented his "rotten taste." Pauline Kael excoriated his "brazen contempt for people." *Ace in the Hole* (1951, also known as *The Big Carnival*) presents such an acid picture of humanity that it failed dismally at the box office. Like several of Wilder's darker works, however, the movie was a success in Europe. Still reeling from Hitler's Holocaust, European audiences were less naive about the potential for depravity in the human species. Ironically, *Ace in the Hole* is based on a real event which took place in the United States in the 1920s. The film centers on an opportunistic journalist (Kirk Douglas) who exploits a mine accident in order to further his career. He persuades the local police chief to use an inefficient and time-consuming method of rescuing a trapped miner in order to milk the story for its sensational value. Virtually everyone in the film is corrupt. For example, the miner's wife (Jan Sterling) stays around only because she wants to cash in on her husband's tragedy and because she's sexually attracted to the reporter. When he suggests that she pray in the local chapel for a newspaper photo, she snarls, "I don't pray. Kneeling bags my nylons." So much for the milk of human kindness.

Wilder's sensibility was shaped by his early years as an exposé journalist, but he was also influenced by the so-called Lost Generation of American writers in the 1920s, especially Sinclair Lewis, the author of *Babbitt*. Wilder also admires the tradition of skepticism in American letters represented by Mark Twain, Ring Lardner, and H. L. Mencken. The cinematic influences on Wilder's work are more overt, as he has often noted: "I always think of my style as a curious cross between Lubitsch and Stroheim."

Wilder adored Lubitsch and considered him a comic genius. The two became close friends and shared many tastes, especially for French culture. Such graceful romantic comedies as *Sabrina* (1954), *Love in the Afternoon* (1957), and *Avanti!* (1972) are clearly indebted to Lubitsch's work, particularly in their emphasis on sex, money, and *savoir faire*. The satire in these films is softened and more affectionate, the wit more amiable. Wilder's adroitness at story construction is no doubt derived from the French tradition of the well-made play, which also influenced Lubitsch (see Chapter 4). Triangular relationships abound in the works of both artists, though in Wilder's movies they are often given a homoerotic twist, as Stephen Farber has pointed out. Instead of two men in love with one woman or vice versa, Wilder often features a protagonist who is torn between the dangerous sexual attractions of a female versus the affectionate camaraderie of a buddy, as in *Double Indemnity, The Fortune Cookie* (1966), *The Private Life of Sherlock Holmes* (1970), and *The Front Page* (1975). Wilder's clean classical style is also reminiscent of Lubitsch.

The Stroheim influence, which is more pronounced in Wilder's

Figure 13.5. Gloria Swanson in *Sunset Boulevard*, released by Paramount. The mad scene: enter Norma Desmond. Wilder's movie is a stinging exposé of the hypocrisies of Hollywood's studio era. It was received by industry regulars with horrified incredulity. MGM's Louis B. Mayer, who was famous for his near-apoplectic outbursts of emotion, threw a public tantrum at the film's premiere: "We should horsewhip this Wilder!" he bellowed in rage. "He has dirtied the nest! He has brought disgrace on the town that is feeding him!" Seven years later, Mayer was dead, and his funeral was packed with spectators. Quipped Wilder, "It shows that if you give the public what they want, they will come out for it." *Sunset Boulevard* was an enormous hit and received rave reviews. James Agee wrote of the picture, "It is Hollywood craftsmanship at its smartest and just about its best and it is hard to find better craftsmanship than that at this time in any art or country."

harsher movies, can be seen in his unsparing realism and his fondness for the grotesque and the bizarre. During the production of *Sunset Boulevard,* Stroheim made several suggestions for improving his screen character. Wilder accepted some of these gratefully, but he thought the others were too weird even for a Wilder movie, and he tactfully let them drop. The tradition of naturalism represented by Stroheim's oeuvre is essentially fatalistic and pessimistic, qualities which characterize the works of most American filmmakers of Teutonic origins. Stroheim often dealt with characters *in extremis,* as Wilder does in such movies as *A Foreign Affair* (1948), *Stalag 17* (1953), and *Witness for the Prosecution* (1957). Stroheim was also accused of vulgarity and a lurid preoccupation with the animalistic aspects of human nature. Like Wilder too, there is in most of Stroheim's work the unsentimental moral rigor of the social critic.

Wilder's satiric targets—pride, ambition, generational conflicts, political corruption, hypocrisy, gullibility—are in the classic tradition of Jonson, Voltaire, and Swift, who inculcated moral precepts through negative examples. Greed and lust are Wilder's favorite targets, and the two are often combined. "People will do anything for money," he has observed of his antiheroes, "except for some people, who will do *almost* anything for money." Many of his films center on moral weaklings who are only too eager to sell out but in the end choose to reclaim their self-respect. Wilder dislikes sanctimoniousness and preachiness, and at his best he avoids a facile morality. Virtue must be its own reward, for his protagonists are rarely given worldly success merely for acting like human beings, for a change. In fact, a number of his films conclude with the heroes snatching defeat from the jaws of victory: They might manage to salvage their integrity, but that's *all* they salvage. The spoils of their calculations are reluctantly sacrificed when they decide to give up their schemes. In some instances, the hero's reformation ironically leads to his death, as in *Double Indemnity, Sunset Boulevard,* and *Ace in the Hole.*

Though Wilder prefers original screenplays to adaptations, a number of his works are based on stage properties. Generally he retains very little from the original. *Irma la Douce,* for example, was a popular stage musical, and the first change Wilder made was to throw out the music! Most of his adaptations are considerable improvements over the originals, most notably *Sabrina, Stalag 17,* and *Witness for the Prosecution.* Wilder has no theory concerning adaptation. He believes that each property requires a unique approach. For example, he opened up *The Seven Year Itch* (1955) and dramatized many scenes that were only verbally suggested in the original. In *Stalag 17,* on the other hand, he deliberately confined the story to a single setting in order not to relax its claustrophobic tensions.

Wilder's gallery of characters is crammed with offbeat treasures. Most of them are sellouts, burnouts, and other desperate types. They are almost invariably intelligent, if disreputable. Stephen Farber notes that virtually all Wilder's movies hinge on a deception of some kind, usually with larcenous and/or lecherous intent. Many of the protagonists are phonies and con men, but as Farber also has observed, Wilder's attitude toward them is mixed: If their schemes are sufficiently brazen, he treats

Figure 13.6. Audrey Hepburn in *Sabrina* (1954), released by Paramount. Like almost everyone, Wilder was enchanted by that exquisite sprite, Audrey Hepburn: "After so many drive-in waitresses in movies—it has been a real drought—here is class, somebody who went to school, can spell and possibly play the piano."

them with a degree of sympathy and pays tribute to the imaginative audacity behind their fraudulence. In this respect Wilder resembles the Elizabethan satirist, Ben Jonson, who was more drawn to his demonic swindlers than to the clods who are gulled. One of Wilder's most endearing chiselers is Whiplash Willie, the shyster lawyer in *The Fortune Cookie,* a role that catapulted Walter Matthau to stardom after he had spent years as an obscure character actor. Wilder is fond of paradoxes of character, and one of his favorite ploys is to exaggerate the compelling allure of vice and the dreary respectability of virtue. Innocence is often portrayed as a beguiling form of stupidity. Sometimes this innocence is sexual, as in *The Seven Year Itch* and *Some Like It Hot.* Other times it's political, as in *A Foreign Affair* and *One, Two, Three* (1961). A number of works explore culture clashes between American characters and Europeans, as in *Love in the Afternoon* and *Avanti!*

Many of Wilder's movies are love stories. His lovers are often portrayed as opposite extremes—a virginal character is paired with a dissipated one, for example, or young characters are drawn to older ones—relationships Farber refers to as Wilder's Oedipal euphemisms. Farber also notes that love is seldom a goal for Wilder's characters; it's something they stumble over while pursuing something else, as in *A Foreign Affair, Some Like It Hot,* and *The Apartment.* In *Double Indemnity* the

Figure 13.7. Tom Ewell in *The Seven Year Itch* (1955), released by 20th Century-Fox. Wilder's movies are filled with jokey cinematic allusions. Shown here is a delicious parody-homage to Wilder's longtime friend, Fred Zinnemann. The Walter Mittyish protagonist daydreams that he's making love to a beautiful woman in the same manner as the lovers in *From Here to Eternity* (see Fig. 15.7). His middle-age spread presents an absurdly comical contrast to Burt Lancaster's manly physique, and when the startled Ewell is kissed passionately, it is *he* who exclaims preposterously, "Oh, I never knew it could be like this!"

treacherous Phyllis Dietrichson (Barbara Stanwyck) is sexually aroused by her gullible accomplice (Fred MacMurray) only when he's pressing a revolver into her stomach—just moments before he pumps her full of lead. Love in Wilder's universe is not usually a many-splendored thing, but it does have its kinky highs. "Unless she's a whore, she's a bore," Wilder has said of his favorite female characters. (The same could be said of many of his males.) But not all his women are vicious and futile. Many of his heroines embody such positive values as emotional honesty and trust. Those portrayed by Marilyn Monroe, Audrey Hepburn, and Shirley MacLaine are particularly warm and open—though of course this is also what makes them easy prey for predatory males.

Most of his characters are obsessive personalities. Indeed, some are pushed to the edge of caricature, and a few are almost gargoylelike in their grotesqueness. For example, *Sunset Boulevard* centers on a former silent movie queen (Gloria Swanson) whose career was destroyed by the advent of sound. She is so steeped in vanity and self-delusion that she scarcely deigns to acknowledge the world Since Then—the talkie revolution. When the protagonist (William Holden) stumbles accidentally into her private world, he suddenly realizes who she is. "You're Norma Desmond. You used to be big," he grudgingly admits. "I *am* big," she hisses, "it's the pictures that got small." Though such characters are individualized to an indelible degree, they can also be viewed as personifications of such vices as pride, hypocrisy, and lust.

Wilder is a literary filmmaker. Unlike many Hollywood scenarists, he was not a frustrated novelist or dramatist. He preferred writing directly for the screen. He has always taken pride in the scenarist's art and regards filmmaking as 80 percent writing. A number of his characters

Figure 13.8. Publicity photo of Jack Lemmon and Tony Curtis in *Some Like It Hot* **(1959), distributed by United Artists.** Wilder has been able to mine comedy from the unlikeliest sources: prostitution, fraud, pimping, adultery, the cold war, suicide, prisoners of war, and pictured here, transvestism. Forced to don women's clothing while on the lam from the mob, the musician heroes of this film join an all-girl band to escape detection. Most of the gags revolve around the incongruity of two virile men trying to cope with the agony of womanhood—Lemmon, for example, keeps losing one of his chests.

Figure 13.9. Marilyn Monroe and Tony Curtis in *Some Like It Hot*. The production of this film was total chaos. Marilyn's private life was in a shambles. Repeatedly she needed thirty, forty, even fifty takes before she could warm up to a scene. As co-star Curtis got progressively exhausted, she got better, and Wilder usually had to go with the later takes. In one shot, she had only one line—"Where's that bourbon?"—and she was so disorganized that she had to go through fifty-nine takes before she got the line straight. As usual, she came out smelling like a rose: Her performance is radiant, and she's at the height of her loveliness. "I'm the only director who ever made two pictures with Monroe," Wilder said after the completion of the project. "It behooves the Screen Directors Guild to award me a Purple Heart."

are writers, including Joe Gillis, the scenarist-cum-gigolo in *Sunset Boulevard,* who remarks sardonically, "Audiences don't know that somebody sits down and writes a picture. They think the actors make it up as they go along." A lifelong devotee of literature, Wilder is an avid reader, averaging about ten books per week in three languages. His adaptations have been praised by such original authors as James M. Cain and Agatha Christie, who regarded *Witness for the Prosecution* the finest of all adaptations of her work. Wilder has received eight Writers Guild Awards for his scripts, and in 1957 that organization presented him with their prestigious Laurel Award.

"It's such an ordeal to write, and such a pleasure to direct," Wilder has observed, even though he became a director only in self-defense. "I am not alone in taking this defensive action," he pointed out; "most of the creative film-making in Hollywood (and other world studios) is the result of the writer-director autonomy." All his scripts have been written in collaboration, usually with one other scenarist, one who can keep

Wilder from going off the deep end. Before beginning the actual writing, he first decides on the cast, for he believes that characterization is a collaborative enterprise between the actor and the writer-director. He always starts production with the scenario only two-thirds completed, a practice he developed early in his directing career: "If you give the bosses the third act in advance, they can fire you anytime." He shoots scenes in chronological sequence as much as possible, and though he and his coscenarists usually agree in advance on how the picture will end, the actual scripting of the final act is completed only after production is well underway.

Wilder is touchy about the integrity of his scripts, which are shot exactly as written 95 percent of the time. Actors are not allowed to change a syllable. If a scene repeatedly fails to ignite as written, he and his coscenarist will revise it, grudgingly. "You can be as witty as you like in a script, but if it doesn't show on the screen, it doesn't mean a damned thing," he admits. However, he refuses to make alterations for any other reason. He is regarded as a master of economy in story construction: Each detail has a precise interlocking function. "In a good script, *everything* is necessary or it ain't good," he insists. "And if you take out one piece, you better replace it with a different piece, or you got trouble." He dramatizes situations and characters in terms of images, movement, and iconography, not just dialogue alone. For these reasons, he doesn't think of a scenario as an autonomous literary work. "Giving the average reader a script is like giving him blueprints and asking him to imagine the finished building," he has said.

Wilder often retorts to military metaphors in describing the process of production: "To be a good director, one has to know the script, and then, to be like a general under fire. The screenplay is the battle plan. The filming is when the bullets are flying." Most of the flack comes from actors. He insists that the players recite their lines letter-perfect. In *The Apartment,* Shirley MacLaine had to repeat an entire scene because she forgot one word. Wilder never allows actors to improvise, even at the risk of dissipating their spontaneity. In the complicated shoeshine scene in *One, Two, Three,* James Cagney went through fifty-two takes before he was able to execute all his movements in synchronization with a long speech which had to be delivered at a breakneck tempo. Unfortunately, the results look mechanical and forced, which can be said of very few of Cagney's other performances.

Most actors enjoy working with Wilder because his directions are precise and specific and the atmosphere on his set is usually festive. "I learned more from Billy Wilder than anyone else in the business," MacLaine has stated. She regards him as an excellent judge of performance, functioning more like an editor than a martinet. Others have been less lauditory. Humphrey Bogart loathed him, thinking him authoritarian and inflexible. During the production of *Sabrina,* he needled the director sadistically, referring to him as "that Nazi." Wilder's problems with Marilyn Monroe became legendary. *The Seven Year Itch* ran three weeks over schedule and $1,800,000 over budget because of her fits of moodiness and almost total lack of discipline. "She was never on time once," Wilder complained. Then, adding with a sigh, "On the other hand, I

Figure 13.10. Jack Lemmon in *The Apartment* (1960), art direction by Alexander Trauner, released by United Artists. Wilder has always been a stickler for authenticity in his sets, and Trauner has always delivered—though sometimes he's had to cheat a little. For example, to convey an endless succession of desks receding into the horizon, Trauner used the principle of a diminishing scale for this vast office set. At the rear were placed small-scale desks, with dwarfs as extras.

have an Aunt Ida in Vienna who is always on time, but I wouldn't put her in a movie."

Wilder's close friend, Walter Matthau, believes that the director resents actors and regards them as necessary evils. Nonetheless, Wilder goes to considerable lengths to keep them in good spirits, for in the final analysis, he realizes he's utterly dependent on them. "A movie is a star vehicle," he concedes. "One moment the director is forced to be a nurse-maid, the next a Marquis de Sade. You've got to be a psychoanalyst. You've got to demean yourself. You've got to charm them. You've got to whip them. You've got to bring them the bed pan personally." However, there are some things Wilder refuses to do. He won't light or shoot a scene to heighten a star's glamor if glamor is inappropriate to the role, nor will he conceal physical defects to gratify one's vanity. He never takes extra closeups, for he thinks they should be used sparingly, like a trump in bridge.

At the beginning of his career, Wilder found it difficult to convince stars to accept roles in his films, for his antiheroes were a far cry from the moral paragons that most leading men of that era regarded as suitable material. MacMurray repeatedly refused the lead in *Double Indemnity* because he was afraid his image as a happy-go-lucky nice guy would be destroyed by the part. Wilder badgered him into it. He also hounded Ray Milland until he agreed to play the drunk in *The Lost Weekend.* Holden was virtually blackmailed into *Stalag 17,* and like Milland, was rewarded with an Oscar for best actor. Once Wilder was established, most ambitious actors agreed to work in his movies script unseen—a rare compliment for any filmmaker. He has always tailored his dialogue to fit the personality of his stars. When Montgomery Clift backed out of playing the lead in *Sunset Boulevard,* Wilder rewrote the part to fit William Holden, who brought totally different character nuances to the role. Similarly, when Paul Douglas died two weeks before production was to begin on *The Apartment,* MacMurray was asked to take over the part, which was completely revised to exploit his personality.

Jack Lemmon has starred in seven of Wilder's films. His brilliant performances in *Some Like It Hot* and *The Apartment* established him as a star of the first rank. He regards Wilder as a genius and credits him with suggesting many of the actor's details in characterization. Lemmon's roles might be regarded as variations on the quintessential Wilder protagonist—the weak compromiser who's not as smart as he thinks he is. Neurotic and fussy, the Lemmon character is usually sucked into conspiracies that promise easy success but somehow turn rancid. Paralyzed with indecision, he thrashes and frets and sighs and occasionally explodes into paroxysms of self-loathing. His character abounds with contradictions. He's both a schnook and an opportunist, a victim and a victimizer. But in the end, he prefers being a *mensch* to a swine. He's Wilder's portrait of the loser as a winner, with more class than he realizes.

"I admire elegant camerawork, but not fancy stuff," Wilder has said. He dislikes virtuoso techniques, considering them arty. He believes that a filmmaker is above all a storyteller, and anything that interferes with telling a story is self-indulgence: "I would like to give the impression that the best directing is the one you don't see. The audience must forget that they are in front of a screen—they must be sucked into the screen to the point when they forget that the image is only two-dimensional." The hallmark of his style is simplicity: "I like to tell my stories with a minimum of camera interruption—camera movement, closeups, quick cuts, must be used like punctuations in a novel. They must emphasize and not distract, surprise but not weary by overemphasis." He is a classicist.

This is not to say that Wilder's mise-en-scène is plain or lacking in textural richness, which is far from the case. He is sensitive to visual nuances and insists on approving every detail of his sets, costumes, and props. His regular set designer, Alexander Trauner, is one of the most admired in the world and is particularly respected for his authenticity. Wilder has the proverbial painter's eye for composition, and in fact is the foremost art collector in the film colony. (His collection boasts over three hundred pieces, many of which must be stored in a warehouse, if they're not out on loan to museums. He owns eight Picassos and paintings by Klee, Kirchner, Chagall, Dufy, Renoir, Rouault, Braque, Pissarro, and Bonnard. He was collecting works by Schiele and Klimpt long before they became fashionable. Wilder also owns sculptures by Henry Moore,

Figure 13.11. Jack Lemmon and Shirley MacLaine in *The Apartment*, music by Adolph Deutsch. "Fluffy comedies about New York working girls who earn $60 a week and manage to live in all white apartments and wear designer clothes will always continue to be popular, no doubt," Wilder observed. "But not with me. I want to go beyond the powder-puff school and find humor in a situation that is normally treated with solemnity." He believes that comedy needs a strong story line to be compelling, that with only a slight shift in emphasis, a good comedy could be played as a straight drama. He has also succeeded in fusing satire with romanticism, perhaps most effectively in this film, thanks in part to Deutsch's lush, Gershwin-like score.

Giacometti, and Noguchi and paintings by such American artists as Ben Shahn, Larry Rivers, and Saul Steinberg.) The visual style of each of Wilder's movies is unique and is geared to the materials. He dislikes shooting in color and thinks black-and-white photography is more subtle. Even in the 1960s, when virtually every filmmaker converted to color cinematography, Wilder was a holdout. He also disliked cinemascope, though in fact such widescreen movies as *The Apartment,* despite its confined intimacy, is exquisitely composed.

Wilder prefers working with a crew of regulars, like his longtime associate, Doane Harrison, who was his production assistant for over twenty-five years. Working on a Wilder project is considered a plum assignment by most technicians, for his salaries are traditionally among the highest in the industry, not to speak of frequent gifts, bonuses, and location amenities. Wilder is much admired by crews for his efficiency and professionalism. Almost all his movies were completed on schedule and within budget. He dislikes wasting time, money, and footage. He knows exactly what he wants for each shot, and he cuts in the camera as much as possible. His films average about four minutes' worth of outtakes—which requires an extraordinary degree of control. In his studio days this economy also prevented front-office meddlers from tampering with his footage. Ever since the teens, sneak previews were considered mandatory in Hollywood, especially for comedies. Wilder was one of the first to question this practice, for a number of his most popular works elicited hostile reactions from sneak preview audiences, including *Double Indemnity, The Lost Weekend, Sunset Boulevard,* and even the exhilarating *Some Like It Hot.*

Up until 1963, almost all Wilder's movies were popular with the public. After that, none were. *Kiss Me, Stupid* (1964) was ravaged by critics, and Wilder was shaken by its poor public reception. Shortly after its release, a sympathetic friend visited him and Diamond at their office. He found them both deeply depressed and unable to work. "We feel like parents who have given birth to a mongoloid child," Wilder explained. "Now we keep asking ourselves—do we dare screw again?" Ironically,

Figure 13.12.   Kim Novak, Dean Martin, and Ray Walston in *Kiss Me, Stupid* (1964), distributed by Lopert Pictures. This film created a furor when it was first released. Reviewers vied with one another in the racy censoriousness of their adjectives: "squalid," "sleazy," "smutty," "coarse," "the slimiest movie of the year," and so on. The Catholic Legion of Decency, which hadn't awarded a Condemned rating since Kazan's *Baby Doll* in 1956, denounced Wilder's film for its "crude and suggestive dialogue, a leering treatment of marital and extra-marital sex, and a prurient preoccupation with lechery." Wilder has never denied his cynicism, but he believes that his films are an accurate reflection of American society: "We are a nation of hecklers, the most hardboiled, undisciplined people in the world."

just as the mainstream American cinema veered into a stridently self-critical cycle in the late 1960s (see Chapter 16), Wilder's movies grew mellow and more romantic. Also ironically, critics increasingly expressed admiration for the creator of such elegant entertainments as *The Private Life of Sherlock Holmes* and *Avanti!*

Widespread critical approval came late in Wilder's career, after he had completed the bulk of his work. The Museum of Modern Art held a retrospective in 1964, when curator Richard Griffith described the filmmaker as "the most precise, indeed relentless, chronicler of the postwar American in shade as well as light, that the motion picture has produced." Other important retrospectives followed in Paris, Los Angeles, and Berlin. In London the British Film Institute sponsored a Wilder series which was greeted with thunderous applause. "In a world all too obsessively infected with the cult of ghastly good taste," said the majesterial London *Times,* "thank heavens for Mr. Billy Wilder."

BIBLIOGRAPHY

BAXTER, JOHN.   *The Hollywood Exiles.* New York: Taplinger Publishing, 1976. Contains several chapters on the German colony in pre-World War II Hollywood. See also Paul Monaco, *Cinema & Society* (New York: Elsevier North-Holland, 1976): the German film industry in the 1920s.

"Charming Billy," in *Playboy* (December, 1960). Other interviews include "Billy Wilder," in *The Celluloid Muse,* Charles Higham and Joel Greenberg, eds. (New York: Signet Books, 1972); "An Interview with Billy Wilder," in *Playboy* (June, 1963); and "Billy Wilder," an interview with Gene D. Phillips, in *Literature/Film Quarterly* (Winter, 1976).

FARBER, STEPHEN.   "The Films of Billy Wilder," in *Film Comment* (Winter, 1971–1972). An excellent critical study. See also Robert Munday, "Wilder Reappraised," in *Cinema* (Great Britain, October, 1969).

FROUG, WILLIAM, ed.   "I.A.L. Diamond," in *The Screenwriter Looks at the Screenwriter.* New York: Delta Books, 1972. Interview. See also "Billy Wilder and I.A.L. Diamond," in "Dialogue on Film," in *American Film* (July-August, 1976); and "Billy Wilder" and "Charles Brackett," in *Talking Pictures,* Richard Corliss, ed. (New York: Penguin, 1975).

MADSEN, AXEL.   *Billy Wilder.* Bloomington: Indiana University Press, 1967. Biography and critical study, with filmography.

SEIDMAN, STEVE.   *The Film Career of Billy Wilder.* Boston: G. K. Hall, 1977. Critical study, and the most extensive bibliography and filmography.

WILDER, BILLY.   "One Head is Better Than Two," in *Hollywood Directors: 1941 – 1976,* Richard Koszarski, ed. New York: Oxford University Press, 1977. An article on his views about filmmaking.

———, AND I. A. L. DIAMOND.   *The Apartment* and *The Fortune Cookie.* New York: Praeger, 1971. Reading versions of screenplays. See also the *Ninotchka* entry in the bibliography of Lubitsch.

WOOD, TOM.   *The Bright Side of Billy Wilder, Primarily.* New York: Doubleday, 1970. Biography, with filmography.

ZOLOTOW, MAURICE.   *Billy Wilder in Hollywood.* New York: Putnam's, 1977. A lively and perceptive biography.

Figure 14.1. Elia Kazan, during the production of *The Arrangement* (1969), distributed by Warner Brothers. From the time he was a zealous member of the American Communist party as a youth, Kazan considered himself a revolutionary artist. Though he eventually turned against communism, he never abandoned Marxism; he merely modified it to fit his own temperament and the realities of American life. Of course yesterday's radicalism has a way of becoming today's centrism. The Marxist influence in Kazan's movies might seem less apparent from the perspective of the present. However, the following characteristics of his oeuvre might be regarded as essentially Marxist in origin: (1) the use of art as a tool for social change and the belief that all art is at least implicitly ideological, affirming or challenging the status quo; (2) a demystification of power: how it's actually wielded and who it benefits; (3) the assumption that capitalism exploits the working class to further the interests of a small ruling class; (4) an identification with oppressed minorities; (5) the belief that environment largely determines human behavior; (6) a rejection of religion and the supernatural in favor of a strict scientific materialism; (7) a belief in the equality of the sexes and races; and (8) a dialectical view of history and knowledge, in which progress is the result of a conflict and ultimate synthesis of opposites.

A child of the New Deal, Kazan is one of the most political filmmakers of the American cinema and one of its most disruptive forces. His exposure to the ideas of Marx and Freud in the live theatre of the 1930s exerted a strong influence on his postwar cinematic output, a period in which he was also caught up in the political hysteria of the cold war. At the height of his success (roughly from 1947 to 1961) he was called a "two-coast genius," mounting the premiere productions of such distinguished dramatists as Tennessee Williams and Arthur Miller on the New York stage, and directing such important movies as *On the Waterfront* and *East of Eden,* which were huge box office hits. None of his twenty or so movies was considered safe, and many of them lost money. His brilliance with actors is undisputed: Twenty-one of his performers have been nominated for Academy Awards, and nine of them have won. Kazan spearheaded a revolution in acting styles in the 1950s. The Method has since become the dominant tradition of acting in American movies as well as in the live theatre. His range is narrow: mostly literary and dramatic adaptations and social dramas. Within these genres, he is capable of projecting an extraordinary virility while still capturing the poetry of everyday life. His themes almost invariably revolve around conflicts between the individual and society, but few filmmakers have explored this topic with such ambivalence and emotional intensity.

This is my relationship with America: I really love it and have great resentment against it.

—Elia Kazan

Elia Kazanjoglou was born in 1909 near Istanbul. Like other displaced Greeks living in Turkish Asia Minor, his family had endured the most appalling persecution. They survived by their wits, keeping a low profile whenever the Turks embarked on their murderous rampages. To circumvent the quotidian tyranny of their masters, the Greek minority employed guile and cunning. To this day, Kazan speaks both Greek and Turkish—the languages of the oppressed and of the oppressors. When the family fled to America in 1913, shortening their name to Kazan, they moved into a Greek ghetto in New York City, where they prospered as rug merchants. Suspicious of assimilation, Kazan's father taught him to be sly and crafty if he hoped to survive in an alien environment. The youth grew up in an atmosphere of paranoia, and he had no friends until he was eleven years old.

When he attended Williams College in the late 1920s, Kazan felt more isolated than ever. He viewed Williams as a bastion of WASP exclusiveness, and he resented his classmates' air of superiority. The crash of 1929 wiped out his family's modest holdings, and he had to wash dishes and wait on tables in order to stay in school. Throughout this period, he smoldered in anger, but his sense of alienation made him tough and tenacious. Since childhood he had been attracted to the arts, an interest his cultivated mother had encouraged as much as his father had ridiculed. Upon graduating from college in 1930, young Kazan decided to attend Yale University's School of Drama. The training he received there was comprehensive, and he felt less disaffected, for his classmates were mostly bohemian types who judged him on the basis of his talent rather than his pedigree. They too washed dishes and waited on tables.

"I'm a child of the thirties," Kazan has stated. During the Great Depression he converted his anger into an intense political activism. Karl Marx was his god. Kazan was also influenced by the ideas of Freud and by the revolutionary movies of such Soviet artists as Eisenstein and Dov-zhenko. Kazan's feelings for his adopted country also began to change. He identified strongly with the American working class and adopted the rough clothing of laborers as a symbolic repudiation of bourgeois values. In his travels across the country, he was intoxicated by its color, romance, and excitement. What he still lacked, however, was an artistic outlet for these enthusiasms. He was not long in waiting. "All of these trends came together in the Group Theatre," Kazan has recalled, "the political Left, the introduction to Freud and Marx, the absolute, idealistic dedication and determination towards a new world."

The Group Theatre was founded by Lee Strasberg and Harold Clurman, who wanted a theatre of social relevance. It was only one of many leftist theatre organizations in the 1930s (see Chapter 11). The Group Theatre was even a collective for a brief period: Its members cooked, lived, and worked together. Kazan joined in 1932 as an actor, and eventually he became a writer and director as well. Even by depression standards, his $18 a week salary was low. Like most of his comrades, Kazan also joined the American Communist party, and he made many political speeches on streetcorners. He wrote several agit-prop (agitation propaganda) plays to awaken blue-collar workers to their collective power. He idealized the U.S.S.R. and such Soviet theatre artists as Meyerhold, Vakhtangov, and Stanislavsky.

The Group Theatre's ideal was to discover the poetry in the common things of life. It was influenced by the psychological theory of acting promulgated by the Soviet stage director, Constantine Stanislavsky. "Stanislavsky was also peculiarly suited to us because he emphasized not the heroic man but the hero in every man," Kazan recalled. "That Russian idea of the profound soul of the inconspicuous person also fits the American temperament." He adhered religiously to the strict regimen of exercises of Stanislavsky's method, or the Method, as it was commonly called in America. As an actor, Kazan was fiery and intense (one reviewer called him "the proletarian thunderbolt"), but his range was narrow.

His disillusionment with communism took place in 1935. He and other Communist party members of the Group Theatre were instructed to go on strike and wrest control of the organization from Strasberg and Clurman, who were not Communists. Kazan refused to take part in this treachery. He was tried for failing to follow orders and expelled from the party. Bitter as he was, he still had faith in the U.S.S.R. "We believed the lies they told," he recalled in later years. When he heard rumors of the mass killings of Stalin's purges, Kazan's faith waivered, and with the Hitler-Stalin pact of 1939, he gave up entirely on the U.S.S.R. Although still a leftist, he was passionately opposed to the totalitarian and repressive form of communism which came to be known as Stalinism.

The New Deal ushered in an era of hope. Like many leftists, Kazan originally feared that Roosevelt's relief program was merely a Band-Aid remedy for the serious economic ills of that era. Eventually, he came to believe that FDR's selective use of Marxist principles to bolster the capitalistic system was what most Americans really wanted. To this day, Roosevelt is his political idol. Furthermore, Kazan believes that social equality is likely to be evolutionary rather than revolutionary: "I believe that socialism will win in the world—maybe not fast enough in every way, but it is going that way." During this same period, Kazan began to develop doubts about the political efficacy of the Group Theatre, whose patrons, like himself, were mostly left-wing intellectuals aspiring to be proletarian. Working-class audiences were going to the movies. More and more, he was drawn to film as the best medium for communicating his views.

Kazan believes that the influence of Marxism hasn't been entirely salutary in his work. For example, he considers his early movies excessively dogmatic: The ideas are too glib and clear, uncontaminated by the contradictions of life. He believes that many Marxists are not truly dialectical. His own works are profoundly so. He's fascinated by self-contradiction, paradox, and ambivalence. His characters are often attracted to their opposites, even at the risk of self-destruction. He believes that life is a process of constant renewal: "I always felt that one had to turn against oneself, to turn against one's past." *Wild River* (1960) is a good example of Kazan's dialectical method at work. The movie doesn't pit good against bad so much as one kind of good against another kind. The story is set in Tennessee during the depression and concerns the conflict between a TVA official (Montgomery Clift) and an old matriarch (Jo Van Fleet), who refuses to move from her island home even though it will be submerged after the dam is completed. Kazan treats both sides sympathetically: The matriarch's stubborn individualism is accorded the same respect as the official's bewildered idealism. The film's tone is characteristically ambivalent. On the one hand, Kazan recognizes that the TVA relieved the misery of hundreds of thousands of Americans; on the other hand, he laments the passing of a certain kind of innocence and grandeur of spirit. The movie is an elegaical lament for a lost individualism—a casualty of progress.

In the late 1930s, Kazan finally got a chance to work in film. A number of leftist artists, including the photographers Leo Hurwitz, Paul Strand, and Ralph Steiner, had established their own company, Frontier Films, in order to make documentaries with a strong emphasis on social reform. Kazan's *People of the Cumberland* (1937) was a twenty-minute film about coal miners, shot entirely on location, with nonprofessionals in the cast. "That experience showed me that before and beyond a script there was life itself to photograph," Kazan said, an attitude that was to exert an influence on his fiction filmmaking as well.

He came into his own in the decade of the 1940s. His first big break came when he directed the premiere stage production of Thornton Wilder's *The Skin of Our Teeth* (1942). From then onward, he was one of Broadway's busiest directors, with four productions playing simultaneously for a brief period. On the basis of his success as a stage director, he received several offers to go to Hollywood, primarily from Warner Brothers and 20th Century-Fox. Both studios had made many movies revolving around contemporary social problems. In 1944 he finally signed with Fox. His contract called for one picture per year for five years, with no final-cut privileges. It wasn't a great contract compared to the one RKO had given Orson Welles, but at least Kazan was free to direct other movies and plays provided he fulfilled his obligations to Fox. [Kazan was not to abandon the New York theatre for another twenty years, and throughout much of this period, he was the most eminent stage director in the United States as well as a filmmaker. His productions included such classics of the American theatre as Arthur Miller's *All My Sons* (1947), Tennessee Williams's *A Streetcar Named Desire* (1947), Miller's *Death of a Salesman* (1949), Williams's *Camino Real* (1953) and *Cat on a Hot Tin Roof* (1955), William Inge's *The Dark at the Top of the Stairs* (1957), Archibald McLeish's *J.B.* (1958), Williams's *Sweet Bird of Youth* (1959), and Miller's *After the Fall* (1964).]

The cocky and diminutive Darryl F. Zanuck headed 20th Century-Fox. Most of the moguls were politically conservative, and some, like MGM's Louis B. Mayer, were outright reactionaries. Zanuck was perhaps the most liberal—in theory, if not always in practice. Though the studio's pictures were diversified, he tended to favor topical and controversial subjects, with an emphasis on story values rather than stars. Energetic, strutting, and competitive, he liked to put his personal stamp on his pictures, but as Kazan was to discover, the mogul's contributions were by no means contemptible. When World War II broke out, Zanuck—who was intensely patriotic—enlisted in the Army and became a producer of documentaries. In the postwar era he was one of the first to sense that American audiences had changed as a result of the war. Fox became the leading producer of films of social commentary, and it also was the first to abandon the soft, romantic style of photography which had typified the prewar era. The movies at Fox were usually shot in razor-sharp focus. Kazan respected Zanuck and thought him a decent, honest man, though perhaps too eager to curry favor at the box office at the expense of truth. Kazan also thought the mogul was tuned in to American society: "Zanuck was always a man of the people. If something was being felt, he felt it."

Kazan's first assignment at Fox was *A Tree Grows in Brooklyn* (1945), which was a modest success at the box office. He wanted to shoot the movie on location, but Zanuck insisted on studio sets. Kazan believes that the picture's glossiness is at odds with the harsh realism the story required. *Boomerang!* (1947), a story of civic corruption based on an actual event, was made on location with a largely nonprofessional cast—only its five principals were trained actors. Its photographic style was matter-of-factly plain. Kazan's next project, *Gentleman's Agreement* (1948), dealt with anti-Semitism, which was still a taboo theme in Hollywood. Zanuck, a Gentile, thought the film should be made, even against the objection of the other moguls, who preferred keeping a low ethnic profile. The movie won the Academy Award for best picture, as well as an Oscar for Kazan's direction. He went on to direct another social exposé, *Pinky* (1949), which dealt with American racism and was one of Fox's biggest grossers. As a result of these films, Kazan was admitted to the forefront of American directors. He initiated most of his subsequent projects and had total or near-total artistic autonomy.

During this same period, Kazan was involved in one of the most bizarre chapters of American history—the Red scare. In Hollywood the anti-Communist hysteria began in 1947, and its effects could still be felt

Figure 14.2. Gregory Peck and Dorothy McGuire in *Gentleman's Agreement* **(1948), produced by 20th Century-Fox.** Kazan regards this and its companion film, *Pinky*, as Zanuck's pictures. Although not denying the courage it took to make such movies, Kazan finds them slick and compromised. The characters are excessively heroic and lacking in psychological complexity. The social problems are oversimplified, resolved with pious clichés. He believes that the rough contradictions of life were ironed out in the scripting and prettified in the casting, over which he had little control.

until the late 1950s. It was flamed by Stalin's takeover of eastern Europe and by the Korean War, in which 50,000 Americans were killed. The Congressional House Un-American Activities Committee (HUAC) set out to investigate Communist propaganda in American movies. (A handful of pro-Soviet films had been produced during World War II, ironically at the request of the U.S. government, to bolster the image of our wartime ally. Most of these pictures failed at the box office.) HUAC was chaired by J. Parnell Thomas, a notorious Red-baiter who considered the New Deal to be Communist inspired and who opposed the Congressional antilynching bill, as well as fair employment legislation. Other HUAC members included John E. Rankin, an admitted racist and anti-Semite, and young Richard M. Nixon, who learned a great deal during the proceedings. Many careers were launched as a result of the HUAC hearings. Many more were destroyed. "Friendly" witnesses were allowed to make opening statements and were granted immunity from prosecution for libel. There followed an orgy of character assassination, almost all of it based on hearsay and malice. Many of the fingered victims were writers, many of them Jewish, with roots in the New York theatre of the 1930s. Friendly witness Ayn Rand went so far as to brand Louis B. Mayer as "not much better than an agent of Communism," because

MGM (the least political of the majors) had produced *Song of Russia,* which actually showed Russian peasants smiling. "Unfriendly" witnesses, who were mostly liberals and not Communists, were not allowed to make opening statements nor to cross-examine their accusers. Unfriendly witnesses were widely branded as Communists because they challenged the legality of a committee that violated the First Amendment's guarantee of freedom of speech and conscience. Witnesses were coerced into revealing not only their own political pasts but those of their associates as well. Actor Larry Parks was reduced to tears when he was forced to inform on his friends, most of whom had long abandoned their interest in politics. (Being left was chic in the 1930s.) Their careers were ruined. Ten witnesses, mostly scenarists, refused to cooperate entirely, and they served prison sentences for contempt of Congress. The famous Hollywood Ten were Alvah Bessie, Herbert Biberman, Lester Cole, Edward Dmytryk, Ring Lardner, Jr., John Howard Lawson, Albert Maltz, Samuel Ornitz, Adrian Scott, and Dalton Trumbo. When they were released from jail, they found themselves blacklisted in the industry, along with an estimated 400 others. Senator Joseph McCarthy joined in the hunt and upped the stakes. He produced a list of 324 "known Communists" within the industry. The American Legion provided 356 more names. None of

Figure 14.3. Marlon Brando and Vivien Leigh in *A Streetcar Named Desire* (1951), script by Tennessee Williams, distributed by Warner Brothers. The original Broadway cast re-created their roles for the movie version of Williams's play except for Vivien Leigh, who played the role of Blanche du Bois in the original London stage production. Audiences were electrified by the sparks thrown off in the scenes between Leigh and Brando. *Streetcar* is that rarest of species—a movie masterpiece based on a literary masterpiece.

the accusations was substantiated, nor did HUAC ever deign to offer the title of a single movie that was Communist inspired.

The industry was paralyzed with fear, for the Hearst press and others had been calling for stringent federal censorship of films. To show their good faith, the studios produced a spate of blatantly anti-Communist movies, most of which failed at the box office. Such industry liberals as Wyler, Huston, Bogart, and Lauren Bacall helped form the Committee for the First Amendment, which publicized the Constitutional violations of HUAC and McCarthy. The Writers Guild strongly opposed the blacklist, which was condemned by a vote of four hundred to eight. Eventually even industry conservatives, like John Ford, spoke out against the witch-hunts. In 1954, the televised Army-McCarthy hearings revealed the senator for what he was, and public sentiment veered sharply against him. Later he was censured by the Senate. The hysteria began to subside—very slowly. A number of blacklisted writers were still working, at vastly reduced wages, during this period, but they were forced to use pseudonymns. By the end of the decade, such producer-directors as Otto Preminger and Stanley Kramer were the first to defy this practice, and blacklisted writers were finally allowed public credit for their work.

Kazan was a friendly witness. And he named names—twelve of them. He had strong misgivings about his collaboration with HUAC, for though he hated Stalin (whom he considered as evil as Hitler), Kazan also hated McCarthy and other elements of the extreme right. Nor did he lie to the committee: He made it plain that he favored a strong non-Communist left in the United States. During this same period, of course, he continued making movies that were critical of America's social hypocrisies. The studios exploited Kazan's vulnerability by cutting his salary in half after he testified: He was now damaged goods. He was harshly criticized by the liberal press for cooperating with HUAC. Filmmaker Abraham Polonsky, who was blacklisted for many years, claimed that Kazan's subsequent work was "marked by bad conscience." Others have interpreted such movies as *Viva Zapata!* (1952), *Man on a Tightrope* (1953), and *On the Waterfront* (1954) as rationalizations for informing.

Kazan doesn't deny the autobiographical element in his work. Indeed, he insists upon it: "Every film is autobiographical," he claims. "A thing in my life is expressed by the essence of the film. I've got to feel that it's in some way about me, some way about my struggles, some way about my pain, my hopes." He identified strongly with Terry Malloy (Marlon Brando) in *Waterfront*. The dupe of a paternalistic labor racketeer, Malloy decides, after agonizing with his conscience, to cooperate with a government investigating committee and is subsequently spurned by the fellow longshoremen he wanted to help. Similarly, *East of Eden* (1955) involves a clash of moral values between a rebellious son (James Dean) and his strong-willed and righteous father (Raymond Massey). "It's really the story of my father and me," Kazan has observed of the film, "and I didn't realize it for a long time."

Except for his early Zanuck pictures, Kazan has been able to work with few compromises to his artistic integrity. After the enormous suc-

Figure 14.4. Marlon Brando in *Viva Zapata!* (1952), with Joseph Wiseman (center) produced by 20th Century-Fox. An epic tale of Marxist idealism betrayed, this film has the unusual distinction of having been denounced by the extreme left and the extreme right. The character of Aguire (Wiseman) is a portrait of a Stalinist. Kazan said of him, "He typifies the men who use the just grievances of the people for their own ends, who shift and twist their course, betray any friend or principle or promise to get power and keep it."

cess of *Waterfront* in 1954, he produced most of his own movies. His company, Newtown Productions, is New York based, for he has always disliked the cultural and political atmosphere of the Los Angeles area. A number of other filmmakers followed suit by using New York as their base of operations: Sidney Lumet, Arthur Penn, Brian De Palma, and Woody Allen, among others. Kazan has always been confident of his artistic powers and has been willing to fight for his ideas. Not that he wants to be surrounded by zombies. He finds disagreements stimulating, and he believes that the chief enemy of art is indifference. He has even praised some of his producers. For example, he regards Sam Spiegel, who produced *Waterfront* and *The Last Tycoon* (1976), as one of the most creative people he has worked with. Although he is a harsh self-critic, Kazan's critiques of his work usually involve errors in execution. He has never disavowed a film for its ideas or values.

"I think a work of art is good when it has trailing roots that go into society," Kazan has stated, "and through it, you get a clearer view of the society. That's what I've always tried to do in films." A number of critics have pointed out that his movies might be viewed as spiritual barometers

Figure 14.5. Marlon Brando and Eva Marie Saint in *On the Waterfront* (1954), distributed by Columbia Pictures. "At his best," Kazan said, "Brando was the best actor we've had in this country in my time." Many regard this performance as his very best—emotionally powerful, tender, poetic. It won him his first Academy Award for best actor, as well as the New York Film Critics Award and the British Oscar as best foreign actor—his third year in a row. Kazan was often surprised by his gifted protégé, because he came up with ideas so fresh and arrived at in so underground a fashion that they seemed virtually discovered on the spot. See Joe Morella and Edward Z. Epstein, *Brando: The Unauthorized Biography* (New York: Crown Publishers, 1973).

of the national psyche. He has always believed that it was his responsibility as a citizen-artist to speak out against injustice and to exert pressure on public policy as strongly as possible. "I was born in another country, and I have been in many countries and therefore, more than most American men I know, I appreciate and value what we have here, while at the same time not closing my eyes to our faults and differences," he's observed. Throughout most of his career, he believed that American society was basically healthy and that justice would eventually prevail. However, like John Ford, who influenced him more than any other American filmmaker, Kazan grew more pessimistic with age. During the Vietnam era especially, his faith in American institutions wavered. *The Arrangement* (1969) and *The Visitors* (1971) reflect this darker vision. Nonetheless, he saw great moral strength in the protest movement of this same era (see Chapter 16), and he was heartened by the revival of interest in Marxism. He considered the New Left less dogmatic and authoritarian than the old left of the 1930s.

"Kazan's career can be seen as a set of variations on the basic theme of the individual as victim of social pressures that demand a caricature of the self and betrayal of the past," Jim Kitses has pointed out in his perceptive analysis of Kazan's work. Most of his movies deal with a conflict of loyalties, in which the protagonist struggles inarticulately to find his essential nature. His struggle is usually dialectical, cutting across cultural boundaries, impelling him to adapt to an alien world, whose values are both alluring and repugnant. In order to fit in, he initially believes that he must repudiate his family, his past, and his cultural origins. He becomes, in effect, a spiritual exile, devoured by guilt and feelings of ambivalence. Only those characters who are able to synthesize the best of both worlds survive with their souls intact. The dialectical tensions between the values of the individual and those of society in Kazan's work might be schematized by the following sets of polarities:

Individual	Society
Past	Future
Instincts	Principles
Freud	Marx
U.S.	U.S.S.R.
Female	Male
Subculture	Establishment
Innocence	Experience
Youth	Adulthood
Victims	Oppressors
Skepticism	Idealism
Self-interest	Solidarity
Tennessee Williams	Arthur Miller
Constantine Stanislavsky	John Ford
Psychological drama	Epic drama
Cinema	Theatre

Many of Kazan's movies deal with the theme of power and its abuses. For example, when the revolutionary hero of *Zapata* is finally able to seize power, he's mired in indecision, unable to wield his power justly, and is ultimately martyred by it. *A Face in the Crowd* (1957) was one of the first movies to deal with the power of television, and it centers on a popular television personality who's destroyed by his own fascist impulses to manipulate the public. A number of Kazan's films deal with the success ethic and the compromises and sellouts that are required to get to the top: *America America* (1963) and *The Arrangement* are virtually parodies of the Horatio Alger myth. In order to acquire or preserve power, Kazan's characters frequently resort to desperate acts of violence—and self-violence.

The image of the family in Kazan's films is at best ambivalent. Beginning the the early 1950s, American movie audiences no longer consisted of the monolithic family trade of the prewar era but of smaller, more specialized audiences. By far the largest of these was the so-called youth audience, which responded enthusiastically to films that pleaded the cause of adolescents. Two of Kazan's biggest hits dealt with the

Figure 14.6. *On the Waterfront,* **with (left to right) Tony Galento, Lee J. Cobb, Karl Malden, Eva Marie Saint, and John Hamilton.** Among other things, this movie is a milestone of cinematic realism. The script was based on a series of articles by Malcolm Johnson, exposing labor racketeering in the longshoreman's union. Like most of Kazan's best works, it was shot on location. Boris Kaufman's gritty photographic style was startlingly deglamorized in comparison to most fiction films of this era. Costumer Anna Hill Johnstone found most of the actors' clothing in second-hand stores in the neighborhood. The cast was virtually a showcase for the "new" acting style called the Method—so naturalistic that traditional styles looked studied in comparison. All the players look as though they had spent their lives on real streets, not sound stages.

problems of young people with their parents: *East of Eden* and *Splendor in the Grass* (1961). Tortured relationships within families abound in his works, as Kitses and Estelle Changas have pointed out. Some of these conflicts are between brothers (*Zapata, Eden, Waterfront*), between generations (*Pinky, Eden, Splendor, America, Wild River*), and often between sons and fathers or father-figures (*Zapata, Waterfront, Eden, Splendor, America, Arrangement, Visitors,* and *Last Tycoon*).

Like his contemporaries, Huston, Wilder, Zinnemann, and Welles, Kazan has a literary sensibility. In interviews he's highly articulate. He has written several popular novels, which served as bases for his movies. *The Arrangement* was the top bestseller in the United States for thirty-seven weeks. Kazan has collaborated on most of his screenplays and even on some of his stage plays. For example, he helped rewrite two of Williams's plays, *Sweet Bird of Youth* and *Cat on a Hot Tin Roof.* He is close friends with Williams and Arthur Miller, who have both had a strong influence on Kazan's filmmaking. He feels closer to Williams than to any other dramatist. Kazan agreed to film *Streetcar* at the author's request.

It's the finest of all of Williams's adaptations. Budd Schulberg, the novelist and scenarist who scripted *Waterfront* and *Face in the Crowd,* has praised Kazan's rapport with writers and writing: "He's been a pioneer, sometimes I think the *only* pioneer, in treating screenplays with the same respect that he would give a work written for the stage." Because of his theatre experience, Kazan refused to separate writing from directing. When he first went to Hollywood, he was appalled by the shabby way writers were treated. He has always preferred working with novelists and dramatists rather than professional scenarists. His relationship with his writers is usually close and personal as well as professional. Whenever possible, he prefers them to remain on the set, in case of last-minute adjustments in the script.

Kazan believes that some of his early movies suffered because he was *too* respectful of scripts. He thinks that a screenplay's worth is measured less by its language than by its architecture and how it shapes and dramatizes the theme. In most cases, a script is not a piece of writing so much as a construction. The director's job is to learn to feel for the skeleton under the skin of words: "I always try to leave the script free enough, open enough so that the human material that's being photo-

Figure 14.7. Julie Harris and James Dean in *East of Eden* (1955), distributed by Warner Brothers. This movie catapulted Dean to stardom. Millions of young people identified with his tortured sensitivity. "His face is so desolate and lonely and strange," Kazan said of the young actor. He soon developed a reputation for being neurotic and self-destructive. He died in an auto crash at the age of twenty-four, shortly after the release of this film. He was virtually deified by his cult followers, mostly young people, who idealized him as a symbol of misunderstood youth. Kazan regarded these cult followers as misguided: "What I disliked was the Dean legend. He was the glorification of hatred and sickness. When he got success he was victimized by it."

graphed is not rigidly arranged to the point of choking out surprises, any unexpected possibilities." Kazan derived the idea of a subtext from Stanislavsky:

> The film director knows that beneath the surface of his screenplay there is a subtext, a calandar of intentions and feelings and inner events. What appears to be happening, he soon learns, is rarely what is happening. The subtext is one of the film director's most valuable tools. It is what he directs. You will rarely see a veteran director holding a script as he works—or even looking at it.

The subtext involves what's beneath the language of the script: not what people say, but what they really want but are afraid to ask. Spoken dialogue is always secondary to Kazan. His concern is with an inner dialogue, and in order to capture this, he sometimes allows his actors to throw away their lines, to choke on them, or even to mumble. (Throughout the 1950s, Method actors like Brando and Dean were ridiculed by some critics and industry regulars for mumbling their lines.)

Kazan's interest in character is strong. He dislikes conventional leading men and leading lady roles, and he was one of the first postwar filmmakers to reject sexual stereotypes in favor of a more dialectical approach to characterization. His males are generally played by sexually magnetic actors such as Brando, Dean, and Warren Beatty. Yet these obvious studs are allowed many "feminine" characteristics, like tenderness, eroticism, indecisiveness. They cry under intense emotional pressures. (On the other hand, while making *Gone with the Wind* in the prewar era, Clark Gable refused to play in a scene in which Rhett Butler cries over his child's death. The actor thought it would compromise his masculine image. Under pressure, he finally submitted.) Kazan's female characters are usually strong, articulate, and mature. They often act as moral catalysts, impelling the men they love to face up to their self-deceptions and fears. Rarely are Kazan's females characterized as sex objects—though they can be sexy, girlish, and even maternal. Their strength can be surprising because they are generally played by actresses who are vulnerable and feminine, such as Eva Marie Saint in *Waterfront,* Julie Harris in *Eden,* and Lee Remick in *Wild River.* Kazan believes that women bring out the more sensitive side of his talent, and like Ford, he regards them as a civilizing force. He has always been attracted to honest and direct female characters, and he tends to cast actresses who are not conventionally glamorous to play them. While working on a movie, Kazan keeps a notebook describing all his characters—their essential natures, their self-contradictions, the way they relate to others and to the theme. He believes that people reveal themselves most fully under duress, with their backs against the wall. But he dislikes characters who are too definitive, and he tries to preserve in them an air of mystery, of the unknowable: "I try to be critical but loving, privately uncertain, with my characters."

Throughout the 1950s Kazan was said to have "invented" the Method, which he repeatedly pointed out was not new and was not his. It was an off-shoot of Stanislavsky's system of training actors and rehears-

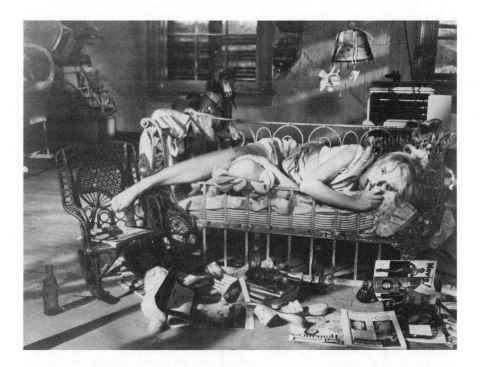

Figure 14.8. Carroll Baker in *Baby Doll* (1956), distributed by Warner Brothers. Most of this film was shot in Kazan's favorite region, the American South. He wanted the movie to be irreverent, playful, and grotesque, with elements of the real and the fantastic spilling over each other. "The highest form of art," he believes, "is when there's no formalistic 'genre' difference between the comedy, the farce, the tragedy, the social meaning, the symbolism. It's one piece." The picture provoked a controversy by its frank depiction of sexual tensions. Quipped Billy Wilder after seeing the film, "Why, the times are almost ripe for a movie about a young man who has a passionate love affair with his mother. At the end he learns that she is not his mother and he commits suicide."

ing, which he had developed at the Moscow Art Theatre. His ideas were adopted by Strasberg and Clurman at the Group Theatre, which folded in 1941. In 1947 Kazan and his associates Cheryl Crawford and Robert Lewis founded the Actors' Studio, which received much publicity during the 1950s because it had developed such well-known graduates as Brando, Dean, Julie Harris, Karl Malden, and Rod Steiger. "The Actors' Studio was my artistic home," Kazan has said. He continued there as a teacher until 1954, when he asked his old mentor, Strasberg, to take over the organization. Within a short period, Strasberg became the most celebrated acting teacher in the country, and his former students were—and still are—among the most famous performers in the world.

The central credo of Stanislavsky's system was "You must live the part every moment you are playing it." He rejected the tradition of acting that emphasized externals—declamatory vocal techniques, stylizations, "correct" body positions, and so on. He believed that truth in acting can only be achieved by exploring a character's inner spirit, which

Figure 14.9. Lee Remick in *Wild River* (1960), distributed by 20th Century-Fox. "I got more from Ford than anybody else," Kazan said of the influences on his work; "John Ford had soul." In his early years at 20th Century-Fox, Kazan often watched Ford at work and barraged him with questions: "I used to hang around Ford and get his goddamned sour answers, which I adored. I began to say, I must learn from Ford. I must learn to hold the long shot and trust the long shot, not cut into it." Kazan especially admired the poetry, loneliness, and longing in Ford's movies. Most of Kazan's favorite filmmakers are in the humanist tradition: Ford, Jean Renoir, and Satyajit Ray, artists who are concerned with making audiences feel the humanity of others.

must be fused with the actor's own emotions. One of the most important techniques he developed is emotional recall, in which an actor delves into his or her own past to discover feelings which are analogous to those of the character. "In every part you do," Julie Harris explained, "there is some connection you can make with your own background or with some feeling you've had at one time or another." Stanislavsky's techniques were strongly psychoanalytical: By exploring their own subconscious, actors are able to trigger real emotions, which are recalled in every performance and transferred to the characters they are playing. He also devised techniques for helping actors to focus their concentration on the "world" of the play—its concrete details and textures. In some form or another, these techniques are probably as old as the acting profession itself, but Stanislavsky was the first to systemize them with exercises and methods of analysis; hence the terms *the System* and *the Method*. Nor did he claim that inner truth and emotional sincerity are sufficient unto themselves. He insisted that actors must master all the externals as well, particularly for classic plays, which require a somewhat stylized manner of speaking, moving, and wearing costumes. He was famous for his lengthy rehearsals, in which performers were encouraged to improvise with their roles in order to discover the resonances of the text—the subtext, which is analogous to Freud's concept of the subconscious. Stanislavsky condemned individual virtuosity and the star system. He insisted upon ensemble playing, with genuine interactions among the actor-characters. Players are encouraged to analyze all the specifics of a scene: What does the character really *want?* What has happened before the immediate moment? What time of day is it? And so on. When presented with a role utterly foreign to their experience, actors were urged to research the part so that it would be understood in their guts as well as their minds. For example, in order to play a prison inmate, an actor might actually ask to spend some time in a prison cell, studying its smells, sounds, and textures.

Kazan is famous for bringing out the emotional intensity of his players. His working-class protagonists especially have "the frenzied smell of crotch and armpit about them," to use Charles Silver's memorable phrase. The violent outbursts of passion in such movies as *Waterfront* and *Eden* were unprecedented in the American cinema. Even in ostensibly quiet scenes, Kazan is able to achieve an underlying sense of tension and repressed anger. His eight years' experience as an actor has made

Figure 14.10. Warren Beatty and Natalie Wood in *Splendor in the Grass* (1961), distributed by Warner Brothers. Kazan often deals with sexual tensions in his movies. Like Freud, he believes that many adult neuroses are caused by the traumatic effects of sexual repression. His protagonists are often torn by Oedipal conflicts and by a sense of guilt about the sex drive. This film explores the effects of American puritanism with rare candor and compassion.

him especially sensitive to actors' needs and insecurities. He believes that a person must have a character's experience within him, and he goes to considerable lengths to learn about the personal lives of his players in order to use such details for characterization. He cast the unknown James Dean in *Eden* on sheer instinct: "I thought he was an extreme grotesque of a boy, a twisted boy. As I got to know his father, as I got to know about his family, I learned that he had been, in fact, twisted by the denial of love." He considers Brando as close to a genius as he has ever encountered among actors—a view that's widely shared by others, especially other actors, to whom Brando is an idol. Kazan usually has a close rapport with his actors. With Brando and Montgomery Clift, the relationship was loving and paternal. Kazan tries to build up an atmosphere of trust and mutual respect on the set and often socializes with his players in their off-hours. Sometimes he casts nonprofessionals, especially in minor roles, to enhance a sense of authenticity: "There's something about almost all actors that is well-fed looking. If you have a scene

Figure 14.11. *America America* (1963), with Stathis Giallelis (center), distrubuted by **Warner Brothers.** *America America* is Kazan's favorite work and one of his most personal. The story is based on family history, dealing with how his uncle came to America from Turkish Asia Minor. An indictment of U.S. capitalism, the movie explores how America turned its immigrant dreamers into cynics. The film is deglamorized and like a documentary in its visual style. The cast is composed mostly of nonprofessional players. Kazan realizes that a movie is a collective enterprise and is subject to a variety of interpretations, but in the end, his films reflect *his* obsessions: "I think there should be collaboration, but under my thumb! I think people should collaborate with *me*. I think any art is, finally, the expression of one maniac. That's me."

Figure 14.12.   Robert De Niro in _The Last Tycoon_ (1976), with Ingrid Boulting, script by Harold Pinter, based on the novel by F. Scott Fitzgerald, distributed by Paramount. This is one of Kazan's most romantic works, an accurate reflection of Fitzgerald's famous novel, which was loosely based on the life of MGM's production chief, Irving Thalberg. (Thalberg was one of the few Hollywood bigwigs who had been kind to the broken novelist in the 1930s, when he worked as an occasional scenarist. Not surprisingly, Fitzgerald's portrait of the mogul is strongly sympathetic.) Throughout the production, Kazan deliberately kept De Niro away from Boulting to give their love scenes a tentative awkwardness and to enhance her ethereal air. Photo: Gary Engle.

of either a working-class person or a person deprived by life or a person who is hard up, it's much better sometimes to get a face."

He uses many techniques derived from Freud in the analysis of a character, and he encourages his actors to do the same. He has undergone psychoanalysis twice and believes that it made him more self-perceptive and responsible. He also thinks that it made him more articulate and helped him as an artist. He believes in confronting the unthinkable, the embarrassing, the shameful in oneself, however fearful or chastening. Usually he gives his players the basic objectives of a scene, then leaves them enough room to explore the character within these parameters. He prefers actors who are creatively independent, who discover surprises and nuances that even he hadn't seen.

Critics have generally lumped Kazan with such postwar realists as Fred Zinnemann, but Kazan's realism is generally less austere and matter of fact. There is a pronounced lyric and epic quality in his style, especially in his long shots, which he derived from that old fox at Fox, John Ford. Like most classicists, Kazan has no single visual signature but adjusts his form of expression to fit the nature of the materials. The visuals in *Zapata,* for example, were based on actual photographs of the Mexican Revolution. (The musical score by Alex North was likewise based on tunes popularized by peasant brass bands of the revolutionary era.) The sun-bleached exteriors of the New Orleans setting in *Panic in the Streets* (1950) recall the movies of the Italian neorealists. *Streetcar* on the other hand is almost Sternbergian in its diaphanous lighting effects. Kazan rarely moves his camera, and he avoids virtuoso editing. His concern is always with the human material. His mise-en-scène rarely suggests an overt manipulation of visual forms. He considers the long shot one of the richest forms of expression, however, and in lyrical scenes he uses such shots with considerable power.

Kazan's main fault as a director is his tendency to overheat his materials, to hype up the action with explosive effects. "My problem is that I can always make things forceful," he has admitted. "I used to make every scene GO GO GO! mounting to a climax, and if I had sixty minutes in a picture there were sixty climaxes." In his later works he learned to relax more, to allow the emotional moments in the action to assert themselves without overstatement. Estelle Changas has also pointed out that Kazan has difficulty offering endings that are dramatically satisfying. For example, she finds the hopeful ending of *Waterfront* unconvincing and contrived, as do a number of other critics.

After the success of *Splendor* in 1961, Kazan's career as a filmmaker began its slow decline. None of his movies after that date was popular, perhaps because they became increasingly more personal. During this period he gave up his stage work and cut back on his film projects in order to devote more time to writing novels. Previously, Kazan had often been singled out by critics for his seriousness of purpose as an artist, but he's had few defenders among American critics since his halcyon days of the 1950s. His most fervent champions have been associated with the French Marxist journal, *Positif.* One of their finest critics, Michel Ciment, regards Kazan as a seminal force in the postwar American cinema. "Few directors of the younger generation would deny Kazan's influence on their work," Ciment has pointed out. Among the most conspicious of Kazan's spiritual heirs are such filmmakers as Arthur Penn, Sidney Lumet, John Cassavetes, Martin Scorsese, Francis Ford Coppola, Robert Altman, and Michael Cimino.

BIBLIOGRAPHY

CIMENT, MICHEL. *Kazan on Kazan.* New York: Viking, 1974. An excellent book-length interview, with filmography and bibliography. Other interviews include, "Elia Kazan," in *Directors at Work* (New York: Funk & Wagnalls, 1970) Bernard R. Kantor, Irwin R. Blacker, Anne Kramer, eds.; "Elia Kazan," in "Dialogue on Film," *American Film* (March, 1976); and

"Visiting Kazan," an interview with Charles Silver and Joel Zuker, in *Film Comment* (Summer, 1972).

Dow, GORDON. *Hollywood in the Fifties.* Cranbury, N.J.: A. S. Barnes, 1971. See also Andrew Dowdy, *The Films of the Fifties* (New York: Morrow, 1973); and Gary Collins, "Kazan in the Fifties," in *The Velvet Light Trap* (Winter, 1974): cultural studies.

GUSSOW, MEL. *Don't Say Yes Until I Finish Talking.* New York: Doubleday, 1971. Biography of Darryl F. Zanuck.

HURT, JAMES, ed. *Focus on Film and Theatre.* New York: Prentice-Hall, 1974. See also Harold Clurman, *The Fervant Years* (New York: Hill and Wang, 1945): the story of the Group Theatre and the 1930s.

KAHN, GORDON. *Hollywood on Trial.* New York: Boni & Gaer, 1948. See also John Cogley, *Report on Blacklisting* (New York: Fund for the Republic, 1956); "Hollywood Blacklisting" issue of *Film Culture* (Summer-Fall, 1970); and Peter Biskind, "The Politics of Power in *On the Waterfront,*" in *Film Quarterly* (Fall, 1975): studies in the Red scare.

KAZAN, ELIA. *On What Makes a Director.* Pamphlet published by the Directors Guild of America, 1973. Kazan's novels include *America America* (1962), *The Arrangement* (1967), and *The Assassins* (1972) (New York: Stein & Day).

KITSES, JIM. "Elia Kazan: A Structural Analysis," in *Cinema* (Winter, 1972–73); and Estelle Changas, "Elia Kazan's America," in *Film Comment* (Summer, 1972). Two excellent critical studies.

MOORE, SONIA. *The Stanislavski System.* New York: Viking, 1974.

SCHULBERG, BUDD. *A Face in the Crowd.* New York: Random House, 1957. The screenplay, with an introduction by Kazan. See also John Steinbeck, *Viva Zapata!* (New York: Viking, 1975); and Tennessee Williams, *Baby Doll: The Script for the Film* (New York: New Directions, 1956).

WHITE, DAVID MANNING, AND RICHARD AVERSON. *The Celluloid Weapon.* Boston: The Beacon Press, 1972. A history of social comment in the American cinema.

15

Films of Conscience

The Cinema of Fred Zinnemann

Figure 15.1. Publicity photo of Fred Zinnemann and Julie Harris during the production of *The Member of the Wedding* (1953). There is more of the college don in Zinnemann than the stereotyped industry regular. He is polite, tactful, and respectful of the opinion of others. His sets are well organized and efficient, the morale high. Trained as a cinematographer, Zinnemann is sophisticated in his knowledge of the camera, and his instructions to his crews are precise and authoritative. A team man, he doesn't hold his judgments infallible, and he accepts suggestions from his collaborators without resentment and with thanks.

*Z*innemann is something of a maverick within the American film industry. Repeatedly he shunned the hackneyed wisdom of the studio system which nurtured him, and after its decline in the 1950s he continued his solitary course, making only the kind of movies he wanted to make. Though often praised in retrospect, he had to fight for most of his projects, which were almost routinely dismissed by industry sages as too uncommercial, too depressing, or too highbrow for popular audiences. A documentarist by training, Zinnemann brought to the American fiction film a rigorous authenticity and maturity of subject matter. Though most of his movies fall within the purview of social realism, even his genre films—like the western, *High Noon,* and the thriller, *The Day of the Jackal*—are characterized by an unconventional astringency, a documentary visual style, and an objective tone which is defiantly antiromantic. Virtually all his mature movies might be entitled *No Exit:* Most of his protagonists are trapped in a social crisis which forces them to confront a fundamental paradox of their character. Many of his movies end unhappily—the kiss of death at the box office, according to the strictures of the trade. There's an unyielding quality to most of Zinnemann's movies, a refusal to pander to the audience with reassuring clichés, pop formulas, and moralistic cant. Many of his works, even the popular hits like *From Here to Eternity, The Nun's Story,* and *A Man for All Seasons,* were regarded as offbeat, freakish successes. In short, Zinnemann has taken risks, and he has sometimes suffered the consequences at the box office. His independence of spirit hasn't gone unrewarded, however: He has won four Academy Awards, twice for directing fiction movies, twice for documentaries. The New York Film Critics Circle has also honored his direction four times. He has received three citations from the Directors Guild of America. In 1970, this organization conferred upon him the coveted D. W. Griffith Award for lifelong achievement in film.

The theme that concerns me perhaps more than all others was expressed by Hillel two thousand years ago: "If I am not for myself, who will be for me? And if I am only for myself, what am I? And if not now, when?" This seems to me to be a universal theme.

—Fred Zinnemann

Zinnemann was born in 1907 in Vienna, the son of a prominent Jewish physician. As a youth, he was encouraged to follow in his father's footsteps, for medicine was something of a family tradition. He went to law school instead, though he discovered that this profession wasn't much to his taste either. In the mid-1920s he saw three movies that affected him powerfully: Stroheim's *Greed,* King Vidor's *The Big Parade,* and Eisenstein's *Potemkin,* all classic documents of social realism. Zinnemann now knew what he wanted to do the rest of his life: He wanted to make movies like these. When he announced his plans to his parents, they were far from overjoyed. But the youth persisted, and finally they relented and agreed to finance his education at the Technical School of Cinematography in Paris. He studied there for a year, but upon graduation he was unable to find work in the city.

He moved to Berlin, where prospects seemed more promising (see Chapters 9 and 13). For a time he was an assistant to the cinematographer Eugene Schufftan. In 1929 they photographed the popular *Menschen Am Sonntag (People on Sunday),* which was produced and codirected (with Robert Siodmak) by Edgar G. Ulmer and was written by Billy Wilder. Eventually all of these young men went to America, where they found greater fame and fortune. Though working only in a minor capacity on this movie, Zinnemann learned much about the problems of blending the techniques of the documentary with those of fiction, for the film was shot on location, using mostly nonprofessional performers. But nothing came of the movie for him, and since the political landscape in Germany was darkening, he decided to leave.

In 1930 Zinnemann resolved to try his luck in America. For several years he worked in a variety of jobs in Hollywood, but only when he met Robert Flaherty did his career take another step forward. "Robert Flaherty is probably the greatest single influence on my work as a film maker," Zinnemann has said, "particularly because he was always his own man." The creator of the celebrated documentary, *Nanook of the North* (1922), was a maverick whose brief flirtation with the Hollywood studio system ended in disaster on both sides. Charismatic, gregarious, and conspicuously brilliant, Flaherty attracted many of the intellectually ambitious young artists of Hollywood. Much taken with Zinnemann, he offered the young man a job as an assistant on a documentary that Flaherty had been asked to make in the Soviet Union. They met in Berlin with some Soviet officials, but almost immediately Flaherty ran into difficulties. His sponsors expected a propaganda film dealing with the great technological strides since the 1917 revolution. Flaherty, the archromantic and conservative, wanted to make a movie dealing with the glories of a lost culture. Although the film—like so many of Flaherty's projects—was never made, Zinnemann was profoundly influenced by the old individualist.

By his example, Flaherty taught him two crucial lessons. The first, and ultimately the more important, is the need for the movie artist to be as independent as possible from the people who control the financing of a film. There's not much point in undertaking a project if the director merely executes the ideas of others. Paradoxically, the other lesson Flaherty taught him—albeit unwittingly—is to know how to accommodate the contributions of others without allowing them to corrupt one's artistic integrity. In later years Zinnemann was to fight many stormy battles with the front office, but he also came to recognize that flexibility is an essential survival skill in a collaborative art/business/entertainment like movies. "Carte blanche frightens me," he once remarked, and throughout his career, he has been more than generous in his praise of his collaborators—including producers, whom almost nobody praises.

In 1933 Zinnemann was asked by the still photographer, Paul Strand, to direct a movie he had been commissioned to make by the Mexican government on their revolution. The crew was mostly Mexican, and Zinnemann, Strand, and four other Americans lived for nearly a year in a remote jungle section of the state of Vera Cruz. *Redes* (*The Wave*, 1934) was the result, a sixty-minute semidocumentary dealing with the lives of some impoverished fishermen. Acted by native nonprofessionals, the movie deals with the economic exploitation of the members of a small village. The protagonist is killed after he attempts to organize his fellow fishermen to combat their common oppressor. In directing the movie, Zinnemann was able to put into practice many of the lessons he had learned from Flaherty.

On the strength of the critical admiration inspired by *The Wave*, Zinnemann was offered a contract by Jack Chertok, who headed the short subjects department at MGM, the most powerful and successful studio in Hollywood. During this period, promising young talents usually worked their way up the studio ladder by beginning in B films, which were commonly exhibited on the second half of double bills.

MGM was unique in that it also used its short subjects department for this purpose. Between the years 1937 and 1939, Zinnemann directed a total of eighteen documentaries at MGM, most of them one- and two-reelers. A medical film, *That Mothers Might Live*, garnered an Academy Award as best documentary of 1938. Speed, efficiency, and economy were the watchwords at the MGM unit, though the studio prided itself on the "quality" look of its products. The production values of many of these shorts (especially the *Crime Does Not Pay* series) were sometimes more impressive than the A features of other studios.

Since Zinnemann was restricted to three shooting days per reel, a good deal of painstaking and meticulous preparation was required before the camera began to roll. Virtually every detail had to be pre-visualized and pieced together like a mosaic. But he had already learned the lesson of exhaustive research from Flaherty, and the rigorous discipline required in these shorts Zinnemann considered an artistic challenge. Perhaps the most valuable lesson he learned was the need to tell a story as economically as possible. Time and footage were limited, so he learned to cut away all superfluities, to intensify the dramatic thrust of a story, and to make the images as densely saturated as possible—techniques he carried over to his later fiction movies as well. In this respect, Zinnemann is somewhat untypical of most realists, who tend to manipulate their narratives less overtly. In most of his movies, the story line is not allowed to slacken. His films are rich in authentic textural details, but generally these are embedded within the mise-en-scène itself, rarely offered separately for their own sake. In such movies as *The Search* (1947), *The Men* (1950), and *Teresa* (1951), he was sometimes at odds with his writers to tighten up the narrative thrust.

In the early 1940s, Zinnemann entered what he calls his "donkey work" period, directing B movies for MGM. There followed a series of well-crafted but conventional genre films, most of which were successful at the box office and praised by B film aficionados. In 1943 he was given an opportunity to make an A feature, *The Seventh Cross*, with Spencer Tracy, one of MGM's most prestigious stars. Despite its success, Zinnemann was sent back to directing routine cheapies. Finally he got disgusted and refused several mediocre scripts in a row, an act of rebellion which gave him the rather impressive distinction of being the first director ever suspended by MGM. Of course like most Hollywood directors during the studio period, Zinnemann was required to pay his dues by directing assembly-line projects. But he viewed his low-budget B-film assignments as necessary stepping-stones for a crack at more important work. Once he got his opportunity to work on more personal projects, the civilized, soft-spoken Zinnemann exhibited a surprising tenacity and combativeness. "I don't like to dictate and I'll be damned if I'll have somebody dictate to me," he once said of meddling producers. He even stood up to the notorious bully, Harry Cohn, the head of Columbia Pictures, when he tried to force his ideas on Zinnemann during the production of *From Here to Eternity* (1953). Those who stood up to Harry Cohn were in a very exclusive minority.

Shortly after World War II, a Swiss company invited Zinnemann to come to Europe to direct *The Search*. MGM eagerly agreed to send their

Figure 15.2. Publicity photo of *The Search* (1947), with Montgomery Clift, distributed by MGM. If the major achievements of the prewar American cinema were in comedy and stylized genre films, the postwar era excelled at realism. Young filmmakers like Zinnemann and Kazan were especially influenced by the Italian neorealist cinema. They wanted their movies to look like newsreels, and accordingly they avoided glossiness and an "arranged" look in their mise-en-scène in favor of authenticity and a sense of discovery. The script to *The Search* was loosely based on an article, "Europe's Children," by Therese Bonney, who also served as technical advisor to the movie. Like his Italian contemporaries, Zinnemann wanted to fuse the conventions of fiction with documentary, emotion with fact, into a form he described as a "dramatic document."

358 Representative Artists

resident "difficult" director, and even put up some of the financing. A story dealing with displaced children in Europe after the war, *The Search* is Zinnemann's first aesthetically mature example of documentary fiction. Employing the Flaherty method he was to use as a standard preparation for his subsequent movies, he and his staff researched the materials in great detail before writing the script:

> We felt that the main thing was to get as much of the elements of the story as possible from first-hand observation: from seeing and studying the locale and talking to a maximum number of people who had been directly involved in the period of history we wanted to portray.

The movie was filmed in the actual ruins of Berlin and the refugee camps of Nuremberg, Munich, and Frankfort. The script was a collaboration, inspired in large part by the horrifying tales of the children who had only recently come out of Nazi concentration camps. Zinnemann also used many of these youngsters as actors: "They alone could understand and project the feeling of animal terror. Normal children could not have comprehended what it was all about." *The Search* was a critical and commercial success, and with it Zinnemann's apprenticeship came to an end.

When his contract with MGM expired in 1949, he signed a three-picture agreement with Stanley Kramer, an independent producer with innovative ideas. He not only shared Zinnemann's liberal values, he also agreed that movies could deal with serious social themes and stories revolving around contemporary problems without a sacrifice in drama, suspense, or excitement. In fact, Kramer was a major contributor to the revival of social realism in the American cinema of the postwar era. Eventually he became a director himself, though most critics and historians believe his main importance was as a producer. Three of his finest properties were directed by Zinnemann: *The Men, High Noon* (1952), and *The Member of the Wedding.*

Social realism is neither a style nor a movement in the usual sense of those terms. Perhaps it would be more accurate to describe it as a set of values, both social and aesthetic, which cuts across national boundries and historical periods. For many years it was the most prestigious branch of the cinema, enjoying wide support among the liberally educated classes of most moviegoing nations. One of the broadest of film classifications, social realism encompasses many movements and styles, including the neorealists of postwar Italy, the films of socialist realism in the Communist countries of the world, the so-called kitchen-sink realism of the British cinema in the late 1950s and early 1960s, and many individual moviemakers who are concerned with themes of social anxiety and change: Eisenstein, Satyajit Ray, and Yasujiro Ozu, to name only a few. In America, some of the most respected directors have made major contributions in this area: Griffith, Stroheim, King Vidor, Ford, Kazan, Sidney Lumet, Martin Ritt, Hal Ashby, Michael Ritchie, and of course, Zinnemann. Social realism tends to emphasize the documentary aspects of the medium, its ability to photograph authentic people, details, and places. Sometimes these movies use nonprofessional performers rather

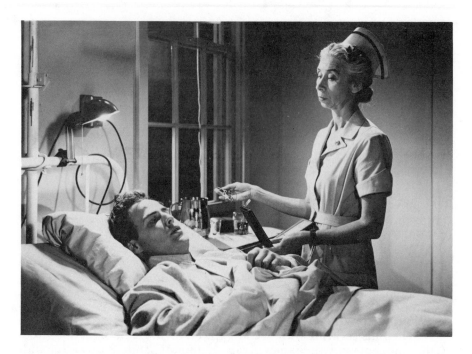

Figure 15.3. Marlon Brando in *The Men* (1950), distributed by United Artists. This was one of many postwar movies exploring the problems of civilian readjustment. It centers on the attempts of a young veteran (Brando) to come to grips with a war wound that has left him a paraplegic. Zinnemann's emphasis is on a hardnosed documentary objectivity. He and his crew spent weeks at Birmingham Veterans Hospital, observing and researching. Brando spent a month confined in a paraplegic ward, undergoing the same grueling physical regimen as the actual paraplegics of the hospital. "It was one of the most dedicated and effective jobs of preparation I have ever seen an actor do," Zinnemann observed. The director also cast about twenty actual paraplegic veterans in the film. At the time of the movie's release, when the male actors were unknown, audiences had no way of distinguishing the professional performers from the real patients.

than trained actors or stars. Though occasionally a trifle stiff, nonprofessionals seldom seem slick, glamorous, or hammy—qualities that are especially incongruous for working-class characters. Social realism is a view from the left: Filmmakers generally assume a revolutionary or reformist perspective on the narrative materials, and they explore, at least implicitly, the ways in which people near the bottom of the social heap are oppressed. For example, though most of Zinnemann's movies are basically character studies, in *The Nun's Story* (1958) we are also allowed to see how European Christians functioned in a missionized African society. In *The Member of the Wedding*, racism is shown to be essentially economic in its basis. Even in a psychological movie like *From Here to Eternity*, Zinnemann places the two love stories within a clearly defined economic context. Though he's sympathetic to the romantic yearnings of his characters, he's objective and analytical in his treatment of their social milieu. People never live on love in Zinnemann's movies, for one of his major preoccupations is with who pays the bills. He's concerned with the cost of love as well as its value.

Some social realists—most notably Eisenstein—are relatively unconcerned with the subtleties of character and concentrate more on stylistic matters, sociological details, or a didactic theme. This lack of interest in character is far from universal, however. Most of Zinnemann's movies, for example, are psychological in emphasis, though they're seldom only that. Furthermore, when he deals with social problems, like the plight of paraplegic veterans (*The Men*), heroin addiction (*A Hatful of Rain*, 1957), or the lives of migrant laborers (*The Sundowners*, 1960), his characters are presented in individualized terms, seldom as general types who are supposed to symbolize an entire class of people. Zinnemann's movies don't end with a universalized, cheaply comforting solution. Implicit in his realistic treatment is the assumption that all

Figure 15.4. Gary Cooper (right) in *High Noon* (1952), with Grace Kelly, distributed by United Artists. Almost all westerns have an obligatory shootout, and *High Noon* is no exception. What was new about the film was its startling realism. The hero, Will Kane (Cooper) is a mere mortal, not a superman, and must use cunning and stealth to outwit four killers. We see him sneaking down alleyways and behind buildings, where he manages to pick two of the killers off. There is a great deal of firing, missing, and reloading during the ensuing violence. In the confusion, Kane is able to kill another henchman. Terrified by the sound of bullets, his bride rushes back to the scene, where the villain surprises her and uses her as a shield. But she claws at his face and pulls away, at which time both men fire their guns (pictured). The villain falls to the ground lifeless, and Kane is wounded. The two gasping lovers cling to each other, totally exhausted.

individuals are unique and must contend with like problems in light of their own psychological and spiritual resources.

In fact, Zinnemann carries this principle of individuation even into his genre movies. *High Noon,* one of the first of the so-called "psychological" or "adult" westerns of the early 1950s, began a trend in the demythologizing of genres. Many of the simpler prewar myths increasingly were being viewed from an ironic and skeptical perspective. *High Noon* was criticized by such conservative genre purists as Robert Warshow, who believed that the western hero ought to be stylized and conventionalized. Instead, Zinnemann treated his western hero (Gary Cooper) as though he were a real human being, one who feels panic, fear, and even some moments of cowardice. We're allowed to see his bruised and bloodied hands as he soothes them in a pan of water after a fistfight. He sweats profusely under the glare of the sun. He gets dirtier, more stooped, and haggard as the urgency of his situation increases. Before entering the final shootout, he writes his last will and testament, unheroically assuming that he'll probably be killed since he's outnumbered and alone. After the violently unpredictable shootout, he gasps for breath and is hardly able to speak. Zinnemann's realistic innovations helped to bring about a new attitude toward the genre, setting the stage for such later "revisionist" westerns as Peckinpah's *The Wild Bunch,* Penn's *Little Big Man,* and Altman's *McCabe and Mrs. Miller.*

Because the subject matter of the social realist cinema is innately important, many naive viewers feel coerced into accepting all movies of this type as likewise important—as though it were the subject itself and not its sensitive treatment that determines artistic excellence. It was not until the 1950s that several astute French critics pointed out that there are as many mediocre directors working within this tradition as there are in any other genre, style, or movement. A movie can be accurate sociology, edifying in its high-mindedness, and still be tiresome as art. Some social realist movies are self-congratulatory, psychologically dishonest, and patronizing in their attitude toward the Little People and their dull, drab lives. Films of this sort are sometimes called message movies because their preachments take precedence over most aesthetic and psychological considerations. Few of Zinnemann's films could be thus dismissed. Even his movies dealing with children—an acid test—betray no air of condescension, invoke no knee-jerk sentimental platitudes. Most of his works are tough as well as honest, powerful in their emotional impact without being a "deeply moving experience not to be missed." The emotion, in short, is artistically earned, not piously extorted.

In fact, if it weren't for the emotional intensity of Zinnemann's movies, they might well strike audiences as too drily objective. Precisely because his general tone is unsentimental, the outbursts of feeling are never forced or melodramatic. In *The Member of the Wedding,* for example, Frankie Addams (Julie Harris), a precocious twelve-year old girl, announces to all who'll listen that she's going to travel with her soldier brother and his bride after they get married. The only adult who bothers to listen is Bernice (Ethel Waters), a housekeeper who serves as Frankie's surrogate mother. (Zinnemann's movies are filled with symbolic parental

Figure 15.5. Ethel Waters, Julie Harris, and Brandon de Wilde in *The Member of the Wedding* (1953), distributed by Columbia. Superficially, the role of Bernice (Waters) appears to be a mammy stereotype, but the character is founded on life, not convention. She loves the two children in her charge, but she also has a separate life of her own, which they aren't permitted to enter. As the only adult of the kitchen trio, she often makes private jokes. The irony of her remarks eludes the children, but not us. Waters's performance in this film was an inspiring event for black viewers. It marked the first time a black actress was allowed to carry a white production by a major studio. "For black audiences," film historian Donald Bogle has observed, "Ethel Waters was the personification of the black spirit they believed had prevailed during the hard times of slavery, and they felt she brought dignity and wisdom to the race." See Donald Bogle, *Toms, Coons, Mulattoes, Mammies, & Bucks: An Interpretive History of Blacks in American Films* (New York: Bantam, 1974).

figures but few actual parents.) When Bernice tries to talk sense to the child, she refuses to listen, for she has a desperate need to be a "member" of something larger than herself. As soon as the wedding is concluded, Frankie takes her suitcase to the honeymoon car and waits in the back seat. The ensuing scene is photographed mostly through the windows of the car, preserving the film's characteristic motif of entrapment. (Zinnemann's movies are profuse in images of doors and windows, usually suggesting exclusion or confinement.) The brother and his bride, a pleasant but commonplace couple, try to reason with Frankie to get out, but she refuses, insisting that she "belongs" with them. In exasperation, her no-nonsense father yanks her out, and she falls down on the dusty road, screaming, "Take me! Take me!" As the music rises to a shrieking crescendo, the high-angled camera cranes down to a tightly framed shot of the hysterical child. In the background we can see the lower bodies of the bewildered wedding guests surrounding her. Suddenly two strong arms reach down and help her up. We don't need to guess whose arms reach into the frame: Only Bernice can understand the child's anguish. Zinnemann's movies are filled with such rituals of humiliation.

Sometimes the austerity of his camerawork produces an understated emotional impact, as in the final scene of *The Nun's Story*. The movie centers on a missionary nursing nun, Sister Luke (Audrey Hepburn). For years she fights an almost constant battle to remain true to both herself and her religious vows, especially the vow of obedience. When she returns to her native Belgium during World War II, her religious superiors warn her to preserve a strict neutrality toward the Nazi occupiers of her homeland, for otherwise the Catholic hospital would not be allowed to provide its essential services. Zinnemann's protagonists are not very good at compromises, especially moral compromises. When she learns that the Nazis have killed her father, Sister Luke is unable to act the forgiving Christian. Despite years of rigorous self-discipline, she realizes she can't remain a nun with a heart filled with hatred. She asks for and receives dispensation to leave religious orders, a rare occurrence at this time. Zinnemann photographs the final scene in one of his superb deep-focus lengthy takes. The camera is placed at the further end of a small room, where it tactfully remains for the duration of the scene. Alone inside, Sister Luke removes her ring, beads, and veil. For the first time since the beginning of the film, we see her hair; except then it was long and healthy; now it's bluntly shorn and grayed. She changes into a shapeless suit, several sizes too large for her—hardly an improvement on her haggard appearance. Throughout the scene the soundtrack is silent, suggesting a vacuum. She presses a buzzer, and an outer door mysteriously snaps open for her. It's almost as though she were a contaminated creature, to be released without further human contact. Outside the door is an alleyway leading to a city street which we can see in the distance. Slowly she walks down the alley: The distant sounds of city traffic are all that can be heard. The year is 1944. The members of her family have been killed or dispersed. The Nazis occupy her country, and she can no longer count on the protection of religious orders. We watch her stop in the distance at the end of the alley. Then, turning toward the street, she disappears from view, to confront her uncertain destiny alone.

Zinnemann's movies often deal with a conflict of conscience, in which an individual strives to preserve his or her integrity in the face of increasingly constrictive pressures. As he has pointed out, this conflict can be social, psychological, or both: "It applies to the—sometimes tragic—clash of an individual with the community of which he is a part; an individual who is trying to follow his own personal conscience against all kinds of odds. It applies equally to a purely interior dilemma, where the conflict of conscience is not directed against an opponent, but rages within the soul of the individual himself." Raymond Rohauer has noted that the Zinnemann protagonist is usually intelligent, proud, and articulate, slow to act yet finally aroused to pursue a defiant course which sometimes leads to defeat. Sir Thomas More in *A Man for All Seasons* (1966) and the title character of *Julia* (1977) are perhaps the ultimate examples, for the stakes in these films are unreasonably dear: life itself. Most of the protagonists are reluctant loners, men and women who long to be part of a larger social unit yet are unable in the end to pay the price—a yielding of personal identity.

Not that Zinnemann has this conflict in mind beforehand, for he's seldom attracted to a story simply because it happens to illustrate a recurring theme or a personal belief. Individualism is hardly a novel topic in the American cinema of course, but Zinnemann is unusual in that he dramatizes its devastating spiritual cost and few of its pleasures. He's sympathetic to the need of an individual to be part of a larger community, but the price of communal admission is steep. Generally his protagonists choose solitude over a corrupted solidarity. Hence, many of Zinnemann's movies end on a note of disintegration, loneliness, and shattered hope. For that matter, even those films that end less harshly, like *The Men* and *A Hatful of Rain,* don't conclude with a resolution of the crisis so much as a decision to finally confront it. Zinnemann's "happy endings" are among the most equivocal of the American cinema.

His plots are generally constructed like traps, which close in menacingly until the protagonists have no other choice but to flee or confront

Figure 15.6. Montgomery Clift (center) and Burt Lancaster (left rear) in *From Here to Eternity* (1953), produced by Columbia Pictures. Unlike most realists, Zinnemann often uses closed forms in his mise-en-scène to convey his characteristic theme of entrapment. In this shot, the willfully individualistic Prewitt (Clift) is allowed no visual avenue of escape in a scene in which he's being interrogated by his commanding officer. Zinnemann fought hard to get Clift for the role of Prewitt. The director believed no other actor could convey the character's quiet indomitable strength. See also Robert La Guardia, *Monty* (New York: Arbor, 1977).

the inevitable. Since they're portrayed as mere flesh and blood, they sometimes attempt to run away in their moments of panic. But destiny is self in Zinnemann's universe, and his fugitives always return. (One of his major projects of the 1960s was an adaptation of André Malraux's powerful novel, *Man's Fate,* but unfortunately the project fell through at the last moment because of financing difficulties.) Even a casual examination of his mature movies reveals a persistent preoccupation with the motif of entrapment. A number of his works are set in police states, occupied countries, and other kinds of repressive societies. Several films even feature literal prisons. Others deal with aliens and exiles, who are trapped in foreign countries, as in *The Search, Teresa, Behold a Pale Horse* (1963), and *Julia.* There are protagonists imprisoned by the pressures of time, as in *High Noon* and *The Day of the Jackal* (1973). Some of his characters are metaphorically trapped by severe illness, by their own bodies, as in *The Men;* in *Hatful of Rain* (the protagonist is a heroin addict); and in the Academy Award-winning medical documentary, *Benjy* (1951). Institutions are sometimes viewed as prisons: marriage and the U.S. Army in *Eternity,* the Catholic Church in *Nun's Story,* the family in *Julia.*

Unlike most realists, Zinnemann's techniques emphasize closed forms, with many claustrophobic medium and close shots and tightly framed compositions which permit little freedom of movement. The edges of his frame are often sealed off, and the ceilings are oppressively low, visually reinforcing the sense of confinement. Since Zinnemann's movies usually deal with characters who are estranged from a community, he uses many closeups to emphasize their isolation. Even in *High Noon* he favors the psychological landscape of his protagonist's face to shots of the spacious locale, of which there are very few. Zinnemann also uses many anticipatory setups, suggesting fatality, for the camera seems to be waiting for the protagonist to enter a preordained visual design. In *Member of the Wedding,* a faithful adaptation of Carson McCullers's stage play, he resisted the temptation to open up the story with lots of exterior settings. Instead, most of the action takes place in the cramped kitchen of the Addams household. The director's famous lengthy takes, like the alley fight in *Eternity* and the murder of the shy homosexual in *Day of the Jackal,* are unnerving precisely because Zinnemann refuses to dissipate the tension by cutting to a variety of shots. In other words, the unedited shot itself can be a kind of spatial and temporal prison from which there's no escape.

Zinnemann is one of the few directors who discusses the moviemaking process in the first-person plural, though in fact he's enjoyed more creative autonomy than the vast majority of American filmmakers. "I like to work as a team," he has stated, "rather than to dominate everybody around me. I don't believe in that. If people are not talented enough to contribute anything in the first place, I don't want them around." His collaborators have often remarked on the director's generosity in allowing them to realize their fullest artistic potential. Writer Stewart Stern praises him not only as a collaborator but also as a teacher: "I learned through Zinnemann where drama lay, that you have to go to the source. And he taught me to write 'in grunts': use images and

Figure 15.7. Deborah Kerr and Burt Lancaster in *From Here to Eternity*. The censorship of the period prevented Zinnemann from using much of the steamy sexuality in James Jones's novel. The love scenes in the movie acquire their power indirectly, through symbolic suggestion. In the celebrated beach scene between Warden and Karen (pictured), the sexuality is aestheticized. Zinnemann's style is rarely lyrical, but here he used a rapturous crane shot to suggest an emotional release. With the melancholy title song playing softly, the camera floats in from a high-angle extreme long shot to a closer view of the two lovers, kissing passionately on a deserted beach. An ocean wave sweeps over their bodies as they continue to cling to each other. The rhythmical pounding of the waves, the slowly penetrating camera, and her exclamation, "Oh, I never knew it could be like this," combine to produce one of the most erotic love scenes ever filmed up to that time.

behavior when you can, words as a last resort, *few words*—grunts." In addition to Stern, who worked on three of Zinnemann's projects, the director has also been associated with such respected scenarists as Carl Foreman, Daniel Taradash, Robert Anderson, Robert Bolt, and Alvin Sargent.

Though he seldom allows language to do more work than is necessary, Zinnemann has a high regard for well-written, even literary, scripts. Many of his scenarists are independent novelists and dramatists. He prefers to use short stories as a basis for movies, although several are adaptations of distinguished novels, most notably James Jones's *From Here to Eternity*. Plays, with their reliance on dialogue, Zinnemann likes least as a platform for launching movies. Sometimes he makes considerable alterations in his stage properties, as in such works as *Hatful of Rain* and *Man for All Seasons*. However, *Member of the Wedding* preserves most of McCullers's brilliant dialogue intact—a rare instance of an American movie artist respecting the talent of a literary colleague. After extensive

Figure 15.8. Audrey Hepburn and Peter Finch in *The Nun's Story* (1958), distributed by Warner Brothers. Zinnemann is a master of subtexts. The love that grows between Sister Luke (Hepburn) and the nonbeliever, Dr. Fortunati (Finch), is never spoken of in the movie. Zinnemann neither sentimentalizes nor sensationalizes his subject. Nor does he stoop to characterizing the women as adorable little nunlets. Sister Luke and the other nuns are treated as intelligent and hard-working women who have dedicated their lives to God. Apparently no one before Zinnemann ever bothered to find out precisely what nuns *do,* and among the most compelling aspects of this movie are the purely documentary sequences detailing the arduous discipline that goes into the making—and in some cases the unmaking—of a nun.

research, in which the writers are often involved, Zinnemann usually outlines what he wants in his scenario. He generally prefers the writers to write the first draft of the script by themselves. Then he shapes it to whatever extent it needs to be reworked, before production if possible, but during the actual shooting if necessary.

Few American directors are so respectful of the art of acting. His players have rewarded him in turn with performances that are almost routinely nominated for Academy Awards. He is the only major director of Germanic origins who doesn't have a reputation as an authoritarian with his players. Quite the contrary. Actors have frequently praised his patience, understanding, and critical insight. When asked about the notoriously neurotic Montgomery Clift, who played in two of Zinnemann's movies, the director refused to criticize his gifted collaborator: "What difference does it make whether he was easy or difficult to work with? Personal comfort or discomfort of this kind doesn't enter into the making of a picture." Whether working with powerful stars, trained unknowns, or nonprofessionals, the director's handling of his players is almost invariably impressive. There are few hammy performances in his movies, for above all, Zinnemann emphasizes naturalness. Instead of having the actors project out to the audience, the audience is allowed to tune in on them. We watch them behaving rather than performing. As Zinnemann was rising to prominence in the movies, the new interior style of acting known as the Method was also growing in popularity (see Chapter 14). Kazan is generally credited with introducing it to American movies, but it was Zinnemann who introduced several of the performers who were most associated with this style: Clift, Marlon Brando, and Julie Harris, to name only the most prominent. Unlike Kazan, who derived his acting theories from the Soviet stage director, Stanislavsky, Zinnemann developed the same passion for authenticity and emotional sincerity by way of the documentary.

In his early movies, like *The Search* and *The Men,* Zinnemann favored using nonprofessional and unfamiliar actors, thus forcing the audience to suspend immediate judgment and evaluate the characters as

Figure 15.9 Deborah Kerr and Robert Mitchum in *The Sundowners* (1960), with Peter Ustinov, released by Warner Brothers. Zinnemann in this film extols the virtues of family life. Ida and Paddy Carmody (Kerr and Mitchum) have been married fifteen years, have a fourteen-year old son, and own almost nothing. They are "sundowners," people who follow the sun in search of temporary employment. Ida combines the roles of wife, mother, friend, and general manager with flexibility and grace. In an era when America's screens were dominated by Jayne Mansfield's cleavage and the state of Sandra Dee's chastity, Zinnemann refused to trivialize his female characters. Women are often the protagonists in his movies, and he treats them as productive human beings, without any sacrifice to their femininity. They are warm, generous, thinking adults who not only enjoy each other's company but also actively seek it out.

their situations unfold. Later in his career, when he used stars in several movies, the director often cast them against type and discouraged them from using familiar mannerisms, thereby creating surprising tensions between what we expect and what we actually see them do. For example, he cast Deborah Kerr in *Eternity* because he thought her ladylike gentility would provide a provocative foil to the character's sordid past. In other cases, he simply asked his stars to behave as naturally as possible, like Gary Cooper in *High Noon* (whose Academy Award as best actor for this movie was viewed as something of a joke by critics, for Cooper's range was among the most narrow of all the great stars). Yet there's not a false note in his performance as the sheriff of a scared frontier town, largely because Zinnemann asked him to be himself: "Cooper is first of all a tremendous personality," the director observed. "He is best when he doesn't act. His just being on the screen exerts something that is very powerful." Zinnemann shrewdly exploited Cooper's iconographical value, for in the public's mind, the star personified both the social idealism of Capra's Mr. Deeds and John Doe and the laconic, fearless westerner of *The Virginian* and *The Plainsman*. Much of the impact of *High Noon* results from the humiliation its hero/star must endure. Audiences are genuinely shocked—and moved—by Cooper's profound vulnerability.

Zinnemann is a fine "woman's director," though seldom at the expense of the males in his movies. His female characters come from a wide variety of social backgrounds, yet it's still possible to speak of a Zinnemann heroine without too much violence to the uniqueness of each. In the first place, the actresses playing his heroines—always excellent performers—are spiritual rather than sensual in their appeal: Teresa Wright, Pier Angeli, Grace Kelly, Julie Harris, Ethel Waters, Deborah Kerr, Eva Marie Saint, and Audrey Hepburn, to mention only some of the leading ladies. Intelligent and serious, the Zinnemann heroine is never portrayed in stereotypically "adorable" terms. Feminist film critics have singled out the decade of the 1950s as the nadir of sexist stereotyping in the American cinema. Whereas this is probably true in general, there are some important exceptions—most notably the female characters of Kazan and Zinnemann. They are as courageous and principled as the males and are often more perceptive. They seldom define themselves in terms of a man, and in Zinnemann's case especially, they sometimes prefer the single state. Despite their strength, all of them are characterized by a certain poetic vulnerability.

The production values of Zinnemann's movies are impressive for their authenticity. "I'd be perfectly happy to stay at home with moderate crews and things like that," he's said, "but I find that I have to go where the story is." Nor does he fake such matters with reasonable approximations, for like Stroheim, he's acutely sensitive to the "feel" of authenticity. In *From Here to Eternity,* for example, he insisted that all the extras be played by real soldiers, whose military bearing couldn't easily be duplicated by actors. Photographed on location in Hawaii, the movie seldom offers us any picturesque shots of the locale: It's enough that it's palpably *there,* lending the drama a documentary veracity. *The Sundowners* takes place in the outback regions of Australia, and Zinnemann refused to cut corners by shooting the movie in a similar location, like Texas, with a few kangaroos thrown in for "atmosphere." He was afraid if he did, the movie would look like a western: "There is an enormous—though largely subconscious—difference between a pub and a saloon. Besides, Australians don't carry guns, and this makes a tremendous difference in their psychology." Zinnemann's obsession with nuance is characteristic of many realists in the cinema.

Even his genre movies are characterized by this insistence on authenticity. In *The Day of the Jackal,* the director was required to reconstruct the façade of an enormous public building that had been torn down after the period in which the movie is laid. Probably no one but a Parisian would have noticed the anachronism, but nonetheless, Zinnemann insisted on an historically accurate set. This blending of documentary with genre conventions is what impressed critics about *High Noon* as well. There are no sweeping vistas of open spaces and majestic natural monuments in this western, only plain cramped interiors, lacklustre buildings, and white textureless skies. Floyd Crosby's cinematography was worked out in advance with the director, who wanted the movie to look like a "contemporary newsreel." They avoided

Figure 15.10. *A Man for All Seasons* **(1966), with Paul Scofield (right) and Robert Shaw, cinematography by Ted Moore, distributed by Columbia.** This is Zinnemann's most handsomely mounted movie, yet he doesn't overwhelm us with production values: There is a certain austerity in the mise-en-scène, suggesting a reconstructed documentary, Moore's cinematography is richly textured, yet very English in its restraint and quiet modulations. The photography of the countryside suggests the misty canvasses of nineteenth-century British landscape artists.

Figure 15.11. Publicity photo of *The Day of the Jackal* (1973), distributed by Universal.
This film deals with a right-wing conspiracy to assassinate President Charles de Gaulle of
France in 1963. Zinnemann shot it as a virtual documentary. For example, he went to
considerable lengths to find an actor, Adrian Cayla-Legrand (right), who resembled de
Gaulle (left). Despite the fact that everyone knew Le Grand Charles died of natural causes
in his bed, Zinnemann makes the materials compelling by concentrating on the hows and
whys of the conspiracy rather than its outcome. This is perhaps his most flashily directed
film, in the sense that the audience is encouraged to enjoy the virtuosity of the cutting, the
tautness of the exposition, and the authoritative control over the complexities of the
narrative.

the striking, romantic cinematography popularized by Ford's *Stagecoach.*
The mythic, lyrical West typified by such painters as Frederic Remington
is what influenced the visual style of Ford's westerns, but Zinnemann
consciously modeled his style on the photographs of Mathew Brady.
Accordingly, the director allowed the use of no prettifying filters in the
movie. The lighting style is flat and matter of fact, emphasizing the
gritty, stark, bleached-out look of nineteenth-century photos of the actual frontier.

Zinnemann's shortcomings as an artist might be viewed as the vices
of his virtues. There is in all of his mature works the air of a serious,
thoughtful man—not altogether a desirable trait in an expensive, popular medium like the movies. Though he's too fine a technician to bungle
a project, some of his films, like the musical *Oklahoma!* (1955) are rather
perfunctory, for Zinnemann lacks the necessary spontaneity, humor,
and lyricism for this genre. His avoidance of vulgarity, in short, isn't

always an artistic virtue. Some of his films are overwritten, and a few are frankly dull, if earnest. Not even his staunchest champions can muster much enthusiasm for *Behold a Pale Horse,* which suffers from many of the vices of social realism and boasts few of its strengths.

The American cinema is nothing if not romantic. Most of our major moviemakers have dealt with mavericks, outsiders, and rebels. Zinnemann is no exception. But he refuses to treat such characters from a romantic perspective, insisting on the validity of the head as well as the heart, of objective analysis as well as passionate commitment. If his movies lack the bravura of the romantic cinema, they're also free of its vices: grandiosity, the glorification of violence, antiintellectualism, naiveté, sentimentality, and formulaic characterizations. Zinnemann is almost always sympathetic to our romantic aspirations; he simply refuses to pander to our romantic follies. There is a sincerity and absence of hokum in his movies. Without sanctimoniousness, he has championed such values as generosity, integrity, and idealism. But he has also shown that these virtues aren't cheaply acquired through miraculous interventions in the final reel. Above all, he's unsurpassed in the American cinema in his ability to dramatize the awesome toll that conscience can exact.

Figure 15.12. Jane Fonda and Vanessa Redgrave in *Julia* (1977), released by 20th Century-Fox. Fonda and Redgrave are among the foremost Marxist artists of the contemporary cinema, and this project was a labor of love for them as well as for Zinnemann. Fonda was radicalized in the 1960s, and became an outspoken critic of America's involvement in Vietnam. She is also a feminist, and she insists that her screen roles reflect these values. For a time her politics adversely affected her box office popularity, but eventually her tenacity and fighting spirit endeared her to audiences. She has since become an icon of Americanism, and like Zinnemann, an artist of conscience.

BIBLIOGRAPHY

FOREMAN, CARL. *High Noon,* in *Film Scripts Two,* George P. Garrett *et al.,* eds. New York: Appleton-Century-Crofts and Irvington Publishers, 1971. The original film script, without Zinnemann's changes.

"Fred Zinnemann Talking to Gene Phillips," in *Focus on Film* (Spring, 1973). The most revealing and lengthy interview, with the most complete filmography.

GIANNETTI, LOUIS D. *"The Member of the Wedding,"* in *Literature/Film Quaterly* (Winter, 1976); and "Fred Zinnemann's *High Noon,"* in *Film Criticism* (Winter, 1976–77). Critical analyses.

GRIFFITH, RICHARD. "Fred Zinnemann." New York: Museum of Modern Art, 1958. A brief appreciation and analysis by one of America's most respected social realist critics.

LIGHTMAN, HERB. "Shooting Black and White in Color," in *American Cinematographer* (August, 1959). On Franz Planer's cinematography in *The Nun's Story.*

MACCANN, RICHARD DYER. "The Problem Film in America," in *Film and Society.* New York: Scribner's, 1964. A useful survey of American social realism and its influences.

REID, JOHN HOWARD. "A Man for All Movies," in *Films and Filming* (May, 1967). A discussion of Zinnemann's range as an artist, with some remarks on his documentaries and B films. See also Alan Stanbrook, "A Man for All Movies," in *Films and Filming,* part 2 (June, 1967): a thematic study of Zinnemann's movies, with emphasis on the ideas of identity and individualism.

ROHAUER, RAYMOND. "A Tribute to Fred Zinnemann." New York: Gallery of Modern Art, 1967. A brief appreciation and interview, with an appended filmography.

"Stanley Kramer," in *Dialogue on Film* (July, 1973). Pamphlet published by the American Film Institute. An interview with America's best-known producer (and later director) of social realist movies.

ZINNEMANN, FRED. "Different Perspective," in *Sight and Sound* (Autumn, 1948). Remarks on documentary fiction. See also Zinnemann's other articles, "A Conflict of Conscience," in *Films and Filming* (December, 1959); and "Revelations," in *Films and Filming* (September, 1964).

Figure 16.1. Publicity photo of Penn and Marlon Brando during the production of *The Chase* (1965). Quiet and soft-spoken, Penn is usually receptive to suggestions by his casts and crews. The atmosphere on his set is generally calm, relaxed, and professional. He is admired by actors, who have praised his sympathy for their problems. Himself a graduate of the Actors Studio, Penn tends to prefer Method-trained actors, who he believes are more creative and analytical than conventional players.

Like many filmmakers of his generation, Penn began as a television director during its golden age, the 1950s. By the end of that decade he was working in three mediums: Television, the New York stage, and the movies. Though he is still in mid-career, his cinematic output has been small: To date he has completed only ten films. The theories and movies of the French New Wave directors exerted a strong influence on Penn, who has been described as "the American Truffaut." Like Kazan (and Capra before him), Penn is acutely attuned to the spiritual crises of his generation. His films could be viewed as artistic gauges of the national spirit, especially those of the Vietnam and Watergate eras: *Bonnie and Clyde, Alice's Restaurant, Little Big Man,* and *Night Moves.* Though he is a pacifist by inclination, Penn might almost be regarded as the poet laureate of America the Violent. The immensely popular *Bonnie and Clyde* became a *cause célèbre* among film critics and public commentators, for it ushered in an era of unprecedented brutality in the American cinema. Penn insisted that his movie was in fact a mirror of the times: "We undergo a sort of contract with violence during our own lives." Most of his films are characterized by a sense of loss and moral drift, a coming apart of the American social fabric. He offers little hope for the future: "We're part of a generation which knows there are no solutions."

> *I think violence is a part of the American character. It began with the Western, the frontier. America is a country of people who act out their views in violent ways—there is not a strong tradition of persuasion, of ideation, and of law.*
> —*Arthur Penn*

Penn was born in Philadelphia in 1922. Less than four years later, his parents divorced, and he went with his mother to New York City. He rarely speaks of his early youth in interviews, except to say that he had an unhappy childhood and felt alienated from his surroundings. Because of financial difficulties, he and his mother were often forced to move to cheaper housing. When he was five he was frightened by a film whose title he can't even recall; he stayed away from movies until he was a teenager. At the age of fourteen he went back to Phildelphia to live with his father, who was a clockmaker. In high school the youth had no specific goals in life. Eventually he drifted into amateur theatrics. For a brief period after high school he took up his father's trade, but he lost interest.

He joined the Army in 1943, when he turned twenty-one. While he was in the service he met Fred Coe and joined Coe's small military theatre company, which played to Army personnel across Europe. Penn was later transferred to a military theatrical group run by the stage director, Joshua Logan. Throughout the 1940s, Penn's intellectual horizons expanded. He was influenced by the ideas of Freud and Marx, and his interest in all the arts deepened. His values became increasingly political and communal. "In my case," he explained, "the idea of divorce was so intolerable that I tried to make up a new kind of family, a new structure." He believes that the leftist idealism of his youth was rather simple-minded: Labor was good, capital bad, community action best. "The shape of our protests was collective," Penn recalled. "The suspicion of groups was not strong. The Soviet ideal was the one ideal, for better or worse. It got worse." Like Kazan, Penn became disillusioned with the U.S.S.R., though his political values have remained left of center. He believes that social anxiety is the underlying basis for much of his art: "What frightens you and concerns you is also a very good source of materials."

After he was discharged from the Army in 1946, Penn decided to use his G.I. Bill to pursue his academic studies. He attended Black Mountain College in North Carolina, struggling on a $75-a-month stipend. But he loved the communal atmosphere of the school, which was an experimental college of only sixty-five or so students. Some of the finest artists in America served as visiting scholars to the school, but after a few years it folded for lack of funds. Penn decided to go on to Italy, where he studied literature at the Universities of Perugia and Florence. At this time he was interested in pursuing a career in writing, but eventually he veered back to theatre arts. When he returned to New York in the late 1940s, he enrolled in courses at the celebrated Actors Studio (see Chapter 14).

In 1951, his Army mentor, Fred Coe, was working as a television producer for NBC, and he managed to get Penn a job at the network. He began as a lowly go-fer and quickly worked his way up to floor manager for a variety of shows. At this time, virtually all network television was New York based and was expanding rapidly, offering many opportunities for young talent. Some of the most accomplished filmmakers of Penn's generation began in television, including Delbert Mann, Sidney Lumet, John Frankenheimer, Robert Mulligan, Franklin Schaffner, and Sam Peckinpah. In 1953, Penn got a chance to direct on Coe's experimental dramatic series, *First Person.* Penn and Coe went on to such prestigious assignments as *The Philco Playhouse* and *Playhouse 90,* which employed some of the best acting and writing talent in New York.

Television directing was closer to theatre than to movies during this period because productions were live, and editing from shot to shot had to be accomplished during performance, with no opportunity for retakes. In most of the teleplays he directed, Penn used four cameras in order to cut from long to close to group shots. Television was regarded as a writer's and actor's medium, less a director's, because most teleplays of this era emphasized spoken dialogue within a confined playing area, with the camera acting as neutral recorder. Penn's experiences in live television influenced him as a filmmaker, particularly in his handling of actors. He often uses multiple cameras in his movies in order to photograph the action from a variety of distances. This gives him a great deal of footage, with many covering shots, and allows him maximum flexibility and creativity at the editing bench.

Though Penn continued directing for television as late as 1968, his real goal was the New York stage, which was enjoying a renaissance during the 1950s. His first opportunity to direct in the legitimate theatre came in 1954, with *Blue Denim.* In the following years, he directed a string of hits on Broadway, including *Two for the Seesaw, The Miracle Worker, Toys in the Attic, An Evening with Mike Nichols and Elaine May, All the Way Home,* and *Fiorello!* Penn still alternates between stage and screen directing, but he believes that since the 1960s he has been able to do truer, more serious work in movies. He thinks that Broadway audiences are complacent and don't want to be upset or shocked by anything so radical as an idea: "The so-called serious play has the air of being stately and literary, but it does not really assault any of the fundamental values of its audience. Movies do—they move in on a highly personal level in the way that a book or a poem does." Cinema has been his first love since *Bonnie and Clyde.*

Penn's first experience as a movie director was *The Left-Handed Gun* in 1957. He agreed to the project as a favor to Coe, for the director's chief ambitions were still with the New York theatre. *The Left-Handed Gun* was made on a relatively small budget (Penn received only $17,000 for directing) and was shot in a breathless twenty-three days. Penn rewrote much of the script, and all the shots were worked out in advance. He used two cameras for most of the scenes. The film was cut by studio editors without consulting him, and though it's substantially in the form he envisioned, he thinks its conventional editing style destroys the internal rhythms of some of the scenes. He was repelled by the experience,

Figure 16.2. Publicity photo of Paul Newman in *The Left-Handed Gun* (1957), distributed by Warner Brothers. The role of Billy the Kid was one of Newman's first challenging parts. His best performances suggest a touch of the cynic and have an anti-Establishment bravado that made him a great favorite with the public. Since the 1960s he has been a top box office attraction in America and one of the most admired stars of his generation. "Paul Newman is the last star," observed George Segal. "He's the link. We're just actors."

and he returned to New York, vowing never to direct another movie unless he received final-cut privileges.

It was five years before he returned to filmmaking, with *The Miracle Worker* (1962). When he did, he had a lot more clout, for he was now one of Broadway's most respected directors. He had originally directed William Gibson's teleplay in 1956 for *Playhouse 90*. The show was so popular that Penn, Coe, and Gibson decided to adapt it for Broadway, where it was also very successful. Penn agreed to direct the movie version only if he had artistic control and final-cut rights. The film was shot in New York, with Anne Bancroft and Patty Duke re-creating their highly praised performances as Annie Sullivan and Helen Keller. The movie was a hit, and Bancroft and Duke both won Academy Awards for their acting. Since that time, Penn has enjoyed artistic autonomy on all of his films except *The Chase*(1965).

The Hollywood studio system was in its terminal throes when Penn began his movie career. He believes that television and the Red scare (see Chapter 14) wiped out the old establishment. By the 1960s, the industry had been taken over by younger executives who were more attuned to audience tastes and willing to allow filmmakers somewhat more independence. Penn regards the big studios as film investment organizations primarily and as places to get technical equipment. He has never signed a long-term contract, preferring to finance his projects one at a time. He dislikes producing his own films, which he considers enervating and boring. He usually prefers to work with producers who limit their activities to financial rather than artistic decisions. However, Penn is one of the most receptive of filmmakers, and he accepts suggestions from any source if he thinks they're helpful.

Figure 16.3. **Anne Bancroft and Patty Duke in *The Miracle Worker* (1962), released by United Artists.** "I have always equated the American temperament with the kinetic temperament," Penn has said. "I like kinetic behavior; I think that's good for cinema. Kinetic-Cinema: the two words have the same source." Penn's most memorable scenes are usually his most kinetic, like the flour-sack fight in *The Left-Handed Gun,* the slow-motion balletic massacre in *Bonnie and Clyde,* and the explosive climax of *Night Moves.*

Penn was strongly influenced by the *nouvelle vague,* or the New Wave, as Anglo-American critics referred to the revolution that revitalized the French cinema of the 1960s. In fact, Penn was "discovered" by the critics of *Cahiers du Cinéma.* *The Left-Handed Gun* had not been popular with American audiences, and critics in the United States had scarcely acknowledged its release—it was just a western, made without important stars, by a mere television director. In Europe, and especially in France, the film was much better received. Truffaut, Godard, and André Bazin had strong praise for its young director. Penn was soon a favorite with the Marxist critics at *Positif* as well. *The Left-Handed Gun* went on to win the Grand Prix at the Brussels Film Festival. Penn was a bit bewildered by it all, though of course he was pleased that European audiences and critics seemed so receptive to what he was trying to do.

The movies of the New Wave had a major influence on Penn's work, both in terms of style and philosophical outlook. He especially admired the works of Truffaut and Godard, which were dazzling in their technical virtuosity. Both used the newly perfected hand-held camera to create an air of playful spontaneity. The tone shifts in their movies were breathtaking, veering from comedy to tenderness to violence even within a single scene. Stylistically the New Wave was eclectic and revived such techniques as irises, freeze frames, fast and slow motion. Some scenes were edited in languorously lyrical rhythms. Others were jump cut in staccato explosions. The New Wave filmmakers weren't story-oriented. Godard pointed out—correctly—that the French rarely are. Their real concern was with ideas and character, with revealing the poignant absurdities of the young and romantic. Penn absorbed many of these ideas. [So did Newman and Benton, who wrote the original script of *Bonnie and Clyde* (1967). In fact, they initially approached Truffaut with the property, and he agreed to direct it until a prior commitment prevented him. Truffaut recommended Godard, and he too responded with interest. But his deal also fell through. Warren Beatty finally bought the script, and he persuaded his friend Penn to direct it.]

Another major influence on Penn are the movies of Elia Kazan. Both filmmakers are concerned with the conflict between the individual and society. Both deal with characters driven to violence by repressive social institutions—a conflict explored from the perspectives of Freud and Marx. Both believe in challenging the complacency of the status quo: "I think one of the functions of art is to purge or exorcize the crap that encrusts society," Penn has stated. He believes that there is "a hidden Freudian impulse in all of us which is to, somehow, bring the forces of authority at least one rung down the ladder." Kazan and Penn also experienced a progressive disenchantment with American institutions.

But there are important differences between these two artists. Penn is more instinctive, less cerebral, than Kazan. Penn's movies are generally looser and pocked with ambiguities and private ideas. Kazan's works, autobiographical as they are, are more externalized aesthetically. Kazan is also more objective and optimistic: His belief in a dialectical fusion of opposites presupposes a moral teleology. Kazan's universe, however dark, is essentially coalescent, a coming together. In Penn's

Figure 16.4. Warren Beatty in *Mickey One* (1964), distributed by Columbia. Penn referred to this movie as an allegory of a man's trip through purgatory. It centers on a stand-up comedian (Beatty) who is being pursued by a mysterious mob for a nameless crime. The film resembles Welles's *The Trial*, with its nightmarish atmosphere of paranoia and its surrealistic visual style. Like Welles's protagonist, Mickey is "guilty of not being innocent."

universe, the center doesn't hold, to use Yeats's famous metaphor. Like other modernist artists, Penn is essentially pessimistic. (For a discussion of modernism, see Chapter 18.) Structurally and thematically, his movies portray a coming apart. Unlike Kazan, he doesn't believe a *rapprochement* between society and its outcasts is possible, though Penn does believe that society in a given era has its mirror in its outcasts: "A time creates its own myths and heroes. If the heroes are less than admirable, that is a clue to the times." However ambivalently, Kazan's movies ultimately reaffirm the myth of the American melting pot. In Penn's works, subcultures are not absorbed into the Establishment; they're alternatives to it, they're countercultures. If these alternative communities are doomed to failure, as in *Alice's Restaurant* (1969), he presents them nonetheless as noble failures.

He believes that when society refuses to provide a vent for the frustrations of its outcasts and misfits, violence is the inevitable outcome. Penn also feels that the assassinations of John F. Kennedy, Martin Luther King, and Robert Kennedy were the irrational manifestations of social and sexual repression. He attempted to dramatize these ideas in the whirlwind violence of *The Chase*:

Figure 16.5. Marlon Brando (center forward) and Robert Redford (center rear) in *The Chase* (1965), distributed by Columbia. This was Penn's most violent movie to date, culminating in the hysterical auto graveyard sequence (pictured). Penn believes that the assassination of the Kennedy brothers and Martin Luther King triggered off an atmosphere of hysteria in the United States. As the 1960s wore on, the country veered increasingly toward anarchy.

The way those people shoot at each other in that film: it is not that they hate so much, it is more an extension of a kind of violence that they don't know where to deposit. They feel this kind of rage and impotence, and in a culture which uses weapons as freely as our culture does, there are very many unbalanced people who can, as we have seen all too painfully in the last few years, kill very fine men. I was television adviser to President Kennedy and then I worked with Robert Kennedy. I knew them just before they were killed.

Bonnie and Clyde triggered off a furious controversy among commentators. Of course violence was hardly something new in the American cinema. (Anthropologist Hortense Powdermaker wryly noted that even in the silent era, South Sea Islanders divided American movies into two genres: Kiss-Kiss and Bang-Bang.) What was new in Penn's film was the visceral intensity of the violence, which "puts the sting back into death," to quote from Pauline Kael's panegyric on the movie. *Newsweek's* Joseph Morgenstern was totally repelled by the film's gore. Then, in an impressive instance of public candor, he retracted his earlier opinion in a subsequent column, admitting that he had misinterpreted the film's explicitness for exploitiveness. Bosley Crowther of the *New York Times* condemned the movie in the harshest terms and conducted a crusade against the increasing brutality of American movies. Penn was dismayed that most of the film's detractors had missed the point. He regarded the "tasteful" presentation of violence and killing as an obscene hypocrisy and an evasion of our national heritage:

> It's absurd to suggest that the film is *the* central issue in violence in a violent society which has been repressing the black race for two hundred years and which has been ridden with prejudice and violence of the most flagrant character through all its history—the West, the 20s and 30s. It's a violent society engaged in a violent and ridiculous war.

Many critics also misinterpreted the function of comedy in *Bonnie and Clyde,* assuming that it was meant only to glamorize crime and ridicule the law. The unpredictable shifts of tone in the film, clearly indebted to the New Wave, were intended to keep the audience off balance and to make the characters less threatening—'jes folks. "We used laughter to get the audience to feel like a member of the gang," Penn explained, "to have the feeling of adventure, a feeling of playing together." One of the bank robbery sequences begins almost like a Keystone comedy. While Bonnie and Clyde are robbing the bank, their accomplice, C. W. Moss (Michael J. Pollard), who's as endearing as he is

Figure 16.6. Warren Beatty and Faye Dunaway in *Bonnie and Clyde* (1967), distributed by Warner Brothers. The influence of Freud is pronounced in Penn's work. He has undergone intensive psychoanalysis and believes that it helped him as an artist. "Everything in life comes out of the bedroom," he has observed of his sexually neurotic characters. Violence is often the expression of their sexual problems, like Clyde's impotence and Bonnie's fascination with his gun, with its obvious phallic symbolism. Sex is rarely suave and romantic in Penn's movies. Most of his lovers are groping, and sometimes outright funny.

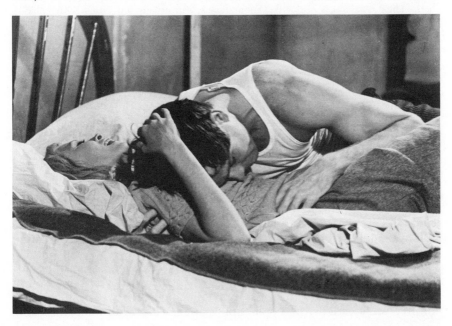

Figure 16.7.   Warren Beatty in _Bonnie and Clyde_. "The only people who really interest me are the outcasts from society," Penn has said. "My sympathies lie with that person who cannot accommodate himself to society and may have to lose his life to change it." Penn's outsiders and misfits rarely analyze their actions. Ideology is a foreign concept to most of them. Their rebellion is instinctive, spontaneous, and usually unfocused. Often they're swept up by the immediacy of the moment and are unable to anticipate the apocalyptic destiny that awaits them.

cretinous, waits outside in the getaway car, primed for action. When he observes another car leaving its parking space, C. W. decides to take it over. His partners rush out to the street to make their getaway: They find themselves stranded without transportation. Nearby, C. W. furiously rams and batters the two cars abutting the getaway vehicle. Miraculously, the three gangsters just barely manage to escape. To heighten the comic exhilaration of the scene, Penn accompanies his visuals with the jolly banjo music of Flatt and Scruggs. As the getaway car pulls away from the scene, an elderly bank teller impulsively leaps on the vehicle, clinging to it as it roars through town. Seeing the old man's face in the window, Clyde panics and shoots him point blank. In a shocking close shot of the teller's bloodied face, the screen erupts in red. The transition from comedy to tragedy is swift as a gunblast.

Young people were instinctively drawn to _Bonnie and Clyde,_ in part because it captured their own feelings of anger about Vietnam. America's youth and its minorities grew more alienated in the years ahead. The country was headed for a crackup. When social conditions worsened, college campuses were thrown into chaos. Militant students vented their fury at the Establishment through strikes, confrontation tactics, and rampages of vandalism. Black Americans were no longer asking for their civil rights; they were demanding them—and fighting for them. As the official violence escalated, so did that of the protest movement. The 1968 Democratic Convention in Chicago resembled an armed camp. Outside its bastions, police and taunting demonstrators clashed like savage armies. "The whole world is watching! The whole world is watching!" the protesters chanted, while the television cameras rolled. The footage was ritualistically unreeled each night on the evening news, along with the latest carnage from Vietnam and reports of America's ghettos in flames.

For the first time in history, American movies with downbeat and pessimistic themes became the rule rather than the exception. Violence, sex, and race were the big box office draws during this era. "People are used to seeing the war on television," said Philip D'Antonio, producer of *Bullitt* (1968) and *The French Connection* (1971). "They know what the real thing looks like. So, how can you fake it? Audiences won't buy that anymore." What they were buying was an unparalleled profusion of gore, despair, and sexual explicitness, in such important movies as *Midnight Cowboy, Easy Rider, Medium Cool, The Wild Bunch, Five Easy Pieces, M*A*S*H, A Clockwork Orange, Klute, McCabe and Mrs. Miller, Carnal Knowledge, The Godfather, Cabaret,* and *Straw Dogs,* and many others. The old censorship code was scrapped in favor of the present rating system, ushering in the pornographic revolution. The American screen was now the frankest and freest in the world. By 1972, there were over seven hundred theatres in the United States exhibiting only hardcore porn. Melvin Van Peebles's *Sweet Sweetback's Baadasss Song* (1971) popularized a new genre, the so-called blaxploitation picture—primarily urban melodramas and detective thrillers, reflecting the new black militancy. The early 1970s saw the release of over sixty of these films, most of them venting a murderous resentment against the white majority.

Movies, like rock music, provided an artistic outlet for the dissenting values of the young, and in their own idiom. Cultural commentators increasingly spoke of "the film generation," more sophisticated than any in history, and often as open to the works of Bergman, Fellini, Kurosawa, and the New Wave as they were to their native cinematic traditions. Movie courses proliferated in colleges and universities across the country. By 1975, the American Film Institute (itself created in 1967) reported that there were at least 3,000 film courses at more than 600 colleges and universities across the United States. This cinematic self-consciousness gave rise to an unprecedented number of serious movie critics and scholars. More critical studies about movies were published during this era than in all previous periods combined.

Penn followed his most violent film with his most gentle, *Alice's Restaurant,* which is loosely based on a popular recording by Arlo Guthrie, the son of the folk singer Woody Guthrie, who was the creator of many protest songs of the old left in the 1930s. *Alice's Restaurant* affectionately celebrates the values of the protest movement—its rejection of racism, militarism, materialism, and authoritarianism. The film's tone

Figure 16.8. *Alice's Restaurant* **(1969), with Arlo Guthrie (holding hat), released by United Artists.** Penn made this movie as a tribute to the protest movement, which was dominated by young people. But the film is by no means a mindless endorsement of the hippie counterculture. "Some movies are creating the myths of the young," he complained. "They promote the notion that freedom from all authority is an unqualified good, that mobility as a lifestyle is superior to permanence, that the older generation is totally corrupt, that cool is the only legitimate response. And what's worse about these films is that they patronize young people. They reduce them to their accouterments—their grass, their bikes, their music—all their labels."

swings abruptly from slapstick comedy to moments of poignant anguish. It also contains a few brutal sequences, mostly centering on the heroin-addicted motorcyclist, Shelly (Michael McClanathan). Penn wanted to pay tribute to the young men who defied the military draft for reasons of moral conscience. Youthful audiences delighted in the movie's raucously comic sequence in which Arlo is convicted of littering, and is therefore subsequently judged unfit for military service. "You wanna know if I'm moral enough to join the Army, burn women, kids, houses and villages, after being a litterbug?" Arlo asks with mock incredulity. An Army regular replies stonily: "Kid, we don't like your kind."

Actually, the movie centers on the quasi-fictionalized characters of Alice and Ray Brock (Pat Quinn and James Broderick), who are in their thirties and act as surrogate parents for the young people. Alice and Ray are dropouts from straight society and have established their own community in an abandoned church in Stockbridge, Massachusetts. Their idealism—and their marriage—begins to come apart when they discover that the simple life isn't all that simple. Alice feels like a bitch who's being milked by too many pups. Ray—the least self-aware character in the film—lives only for the pleasure of the moment and is unable to cast off his authoritarian impulses. After Alice leaves him, he promises to change, to be less selfish and domineering. He suggests that they get married again, this time in an elaborate hippie ceremony to recement their relationship. But as the final sequence of the film shows, their second marriage vows are as fragile as their first. The sequence begins festively, with hoards of colorfully garbed hippies enjoying the rituals of their subculture. Gradually the tone darkens, as most of the wedding guests depart to travel their separate ways. In a drunken flight of fancy, Ray talks to a few stragglers about selling the church and starting over again in Vermont. But no one really listens, except Alice, who slowly begins to realize that nothing has changed—least of all Ray. He stumbles back into the church, leaving her standing outside its doors, her hair

Figure 16.9. *Alice's Restaurant,* **with Pat Quinn and James Broderick.** Penn's movie was one of the few of its era to explore the hippie counterculture in an honest manner. Their music, rituals, and clothing are authentic depictions of their laid-back life-style and innocent (and sometimes not so innocent) hedonism. But Penn refused to sentimentalize his characters. The Children in the Age of Aquarius—Godard dubbed their French counterpart "The Children of Marx and Coca-Cola"—are sometimes unable to handle the responsibility of their freedom.

garlanded with flowers, her wedding dress slightly crumpled. As she looks past the camera, her face reflects an ambiguous mixture of anxiety and desolation. Never has she seemed so totally vulnerable. On the soundtrack, the cheery lyrics of Arlo's title song ("You can get anything you want at Alice's Restaurant") are distorted into a lonely ironic mockery by the use of an echo chamber. As the song continues, the camera dollys to the left, while occasional intervening tree trunks obliterate our view of Alice. A cloud slowly snuffs out the bright sunlight, and she is shrouded in a grayish semidarkness. As the camera dollys out to the left, it also zooms in slowly to the right, producing an eerie sense of movement toward and away from Alice simultaneously. Penn said of this shot, "No matter what the sense of motion might be, the final condition is one of paralysis." It's one of Penn's most celebrated "privileged moments." The moving camera tends to suggest the idea of time passing and the impermanence of things. The slow zooming in suggests Alice's gradual realization that the quality of her life won't improve, but instead, will probably deteriorate. It's a poetic and moving conclusion, charged with bittersweet ambiguities—and forebodings of futility.

Penn's vision grew darker as the war dragged into the 1970s. *Little Big Man* (1970) was an oblique comment on the American military presence in Vietnam. The movie is one of several "revisionist" westerns of this period—so-called because the genre had veered into an ironic mode, mocking many of the ideals of such classical westerns as Ford's *Wagon Master* and *She Wore a Yellow Ribbon*. Penn's symbolism wasn't missed by many when he cast an oriental actress (Amy Eccles) to play the hero's Indian wife, Sunshine. The sequence in which their quiet Indian community is wiped out by Custer's cavalry was intended to suggest the search-and-destroy missions in the villages of Vietnam. One of the most horrifying scenes is when Sunshine and her infant are brutally cut down by the soldiers' bullets.

Penn was among the first of his generation to reject many of the time-honored conventions of the classical American cinema. Most of his early works fall within its purview, but with *Bonnie and Clyde* he began to adopt other options, mostly from the tradition of modernism which dominated the New Wave and other European filmmakers. For example, Penn's earlier movies tend to be story-oriented, but after *Bonnie and Clyde* his narratives became looser, more exploratory. The earlier works are structured around a chase of some kind; the later works, around a search. In the earlier movies the characters pursue a specific goal; in the later movies, they drift rudderlessly. All of them tend to get swept up by events beyond their control. The later films are generally unified by tone and by a symbolic concept. For example, the quasi-discrete vignettes of *Alice's Restaurant* are connected by the motif of roads. The movie is profuse in road images, and often this term is used metaphorically to suggest alternative life-styles. *Little Big Man, Night Moves* (1975), and *The Missouri Breaks* (1976) are unified in part by the expectations of their genres. We expect the western hero and the private eye to succeed because they almost always do in the classical cinema. But revisionist genres are ironic by definition. The contrast between what is expected and what actually happens (or doesn't happen) dislocates the neat

Figure 16.10. Dustin Hoffman in *Little Big Man* (1970), distributed by Cinema Center.
Stylistically this was Penn's most audacious movie to date, alternating farcical sequences
with scenes of brutality and touches of whimsical absurdity. It ends on a note of disillusionment and shattered hope. Drawing his materials from the myth of Custer's last stand,
Penn rejected its heroic dimensions and converted it into a tragic parable of American
racism and genocide.

symmetries—both aesthetic and moral—of classical structures. Subversion of genre is also an implicit rejection of the classical *Weltanschauung*.
There's a low degree of predictability in Penn's later films, a sense of
mystery and ellipsis. Character relationships aren't always sharply defined, plot strands are abruptly dropped or allowed to wear out, and it's
difficult to guess how the stories will end. Several end inconclusively,
with a gnawing sense of irresolution, as in *Alice's Restaurant* and *Night
Moves*.

Myth and ritual are important in genre movies even in their revisionist phase. Penn exploits myths as ironic analogues to contemporary
issues, as a way of focusing and sublimating public anxieties. "Being a
director is a reorganization of the material of living into a better form
than one can experience," he has explained. He often grafts nationalistic
myths with those of Freudian psychology. For example, he described
Billy the Kid in *The Left-Handed Gun* as "Oedipus in the West." Similarly,
Helen Keller—a legendary figure for many American schoolchildren—
can find meaningful articulation only when she symbolically rejects her
literal parents in favor of a parental surrogate, Annie Sullivan. Penn

Figure 16.11. Gene Hackman (extreme right) in *Night Moves* (1975), distributed by Warner Brothers. This is a detective thriller in which the hero, Harry Moseby (Hackman), can't solve a single problem. As originally written, the script was a straight genre story, but Penn rewrote it to reflect his personal beliefs and his feelings about the Watergate disclosures: "I really think we're bankrupt, and that the Watergate experience was just the *coup de grâce*. We've been drifting into this state for the last twenty years." Penn's mise-en-scène embodies a sense of alienation. In this photo, for example, each character is imprisoned in his or her own space cubicle: They look buried alive.

treated Bonnie and Clyde not only as folk heroes of the depression but also as mythic archetypes for posterity: "I think some people have had to fight and lose the fight, to create a kind of conscience that is part of the rest of us for the rest of our lives." The famous slow-motion dance of death which concludes *Bonnie and Clyde* is paradoxically repellant in its savagery and riveting in its lyricism. By aestheticizing their slaughter, Penn was trying to transform the materials of life into myth. *Alice's Restaurant* is filled with communal rituals, like the deconsecration of the church, the Thanksgiving Day feast, and the hippie remarriage of Alice and Ray. *Little Big Man* mocks the classical western hero by portraying General Custer as a pompous fraud and psychopath. Penn also accompanies a scene of Indian genocide with the bagpipe music of the famous U.S. 7th Cavalry—Ford's favorite military unit.

Penn's themes are similar to Kazan's. In addition to conflicts between the individual and society, they revolve around problems of identity, the creation of deceptive images by the media, the disintegration of the family, and the centrality of sex in determining human behavior. *Mickey One* (1964) combines many of these themes. Like most of Penn's protagonists, Mickey wants "to be somebody" and hungers for a sense of identity, but he's unable to function without the approval of society. In

Alice's Restaurant, Arlo realizes that he must reject his parents (and their successors, Alice and Ray), even though he admires and loves them. He must travel his own road in order to discover what his "thing" in life will be. Many of Penn's movies explore the ironic contrast between an image and reality. The neurotic Moultrie in *The Left-Handed Gun* writes pulp fiction about his hero, Billy the Kid, and is embittered when William Bonney fails to live up to this idealized image. Bonnie and Clyde religiously check out the newspaper accounts of their exploits and wax indignant at the press's exaggerations and lies. To enhance its public image, the FBI transforms these redneck amateurs into "the Bloody Barrow Gang"—which doesn't altogether displease them. Often this theme is treated comically, as in *The Missouri Breaks*, when a train robber asks, "I'd like you to refer to me from now on as The Lonesome Kid. Especially in front of outsiders." The image of the family as an eroded institution is common in Penn's works. Many of his characters turn away from their families and attempt to find substitute relationships. When Bonnie realizes that she's cut herself off from her roots by her life of crime, Clyde tries to comfort her by saying, "I'm your family."

Penn's collaborators have strongly praised his openness and flexiblity as a director. He regards his movies as expressions of his own feelings and ideas, but he also insists that cinema is a collective art. Generally he likes to rework his scenarios to reflect his personal obsessions, but without violating the spirit of the original. Unlike the live theatre, in which the script is virtually Holy Writ, Penn believes that dialogue in the cinema serves only as a guide to visualization: "I try to take as much of the literary value away from the script as possible." He believes that in film there ought to be a constant contradiction between what's said and what's done: "Movies are not necessarily about literary utterances in the way that the stage is."

Penn believes that actors as well as writers are the creators of meaning in the cinema: "Film is the exquisite medium for expressing ambivalence. A man says one thing, but his eyes are saying another thing." Like most artists who have been trained in the Method, he believes that the subtext is where the real drama lies. "Arthur Penn is a great director because he sees the special human moment in a scene, outside the dialogue, outside the scenery," Gene Hackman has noted. Penn regards Kazan as the finest director of actors, and like Kazan, he believes that sincerity, spontaneity, and the unexpected are what produce great performances. He tries to create an atmosphere of "controlled accident" on his sets and encourages his players to improvise with their roles. In *Alice's Restaurant*, for example, he urged his performers to rephrase their dialogue in their own idiom if they were uncomfortable with the wording of the script.

Penn's visual style varies from film to film. Even within a single work he's fond of juxtaposing contrasting styles. Before *Bonnie and Clyde*, he was not very interested in camera technique, and he allowed his cinematographers to determine much of the look of his movies. For example, both *The Left-Handed Gun* and *The Miracle Worker* are photographed according to classical conventions. With *Bonnie and Clyde* Penn's style became more self-conscious and personal: His use of color is more sensuous; there's more experimentation with lenses and filters, and a greater interest in landscape and décor as symbols of spiritual states. Unlike most filmmakers of his generation, Penn doesn't always desaturate his colors to produce a sense of tasteful restraint. The colors in *The Chase* were deliberately heightened to suggest a vulgar brashness, which is in keeping with the nature of the materials. *Alice's Restaurant* alternates styles. The scenes involving Alice and Ray tend to emphasize pale, washed-out colors and a documentary visual style; the farcical scenes involving Arlo's encounter with the police and the Army have a pop, comic-book flavor. Similarly, in *Little Big Man,* many of the Indian scenes are photographed to look like newsreel footage; the scenes involving white people, on the other hand, tend to be cartoonlike in their candy-colored stylization. Bruce Surtees' cinematography in *Night Moves* has a deliberately garish fluorescence, dominated by sickly hues. Penn's mise-en-scène in this movie emphasizes murkiness, clutter, glassy reflections, and enclosures within enclosures—all suggesting deceptive surfaces and a labyrinthine impenetrability. In Penn's later works, scenes are often staged obliquely, producing a sense of frustration in the viewer, since the significance of the action is not self-evident. For example, in the lyrical opening shot of *The Missouri Breaks,* we see three horsemen in the distance, casually riding through some lovely tall grass. Their low-keyed, barely decipherable conversation revolves around indifferent topics. They could be three ol' boys out for a ride and a breath of fresh air. Only when they lope into the proximity of the camera do we realize that they're coming to a hanging—and one of the three is the man who's going to be hanged.

Penn believes that his stylistic signature is most apparent in his editing, which is indebted to the practices of the New Wave directors, especially Truffaut, Godard, and Alain Resnais. Penn's style of cutting represents a considerable departure from the classical paradigm. Of course classical cutting is a term of convenience, encompassing a considerable diversity of styles—from the seamless elisions of Capra, to the austere minimalism of Wyler, to the no-fuss functionalism of Hawks, to the nervous edginess of Zinnemann. But they are all classicists. The way they connect their shots is determined by the continuity of the narrative and the logical breakdown of the action into its component parts. Many of Penn's movies are so loosely structured that the narrative is weakened in its logic. His shots are linked more arbitrarily and instinctively and are determined by the subtext rather than the action per se. "Editing is a very refined process in which your own viewpoint comes through in a more subtle way," he has explained. He regards his footage as raw material from which the movie is extracted. He often shoots a scene from a variety of angles and distances and with different lenses to give him a vast amount of footage. He often escalates the violence of a scene by bombarding the viewer with a barrage of closeups. His cutting style is usually tense and jittery, but occasionally he will use lengthy takes. As in the early movies of the New Wave, his cutting dazzles with abrupt transitions, jump cuts, and shocking juxtapositions. His favorite editor, Dede Allen, is widely regarded as the most brilliant of contemporary American editors. She and Penn are close personal friends as well as profes-

Figure 16.12. Marlon Brando in *The Missouri Breaks* (1976), distributed by United Artists. Penn's presentation of violence is always shocking and grotesque. In this film, Brando plays a regulator, whose job it is to hunt down and kill cattle rustlers for a fee. One of his victims is shot out of a toilet; another is drowned in the middle of a conversation. Another rustler is shot while trying to make love. The last victim is shot in the head after escaping from a burning shack. The tools of the killing trade can be exotic, like this terrifying medieval implement. Photo: Gary Engle.

sional colleagues. They go over the footage together, deciding jointly on how it will be edited.

Penn's artistic shortcomings might be viewed as the obverse side of his virtues. He is a master of the intimate privileged moment (hence his affinity with Truffaut), but he's not much of a storyteller. Some of his narrative structures seem to come apart before our very eyes. *Mickey One* is so personal and elliptical that it could mean almost anything. There are uneven sections in almost all his movies. Sometimes he gets so swept up by the explosiveness of the moment that the overall action of a scene—like Custer's last stand in *Little Big Man*—is clumsily laid out. *Night Moves* attempts to untangle a densely textured mystery in the final few minutes, but for all its visual and kinetic brilliance, the denouement confuses many viewers. *The Missouri Breaks* contains a number of excellent scenes, but some critics thought its structure verged on incoherence because of its isolated groups of characters, divergent tones, and drifting plotlines. Even critics who were sympathetically drawn to the movie's bizarre charm were thrown by its formlessness. "What's this thing *about?*" critic Charles Michener asked himself toward the end of the film. It's a question that was asked by many.

But despite his limitations as an artist, Penn's movies are regarded as important cultural events by the *cognoscenti*. He is admired by such diverse European filmmakers as Ingmar Bergman, Lina Wertmüller, and of course, the French. He is rarely criticized for his violence anymore, in part because audiences can now accept the idea of an artistically responsible use of violence: In Penn's movies, the brutality is usually perpetrated against the people we care the most about. "You look at *Bonnie and Clyde* now and it's like a ladies' tea party compared to what Peckinpah and quite a few other guys have done," Penn has observed. He has influenced an entire generation of young American filmmakers, who might be regarded as the disciples of violence: Martin Scorsese, John Milius, Brian De Palma, Paul Schrader, and Francis Ford Coppola, to name a few. Like Penn, these artists believe that America is a violent society. Like him, they seek to explore the reasons why.

BIBLIOGRAPHY

BARNOUW, ERIK. *Tube of Plenty.* New York: Oxford University Press, 1975. The evolution and history of American television.

BAXTER, JOHN. *Hollywood in the Sixties.* Cranbury, N.J.: A. S. Barnes, 1972. Survey of the decade, mostly by genre.

CAWELTI, JOHN G., ed. *Focus on Bonnie and Clyde.* New York: Prentice-Hall, 1973. Reviews, critical essays, and interview with Penn.

HERNDON, VENABLE, AND ARTHUR PENN. *Alice's Restaurant.* New York: Doubleday, 1970. Script, with forewords by the authors.

KAEL, PAULINE. "*Bonnie and Clyde,*" in *Kiss Kiss Bang Bang.* New York: Bantam, 1968. A reprint of her celebrated piece in *The New Yorker.*

MONACO, JAMES. *The New Wave.* New York: Oxford University Press, 1976. See also Peter Graham, ed., *The New Wave* (London: Secker & Warburg, 1968).

SHERMAN, ERIC, AND MARTIN RUBIN, eds. "Arthur Penn," in *The Director's Event.* New York: Signet Books, 1969. Other interviews include Curtis Lee Hanson, "An Interview with Arthur Penn," *Cinema* (1967); Joseph Gelmis, ed., "Arthur Penn," in *The Film Director as Superstar* (New York: Doubleday, 1970); Gordon Gow, "Metaphor: Arthur Penn in an Interview," *Films and Filming* (July, 1971); Tag Gallagher, "*Night Moves,*" in *Sight and Sound* (Spring, 1975); and "What *Is* a Western?" interview with Stuart Byron and Terry Curtis Fox, in *Film Comment* (July-August, 1976): This issue also contains a piece by Charles Michener on *The Missouri Breaks.*

VAN DEN BERGH, LILY. "*Alice's Restaurant,*" in *Sight and Sound* (Spring, 1969); and Louis D. Giannetti, "*Alice's Restaurant* and the Tradition of the Plotless Film," in *Godard and Others: Essays in Film Form.* Cranbury, N.J.: Fairleigh Dickinson University Press, 1975.

WAKE, SANDRA, AND NICOLA HAYDEN, eds. *The Bonnie & Clyde Book.* New York: Simon & Schuster, 1972. Includes the screenplay, interview, critical articles about the film, and script changes by Penn, Warren Beatty, and uncredited writer Robert Towne.

WOOD, ROBIN. *Arthur Penn.* New York: Praeger, 1970. A perceptive critical study. Filmography.

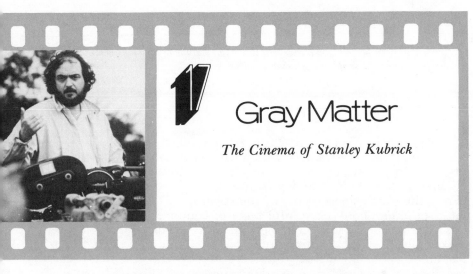

Gray Matter

The Cinema of Stanley Kubrick

Figure 17.1. Stanley Kubrick on the set of *Barry Lyndon* (1975). Kubrick's projects tend to be complex enterprises, requiring a high degree of organization. His sets are usually disciplined and efficient, and his assistants regard his monomania for perfection with good-humored stoicism. His technical instructions to his crew are fast, precise, and confident. He is polite to everyone, and rarely raises his voice. One aide recalled that in his five years with Kubrick he never once saw the director lose his temper. His collaborators think he's a bit weird, but their admiration for him verges on awe. Even George C. Scott, who's not easily awed, conceded, "He is most certainly in command, and he's so self-effacing and apologetic it's impossible to be offended by him."

ew filmmakers can match the originality of Kubrick's mind. He has created some of the most audacious movies of the contemporary cinema, including such classics as *Dr. Strangelove, 2001,* and *A Clockwork Orange.* He is perhaps the least romantic of American filmmakers. His tone is cold, ironic, detached. He is unsentimental about the human species, regarding man as more akin to the beasts than the angels. His output to date has been small—fewer than a dozen features in more than twice that number of years—in part because he insists on handling every aspect of his work personally. Kubrick's movies often explore ideas, not explicitly but ambiguously, through the sensuousness of his medium: "Film operates on a level much closer to music and to painting than to the printed word," he believes. "The feel of the experience is the important thing, not the ability to verbalize or analyze it." He is a bravura technician, and his stylistic virtuosity has left audiences spellbound in astonishment. "To be boring," he thinks, "is the worst sin of all." It's a sin he's rarely accused of committing.

> *A truly original person with a truly original mind will not be able to function in the old form and will simply do something different.*
>
> *—Stanley Kubrick*

Kubrick was born in 1928 in the borough of the Bronx in New York City. His father was a physician whose pet hobbies were chess and photography. At an early age his son also adopted these enthusiasms. He became a chess fanatic and was also his high school photographer. "From the start I loved cameras," he recalled. "There is something almost sensuous about a beautiful piece of equipment." Young Kubrick was a below-average student in high school. When his concerned parents took him to Columbia University to be tested, they discovered that he had an exceptionally high IQ but was bored by school; at that time this was apparently regarded as an odd phenomenon. "I never learned anything at all in school and I didn't read a book for pleasure until I was nineteen years old," Kubrick has said. Because of his low grade-point average, he was unable to go to college.

But he had plenty of nerve and confidence, and he was a good talker. In 1945, at the age of seventeen, he persuaded *Look* magazine to hire him as a staff photographer; they did so "out of pity," according to Kubrick. For the next four-and-a-half years, he traveled across the country as a photojournalist for *Look*. During this period, Kubrick also began to expand his cultural horizons. He audited courses at Columbia, primarily in literature. He became a voracious reader and has remained so ever since. As a child he was often taken to the movies by his mother, and by the time he was nineteen, he was a hardcore film freak. Five nights a week he attended the retrospectives offered by the Museum of Modern Art. He studied these films carefully, and he was especially impressed by the visual genius in the movies of Welles, the editing style of Eisenstein, and the dazzling traveling shots of Max Ophüls. On weekends, Kubrick spent his time by going to recently released movies.

The bad films he saw gave him the courage to make a movie of his own. "The best way to learn is to do," he believes, and in 1950 he made *Day of Flight,* a sixteen-minute documentary about a prizefighter, Walter Cartier. It cost $3,800 of Kubrick's own money, and he sold it to RKO for $4,000. He quit his job at *Look* soon after and turned to filmmaking full time. *Flying Padre* (1951), a nine-minute documentary, was also sold to RKO, with no profit. Next came *The Seafarers* (1953), a half-hour color documentary. This too made no money. Kubrick decided to move into fiction films. At the age of twenty-five, he made *Fear and Desire* (1953), an allegory about war, on a sorry budget of $39,000—mostly borrowed from his father and uncle. His second independent feature was *Killer's Kiss* (1955), a B thriller in the stylistic vein of *film noir.* Kubrick regards both these movies as "inept and pretentious," but they were valuable learning experiences, enabling him to master his craft with exceptional thoroughness: He produced, wrote, directed, photographed, edited, and mixed the sound. Neither film prospered

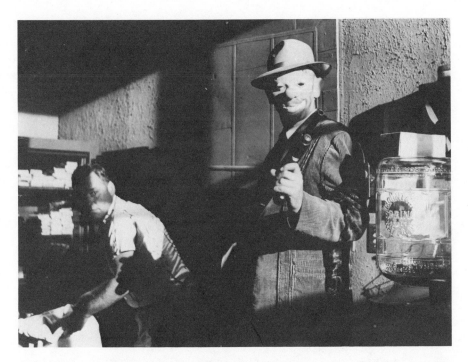

Figure 17.2. *The Killing* (1956), distributed by United Artists. This caper film deals with some penny-ante crooks who attempt a major-league hoist, a racetrack robbery. Mostly because of their human frailties, but also the intervention of fate, the robbers bungle the job, and they all go down in defeat. Except for the racetrack scenes, the movie was shot in the studio, in the *noir* style. (For a discussion of *film noir,* see Chapter 9.)

at the box office and neither excited much critical notice, though a few reviewers praised their technical inventiveness.

His first professional film was *The Killing* (1956). Sterling Hayden agreed to act in it on the basis of Kubrick's well-constructed and suspenseful screenplay. The young producer-director then persuaded UA to finance the project with a modest budget of $320,000. The cast also included those B-film stalwarts, Marie Windsor (playing a slut, as usual) and Elisha Cook, Jr. (playing a sad little gangster, also as usual).

Kubrick's first important movie was *Paths of Glory* (1957), which UA again agreed to finance (to the tune of a million dollars) because Kirk Douglas was enthusiastic about the script. The story is based on an actual event which took place during World War I, a French infantry attack against an impregnable German hill fortification—the futile scheme of two cynical French generals who cared more about advancing their careers than protecting the lives of their troops. The movie's liberal idealism is considerably undercut by its pessimistic ending, in which three trench soldiers are arbitrarily chosen to be shot by a firing squad for their presumed cowardice under fire. The film is still banned in France. It was made primarily on location in Germany and has been highly praised for its authenticity of detail. The battle scenes, photographed mostly by Kubrick himself, are stunning in their power and technical brilliance. The movie was praised by many critics, but it failed at the box office.

None of Kubrick's first four features had shown a profit, and by the age of thirty, he was still not able to support himself as a filmmaker. (He had agreed to a deferred salary with his UA pictures, which meant he would be paid for his work only after the films broke even; but since they returned no profits, he had to forfeit his salary.) His next picture, *Spartacus* (1960), inaugurated a reversal of fortunes, for it was a big hit and allowed him to work independently from then on. Kubrick thought that Dalton Trumbo's screenplay was sentimental, its spear-and-sandal clichés smacking of the De Mille school of grandiosity. The director was told he would be able to change the script, but during production he was overruled. *Spartacus* is considerably superior to most examples of its genre, thanks primarily to Kubrick's action footage, but it's his least favorite work. "If you don't have legal authority," he discovered, "you don't have any authority at all."

But *Spartacus* set him free. Ever since then, Kubrick has worked only for himself. In fact, his mania for control is as legendary as Hitchcock's. In addition to making all financial and artistic decisions, Kubrick also handles his own publicity campaigns—making television commer-

Figure 17.3.   Kirk Douglas in *Paths of Glory* (1957), distributed by United Artists. Failure is the rule, not the exception for Kubrick's characters. Almost all of them are loners: isolated, melancholy, with no intimate human contacts to solace them in defeat. Kubrick has always been fascinated by war as the ultimate expression of human violence.

Figure 17.4. Kirk Douglas in *Spartacus* (1960), distributed by Universal. The director claims he was merely a "hired hand" for this project, the only movie in which he didn't have total artistic control. Like many of Kubrick's other works, however, it deals with class exploitation and how power is inevitably abused by members of a ruling class.

cials and theatrical trailers, designing posters and artwork. He also supervises the dubbing for foreign-language versions of his movies and carefully researches which theatres they ought to play in. He has never geared his mature works toward industry or audience trends, assuming that if he found a subject interesting, other people would too: "Though success is pleasing, I don't conduct a market survey. If I were to concern myself with that, I might as well be doing *Hawaii Five-O*."

For financial reasons, Kubrick went to England for his next project, and he liked it so much he decided to stay. All his movies since 1961 have been officially produced in Great Britain, but he regards himself as an American artist, and his financing still comes from the American studios. He has the *New York Times* airmailed in every day and doesn't consider himself an expatriot. He lives in a rambling country manor with his third wife, the German-born painter, Christiane Harlan, their three daughters, and an assortment of noisy pets. Their home is isolated, yet within a half-hour's drive from London, which Kubrick regards as second only to Hollywood in its technical expertise. He loathes traveling, and though he has a pilot's license, he refuses to commute by air. In his trips to the United States and the Continent, he travels by ocean liner and by train. He tries to do as much of his work as possible at home. His art and life are fused, so much so that he's been said to be "like a medieval artist, living above his workshop." His home is equipped with editing facilities, cameras, a computer, and a thirty-five-millimeter projector.

Kubrick is one of the most interesting personalities of the contemporary cinema. He is totally indifferent to fashion, elegant living, social status, or money (which he views only as a necessary evil for his art). He usually wears nondescript casual clothing and hasn't had a vacation since 1961. He occasionally grants interviews (usually in his home) but only to serious critics, who are invariably treated with courtesy. He never discusses his private life with interviewers but is highly articulate about his work. Kubrick has an immense intellectual curiosity, and he loves to immerse himself in researching a topic for a movie. He used to keep cross-indexed notebooks on his findings, but now he computerizes the information. He's fascinated by abstract ideas and discusses them with authority. His interviews are profuse in references to the arts, science, politics, and history. He has a retentive memory and can quote facts and figures from military treatises and arcane scientific journals, as well as the poetry of Matthew Arnold, the literary essays of T. S. Eliot, the philosophical writings of Jean-Paul Sartre, and the psychological theories of Carl Jung. Kubrick has a high respect for reason, logic, and precision. He dislikes all forms of intellectual and artistic carelessness. He has been described as a "demented perfectionist," and there are famous tales of how his obsessive punctiliousness has driven his associates up the wall. Arthur C. Clarke, his coscenarist on *2001* (1968), said of him, "Every time I get through a session with Stanley, I have to go lie down."

Beginning with *Lolita* (1961), Kubrick advanced to the forefront of American directors, and his movies were regarded as important cultural events. Even within the more permissive world of the publishing industry, Vladimir Nabokov's brilliantly written tale of sexual obsession was regarded as controversial. The novel had been rejected by several publishers as too raunchy to handle, until it was finally accepted by the Olympia Press in Paris, a publishing house specializing in erotic literature. The story revolves around the tragicomic character of Humbert Humbert, a middle-aged college professor who's smitten by a jaded thirteen-year-old "nymphet." When Kubrick decided to adapt the novel, he realized that the censorship code would not permit him to dramatize the sexual scenes explicitly, but he thought the bizarre relationship between Humbert and Lolita could be evoked indirectly, through symbolic suggestion. In the credit sequence, for example, we see Lolita's imperiously thrust foot fondled by Humbert's hand before he tenderly inserts cotton wads between the divine digits, a prelude to his painting her toenails. Several critics complained that Sue Lyon was too old to play Lolita, but in fact she was about the same age as the character in the book. Kubrick believes that the basic problem with the movie is that it's not erotic enough, and hence the shocking incongruity of the central relationship is weakened.

The difficulty of adapting a first-person novel into a film presented many challenges. In the book, Humbert narrates his own story, and the degrading urgency of his *idée fixe* is conveyed by his ludicrous choice of words. In the movie, his sexual obsession is externalized; and its effec-

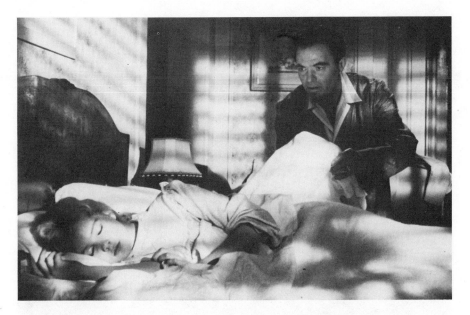

Figure 17.5. James Mason and Sue Lyon in *Lolita* (1961), distributed by MGM. Male-female relationships in Kubrick's movies are doomed to failure. His characters are often obsessed with sex, but there's not much love in his films, and usually it comes too late, too early, or leads to grief.

tiveness is due in no small measure to James Mason's performance as Humbert. Mason manages to convey the character's comic absurdity while still suggesting a sense of desperation and deepening despair. Nabokov wrote the first draft of the screenplay, but it was much too long. Kubrick and his producer, James B. Harris, rewrote it extensively, preserving about 20 percent of the original. Perhaps as a result of this condensation, the film's story line tends to be choppy and the connections between scenes occasionally unclear. The narrative thrust is also blunted by the reappearing character of Quilty (Peter Sellers), Humbert's sleazy rival, whose function in the story is left somewhat undefined until late in the movie. Despite these flaws, Nabokov considered it a first-rate film, with magnificent actors, and he called Kubrick "a great director." *Lolita* was a hit with the public, which delighted in its outlandish black comedy.

Dr. Strangelove (1963), Kubrick's next movie, was even more popular and received virtually unanimous raves from critics. He had originally intended to make a straightforward film about a nuclear holocaust, based on Peter George's taut thriller, *Red Alert*. While working on the screenplay, however, Kubrick found that the story kept veering into black comedy. He decided to scrap his original plans and make an out-and-out satire on the cold war and the nuclear follies of the United States and the U.S.S.R. The premise of the film is dead serious, but it is treated from a farcical perspective. The catastrophe is triggered off by a SAC commander, General Jack D. Ripper (Sterling Hayden), a certifiable

Figure 17.6. Peter Sellers (facing left) in *Dr. Strangelove, or How I Learned to Stop Worrying and Love the Bomb* (1963), distributed by Columbia. Much of the action of this movie is confined to the War Room of President Merkin Muffley (Sellers). The computerized maps on the wall might be giant pinball machines, and each time there's a dramatic shift in the crisis, the spectators in the War Room let out a hoop an' holler of victory. Sometimes the boys get a bit carried away, such as the altercation between the Soviet ambassador and an overzealous American general. "Gentlemen!" pleads President Muffley, "You can't fight in here—this is the War Room."

loon and paranoid, who believes that his "precious bodily fluids" were contaminated by a Commie conspiracy—the fluoridation of the American water supply. To save the nation, he decides to launch a nuclear attack on the Soviet Union by setting off the red-alert mechanism. The remainder of the movie is a grotesque parody of the domino principle: Hundreds of B-52s, armed with hydrogen warheads, are diverted from their peacetime manoeuvres to preordained targets in the Soviet Union. After a series of spooky twists and turns in the plot, all the planes except one are recalled. Thanks to its deviously resourceful pilot, Major T. J. "King" Kong (Slim Pickens), the remaining B-52, cut off from all communications, manages to slip through every failsafe mechanism, and in a burst of glory, the aircraft releases its deadly load, thus detonating the Soviet Doomsday Machine—an automatic "ultimate weapon" which convulses the globe into nuclear Armageddon. The movie concludes with a lyrical montage of mushroom-shaped explosions, accompanied by the voice of Vera Lynn singing "We'll Meet Again" ("We'll meet again . . . don't know where . . . don't know when . . . ,").

Kubrick intensifies the suspense of the crisis through his jittery crosscutting to the movie's three isolated locations: Burpelson Air Base, where General Ripper has barricaded himself with the recall code;

Major Kong's stricken but persevering B-52; and the War Room of the President of the United States, who is surrounded by his military aides and his special advisor, the ex-Nazi scientist, Dr. Strangelove. The movie features a bizarre menagerie of characters, most of whom have funny names, like the dumb gung-ho General Buck Turgidson (George C. Scott); the macho Colonel Bat Guano (Kennan Wynn); and Soviet Ambassador De Sadesky (John Bull), who secretly snaps photos of the War

Figure 17.7. Publicity photo of Sterling Hayden in *Dr. Strangelove*. Ordinarily, Kubrick is skeptical of Freudian explanations of character, but sexual neurosis is the mainspring of this film's action. Most of the men use war as a substitute for sex. General Jack D. Ripper (Hayden) reinforces his macho image by comforting himself with such phallic props as cigars and guns. It's Freud according to *Mad* comics.

Room even while the planet is on the brink of extinction. In a tour-de-force performance, Peter Sellers plays three roles: a stiff-upper-lipped British aide to Ripper; the ineffectual liberal President, Merkin Muffley; and the evil genius, Dr. Strangelove, who is confined to a wheelchair and has a mechanical arm which seems to want to strangle him. (Near the film's conclusion, Strangelove is so intoxicated by the possibility of outwitting the Doomsday Machine that he struggles to his feet, screaming to the President, "*Mein Führer,* I can walk!" while his metal arm snaps wildly into a Nazi salute.) Kubrick was criticized by a few literalists for displaying a frivolous attitude about the arms race. "A recognition of insanity doesn't imply a celebration of it," he patiently explained, "nor a sense of despair and futility about the possibility of curing it."

His next film, *2001,* was more than four years in the making, and the originality of its concept created a sensation with the public. Youthful audiences especially were astonished by the movie's special effects and its provocative mysticism. Kubrick set out to make a new kind of film—nonverbal, ambiguous, and mythical. He wanted to create a *visual* experience about ideas, an experience that reached the mind through the feelings and penetrated the subconscious with its emotional and philosophical content. In order to accomplish this, he discarded the concept of plot almost completely—an audacious decision, considering the movie's 141-minute length and the longstanding addiction of American audiences to a story line.

Figure 17.8. *2001: A Space Odyssey* **(1968), with Keir Dullea and Gary Lockwood, special effects by Wally Veevers, Douglas Trumbull, Con Pederson, and Tom Howard, distributed by MGM.** The special effects in this movie took eighteen months to create, cost $6,500,000 (out of a total budget of $10,500,000), and were carefully researched to conform to actual scientific predictions. The director's aide, Roger Caras, was staggered by Kubrick's preparations. "He called up and told me to get him copies of everything that had been written about space, and I mean everything. I did, and he read all of it." Kubrick also viewed hundreds of other sci-fi movies and consulted with over 70 aerospace specialists and research corporations. His production unit consisted of 106 people, including 35 artists and designers and 20 special-effects technicians to create the animation shots, miniatures, matte shots, and front and rear projections. A centrifuge, to create a realistic weightless atmosphere, cost $750,000; 16,000 separate shots had to be taken for the 205 composite special-effects shots in the movie.

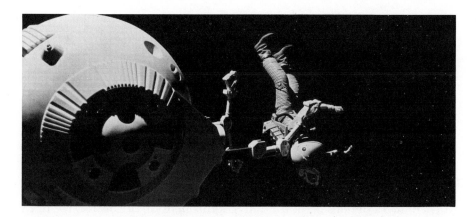

Figure 17.9. *2001.* "The God concept is at the heart of *2001*," Kubrick told interviewer Eric Norden, "but not any traditional anthropormorphic image of God. I don't believe in any of Earth's monotheistic religions, but I do believe that one can construct an intriguing *scientific* definition of God. When you think of the giant technological strides that man has made in a few millennia—less than a microsecond in the chronology of the universe—can you imagine the evolutionary development that much older life forms have taken? They may have progressed from biological species, which are fragile shells for the mind at best, into immortal machine entities—and then, over innumerable eons, they could emerge from the chrysalis of matter transformed into beings of pure energy and spirit. Their potentialities would be limitless and their intelligence ungraspable by humans." [Quoted from "Playboy Interview: Stanley Kubrick," *Playboy* (September, 1965).]

The film is divided into three periods. The first section, "The Dawn of Man," takes place in primordial times and depicts the harsh existence of a tribe of apes. They awake one morning to discover a large rectangular monolith in their midst. The apes are excited by the mysterious black slab, and soon after its appearance, the leader of the tribe discovers that an animal thigh bone can be used as a weapon, as a primitive machine. Soon the other apes learn how to use these weapons, and they are now able to slaughter game and defend their territory from outsiders. Exhilarated by the tribe's new-found power, the ape leader joyously hurls his bone cudgel in the air. As it falls back to earth, Kubrick cuts to a shot of a satellite, shaped like the bone, floating effortlessly through space.

It's now four million years later, in the year 2001, and machines have become considerably more sophisticated. This is the lengthiest section of the movie, and it is devoted mostly to a lyrical celebration of the technology in the space age of man. An American scientist is on a secret mission to the moon, where a mysterious black monolith has been excavated. When he and his associates approach it, they too are baffled, frightened, and oddly transformed. Without explanation, a title now informs us that it's eighteen months later, on a mission to Jupiter, deep in space. Aboard the launch *Discovery* are two astronauts, Dave Bowman (Keir Dullea) and Frank Poole (Gary Lockwood). Three other scientists are kept in hibernation chambers, to be revived when the spaceship approaches Jupiter. The *Discovery* is controlled by a talking computer,

HAL 9000—easily the most interesting personality in the film. Before long, the astronauts discover that HAL is malfunctioning. A computer of immense sophistication, HAL has been programmed with feelings and perceptual abilities as well as data. Realizing that the two astronauts have doubts about the machine's accuracy, HAL "terminates" all the humans in the spacecraft except for Bowman, who manages finally to disconnect the computer. Upon doing so, a prerecorded message informs him of the true purpose of his odyssey: to investigate a mysterious signal which is being beamed to Jupiter from the recently discovered monolith on the moon.

The third section of the film is entitled "Jupiter and Beyond the Infinite." Bowman sees a monolith floating in space, and while pursuing it, the time-space continuum suddenly goes beserk: His spacecraft is sucked into a dimension beyond his comprehension or control. He finds himself in an eerie laboratory-bedroom, decorated in an incongruous eighteenth-century style. Bowman seems to be under some kind of observation, while he rapidly ages before our (and his own) eyes. Within minutes he's an old man, dying in his bed. Suddenly the monolith reappears, and he calmly gazes up at it. The final image of the movie shows us a star-child floating in space like a new planet: The embryo's features bear a marked resemblance to those of Bowman.

Obviously, the question everyone asked was "What does it all mean?" The movie is loosely based on a short story, "The Sentinel," by Arthur C. Clarke, who also helped write the screenplay. After the film's release, Clarke published a novel based on the ideas he and Kubrick discussed while working on the script. The book demystifies many of the film's ambiguities. For example, Clarke explains that the eighteenth-century room on Jupiter is merely Bowman's mental construct, to help him to understand his experiences in terrestrial terms. (The eighteenth century is commonly referred to by historians as the Age of Reason and the Enlightenment.) The novel sold over a million copies, but it lacks the mysticism and symbolic resonance of the movie. Nor are Clarke's interpretations necessarily those of Kubrick, for the filmmaker often departs from the spirit of his sources. For instance, in the movie, HAL degenerates into a sinister nemesis, but in the book the computer is treated in a rather sympathetic fashion. Some critics interpreted the film pessimistically, emphasizing the dehumanization of the characters and the puniness of man compared to the intelligence on Jupiter. Others thought it was an optimistic statement about technological progress and Kubrick's only hopeful film. Critic Alexander Walker believes that Kubrick's theme is the evolution of intelligence: "He roots intelligence in the mythological past, before man has begun to use it; and he ends intelligence in the metaphysical future, where man cannot yet grasp its latest transformation."

Kubrick refused to explain the movie's meaning, insisting that he intended its significance to reach beyond reason and language: "If the film stirs the emotions and penetrates the subconscious of the viewer, if it stimulates, however inchoately, his mythological and religious yearnings and impulses, then it has succeeded." He compared the movie to music and painting, pointing out that our emotional responses to these mediums aren't contingent upon written explanations by the composer or painter. "Once you're dealing on a nonverbal level," he added, "ambiguity is unavoidable." (*2001* has only forty minutes of dialogue, none of it very important.) He intended the monoliths to symbolize a Jungian archetypal experience: When they appear in the film they're accompanied by a shot of the earth, moon, and sun in orbital conjunction, suggesting a kind of magical alignment, a mystical leap in intelligence. But Kubrick refused to say whether the star-child symbolically heralds the birth of a superior species or the debasement of the human intellect to an embryonic level—a mere satellite to Jupiter. Throughout the film, technological advancement is presented ambivalently: The bone cudgel is used to destroy as well as preserve life; the magnificent machines in the year 2001 have also reduced the humans to brainy zombies. The parallelism of the film's three sections suggests that the star-child might likewise represent a mixed blessing.

The film was one of the top-grossing movies in history, garnering over $31 million in its first year of release. The critical response was overwhelmingly enthusiastic, though a few reviewers complained of the film's length, its lack of plot, and especially its lack of clarity. Kubrick wasn't bothered by most of these objections, claiming that they were based on passé literary conventions which simply weren't relevant. The desire for clarity is understandable, he conceded, but not all questions have answers. Furthermore, he believes that explanations of works of art are valued primarily by critics and teachers, who earn their living this way, but reactions to art are different because they're always deeply personal.

The striking originality of Kubrick's next movie, *A Clockwork Orange* (1971), was also somewhat misunderstood. Based on a novel by Anthony Burgess, the story is set in England in the future—though closer to 1984 than to 2001. Kubrick preserved the fablelike symmetry of the novel's plot, but he departed considerably from the spirit of its traditional Christian values. The film opens in a futuristic milkbar, where we're introduced to its young punk protagonist, Alex (Malcolm McDowell). He and his three underlings, or "droogs," juice up on liquid refreshments laced with drugs, then embark on a rampage of "ultra-violence," their favorite recreation. They beat up an old wino; brawl with a rival gang, which is in the process of gang-raping a terrified girl; steal a car; then force their way into the home of a writer and his wife, where they gleefully rape her and beat him so viciously that they cripple him for life. Eventually Alex's treacherous droogs betray him, and he's sent to prison for the murder of the Catlady, whose face he smashed with a pop-art plastic phallus. While in prison, Alex hypocritically volunteers to be the first to undergo a new criminal "cure" called the Ludovico Technique—a behavior modification treatment based on the theories of B. F. Skinner. Within two weeks, Alex is returned to society "a perfect Christian," for whenever he's confronted by sex or violence, he has a painful avoidance reaction.

The second half of the movie is a reverse recapitulation of the first. Alex is now defanged, and hence utterly without defenses in the jungle world outside. He meets all his former victims: The old drunk and his

Figure 17.10.   Malcolm McDowell in *A Clockwork Orange* (1971), distributed by Warner Brothers. Kubrick wanted *Clockwork* to have a pop, comic-book style. The mise-en-scène is dreamlike, detached, with the furnishings floating eerily before a black backdrop. The décor seems temporary, as though it could be whisked off in a matter of minutes. The erotic art is merely chic pornography: It doesn't celebrate sexuality but degrades it. Most of the artwork defiles women in particular. The rooms exist in a kind of physical limbo—sealed off, airless. Nothing connects: We seldom have a sense of place in the movie. Despite his widescreen format, Kubrick's mise-en-scène is densely packed, claustrophobic, yet totally lacking in intimacy. The camera is close in, and we're seldom permitted to see much of the surrounding milieu. These visual techniques reinforce the themes of fragmentation, loneliness, and alienation.

cronies pounce upon him, and his former droogs (who are now policemen) drag him out to the country where they beat him mercilessly and almost drown him. He manages to stagger to—of all places—the home of the writer, where Alex is not immediately recognized. Now confined to a wheelchair, the writer wants to publicize Alex's victimization at the hands of the repressive right-wing government. But his compassion turns to hatred when he accidentally discovers that Alex is the sadist who crippled him and caused his wife's death. The writer imprisons Alex in an attic, where he's tortured. Unable to endure his agony, the youth attempts to commit suicide. But he survives, and his case creates a scandalous sensation in the liberal press. In the hospital, he is secretly deprogrammed, and when the cynical minister of the interior bribes him, the youth agrees to string along. In short, we're right back where we started, except now Alex will have unobstructed liberty to do his worst.

Kubrick exploits the narrative to create an escape-proof labyrinth—a moral dilemma which has no solution. Burgess intended his novel to be a cautionary parable about the sanctity of free will: "To meddle with man, condition him, is to turn him into a mechanical creation," the Catholic novelist explained. Hence, the title: Alex is transformed into a "clockwork orange," a human robot without choice, without will, without a soul. This sentiment is most overtly expressed by the prison chaplain, who warns Alex, "When a man cannot choose, he ceases to be a man." Virtue is meaningful only when it's freely willed. But of course if a man must be free to choose virtue, he must also have the option to choose evil—as Alex repeatedly does. The presence of evil is the price a Christian society must pay if it truly believes in the freedom of the will.

But Burgess didn't write the screenplay, nor did he direct the movie. Characteristically, Kubrick is far more ambivalent and ambiguous in his views. Because of its visual immediacy, the film tends to emphasize the comic incongruity of the chaplain's words within the context of the prison. Is his "flock" in jail any freer than Alex after he's been programmed and released? It's easy for the chaplain to preach about freedom to a captive audience, since he's not threatened. But how would he react, one wonders, if *he* were the victim of Alex's viciousness? As the writer later discovers, when one's own freedoms are brutally violated, it's difficult to continue defending the sanctity of choice with quite the same glibness. The novel, for all its literary brilliance, tends to explore this paradox on a somewhat abstract level; but the movie's impact is more visceral, thus undermining much of the conviction of these liberal sentiments. The chaplain and the writer, in fact, are the butts of Kubrick's most sardonic irony: They're such *theoretical* idealists. Is the alternative then the "law and order" represented by the minister of the interior?

Figure 17.11. *A Clockwork Orange*, **with Mariam Karlin.** Throughout *Clockwork*, Kubrick uses steep angles, violent juxtapositions of shots, dramatic lighting and color clashes, and a raucous soundtrack to create the hellish world of the film and to produce an almost palpable sense of assault on the viewer. Many scenes are photographed with extreme (9.8 mm) wide-angle lenses, which cause radical distortions in the screen image. In closeup, these lenses warp the human face into twisted masks. Shown here, the high-angle closeup of the Catlady just before she is murdered by Alex is Dantean in its grotesqueness. In traveling shots, wide-angle lenses kineticize the visual materials with a terrifying quicksilver instability.

Hardly. In totalitarian societies, there's not much freedom, but there generally *is* order. Kubrick's world has neither. It's paralyzed in the crossfire of the center, assaulted by both extremes.

Like most modernist artists, Kubrick has little faith in traditional value systems, and he's strongly inclined toward a pessimistic view of the human condition. (For a discussion of modernism, see Chapter 18). "The most terrifying fact about the universe is not that it is hostile but that it is indifferent," he has observed. "The very meaninglessness of life forces man to create his own meaning." Kubrick believes that in order to give purpose to our existence, we must have something to care about, something more important than our grubby selves. In his youth, he was liberal and humanist in his values, but his vision has grown darker over the years. He believes that most people are irrational, weak, and incapable of objectivity where their own interests are involved. Most of his films portray man as corrupt and savage, and each movie contains at least one killing. "I'm interested in the brutal and violent nature of man because it's a true picture of him," he has stated frankly. Like most modernists, however, Kubrick has not given up on humanity, or he obviously wouldn't go on making movies: "You don't stop being concerned with man because you recognize his essential absurdities and frailties and pretentions. To me, the only real immorality is that which endangers the species; and the only absolute evil, that which threatens its annihilation. In the deepest sense, I believe in man's potential and in his capacity for progress."

But Kubrick is not a didactic artist, and he refuses to be the purveyor of a false cheer. He presents his values obliquely, forcing the viewer to analyze them on his own. "I have found it always the best policy to let the film speak for itself," he has said. Like his spiritual antecedents, Lang, Welles, and Wilder, Kubrick tends to be fatalistic. He often uses narration in his movies, suggesting an ironic double perspective. In *Barry Lyndon* (1975), for example, the narrator tells us in advance what will happen to the protagonist, thus emphasizing an air of predestination. In *Lolita,* Kubrick scrambled the chronology of Nabokov's novel by beginning the film with Humbert's murder of Quilty, followed by the title, "Four Years Earlier." A flashback then presents us with the events leading up to this fatal climax.

Alexander Walker has pointed out that Kubrick's themes often revolve around the concept of intelligence, which he treats ambivalently—as gray matter in more ways than one. *Strangelove, 2001,* and *Clockwork* all explore the abuses of science and technology. Kubrick is not opposed to machines per se. He has a house filled with them and believes they can be immeasurably beneficial to society. Though he admires the intelligence that can create a HAL 9000—described in the movie as "by any practical definitions of the words, foolproof and incapable of error"—Kubrick is deeply skeptical of man's ability to control his technology. Walker has noted that even Kubrick's earlier works are structured around machinelike plots which go awry: "While a 'flawless' scheme is pushed forward step by predetermined step, at the same time chance, accident, and irrational forces lodged in its executors are bringing about its failure."

Figure 17.12. ***Barry Lyndon,* distributed by Warner Brothers.** "What I'm after is a majestic visual experience," Kubrick has said of his movies. Few costume pictures can stand comparison with the majesty of *Barry Lyndon.* Its visual style was modeled on the paintings of the eighteenth-century masters, especially Gainsborough and Watteau. As usual, Kubrick insisted that every detail be absolutely authentic. Since candlelight was the main source of interior illumination in the eighteenth century, he asked the Zeiss Corporation to adopt a very fast (F 0.7) 50 mm still camera lens for the motion picture camera. The Zeiss Lens is the fastest in existence, allowing scenes to be shot by candlelight. Kubrick had to have a special movie camera built for its use. But he got what he wanted: The warm, glowing interiors of *Barry Lyndon* are ravishing in their beauty.

But Kubrick is equally ambivalent about control. In *Clockwork,* for example, most of the characters are instinctive fascists, intent upon imposing their will on others. *Control* is a word used by many of them. Alex refers to his droogs as *sheep.* The writer speaks contemptuously of "the common people," who must be "led, pushed, even driven!" The minister wants to restore control through the Ludovico Technique—though of course *he* wants to decide who's dangerous to the social order. The police and criminals vie with each other in their sadism. The world of the film is an absurd pop inferno, where the degree of depravity correlates with the degree of control and power. Everybody loses.

Despite his reputation as an intellectual artist, Kubrick regards filmmaking as primarily intuitive. Only in retrospect can he explain why he was attracted to a story. He has been influenced by the theories of Jung, and he believes that myths have an energizing power, connecting directly to childhood experiences and the subconscious. For example, he considers Alex's adventures in *Clockwork* a kind of psychological myth: "Our subconscious finds release in Alex, just as it finds release in dreams. It resents Alex being stifled and repressed by Authority, however much our conscious mind recognizes the necessity of doing this."

2001 is indebted to the mythic quest structure of Homer's *Odyssey*. The movie also alludes to Nietzsche's *Thus Spake Zarathustra,* in which the German philosopher traced the evolution of ape to man to Superman—a tripartite structure Kubrick also employed. His use of Richard Strauss's *Thus Spake Zarathustra,* a musical composition inspired by Nietzsche's philosophical tract, reinforces this mythic parallel. (Hitler's concept of a master race was also derived from the ideas of Nietzsche. Kubrick, whose ethnic heritage is Jewish, no doubt savored this sardonic ambiguity.)

Kubrick's early movies were story-oriented. A number of them contain multiple subplots and flip back and forth to different sets of characters. After *Strangelove,* his narratives loosened considerably. Except for *Spartacus,* he has written or co-written all his films, though his coscenarists have generally disclaimed major contributions. For example, Clarke said that *2001* was 90 percent Kubrick's imagination, 5 percent the genius of the special-effects unit, and 5 percent the contributions of Arthur C. Clarke. Kubrick likes his scripts to be as complete as possible before production. He is open to suggestions, however, especially from actors, whose improvisations during rehearsals are often incorporated into the final shooting script. "The screenplay is the most uncommunicative form of writing ever devised," he has said, and he claims that its literary value decreases in direct proportion to a movie's cinematic flair. Nonetheless, his sensibility has its literary side, and he has demonstrated a knack for preserving the flavor of his sources without compromising his visual and kinetic expression. For example, one of the triumphs of *Clockwork* is Alex's voice-over commentary, which is taken from the first-person narration of Burgess's novel. Alex's peculiar manner of speech, which Burgess called Nadsat, is a witty concoction of Russian, Cockney slang, and Gypsy. The film's voice-over monologues help the audience to understand the devious workings of Alex's mind. Like Richard III's soliloquies, these "O My Brothers" confidences tend to bind us (however unwillingly) to the protagonist, even implying a sense of complicity with his actions.

Kubrick's relationship with actors varies from film to film. In *2001,* for instance, the players were asked to keep their acting to a minimum, and the director used them primarily as aspects of his mise-en-scène. Keir Dullea regarded HAL as much more personable than Bowman: "To play a 21st century astronaut, I tried to show him as a man without emotional highs and lows—an intelligent, highly trained man, lonely and alienated, not too imaginative." On the other hand, Kubrick claims that he wouldn't have attempted *Clockwork* unless Malcolm McDowell agreed to play Alex, so crucial was his performance to the film's totality of impact. Kubrick admires such disciplined actors as George C. Scott, who can produce the same effect in take after take; yet one of his favorite players was Peter Sellers, who was radically inconsistent but managed to hit upon brilliant comic surprises: "Peter has the most responsive attitude of all the actors I've worked with to the things I think are funny. He is always at his best in dealing with grotesque and horrifying ideas."

Kubrick has been strongly influenced by the acting theories of Stanislavsky (see Chapter 14). He likes to rehearse extensively, using many improvisational techniques, on the actual sets if possible. He alters his direction to suit the needs of his players and tries to avoid locking up any ideas about staging or camera or even dialogue before working with the actors. He regards camerawork as easy compared to the hard work in these crucial rehearsal periods, which he thinks either make or break a scene. He often asks his players to repeat a take, for he likes to have maximum flexibility at the editing bench, and he often synthesizes a final performance from a variety of takes. There are very few arguments on his sets, and those few are always won by Kubrick.

He is a master of the moving camera and uses traveling shots in most of his movies. A former member of the American Society of Cinematographers, Kubrick still executes most of his hand-held shots. *2001* is filled with lyrical ballet sequences in which the camera swirls around the satellites glissading through space. In *Paths of Glory,* he uses traveling shots as kinetic metaphors, paralleling the film's title, which comes from a line in "Elegy in a Country Churchyard," a poem by Thomas Gray: "Paths of glory lead but to the grave." On the day that some conscripted soldiers are to execute a futile military mission, the general who masterminded the scheme comes to wish them luck. In an incredibly lengthy dolly shot, the camera sweeps efficiently through the winding trenches, as he whisks past his troops, patronizing them with bad jokes and fatuous predictions of success. The smooth elegant dollying through the trenches represents the general's real path of glory— safely behind the front lines. The camera then leaves the trenches with the soldiers as they venture out on the raging battlefield—a bomb-pocked landscape littered with abandoned equipment, twisted barbed wire, and blasted corpses. The camera doggedly stays with the soldiers, as they zigzag around explosions, inch ahead slightly, retreat, then go forward again. Through the drifting smoke we see soldiers dropping everywhere, and the roar of the guns is stupifying. The troops are decimated as they push forward bravely, hopelessly, absurdly. Only a few tattered men are left alive. These few decide to turn back, and with their retreat, the camera turns back as well, as they crawl to the protection of the trenches. This path of glory turns out to be as meaningless as the first.

"I love editing," Kubrick has admitted, "I think I like it more than any other phase of filmmaking." He has edited all his movies, and during this phase of his work he adheres to a seven-day-a-week schedule, beginning with ten hours a day and escalating to fourteen and sixteen hours. The transitions between his shots are often unpredictable and jolting, a technique he doubtless derived from Eisenstein. Often Kubrick will establish a sequence with a closeup rather than a long shot, thus catching the viewer off guard, for we mistakenly assume that the shot is a part of the preceding continuity. This technique is especially effective in violent and suspenseful sequences. By depriving us of the context of a shot, Kubrick is able to disorient us and intensify our sense of anxiety. In his do-it-yourself youth, he was strongly influenced by Pudovkin's theoretical treatise, *Film Technique,* which stresses editing as the foundation of film art (see Chapter 12). Pudovkin believed that by juxtaposing shots expressively, the filmmaker can synthesize an event that never actually occurred. The murder of the Catlady in *Clockwork* is an example of Pudovkin's associational technique. Alex grapples with the Catlady in her living room, which is filled with erotic pop art. He knocks her down on the floor, wielding an enormous plastic phallus as a weapon. We see a high-angle closeup of her terrified features (see Fig. 17.11). This is intercut with a low-angle shot of Alex crashing the phallus down toward the camera, simulating the point of view of the collapsed woman. This is juxtaposed with a number of split-second shots of extreme closeups of a pop-art lipsticked mouth. Despite the obvious artificiality of these mouth images, we almost imagine that we've seen the Catlady's face being pulverized. But Kubrick also uses lengthy takes on occasion. The scene where Alex's former droogs nearly drown him, for example, is taken with a single setup, to emphasize the sheer agonizing duration of the torture.

Kubrick has been a bold innovator in his use of music. The jokey title seqeunce of *Strangelove* introduces the war-as-sex motif, which is continued throughout the movie. A Muzak rendition of "Try a Little Tenderness" is accompanied by an undulating aerial shot of a nuclear bomber being refueled in midair by another plane, photographed in such a manner as to suggest a kind of celestial copulation. In *2001*, he wanted to avoid sci-fi bromides in his music and decided to use classical compositions for many of the sequences. Shots of an immense satellite gliding through space are accompanied by "The Blue Danube Waltz." Strauss's *Thus Spake Zarathustra* was such a stirring theme that it soon degenerated into a television cliché to sell salad dressing and deodorants. An otherwise brutal gang fight in *Clockwork* is rendered comical by the accompaniment of Rossini's elegant and witty overture to *The Thieving Magpie*. The terrifying attack on the writer and his wife is made bearable by Alex's ludicrous song and dance routine to the tune of "Singin' in the Rain." This is chillingly reprised (in the original Gene Kelly version) at the end of the film, when Alex looks directly at the camera—at us—and we hear his voice-over realization: "I was cured all right." *Barry Lyndon* is profuse in the majestic music of such eighteenth-century composers as Mozart, Handel, and Vivaldi. For a touch of literal majesty, Kubrick even uses a composition by Frederick the Great.

Kubrick is still in mid-career, and on the basis of his past performances, it's impossible to predict his future except to say that his movies are likely to be brazenly original. His influence on other filmmakers has been slight, for his work is too unique to inspire copies. Perhaps his greatest influence has been inspirational, particularly on such artists as Woody Allen and Terrence Malick, whose films are also deeply personal and original. Whatever his future, Kubrick's place in the American cinema has been firmly established for years. In his review of *Clockwork*, critic Hollis Alpert concluded, "It can be said, without question, that he is this country's most important filmmaker, fit to stand on a pedestal beside Europe's best, Bergman and Fellini."

BIBLIOGRAPHY

AGEL, JEROME, ed. *The Making of Kubrick's 2001*. New York: New American Library, 1970. An excellent collection of articles, reviews, and photos, including Kubrick's *Playboy* interview.

CLARKE, ARTHUR C. *2001: A Space Odyssey*. New York: New American Library, 1968. The novelized version of the screenplay. See also Clarke's *The Lost Worlds of 2001* (New York: New American Library, 1972), which contains the first version of the script, the screenwriters' log, and three alternate endings to the film; and Carolyn Geduld, *Filmguide to 2001: A Space Odyssey* (Bloomington: Indiana University Press, 1973): critical study, bibliography, filmography.

DE VRIES, DANIEL. *The Films of Stanley Kubrick*. Grand Rapids, Mich.: William B. Eerdmans Publishing Company, 1973. Critical study, bibliography, and filmography.

JOHNSON, WILLIAM, ed. *Focus on the Science Fiction Film*. New York: Prentice-Hall, 1972. Collection of articles. See also John Brosnan, *Movie Magic: The Story of Special Effects in the Cinema* (New York: New American Library, 1974): copiously illustrated.

KAGAN, NORMAN. *The Cinema of Stanley Kubrick*. New York: Grove Press, 1972. Critical study, filmography.

NABOKOV, VLADIMIR. *Lolita: A Screenplay*. New York: McGraw-Hill, 1974. Includes many scenes cut out of the film version.

NORDEN, ERIC. "Playboy Interview: Stanley Kubrick," in *Playboy* (September, 1968). The longest and most revealing interview, mostly about *2001*. Other interviews include Jeremy Bernstein, "Profile: Stanley Kubrick," in *The New Yorker* (November 12, 1966); Joseph Gelmis, ed., "Stanley Kubrick," in *The Film Director as Superstar* (New York: Doubleday, 1970); and Philip Strick and Penelope Houston, "Interview with Stanley Kubrick," in *Sight and Sound* (Spring, 1972).

PHILLIPS, GENE D. *Stanley Kubrick: A Film Odyssey*. New York: Popular Library, 1975. Critical study, filmography, bibliography.

Stanley Kubrick's A Clockwork Orange, Based on the Novel by Anthony Burgess. New York: Ballantine, 1972. The text of the movie, copiously illustrated with uncropped stills, supervised by Kubrick and his associates, Andros Epaminondas and Margaret Adams.

WALKER, ALEXANDER. *Stanley Kubrick Directs*. New York: Harcourt Brace Jovanovich, Inc., 1972. A perceptive critical study, copiously illustrated with frame enlargements. Filmography.

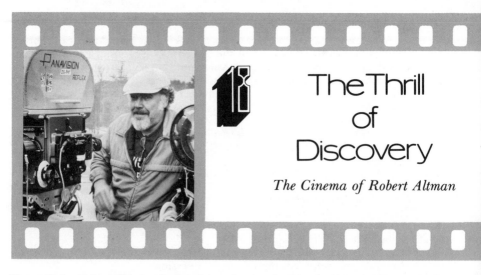

Figure 18.1. Robert Altman, during the production of *Thieves Like Us* (1974). Altman's sets are usually festive, with a good deal of camaraderie among the members of the company. "He's like a host at a party," said actor Michael Murphy. Altman believes that making a movie should be fun and liberating, with a maximum of creative freedom for everybody involved.

Altman is the Thoreau of the American cinema, marching to the beat of a different drummer. He was catapulted to fame in 1969, with his popular antiwar comedy, *M*A*S*H*. Since that time, he has averaged better than a movie per year, but he's been unable to recapture the mass audience—not even with such acclaimed masterpieces as *McCabe and Mrs. Miller* and *Nashville*, which were only modestly successful at the box office. He is much admired by intellectuals, artists, and film critics, especially those who share his modernist sensibility. Altman has worked within a variety of genres, but his treatment is always idiosyncratic, steeped in private ideas and mysterious ambiguities. He has been influenced by the documentary movement, *cinéma vérité*, with its emphasis on immediacy, spontaneity, and surprise. The flexible technology of *vérité* has allowed him to create a kind of conceptual cinema, based on the principle of chance combinations. He's arguably the most collaborative of major filmmakers, and he insists that his actors and writers are full partners in the communal enterprise of making a movie. He is also deeply instinctive, refusing to diminish the complexity of his vision by pinning labels on his feelings. He is a master of the cinema of the privileged moment. His revelations of humanity can be funny or saddening, but rarely hackneyed. Like Chekhov and Vermeer, his artistry is found primarily in "little things": not with plots or articulated themes, but with the poetry—and prose—of people.

> *I think art is a reflection of life. I think it's learning somehow, it's learning something. You say "Oh!" I think it has something to do with discovery. We react to a piece of art, any individual, and I think the thrill of it is really a kind of discovery.*
> *—Robert Altman*

Altman was born in 1925 in Kansas City, Missouri. In his many interviews he rarely discusses his childhood, except to say that it was constricting and rather regimented. His parents were middle-class Catholics and they wanted their first-born child to be educated in Jesuit schools. (He also spent two years at a military academy.) Though Altman left the church at the age of eighteen, a number of critics believe that his religious background has influenced his art, a theory he regards as far-fetched. He was a B-24 pilot during World War II and logged forty-five bombing missions in the Pacific theatre.

Altman was fascinated by movies even as a child, and in the early 1940s he wrote several story treatments that had been purchased but never made into films by Hollywood producers. After the war, he stopped in Los Angeles to collaborate with a friend, George W. George, on original screen stories. Several of these were sold, but only one was produced—*Bodyguard,* by RKO in 1948. It flopped. Altman subsequently scratched out a living by writing for magazines and radio shows. He then spent a year in New York, writing novels and plays, though not with much success. Finally he decided to return to Kansas City, where he accepted a job with the Calvin Company, which produced industrial documentaries and public relations films. Though almost totally without experience, he soon learned every aspect of his craft. He wrote, produced, directed, photographed, edited, and even decorated his sets and sold his products. He remained with the company for eight years.

Twice during this period he tried his luck in Hollywood, but both times he had to return when his money ran out. After his third trip west in 1955, he wrote, produced, and directed his first feature for United Artists, *The Delinquents,* with Tom Laughlin. It was a failure. Two years later Altman and his former collaborator George made *The James Dean Story,* a documentary that explored the fanatical cult that had developed around the recently deceased young star. Alfred Hitchcock offered Altman a television contract on the basis of the film, but he chose to do individual shows instead and directed two half-hour episodes for the famous television series (see Chapter 12).

For the next decade, Altman was one of television's busiest all-purpose talents. He wrote, directed, and/or produced segments for such programs as *The Roaring Twenties, Bonanza, The Millionaire, Bus Stop,*

Whirlybirds, Combat, and *Kraft Theatre,* as well as the pilot films for *The Gallant Men* and *The Long Hot Summer.* But he considered television an inflexible medium, and though he was earning as much as $125,000 a year, he thought his commercial success was corrupting him artistically. Whenever he tried to experiment—usually by overlapping his dialogue to produce a more realistic sound texture—he was fired by his bosses. Disgusted by television's stifling formats, Altman finally quit. He set up his own production company, Lion's Gate Films, and eventually managed to produce and direct *Countdown* (1968), with James Caan, and *That Cold Day in the Park* (1969), with Sandy Dennis. His gamble at independence didn't pay off: Both movies were failures. He was now forty-five years old.

Producer Ingo Preminger had been circulating Ring Lardner, Jr.'s, script of *M*A*S*H* (1969) for some time, but no one wanted to direct it, apparently because of its parallels to the war in Vietnam. (Unlike previous wars, the Vietnam adventure was box office poison.) Reputedly, Altman was Preminger's fifteenth choice. When the director agreed to the project, he did so with the provision that he could make changes in the screenplay, which was a more conventional service comedy written along traditional genre lines. Much of what was later praised in Lardner's Academy-Award-winning script was actually improvised by Altman and his actors. The movie is his first mature work and contains many trademark characteristics: the deemphasis of plot in favor of aleatory structures, a strong concern with characterization, a subversion of genre expectations, a throwaway style of acting, a documentary visual style, and the use of overlapping dialogue. (A popular television series based on the film duplicated many of these characteristics, and though the series was considerably laundered in comparison with the movie, it was nonetheless one of the most sophisticated sitcoms ever offered on American television. The movie was ideally suited for adaptation, consisting of a series of quasi-independent skits, a variety of offbeat characters, and a confined geographical location.)

The film is unified by theme rather than narrative. Each episode is a variation of the same conflict, the clash between a flexible humanism on the one hand and an authoritarian rigidity on the other. The Good Guys are represented primarily by its three oversexed surgeon-officers: Hawkeye (Donald Sutherland), Trapper John (Elliott Gould), and Duke (Tom Skerritt). The Bad Guys are the two "regular Army clowns," Major Frank Burns (Robert Duvall), a psalm-singing hypocrite, and Major Margaret O'Hoolihan (Sally Kellerman), a gung-ho bore who's later dubbed Hotlips.

Altman's genre films are revisionist: They ironically undercut an implied classical ideal. *M*A*S*H* is no exception. Most military comedies are detoxified: We aren't permitted to see any battle scenes, unless they are treated comically. Gore, dismemberment, and death are scrupulously avoided. The professional bureaucrats in conventional service comedies are generally lovable buffoons. They present no real threat, for their stupidity is placed within a context of a farcical never-never land, where no one is seriously endangered by incompetence, merely inconvenienced. *M*A*S*H* contains no battle scenes, it's true, but the

Figure 18.2. Publicity photo of _M*A*S*H_ (1969), with Elliott Gould, Tom Skerritt, and Donald Sutherland, distributed by 20th Century-Fox. Though ostensibly about the Korean War of the early 1950s, Altman photographed _M*A*S*H_ in a television documentary style which couldn't help but remind viewers of the grim evening news of the late 1960s. The movie struck a responsive chord in the American public. It became the most successful antiwar comedy ever made, and won the Grand Prix at the Cannes Film Festival. It also grossed an astonishing $40 million.

surgical scenes in the tents are filled with blood, blasted limbs, and discarded corpses. We're always kept aware of the larger human stakes behind the comic chaos. Major Burns is the heavy in the piece, not only because he's a bully and a sanctimonious prig, but also because he's a bad surgeon whose bungling costs men their lives. O'Hoolihan is an excellent nurse, and hence is morally salvagable.

The scenes in *M*A*S*H* are not neatly dovetailed but are randomly interspersed with what Altman calls *open spaces*—jokey character vignettes and sight gags that don't relate directly to the action. Altman is fond of this technique of punching holes in his structures, and he has used it in many of his films. He often deliberately allows for open spaces during shooting, then adds materials in the editing and sound-mixing stages. The most prominent additions of this sort in *M*A*S*H* are the funny public address announcements on the camp loudspeakers. Included among the more absurd announcements are the movies that are shown every evening: All of them are old war films, like *Glory Brigade,* and the inept announcer usually describes them in Hollywood press-release jargon, like "those lovable lugs of World War II." At other times the speakers blare out popular American songs, only incongruously crooned by Japanese singers.

M*A*S*H is Altman's most overtly funny movie to date. It's steeped in black comedy and locker-room raunchiness, as in the scene depicting the sexual encounter between the two majors. Burns has been silently lusting after O'Hoolihan for some time. Finally he decides to make his move. He stumbles into her tent and announces, "God meant for us to find each other." Quick to enter the religious spirit of the occasion, O'Hoolihan opens her robe wide and hosannas, "His will be done!" They grapple with each other in the dark, spewing *True Romance* clichés of ardor. In a pseudorapture of abandonment, she hisses "Kiss my hot lips!" Hence her nickname for the remainder of the movie, for unbeknownst to them, their enemies have placed a microphone under the bed, and their passion is being broadcast to the entire camp over the loudspeakers.

For all its comic verve, *M*A*S*H* is also undercut by a melancholy ambiance which became more pronounced in Altman's work. The opening credit sequence introduces this mournful note, for while the gently urgent tune, "Suicide is Painless," is playing, we see on the screen a choreographed fleet of helicopters gliding lyrically in the sky. As the camera zooms to a closer view of one of these helicopters, we realize that each of them is laden with the wounded bodies of American soldiers. The conclusion of the movie is also characterized by this Altmanesque melancholia. Duke and Hotlips (who are now lovers) are operating on a patient. Both of them are wearing surgical masks. When they hear the announcement that his tour of duty will soon conclude, they exchange stunned glances: Their relationship has obviously gone beyond the merely lustful stage. Duke has a momentary mental flash in which we see him being welcomed home at the airport by his wife and children. Hotlips and Duke remain speechless, but their eyes reveal a piercing awareness that their love must end. Similarly, the groping farewell scene between Hawkeye and Trapper John is underlined by a sense of the fragile impermanence of all human relationships. In the Altman universe, even the winners lose.

"You always lose in the long run because of the percentages," Altman has observed about his habit of gambling. The same could be said of his view of life in general. Most of his movies have desolate or violent endings, and a sense of futility hovers even over his more comic works, like *Brewster McCloud* (1970), *California Split* (1974), and *A Wedding* (1978). Altman's pessimistic vision is the hallmark of the modernist *Weltanschauung*. Modernism is a vague but convenient critical term defining a kind of sensibility, rather than a specific movement or style. It cuts across all the arts, of different periods and various nationalities, though it's especially associated with the cultures of western Europe since the early twentieth century. The roots of modernism extend back to the nineteenth century, with the rejection of romanticism and the dissemination of the ideas of Darwin and Marx. The bleak view of the human condition which typifies this sensibility was intensified by the loss of innocence and disillusionment with social causes that followed World War I in Europe. It was originally a philosophy of revolt against absolute values and traditional systems of order.

The modernist universe is oppressive and empty, and man is condemned to it in a state of alienation. Civilization is a sentimental illusion or a cynical contract of expedience. The only possibility for heroism is to

Figure 18.3. *Brewster McCloud* (1970), with Bud Cort (flying), distributed by MGM. This is Altman's personal favorite among his movies—not because he considers it his best work, but rather his most adventurous. It's a comic allegory that interweaves a variety of characters and stories and is loosely unified by the symbolic motif of man's eternal aspiration to fly. The movie reflects Altman's distaste for confinement and restraint. He is suspicious of all social institutions that demand a denial of the self: family, church, school, military, big business, politics. He believes that ultimately the only valid truth is the truth of the self.

cultivate a sense of irony and stoicism. The philosophy of existentialism, which was propounded in the post-Holocaust era by the French intellectual, Jean-Paul Sartre, reinforced many of these grim sentiments. In a world steeped in cosmic indifference, nothing is intrinsically meaningful, Sartre argued. God is dead, and man must create his own sense of purpose—it's not something "out there." Meaning must be individually—and arbitrarily—willed into existence out of the absurd void we're confronted with. Probably no single modernist embodies all these philosophical assumptions. There are also many hybridizations. In the area of movies, for example, the Frenchman, Robert Bresson, fuses this sensibility with Christian mysticism. Similarly, the Italian filmmaker, Michelangelo Antonioni, combines modernism with Marxism. Altman tends to be more romantic and humanist in his emphases.

There is also no aesthetic uniformity to modernist art, though it tends toward complexity of form, irony, and an appeal to the intellect over the emotions. One way of creating meaning is through the order of art itself—art for its own sake. Technical excellence and aesthetic self-sufficiency are values in themselves. Artists often reflect upon their artwork while they're creating it, and allusions to other works are common. Most modernists insist that art is an *experience*, something unparaphrasable, not a collection of explanations. Its didactic function is deemphasized, oblique. Preaching is regarded as presumptuous, since it implies a secure (and hence fatuous) set of values. Modernist art is ambiguous and ambivalent, its values relative. Multiple meanings embody both conscious and subconscious elements—the influence of Jung and Freud. Myths are often used as ironic metaphors, as in Joyce's novel, *Ulysses*, and T. S. Eliot's poem, *The Waste Land*. The nature imagery that dominated romantic art is replaced by pop images, the ugliness of kitsch, and an emphasis on urban and mechanistic motifs, as in the German expressionist movement (see Chapter 9). The tone of modernist art often flips from mockery to tragedy to nihilism, as in the fiction of Franz Kafka. Realism is generally rejected in favor of symbolic distortion. Time and space are fragmented and subjectivized, as in the paintings of Picasso and Braque and the novels of Proust and Faulkner. Modernist art is frequently sober, like the movies of Ingmar Bergman. What comedy does exist tends to be grotesque and mock-heroic. Modernism began to make inroads into the American cinema in the 1940s, particularly in the movies of Welles and the works of such expatriot directors as Lang and Wilder. After the Vietnam and Watergate eras (see Chapter 16), it became a dominant mode in American filmmaking, and virtually every important young director since that time has come under its influence. The Hollywood studio establishment traditionally shied away from such unhappy ideas because they were thought to be depressing, lacking in entertainment values, and hence the kiss of death at the box office. But nothing succeeds like success: The Vietnam era ushered in a revolution in taste, and movies reflecting modernist values suddenly became commercially viable in the United States.

As a result of the enormous profits reaped by *M*A*S*H*, Altman was deluged with offers from the big studios. He would have made more money if he had directed their projects, but he preferred his independence. He believes too much security is artistically deadening, and he has expressed contempt for the corrupt values of most industry regulars. Despite a mutual antipathy, most of Altman's films have been financed by the studios. His projects are generally low cost (under $2 million in most cases), and he's usually on schedule and within budget. Even when his films fail at the box office, the investment is generally recovered through television rentals and other ancillary revenues. Producers have not been insensitive to the prestige value of financing an Altman movie. He has suffered very few problems of interference and has personally edited all his major works. For the most part, he preserves a distance from the big studios, working out of his own Lion's Gate Films, which doesn't make huge profits, only enough to maintain a cash flow and to keep him and his regulars steadily employed without hassles. The company has its own editing and sound equipment, which helps to keep costs down. Altman has also proved to be a generous friend and has produced several of the movies of his colleagues, including such accomplished works as Alan Rudolph's *Welcome to L.A.* and Robert Benton's *The Late Show.*

Some critics have attempted to superimpose a thematic unity on Altman's films, but he claims that they've been distorted considerably in the process. His feelings about his materials, he insists, are ambivalent and aren't usually amenable to verbal formulations. He aims at engaging the audience's emotions rather than its intellect. He believes that a movie is a private experience, not a platitudinous paraphrase: "I don't want anybody to come out with the right answer, because I don't think there is any right answer." Altman does, however, return to certain ideas, motifs, and strategies, though not in a very systematic manner. For example, a number of his movies deal with characters who have mental breakdowns: the Sandy Dennis character in *A Cold Day in the Park,* Robert Duvall in *M*A*S*H,* Susannah York in *Images* (1972), Sissy Spacek in *3 Women* (1977). Judith Kass has pointed out that several of Altman's films deal with show-business motifs and theatricalizations, most notably *Brewster; Nashville* (1975); *Buffalo Bill and the Indians, Or, Sitting Bull's History Lesson* (1976); and *A Perfect Couple* (1979). Another persistent motif is the brutalization and humiliation of women.

Mostly Altman is interested in character. At his best, he doesn't coerce us into responding to his characters in any one given way. Some of them manage to be funny, repellent, and endearing at the same time. In *Nashville,* for example, one of the major characters is the rich and powerful Haven Hamilton (Henry Gibson), a country and western singer and self-appointed city father. An unctuous egomaniac, Hamilton lards his talk with homilies on family, country, and God. He has risen to the top by pandering to his audience's most banal sentiments. His opening tune, "200 Years," is a pseudoreverent homage to America's Bicentennial, oozing with self-congratulation. He has been speaking in clichés for so long that he doesn't even hear them any more, as in the party scene, where he coos to a visiting celebrity, "Welcome to Nashville and my lovely home." He can slip from folksiness to bitchery with a mere turn of a phrase, as in the scene where he introduces Connie White (Karen Black), whom he obviously dislikes, by telling an audience that she just "got out of the dentist's chair this morning, where she was having some root canal work done," adding, "she's a wonderful singer, in her own way." Yet near the end of the film, when an assassin's bullet cuts down one of his dearest friends, this same strutting pipsqueak is the only person with presence of mind to try to calm the audience and prevent panic, even though he's wounded himself.

Altman seldom provides us with much background on his characters. He usually sets them out of their element: They're strangers to a situation and must discover their way as best they can. Disregarding traditional methods of exposition, Altman forces us to make certain discoveries as well. Like people in real life, his characters are unpredictable, inconsistent, and beyond our complete understanding. We must judge them on the basis of what they do here and now. In *McCabe and Mrs. Miller* (1970), for example, characters aren't "presented" to us as they are in classical westerns, with clear and efficient exposition. Instead, they emerge unobtrusively from the fabric of the community. Throughout the first third of the movie, the viewer is engaged primarily in trying to find its dramatic focus. The early scenes are deliberately elliptical, offering us tantalizing glimpses of the characters but nothing definitive, nothing we can follow. There are many subsidiary characters, but they appear briefly, disappear, then reemerge, like elusive threads in a subtle tapestry. We never have the sense that a given character can be finally

Figure 18.4. Warren Beatty and Julie Christie in *McCabe and Mrs. Miller* (1970), distributed by Warner Brothers. Many of Altman's characters are dreamers who are more than a little self-deluded in their expectations. When asked why he preferred dealing with foolish heroes, Altman replied: "Can you find somebody who isn't somewhat of a fool?"

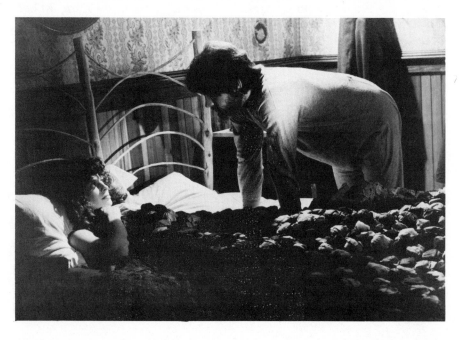

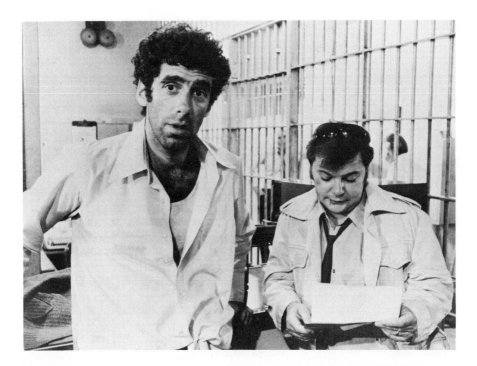

Figure 18.5. Elliott Gould in *The Long Goodbye* (1973), distributed by United Artists.
Based on a 1953 Raymond Chandler novel, this film dramatizes how its detective hero,
Philip Marlowe (Gould), is a man out of his time—that his tough romanticism, pride,
honesty, and independence are what make him a total loser in terms of contemporary
American values. He was referred to as "Rip Van Marlowe" throughout production be-
cause he seemed to have slept through twenty years of American history.

summed up, for there are too many surprises and too much that's left
deliberately muted. Motivations are seldom spelled out, and in many
instances Altman avoids the suggestion of causality. Things happen and
then other things happen, but he tends to avoid suggesting things happen *because* other things happen. More than any other American
filmmaker, Altman cuts us adrift, suggesting possible explanations here
and there but never forcing them on us. He is one of the least manipulative directors of the contemporary cinema. He prefers to explore groups
that are in a state of flux, where human affections are transitory and
provisional. Friendships in these communities are based on considerations of expedience and momentary needs, but eventually, inevitably,
they are short-circuited. In the harsher films, like *McCabe, Thieves Like Us*
(1974), and *Nashville,* the characters are left with their dreams dispersed,
the fragile strands of love and affection blasted by a ritualized death.
The survivors seldom have permanent roots to solace them. Almost
invariably, the movies conclude on a note of loss, disintegration, and
defeat.

Altman divides the filmmaking process into four stages: (1) con-
ceptualization, (2) packaging and financing, (3) shooting, and (4) editing.

Figure 18.6. **Keith Carradine and Shelley Duvall in** *Thieves Like Us* **(1974), distributed by United Artists.** Altman's Bonnie and Clyde, who are called Keechie and Bowie in this movie, are a couple of hicks—inarticulate, drab, and dumb. Rather than concentrating on the dramatic highlights of the story and discarding the dull intervening stretches, Altman often reverses this procedure. He deliberately de-theatricalizes the materials, emphasizing the ordinary, the everyday, the commonplace. Typically, the materials that most directors would discard as irrelevant to the story are precisely those that Altman dwells on most lovingly, whereas the dramatic materials—like the bank holdups—are casually thrown away.

The first stage involves story and characters, but Altman rarely uses shooting scripts, preferring to be guided by a general concept. Joan Tewkesbury, writer for *Thieves Like Us* and *Nashville*, explained: "What you have to do for a director like Bob is to provide an environment in which he can work." For example, he wanted to make *Nashville* as though it were a documentary rather than a conventional fiction film. The movie is structured mosaically, tracing the activities of twenty-four eccentric characters over a five-day period in· the city of Nashville, the heart of the country-music industry. One wag referred to the film as "twenty-four characters in search of a movie." Altman never used a script. He instructed Tewkesbury to research the materials (several of the characters are based on actual country-music personalities), stipulating only that the movie should end with a killing. She created many of the characters in sketch form, then mapped out what each major character would be doing at any given time. Altman added some characters, deleted others. Most of the dialogue and details for the actions were created by the actors. They even composed their own songs. Some episodes were staged as though they were actual occurrences. For example, a political campaign was conducted while the movie was being made. Many of the citizens of Nashville had no idea that the campaign was especially created for the film. The baton twirlers, majorettes, and marching bands are the genuine articles. A variety of cameramen, some unsupervised by Altman, recorded the political rallies and parades documentary fashion, without special setups and retakes. Later, Altman intercut this footage with the fictional scenes. "It's like jazz," he explained. "You're not planning any of this that you film. You're capturing. You can't even hope to see it, you just turn on the camera and hope to capture it." Several of Altman's other films utilize this Grand Hotel formula (so-called for the 1932 MGM picture, which featured a gallery of unrelated characters from various walks of life, unified by their brief presence in a single location, a luxury hotel). The formula is especially suited to anthology genres and has been used in such diverse works as Chaucer's *Canterbury Tales,* Sherwood Anderson's *Winesburg, Ohio,* and in many television series.

Altman is fascinated by the artistic chemistry of aleatory structures. Chance theories are commonplace in the avant-garde cinema, where subject matter is usually abstract; and in the silent era, of course, impro-

Figure 18.7. George Segal and Elliott Gould in *California Split* (1974), distributed by Columbia Pictures. This film centers on two obsessive gamblers. In a movie about chance, Altman's random, unpredictable structure is totally appropriate: Characters meet by chance, connect briefly, then go off in search of more excitement. Despite its surface comedy, the film explores the lonely rootlessness of people who can't be satisfied with a life of routine commitments.

visation was far from unusual. After the talkie revolution, however, fiction filmmaking became less flexible, in part because of the cumbersome technology that accompanied the arrival of sound. In the 1950s, television journalism introduced a more versatile technology (hand-held cameras, portable sound equipment, zoom lenses), which gave birth to the *cinéma vérité* movement, or *direct cinema* as it's sometimes called. The French New Wave directors popularized the use of this technology in the fictional cinema during the 1960s. Altman believes that it could revolutionize the medium. "I don't think we've found a format for movies yet," he has said. "I think we're still imitating literature and theatre. I don't believe film should be limited to photographing people talking. Or walking from a car to a building, the kind of stuff we do. It can be much more abstract, impressionistic, less linear. Music changes form all the time. I think if you just establish a *mood* with a film, it might have more impact than anything we've done, just a *mood*." His frequent comparison of cinema to music is especially appropriate to *Nashville*, for music is at the heart of the film's form as well as its subject matter. "This is written like a piece of music," Tewkesbury said, "where things go out and recur."

Figure 18.8. *Nashville* (1975), with Ronee Blakley, Henry Gibson, and Barbara Baxley. "I wanted to do *Nashville* to study our myths and our heroes and our hypocrisy," Altman said. He explores political ideas from a skeptical, though not despairing, perspective. "My attitude and my political statements aren't nearly as harsh as people seem to think," he has pointed out. At its Washington, D.C., premiere, Senator George McGovern responded, "I can't say it left me in high spirits. It had that combination of tragedy and comedy which characterizes both good drama and the poignant condition of our lives in the Seventies. It looked into the soul of the country and it ended without any answers."

Figure 18.9. *Nashville,* **with Lily Tomlin and Robert Doqui, distributed by Paramount.**
Altman is obsessed with "the edges of things." Some of the most poetic effects in his movies
are candid reactions of onlookers at the periphery of the action. In this scene, for example,
he used multiple cameras equiped with zoom lenses, which allowed him to pick up intimate
shots even in a crowded location. The performers were unsure of what was being photographed, and hence were required to remain constantly in character. These aleatory techniques are rich in surprises. "Sometimes I look at a scene afterwards and see that I missed
entirely what I wanted, but that I got something much better instead," Altman said.
Throughout *Nashville,* incidental characters stream in and out of view, temporarily
obstructing the action. The images are overflowing—life is constantly spilling over the
edges of the frame. Often we can hear two, and sometimes three or four, different conversations at the same time. Most scenarists get disgruntled when their dialogue is obscured,
but Joan Tewkesbury viewed her role differently: "I don't mind the overlapping dialogue,
the improvisation, the noise drowning out my words. That's how life is, there is mostly no
dialogue in life."

Altman employs aleatory principles even in his genre films, which
tend traditionally to be less flexible in terms of form. In fact, his exploitation of genre is so radically revisionist that the movies scarcely qualify as
such: *McCabe* looks like no other western ever made. *Thieves* is probably
the weirdest gangster film of the contemporary cinema. *Images* and *3
Women* are some kind of women's pictures. *Nashville* can be viewed as a
revisionist musical, and so on.

"I like a community of people rather than to be alone with the
film," Altman has stated. He insists that his art is always collaborative,
and he generally talks about it in the first person plural. He describes
Lion's Gate Films as "controlled chaos," where no one has an assigned
job but everybody finds something useful to do. He claims that often he
doesn't have to say a thing to his regulars: He simply shows up, and they

move into action. The researching of a movie is far more important than a shooting script, and he once observed that each of his pictures was like getting a master's degree in a given period or subject. After a project has been researched, cast, and its conceptual limits established, it takes on a life of its own. All he has to do is let it happen. During production he welcomes suggestions from actors, writers, assistants, and friends. "I rarely do any pre-planning on what I'm going to shoot, how I'm going to shoot it until I actually see it happen in front of me," he has said. Of course Altman makes the ultimate decisions about what will be kept in the finished work, usually in the editing and sound-mixing stages, which can take as long to complete as the shooting—sometimes longer.

He is able to work in this unorthodox manner because he uses many of the same actors, technicians, and assistants from film to film. The Altman regulars are virtually a repertory company-cum-social club, strongly devoted to their director and proud of their contributions to his movies. As in most repertory groups, they are close friends as well as professional colleagues. They trust each other and are willing to take risks that conventional movie people probably wouldn't hazard for fear of public humiliation. Altman is like a benevolent patriarch, and most of his regulars affectionately refer to him as the *commander*. Included among his regulars are writer Tewkesbury, cinematographers Vilmos Zsigmond and Paul Lohmann, art director Leon Ericksen, associate producer Robert Eggenweiler, assistant director Tommy Thompson, editor Lou Lombardo, and such actors as Elliott Gould, Shelley Duvall, Keith Carradine, René Auberjonois, Michael Murphy, and Bert Remsen.

Altman is admired by actors because he allows them an unprecedented degree of creativity. He has always had control of his casting and tends to favor skillful improvisers for his leads. He rarely uses professionals as extras, because he thinks they can't compete with the real thing: "What I'm looking for instead of actors is behaviors." A few of his projects, like *Buffalo Bill and the Indians,* required an important star in the lead; but for the most part he prefers players without an established iconography, who are more likely to surprise the audience. He bitterly resents the imputation that his players aren't acting but are merely being themselves—a misconception probably inspired by their unactorish style of acting. They're never "on" unless it's part of the character's personality. Usually they're just like us. For example, the characterizations of Shelley Duvall are so low-keyed and natural that they hardly seem like performances at all, until we consider her range. She has been equally at home as a mousy widow turned whore in *McCabe,* a gawky provincial in *Thieves,* a mindless rock groupie in *Nashville,* a perfect Cosmo Girl and would-be swinging single in *3 Women,* and Olive Oyl in *Popeye* (1980).

"An actor is the bravest of all artists," Altman told interviewer Carmie Amata, "because he cannot hide behind the canvas or stand in the back of the theatre like I can. He's right up there and he's showing his body and he's saying, 'This is my art. I'm showing you my bad leg, my bad teeth, my bad whatever it may be.' As far as I'm concerned, actors have to really, really be dealt with and paid tribute to." A number of his regulars could work for higher pay with other directors, but they prefer the challenges of Altman's approach. He is one of the few directors who almost boasts of losing arguments with his actors. For example, during the production of *Images* (which Altman wrote as well as directed), he repeatedly yielded to the ideas of his star, Susannah York, because he felt that she understood the character better than he did. Furthermore,

Figure 18.10. Publicity photo of Barbara Baxley in *Nashville*. Altman's privileged moments can take the viewer by surprise, revealing depths of character we wouldn't have expected. When we first see Lady Pearl (Baxley), she looks like a Barbie Doll gone to seed—coarse and vulgar, her voice raspy from too much booze and cigarettes. But in this scene, she speaks of her great devotion to "the Kennedy boys" and how hard she worked for their political campaigns, first for John, then for Robert, who was "more puny-like" she recalls, without conscious humor. Grieved over their deaths, she's disillusioned with politics now and has drifted without purpose since the assassination of her two idols. The movie is filled with such tender revelations, often as funny as they are moving. Altman isn't concerned with scoring points in these scenes; he simply wants to reveal the transience and beauty of his discovery: "I have no philosophy. All I'm trying to do is paint a picture and show it to you. It's like a sand castle. It's going to go away."

he thinks the movie was improved as a result. He has berated himself for not always preserving this openness of attitude. During the production of *Nashville,* actress Ronee Blakley wanted to show him a scene she had written, but Altman was in a rare foul humor and told her there was no time, to perform the scene as they had previously agreed. But he began to feel guilty about his peremptory manner, so he asked her to play it her way. The scene takes place in an outdoor auditorium, where the frail Barbara-Jean (Blakley) is to perform after a long illness. Repeatedly she interrupts her musical number to reminisce about her childhood. While her mind flutters distractedly, the audience looks on in confusion and growing resentment. Finally, dazed and stumbling, she's led off the stage by two attendants. Altman was thrilled by the impact of the scene. (Originally Barbara-Jean simply fainted on stage.) Had he not relented at the last moment, he would have lost one of the finest passages in the movie.

He is a brilliant practitioner of Stanislavsky's improvisational methods (see Chapter 14). Actually, improvisation is a term that's used to describe several techniques he uses. Sometimes the actors are given scenes written by Altman or his scenarist and are then urged to rewrite their parts to suit their own personalities. Some of the improvising takes place during rehearsals, though usually nothing is fixed or set until just before shooting. Altman and his writers normally have backup material

Figure 18.11. Sissy Spacek and Shelley Duvall in *3 Women* (1977), distributed by 20th Century-Fox. According to Altman, this movie came to him in a dream, but its finest sections are the most realistic and satirize the swinging singles scene. Millie (Duvall) and Pinky (Spacek) are roommates, trying desperately to be "with it." Millie is the self-appointed arbiter of style: "You don't drink, you don't smoke, you don't do anything you're supposed to do," she complains of her shy disciple, who eventually becomes her double. Duvall's twenty monologues, written by the actress herself, are fiendishly funny. She and Spacek shared the top acting awards at Cannes, where the picture premiered.

in case an actor's improvisations don't ignite. Generally the players are given a description of their characters and then told to reconstruct their histories and write their dialogue, which is later edited by Altman or the scenarist. "I don't improvise, I just rewrite later," he has quipped about this technique. By using these loose methods, he is able to capture a sense of spontaneity, authenticity, and freshness that's unsurpassed in the contemporary cinema. His approach has been compared to the way jazz musicians interrelate instinctively during a jam session: The artistry is found not in a rigid preordained form but in a process of discovery, mutual exploration, and disciplined self-expression.

"What I am after is essentially the subtext," Altman has declared. "I want to get the quality of what's happening between people, not just the words. The words often don't matter, it's what they're really saying to each other without the words." In *McCabe,* for example, he deliberately muffled the voices of his actors to prevent the audience from being "distracted." A good instance of his subtext approach can be seen in a brothel episode in which McCabe discusses business details with one of his hirelings. A customer enters and asks how much McCabe's partner, Mrs. Miller, charges. McCabe is beginning to fall in love with her, but still, business is business. The customer is told that her fee is $5, and when he agrees to pay it, she accompanies him upstairs. All the while, the soundtrack is occupied exclusively with the dialogue between the protagonist and his assistant; but McCabe's *mind* is preoccupied with Mrs. Miller, as he distractedly watches her and her client disappearing upstairs. The essence of the scene is its divided focus—between sound and image, commerce and love, consciousness and subconsciousness. "Most of the dialogue, well, I don't even listen to it," Altman has admitted. "As I get confident in what the actors are doing, I don't even listen to it. I find that actors know more about the characters they're playing than I do."

Altman allows himself about forty-five days for shooting. He generally ends up using only twenty-five day's worth of material, but he prefers to have a lot of extra footage for maximum flexibility at the editing bench. His visual style varies, depending on the nature of the story materials and the temperament of his cinematographers. For example, the movies photographed by Vilmos Zsigmond [*McCabe, Images, The Long Goodbye* (1973)] are exquisitely composed and lighted. Zsigmond is able to work quickly even in uncontrolled situations and still manage to create images suitable for display in a museum. In *The Long Goodbye,* the camera is almost perpetually in motion, sucking us into each scene. These traveling shots are kinetic analogues to the action: Like the protagonist, the camera is constantly on the prowl, searching for clues, trying to create order in a world of shifting perspectives and deceptive surfaces. The movies photographed by Paul Lohmann have a looser, more improvised look. The images rarely look composed and are deliberately allowed to splash over the edges of the frame. There is a pronounced documentary flavor to Lohmann's cinematography, but he modulates his style to fit the milieu of the story. For example, the gambling scenes of *California Split* have a sickly fluorescence which is indigenous to the sunless world of gambling parlors. The cinematography in *Nashville,* on the other hand, is deliberately garish, with highly saturated colors, like a cheap postcard.

The originality of Altman's visuals is also due in large measure to his gifted art director, Leon Ericksen. Among his many achievements, perhaps *McCabe* is his finest. The story takes place around 1901 in an isolated mining camp, called Presbyterian Church, located in the forested region of the American northwest. Altman and Ericksen carefully researched the photographs of the period, and virtually every detail of the film is authentic. The town was literally constructed from scratch in the middle of the pristine mountain country of Vancouver, where the film was shot. We actually see the community grow from a crude tent camp to a small frontier town. The saloon is little more than a glorified shack—filthy, cramped, and lit by two or three smoky kerosine lamps. The unpainted buildings are constructed out of freshly cut timber, and only the brothel contains any comfortable amenities. Altman includes several new-fangled contraptions—contemporary symbols of progress—like a primitive carpet-vacuuming machine and a fascinating turn-of-the-century jukebox. The men's clothes look as though they were ordered out of the Sears-Roebuck mail-order catalogues of the period, and for once, the whores really look like whores, not aspiring starlets.

Altman is one of the boldest innovators in the use of sound since the heyday of Welles. His earlier works were often criticized for their "muddy" soundtracks, but Altman believes that crisply recorded dialogue sounds phony. "Sound is supposed to be heard, but words are not necessarily supposed to be heard," he insists. He detests postsynchronized sound, which he thinks lacks the richness of life, and produces many dead spots. At Lion's Gate Films he developed an eight-track sound system which can be beefed up to sixteen separate channels if necessary. While a scene is being recorded, he literally separates the sound on different reels. Later these soundtracks are remixed and orchestrated tonally rather than for sense alone. "There's more life to it," Altman has said of this technique. In the saloon and brothel scenes of *McCabe,* for example, we catch wisps of conversations in which only a few key words can be deciphered, but these words are all we need to understand what's going on. The first time McCabe meets the scared, curious miners, for instance, we hear them mumbling among themselves, but from this undifferentiated buzz of noise we're able to hear the words *gun, killed, Bill Roundtree,* and so on. What Altman does in this scene is to dramatize for us how many western "legends" probably began: McCabe's reputation as the famous killer of Bill Roundtree is, in fact, a pastiche of speculation, frontier gossip, and the fantasizing of lonely men who are as fascinated with firearms as they are unused to seeing them. Altman also likes to overlap his dialogue to produce a comic simultaneity, a technique he derived from Howard Hawks, one of his favorite directors.

Altman's editing style is also unorthodox. Because his movies are seldom structured around a clearly articulated plot, he rarely edits according to the conventions of classical cutting. His editing style is more

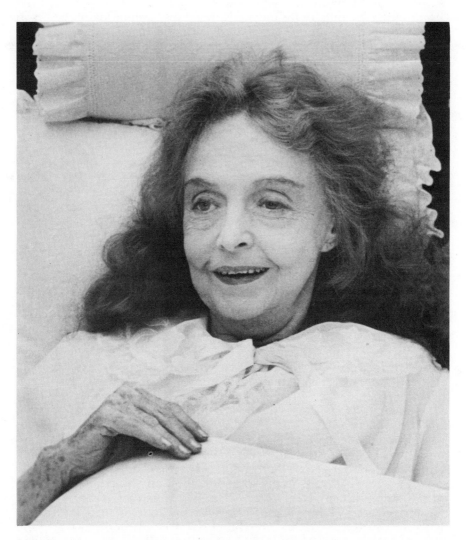

Figure 18.12. Publicity photo of Lillian Gish in *A Wedding* (1978), distributed by 20th Century-Fox. Altman's conceptual premise in this movie is the forced coming together of forty-eight ill-matched people at a formal wedding, where they attempt to put up a front suitable to the loftiness of the occasion. The action takes place within one day, mostly on one location. The formal protocol of the wedding and reception is used to provide the movie with its sequential structure. The actors were given character sketches and encouraged to invent their own details and dialogue. Lillian Gish, no stranger to improvisation since her early years with Griffith, plays the matriarch of one of the families. In a wry allusion to her character in *Birth of a Nation,* Altman's character is a genteel racist, decked out like an old little girl. Photo: Carmie Amata.

intuitive and arbitrary. Unlike the classical paradigm, we can't usually predict what Altman will cut to next. One reason why he employs the Grand Hotel formula in his movies is that it allows him many choices in his editing: Whenever he gets bored with the materials at hand, he simply cuts to another group of characters.

Even within a single scene, his cutting is unpredictable, for his use of multiple cameras provides a vast amount of footage. "When I get to the editing I have a lot of pleasant surprises," he has said. Many of these surprises are the private reactions of onlookers at the periphery of the action. By intercutting these reaction shots, Altman is able to stretch time and explore the emotional depths of an event in detail. In *Nashville*, for example, one of the most powerful scenes takes place in a crowded nightclub, in which we are presented with a variety of privileged moments (see Fig. 18.9). Ostensibly, the only action in the scene is the singing of a song, "I'm Easy," by a jaded country-rock singer, Tom Frank (Keith Carradine). Frank is little more than a windup fornicating machine, and in the audience are four of his former bed partners. While his song provides the scene's ironic continuity, Altman intercuts a variety of shots of the four women in the audience, each of whom thinks—or hopes—that the song is directed at her.

Altman's editing procedures are characteristically personal and instinctive. In the beginning stages, he makes a social ritual of viewing the rushes with his regulars. At this point he's usually in love with all his footage and has no idea how he'll edit it down to a manageable length. He observes his regulars carefully, and after noting where they seemed bored or restless, he constructs a loose preliminary print. He continues this refining process with other groups of friends and associates until he feels confident of what's remaining. Then he sneak-previews the film at a commercial theatre with a cold audience. After observing their reactions, the cutting is often refined even further, and the release print is finally completed.

Altman's main artistic shortcoming is his inconsistency. Some of his movies are flawed by dull stretches in which the materials simply fail to ignite, as in passages from *Buffalo Bill and the Indians.* At other times the subject matter seems too thinly spread to allow anything but a mechanical skimming of character, as in *A Wedding,* which attempts to explore the personalities of forty-eight different people. Obscurity and a tendency to overintellectualize are the chief vices of modernist art, and these are also serious obstacles in such private allegories as *Images* and *Quintet* (1979), which are so impenetrably personal that they're virtual Rorschach tests. A few of his movies begin and develop brilliantly but have contrived endings, like *3 Women,* in which compelling issues are vaporized away by the hot air of its "symbolic" conclusion.

Altman is not one to brood over his commercial and critical failures; he just moves on to his next project. He is the most prolific major filmmaker of the present-day American cinema, perhaps because he was a late bloomer and realizes that time is his most precious commodity: "Sometimes I feel like little Eva, running across the ice cubes with the dogs yapping at my ass. Maybe the reason I'm doing all this is so I can get a lot done before they catch up with me."

BIBLIOGRAPHY

DEMPSEY, MICHAEL. "Robert Altman: The Empty Staircase and the Chinese Princess," in *Film Comment* (September-October, 1975). A discussion of Altman's virtues and vices as an artist, with emphasis on the communities in his movies and his two recurring character types, the dreamers and the realists.

ENGLE, GARY. "*McCabe and Mrs. Miller:* Robert Altman's Anti-western," in *The Journal of Popular Film* (Fall, 1972). *McCabe* as revisionist genre.

HAUSER, ARNOLD. *The Social History of Art.* Vol. 4. New York: Vintage Books, 1951. Contains many perceptive observations about the origins and development of the modernist sensibility, viewed from a Marxist perspective.

HODENFIELD, CHRIS. "Zoom Lens Voyeur: A Few Moments with *Nashville*'s Bob Altman," in *Rolling Stone* (July 17, 1975). Brief interviews with Altman and several of his regulars on the set of *Nashville*. See also "Outlaws, Auteurs, and Actors," eds. Stephen Harvey and Richard Corliss, in *Film Comment* (May, 1974): an interview with Keith Carradine and Shelley Duvall, with emphasis on *Thieves Like Us;* and "Joan Tewkesbury," in "Dialogue on Film," in *American Film* (March, 1979): comments by Altman's former protégée on writing, directing, and the Altman influence in her work.

KASS, JUDITH M. *Robert Altman: American Innovator.* New York: Popular Library, 1978. Critical study. Filmography. See also Neil Feineman, *Persistence of Vision: The Films of Robert Altman* (New York: Arno Press, 1979).

McCLELLAND, C. KIRK. *On Making a Movie: Brewster McCloud.* New York: New American Library, 1971. Cannon's original screenplay, plus daily journal entries during production.

MAMBER, STEPHEN. *Cinéma Vérité in America.* Cambridge, Mass.: M.I.T. Press, 1977. See also Louis Marcorelles, *Living Cinema* (New York: Praeger, 1973); and Alan Rosenthal, *The New Documentary in Action* (Berkeley: University of California Press, 1972). Three studies of *cinéma vérité*.

"Robert Altman," in *Dialogue on Film* (February, 1975). Pamphlet published by the American Film Institute. Altman's most extensive interview. Other interviews include John Cutts, "M*A*S*H, McCloud and McCabe: An Interview with Robert Altman," in *Films and Filming* (November, 1971); Jan Dawson, ed., "Robert Altman Speaking," in *Film Comment* (March, 1974); "Playboy Interview: Robert Altman," in *Playboy* (August, 1976); "The Artist and the Multitude are Natural Enemies," with F. Anthony Macklin, in *Film Heritage* (Winter, 1976–1977); Carmie Amata, "Robert Altman: Maverick Moviemaker," in *The Plain Dealer Weekend Magazine* (July 9, 1976); and "Robert Altman interviewed by Charles Michener," in *Film Comment* (September-October, 1978).

ROSENBAUM, JONATHAN. "Improvisations and Interactions in Altmanville," in *Sight and Sound* (Spring, 1975). A detailed discussion of Altman's improvisational techniques.

TEWKESBURY, JOAN. *Nashville.* New York: Bantam Books, 1976. The screenplay, copiously illustrated with stills from the movie.

Glossary

(T) predominantly technical·terms.
(C) predominantly critical terms.
(I) predominantly industry terms.
(G) terms in general usage.

above-the-line expenses (I).   Expenditures incurred prior to production, such as script costs, salaries of the cast, music, royalties, and so on.

abstract film, absolute film (C).   A nonrepresentational film in which pure forms—for example, lines, shapes, colors—constitute the only content. Abstract movies are often compared to music pieces, which similarly are "about" nothing but pure form. Usually produced independently by the filmmaker, seldom with commercial profit.

actor-star (G).   See *star*.

aerial shot (T).   Essentially a variation of the *crane* shot, though restricted to exterior locations. Usually taken from a helicopter.

aesthetic distance (C).   Viewers' ability to distinguish between an artistic "reality" and external reality—their realization that the events of a fiction film are simulated.

A film (I).   A studio era term, signifying a major production, usually with important stars and a generous budget. Shown as the main feature on double bills.

aleatory techniques (C).   Techniques of filmmaking which depend on the element of chance. Images are not planned in advance but must be composed on the spot by a director who often acts as his own cameraman. Usually used in documentaries or improvisations.

allegory (C). A symbolic technique in which stylized characters and situations represent rather obvious ideas, such as justice, religion, society.

allusion (C). A reference to an event, person, or work of art, usually well known.

animation (G). A form of filmmaking characterized by photographing inanimate objects or individual drawings *frame by frame,* with each frame differing minutely from its predecessor. When such images are projected at the standard speed of twenty-four frames per second, the result is that the objects or drawings appear to move, and hence, seem "animated."

anticipatory camera, anticipatory setup (C). The placement of the camera in such a manner as to anticipate the movements of an action before it occurs. An anticipatory camera often suggests fatality or predestination.

archetype (C). An original model or type after which similar things are patterned. Archetypes can be well-known story patterns, universal experiences, or personality types. Myths, fairy tales, *genres,* and cultural heroes are generally archetypal, as are the basic cycles of life and nature.

art director, also **production designer** (G). The individual responsible for designing and overseeing the construction of sets for a movie and sometimes its interior decoration and overall visual style.

art house (I). A theatre specializing in sophisticated fare, especially classic, experimental, and foreign movies.

aspect ratio (T). The ratio between the horizontal and vertical dimensions of the *frame.*

auteur theory (C). A theory of film popularized by the critics of the French periodical, *Cahiers du Cinéma,* in the 1950s. The theory emphasizes the director as the major creator of film art. A strong director (an *auteur*) stamps the material with his personal vision, even when working with an externally imposed script or *genre.*

available lighting (G). The use of only that illumination that actually exists on a location, either natural (the sun) or artificial (house lamps). When available lighting is used in interior locations, generally a sensitive *fast film stock* must also be used.

avant-garde (C). From the French, meaning "in the front ranks." Those minority artists whose works are characterized by an unconventional daring and by obscure, controversial, or highly personal ideas.

back lot (I). During the studio era, standing exterior sets of such common locales as a frontier town, a turn-of-the-century city block, a European village, and so on. MGM boasted the largest number of back lots.

beefcake (I). Visual publicity emphasizing an actor's sex appeal, usually with his chest bared or otherwise scantily attired.

below-the-line-expenses (I). The costs incurred during production and postproduction: set construction, salaries of technical personnel, equipment rental, transportation, location expenses, and so on.

B film (G).   A low-budget movie usually shown as the second feature during the big studio era. B films rarely included important stars and took the form of popular *genres,* like thrillers, westerns, horror films. The major studios used them as testing grounds for the raw talent under contract.

bird's eye view (G).   A shot in which the camera photographs a scene from directly overhead.

black comedy (C).   Cruel, bitter, and grotesque humor that often revels in its own bad taste. Best represented in the American cinema by the movies of Billy Wilder.

blacklist (I).   The names of people who are or have been refused employment in the movie industry, usually because of their political beliefs.

blimp (T).   A soundproof camera housing which muffles the noise of the camera's motor so that sound can be clearly recorded on the set.

blind booking (I).   When an *exhibitor* agrees to rent a movie sight unseen, often before its completion—a common practice during the studio era and not uncommon now.

block booking (I).   During the studio era, the practice of forcing an *exhibitor* to rent a desirable movie as part of a package which includes less attractive films produced by the same studio. Though declared illegal in the late 1940s, this practice is by no means extinct.

blocking (T).   The movements of the actors within a given playing area.

boom, mike boom (T).   An overhead telescoping pole which carries a microphone, permitting the *synchronous* recording of sound without restricting the movements of the actors.

box office (G).   Literally, the ticket office of a movie theatre. Figuratively, the drawing power of a performer, genre, or individual movie.

buddy-buddy film, buddy film (I).   An offshoot of the *action picture,* emphasizing the camaraderie between two adventurous males. The genre is antidomestic and usually excludes important female characters. Popular during the late 1960s and early 1970s.

cels, also **cells** (T).   Transparent plastic sheets which are superimposed in layers by animators to give the illusion of depth and volume to their drawings.

character roles (G).   Secondary rolès in a movie, usually lacking the glamor of the leading parts.

cheesecake (I).   Publicity photos stressing the sex appeal of an actress, who is usually scantily clad in provocative poses.

cinematographer, also **director of photography, lighting cameraman** (G).   The artist or technician responsible for the lighting of a shot and the quality of the photography.

cinéma vérité, also **direct cinema** (C).   A method of documentary filming, using *aleatory* methods that don't interfere with the way events take place in reality. Such films are made with a minimum of equipment, usually a hand-held camera and portable sound apparatus.

classical American cinema (C).   A vague but convenient term used to designate the mainstream of fiction films produced in Hollywood, roughly from the maturity of Griffith in the mid-teens till the late 1960s. The classical paradigm is a movie strong in *story, star,* and *production values,* with a high level of technical achievement and edited according to the conventions of *classical cutting.* The visual style is functional and rarely distracts from the characters in action. Movies in this mold are structured narratively, with a clearly defined conflict, complications that intensify to a rising climax, and a resolution that is usually optimistic.

classical cutting, découpage classique (C). A style of editing developed by Griffith, in which a sequence of shots is determined by a scene's dramatic and emotional emphases rather than by its physical action alone. The sequence of shots represents the breakdown of the event into its psychological as well as logical components.

closed forms (C). A visual style which inclines toward self-conscious designs and carefully harmonized compositions. The *frame* is exploited to suggest a self-sufficient universe which encloses all the necessary visual information.

closeup, close shot (G). A detailed view of a person or object, usually without much context provided. A closeup of an actor generally includes only his head.

content curve (C). The amount of time necessary for the average viewer to assimilate most of the information of a shot.

continuity (T). The kind of logic implied between *edited* shots, their principle of coherence. *Cutting to continuity* emphasizes smooth transitions between shots, in which time and space are unobtrusively condensed. *Classical cutting* is the linking of shots according to an event's psychological as well as logical breakdown. In *radical montage,* the continuity is determined by the symbolic association of ideas between shots rather than any literal connections in time and space. Continuity can also refer to the space-time continuum of reality before it's broken down into fragments (shots).

convention (C). An implied agreement between the viewer and artist to accept certain artificialities as real in a work of art. In movies, editing—or the juxtaposition of shots—is accepted as "logical," even though a viewer's perception of reality is continuous and unfragmented. *Genre* films contain many preestablished conventions. In musicals, for example, characters express themselves most forcefully through song and dance.

costume picture (G). A movie set in an historical period, requiring elaborate and colorful costumes, such as *Birth of a Nation, Gone With the Wind,* and *Barry Lyndon.*

coverage, covering shots (T). Extra shots of a scene which can be used to bridge transitions in case the planned footage fails to edit according to expectations—usually long shots which preserve the overall continuity of a scene.

crane shot (T). A shot taken from a special device called a crane, which resembles a huge mechanical arm. The crane carries the camera and the cameraman and can move in virtually any direction.

creative producer (I). A producer who supervises the making of a movie in such detail that he is virtually its artistic creator. During the studio era, the two most famous creative producers were Selznick and Disney.

crosscutting (G).   The alternating of shots from two sequences, often in different locales, suggesting that they are taking place at the same time.

cutting in the camera, editing in the camera (I).   The practice of shooting only what's necessary for the individual shots of a film, with virtually no leftover footage. In effect, the film is precut: The editor needs only to splice the shots in their proper sequence.

cutting to continuity (T).   A type of editing in which the shots are arranged to preserve the fluidity of an action without showing all of it—an unobtrusive condensation of a continuous action.

day-for-night shooting (T).   Scenes that are filmed in daytime with special filters, to suggest nighttime settings in the movie image.

découpage (C).   From the French, "to cut up"—the breakdown of a dramatic action into its constituent shots. See *editing*.

découpage classique, see **classical cutting** (C).

deep focus (T).   A technique of photography which permits all distance planes to remain clearly in focus, from closeup ranges to infinity.

direct cinema, see **cinéma vérité** (C).

dissolve, lap dissolve (T).   These terms refer to the slow fading out of one shot and the gradual fading in of its successor, with a superimposition of images, usually at the midpoint.

distributor (I).   Those individuals who serve as middle men in the movie industry, who arrange to book the producer's product in the exhibitor's theatre. During the big studio era, these three branches of the industry were combined.

dolly shot, tracking shot, trucking shot (T).   A shot taken from a moving vehicle. Originally tracks were laid on the set to permit a smoother movement of the camera. Today even a smooth hand-held traveling shot is considered a variation of the dolly shot.

dominant contrast, also **dominant** (C).   That area of the film image, which because of a prominent visual contrast, compels the viewer's most immediate attention. Occasionally the dominant can be aural, in which case the image serves as a *subsidiary contrast.*

double exposure (T).   The superimposition of two literally unrelated images on film. See also *multiple exposure.*

double feature, double bill (G).   The practice, primarily in the 1930s and 1940s, of exhibiting two feature-length movies for a single admission, usually an *A production* followed by a *B film.*

dubbing (T).   The addition of sound after the visuals have been photographed. Dubbing can be either *synchronous* with the image or *nonsynchronous.* Foreign language movies are often dubbed in English for release in this country.

editing (G).   The joining of one shot (strip of film) with another. The shots can picture events and objects in different places at different times. Editing is called *montage* in Europe.

epic (C).   A film *genre* characterized by bold and sweeping themes, usually in heroic proportions. The protagonist is generally an ideal representative of a culture—either national, religious, or regional.

The tone of most epics is dignified, the treatment larger than life. The western is the most popular epic genre in the United States.

establishing shot (T). Usually an *extreme long shot* or *long shot* offered at the beginning of a scene, providing the context of the subsequent closer shots.

exchange (I). The original *distributors*, primarily in the early silent era, who provided a clearing house where, for a fee, theatre owners could swap their used movies for those of other exhibitors. This crude system of distribution was abandoned by the mid-teens.

exhibitor (I). The individual or company owning a movie theatre or chain of theatres.

exploitation film (I). A low-budget movie capitalizing on a current fad or popular trend, usually aimed at youthful audiences.

expressionism (C). A style of filmmaking which distorts time and space as ordinarily perceived in reality. Emphasis is placed on the essential characteristics of objects and people, not necessarily on their superficial appearance. Typical expressionist techniques are fragmentary editing, a wide variety of shots, extreme angles, dramatic lighting effects, and distorting lenses.

extra (I). A minor screen performer, usually hired by the day to play a nonspeaking role, often as a member of a crowd.

extreme closeup (G). A minutely detailed view of an object or person. An extreme closeup of an actor generally includes only his eyes or his mouth.

extreme long shot (G). A panoramic view of an exterior location photographed from a great distance, often as far as a quarter-mile away.

eye-level shot (T). The placement of the camera approximately five to six feet from the ground, corresponding to the height of an observer on the scene.

factory system (G). During the studio era, a method of mass production based on the principle of the assembly line, in which movies are created not by a single artist and his collaborators but by specialized departments which perform the same function for all films produced by the studio. Except for an executive overseer—usually the producer—no single individual handles a movie from conception to release. The term is generally used in a pejorative sense.

fade (T). The *fade-out* is the snuffing of an image from normal brightness to a black screen. A *fade-in* is the slow brightening of the image from a black screen to normal.

faithful adaptation (C). A film based on another medium (usually a work of literature) which captures the essence of the original and uses cinematic equivalents for specific literary techniques.

fast motion, accelerated motion (T). If an action is photographed at a slower rate than twenty-four frames per second, when the film is projected at the standard rate, the action will appear to be moving at a faster rate than normal and will often seem jerky.

fast stock, fast film (T). Film stock that's highly sensitive to light and generally produces a grainy image—used often by documentarists who wish to shoot only with *available lighting*. See also *slow stock*.

feature, feature-length film (G). A movie of over an hour's duration and generally under two.

filters (T). Pieces of glass or plastic placed in front of the *lens* which distort the quality of the light entering the camera, and hence, the movie image.

final cut, also **release print** (I). The sequence of shots in a movie as it will be released to the public.

first cut (I). The initial sequence of shots in a movie, often constructed by the director; also called a *rough cut.*

first run (I). One of several types of film distribution, usually the opening engagement of a movie at a limited number of important theatres.

first-run house (I). A prestigious movie theatre, usually located in a city, commanding the best films, the highest ticket prices, and the biggest audiences.

fish-eye lens (T). An extreme wide-angle lens, which distorts the image so radically that the edges seem wrapped into a sphere.

flashback (G). An editing technique that suggests the interruption of the present by a shot or series of shots representing the past.

flash-forward (G). An editing technique that suggests the interruption of the present by a shot or series of shots representing the future.

flash pan. See *swish pan* (T).

focus (T). The degree of acceptable sharpness in a film image. *Out of focus* means the images are blurred and lack acceptable linear definition.

footage (T). Exposed film *stock.*

frame (T). The dividing line between the edges of the screen image and the enclosing darkness of the theatre. Can also refer to a single photograph from the filmstrip.

freeze frame, freeze shot (T). A shot composed of a single *frame* that is reprinted a number of times on the filmstrip, which when projected gives the illusion of a still photograph.

front office (I). The executive branch of a studio. During the big studio era, the front office consisted of the studio head, the *production chief,* the producers, and their assistants. The front office made virtually all the major decisions concerning what movies to make and how. In short, it was the center of power.

f-stop (T). The measurement of the size of the lens opening in the camera, indicating the amount of light that's admitted.

full shot (T). A type of *long shot* which includes the human body in full, with the head near the top of the frame and the feet near the bottom.

gauge (T). The width of the filmstrip, expressed in millimeters (mm). The wider the gauge, the better the quality of the image. The most common gauges are 8 mm, 16 mm, 35 mm, and 70 mm. The standard in theatrical exhibitions is 35 mm; in most college and museum showings, 16 mm. 70 mm is usually reserved for big-budget *spectacle films.*

genre (C). A recognizable type of movie, characterized by certain preestablished conventions. Some common American genres are westerns, musicals, thrillers, and comedies.

heavy (I).   The villain, so called because early movie villains were often fat.

high angle shot (T).   A shot in which the subject is photographed from above.

high contrast (T).   A style of lighting emphasizing harsh shafts and dramatic streaks of lights and darks—often used in thrillers and melodramas.

high key (T).   A style of lighting emphasizing bright, even illumination, with few conspicuous shadows—used generally in comedies, musicals, and light entertainment films.

homage (C).   A direct or indirect reference within a movie to another movie, filmmaker, or cinematic style; a respectful and affectionate tribute.

hyphenate (I).   A person who engages in more than one important function in the filmmaking process, such as a writer-director, producer-director, star-producer, and so on.

iconography (C).   The use of a well-known cultural symbol or complex of symbols in an artistic representation. In movies, iconography can involve a star's *persona*, the preestablished conventions of a *genre*, the use of *archetypal* characters and situations, and such stylistic features as lighting, settings, costuming, and props.

independent cinema, underground films (C).   An avant-garde movement which began in the United States in the mid-1950s, emphasizing film as pure form and the filmmaker's self-expression over considerations of subject matter alone; mostly short, nonnarrative movies, produced outside the industry.

independent producer (G).   A producer not affiliated with a studio. Many stars and directors have been independent producers to insure their artistic autonomy.

intrinsic interest (C).   An unobtrusive area of the film image which nonetheless compels the viewer's most immediate attention because of its dramatic or contextual importance. An object of intrinsic interest will take precedence over the formal *dominant contrast*.

iris (T).   A *masking* device that blacks out portions of the screen, permitting only a part of the image to be seen. Usually the iris is circular or oval shaped and can be expanded or contracted.

jump cut (T).   An abrupt transition between shots, sometimes deliberate, which is disorienting in terms of the *continuity* of space and time.

key light (T).   The main source of illumination for a shot.

kinetic (C).   Pertaining to motion and movement.

leftist (C).   A political term used to describe the acceptance, at least in part, of the economic, social, and philosophical ideas of Karl Marx.

lengthy take, long take (C).   A shot of lengthy duration.

lens (T).   A ground or molded piece of glass, plastic, or other transparent material through which light rays are refracted so that they converge or diverge to form the photographic image within the camera.

literal adaptation (C).   A movie based on a stage play, in which the dialogue and actions are preserved more or less intact, though subtly altered by the director's uniquely cinematic techniques, like *editing* and *mise-en-scène.*

loan-out (I). During the studio era, when a contract employee (usually a star) was allowed to work for an outside producer, with a handsome profit for the studio holding the contract.

long lens (T). See *telephoto lens.*

long shot (G). Includes an area within the *frame* which roughly corresponds to the audience's view of the area within the proscenium arch in the live theatre.

loose adaptation (C). A movie based on another medium (usually literary), in which only a superficial resemblance exists between the two versions.

loose framing (C). Usually used in longer shots. The *mise-en-scène* is so spaciously distributed that the people photographed have considerable freedom of movement.

low-angle shot (T). A shot in which the subject is photographed from below.

low key (T). A style of lighting emphasizing diffused shadows and atmospheric pools of light; often used in mysteries, thrillers, and *film noir.*

majors, the (I). The principal film-producing companies in the United States. During the studio era, the majors consisted of the so-called Big Five: MGM, Warner Brothers, Paramount, RKO, and 20th Century-Fox. Sometimes the Little Three were also considered majors: United Artists, Columbia, and Universal Pictures.

Marxist (C). A person who subscribes to the economic, social, political, and philosophical theories of Karl Marx; any artistic work reflecting these values.

masking (T). A technique whereby a portion of the movie image is blocked out, thus temporarily altering the dimensions of the screen's *aspect ratio.*

master shot (T). An uninterrupted shot, usually taken from a long- or full-shot range, which contains an entire scene. Later, the closer shots are photographed, and an edited sequence, composed of a variety of shots, is constructed on the editor's bench.

matte shot (T). A process of combining two separate shots on one print, resulting in an image that looks as though it had been photographed normally; used mostly for special effects, such as combining a human figure with giant dinosaurs.

medium shot (G). A relatively close shot, revealing a moderate amount of detail. A medium shot of a figure generally includes the body from the knees or waist up. French critics called it *le plan amèricain,* the American shot, because it's so characteristic of the *classical American cinema,* particularly for dialogue scenes.

metaphor (C). An implied comparison between two otherwise unlike elements, meaningful in a figurative rather than literal sense.

metteur-en-scène (C). The artist or technician who creates the *mise-en-scène;* that is, the director. Used pejoratively, this term refers to a hired hand who doesn't impose his personal vision on his materials but merely stages the action mechanically.

mickeymousing (T).   A type of film music which is purely descriptive and attempts to reproduce the visual action with musical equivalents; often used in animation.

miniatures, also **model** or **miniature shots** (T).   Small-scale models photographed to give the illusion that they are full-scale objects, for example, ships sinking at sea, giant dinosaurs, airplanes colliding.

minimalism (C).   A style of filmmaking characterized by austerity and restraint, in which cinematic elements are reduced to the barest minimum of information.

mise-en-scène (C).   The arrangement of visual weights and movements within a given space. In the live theatre, the space is usually defined by the proscenium arch; in movies, by the *frame* which encloses the image. Cinematic *mise-en-scène* encompasses both the staging of the action and the way that it's photographed.

mix (T).   The process of combining separately recorded sounds from individual soundtracks onto a master track.

mogul (I).   The name given to the powerful chief executives of the studios during the supremacy of the studio system in Hollywood. Generally the term was reserved only for presidents, vice-presidents, and the most prestigious producers, such as Selznick and Goldwyn.

montage (T).   Transitional sequences of rapidly edited images, used to suggest the lapse of time or the passing of events; often employs *dissolves* and *multiple exposures.* In Europe, montage means the art of editing.

motif (C).   Any unobtrusive technique, object, or thematic idea that's systematically repeated throughout a film.

multiple exposure (T).   A special effect produced by the *optical printer,* which permits the superimposition of many images simultaneously.

negative cost (I).   The amount of money necessary to produce a completed film, the combined total of *above-the-line* and *below-the-line expenses.*

negative image (T).   The reversal of lights and darks of the subject photographed: Blacks are white, and whites are black.

New Wave, nouvelle vague (C).   A group of young French directors who came to prominence during the late 1950s. The most widely known are Jean-Luc Godard, François Truffaut, Claude Chabrol, and Alain Resnais, who all began as movie critics at *Cahiers du Cinéma.*

nickelodeon (G).   The earliest movie theatres, primarily between the years 1895–1908, which were crudely converted from vacant stores and charged a nickel admission.

nonsynchronous sound, also **commentative sound** (T).   Sound and image are not recorded simultaneously, or the sound is detached from its source in the film image. Music, for example, is usually nonsynchronous in a movie.

oblique angle (T).   A shot photographed by a tilted camera. When the image is projected on the screen, the subject itself seems to be tilted on a diagonal.

oeuvre (C).   From the French: *work*. The complete works of an artist, viewed as a whole.

omniscient point of view (C).   In literature, this refers to an all-knowing narrator who provides the reader with all the necessary information. Most movies are omnisciently narrated by the camera.

one-reeler (G).   A movie fitting on a single reel, lasting about ten to fourteen minutes, used primarily in the pre-World War II era.

open forms (C).   Used primarily by *realist* filmmakers, these techniques are likely to be unobtrusive, with an emphasis on informal compositions and apparently haphazard designs. The *frame* is exploited to suggest a temporary masking which arbitrarily cuts off part of the action.

open up (I).   A term used in adapting a play to film, in which the action is transferred to a variety of locations, often exteriors, in order to make the story appear less stagey and confined.

optical printer (T).   An elaborate machine used to create special effects in movies, for example, *fades, dissolves, multiple exposures*.

outtakes (I).   Shots or pieces of shots that are not used in the *final cut* of a film; the leftover footage.

overexposure (T).   Too much light enters the aperture of a camera lens, bleaching out the image; useful for fantasy and nightmare sequences.

over-the-shoulder shot (T).   Usually a *medium shot,* useful in dialogue scenes, in which one actor is photographed head on from over the shoulder of another character.

pan, panning shot (T).   Short for panorama, this is a revolving horizontal movement of the camera from left to right or vice versa.

parallel editing (G).   See *crosscutting*.

persona (C).   From the Latin for mask: an actor's public image, based on his or her previous roles, and often incorporating elements of their actual personality as well.

personality-star (G).   See *star*.

pilot film (I).   A made-for-television movie which is used to test audience reaction to a planned series. Pilot films are sometimes released abroad as theatrical features.

point-of-view-shot, also **pov shot, first person camera,** and **subjective camera** (T).   Any shot that is taken from the vantage point of a character in the film.

Poverty Row (I).   An area in Hollywood where most of the lesser studios were located. Such Poverty Row studios as Monogram and Republic produced low-budget B films almost exclusively.

process shot, also **rear projection** (T).   A technique in which a background scene is projected onto a translucent screen behind the actors so it appears as if the actors are on location in the final image. Kubrick developed a front projection system for *2001*.

producer (G).   An ambiguous term referring to the individual or company that controls the financing of a film, and often the way it will be made. The producer can concern himself solely with business matters or with putting together a package deal (such as script, stars, and director), or he can function as an expeditor, smoothing over problems during production. During the studio era, producers were usually the most powerful figures associated with the making of a movie.

producer-director (I). A filmmaker who finances his projects independently, to allow himself maximum creative freedom.

production chief, also **vice-president in charge of production** (I). In the studio era, the executive of a studio who made most of the major decisions concerning which movies to make and how. In major studios, he supervised about fifty films per year, allocating budgets and assigning key personnel for each project, including producer and director.

Production Code, also **Motion Picture Production Code,** and **The Hays Office,** or **The Johnston Office** (I). The film industry's censorship arm, the Code was introduced in 1930 but not enforced until 1934. It was revised in the 1950s and scrapped in favor of the present rating system in 1966.

production number (I). An elaborate sequence, often in a musical, which involves a large cast and complicated technical maneuvers.

production values (I). The box office appeal of the physical mounting of a film, such as sets, costumes, props. *Spectacle pictures* are generally the most lavish in their production values.

program films. See *B films*.

prop (T). Any movable item included in a movie: tables, guns, books, and so on.

property (I). Anything with a profit-making potential in movies, though generally used to describe a story of some kind: a screenplay, novel, short story, and so on. Contract actors are sometimes referred to as properties.

proxemic patterns (C). The spatial relationships among characters within the *mise-en-scène* and the apparent distance of the camera from the subject photographed.

pull-back dolly (T). When the camera withdraws from a scene to reveal an object or character that was previously out of *frame*.

rack focusing, selective focusing (T). The blurring of focal planes in sequence, forcing the viewer's eye to travel with those areas of an image that remain in sharp focus.

radical montage (C). A type of editing propounded by the Soviet filmmaker, Sergei Eisenstein, in which separate shots are linked together not by their literal continuity in reality but by symbolic association. A shot of a preening braggart might be linked to a shot of a toy peacock, for example. This type of editing juxtaposes shots to produce a sense of collision.

reaction pan (T). Similar to a reaction shot, only instead of cutting, the director *pans* to a character's response.

reaction shot (T). A cut to a shot of a character's reaction to the contents of the preceding shot.

realism (G). A style of filmmaking which attempts to duplicate the look of reality as it's commonly observed, with emphasis on authentic locations and details, long shots, lengthy takes, eye-level camera placements, and a minimum of editing and special effects.

reestablishing shot (T). A return to an initial *establishing shot* within a scene, acting as a reminder of the physical context of the closer shots.

release print (I). See *final cut.*

reverse angle shot (T). A shot taken from an angle 180 degrees opposed to the previous shot; that is, the camera is placed opposite its previous position.

reverse motion (T). A series of images are photographed with the film reversed. When projected normally, the effect is to suggest backward movement—an egg "returning" to its shell, for example.

rough cut (T). The crudely edited footage of a movie before the editor has tightened up the slackness between shots; a kind of rough draft.

rushes, dailies (I). The selected footage of the previous day's shooting, which is usually evaluated by the director and cinematographer before the start of the next day's shooting.

scene (G). An imprecise unit of film, composed of a number of interrelated shots, unified usually by a central concern—a location, an incident, or a minor dramatic climax.

script, screenplay, scenario (G). A written description of a movie's dialogue and action, which occasionally includes camera instructions.

second-unit director (I). A director who specializes in complicated action scenes, stunt work, or location sequences which don't usually involve the main actors.

semiology, semiotics (C). A theory of cinematic communications which studies signs or symbolic codes as minimal units of signification. Influenced by the methodology and theory of structural linguistics, semiological theories are descriptive rather than normative and are concerned with the systematic identification and classification of cinematic signs.

sequence (G). An imprecise structural unit of film, composed of a number of interrelated scenes and leading to a major climax.

sequence shot, also plan-séquence (C). A single lengthy take, usually involving complex staging and camera movements.

serial (I). A story told in weekly episodes, emphasizing cheap thrills and suspense. Each segment concludes with a cliffhanging situation that's fortuitously resolved at the beginning of the next episode. All ends happily in the final installment. These were popular from the silent period to the 1950s, when the big studios ceased producing them.

setup (T). The positioning of the camera and lights for a specific shot.

shooting ratio (I). The amount of film stock used in photographing a film in relation to what's finally included in the finished product. Some directors, like Hitchcock, have very low shooting ratios; others, like Altman, very high.

shooting script (I). A written breakdown of a movie story into its individual shots, often containing technical instructions; used by the director and his staff during production.

short lens (T). See *wide-angle lens.*

shot (G).   Those images that are recorded continuously from the time the camera starts to the time it stops, that is, an unedited strip of film.

shtick (I).   A characteristic gesture or piece of business that's associated with a given performer, especially comedians.

slapstick (G).   A type of comedy, popular in the silent era, involving pantomime and broad physical actions, such as pratfalls and auto collisions.

slow motion (T).   Shots of a subject photographed at a faster rate than twenty-four fps, which when projected at the standard rate produce a dreamy dancelike slowness of action.

slow stock, slow film (T).   Film stocks that are relatively insensitive to light and produce images of great crispness and sharpness of detail. When used in interior settings, these stocks generally require considerable artificial illumination.

sneak preview (I).   A trial exhibition of a movie, usually unadvertized, in order to gauge an audience's response before the film's official release. If the reaction is unfavorable, the movie is often reedited to conform to the criticisms—inferred or explicit—of the sneak-preview audience.

soft focus (T).   The blurring out of focus of all but one desired distance range; can also refer to a glamorizing technique which softens the sharpness of definition so that facial wrinkles can be smoothed over and even eliminated.

spectacle picture (G).   A movie set in an historical period (biblical times, the Roman Empire, etc.), emphasizing *epic* clashes. Such films feature large casts and lavish *production values*.

star (G).   A film actor or actress of great popularity. A *personality-star* tends to play only those roles that fit a preconceived public image, which constitutes his or her *persona*. An *actor-star* can play roles of greater range and variety. Barbra Streisand is a personality-star; Robert De Niro, an actor-star.

starlet (I).   During the studio era, a promising young female who was being groomed by the studio as a potential star.

star system (G).   The technique of exploiting the charisma of popular players to enhance the box office appeal of films. The star system has been the backbone of the American cinema since the mid-teens.

star values (I).   The box office appeal of the stars in a movie, independent of its *story* and *production values*.

star vehicle (G).   A movie especially designed to showcase the talents and charms of a specific star.

stock (T).   Unexposed film. There are many types of movie stocks, including those highly sensitive to light (*fast stocks*) and those relatively insensitive to light (*slow stocks*).

storyboard (T).   Continuity sketches resembling a comic strip, showing the design and sequence of each shot in a scene. The term can also be used as a verb, that is, "to storyboard" a sequence.

story editor (I).   During the studio era, the person who headed the story department, whose main responsibility was scouting and evaluating literary properties.

story values (I).   The narrative appeal of a movie, which can reside in the popularity of an adapted property, the high craftsmanship of a script, or both.

structuralism, cine-structuralism (C).   Cinematic theories employing various *semiological* methods to determine how certain codes and signs are synthesized in a single film, *genre,* or *oeuvre* of a filmmaker.

studio (G).   A large corporation specializing in the production and/or distribution of movies, such as Paramount, Warner Brothers, and so on; also, any physical facility equipped for the production of films.

studio era (G).   That period (roughly from 1925 to 1955, but especially the 1930s and 1940s) when most American fiction movies were produced under the auspices of the big studios, such as MGM, Warners, and Paramount.

subjective camera.   See *point-of-view shot.*

subsidiary contrast (C).   A subordinated element of the film image, complementing or contrasting with the *dominant contrast.*

subtext (C).   A term used in drama and film to signify the dramatic implications beneath the language of a play or movie. Often the subtext concerns ideas and emotions that are totally independent of the language of a text.

Surrealism (C).   An avant-garde movement in the arts stressing Freudian and Marxist ideas, unconscious elements, irrationalism, and the symbolic association of ideas. Surrealist movies were produced roughly from 1924 to 1931, primarily in France, though there are still surrealist elements in the works of many directors, most notably those of Federico Fellini and Luis Buñuel.

swish pan (T).   Also known as a *flash* or *zip pan.* A horizontal movement of the camera at such a rapid rate that the subject photographed blurs on the screen.

symbol, symbolic (C).   A figurative device in which an object, event, or cinematic technique has significance beyond its literal meaning. Symbolism is always determined by the dramatic context. A raging fire between two lovers, for example, can symbolize sexual passion. Otherwise a fire is just a fire, unless the context suggests other symbolic ideas.

synchronous sound (T).   The agreement or correspondence between image and sound, which are recorded simultaneously or seem so in the finished print. Synchronous sounds appear to derive from an obvious source in the visuals.

take (T).   A variation of a specific shot. The final shot is often selected from a number of possible takes.

telephoto lens, long lens (T).   A lens that acts as a telescope, magnifying the size of objects at a great distance. A side effect is its tendency to flatten perspective.

three-shot (T).   A *medium* shot, featuring three actors.

tie-in (I).   Any commercial product connected with the release of a movie, for example, original soundtrack recordings, tee-shirts, novelizations.

tight framing (C).   Used usually in close shots; the *mise-en-scène* is so carefully balanced and harmonized that the people photographed have little or no freedom of movement.

tracking shot, trucking shot (T).   See *dolly shot.*

trailer, preview (I).   A short film used to advertize a coming attraction to a theatre, highlighting the movie's most compelling features.

treatment (I).   A written description of a film story, longer and more detailed than an outline but briefer than a screenplay.

two-shot (T).   A *medium shot,* featuring two actors.

vaudeville (G).   Stage entertainment, especially popular with middle-class audiences in the early twentieth century, offering a variety of short acts, such as slapstick comedy, song and dance, stand-up comedy, juggling, parodies, and impersonations.

vertical integration (I).   During the studio era, combining all three phases of the film industry—production, distribution, exhibition—under one organization; declared an illegal monopoly by the Supreme Court in the late 1940s.

viewfinder (T).   An eyepiece on the camera which defines the playing area and the framing of the action to be photographed.

vignetting (T).   A technique used to round off the corner edges of a movie image with a soft blurring effect.

voice-over (T).   A nonsynchronous spoken commentary in a movie, often used to convey a character's thoughts or memories.

wide-angle lens, short lens (T).   A lens that permits the camera to photograph a wider area than does a normal lens. A side effect is its tendency to exaggerate perspective. Also used for *deep-focus* photography.

wide screen, also **CinemaScope** and **scope** (G).   A movie image which has an *aspect ratio* of approximately 5 by 3, though some wide screens possess horizontal dimensions that extend as wide as 2.5 times the vertical dimensions.

wipe (T).   An editing device, usually a line that travels across the screen, "pushing off" one image and revealing another.

woman's picture (I).   A genre in the domestic mode, primarily in the big studio era, centering on a top female star and emphasizing such emotion-laden scenes as painful separations, noble sacrifices, and tearful reconciliations. Known pejoratively as *weepies, weepers,* and *soap operas.*

zip pan (T).   See *swish pan.*

zoom lens, zoom shot (T).   A lens of variable focal length which permits the cameraman to change from *wide-angle* to *telephoto shots* (and vice versa) in one continuous movement, often plunging the viewer in or out of a scene rapidly.

Index of Film Titles and Personalities